The Palgrave Handbook of Toleration

Mitja Sardoč
Editor

The Palgrave Handbook of Toleration

Volume 2

Editor
Mitja Sardoč
Educational Research Institute
Ljubljana, Slovenia

ISBN 978-3-030-42120-5   ISBN 978-3-030-42121-2 (eBook)
ISBN 978-3-030-42122-9 (print and electronic bundle)
https://doi.org/10.1007/978-3-030-42121-2

© Springer Nature Switzerland AG 2022
This work is subject to copyright. All rights are reserved by the Publisher, whether the whole or part of the material is concerned, specifically the rights of translation, reprinting, reuse of illustrations, recitation, broadcasting, reproduction on microfilms or in any other physical way, and transmission or information storage and retrieval, electronic adaptation, computer software, or by similar or dissimilar methodology now known or hereafter developed.
The use of general descriptive names, registered names, trademarks, service marks, etc. in this publication does not imply, even in the absence of a specific statement, that such names are exempt from the relevant protective laws and regulations and therefore free for general use.
The publisher, the authors, and the editors are safe to assume that the advice and information in this book are believed to be true and accurate at the date of publication. Neither the publisher nor the authors or the editors give a warranty, expressed or implied, with respect to the material contained herein or for any errors or omissions that may have been made. The publisher remains neutral with regard to jurisdictional claims in published maps and institutional affiliations.

This Palgrave Macmillan imprint is published by the registered company Springer Nature Switzerland AG.
The registered company address is: Gewerbestrasse 11, 6330 Cham, Switzerland

Preface

"The safest general characterization of the European philosophical tradition," as Alfred North Whitehead accentuated in *Process and Reality* (based on his *Gifford Lectures Delivered in the University of Edinburgh During the Session 1927–28*) "is that it consists of a series of footnotes to Plato" (1978, p. 39). If one would follow Whitehead's footsteps, contemporary discussions of toleration might best be depicted as didaskalia to the writings of John Locke. Seminal intellectual figures such as Plato and Locke alongside other luminaries from the philosophical tradition provide us with a (giant's) shoulder on which to stand on, while grappling with whatever the task of scholarly research one is focusing on.

As a repository of knowledge on a particular topic, reference works including encyclopedias, handbooks, and companions provide another such shoulder on which to stand upon. Yet, the main goal of this publishing project is not only one of customary purpose reference work has been usually associated with. Ultimately, any author or editor has its own overall plan on how the volume one is either writing or editing should turn out at the end. For example, Ian Fleming supposedly wrote *Casino Royale*, the first of a series of novels on what turned out to be the global franchise of James Bond, to end all spy stories. This reference work obviously does not point in this direction.

The overall aim of this handbook has been to bring together a set of contributions presenting some of the most distinctive, complex, and controversial aspects associated with the idea of toleration. Interestingly enough, there are plenty of these issues around, making the navigation in this area of scholarly research particularly distressing. Its ambivalent character and its enigmatic nature together with its allegedly exotic origins and complex legacy are just some of the character traits toleration has been associated with. The immediate impulse one encounters when faced with the scholarly literature on toleration would most probably resemble Winston Churchill's puzzling observation summed up in the parable of "a riddle wrapped in a mystery inside an enigma." This handbook therefore aims to provide a conceptual cartography that would enable anyone making use of it a safe journey through the many tumultuous issues this area of scholarly research is replete with.

In contrast to some of the other concepts from the pantheon of political ideas, toleration has been graced with a number of monographs, articles, journal special issues, and edited collections that have popped up around the globe. Nevertheless, despite a steady supply of scholarly output, no reference work on toleration has been available to this date. This publishing project aims to fill this gap in the academic market by bringing together more than 50 chapters by leading academics in this area of scholarly research on some of the most pressing and timely issues toleration has been associated with.

Like any scholarly publication, this reference work has its fair share of lost opportunities. They would have been much more numerous if it wouldn't be for the editorial team at Palgrave. In particular, I would like to thank Ambra Finotello, senior commissioning editor in politics at Palgrave, and Michael Hermann, chief editor of the MRW series at Springer, for supporting the idea of this handbook and for helping out in the transition from "book proposal" to "book contract" for this publishing project (usually a distressing period for any author or volume editor). My most profound thanks go to Eleanor Gaffney, editor at Palgrave, for her superb editorial skills, patience, care, and dedication to this handbook. Any author or volume editor could not find better editorial cooperation than Eleanor has provided both to me as volume editor and, I believe, to each of the contributors to this handbook.

Last but not least, I would like to dedicate this handbook to my wife Mojca and our two sons, Žiga and Jakob. It is in their company that the idea for this handbook arose during a summer holiday back in 2018 on the island of Mljet in Croatia. Perhaps more than anyone else, they exemplify a form of "liberal expectancy" the idea of toleration has been associated with. Describing the many nuances of their toleration (alongside their unfailing support and encouragement) would take another volume to straight out.

September 2021   Mitja Sardoč

References

Whitehead N (1978 [1929]) Process and reality (Gifford lectures delivered in the University of Edinburgh during the session 1927–28). Free Press, New York

Contents

Volume 1

1. **The Trouble with Toleration** 1
   Mitja Sardoč

2. **Toleration: Concept and Conceptions** 11
   Rainer Forst

3. **Defining Toleration** 23
   Andrew Jason Cohen

4. **What Toleration Is Not** 53
   David Heyd

5. **Toleration** 71
   Anna Elisabetta Galeotti

6. **Paradoxes of Toleration** 93
   Peter Königs

7. **The Epistemic Justification for Tolerance** 109
   Joshua C. Thurow

8. **Political Toleration Explained** 129
   Peter Balint

9. **Toleration, Respect for Persons, and the Free Speech Right to Do Moral Wrong** 149
   Kristian Skagen Ekeli

10. **Toleration and Political Change** 173
    Lucia M. Rafanelli

11. **Toleration and the Law** 189
    Stijn Smet

12. **Toleration and Domination** 209
    Monica Mookherjee

13	**State Responses to Incongruence: Toleration and Transformation**	229
	Paul Billingham	
14	**Toleration and State Neutrality: The Case of Symbolic FGM**	249
	Federico Zuolo	
15	**Toleration of Moral Offense**	263
	Thomas E. Hill Jr	
16	**Moralism and Anti-Moralism in Theories of Toleration**	277
	John Christian Laursen and Zachary Dorson	
17	**Toleration and Neutrality**	299
	Peter Jones	
18	**Political Toleration as Substantive Neutrality**	325
	Bryan T. McGraw	
19	**Conscientious Exemptions: Between Toleration, Neutrality, and Respect**	341
	Yossi Nehushtan	
20	**Toleration and Its Possibilities: Relativism, Skepticism, and Pluralism**	363
	John William Tate	
21	**Toleration, Reasonableness, and Power**	397
	Thomas M. Besch and Jung-Sook Lee	
22	**Toleration and Reasonableness**	419
	Roberta Sala	
23	**International Toleration**	439
	Pietro Maffettone	
24	**Toleration and Tolerance in a Global Context**	455
	Vicki A. Spencer	
25	**Two Models of Toleration**	477
	Will Kymlicka	
26	**Modus Vivendi Toleration**	499
	Manon Westphal	
27	**Multiculturalism and Toleration**	519
	Sune Lægaard	
28	**Recognition and Toleration**	541
	Cillian McBride	
29	**Toleration and Dignity**	563
	Colin Bird	

30	**Toleration and Respect** John William Tate	583

Volume 2

31	**Toleration and Justice** Fabio Macioce	615
32	**The Logic of Intolerance** Richard Dees	635
33	**Intolerance and Populism** Nenad Miščević	653
34	**Fear and Toleration** Robert Paul Churchill	673
35	**Toleration, "Mindsight" and the Epistemic Virtues** Colin Farrelly	699
36	**Tough on Tolerance: The Vice of Virtue** Thomas Nys and Bart Engelen	719
37	**Toleration and Close Personal Relationships** Michael Kühler	737
38	**Hospitality and Toleration** Andrew Fiala	757
39	**Toleration and Compassion: A Conceptual Comparison** Yossi Nehushtan and Emily Prince	777
40	**Toleration and Religion** John William Tate	797
41	**Toleration and Religious Discrimination** Andrew Shorten	827
42	**Religious Toleration and Social Contract Theories of Justice** Phillip J. Donnelly	853
43	**Toleration and the Protestant Tradition** Manfred Svensson	873
44	**Atheist Toleration** Charles Devellennes	887
45	**Toleration and the Right to Freedom of Religion in Education** Zdenko Kodelja	905
46	**Education and Toleration** Johannes Drerup	925

47	**Toleration, Liberal Education, and the Accommodation of Diversity** 951
	Ole Henrik Borchgrevink Hansen
48	**Toleration Before Toleration** 969
	Cary J. Nederman
49	**Early Modern Arguments for Toleration** 993
	Andrew R. Murphy
50	**Thomas Hobbes and the Conditionality of Toleration** 1009
	J. Judd Owen
51	**John Locke and Religious Toleration** 1023
	John William Tate
52	**"Stop Being So Judgmental!": A Spinozist Model of Personal Tolerance** 1077
	Justin Steinberg
53	**Toleration and Liberty of Conscience** 1095
	Jon Mahoney
54	**Tolerating Racism and Hate Speech: A Critique of C.E. Baker's "Almost" Absolutism** 1115
	Raphael Cohen-Almagor
55	**Toleration of Free Speech: Imposing Limits on Elected Officials** 1139
	Amos N. Guiora
Index	 1161

About the Editor

Mitja Sardoč (PhD) is senior research associate at the Educational Research Institute in Ljubljana (Slovenia). His research interests and expertise include philosophy of education, political philosophy, and education policy. Over the last two decades he has been member of several (national and international) research projects on multiculturalism, diversity, equality of opportunity, patriotism, citizenship education, etc. During the last few years, his research interest has moved to some of the conceptual and policy-oriented issues associated with radicalization, violent extremism, and conflicting diversity. Between 2018 and 2021, he carried out a research project "Radicalisation and Violent Extremism: Philosophical, Sociological and Educational Perspective(s)" funded by the Slovenian Research Agency as part of its "basic research projects" program (the most selective research funding scheme for basic research in Slovenia). He is author of more than 40 scholarly articles and editor of a number of journal special issues on radicalization and violent extremism, citizenship education, multiculturalism, toleration, the American Dream, equality of opportunity, and patriotism. He acted as an expert for various research initiatives including the Organization for Security and Co-operation in Europe (OSCE), the Council of Europe, and the Slovene Ministry of Foreign Affairs. He also carried out consultancy work for other international institutions (e.g., Cardiff University, ODIHR). He is Managing Editor of *Theory and Research in Education* (http://tre.sagepub.com/), Editor-in-Chief of *The Handbook of Patriotism*, and editor of *The Impacts of Neoliberal Discourse and Language in Education* published by Routledge. Between September and December 2019, he was a visiting fellow at the Robert Schuman Centre for Advanced Studies at the

European University Institute in Florence (Italy). Additional information (including the list of publications) is available at the website: https://www.researchgate.net/profile/Mitja_Sardoc

Contributors

Peter Balint School of Humanities and Social Sciences, UNSW Canberra, Canberra, ACT, Australia

Thomas M. Besch School of Philosophy, Wuhan University, Wuhan, Hubei, China Department of Philosophy, The University of Sydney, Sydney, NSW, Australia

Paul Billingham Department of Politics and International Relations and Magdalen College, University of Oxford, Oxford, UK

Colin Bird Department of Politics, Program in Political Philosophy, Policy, and Law, University of Virginia, Charlottesville, VA, USA

Robert Paul Churchill Department of Philosophy, George Washington University, Westminster, MD, USA

Andrew Jason Cohen Georgia State University, Atlanta, GA, USA

Raphael Cohen-Almagor University of Hull, Hull, UK

Richard Dees University of Rochester, Rochester, NY, USA

Charles Devellennes University of Kent, Canterbury, UK

Phillip J. Donnelly Baylor University, Waco, TX, USA

Zachary Dorson University of California, Riverside, Riverside, CA, USA

Johannes Drerup Technische Universität Dortmund, Dortmund, Germany

Kristian Skagen Ekeli University of Stavanger, Stavanger, Norway

Bart Engelen Tilburg University, Tilburg, The Netherlands

Colin Farrelly Queen's University, Kingston, Canada

Andrew Fiala Department of Philosophy, California State University, Fresno, CA, USA

Rainer Forst Goethe University, Normative Orders Research Centre, Frankfurt/Main, Germany

Anna Elisabetta Galeotti Università del Piemonte Orientale, Vercelli, Italy

Amos N. Guiora S.J. Quinney College of Law, University of Utah, Salt Lake City, UT, USA

Ole Henrik Borchgrevink Hansen Ostfold University College, School of Education, Ostfold, Norway

David Heyd The Hebrew University of Jerusalem, Jerusalem, Israel

Thomas E. Hill Jr Department of Philosophy, University of North Carolina, Chapel Hill, NC, USA

Peter Jones Newcastle University, Newcastle upon Tyne, UK

Zdenko Kodelja Educational Research Institute, Ljubljana, Slovenia

Peter Königs Human Technology Center, Applied Ethics, RWTH Aachen University, Aachen, Germany

Michael Kühler Department of Philosophy, University of Münster, Münster, Germany

Will Kymlicka Department of Philosophy, Queen's University, Kingston, ON, Canada

Sune Lægaard Department of Communication and Arts, Roskilde University, Roskilde, Denmark

John Christian Laursen University of California, Riverside, Riverside, CA, USA

Jung-Sook Lee School of Social Sciences, UNSW Sydney, Sydney, NSW, Australia

Fabio Macioce Law School, Lumsa University, Rome, Italy

Pietro Maffettone Political Science Department, University of Napoli, Federico II, Naples, Italy

Jon Mahoney Department of Philosophy, Kansas State University, Manhattan, KS, USA

Cillian McBride Queen's University Belfast, Belfast, UK

Bryan T. McGraw Wheaton College, Wheaton, IL, USA

Nenad Miščević University of Maribor, Maribor, Slovenia

Monica Mookherjee School of Social, Political and Global Studies, Keele University, Stoke-on-Trent, Staffordshire, UK

Andrew R. Murphy Department of Political Science, Virginia Commonwealth University, Richmond, VA, USA

Cary J. Nederman Department of Political Science, Texas A&M University, College Station, TX, USA

Yossi Nehushtan Keele University, Newcastle-Under-Lyme, UK

Thomas Nys University of Amsterdam, Amsterdam, The Netherlands

J. Judd Owen Department of Political Science, Emory University, Atlanta, GA, USA

Emily Prince University of Sheffield, Sheffield, UK

Lucia M. Rafanelli The George Washington University, Washington, DC, USA

Roberta Sala Faculty of Philosophy, Vita-Salute San Raffaele University, Milan, Italy

Mitja Sardoč Educational Research Institute, Ljubljana, Slovenia

Andrew Shorten Department of Politics and Public Administration, University of Limerick, Limerick, Ireland

Stijn Smet Faculty of Law, Hasselt University, Hasselt, Belgium

Vicki A. Spencer Politics, School of Social Sciences, University of Otago, Dunedin, New Zealand

Justin Steinberg Brooklyn College and CUNY Graduate Center, New York, NY, USA

Manfred Svensson Department of Philosophy, Universidad de los Andes, Santiago, Chile

John William Tate Discipline of Politics and International Relations, Newcastle Business School, College of Human and Social Futures, University of Newcastle, Newcastle, NSW, Australia

Joshua C. Thurow University of Texas at San Antonio, San Antonio, TX, USA

Manon Westphal Institute of Political Science, University of Münster, Münster, Germany

Federico Zuolo Department of Classics, Philosophy and History, University of Genova, Genova, Italy

Toleration and Justice

31

Fabio Macioce

Contents

Introduction	616
Toleration and Justice: The Liberal Paradigm and its Critics	617
Rawls on Toleration and Justice	620
Forst: Toleration, Justice, and Reason	623
Toleration, Justice, and the Political Inclusion of the Other	626
Summary and Future Directions	631
References	632

Abstract

In this chapter, the relation between toleration and justice is analyzed starting by discussing the liberal perspective, and taking into consideration both its historical roots and its more recent developments. Within this approach, toleration provided a viable strategy for the coexistence of the beliefs, values, and ways of life of all citizens, by dividing the political sphere from the private realm, and neutralizing both these areas. The chapter also analyzes the criticisms that have been addressed to the liberal account of toleration, like the fact that the neutrality principle reflects the values and the conception of the dominant majority, in so neglecting power imbalances, and does not consider social advantages and disadvantages related to the public/private distinction. In the second part, the chapter discusses two perspectives on the relation between toleration and justice, those of John Rawls and Rainer Forst, which are considered as partially answering these criticisms. While Rawls' theory does not precisely define the relation between toleration and justice, and it has been considered as excessively linked to an ideal and initial situation, the theory of Rainer Forst takes power relations explicitly into account, by distinguishing different conceptions of toleration. The analysis of both the theories highlights that the role played by reason in questions concerning toleration may overshadow the fact that reason and reasonableness are

F. Macioce (✉)
Law School, Lumsa University, Rome, Italy

always exercised within specific power relations. Therefore, in the final part of the chapter, accounts of toleration that start from the recognition of specific intergroup relations, and that are aimed at counterbalancing them as a political objective, are discussed. In these accounts, toleration is understood as delivering justice through social and political inclusion, and as counterbalancing political asymmetries, being given in cases that are beyond the range of what we can recognize and accommodate.

Keywords

Justice · Liberalism · Rawls · Forst · Recognition · Political inclusion · Asymmetry

Introduction

While no one wants to live in a society where either justice or toleration is denied, the relation between toleration and justice is not completely clear: on the one hand, it is possible to say that justice has priority over toleration, because toleration is both grounded on justice, which provides the reasons for it, and is also limited by it, because justice is taken as the criterion for deciding what one shall tolerate, and what one shall not. On the other hand, a tolerant society is the basis (that is, it is either the ideal framework, or the necessary condition) to deliver a just society: only to the extent to which people accept to tolerate each other, they may live together and discuss peacefully, therefore establishing mutually acceptable rules and principles to design a just society.

Therefore, and aside from their being allocated a logical or axiological priority, it is necessary to clarify the sense in which toleration and justice are spoken of. For instance, it is not the same to talk about religious toleration in countries where religious freedom and equality among religions are sanctioned by the national Constitutions, and attempt to do the same when referring to countries where such a liberty is not affirmed, or is even expressly denied. At the same time, it is not the same to discuss toleration by referring to social practices, and to forms of social discrimination (that are unfortunately possible, and even frequent, even in countries where freedom of religion is recognized by the constitution), or to do the same by considering public institutions and how they deal with this issue. Similarly, if one considers the limits to hate speech, it is not necessary – in some countries – to call toleration into question, rather a (more or less) difficult interpretation of existing norms concerning freedom of speech: not only does much depend on the specific legal system that is considered, and on the kind of speech that is under scrutiny, so that different answers are possible for the US, France, Germany, etc. What is at stake, is that in all these cases the answers will depend on the enforcing of existing rules (and, of course, on the case law of local courts), but not on the appeal to the virtue of tolerance, with regard to behaviors one disapproves of (Heyd 2008, 178). Therefore, in the analysis of relations between toleration and justice, it is useful to distinguish between forms of toleration that have already been translated into principles and rules, and the challenges arising within a gray area where intolerant behaviors are indeed possible, for both single individuals and public authorities, but there are sound reasons not to do so, opting instead for toleration.

Unfortunately, many theories on toleration, and many analyses of the relation between toleration and justice, often concern either a hypothetical initial situation, or an idealized social framework (that is, not situated in any place and at any time). In these cases, toleration is a specific virtue that agents must display to deliver a system which may be just, fair, liberal, and peaceful. But if the social system is already in place, and an existing setting (this or that country, nowadays) is analyzed, the framework is complicated by the existence of a settled "we," and by the fact that such a "we" is allowed to decide whether or not to tolerate a specific "other," starting from a power imbalance. In the real world, the existence and the authority of the state must be presupposed: "it is already established that there is a «we» who are faced with the problem of determining how far to tolerate particular groups in «our» midst" (Kukathas 1997, 71). For this reason, it has rightly been argued that the notion of tolerance itself can be used to stress the distinction, and the subsequent power imbalance, between "us, the tolerant," and "them, the intolerant" and thereby the morally inferior: values such as equality, freedom, and tolerance may be used – even unintentionally – to compare "our" social practices and values with the alleged intolerance of some immigrant groups (for instance, Muslims), and to draw the line between us and them, in so reinforcing segregation and misrecognition (Van der Veer 2006). Analogously, in the international realm, the "identification of liberal democracies with tolerance and of non-liberal regimes with fundamentalism discursively articulates the global moral superiority of the West," and may also legitimize forms of political or economic exploitation toward the non-West (Brown 2006, 37). Therefore, it may be useful to call into question these power asymmetries, by asking to what extent toleration is consistent with them, and to what extent it could even be counterbalancing them.

In this chapter, the relation between toleration and justice will be analyzed starting by discussing the liberal perspective. Within this approach, toleration *delivers* justice, because it is affirmed as one of the basic features of a political system, which is just because individual liberties are affirmed; however, power imbalances are not always taken into account, and toleration partially overlaps both the enforcement of already existing rules and the respect of legal principles. Two perspectives on the relation between toleration and justice will be analyzed, those of John Rawls and Rainer Forst, discussing their respective merits and shortcomings: the role that reasonableness plays within these theories will also be analyzed. Finally, the relationship between toleration, justice, and the need to preserve social cohesion among different groups will be discussed.

Toleration and Justice: The Liberal Paradigm and its Critics

Toleration is a typical feature of liberal political theories: more precisely, it is one of the fundamental values that distinguish a liberal society, along with equality and freedom. Liberal thinkers agree on the fact that enforcing toleration is a political priority: the fact of pluralism, and recognition at the political level that it is legitimate for individuals to differ on issues concerning values, religion, morality, political ideologies, and good, makes toleration necessary in order to permit a wide range of lifestyles, religious and moral communities, and practices to coexist in peace (McKinnon 2006, 16).

The historical reasons for such a strict connection between toleration and liberalism are known. Toleration emerged as the best political solution to the devastating religious wars that took place in Europe after the Reformation, and it provided a viable strategy for the coexistence of the beliefs, values, and ways of life of all citizens, without sacrificing individual freedoms through state coercion. And given the fact that the main goal of liberalism has been precisely that of limiting any justifiable coercion on the part of the state, in so fostering individual freedom and autonomy, toleration appeared to be an essential feature of the liberal project (Galeotti 2002, 23). Therefore, even if many accounts of toleration have been given within the liberal perspective, the demarcation of society into two areas appears to be a common pattern, through which toleration becomes a practical political strategy: on the one hand, the political sphere, subject to public authorities and where coercion may be exercised in order to secure order and peace; on the other hand, the private sphere, where any political interference must be suspended, and therefore toleration is mainly located.

Therefore, first, toleration meant the neutralization of the private realm, in a political sense. The private sphere has been recognized as the realm of autonomy and conscience, a space where protection against political intervention was granted, and at the same time the place where beliefs and values are circumscribed, not being allowed to interfere with political decisions. Second – but also later on (Galeotti 2002, 25) – toleration entailed the neutralization of the public, political area. The secularization of the state led to the neutralization of the public realm, and to the full enforcement of toleration also in this area. Within the secular state not only is any interference in the private realm (that is, in matters of religious and moral doctrine) banned, but it is also affirmed the refusal of any form of public favor directed toward one among the many religious (or moral) views: toleration becomes a criterion for any legitimate political action, not allowing citizens to be discriminated because of their views, more than merely protecting them against positive interference in religious matters.

Within the public area, individual differences must be ignored, at least those that are linked to beliefs, value choices, and religious views. Other factors matter, such as merit, talent, effort, actions, and so on. However, state neutrality simply means that the rules governing the public sphere can be justified by reasons that must not be biased, and that heretic or deviant practices are only permitted within the private realm: "Every man has commission to admonish, exhort, convince another of error, and, by reasoning, to draw him into truth; but to give laws, receive obedience, and compel with the sword, belongs to none but the magistrate. And, upon this ground, I affirm that the magistrate's power extends not to the establishing of any articles of faith, or forms of worship, by the force of his laws. For laws are of no force at all without penalties, and penalties in this case are absolutely impertinent, because they are not proper to convince the mind." (Locke 2016, 129). In this perspective, toleration is the basic feature of a political system where individual liberties are affirmed and protected, and where any individual is allowed to pursue his/her objectives, provided he/she does not harm others, and does not claim public endorsement of his/her own views.

A number of criticisms have been addressed to the liberal account of toleration. For instance, it has been argued that the private/public distinction is not neutral in itself, with respect to the plurality of beliefs and practices found in diverse societies, but it reflects the values and the conception of the dominant majority (Bader 1997; Kymlicka 1989; Taylor 1994). Additionally, the neutrality principle "simply overlooks the public/private dimension that regulates the very working of the neutrality principle" (Galeotti 1993, 592): as long as citizens are free to pursue their own ideals and to practice their culture in the private realm, and as long as they "should disregard their particular membership and be 'just citizens' on an equal basis" in the public sphere (ibidem), the fact of holding the power to draw the line between the public and the private realm is pivotal. As Galeotti states, not only modern democracies need to allow minority members freedom of expression or freedom of religion, but liberal states should also "counter the advantages or disadvantages that (they) have accumulated over a long period of discrimination" (Galeotti 2002, 65). If minority members' beliefs and practices are tolerated in the sense of mere permission, and if they are relegated into the private realm, without allowing them any form of public recognition, substantial equality is lacking: members of these groups are not equal to members of the majority, because they do not enjoy public respect. Moreover, the withdrawal of (his/her own) personal membership is not equally easy for everyone: the pressure of the state can be different for those who belong to minority groups, that is for those who experience the pressure of other loyalties and other memberships, in addition to that of the state. Such a kind of pressure is not exclusively experienced by cultural minorities: as Young correctly observed, "dominant institutions support norms and expectations that privilege some groups and render others deviant. Some of these are cultural norms, but others are norms of capability, social role, sexual desire, or location in the division of labor" (Young 1999, 415). If a given diversity (for instance, a religious diversity) is relegated to the private realm, it is denied equal public legitimacy with other forms of belonging (for instance, political identity) and with other creeds (Jones 2006, 123). Therefore, in so far as that diversity is related to a minority, and it is part of the minority's identity, the group associated with it does bear a social stigma: its members lack a crucial condition for self-esteem and well-being (Galeotti 1993, 597).

In sum, liberal conceptions overestimate the neutrality principle, and underestimate power imbalances. On the one hand, they tend to neglect the fact that the neutrality principle reflects the values and the conception of the dominant majority, being not neutral in itself. On the other hand, they do not consider social advantages and disadvantages related to such a distinction, in addition to the political exclusion it entails, for those who are members of minority groups. Therefore, even if toleration is correctly understood as the necessary political premise of a just society, at least within what has been called the Westphalian project (Floridi 2015), it is understood in an overly idealized fashion, neglecting power relations between groups, and over-emphasizing the neutrality of the public sphere as a trump card for moral conflicts in a pluralistic society.

Rawls on Toleration and Justice

Within the liberal paradigm, Rawls' conception partially answers the above mentioned challenges, both by recognizing that toleration requires its being grounded in a conception of justice, and by arguing that the line dividing what may or may not be tolerated shall be drawn accordant with a reasonable agreement between all the subjects involved, on an equal basis, rather than adhering to the will of a majority. However, Rawls' conception of toleration has been criticized for different reasons: first, it rests on a certain circularity between toleration and justice; second, it is not really freestanding, being grounded on certain values that are culturally embedded; third, it is excessively linked to an ideal and initial situation, without adequately considering challenges arising in a setting where power relations are already in place.

Rawls' main goal is to discuss a conception of justice, which is viable in contemporary pluralistic democracies (Rawls 1993). In *Political Liberalism* the question of toleration is clearly stated: "How is it possible for there to exist over time a just and stable society of free and equal citizens who still remain profoundly divided by reasonable religious, philosophical, and moral doctrines?" (Rawls 1993, 47). The answer, according to Rawls, is not that of neutralizing the public sphere, and of relegating individual beliefs and creed in the private realm; for a liberal and pluralistic society to be possible, its structure must be effectively "regulated by a political conception of justice that is the focus of an overlapping consensus of at least the reasonable comprehensive doctrines affirmed by its citizens" (p. 48).

Therefore, at least at first glance, justice (as equity) *delivers* a tolerant and liberal society: a political conception of justice, which is freestanding (not derived from a comprehensive moral doctrine applied to the basic structure of society), which can be supported by various reasonable comprehensive doctrines, and which is developed on the common ground of certain fundamental ideas that command widespread agreement, is the basis of an overlapping consensus, and may be accepted by people who affirm different comprehensive moral/religious doctrines.

This is also why toleration is not understood by Rawls as a mere modus vivendi. First, it requires (being both delivered by and limited by) a conception of justice. Second, all those who participate in the consensus "accept that conception for moral reasons of one sort or another" (Scheffler 1994, 7). Additionally, it is not liable to be affected by changes in power relations among groups within the society itself, in so providing a greater stability for the structure of the society (Scheffler 1994, 7–8). The duty of toleration comes from the duty to treat other fellow citizens reasonably in the public arena, not from the mere desire to preserve the conditions for order and peace: as long as citizens with different views are reasonable, they can consent to principles of justice, and therefore accept to tolerate each other (insofar as toleration is one feature, among others, of a just social order). The difference between a mere modus vivendi and toleration grounded on justice (as fairness), is that in the first hypothesis the existing balance of power determines the condition for toleration, and its eventual abandonment (if the power imbalance changes, the reasons for toleration change too), while in the second people will remain committed to the principles of justice (McKinnon 2006, 69). Whether and to what extent a certain practice or belief must be tolerated, depends on its compatibility with such a conception of justice: "The aim of a well-ordered society, is to preserve and strengthen its institutions of justice. If a religion is denied its full expression, presumably it is because it is in violation of the equal liberties of the others" (Rawls 1999a, 370).

However, three main questions arise: first, the relation between toleration and justice is less clear cut than one might think, and it is possible to highlight a certain circularity between the two poles, which undermines the reasoning itself. On the one hand, as Floridi rightly observes (Floridi 2015), within Rawls' political liberalism toleration is also a necessary condition for justice (and not only vice versa), because it can make the latter more likely. It is only among reciprocally tolerant agents that principles of justice may be determinate: insofar as persons are deemed reasonable (persons that, however convinced of their views, admit that other people may rationally disagree, and refrain from using state power to impose their preferred political principles on others), they will reject imposition of their values on others, being committed to the use of public reason to solve problems of justice (Rawls 1993, 61). On the other hand, Rawls sets the limit of toleration with regard to those doctrines, which are "incompatible with the essentials of public reason and a democratic polity" (Rawls 1999b, 576). A society is justified in excluding and not tolerating them, so that they do not undermine the very possibility of the society: "Let us now consider whether justice requires the toleration of the intolerant, and if so under what conditions. There are a variety of situations in which this question arises. Some political parties in democratic states hold doctrines that commit them to suppress constitutional liberties whenever they have the power. Again, there are those who reject intellectual freedom but who nevertheless hold positions in the university. It may appear that toleration in these cases is inconsistent with the principles of justice, or at any rate not required by them" (Rawls 1999a, 190). As one can see, here justice delivers toleration, at least in the sense that it determines both its limits and criteria of applicability.

Second, Rawls' conception of toleration and justice is not completely freestanding, being rather grounded both on the value of autonomy (Kukathas 1997, 74), and on a very specific conception of reasonableness (Waldron 2003, 21). Both are necessary to admit Rawlsian toleration, but none of them are really self-booting. Toleration and justice are grounded – more evidently in Theory of Justice, but also in Political Liberalism – on the value of individual autonomy. When Rawls argues that a civic education for children is necessary, and that it should "prepare them to be fully cooperating members of society and enable them to be self-supporting; it should also encourage the political virtues so that they want to honour the fair terms of social cooperation in their relations with the rest of society," he is admitting ("often with regret," he writes politely) that a liberal society must educate citizens into a comprehensive liberal conception. And since a liberal society needs to be protected against non-liberal doctrines, imposing a liberal conception of the good (autonomy, in our case) on individuals is necessary, against non-autonomy supporting ways of life (Fitzmaurice 1993, 13). In this sense, this conception is not completely consistent with Rawls' aim of remaining silent on questions concerning values, and of making use only of ideas of justice not unique to any particular view or way of life.

Third, Rawls conception is strongly connected to the concept (and the value) of reasonableness. Both the reasons for toleration and its limits are grounded on the premise of subjective reasonableness. The very initial question is: how is it possible for there to be a just and stable society of free and equal citizens who still remain profoundly divided by *reasonable* religious moral and philosophical doctrines? Similarly, the overlapping consensus is reached among *reasonable* comprehensive doctrines affirmed by citizens. Finally, a society is justified in excluding aims and views that are *unreasonable* (conceptions of the good that are not intelligible in light of "the burdens of judgment"), so that they do not undermine the unity and justice of the society (Waldron 2003, 22). Such a conception has been criticized, for two main reasons: first, because it excludes from the range of toleration those doctrines which are more distant from the liberal-democratic framework (in so reducing toleration to what is so easy to tolerate, that it would not be necessary to tolerate); second, because it excludes passions and feelings from the political domain (Mouffe 2000), in so giving an unrealistic and idealized view of the political debate, as well as of decisions concerning toleration.

On the one hand, Rawls draws the line between tolerable and intolerable by using the principle of reasonable justification: any conception of the good is allowed to participate in the public debate, interacting with each other within a framework of rules that give to each actor equal chances to raise claims (that is, to both minorities as well as to the majority). Therefore, according to the principle of reasonable justification, arguments for and against any conception must be mutually justifiable, and not based on a prejudicial denial of what is different. The acceptance of this principle draws the limits of the tolerable, thus defining what may be recognized, and what may not, for those who deny it also deny the basic norms of dialogue and democratic coexistence (Calhoun 2002).

However, the risk of overemphasizing the principle or reasonableness is that of limiting recognition of these differences that in a pluralistic society are already allowed (by the freedom of religion, worship, and conscience, by freedom of association, by the principle of nondiscrimination, etc.. . .). As Habermas recognized in a widely known article, the liberal state can neither expect of all citizens that they justify their claims independently of their religious convictions or world views, nor that every participant to the public discourse is obligated to supplement his/her public statements of cultural and religious convictions by equivalents in a generally accessible language. (Habermas 2006, 9). This would mean imposing an undue psychological burden on those citizens, whose practices and world views are rooted in a faith, or in a traditional culture, allowing them to express and justify their convictions only by translating them into rationally understandable arguments. On the contrary, we need not to "estrange 'mono-glot' citizens from the political process," even if their religious or traditional language is the only one they can speak in public, and they should be fully perceived as members of the community, because "we should not over-hastily reduce the polyphonic complexity of public voices" (Habermas 2006, 10). To treat other fellow citizens reasonably in the public arena may not be enough, if some are not able to take part in it, otherwise we "violate the democratic commitment to political egalitarianism" (Bohman 2003, 118). In sum, as Raimon Panikkar correctly stated, toleration arises in the area of what is *not negotiable* for us: all the rest is a matter of acceptance, or compromise, or savoir-faire (Panikkar 1979, 207). Limiting toleration with the proviso of the acceptation of discourse ethics, and/or of basic principles of our constitutional charters, does mean limiting toleration to what is internal to the current power imbalance between majority and minorities, between the settled "we" (who draw the line of what is reasonable and acceptable) and the "others": toleration does not end here, rather it begins here.

On the other hand, a second limit of the Rawlsian approach is to underestimate the weight of passions and feelings in the political domain, being curtailed in an idealized framework. On the contrary, since the relationship between alternative views becomes relevant in the public sphere, we cannot neglect how much passions and feelings shape it. In writings about the role of shame and disgust in the process of group-formation and social intolerance, for instance, Nussbaum highlights how these feelings are grounded in a kind of child pain of imperfection and incompetence that are projected outward onto subordinate groups (Nussbaum 2006). Similarly, recent research on intergroup toleration show how practical decisions concerning toleration may depend on people's own ideologies and motivations (Jost 2017), and how initial attitudes (prejudices, unmotivated beliefs, etc.) condition the effective implementation of tolerant social rules. Moreover, the impact of rigid attitudes has been analyzed, such as cognitive inflexibility, close-mindedness, and a desire for simplicity and certainty, on subjective openness to toleration and disposition toward dissenting beliefs and practices (Verkuyten 2019, 13). Of course, subjective attitudes may change: the very fact of living with cultural diversity may (hopefully, but not necessarily) lead to gradually adapt to it, and accept new behaviors and norms. What is at stake, however, is that a too stark connection between toleration and reasonableness may both cloud the role played by these feelings, and the role played by unreasonable factors (attitudes, prejudices, passions, emotions, etc.) in determining public policies and decisions concerning intergroup toleration (Verkuyten 2019, 14).

Forst: Toleration, Justice, and Reason

Differently from Rawls, toleration is clearly understood by Rainer Forst as a virtue of justice (that is, toleration is grounded on justice, as well as limited by it), in so resolving the circularity between the two; additionally, power relations are explicitly taken into account, by distinguishing different conceptions of toleration; finally, the question of toleration is set in nonutopian terms, by considering existing legal systems and established rules in order to understand its meaning and its limits. However, Forst' view of toleration is still firmly grounded on the role of reason and reasonableness: when Forst argues that toleration must be grounded on intersubjectively justifiable reasons, he is drawing the threshold of toleration on something that is not evident, being rather the object of the debate in pluralistic societies. Additionally, his conception of toleration as respect blurs intergroup power imbalances, over-emphasizing the equal moral-political standing of the parties, and neglecting the asymmetry between tolerator and tolerated.

In Forst' view, the analysis of toleration is developed from a nonutopian perspective. Differently from Rawls, he precisely defines when, and under what conditions, we may talk of toleration, and what its characteristics are (Forst 2004, 2012), in so distinguishing cases where referring to toleration is appropriate, and cases where it is not, due to the characteristics of the legal system. As a consequence, the vertical and/or horizontal relationship between tolerator and tolerated should be specified, as well as the object (beliefs, practices, etc....) of toleration. Second, according to the *objection component*, we tolerate only practices, beliefs, or acts that we disapprove of, thereby distinguishing toleration from a generic non-interference. Third, there must be a number of (practical or theoretical) factors that provide reasons for acceptance, encompassing the action and beliefs tolerated, and making them acceptable though not positively evaluable (King 1976). At the same time, fourth, any form of toleration is accompanied by the idea of a limit: we can tolerate objectionable things, provided we make clear what lies beyond such a sphere of toleration, what is to be rejected because reasons for acceptance and tolerance are not strong enough (Forst 2003, 72). Fifth, the exercise of toleration must be voluntary, since otherwise we should talk of suffering, endurance, or patience, rather than of toleration. This is the reason why citizens of any European country do not properly tolerate those who are of a different religion, because legal systems, in granting to anyone freedom of religion and conscience, compel them to "accept" those who are – in their eyes – heretics or nonbelievers (Churchill 1997): they may suffer, or abstain from illegal behaviors (such as interfering with freedom of worship or the religion of other people), but they do not tolerate anything.

Additionally, Forst takes intergroup relations seriously into account, considering power imbalance as an element for distinguishing between different conceptions of toleration. Even if all these conceptions are valid examples of toleration, according to Forst the respect conception is superior to the others in terms of justice (Forst 2003), being grounded on moral reasons, rather than on mere opportunity or permissiveness. Toleration may in fact be given in asymmetrical relations of power, for instance, where the most powerful group tolerates a powerless minority, but only to the extent that the tolerated party accepts the dominant position of the majority (permission conception). Alternatively, toleration may be more reciprocal (co-existence conception), where intergroup relations are characterized by roughly equal power: in these cases, toleration is a kind of "modus vivendi," i.e., a pragmatic solution to end or avoid conflict. Third, in the respect conception, toleration is grounded on moral/principled reasons: parties respect each other "as moral-political equals in the sense that their common framework of social life should (...) be guided by norms that all parties can equally accept" (Forst 2003, 74), though reciprocally objecting to the others' ethical ways of life. Fourth, and even more demanding, toleration may be understood as the outcome of mutual recognition: parties positively value and appreciate other cultural forms of life or religions, in that they find them ethically attractive and held for good reasons, even if different from their own conception and beliefs.

In Forst' conception, toleration as respect is superior to others precisely in terms of justice: it is more consistent and more plausible than the others, within a legal and political structure that is mutually justifiable for a pluralistic political community of citizens with different ethical beliefs (Forst 2003, 76). In such a framework, to tolerate is the right thing to do, and claims for toleration are raised as claims for justice; on the contrary, intolerance is perceived and portrayed as a form of political injustice.

However, some scholars highlighted that such a connection with justice requires determining the content of justice *before* deciding whether or not to tolerate, even if disagreements on justice are precisely the setting within which we decide whether or not to tolerate anything. Therefore, as Laegard rightly points out, Forst's conception is not helpful in practice, because "it is impossible to determine whether a specific act or policy is an instance of toleration out of respect without first having answered the substantial normative question about what morality or justice requires" (Laegaard 2013, 529). And the criteria Forst provides, that toleration is out of respect (and a virtue of justice) being grounded on inter-subjectively justifiable reasons, is in itself debatable. To say that (in order to be a form of respect) toleration should be grounded on reasons that "all parties can equally accept, and that do not favour one specific 'ethical community'" (Forst 2003, 74; 2012, 56), calls for a standard of generality and/or objectivity, in order to determine the threshold between moral norms that can be justified to all, and ethical values that cannot (Forst 2012, 61). However, as Laegaard argues, this argument seems to be more a question than an answer: given the fact that mere consensus (of the majority, of course) is not enough, the criterion of general acceptability in itself does not determine which norms pass such a threshold, precisely because in contexts of deep pluralism every party can claim that its own norms have got it right. Every party, in other word, starts from the assumption that the norms they are proposing are in fact not reasonably rejectable (Laegaard 2013, 532).

On the other hand, the pivotal role played by reason still remains in Forst's conception. Forst argues that the threshold of toleration must be settled by reason: what is reasonably rejectable is beyond the threshold, whereas what may be reasonably justifiable by arguments that all parties can equally accept, is tolerable. What is not convincing is the assumption that reasons may be generalized and accepted (at least potentially) by any person. Even if reasons are important to determine the objection component, they are at the same time largely subjective: taking pluralism seriously means recognizing that reasonableness is everything but an objective dimension, and that on a number of topics we simply disagree, for reasons we reciprocally find unacceptable. If some people find that there are good reasons to tolerate the headscarf, even if they deem it at odds with their conception of gender equality, they are arguing – for instance – that respect for both freedoms of conscience and religion are reasons that encompass this deviant action, and urge them to accept it, however wrong they may find it. However, these reasons for accepting are *their reasons*, in the sense that they are subjectively acceptable: in the context of a super-diverse society, which is the current starting point for any current discourse concerning toleration, therefore they will not be inter-subjectively acceptable, being rather unconvincing for other people.

Toleration, Justice, and the Political Inclusion of the Other

The role played by reason in questions concerning toleration may overshadow the fact that reason and reasonableness are always exercised within specific power relations. As Forst rightly argues (Forst 2003, 71), reasons for toleration and its limits may change depending on the context (a family, between citizens, between insiders and outsiders, etc.) within which it happens, precisely because power imbalances are different. For this reason, a conception of toleration that starts from the idea of reciprocity, of mutuality, and of horizontal recognition is, or might be, an illusion, not recognizing the framework where toleration takes place. On the contrary, toleration may effectively be understood as delivering justice, but not by anchoring it to reason, or to a certain conception of reasonableness. Rather, it may be understood as a virtue of justice (as Forst does), starting from the recognition of the specific intergroup relations, and aiming at counterbalancing them, as a political objective.

Unfortunately, many discussions on toleration leave completely unaddressed the question of how communities and groups relate to one another, aiming rather at producing an idealized social unity (for instance, under the umbrella of constitutional principles, or of discourse ethics, or reasonableness, etc.). Contrariwise, "many contexts of moral interaction and political conflict involve members of socially and culturally differentiated groups that also stand in specific relations of privilege and oppression with respect to one another (. . .) and this is also part of the definition" (Young 1997, 349). According to Young, it would be impossible to discuss about the just toleration between groups, without analyzing whether intergroup relations are just in themselves, and without considering how power imbalances are linked to oppression and/or privilege. Therefore, in order to take intergroup power balance into account, one should ascertain the specific nature of the society that is under analysis and of its intergroup relations, before debating limits and reasons for toleration.

What is at stake is that toleration may foster social cohesion and political inclusion: as perfectly remarked by Hans Kelsen in his work on democracy (Kelsen 1929, 57), with a play on words that is unfortunately untranslatable in many other languages, there is a deep connection between the social contract (Vertrag), and mutual toleration by the associates (sich vertragen). In other words, toleration *delivers* justice not because it is grounded on (and limited by) reasonableness, that is, on reasons that all parties can equally accept, that do not favor one specific ethical community, and that are beyond the threshold of generality and/or objectivity. Rather, toleration is grounded on the necessity of preserving social cohesion among different groups and people holding different moral and religious views, *even if* they are unable to correctly participate in a democratic debate (that is, to provide arguments within the bounds of reciprocity and generality).

To be more precise, toleration should be understood as being entwined with social and political inclusion. Therefore, a specific regime of toleration (specific political decisions, or specific policies toward minorities) may deliver justice, to the extent it permits to those who are tolerated to contribute to the definition of the society within which they live (Bohman 2003, 121). The aim of a politics of toleration is not (merely) permitting minorities to display the reasons underpinning their practices (this should rather be the aim of any democratic debate under conditions of pluralism): much before, the goal is to include them in the political realm, protecting the very possibility of achieving communication between strangers, even if they are unable to perform such communication in the ways we (the majority) deem fitting. Conflicts and disagreements about reasons "are the normal business of public deliberation, and public communication over such first-order disagreements is preserved by respectful and mutual criticism and scrutiny" (Bohman 2003, 122). Much more than this, what is at stake is the inclusion of strongly different perspectives (ways of living, beliefs, traditions...) within the realm of what is worthy of consideration and scrutiny, in order to grant all citizens equal standing as members of a community. As Scanlon rightly argues, toleration expresses the recognition of a "common membership that is deeper than these conflicts," being rather the recognition of others as entitled (just as we are) to contribute to the definition of our society (Scanlon 1996, 231).

As a consequence, toleration delivers justice through social and political inclusion: to be more precise, it delivers a society which is just, not because its principles and its rules are morally right (from a specific, or even majoritarian, moral point of view), nor because they are accepted as just (as the outcome of a fair procedure, which is deemed rational and reasonable by all those who participated in the deliberative process). First and foremost, toleration delivers a *decent* society (Margalit 1998), a society where everyone is not excluded by that context of recognition that is the basis for self-esteem and respect. To ask some individual to decide between his/her personal belonging, or identity, and participation in public life as a full member of the whole community, is not consistent with such a standard of decency. On the contrary, a decent society is a place where membership is allowed by virtue and not *in spite of* individual identity, being therefore the premise of any possible debate concerning justice.

Thus, first, such a form of toleration obliges us to consider "others" as partners in a relationship of recognition. Those whose beliefs and practices are "different," are recognized as equals, even if they hold in many respects a number of incompatible views: not only are they free and equal in the public sphere, in the sense that they are entitled to the same set of rights as anyone else, but they are equal because society is willing to open to forms of adaptation in order to leave room to them. Diversities are not simply confined to the private realm, and individuals who belong to a minority group do not bear any kind of social stigma, but they are accepted so as to symbolically recognize their public presence (Lukes 1997, 215). Therefore, toleration always involves a "perceptual shift: from beliefs to the subject holding them, or from actions to their agent" (Heyd 1996, 11), being granted not because the practices and beliefs at stake are deemed to be intrinsically valuable, but because the majority acknowledges the agent's intrinsic attachment to these values, it takes his/her specific identity into consideration, and symbolically recognizes its public presence. In a similar vein other scholars argue for a necessary consideration of the political value of emotions that support equal respect, and stress the relation between the specific social ethos, and the kind of tolerating response to minorities' claims (Nussbaum 2006; Wolff 2003, p. 151). Toleration is linked to attitudes, to the willingness to include and respect otherness (or not to do so), and not only to the respect of reasonable claims.

Second, in order to counterbalance the asymmetry of power between groups, toleration is to be enacted as the outcome of an asymmetric burden: something that the majority group should do, even if it may ask nothing (or little) in return. Toleration overlooks the dialectic of reciprocity: it is given in cases that are beyond the range of what we can recognize and accommodate, being something the majority should grant, even without asking for reciprocal forms of accommodation in return (Macioce 2017, 241). Such a conception is similar to that of vertical permission: the main difference is that while toleration as a permission is given, according to Forst, "on the condition that the minority accepts the dominant position of the authority (or majority)" (Forst 2003, 74), it is also possible to argue that such a dominant position must simply be taken as a starting point (as an empirical fact), to be partially balanced by an asymmetrical burden in a relation of recognition. It is precisely because "we" (the majority group) start from a dominant position that we *ought* to tolerate the radical otherness of minority groups, asking nothing or little in return. Differently to the permission conception, here toleration is not given on the premise that tolerated groups will accept their subordination or their political exclusion; rather, it is given on the premise that such a subordinate status has to be balanced (Macioce 2017, 245).

What is at stake is the identification of the reasons for toleration. To determine under what conditions we have reasons to tolerate, and to tolerate even what we deem unreasonable in itself, is necessary. As already mentioned, the general motivation is the inclusion of people and groups in the political realm, not excluding them in virtue of their identity (and the traditions and beliefs that display such an identity). However, we need to identify the specific factors we have to consider in order to know whether to tolerate or not: we need to determine the limits of toleration, that is, those behaviors and practices we cannot tolerate, even for the sake of including minority groups in the political realm. Sociopolitical inclusion may work well as a criterion, both in order to establish what to tolerate, as well as to determine the limits of toleration. As a criterion for delivering toleration, the need for sociopolitical inclusion means that toleration begins where full recognition of diversity is neither possible nor desirable: toleration works in the area between what may be fully recognized, and what is to be forbidden.

Nowadays, in diverse societies the demand for recognition takes the place of what in past centuries was a request for toleration. The state is (or is expected to be) neutral toward religious beliefs, as well as toward other conflicts of value, and it has to treat with equal respect different conceptions of the good, rather than merely tolerate them (Heyd 2008, 175). Besides this, policies of accommodation are aimed at granting full participation of ethno-cultural minorities in the public sphere, by shaping it so as to permit such a participation. Policies of accommodation may be distinguished (Murphy 2012; Modood 2007) between policies of autonomy (by granting minorities a voice in the decision-making processes), policies of symbolic recognition (apologies for injustice in the past, or inclusion of minority cultures in school curricula), policies of protection (e.g., measures to preserve cultural and linguistic minorities from assimilation, through specific measures of support), exemptions from specific legal requirements (for instance, the exemptions concerning the wearing of Sikh turbans), and policies of direct assistance (through funding or through affirmative actions). However, all these policies are not proper exempla of toleration, being rather solutions (precarious though they may be) to conflicts between the rules followed by a specific minority, and the rules of the national legal system. Moreover, even if they display a more or less extensive recognition of minority claims, all of them provide solutions to the conflict between specific practices and the legal system, displaying *acceptance* rather than toleration: to be more precise, in all these cases the legal system (which we can label as the "basic" normative system) is re-shaped, or adapted, in order to accommodate the diversity at stake. No toleration is needed, because what was *deviant* becomes allowed, and what was irregular is now recognized as lawful.

However, if equality before the law and minority groups tend to make toleration rare, it is not "politically redundant," as Heyd argues (Heyd 2008, 175). There are situations in which toleration is still possible, and even just, but the above mentioned policies of recognition are not enforceable. They are, so to say, weaker forms of recognition, which arise from the same kind of claims. In these other cases, the rules of the basic normative system are neither modified not replaced by new ones: what is allowed is either a *provisional suspension* of the rules prohibiting the specific behavior at stake, or a *different interpretation* of these rules for specific cases, more compatible with the diversity claimed by individuals or groups. In other word, one cannot simply dismiss the question of toleration by saying that the law either permits or prohibits certain practices: it is possible that what is prohibited for the majority may be tolerated for a small group of people, or for single individuals, by suspending the enforcement of existing rules, or interpreting them differently and in a more welcoming manner. And the reason for this suspension (or this different interpretation) is fully political: the achievement of social cohesion and political inclusion in super-diverse societies.

The shift from accommodation to toleration is not clear-cut. It may be said that reasons for toleration are similar to those underpinning policies of accommodation, but they are *less relevant*, that is, not strong enough to justify a change of the basic normative system. In both cases, a number of claims arise from inequalities between groups, and from the fact that these group identities are excluded from the public sphere in liberal societies. The difference is that in a number of cases minority claims are deemed strong enough to modify the basic normative system, so as to be fully recognized, while in other cases they are not, even if not completely undeserving.

This kind of perceptual shift has been repeatedly expressed by the European Court of Human Rights, when it affirmed – for instance – that "the vulnerable position of gypsies as a minority means that some special consideration should be given to their needs and their different lifestyle both in the relevant regulatory framework and *in reaching decisions in particular cases*" (Connors v. United Kingdom, App. No. 66746/01, par. 84 (my italics); see also Smith v. United Kingdom, App. No. 25154/94; Beard v. United Kingdom, App. No. 24882/94). According to the Court, due to the ascertained vulnerability of the Roma, States are to a certain extent under the obligation to *facilitate* their lifestyle: it does not mean that States are compelled to accommodate all aspects of Roma lifestyle, but that public authorities must show how, and to what extent, they have taken into account the specific cultural situation both in policy-making and judicial interpretation (Peroni and Timmer 2013, 1077). Facilitating Roma lifestyle (a number of cases have concerned the fact of living in caravans, for instance), is not, therefore, a form of recognition: it does not mean that the legal system has been modified (through an exemption) so as to allow the practices at stake. Rather, it means that the public authorities must give proof that the specific conditions and needs of people belonging to a minority have been considered, in order to appreciate the proportionality and reasonability of their choices.

A further example may be taken from the medical domain. The condition of ethno-cultural minorities facing healthcare issues is often that of partial powerlessness, which is rooted both in broader power relations (between the majority and minorities), and in disempowering practices that originate in the social system (Sadan 2004, 166). The changing of these imbalances and practices, by creating alternative organizational aspects and relationships, is of utmost importance: these alternatives may be good examples of toleration, rather than being understood as forms of accommodation. In this vein, one may consider that national European legal systems and international instruments (e.g., the Oviedo Convention) rule informed consent procedures according to the principles of personal autonomy, individual self-determination, and freedom of conscience. However, members of some minority groups neither really ask for a complete and autonomous control over medical decisions, nor do they want the same information content in disclosures (Blackhall et al. 1995). Accordingly, in order to provide acceptable treatment, the patient's culture should be taken into account when informed consent is required, carrying out a strategy suited to this particular sensitivity. Besides this, the patient's freedom may also be interpreted in a positive sense as freedom *to* treatment, allowing them not merely to give free and informed consent, but also to influence and shape therapies, even asking for personalized treatment paths, which may be partially irrespective of protocols. A broader enforcement of the freedom of treatment principle (Macioce 2014) may leave room for individual perspectives on healthcare and to personal conceptions of health, well-being, and dignity. From this perspective, Art. 8 of the European Convention on Human Rights, recognizing the right to respect for one's private and family life, may also serve (if broadly interpreted) for the protection of a number of claims in the healthcare field, including the patient's right to obtain complete and comprehensible information, which may be interpreted as a requirement for giving information about alternative (i.e., nontraditional) treatment options (Maclean 2009).

These examples may demonstrate that toleration may be given where minority claims are deemed not strong enough to modify the basic normative system, but there is nevertheless the possibility of weaker forms of recognition, either by suspending the enforcement of specific rules, or by interpreting them in a more favorable way. Such a possibility is justified by the need to include people and groups in the political realm, and not to exclude them by virtue of their identity. Additionally, the need for political inclusion may work as a threshold in two directions: upward, between what shall be fully recognized (through a modification in the basic legal system) and what may simply be tolerated; downward, between what would be just to tolerate, and what must be deemed intolerable. If it is just to tolerate a number of behaviors, in order to foster the political inclusion and social cohesion of minorities and vulnerable groups, what is at odds with these sociopolitical objectives must not be tolerated. Both the giving of toleration and its refusal are not arbitrary, even if a wide margin of discretion is unavoidable (and even positive): in both cases, the need to preserve social cohesion and political inclusion may be taken as the criterion, even if it is impossible to draw a sharper line between the realm where toleration may or may not be given. One boundary line, however, can be drawn by making reference to political inclusion: where equality is deliberately disavowed, where the practices at stake are explicitly aimed at excluding some people, where – for instance – there are situations of vulnerable "minorities within minorities" (Eisenberg and Spinner-Halev 2005), which might be negatively affected by the decision to tolerate some practices or behaviors, toleration must be refused. In other words, if political inclusion is the aim of toleration, practices and behaviors that are explicitly oriented at excluding people or groups (women, people with disabilities, people of a different religion, etc....) not recognizing them as morally and politically equal must not be tolerated.

Summary and Future Directions

Toleration has been correctly understood by liberal philosophers as the necessary political premise of a just society. However, it has been understood in a sort of idealized fashion, both neglecting power relations between groups and over-emphasizing the neutrality of the public sphere as a trump card for moral conflicts in a pluralistic society. Within this paradigm, the conceptions of Rawls and Forst partially answer these questions, also taking the relation between toleration and justice seriously into account; Forst' conception, additionally, gives weight to the power imbalances between groups and people, as an important aspect of decisions concerning toleration.

However, the emphasis on reason and reasonableness, which is present in both these authors, may overshadow the fact that reasons for toleration and its limits may change depending on the context, precisely because power imbalances are different.

On the contrary, toleration may effectively be understood as delivering justice, starting from the recognition of the specific intergroup relations, and aiming at counterbalancing them, as a political objective. To summarize, toleration delivers justice because it is aimed at preserving social cohesion among different groups and people holding different moral and religious views, *even if* these subjects are unable to correctly participate in a democratic debate: it is a virtue of justice (as Forst argues) because it delivers a *decent* society, where one is not excluded from those contexts of recognition that are the basis for self-esteem and respect. Moreover, toleration may counterbalance political asymmetries, by overlooking the dialectic of reciprocity: it should be given in cases that are beyond the range of what we can recognize and accommodate, being something the majority grants, even without asking for reciprocal forms of accommodation in return.

Finally, the need for political inclusion may work well as a threshold in two directions: upward, between what shall be fully recognized (through a modification in the basic legal system) and what may simply be tolerated; downward, between what would be just to tolerate, and what must be deemed intolerable. Both the granting of toleration and its refusal are linked with the aim of fostering political inclusion: what is at odds with these sociopolitical objectives (for instance, practices and behaviors that are explicitly oriented at excluding people or groups, and denying them relevance as moral and political subjects, must not be tolerated.)

References

Bader V (1997) The cultural conditions of transnational citizenship: on the interpenetration of political and ethnic cultures. Political Theory 25(6):771–813

Blackhall LJ, Murphy S, Frank G, Michel V, Azen S (1995) Ethnicity and attitudes toward patient autonomy. J Am Med Assoc 274(10):820–825

Bohman J (2003) Reflexive toleration in a deliberative democracy. In: McKinnon C, Castiglione D (eds) The culture of toleration in diverse societies. Manchester University Press

Brown W (2006) Regulating aversion: tolerance in the age of identity and empire. Princeton University Press, Princeton

Calhoun C (2002) Imagining solidarity: cosmopolitanism, constitutional patriotism, and the public sphere. Publ Cult 14(1):147–171

Churchill RP (1997) On the difference between moral and non-moral conceptions of toleration: the case for toleration as an individual virtue. In: Razavi MA, Ambuel D (eds) Philosophy, religion, and the question of intolerance. State University of New York Press, Albany

Eisenberg A, Spinner-Halev J (eds) (2005) Minorities within minorities: equality, rights and diversity. Cambridge University Press, Cambridge

Fitzmaurice D (1993) Autonomy as a good: liberalism, autonomy and toleration. J Polit Philos 1(1):1–16

Floridi L (2015) Toleration and the design of norms. Sci Eng Ethics 21(5):1095–1123

Forst R (2003) Toleration, justice and reason. In: McKinnon C, Castiglione D (eds) The culture of toleration in diverse societies. Manchester University Press

Forst R (2004) The limits of toleration. Constellations 11(3):314–315

Forst R (2012) Toleration. In: Zalta EN (ed) The Stanford encyclopedia of philosophy (summer 2012 edition). http://plato.stanford.edu/archives/sum2012/entries/toleration/

Galeotti AE (1993) Citizenship and equality: the place for toleration. Political Theory 21(4):585–605

Galeotti AE (2002) Toleration as recognition. Cambridge University Press, Cambridge

Habermas J (2006) Religion in the public sphere. Eur J Philos 14(1):1–25
Heyd D (ed) (1996) Toleration: an elusive virtue. Princeton University Press
Heyd D (2008) Is toleration a political virtue? In: Williams MS, Waldron J (eds) Toleration and its limits. New York University Press, New York/London
Jones P (2006) Toleration, recognition and identity. J Polit Philos 14(2):123–143
Jost JT (2017) Ideological asymmetries and the essence of political psychology. Polit Psychol 38(2):167–208
Kelsen H (1929) Wesen und Wert der Demokratie. Mohr, Tübingen
King P (1976) Toleration. St Martin's Press, New York
Kukathas C (1997) Cultural toleration. Nomos 39:69–104
Kymlicka W (1989) Liberal individualism and Liberal neutrality. Ethics 99(4):883–905
Laegaard S (2013) Toleration out of respect? Crit Rev Int Soc Pol Phil 16(4):520–536
Locke J (2016) Second treatise of government and a letter concerning toleration. Goldie M (ed) Oxford University Press, Oxford
Lukes S (1997) Toleration as recognition. Ratio Juris 10(2):213–222
Macioce F (2014) Freedom of treatment. In: Encyclopedia of global bioethics
Macioce F (2017) Toleration as asymmetric recognition. Persona y Derecho 77:227–250
Maclean A (2009) Autonomy, informed consent and medical law: a relational challenge. Cambridge University Press, Cambridge
Margalit A (1998) The decent society. Harvard University Press, Cambridge
McKinnon C (2006) Toleration. A critical introduction. Routledge, Oxon/New York
Modood T (2007) Multiculturalism. A Civic idea. Polity Press, Cambridge, MA
Mouffe C (2000) Politics and passions. Ethical Perspect 7(2):146–150
Murphy M (2012) Multiculturalism: a critical introduction. Routledge, London/New York
Nussbaum MC (2006) Radical evil in the Lockean state: the neglect of the political emotions. J Moral Philos 3(2):159–178
Panikkar R (1979) The myth of pluralism: the tower of babel. A meditation on non-violence. CrossCurrents 29(2):197–230
Peroni L, Timmer A (2013) Vulnerable groups: the promise of an emerging concept in European human rights convention law. Int J Constit Law 11(4):1056–1085
Rawls J (1993) Political liberalism. Columbia University Press, New York
Rawls J (1999a) A theory of justice. Oxford University Press, Oxford
Rawls J (1999b) The idea of public reason revisited. In: Rawls J (ed) Collected papers. Harvard University Press, Cambridge, MA
Sadan E (2004) Empowerment and community planning: theory and practice of people-focused social solutions. Hakibbutz Hameuchad Publishers, Tel Aviv
Scanlon TM (1996) The difficulty of tolerance. In: Heyd D (ed) Toleration: an elusive virtue. Princeton University Press, Princeton NJ
Scheffler S (1994) The appeal of political liberalism. Ethics 105(1):4–22
Taylor C (1994) The politics of recognition. In: Gutman A (ed) Multiculturalism. Princeton University Press, Princeton
Van der Veer P (2006) Pim Fortuyn, Theo van Gogh, and the politics of tolerance in the Netherlands. Publ Cult 18:111–124
Verkuyten M (2019) Intergroup toleration and its implications for culturally diverse societies. Soc Issues Policy Rev 13(1):5–35
Waldron J (2003) Toleration and reasonableness. In: McKinnon C, Castiglione D (eds) The culture of toleration in diverse societies. Manchester University Press
Wolff J (2003) Social ethos and the dynamics of toleration. In: McKinnon C, Castiglione D (eds) The culture of toleration in diverse societies: reasonable tolerance. Manchester University Press
Young IM (1997) Asymmetrical reciprocity: on moral respect, wonder, and enlarged thought. Constellations 3(3):340–363
Young IM (1999) Ruling norms and the politics of difference: a comment on Seyla Benhabib. Yale J Criticism 12(2):415–421

The Logic of Intolerance

Toleration Within the Limits of Trust

Richard Dees

Contents

Introduction	635
The Logic of Distrust	636
Threats	639
Justifications of Toleration	642
Converting to Toleration	645
Conclusion	649
References	650

Abstract

Unfortunately for the advocates of toleration, intolerance has an inescapable logic. Because toleration depends on a modicum of trust, it is hardest to develop in precisely the situations that need it the most. Even the most reasonable of adversaries has plenty of reason not to trust his opponent, and none of the rational or moral arguments we can make need have any effect on him. What is needed to create toleration, then, are changes in the facts on the ground and a leap of faith.

Keywords

Trust · Toleration · Conversions

Introduction

Toleration has taken a beating in recent years. Writing in 2007, Martha Nussbaum could praise Americans for their relatively peaceful reaction to Muslims in the country, even after the devastation of the 9/11 attacks by Islamic radicals:

R. Dees (✉)
University of Rochester, Rochester, NY, USA
e-mail: richard.dees@rochester.edu

© The Author(s), under exclusive licence to Springer Nature Switzerland AG 2022
M. Sardoč (ed.), *The Palgrave Handbook of Toleration*,
https://doi.org/10.1007/978-3-030-42121-2_32

Despite some highly regrettable individual instances of assault against peaceful Muslims, and despite the undoubted existence of religion-based profiling in airports and other places of surveillance, there has been no massive public outcry against U.S. citizens and residents who are Muslims; no public demand that they renounce their distinctive articles of dress; and no claim that their visible difference from others, should they refuse to dress "like everyone else," means that they are somehow threatening or disloyal. (Nussbaum 2008, 346)

By 2016, however, a major party candidate was elected president on a platform that explicitly called for the rejection of Muslim immigrants and increased surveillance of mosques and Muslim residents, including citizens. Muslims as such were now considered suspect. Indeed, Muslim members of Congress were called traitors simply for being elected and then criticizing some aspects of American society (Carlson 2019).

The emergence of intolerance was clearly built upon fear, a fear of terrorism that has been turned into a fear of beliefs and cultures that are not readily understood. Politicians and others can easily incite fear, and they frequently do so to stoke up their supporters. In doing so, they deliberately foster anxiety and antagonism in those already wary of others. Unfortunately, fear quickly dissolves tolerance, and, even more unfortunately, that fear has a certain kind of logic. Fear breeds distrust, and distrust undermines the relationships on which toleration depends. Toleration is always a fragile achievement.

Philosophical justifications of toleration tend to gloss over the logic of intolerance and ignore that element of fear. Instead, they focus on the grand ideas of recognition and mutual respect as the basis for toleration, and they are not wrong to do so. But we must begin with the fear and work from there. When we do so, we understand better the structure of toleration, and we can more clearly confront the problems that must be addressed to promote it.

The Logic of Distrust

I once began a presentation on trust and toleration with the sentence, "Toleration surely requires trust," to which one member of the audience objected to every word. He had a point: The relationship between toleration and trust depends on an understanding of both terms, and even when the terms are clear, that relationship is far from obvious. For example, as Sten Widmalm notes, some Hindus in India would say that they trusted Muslims but that they should not have full democratic rights, while others agreed that they should have full democratic rights but that they did not trust them (Widmalm 2016, xvi). Yet there does exist a tight relationship between trust and toleration.

In its classic formulation, toleration is a kind of principled forbearance (see Horton 2011; Cohen 2004). We tolerate a practice only if we disapprove of it and yet refrain from interfering with it even though we have the power to do so. But this view is too narrow. On such a view, a society that celebrated diversity is not tolerant at all since there is no disapproval of those who act differently. But common sense suggests that a diverse society is a paradigm of toleration, so a better view of toleration is that we tolerate any practice that is not our own when we allow it to exist for principled reasons. This broad view of toleration captures the entire spectrum of attitudes from "merely tolerating" differences to reveling in them. Nevertheless, the narrow view makes an important conceptual point, and we should see "mere tolerance" as an important limiting case. We might think trust plays no role in "mere tolerance": If I, as a member of the majority, have the power to prevent the practices of those I dislike, we might think I don't have to trust them to tolerate them. Nevertheless, even here, trust still has an important role: Those I tolerate have to trust *me*, because I might use their open participation in a despised practice as a chance to get them to expose themselves so that I can crack down on them more effectively. Yet the trust cannot be so one-sided for at least two reasons. First, even if I am in a position of power, the point of my toleration is usually to ratchet down hostilities, to create a more peaceful environment for everyone's benefit. Yet in situations in which I merely tolerate, I allow something to occur that I think is, at minimum, unacceptable and probably immoral, and I regard it as possibly detrimental to the community as a whole. I have to trust the other group to show some restraint and not to act in ways that will actually damage the community. Second, a situation in which one party has all the power is relatively unusual; while power imbalances are common, the less powerful almost always have some means to retaliate. Often, two sides acquiesce to toleration because the costs of hostility are too high, and so toleration serves as a crucial part of the peace treaty, even if it is an unequal peace. In this case, the need for trust on both sides is more evident: Each needs to trust the other not to take advantage of the peace to launch a surprise attack, and each needs to trust the other not to undermine the ways of life that each side sees as being at stake in the conflict.

But even getting to the point at which both sides think the costs of hostility are too high is a major achievement. Toleration is most difficult to produce in exactly those situations in which it is needed most. The parties to any long-standing conflict have plenty of reason to distrust each other. Consider the classic rational choice model approach to the situation. "We" should tolerate "them" only if the expected outcome of trust is positive:

(probability that they are trustworthy) x (gains of trust) > (probability that they are untrustworthy [= 1-(probability they are trustworthy]) x (losses of misplaced trust)

In just such situations, our past experiences have taught "us" that "we" have more than enough reason not to trust "them." Typically, each side has years and years of examples of the ways the other side is deceitful, lying, and double-dealing. Each side, thus, has good reason to think that the probability that the other side is trustworthy is quite low. In addition, the same experiences have taught both sides that the costs of misplaced trust are quite high, since "they" have proven willing to exploit any weakness "our" side shows. Thus, "we" have reason to think allowing "them" to have any room to maneuver is only inviting further betrayals, for which we would only have ourselves to blame. In this framework, toleration is pure folly.

Take the situation in England during the reign of James II. James has converted to Catholicism in 1669 (though it remained secret for a while) and succeeded his crypto-Catholic but officially Anglican brother, Charles II. After brutally repressing a rebellion led by Charles II's illegitimate but Protestant son, the Duke of Monmouth, James tried to build an alliance with Dissenters (non-Anglican Protestants like Quakers and Presbyterians), campaigning for a toleration that would include both Catholics and these radical groups. While many prominent Dissenters—like William Penn—joined James's campaign, others were suspicious (Sowerby 2013; Jones 1972). A Catholic had not ruled England since Mary I a century before, and her reign was remembered as one of bloody persecutions, so many Protestants were wary of James. As recently as 1678, the country had been swept by fears of a "Popish Plot," the (completely fictional) plan to assassinate Charles and put James on the throne. (That plot was countered by the less fictional 1683 Rye House Plot by Whig radicals to kill both Charles and James to install Monmouth on the throne [see Marshall 1994].) When James began placing his Catholic friends into administrative positions, promoting Catholic officers in the army, and suspending laws that barred Catholics from holding office, Anglicans feared that James would follow the absolutist policies of his coreligionist in France, Louis XIV. Indeed, Louis inconveniently reinforced the worries a few months after James's coronation by revoking the Edict of Nantes that had granted toleration to France's Protestant minority since 1598 but which had gradually ceased to have much more than symbolic value. The fact that many of these bitter and now-vehemently-anti-Catholic Huguenots landed in England cemented the impression. In a word, most Protestants, Anglican and non-Anglican alike, did not trust James. And given their past experiences and the example set across the English Channel, they had good reason to be suspicious. Of course, a century's worth of anti-Catholic propaganda did not help either.

Given the propaganda, such distrust would be hard to overcome. But the problem was deeper. Imagine the calculations of a rational Anglican, one not driven by an atavistic hatred of Catholics. Should he (and in this context, it could only be a "he") trust Catholics enough to tolerate them and support James's overture toward Catholics and other nonconformists? On the one hand, doing so might ease some tensions in the country and create unity in a nation that would no longer be divided by religious persecutions. There might even be some economic benefits from increased freedom since it would allow all nonconformists to be more secure in their own goods and therefore stimulate their innovations in other areas besides religion (Sowerby 2013, Chap. 2). And—if he could tear himself from his private interests—there might even be some political benefits. If Catholics and others saw themselves represented in government, they would accept more readily their position in society. On the whole, then, our prudent Anglican would see some real gains for the country from toleration, though they would be modest. On the other hand, the risks of allowing Catholics to rule seemed overwhelmingly high. Given the history of Mary and the example of Louis, the chances were reasonably good that James would seek to consolidate his political power, use it to strong-arm Parliament into more power, and then set up a more absolutist state. The religious downside was likely to be even worse: With his political power, James might then seek to put the

Church of England under the control of the Catholic hierarchy again. From the Anglican's perspective, such a move threatened not only political subordination but also eternal damnation for everyone in Britain. Louis's betrayal of his Protestant subjects gave ample proof that such an outcome was not unlikely. Given these risks, even if our prudent Anglican thought the positive and negative outcomes were equally likely, he would reject toleration. But since he regarded the latter outcome as considerably more likely, it would be positively irrational for him to support toleration.

Notice that this calculation is not based in egoism. The interests of our Anglican gentleman need not be the only ones that are part of his consideration. He will see his logic works whether the interests he takes into account are merely his own, those of his fellow Anglicans, or—importantly—the interests of the country as a whole. The threat he would see in a Catholic ascendency is not limited to himself or his kind; it is to the whole nation.

Notice also that the distrust in this case is not based on a fear of strangers, a fear that Nussbaum rightly notes lies behind so much intolerance (Nussbaum 2008, Chap. 5). Catholics and Anglicans in England were more than familiar with each other. Certainly, Catholics were "othered," treated as unusual and scary, but they were distrusted all the more because of their familiarity. (Similarly, the distrust between Blacks and Whites in the American South is not based on their unfamiliarity with each other.) Anglicans could reason that they were not merely guessing that Catholics were untrustworthy because they were unknown; they *knew* very well that Catholics were untrustworthy. The reason behind this confidence points to another intractable aspect of the dynamic. Even if our rational Anglican and a rational Catholic could agree that they should "give peace a chance," some of their compatriots would not. Indeed, they would regard any rapprochement with the other side as a betrayal of fundamental principles. Worse yet, such a move would be likely to provoke an extreme response from their own side. Some might deliberately provoke the other side with an act of violence to provoke an overreaction to sabotage the peace effort—and therefore demonstrate to everyone that both their side and their opponents cannot be trusted. Or they may simply seek to eliminate the those who commit the ultimate sin of seeking peace, either politically or more literally—as in the cases of Egyptian President Anwar Sadat, assassinated by Islamic fundamentalists in 1981, and of Israeli Prime Minister Yitzhak Rabin, assassinated by an Israeli ultranationalist in 1995—not to mention that of Henri IV of France, who promulgated the Edict of Nantes but was assassinated by a fanatical priest in 1610. Too, too often in these intractable conflicts, progress is undermined by those who prefer conflict to reconciliation.

Threats

Logically, the perception of threats from despised groups undermines toleration for them (Weldon 2006; Gibson 2008; Widmalm 2016). So, we might try to combat the logic of intolerance by thinking about who *really* poses a threat to society. We might think that if we could show our prudent Anglican that Catholics were not really a threat, then we can argue that he *should have* trusted them, even if in fact he would not have.

Consider a more contemporary example. In French public schools, students are not allowed to wear conspicuous religious symbols. This rule has the effect of preventing Muslim girls from wearing headscarves as required by their religion, but it does not prevent Christians from wearing crosses, which can usually be tucked beneath clothes. Thus, this apparently neutral rule places greater burdens on minority groups. Some recent writers on toleration, like Anna Galeotti, have used this case to show that liberal toleration has focused too much on individuals as the locus of choice, and in so doing, it has failed to see the problems that are faced by minorities, who struggle to have their concerns as a group recognized by the society at large (Galeotti 2002, Chap. 4; see also Ceva and Zuolo 2013). Crucial to Galeotti's argument is the claim that, in fact, the headscarves pose no threat to the majority (Galeotti 2002, 127–130).

Whatever threat the headscarves pose is certainly not physical: It "neither picks my pocket or breaks my leg," in Jefferson's memorable phrase (Jefferson 1782, Query XVII). Instead, the threat is *normative*: It "portends a change in one's way of life or in the patterns or rules one expects to govern relationships" (Creppell 2011, 455). In this case, the normative threat is supposed to be to the secular nature of French society, and that threat might take two forms. First, the scarves are supposed to pose a *political* threat because they invade the public space of schools in which all students must be viewed as the same. The thought is that the scarves mark off some students as different and therefore undermine the political equality of persons that is essential to democracy. Second, the scarves are supposed to pose a *cultural* threat because they represent a "foreign" element that undermines the "Frenchness" of the schools. In doing so, they would undermine the unity of the French nation.

But neither threat bears much scrutiny. Wearing headscarves does not threaten the political order in any way; it does not keep anyone from participating in society as such. Opponents worry that the pressure within the Muslim community to wear headscarves creates an atmosphere in which Muslim women feel that they should not participate in politics. But, in that case, banning headscarves would be highly paternalistic: Even though Muslim women have rights and learn about those rights, the assumption is that if they wear a headscarf, they will be unable to exercise those rights, so that the scarves themselves represent a threat to full citizenship. Such an assumption seems not just false but bizarre. Wearing a headscarf does not inhibit the exercise of rights. If women who do wear them are not exercising their rights, the problem lies elsewhere, and a ban on headscarves in schools will not address it. Girls can well learn about their rights whether they wear a headscarf or not. Pretending that the distinctive dress in schools somehow undercuts the ability of the schools to teach equality is disingenuous. Indeed, drawing official attention to the differences does significant damage to the idea that everyone is equal in the country, no matter what they look like.

The argument that headscarves pose a threat to the culture is only marginally more plausible. The claim would have to be that the mere presence of headscarves is alien to French culture, but that argument only gets off the ground if the mere public expression of support for Islam is anti-French. France prides itself as a secular society, where no decision is made for anything like a religious reason (despite a very public and conspicuous presence of Catholicism in the form of national icons like Notre Dame). But even on this conception of French society, headscarves can hardly be said to pose a threat. Just as Christians can walk around Paris wearing large crosses, nun's habits, and monk's cassocks without undermining French society, so can Muslim women stroll around wearing a hijab. Enforcing a uniformity in schools that is not needed in society at large just seems arbitrary.

Note, however, that this defense of headscarves accepts the claim that genuine threats trump toleration. When a phenomenon does threaten the normative order, Galeotti argues, we need not tolerate it. For just that reason, she claims, we need not—and we should not—tolerate racism (Galeotti 2002, Chap. 5). Certainly, the violence and threats of violence implicit in racism violate the rights of others and constitute a threat to public order. But the threats need not be physical to be real. As Jeremy Waldron (2012) notes, calumnies do more than insult their targets. Even "mild" racism harms others precisely because the acts and the public language of racism treat minorities as unfit to participate fully in society. Racists want minorities either to leave or to "know their place"; for them, minorities must never think they should have a voice in how the nation is run. Even in its nonviolent forms, then, racism violates the fundamental principles of democracy. In this way, racists are a threat to society, even when they are not violent. In addition, by undermining the role minorities play in society, racism endangers the public culture of equal citizenship. Thus, racism poses a threat in a way that headscarves do not. The racists cannot be, and should not be, trusted in a democratic society.

Unfortunately, the issue is not so simple. What counts as a threat depends on what we are protecting. Racism certainly poses a threat to any meaningful conception of democracy. The strictures of the Jim Crow South made a mockery of any pretense that the regime was democratic. But Black participation in politics posed a threat to the Jim Crow South. As the *National Review* notoriously argued in 1960:

> In the Deep South the Negroes *are*, by comparison with the Whites, retarded ("unadvanced," the National Association for the Advancement of Colored People might appropriately put it). Any effort to conceal or ignore this fact is sentimentalism or demagoguery. Leadership in the South, then, quite properly rests in White hands. (National Review 1960, 1)

The racists thought that the preservation of civilization itself required White rule. Any attempt to change things by law was not only futile but a threat to order itself (Critchlow 2007, 74). Giving any power to Blacks would simply lead to anarchy:

> In the day-to-day dealings between Whites and Negroes in the deep South there is room for give and take, but the essential relationship is organic, and the attempt to hand over to the Negro the raw political power with which to alter it is hardly a Solution. It is a call to upheaval, which ensues when reality and unbridled abstractions meet head-on. (National Review 1960, 1)

The implication is clear: The relationships between Blacks and Whites at the time were a natural order that might evolve over time, the *National Review* maintained, but only philosophers with their heads in the clouds would attempt to change it. The regime of South would be radically altered if Blacks had any meaningful power, the magazine thought, and not for the better. If racism was a threat to meaningful democracy, anti-racism was a threat to civilization itself (as least as defined by Whites). The *National Review* was clear about which was more important:

> The central question that emerges—and it is not a parliamentary question or a question that is answered by merely consulting a catalogue of the rights of American citizens, born Equal—is whether the White community in the South in entitled to take such measures as are necessary to prevail, politically and culturally, in areas in which it does not predominate numerically. The sobering answer is *Yes*—the White community is so entitled because, for the time being, it is the advanced race…It is more important for any community, anywhere in the world, to affirm and live by civilized standards, than to bow to the demands of the numerical majority. (*National Review* 1957, 149)

Indeed, the editorial—reluctantly—endorses the idea that violence may be necessary to ensure that the "civilized" minority prevails (see Curtis 2019). In some sense, then, both Blacks and Whites could argue that the other side represented a threat. For Blacks, Whites failed to recognize them as persons. For Whites, Blacks were a threat to everything they valued. Because they could regard each other as threats to their fundamental values, they can each then argue that they need not trust nor tolerate the other.

The point is not that these two positions are morally equivalent. They most certainly are not. But if we had hoped to construct an argument for the rationality of toleration based on the claim that intolerance poses a threat to society that everyone can recognize, then we will be disappointed. The situation in the Jim Crow South is another in which both sides view each other as threats, and both sides had—from their own perspectives—plenty of reason not to trust the other and plenty of reason to regard each other as threats.

What constitutes a genuine threat is not, then, a morally neutral claim. To resolve what people should regard as a threat requires a background moral argument that goes beyond assessing claims that each side makes about what they regard as dangerous. Indeed, if both sides accepted the same standards about what constituted a genuine threat, then they would already have a lot of common ground on which to build a more tolerant society. Of course, even so, they might still have little reason to trust one another, so more is needed. But an analysis of whether real threats exist or not does little to change the calculation of whom to trust and whom to distrust.

Justifications of Toleration

To change this calculation, we need to change the views of the people involved. To go back to our rational Anglican, one way to change his view of his relationship to Catholics is not to try to convince him of some neutral fact that Catholics are not really a threat but to demonstrate to him that *morally* he should not view Catholics as a threat and that he is morally *required* to tolerate them. In recent years, justifications for toleration have focused on the reasons we should think of toleration as a positive virtue that people have strong moral reasons to accept. If we can show that our hypothetical Anglican should adopt such a view, then we can show that, rationally, he should tolerate.

Recent justifications for toleration focus on the ideal of respect. So, for example, Nussbaum grounds toleration in Roger Williams's "idea of the preciousness and dignity of individual human conscience" (Nussbaum 2008, 51). Individual consciences are "delicate, vulnerable, living things that need to breathe and not be imprisoned" (Nussbaum 2008, 53). Indeed, Williams talks of persecution as a form of terrorism, a "mind rape" (Nussbaum 2008, 54). No individual ever deserves such treatment. Toleration is needed to allow these delicate consciences to flower. Individuals as such thus deserve respect to pursue their lives in their own way. As Nussbaum recognizes, this view rests on a more fundamental claim that we owe respect to people as moral agents. This respect is what Stephen Darwall calls "recognition respect," the respect owed to people as such, and not the more robust "appraisal respect," which entails an admiration for some feature of the person (Darwall 1977). To respect persons as moral agents, we are morally required to respect their decisions about how they want to live their lives. As Kant famously puts the point: "[T]he ends of any person, who is an end in himself must as far as possible also be my end, if that conception of an end in itself is to have its full effect on me" (Kant 1785, 49). Or, as Rawls puts it, we have to treat people as "self-authenticating sources of moral claims" (Rawls 1993, 32). Politically, to treat people as such requires that we take into account the way they want to live their own lives. We start with the presumption that their choices have value. The default, then, is that we will tolerate whatever they want to do. It does not require that we always do so, but it does require us to have a good reason to interfere with their decisions.

Rainer Forst adds a useful Habermasian twist to these considerations. The idea of moral justification itself, he suggests, serves as the basis for toleration. We have, he claims (citing Pierre Bayle as his inspiration), "an independent duty of justifying one's actions that concern others in morally relevant ways with reciprocally acceptable reasons" (Forst 2017, 421). The principle of justification itself is "a moral principle of mutual respect entailing the duty of reciprocal justification" (Forst 2017, 422). Toleration, then, is grounded in a higher moral principle. Essentially, to recognize someone else as a person is to recognize that we cannot act against her without justification and that the justification must be based on reasons that she would recognize as such, even when she disagrees with them. Toleration, then, arises out of the recognition that reasons that are convincing to me—like the ones that lie behind the Anglican's faith—need not be reasons that others must rationally accept. That division—between what I accept as reasons and what others accept—is the key move, and on this view, that division is required by reflection on the nature of justification itself.

Do these arguments give our rational Anglican a reason to tolerate Catholics? He might claim that he sees the point of regarding each individual as such as worthy of a certain kind of respect, though he might insist that any respect people get must be earned. But he could also accept that every person has dignity of a sort. After all, he would say, we are all God's creatures. He can acknowledge that respect for persons implies that our actions that involve others require justification and that the reasons we have must be good ones. But he need not accept that the reasons we offer must be ones that Catholics would accept. He would reject the idea that respect as such requires him to tolerate their mistakes: Those errors lie on the path to eternal damnation. Those who make them should be treated as children and set a discipline that will show them the right path. Respect for persons and their dignity, he would say, requires us to justify our interference, but saving someone's soul always counts as a good reason to act, even if—indeed especially if—the other does not understand that their salvation is at stake. True respect, he would say, requires us to instill the true religion.

Such a view is, of course, paternalistic and condescending. Yet the moral argument that condemns such an attitude requires a commitment to a kind of recognition respect that would not have seemed plausible to any Anglican in 1688. The concept of respect for persons as moral agents with dignity does not entail the claim that we must leave them to their follies. So, it simply does not entail the recognition respect that Williams, Nussbaum, and Forst champion. Indeed, only in a world that *already* accepts the basic tenets of toleration does the kind of respect they defend make sense.

But the point is not that our Anglican's view of respect is the correct one or that there is no correct view about what respect requires. It is only that the Anglican is not being unreasonable in holding his conception of respect given the context in which he thought and lived. The real challenge here is to think about what would have to change before the arguments that Williams, Nussbaum, and Forst make could gain any traction. To tie dignity and respect to autonomy already requires a conceptual revolution.

We might expect that conceptual revolution to precede the acceptance of toleration, that a new regard for equal respect would drive the adoption of toleration as a political practice. In the West, at least, the historical order of events moved the other way around, from toleration to mutual respect. (For sketches of the history of toleration elsewhere, see Sen 2006, 64–65; Nussbaum 2008, 62; Widmalm 2016, 11–12.) People accepted toleration not because they thought every person deserved respect but because it was a convenient way to end a conflict. The Dutch found it easier to fight a war of independence with a semblance of toleration that united all the Dutch against the Spanish (Israel 1995, Chaps. 9, 16, 27). The French accepted the Edict of Nantes after 40 years of a bitter civil war (Holt 1995). The English accepted toleration both to end 50 years of civil strife between Anglicans and Presbyterians and to solidify the support for the anti-Catholic alliance that William III was fashioning against Louis XIV. In parts of Germany, Catholics and Protestants were forced by treaty to share towns and even churches, and they found workable accommodations—even if those spaces were still contested vigorously (Kaplan 2007, Chap. 8). None of these examples were built on anything like equal respect. In the Netherlands, the toleration frequently took the form of "hidden" churches of Catholics or Mennonites which everyone knew existed but which were allowed to operate only as long as they were not too open about it (Kaplan 2007, Chap. 7). In France, the Edict of Nantes allowed Huguenots to worship in some parts of the country, but they clearly had an inferior status, and they continued to be viewed as dangerous rebels by the French government (Labrousse 1988 and, more generally, Dees 2004, Chap. 4). And in Germany, the squabbles over who could worship where and when would often end in courts of law, where the cases would be decided by who held power in the government. The rules in place often made the prospect of a complete triumph impossible, but both sides were content to squabble in courtrooms rather than battle in the streets (Kaplan 2007, Chaps. 8–10).

Even where it was accepted, toleration was always tenuous. It survived in the United Provinces and England, though not cheerfully in either case. But, as I have already noted, it did not survive in France; indeed, Louis thought he could revoke the Edict of Nantes because he thought he had stamped out Calvinism already. But where toleration was accepted, it set a precedence of allowing people to worship as they saw fit. One of the unintended side effects of the 1689 Act of Toleration in England was that its practice allowed a much broader toleration than intended. Officially, toleration encompassed only Trinitarian Protestants, but since the Anglican Church ceased to have a monopoly on places of worship and since there was no effective bureaucracy to keep track of everyone, few people suffered if they failed to attend either the parish church or an officially sanctioned chapel on any given Sunday (Clark 1985, Chap. 5). So unitarians, deists, Catholics, and even atheists could usually go about their business unmolested. And once the idea became accepted (more or less) that people could worship as they wished in practice, the idea that people should be able to live as they saw fit became much more plausible. Only then does the idea that people as such deserved recognition respect make sense; only then does the ascription of moral agency to persons require us to give presumptive respect to the choices they make for their lives.

Once the antagonists start down this path, it may make sense to continue on it—though, as the French example shows, progress is not inevitable. And nothing in the account shows why they were morally required to take the first step. Toleration requires a leap of faith.

Converting to Toleration

Unfortunately, we cannot prescribe leaps of faith. By definition, they are not rationally required. Typically, we can give causal explanations for why one occurs, but we cannot explain it as a rational progression (Dees 1996). The above account does not even give us a blueprint for how to get antagonists to keep walking down a path toward toleration once they have started, never mind one for the more difficult task of getting them to take that first step.

Nevertheless, we know some practices that help. Many roads to toleration have begun with exhaustion: a long history of conflict, often brutal and violent, sometimes lasting so long that the current participants cannot remember how it started. The identities that characterized the conflict simply became less relevant. So, rather than obliterating the conflicting identities, toleration sometimes emerges from practices in which those identities become less salient. So, for example, in the aftermath of the Glorious Revolution, Anglicans, Presbyterians, Congregationalists, and Quakers united against the absolutist (and Catholic) threat of Louis XIV. Their identity as Britons became more important than their doctrinal differences (Colley 1992, Chap. 1). Voltaire wonderfully points to a different practice that has a similar effect:

> Go into the London Stock Exchange—a more respectable place than many a court—and you will see the representatives from all nations gathered together for the utility of men. Here Jew, Mohammadan and Christian deal with each other as though they were all of the same faith and only apply the word infidel to people who go bankrupt. Here the Presbyterian trusts the Anabaptist and the Anglican accepts a promise from the Quaker. (Voltaire 1734, 41)

For Voltaire, the wonders of capitalism dissolved bigotry. But what is important about Voltaire's observation is less about markets as such but about the way this particular social practice subordinates religious identities to other social roles. In the marketplace, two important factors are at work. First, on a personal level, Jews and Presbyterians and Muslims all interact with each other, and they see that, within this realm, they can trust one another. Participating in the practice helps to generate trust. Second, on an institutional level, the rules of the marketplace encourage a separation of their religious identities from their economic identities. Different religious identities still mattered, just not in the marketplace. As Amartya Sen (2006) has argued, the problem with much of the discourse about religion and religious conflicts is that it flattens people: It squeezes them into only one dimension, all the better to fit them into a file folder. It sees them only as members of a particular religion and fails to respect their "diverse diversities" (Sen 2006, 13). Crude Marxists do the same by seeing everyone exclusively in terms of their relationship to the means of production. A woman is Catholic, and everything else about her is unimportant; a man is a capitalist, and his other relationships cease to matter. Polarizing politics forces people into a single identity, thereby restricting their ability to shape their lives (see Klein 2020). Indeed, whatever the person herself may want, she can be forced into that one identity. The problem is displayed vividly in Ayad Akhtar's play *Disgraced* (2013), in which a Pakistani-American lawyer is forced to foreground his identity as a Muslim, both by the people who want his presence in a courtroom to enlist him into a more active role in supporting civil rights for Muslims accused of terrorism in a post-9/11 world and by his non-Muslim friends, who can only see him as a Muslim once he has done so. The way he is treated, then, changes the way the character acts and leads him to become (inexcusably) violent in ways that he would never have contemplated otherwise. As Locke points out (1689, 52), if gray-eyed people are persecuted, then having gray eyes becomes politically salient and even all-encompassing, and gray-eyed people become much more likely to engage in politically subversive activities. They become a threat to others because they have been threatened. As Sen puts the point:

> What is done to turn that sense of self-understanding into a murderous instrument is (1) to ignore the relevance of all other affiliations and associations, and (2) to redefine the demands of the "sole" identity in a particularly belligerent form. (Sen 2006, 176)

Breaking this cycle, then, is crucial, but breaking it requires concrete practices that help restore the complexities of individual identities.

The liberal strategy for promoting toleration, then, is to foster practices that encourage people to interact in ways that allow them to live these complexities, and as suggested by the marketplace, the strategy has both personal and institutional aspects. First, on a personal level, we must encourage local practices that allow people with different identities to interact. A nice and somewhat surprising example, given its antebellum origins, can be found in *Moby Dick*. When Ishmael first meets Queequeg, a tattooed harpooner from Polynesia, he is frightened of Queequeg's massive frame and strange customs. But because the world of the whalers is one in which shipowners must be most concerned with manning their ships with competent sailors, the members of any crew are expected to get along with everyone well enough to do the work. In that spirit, Ishmael approaches his relationship with Queequeg, and early in their acquaintance, he offers no better soliloquy on toleration:

> I say, we good Presbyterian Christians should be charitable in these things, and not fancy ourselves so vastly superior to other mortals, pagans and what not, because of their half-crazy conceits on these subjects. There was Queequeg, now, certainly entertaining the most absurd notions about Yojo and his Ramadan;—but what of that? Queequeg thought he knew what he was about, I suppose; he seemed to be content; and there let him rest. All our arguing with him would not avail; let him be, I say: and Heaven have mercy on us all—Presbyterians and Pagans alike—for we are all somehow dreadfully cracked about the head, and sadly need mending. (Mellville 1851, 74 [Chap. 17])

Ishmael comes to his live-and-let-live view through a lived experience of whaling that requires different people to work together for a common purpose. He thus allows himself to see Queequeg as more than an exotic stranger, and he comes to respect him and even to love him.

Like a whaling ship, organizations in which people of different backgrounds interact for a common purpose can be crucial. So, as Ashutosh Varshney (2002, 289–297) shows in India, in places where lower class people worked together—either in the grand social movements against the caste system or in local neighborhood groups—more tolerance emerged. The state can sometimes help create such groups, but it can also sabotage them if it tries to usurp their purposes—as was shown with the collapse of civil society in former Communist countries (Varshney 2002, 297–298). Allowing social groups to evolve in their own ways is important.

Second, these efforts need to be supported on an institutional level by what Michael Walzer (1984) calls the "art of separation." For Walzer, the key liberal move is to separate the different spheres of value (see, more generally, Walzer 1983). Each realm should be allowed to operate autonomously, and relations between people in one realm should not affect relations in other realms. Thus, the Catholic and the Quaker, the Jew and the Muslim, the Hindu and the Buddhist, rivals in religion all, can still work together in the stock exchange, they can sell tomatoes and chocolate to one another in the marketplace, and they can all join a bowling league. Likewise, the CEO is not automatically a deacon, the sheriff cannot use his position to intimidate his rival for the presidency of the Rotary Club, and the President of the

United States cannot use the Department of Justice to investigate his political rivals. People cannot exchange money for medals for bravery; indeed, they cannot even use their military rank to obtain them for themselves. More controversially, health care should not be subject to money constraints, and a tycoon's personal fortune should not be able to buy access to power and opportunities for his children. We should not be able to leverage success in one realm into success in another.

As Walzer notes, a challenge for many Western democracies—especially the United States—is that money has become a "dominant good" that converts market success into everything else (Walzer 1983, 10), a point made sharply by Marx in one of his most cogent critiques of capitalism:

> Money is the supreme good, therefore its possessor is good. Money, besides, saves me the trouble of being dishonest: I am therefore presumed honest. I am *stupid*, but money is the *real mind* of all things and how then should its possessor be stupid? Besides, he can buy talented people for himself, and is he who has power over the talented not more talented than the talented? Do not I, who thanks to money am capable of *all* that the human heart longs for, possess all human capacities? Does not all my money therefore transform all of my incapacities into their contrary? (Marx 1844, 103–104)

In our society, money grants people goods that should only be achieved in other ways. Love should not be procured for money, honor should not be purchased, and political power should not be bought. Insofar as money can be converted into all other goods, it violates the separation in the same way that "noble blood" violated the separation in the premodern world. In their own period, each granted almost all unlimited power to those who possessed it and therefore created deep divisions in society, only rivaled by religion and ethnicity.

Besides creating the boundaries, the state has an institutional role in supporting toleration. As noted above, it should allow social groups to flourish. Any state that tries to subsume all of politics almost always stifles such groups, whether in Communist countries or, as Widmalm (2016, Chap. 5) shows in contemporary Uganda, in any other one-party system. Likewise, states can undermine toleration by, say, instituting an educational system that promotes one religion or one ethnicity as the only authentic expression of national identity (Widmalm 2016, Chap. 6).

The art of separation allows people to work together in one sphere without endangering other identities. So, the volunteer umpire at a kickball game need not fear that he will be fired from his part-time city job when he calls the mayor's son out at the plate (Vigdor 2019). A Black need not fear that he will be refused service at a lunch counter. A lesbian knows she will not be fired from her teaching position for marrying her partner. In the art of separation, the role of the state in this regard is to police the boundaries, not to keep the spheres hermetically sealed from one other, but to ensure that they protect the borders in ways that help people. The state ensures that religious groups can operate autonomously—but it also ensures that they do not abuse their members. A church can excommunicate them, but it cannot imprison them or impoverish them—though this question becomes more complicated when the religion itself engages in economic activity as part of its communal efforts, as among the Hutterites (Esau 1999). Markets govern commercial interactions, but the state guarantees that all products sold are safe. The state is also supposed to ensure that voters can't be bribed by politicians and that politicians can't be bribed by Big Pharma or Big Farm, not to mention K Street or Wall Street. And it should not allow people in the marketplace to discriminate against Catholics, Jews, and Muslims or against women, Blacks, and gays.

In this light, Locke's separation of church and state is the quintessential liberal idea (Locke 1689, 26). The point of all this separation is to create multiple spheres in which people interact with each other in many different ways, and so it allows the separate spheres to operate. But by allowing people to interact with different people in different areas, it creates more bonds in the society as a whole. But also, by allowing people to interact with the *same* people, but in different areas of life, it encourages people to see each other as more fully human. George is not just the gay man down the street but the man who sells the best produce in the county and plays a terrible game of bridge. Rachel is the Jewish mom who works at the Jewish Community Center, but she is also volunteer at the blood bank, but she can never keep her lawn cut. Padma is the South Asian software engineer who performs in community musicals but who can't understand local politics. People become complexes of traits rather than caricatures. They become whole people.

As Locke recognizes, the separation depends on a view of the world that does not reduce people to one dimension, while it simultaneously creates the very world in which those different identities are allowed to flourish. Separation creates the space in which people can interact in the different dimensions of their lives, and it therefore creates the space in which the trust on which toleration depends can emerge. But separation itself depends on a kind of trust that identities can be kept within their appropriate spheres. As long as single identities dominate all the others, the kind of trust necessary to sustain the separations can easily collapse.

Fortunately, the separations do not all have to be created at once. Some steps can be taken to create some separations—like the church-state divide that Locke recommends—and then conditions may be created that will allow those separations to become more robust. The society may then find itself in a virtuous cycle in which trust is created that allows a broader toleration, which creates more trust in turn.

Conclusion

Alas, nothing in this account makes toleration rationally required. Our prudent Anglican still has no reason to think that he should accept Catholics as full members of his society. Indeed, he is still likely to see any efforts to create separate spheres of value as a betrayal of his sacred obligation to promote the truths of salvation. In that sense, this account is not an optimistic one. Nevertheless, we can at least see the path that is necessary to achieve the change of hearts that can create trust and toleration. The logic of intolerance may be unanswerable in its own terms, but we may be able to create realities on the ground that build a world in which that logic simply no longer applies. The logic of intolerance cannot be broken by logic; it can only be transformed in the crucible of social practice.

References

Akhtar A (2013) Disgraced. Little, Brown, and Company, New York
Carlson T (2019) Tucker Carlson Tonight, 9 July. https://www.foxnews.com/opinion/tucker-carlson-america-rescued-ilhan-omar. Accessed 31 Jan 2020
Ceva E, Zuolo F (2013) A matter of respect: On majority-minority relations in a liberal democracy. J Appl Philos 30:239–253
Clark JCD (1985) English society 1688–1832: ideology, social structure and political practice during the ancien regime. Cambridge University Press, Cambridge
Cohen AJ (2004) What toleration is. Ethics 115:68–95
Colley L (1992) Britons: forging the nation, 1707–1837. Yale University Press, New Haven
Creppell I (2011) The concept of normative threat. Int Theory 3:450–487
Critchlow D (2007) The conservative ascendency: how the GOP right made political history. Harvard University Press, Cambridge
Curtis J (2019) 'Will the jungle take over?': *National Review* and the defense of Western civilization in the Era of Civil Rights and African Decolonization. J Am Stud 53:997–1023
Darwall S (1977) Two kinds of respect. Ethics 88:36–49
Dees R (1996) Moral conversions. Philos Phenomenol Res 56:531–550
Dees R (2004) Trust and toleration. Routledge, London
Esau A (1999) Communal property and freedom of religion: *Lakeside Colony of Hutterian Brethren v. Hofer*. In: McLaren J, Coward H (eds) Religious conscience, the state, and the law. SUNY Press, Albany, pp 97–116
Forst R (2017) Toleration and its paradoxes: A tribute to John Horton. Philosophia 45:415–424
Galeotti AE (2002) Toleration as recognition. Cambridge University Press, Cambridge
Gibson J (2008) Is intolerance incorrigible?: an analysis of change among Russians. In: Creppell I, Hardin R, Macedo S (eds) Toleration on trial. Rowan and Littlefield, Lanham, pp 257–286
Holt MP (1995) The French wars of religion, 1562–1629. Cambridge University Press, Cambridge
Horton J (2011) Why the traditional conception of toleration still matters. Crit Rev Soc Polit Philos 14(3):289–305
Israel J (1995) The Dutch Republic: its rise, greatness, and fall, 1477–1806. Clarendon Press, Oxford
Jefferson T (1782) Notes on Virginia. https://oll.libertyfund.org/titles/jefferson-the-works-vol-4-notes-on-virginia-ii-correspondence-1782-1786. Accessed 31 Jan 2020
Jones JR (1972) The revolution of 1688 in England. W.W. Norton & Co., New York
Kant I (1785) Foundations of the metaphysics of morals (trans: Beck LW). Bobbs-Merill, New York, 1959
Kaplan B (2007) Divided by faith: religious conflict and the practice of toleration in early modern Europe. Belknap Press of the Harvard University Press, Cambridge
Klein E (2020) Why we're polarized. Avid Reader Press, New York
Labrousse E (1988) Understanding the revocation of the Edict of Nantes from the perspective of the French Court (trans: Whelan Ruth). In: Golden RM (ed) The Huguenot connection. Kluwer Academic Publishers, Dordrecht, pp 49–62
Locke J (1689) Letter concerning toleration, ed. James Tully. Hackett Publishing, Indianapolis, 1983
Marshall J (1994) John Locke: resistance, religion and responsibility. Cambridge University Press, Cambridge
Marx K (1844) Economic and philosophic manuscripts of 1844. In: Tucker R (ed) The Marx-Engels reader, 2nd edn. W.W. Norton and Sons, New York, pp 66–125. 1978
Melville H (1851) In: Parker H (ed) Moby dick or the whale. W.W. Norton and Company, New York. 2018
National Review (1957, August 24) Why the South Must Prevail. National Review 4(7):148–149. Unsigned editorial

National Review (1960, March 19) The South's Travails. National Review Bulletin 8(12):1. Unsigned editorial

Nussbaum M (2008) Liberty of conscience. In: Defense of America's tradition of religious equality. Basic Books, New York

Rawls J (1993) Political liberalism. Columbia University Press, New York

Sen A (2006) Identity and violence: the illusion of destiny. W.W. Norton, New York

Sowerby S (2013) Making toleration: the Repealers and the glorious revolution. Harvard University Press, Cambridge

Varshney A (2002) Ethnic conflict and civic life: Hindus and Muslims in India. Yale University Press, New Haven

Vigdor N (2019) Kickball Umpire Sues South Carolina Mayor, Saying He Was Fired Over Call. New York Times, October 26

Voltaire (1734) Letters on England (trans: Tancock L) Penguin Books, Harmondsworth, 1980

Waldron J (2012) Toleration and calumny. In: Tunstall KE (ed) Self-evident truths?: human rights and the enlightenment. Bloomsbury, New York, pp 209–237

Walzer M (1983) Spheres of justice: a defense of pluralism and equality. Basic Books, New York

Walzer M (1984) Liberalism and the art of separation. Political Theory 12:315–330

Weldon S (2006) The institutional context of tolerance for ethnic minorities: a comparative, multilevel analysis of Western Europe. Am J Polit Sci 50:331–349

Widmalm S (2016) Political tolerance in the global south: images of India, Pakistan, and Uganda. Routledge, London

Intolerance and Populism

33

Nenad Miščević

Contents

Introduction: A New Playground 654
Understanding Populism and Intolerance 656
   Populism 656
   Toleration and Intolerance 657
Populist Intolerance and How to Fight It 662
   Hospitality and the Classical Passive Toleration 662
   Active Toleration in the Service of Inclusion 665
Conclusion 669
   Summarizing the Results 669
   Possible Future Avenues for Research 670
References 671

Abstract

The present-day populist intolerance toward foreigners, in particular migrants and refugees, is an essential element in the new international political playfield. It shares some features with the classical intolerance from the ages of religious wars of early modernity, and the resulting analogies in demands for toleration.

In order to systematize the issue one needs to appeal to a wide, more ordinary, less traditionally philosophical, notion of toleration and intolerance. The first encompasses acceptance and even supports as part of such active toleration; the second then follows suit, and counts non-acceptance, and complete lack of active support as marks of intolerance. What is needed is a two-sided effort: the factual-explanatory work on explaining the new forms of intolerance, and the more theoretical work on proposing the right notions of toleration and its contrary. We argue that the wider notions are the most useful one.

N. Miščević (✉)
University of Maribor, Maribor, Slovenia
e-mail: vismiscevic@ceu.edu

© The Author(s), under exclusive licence to Springer Nature Switzerland AG 2022
M. Sardoĉ (ed.), *The Palgrave Handbook of Toleration*,
https://doi.org/10.1007/978-3-030-42121-2_49

Armed with such notions, we turn to the populist treatment of migrants and refugees. The populist intolerance shows teeth at each stage of migrants-refugees progress toward the normal life away from their home. Interestingly, the main remedies for the populist intolerance have been already formulated in international legal documents. These documents, prominently the Marakesh compact, point to the active toleration (in the sense defended here), as the right kind of treatment, and as protecting human rights of migrants and refugees and offer concisely formulated guidelines for action. The chapter appeals to these guidelines both in diagnosing the ills of intolerance, narrow and wide, and in proposing wide toleration-guided remedies.

Keywords

Populism · Intolerance · Active toleration · Passive toleration · Refugees · Marakesh compact

Introduction: A New Playground

Increasing intolerance toward others, above all migrants and refugees, as well as second of third generation Muslims and Africans living in Europe, often initiated and supported by populist groups, parties, and their leaders, has become a typical phenomenon of the present decade (Thanks go to Mitja Sardoč for inviting me to contribute this chapter, and to Sune Laegard, Petar Popović, Nenad Smokrović, and Boris Vezjak for helpful discussion.). This new situation, characterizing the beginning of the millennium, might remind one of the historical context in which the debate on toleration in the modern age has started. Some prominent philosophers and intellectual historians have noted that the relevant circumstances "obtain as pertinently today as during the sixteenth and seventeenth-century wars of religion that gave way to the European tradition of religious toleration" (Williams and Waldron 2008: 2). Here is their full statement: If the "circumstances of toleration" should be understood as the existence of a plurality of religious faiths with varying degrees of power to oppress one another, then arguably those circumstances obtain as pertinently today as during the sixteenth and seventeenth-century wars of religion that gave way to the European tradition of religious toleration (2008: 2).

Let me illustrate the relevant circumstances of populist intolerance. To start with the linguistic expressions, the neologism "rapefugees," coined in 2016 for refugees, and used in some European countries, is a telling symbol of this new tendency. For instance, the slogan promoted in Cologne on New Year's Eve of 2016, "Rapefugees Not Welcome." A series of race-hate stickers have appeared on lamp-posts and bus stop windows in a coastal town – saying "rapefugees not welcome." One of the race hate stickers which has been posted in South Shields Mirror (21 Sept 2016). Slovenian populist paper "*Demokracija*" claims: "with migrants, arrives the culture of rape" (29 8. 2018).

The hatred is sometimes expressed directly, in terms that leave no place for doubt. "I'd put them up a brick wall, and SHOOT THEM," writes a refugee hater on a wall in Dover (quoted in *Refugees*, 2006, Issue 1. No. 142, Cover). The scope of intolerance is very wide.

On the side of half-crazy extremism one has phenomena like the massacre at Utøya July 22, 2011, in Europe, and the rally in Charlottesville, Virginia, from August 11 to 12, 2017 in the United States. (For Utøya see Indre Bangstad (2016).)

On the side of establishment, one has the promise offered by Donald J. Trump, announcing his candidacy for president of the United States, New York, June 16, 2015.

"I will build a great, great wall on our southern border." Here we shall be addressing this kind of intolerance, and its populist roots. The connection of the two, suggested by the title of the paper, is quite obvious. Reports about Islamophobia, for instance, usually mention populist leaders as initiators. (For a fine overview see Hans-Georg Betz (2017).)

This populist firework of xenophobic propaganda defines, to a large extent, the changed playground in international relations in the last two decades, the playground that reminded Williams and Waldron of the sixteenth- and seventeenth-century wars of religion. The migration crisis brought the suffering of once distant folks from Southern hemisphere to our doors.

There is another change. In Europe and North America the hated Other definitely does not appear in the traditional military form, except for negligible exceptions. The new face of the hated Other is the face of an immigrant, either economic one or a refuge. The dangers normally and traditionally associated with military presence are gone; our national populist has to invent and construct presumed dangers that foreign families, lots of children included, directly bring to the country. Also, the populist identity politics is ready to morph, in a way unimaginable by its classical predecessor. The invention of new enemies, strong enough to mobilize one's "people," requires invention of new solidarities: if the new enemy is Muslim, the traditional rivalry with Christian neighboring states will be pushed into the background, and the brand new Christian identity will replace the ethnic one, or simply cohabitate with it.

Migration crisis and populist intolerance enhance each other: the new migrant arrivals have been fueling waves of populist intolerance, and the reactions have tended to make the crises unresolvable. Of course, this decline of liberal-democratic hopes, theoretical and practical, spread over many parts of the world; in Europe and vicinity it is illustrated by the defeat of liberal efforts in Hungary and Turkey, with other countries threatening to take the same route. Badly enough, this was accompanied with the eclipse of a worldwide functioning arrangement. The UN becomes singularly inefficient, and new multipolar arrangement(s), with Trump's US, Putin's Russia, and Xiaoping's China, appeared at the horizon.

Philosophers have been addressing these issues for some time. We just mentioned the (2008) NOMOS volume. Among the pioneers is also Martha C. Nussbaum with her (2012) *The New Religious Intolerance Overcoming the Politics of Fear in an Anxious Age* (The Belknap Press of Harvard University Press). Others have joined to the pioneers; see for example the papers collected in Dobbernack and Modood (2013) volume. Psychologists are joining in, see Judith Glück (2019) and other papers in the same collection.

We want to approach this growing debate from a clear focus: the role and kinds of intolerance toward migrants and refugees within populist framework, and, symmetrically, the kinds of toleration needed as a remedy. Indeed, what is needed is a two-sided effort: the factual-explanatory work on explaining the new forms of intolerance, and the more theoretical work on proposing the right notions of toleration and its contrary. We shall argue that the wider notions are the most useful ones.

Here is then the preview. The next section discusses our two central items, populism and intolerance; the latter will be contrasted to toleration, and various sub-kinds of both will be proposed and discussed, in a more theoretical context.

Section "Populist Intolerance and How to Fight It" turns to political reality; it is dedicated to the issue of populist intolerance and how to fight it, which is the central section of the chapter. Here, we narrow our focus and choose one direction of populist intolerance to discuss it. The chapter considers the stages of migration and subsequent survival in the host country, focusing at the two opposing forces acting in the context, the populist intolerance, and the tendency to counteract it. The first subsection talks about hospitality and the classical passive toleration needed at two initial stages of the refugees' progress, first at the travel from homeland to the new destination and, second, at the arrival at the host-state border. The second subsection looks at active toleration in the service of inclusion, needed once the newcomers have entered the host-country.

The conclusion summarizes the two lines of research, the more factual-explanatory one on the new populist playground of intolerance, and the more theoretical one on the very notion of (in-)tolerance involved, and shows how the result from both fit each other: the proposed wide notion captures the spirit of actual political debates and of recommendations for action offered in the literature.

Understanding Populism and Intolerance

Populism

The present-day populism is a relatively new anti-cosmopolitan political machine, a specter, to quote Gellner and Ionescu: "A spectre is haunting Europe – the spectre of populism" (Gellner and Ionescu 1969: 1). Leaders like Orban, Trump, Erdogan, Bolsonaro and their likes are to a large extent shaping the global situation; together with the refugee crisis, populism is determining the new playground that is surrounding us. But, how should we think of it? What is it, in the first place?

The first thing to note about the notion of populism is that it is very thin. It covers all sorts of movements and ideologies suspicious toward elites and friendly to the wide masses of "people." Margaret Canovan, in her 1981 book *Populism*, has suggested seven different "types" divided into two major categories:

- *Agrarian Populism*
  - 1. Farmers' radicalism (e.g., the US People's Party) 2. Peasant movements (e.g., the East European Green Rising) 3. Intellectual agrarian socialism (e.g., the Narodniki in Russia)
- *Political Populism*
  - 4. Populist dictatorship (e.g., Peron)
  - 5. Populist democracy (i.e., calls for referendums and "participation")
  - 6. Reactionary populism (e.g., George Wallace and his followers)
  - 7. Politicians' populism (e.g., broad, non-ideological coalition-building that draws on the unificatory appeal of "the people")

Cass Mudde stresses the fact that "...considers society to be ultimately separated into two homogeneous and antagonistic groups, 'the pure people' versus 'the corrupt elite,' and (...) .argues that politics should be an expression of the *volonte generale* (general will) of the People" (2007: 23). He and Kaltwasser note that "T/he term is used to describe left-wing presidents in Latin America, right-wing challenger parties in Europe, and both left-wing and right-wing presidential candidates in the United States." For an excellent recent analysis see Urbinati's (2019) book. The text shall concentrate on right-wing populism, since this is the variety that is responsible for massive intolerance of migrants, refugees, and the like. So, in the sequel, "populism" will mean "right-wing populism."

Here are some of its main characteristics. We noted that the populist identity politics is ready to morph, in a way unimaginable by its classical predecessor. It is clear that the invention of new enemies, strong enough to mobilize one's "people," requires invention of new solidarities. In general, if the new enemy is Muslim, the traditional rivalry with Christian neighboring states will be pushed into the background, and the brand new Christian identity will replace the ethnic one or simply cohabitate with it (see Miscevic 2019).

Take the Balkan example: for a Catholic Balkan people, say, Slovenes or Croats, the identity that will contrast it to the relevant new "enemy" is its Christian identity contrasted to the Muslim one. However, the political conjucture might bring in some tension with the Orthodox neighbors (say Serbs). The common Christian identity will retreat for some time, and the Catholic/Orthodox contrast will dictate the alliances. Similarly, for Albania, the unitary ethno-nationalist framework might be relevant, but an imagined threat from Muslim newcomers will awaken Albanian Christians, in contrast to Albanian Muslims, and vice versa (see Olsi Jazexhi 2019: 60–85).

So much about the notion of populism. Section "Populist Intolerance and How to Fight It" shall passes to its political challenges.

Toleration and Intolerance

The text stays at the conceptual level, and passes to toleration and intolerance. There is no need to insist on the difference between "toleration" and "tolerance." Various authors have understood it in different ways, and there is no consensus about it. So, the text can immediately pass to the main point, contrasting two usages of the term. The official philosophical usage is rather narrow: to tolerate a phenomenon you have to distance yourself from it, but not prevent or forbid it. As T. M. Scanlon puts it in his already classical "The Difficulty of Tolerance"

> Tolerance requires us to accept people and permit their practices even when we strongly disapprove of them. Tolerance thus involves an attitude that is intermediate between wholehearted acceptance and unrestrained opposition. This intermediate status makes tolerance a puzzling attitude. (1996: 226)

Philosophers usually concentrate on this "paradox of toleration." As Bernard Williams puts it in another classical paper

> We need to tolerate other people and their ways of life only in situations that make it very difficult to do so. Toleration, we may say, is required only for the intolerable. That is its basic problem. (1996: 18)

The chapter will not be dealing here with the paradox. The issue of populist intolerance encompasses much wider attitudes, implicit in the popular usage in contrast to the philosophical one. Jan Dobbernack and Tariq Modood in their (2019) chapter note a relevant development happening "across European states and societies." In their view it "articulates the idea that contemporary expressions of cultural difference go 'beyond' toleration. They go 'beyond' because the concerns and desires that underpin the social and political claims of minority groups are insufficiently addressed with tolerance. It is not just non-interference, but respect for and public recognition of ethno-religious diversity that is sought. Toleration contains an element of disapproval and objection that, though balanced out and overridden by reasons for forbearance and acceptance, may be seen to perpetuate a smear on minority groups. If the desire is for the removal of social stigma and for equal accommodation in the public sphere, then toleration may not do the trick" (Dobbernack and Modood 2019: 8).

The description points, however, in the direction of the more relaxed popular usage of the term "toleration." The popular usage is quite wide: it does not involve disagreement or distancing at all. Such loose popular use of the term is present, for instance in proposals by The Office Of The United Nations High Commissioner for Human Rights in its *Questionnaire to member states*: "Identify concrete measures and initiatives for combating and eliminating all manifestations of racism, racial discrimination, xenophobia and related intolerance (...)" (available at www.un.org/en/durbanreview2009/pdf/replies/Slovenia.pdf). It is also formulated in the statement by General Assembly concerning the active character of toleration:

> 1.2 Tolerance is not concession, condescension or indulgence. Tolerance is, above all, an active attitude prompted by recognition of the universal human rights and fundamental freedoms of others. In no circumstance can it be used to justify infringements of these fundamental values. *Final Report on the United Nations Year for Tolerance: Declaration of*

Principles on Tolerance and . Follow-up Plan of Action, 1996, available at http://www.un-documents.net/a51-201.htm#appendix 1

No wonder that philosophers have noticed the relevance of this wider notion. Some of them recommend not calling it "toleration" at all and propose to talk of acceptance, or of accommodation beyond toleration. (Following Veit Bader, Dobernack and Modood mention a sense of "accept," they call it Accept II, which involves "Recognition, respect as equal and admission as normal" (2013: 5).) They place it "beyond toleration" (Ibid.). Sune Laegard goes in the same direction in his (2013). Psychologists similarly talk of "positive tolerance," and link tolerance with "acceptance, respect and appreciation of difference." (See Mikael Hjerm, Maureen A. Eger, Andrea Bohman and Filip Fors Connolly (2019), and Emile Lester and Patrick S. Roberts (2006).) Others, like Iseult Honohan (2013), note that the non-negative sense is widespread, and a popular one: "Toleration strictly speaking – allowing what one disapproves of and could obstruct," and notes in the footnote:

> This strict sense of toleration is distinct from a looser, widespread popular usage of tolerance as broad acceptance that does not contain the negative moment and constraint on action that is characteristic of strict toleration.
> A widespread confusion in this area is indicated by the fact that most people consider it desirable to be tolerant, but not desirable to be tolerated. (2013: 95)

We shall follow Honohan, take the loosest meaning as our starting point, and then distinguish two notions within it, first, the "wide" toleration involving recognition, and help that recognition often requires, and second, the traditional, narrow notion containing the negative moment. However, we have to look at the issue in more detail. The issue has been debated at least since the 1990s (an early collection is *Ratio Juris*. Vol. 10 from 1997).

The two authors who have been arguing for a wide notion of toleration since early 1990s, both represented in the *Ration Juris* collection, are Anna Galeotti and Karl-Otto Apel. The author who is nowadays taken as exemplary in this direction is Ana Galeotti:

> ... the conception of toleration I propose (...) implies a double extension of the liberal notion: first, a spatial extension from the private to the public domain, and, second, a semantic extension from the negative meaning of non-interference to the positive sense of acceptance and recognition. (*Toleration As Recognition*, 2004 Cambridge University Press (1st version 2002), p. 10)

Apel similarly talks about "affirmative tolerance," and, in his (1997) paper argues for it from the viewpoint of his discourse ethics. Richard Bellamy in his 1997 brief paper offers a fine rationale for accepting the notion of positive toleration:

> /t/oleration involves positive as well as negative action. The easiest way to tolerate someone is to ignore them by refraining from actively oppressing them in some way, either by prohibiting their beliefs or activities or by excluding them from benefits or services when there is no reason internal to their views or practices for doing so, such as would debar a

pacifist from serving in the armed forces but not from working in the police. However, when the prevailing social structures and attitudes are biased against the interests and values of certain groups, such negative toleration may simply serve to reinforce existing inequalities and so become, as Marcuse (1965) pointed out, "repressive." (1997: 178)

There is a clear need to include a wide notion in parallel to the narrow notion of toleration, so the text shall continue the line marked here.

The next step is the one from toleration in general or to one limited to individuals to toleration concerning communities. Michael Walzer lists two attitudes that would correspond to our active tolerance. The first, more moderate, includes "openness to the others, curiosity, respect and a willingness to listen and learn" (1997: 166). The other, more extreme, is characterized by the "enthusiastic endorsement of difference" (Ibid.), motivated by aesthetic or moral considerations. And he claims very firmly that people who express such endorsement "possess the virtue of toleration" (1997: 167).

The sources we cited all point on the direction of the wide understanding. Let me, however, note a problem raised by the critics of such understanding. Joseph Raz, for instance, note that "/T/oleration implies the suppression or containment of an inclination or desire to persecute, harass, harm or react in an unwelcome way to a person" (1988: 401). The line is endorsed by many authors, for instance by Ernesto Garzón Valdés in his *Ratio Juris* paper. To illustrate the point I shall use a fine example offered by Paolo Comanducci in his (1997) paper. He notes that some authors, Walzer in particular, "/h/ave to some extent stretched the meaning of "toleration" and of some related words, in comparison with the ordinary-language usage of these words, and goes on to give his counter-example:

For example, Walzer (1997b) defines "toleration" in such a way that it would make sense to utter a very odd sentence like the following: "I am tolerating with enthusiasm a rendez-vous with Kim Basinger! The use of 'toleration' in ordinary language, on the contrary, always implies a prima facie attitude of dislike, of disapproval, completely opposite to the attitude of accepting something with enthusiasm" (1997b: 187). (His reference is to Walzer, Michael. 1997a. "The Politics of Difference: Statehood and Toleration in a Multi-Cultural World." *Ratio Juris* 10: 165–76.)

The counter-example is quite telling! It is indeed odd for one to say that "I am tolerating with enthusiasm a rendez-vous with Kim Basinger"; but why is it so? I propose that positive, active concept of toleration has a link with rejection, pragmatic, or perhaps even semantic, but weaker than the one characterizing the negative one: in order for me properly to claim that "I am actively tolerating X," it should be the case that X is being rejected by someone or some group. Rendez-vous with Kim Basinger is not clearly being rejected by someone or some group. One can say that Benetton is inviting us actively to tolerate the racial difference, not because one hates or despises them, but because there are others who do.

This chapter shall take a step further than Galeotti and Apel and look at the consequences of using the positive notion for understanding of the opposite, the intolerance. To start with toleration, consider the ordinary usage of "toleration" in its widest extent. Suppose the ordinary speaker Jane characterizes John as being "very tolerant of diversity." It looks that she would thereby also imply that John is ready to help his diverse neighbors, not that he is just accepting them in an abstract sense. Test it in the opposite direction. Suppose John is not showing enmity to his "diverse" neighbors, but he never helped any of them, not even in dire need. To say in these circumstances that he is "very tolerant of diversity" would seem a bit too complimentary for his actual behavior.

Staying with this ordinary intuition, one can talk of widest notion of toleration as involving toleration-cum-support, where the initial "toleration" is already a bit wide involving recognition. For John to be tolerant of his diverse neighbors he should do more than just accept the pattern of diversity; he should be ready to help at least in situation that really cry for help. However, widening the notion of toleration entails the corresponding modification of its contrary, the intolerance. This task has not been much addressed in the literature, at least as my knowledge goes.

The classical narrow notion of toleration is the opposite of the idea of active intolerance: not tolerating in the classical sense a group, say, Jews, is to take active measures against them. What is the opposite of wide, acceptance-directed toleration? It seems that both active intolerance and its passive counterpart belong here. Active intolerance case is clear. To stay with the example of Jews, suppose that Jewish colleagues are being discriminated at the workplace in Hungary, and that a non-Jew, call him "Laszlo," is promoting active measures against them. But now, imagine Laszlo's less energetic friend, who is not actively doing anything concerning the matters in question; he just happily supports the discrimination practices, and does not offer and sign of acceptance of his Jewish colleagues. This kind of passive intolerance would equally fit the characterization of wide intolerance, and indeed, it is specific for this wide variety.

	Toleration	Intolerance
Narrow	Classical	Active
Wide	**Recognition and toleration-cum-support**	**Active and passive**

What are the advantages of wide toleration concept? The first advantage is the conservative one: following ordinary usage and enabling systematization of existing debates etc.

The second is unifying the requirements that are normally put forward if one wants to characterize an attitude or act as tolerant or intolerant. To see this consider the problem that faces the "exclusionists," like Raz, Comanducci, and others who want to exclude the attitudes related to negative toleration, but not identical with it. What concept can they offer to characterize them? Respect is the most popular candidate (developed in detail by Galeotti in her (2002) book). However, it is too narrow. It does not capture the ideal of full recognition, that has been proposed by other authors Lukes (1997) or Macioce (2017) as the right "alternative kind" of attitude. But recognition is too strong to capture weaker but still positive attitudes. Similarly, Danilo Zolo (1997) talks about "battle for rights" of relevant groups etc. Again, too narrow.

In brief, no concept proposed captures the unity corresponding to the continuity of attitude-kinds, going from weak positive attitude to a group all the way to the "battle for rights" of such a group. What is the right concept that could capture it? This is the problem of the "other kind" faced by the exclusionist.

The conclusion seems to be that there is no usable alternative to widening; the wide concept of positive toleration covers precisely the ground that the narrow conceptual alternatives (recognition, respect, battle for rights) proposed by the exclusionists fails to cover, and it does it in a unitary and uniform manner. So much about toleration and its contrary.

In applying the present scheme to the case of migrants, refugees (and culturally different others in general) one can be pointing to *The Marakesh global compact* which in a fine, although laconic way, suggests the right tolerant treatments of them, in order to illustrate the important fact that this kind of treatment is not just a moral recommendation of philosophers and activist, but is already gaining legal ground. It is not legally binding, but is proposing the relevant idea as possible future legally binding recommendations. Note that after the initial meeting in Morocco on 10 and 11 December 2018, more than 150 countries have signed the Compact; characteristically, the Pope supported it. Orban and Trump did not. Most importantly, the Compact states that "refugees and migrants are entitled to the same universal human rights and fundamental freedoms, which must be respected, protected and fulfilled at all times" (Preamble, point 4).

The proposals in the Compact are not arranged in any recognizable order; we shall systematize them a bit, following the commonsensical assumptions about the travel, entrance and life in the host countries by the migrants.

Populist Intolerance and How to Fight It

Hospitality and the Classical Passive Toleration

We have noted the new features of the playground in international relations in the last two decades. First, the new proximity of once distant suffering folks; second the absence of traditional nationalistic threats in present-day Europe and North America; and third, the transforming power of the populist identity politics, inventing new enemies, strong enough to mobilize one's "people," and appealing to new solidarities: cultural-religious, wider ethnic and so on. And we noted that migration crisis and populist intolerance enhance each other creating a vicious circle, all this on the background of the eclipse of a worldwide functioning arrangement with the UN becoming singularly inefficient, and with new multipolar arrangement(s) appearing at the horizon.

The framework of change is extremely wide. Here, we have to narrow our focus and choose one direction of populist intolerance to discuss it. So, now consider the stages of migration and subsequent survival in the host country, focusing the attention at the two opposing forces acting in the context, the populist intolerance and the tendency to counteract it. Consider two initial stages, first the travel from homeland to the new destination and, second, the arrival at the host-state border.

The actively intolerant populist side has clear recommendations. To quote the Austrian daily *Kronen Zeitung* (21.06.2017) that entitled and illustrated accordingly a study on immigration and Muslims on the front page as follows: "Close Borders for Muslims" (Report Islamophobia 2017: 58). The paradigmatic populist state president, Viktor Orban, during his visit to Bavaria similarly declared (on 08.01.2018) that "Hungary does not want Muslim invaders." A month later, on the national stage he condemns diversity and claims Hungarians "do not want their colors mixed" (Report, p. 453). Examples can be multiplied *ad nauseam*. They are, of course, meant to be relevant for both initial stages of migration: migrants and refugees should not be helped in traveling to our country, and, if they nevertheless arrive, they should be stopped at the border, with no help offered!

What about the opposite, tolerant side? Here, the classical passive toleration is crucial: the acting side in the relevant host country should not be rejecting the newcomers. Some active toleration is, however, also needed: the refugees need to be let in and helped.

The Marakesh global compact derives the relevant duties from the human rights obligations, and notes that "refugees and migrants are entitled to the same universal human rights and fundamental freedoms," with refugees enjoying "the specific international protection" (Objective 4, here "O" will stand for "Objective"). It requires "availability and flexibility of pathways for regular migration" (O.5); a requirement that now sounds like a far-away ideal for future. And acceptance involves bringing together families that have been separated (Marakesh, O.7, e, f), the opposite of what was done to Mexican immigrant families by the Trump administration in December 2018. It further requires search for missing migrants (O.8), and declares war to smugglers (O.9, 10). Finally, it demands certainty and predictability in migration, of crucial importance to both sides in the encounter, the refugees and the border controls (and allows detention only as an exceptional and short-term measure).

Consider the problems of the first stage. The immediate emergency is assumed psychologically to trigger the Samaritan reaction, and normatively to command it. But can the process start at all? Present-day Greece and Italy are offering the spectacular proof of practical possibility. Greece, an economically heavily burdened country, is showing hospitality to something like 50,000 immigrants (almost a million have passed through the county since 2015). Their life is still difficult, but they do survive, and are getting the necessary minimum. Since 2013, Italy took in over 700,000 migrants! Turkey has taken more than three millions of refugees, but has not offered them the minimum as we see it from our more Western perspective. See Manuel P. Schoenhuber (2018). So, in this case "can" implies "ought," and the antecedent is fulfilled. (For the local example of the Balkan route see the more pessimistic Morvai and Djokovic (2018)), and a more optimistic Nicolas Parent (2018). For the example of Czech republic see Derek Sayer (2018). Of course, the three countries are overburdened. It is clear that potential host states should divide the task; this is the only fair and stable solution (Thanks Boris Vezjak on insisting on the amount of responsibility of host counties!).

The first issue on the list of duties is the very acceptance of refugees, the moral and political duty that has not been respected in many cases. However, at the present time the duties are simply not being fulfilled.

The next set of duties concerns the settlement of the newcomers. One phenomenon is to be avoided at all costs, the very long-term stay in refugee camps; in some cases, big groups of refugees were kept in a camp for something like 17 years. Then comes the task often mentioned in UNHCR documents, of bringing together families, and other closely related group. Finally, there is the two-faced requirement of security. Refugees are sometimes threatened by intergroup violence, and have to be protected. On the other side, some traumatized refugees become violent, and should be restrained.

This brings us to analogous, but more complex demands at the second stage. Here, important changes hopefully take place. On the host side, the initial empathetic reaction connects the local to the (once) distant strangers and to their society and culture. The host person can learn in an empathetic, engaged way what the life is like there, how difficult it is to survive, and so on. (To give a Balkan examples, Bulgarian and Croatian traditions contain sufficiently many multicultural features, most importantly the centuries-long presence of Islam, that might serve as a bridge.)

On the immigrant side, the welcome and the new way of life might produce positive changes. I everything works well, our immigrant learns to appreciate the host country, say Bulgaria, and the community, say of Plovdiv, which has accepted her. Second, she might, after the experiences of both suffering and welcome, develop a better understanding of compassion. And finally, she starts understanding how her new country fits the larger framework. Simon Keller sees the accomplished perspective as "the perspective of the worldly citizen" 2013: 250). But let me go quickly through duties of positive toleration, related to the ones in the first stage, but acquiring new proportions and complexity. The duty of settling the refugees is now transformed and extended to providing decent housing for them. Germany has done a lot in this direction immediately after the 2015 crisis, sometimes securing big, comfortable houses for some lucky newcomers. Here, a very urgent set of duties concerns health care. Physical needs are numerous, and clearly demanding. But these days much work is being done on psychological trauma, for instance the posttraumatic stress disorder (PTSD), common to men and women who are coming from war-ridden countries. Psychologists distinguish simple posttraumatic stress disorder (PTSD) and complex posttraumatic stress disorder (CPTSD). The typical causes of the later are serious neglect, physical assault, and sexual assault, whereas the typical causes of the PTSD are "situational traumatic experiences," for instance, unarmed civilian in a conflict environment and a serious accident (see for example, Rainer Forst (2013), and a thesis by a Syrian student, Rosemary Yachouh (2018)).

The most important requirement is non-isolation: the refugees must have opportunity to mix and interact with the locals, less the isolated areas for foreigners become a source of discrimination, then resentment and then open conflicts.

The duties of health care become more subtle; dramatic emergencies are replaced with the issue of the level of health care, and various obstacles to the high-quality approach. For instance, problems with language often block negotiations about health care and are partly responsible for long-term illnesses of newcomers from Bangladesh or Pakistan (OSI 2010: 154). Some linguistic help has been organized in countries like Great Britain for refugees from former Yugoslavia; the practice should be renewed and extended. Also, the respect for cultural specificities, for example, the availability of healthy halal food, has become central for refugees from Muslim countries (Ibid).

Active Toleration in the Service of Inclusion

The next issue is the inclusion. Can newcomers become full members of the host society? Here, intolerance has been quite visible. To give examples from Austria and Italy in 2017 and 2018 (using data from European Islamophobia Reports for these 2 years) let me not the following: In Austria in spring 2017: the then Chairman Strache declared "No, Islam is not part of Austria" during a FPO party convention in Klagenfurt (04.03.2017). In the fall of the same year the then (and now) OVP Chairman Sebastian Kurz used his Facebook account to legitimize Islamophobic politics with headlines from tabloid media (e.g. 10.08.2017). Also, at the same time, the Identitarian movement placed banners saying "Stop Islamization. Close Islam schools!" on the building of a Vienna school (few months earlier, on 14.05.2018, the OVP General Secretary Karl Nehammer argued that "fasting in Ramadan should be banned for pupils.")

Similar things were happening in Italy. At the beginning of 2018 Matteo Salvini declared in Rome: that nowadays Islam is a danger and his future government would put a stop to the irregular Islamic presence in Italy. (A piece of news from 03.02.2018 from Macerata points to the more practical side: Luca Traini, a supporter of far right movements such as Forza Nuova, shot a group of Nigerian immigrants; six immigrants, five men, and one woman were wounded.) On 08.02.2018 the following news came from Milano: Matteo Salvini declared being against a project for the construction of an Islamic center, claiming that "Islam is incompatible with the Italian Constitution."

And let me conclude the negative part by pointing to one more extremely intolerant reaction. Responding to the Manchester Arena attack, a suicide bombing attack on 22 May 2017, columnist Katie Hopkins tweeted, "We need a final solution."

So much about intolerance. On the side of active toleration, what about the moral duty to accommodate the refugees?

First, preparation for inclusion; here offering decent work to refugees is the *conditio* sine qua non. This third set of duties seems to open a dramatic dilemma for more leftist oriented intellectuals: very often, poor newcomers compete with the poor or low middle-class workers in the host countries. If we want to keep the hardly earned levels of lives the host country workers have, how do we deal with the massive competition of the newcomers? The dilemma is often discussed in the literature; it was also expressed in wonderful talk by Philippe van Parijs, entitled "Just Migration, Within and Into Europe," on January 18, 2019.

The Marakesh Compact is very much on the proactive side of the dilemma, as can be seen from the following quotations:

(18) Invest in skills development and facilitate mutual recognition of skills, qualifications and competences.

And it assumes that all of the following is needed for implementing human rights of migrants!

19) Create conditions for migrants and diasporas to fully contribute to sustainable development in all countries

Of course, the opponents will claim that investment in skills just creates competition with "our" domestic workers, so that solidarity with migrants brings catastrophe for our domestic workers. The most optimistic line of answer, which might work, is offered by sociologists and economists who study the actual developments in various host countries, like the researchers brought together in Arcarazo's and Wiesbrock's (2015) collection *Global Migration: Old Assumptions, New Dynamics* (Praeger). Studies, in particular countries, for instance Spain, suggest that for last few decades the immigrants were really responding to a demand for labor generated by Spanish companies and families. Indeed, it was the demand for unskilled labor launched by economic actors (employers and families) that largely contributed to the generation of immigration; reference to families alludes to the massive demand for persons who would take care of the sick and elderly. Moreover, immigrant labor contributed to the survival (at least temporarily) of economic sectors that would otherwise have succumbed to international competition, in this way generating wealth and helping to maintain higher skilled and better paid jobs for autochthonous workers. And they did this under adverse conditions that often included "open exploitation"!

Other studies suggest that far from taking attractive jobs from the home workers, the newcomers end up in discriminated sectors. As things stand now, even for Muslims who came many years ago, the employment situation is bad: they are not integrated into the labor market to the extent other workers are, and studies suggest the presence of discrimination (OSI 2010: Chap. 5). The dilemma can at the end turn out to be a myth, rather than a burning issue. The Marakesh Compact seems to suggest this option. It encourages all the sides to do the following:

(19) Create conditions for migrants and diasporas to fully contribute to sustainable development in all countries.

The following remark in the Compact can illustrate the way it sees the ways for this objective to be realized (the present text keeps the letters marking each paragraph):

e) Develop targeted support programmes and financial products that facilitate migrant and diaspora investments and entrepreneurship, including by providing administrative and legal support in business creation, granting seed capital-matching, establish diaspora bonds and diaspora development funds, investment funds, and organize dedicated trade fairs.

Let us now pass to inclusion proper. Here come issues of "ideological disagreement" about the extent to which refugee culture should be accommodated (at least in elements that to not threaten elementary human rights). Pro-refugee authors stress positive elements in the refugee culture, above all in Islam, the typical backbone of ordinary identities. Speaking of younger generation of Muslims in Europe, Tariq Modood (2006) notes that for many of them, irrespective of gender, Islam is "a source of educational aspirations and motivations to improve oneself" (250); and that this is particularly important for girls, contrary to what prejudices about Muslims suggest. He compares the motivational force of Islam to Protestant ethics. This kind of results suggests that once Muslims are accepted in the host community, there is a wide ground for negotiations, most importantly about elements in politically understood Islam which go against rights of women and the like. (Compare the advice given by Tariq Ramadan to his fellow Muslims in his well-known (1999, 2004) books. *Western Muslims and the future of Islam* Oxford University Press.)

Now, three decades ago, the social psychologist John W. Berry has offered a picture of varieties of acculturation that fits very much our present needs. Consider a Somali refugee to Norway who intends to stay. One can ask her about her wishes in relation to her Somali identity and to her host country. First, whether she wishes to maintain her Somali identity and characteristics in the new circumstances. If her answer is No, she is giving up on one important strain of her life but is becoming ready to accept a new one. Second, we can ask her how she feels about the host, Norwegian society. Does she want to integrate, find Norwegian friends, possibly a partner, cooperate with Norwegians in her surroundings, narrow or wide, and the like? If No, she is in for separation, Berry proposes. Finally, we have the option he finds best: keeping one's former identity and, at the same time, acquiring the new one. Here is his systematization of "strategies of acculturation":

		Maintaining identity and characteristics?	
		No	Yes
Maintain relation with wider society?	Yes	ASSIMILATION	INTEGRATION
	No	MARGINALIZATION	SEPARATION

He notes that the integrationist or bi-cultural acculturation strategy typically carries with it more positive outcomes than the three alternatives of assimilation, separation, or especially marginalization (1997: 27). The last one can lead to deep stress, even to trauma.

To stay with the Somali example, researchers talk about the need of second generation young Norwegian-Somalis, who continue to feel Somali, to feel included in their surrounding Norwegian society (OSI 2013: 46). One can then follow Barry and take the bi-cultural acculturation to be the true and promising integration. And follow the researchers on the actual life of Muslims in European cities who tell the reader about the deep need of these people for inclusion, and perhaps a built-up of a new identity "on the top" of the old, inherited one. Here the term "integration" will be used in this two-tier copy-paste sense.

Now, here is a conjecture to be proposed. Refugees come with their cultural and ethnic identity each. Assume that many of them are willing to integrate, if, first, offered the possibility of keeping centrally important features of their original identity, and second, offered the chance of inclusion into host society. Of course, there will always be those who find the centrally important features simply incompatible with the host identity, and they will opt for separation. But, one can stay focused upon the first group, on the road to integration. They have been offered active toleration and are accepting it.

Probably, once they are sufficiently integrated, some unacceptable items from their former identity will simply disappear, and that other will become less prominent.

Viewed from the host perspective, there will be a change of persons, and of the way of viewing them. This change might then change the content of their beliefs and actions, so that they look less provocative.

Here is the example of burka that looks inacceptable for many original citizens of Europe. Watching a documentary about young Bosnian women who insist on wearing burka I was surprised by their honest enthusiasm; there was no suggestion of pressure ("we have to, our family demands it from us"). Then, reading interviews with young French Muslim women who favor burka (OSI 2011), one can be even more surprised to learn that they describe their motive as purely religious, the inspiration coming from reading Koran or going to listen to an imam, but strictly with an interest in matters religious. No mention of any pressures of Muslim men in their surroundings, no mention of political motives: they see themselves as French, with Islam as their private religion. "There is your Lord and you, and no other enters. You live for your Lord. You live in permanent adoration, or at least you try so to live" (2011: 87). Viewed as purely religious, almost existential requirement, burka seems less incompatible with our society and culture. Once you see the women as being French, of entertaining this sort of existential choices, you do not see burka as something deeply offending the political morality of our culture!

So, to reiterate the conjecture, successful integration in the strong, two-component sense is a fine product of successful active toleration. Once achieved it makes the person and her beliefs and actions more acceptable, and typically diminishes the need for passive toleration

The section shall end with pointing to a wider problem. The Marakesh compact reminds us, quite unexpectedly (in its Obj. 2), that the international community should go way beyond wide toleration. The Objective suggests that we should "Minimize the adverse drivers and structural factors that compel people to leave their country of origin." Of course, the requirement is extremely wide reaching; no wonder that the comments added to it, fail to address the obvious, namely the fact that people very often leave their country of origin in order to avoid wars and massive and organized violence. The only remedy here is intervention that will first, stop the war, and, second, make sure that no new war will be started. Considerations of human rights of would-be refugees thus lead us way beyond organizing help; they seem to require first, cosmopolitan intervention, and second, cosmopolitan international control strong enough to prevent warfare. This road to cosmopolitanism is an issue worthy of exploring (see Nenad Miščević 2019).

Conclusion

Summarizing the Results

The text started by pointing to an analogy between the present day populist intolerance toward foreigners, in particular migrants and refugees and the classical intolerance from the ages of religious wars of early modernity, and the resulting analogies in demands for toleration. The first question has been how to characterize these populist intolerant attitudes, and their contraries. One might also react to the outcry in the theoretical, mostly philosophical, literature demanding the theoreticians to go beyond toleration, when it comes to the burning issues of the present moment. This is done here by an appeal to a wide, more ordinary, less traditionally philosophical, notion of toleration and intolerance. The first encompasses acceptance, and even support as part of such active toleration; the second then follows suit and counts both non-acceptance, and complete lack of active support as marks of intolerance. The present-day debate invites philosophers to use the wide notions, both of toleration and of intolerance in order, first, to keep in touch with main lines of debate, and second, to have at their disposal a more unitary notions (wider toleration, wide intolerance) capable of organizing the philosophical understanding of the burning issue.

Armed with this wider notions, one can then turn to the main issue for the populist: the treatment of migrants and refugees. Interestingly, international documents like the Marakesh compact point to the active toleration (in the sense defended here), as the right kind of treatment and as protecting human rights of migrants and refugees, and offer concisely formulated guidelines for action. One could thus argue that the main remedies for the populist intolerance have been already formulated in international legal documents.

The text then proposes to appeal to these guidelines both in diagnosing the ills of intolerance, narrow and wide, and in proposing remedies motivated and guided by wide active toleration. The populist intolerance shows is teeth at east stage of migrants-refugees progress toward the normal life away from their miserable home. Here is a summary:

The first stage of interaction at which populist intolerance toward migrants and refugees shows its teeth is the stage of their travel and arrival at the border of the targeted host country. Here it is both passive classical toleration-non-rejection and its more active counterpart that count, and the actual acceptance and admission of the needy, if all goes well, of course.

The next stage, following the admission, involves urgent, short-term help, primarily medical and linguistic and then provisory settlement providing. Populists try to block these urgently needed activities, but international documents already detail the requirements of active toleration, the Marakesh compact grounding them in human rights of the newcomers.

The analogous demands for toleration, active and passive, stay in force at the stage of long(er) term settlement in the host country. Such settlement is the main target of populist indignation.

Finally, the pressing further issue of prevention of the causes of unwanted migration, most spectacularly of violence in countries of origin, clearly shows the need of a more cosmopolitan activity: violence can be prevented only by international control that can be implemented by a more tightly organized international community, but this is the topic for another paper.

To return to the more theoretical issue, concerning the understanding of toleration and its contrary one may hope that the application of wide notions of both offered here illustrates the need for and usefulness of the wide conception. A useful characterization of populist intolerance would appeal both to its narrow *and* its wide variety, so that one needs a unitary term to stress the unity of the phenomenon.

The same is valid for remedies. Their kinds seem to be continuous among themselves, and in the contexts of application just listed their connection shows quite well. Again, unity is extremely useful.

Possible Future Avenues for Research

The area of toleration is enormous, and the present volume testifies to a staggering number of possible future avenues of approach. Here is the right place to add a few words of the narrow topic from the title – the populist intolerance.

On the purely theoretical side, one has witnessed a deepening of the study of populism, where various targets of populist intolerance have been put in context of history of populism. Jason Stanley (2018) and Henry A. Giroux (2018) have recently discussed connections to fascist ideology; the topic is further being developed also in relation to Central and Eastern Europe, for instance Slovenia (personal communication by Boris Vezjak). Other directions of research might bring forward further comparison and further insights.

A further topic is the comparison of left-wing and right-wing populism. Authors like Chantal Mouffe and her collaborators present the left-wing variant as being free of typical populist intolerance; the actual practice of Latin American populist leaders might point in the opposite direction.

On the more practical side an urgent topic is fighting the causes of populism and caused by Trump's populist followers who tried to occupy the Congress, and the reactions to it have provoked, among politicians and among most engaged participants, a search for possible therapies of such intolerance.

At the more general level one can ask about the way from immediate toleration of groups like refugees to a wider cosmopolitan activity; the latter might go to the issues having to do with causes of migrations, like wars in the Third World, dramatic distributional injustice, and the phenomena linked to climate change and the recent pandemics (see papers collected in Brown and Eckersley (2018)). So, besides the problems concerning the immediate presence of needy foreigners, there is the wider question of how to ameliorate the situation in their countries of origin. The first and the most obvious cause of dramatic problems is the spread of violence in the large part of the global South. The Middle East is the closest and most dramatic example, but other examples abound in Africa, in the Sub-Saharan, but also in the northern part, with Libya and Somalia as the obvious dramatic examples. How are the wars to be avoided? The second big group of distal causes has to do with just distribution, and the third, crucially important one, with human rights and global democracy.

This is just a very brief sketch; the area is very rich with problems and issues and discussion about possible avoidance of populist intolerance can bring the researchers quite a long way into the central issues of contemporary political theory.

References

Acosta Arcarazo D, Wiesbrock A (eds) (2015) Global migration: old assumptions, new dynamics. Praeger, Santa Barbara

Apel K-O (1997) Plurality of the Good? The problem of affirmative tolerance in a multicultural society from an ethical point of view. Ratio Juris 10(2):199–212

Bangstad I (2016) Norwegian right-wing discourses: extremism post-Utøya. In: Pratt D, Woodlock R (eds) Fear of Muslims? International perspectives on Islamophobia. Springer, Cham, pp 231–250

Berry JW (1997) Immigration, acculturation, and adaptation. Appl Psychol Int Rev 46(1):5–68

Betz H-G (2017) Populism and Islamophobia. In: Heinisch R, Holtz-Bacha C, Mazzoleni O (eds) Political populism: a handbook. NOMOS, Baden-Baden, pp 375–392

Brown C, Eckersley R (eds) (2018) The Oxford handbook of international political theory. Oxford University Press, Oxford

Comanducci P (1997) Some comments on toleration. Ratio Juris 10(2):187–192

Dobbernack J, Modood T (eds) (2013) Tolerance, intolerance and respect hard to accept? Palgrave Macmillan, Basingstoke

Dobbernack J, Modood T (2019) Tolerance, pluralism and social cohesion: responding to the challenges of the 21st century in Europe (ACCEPT PLURALISM). Robert Schuman Centre for Advanced Studies

Gellner E, Ionescu G (1969) Populism. Macmillan, New York

Giroux HA (2018) American nightmare: facing the challenge of fascism. City Lights Publishers, San Francisco

Glück J (2019) Wisdom vs. populism and polarization: learning to regulate our evolved intuitions. In: Sternberg RJ, Nusbaum HC, Glück J (eds) Applying wisdom to contemporary world problems. Palgrave Macmillan, Cham, pp 81–110

Hjerm M, Eger MA, Bohman A, Connolly FF (2019) A new approach to the study of tolerance: conceptualizing and measuring acceptance, respect, and appreciation of difference. Soc Indic Res:1–23

Honohan I (2013) Toleration and non-domination. In: Dobbernack J, Modood T (eds) Tolerance, intolerance and respect hard to accept? Palgrave Macmillan, Basingstoke, pp 77–99

Jazexhi O (2019) Islamophobia in Albania-2. In: Bayrakli E, Hafez F (eds) European Islamophobia report 2018. SETA, pp 60–85

Laegard S (2013) State toleration, religious recognition and equality. In: Dobbernack J, Modood T (eds) Tolerance, intolerance and respect hard to accept? Palgrave Macmillan, Basingstoke, pp 52–75

Lester E, Roberts PS (2006) Active tolerance as a mean between passive tolerance and recognition. Public Aff Q 20(4):329–362

Lukes S (1997) Toleration and recognition. Ratio Juris 10(2):213–22

Macioce F (2017) Toleration as Asymmetric Recognition PERSONA Y DERECHO número 77 (julio-diciembre), 227–250

Miscevic N (2019) Facing strangers in need, toleration, refugee crisis and cosmopolitanism. Balkan J Philos 11(1):15–30

Modood T, Triandafyllidou A, Zapata-Barrero R (eds) (2006) Multiculturalism, Muslims and citizenship: a European approach. Routlege

Morvai H, Djokovic D (2018) Managing migration: the Balkans united against refugees. N Engl J Publ Policy 30(2 Special issue on Migration):1–7

Mudde C (2007) Populist radical right parties in Europe. Cambridge University Press, Cambridge

Nenad Miščević (2019) We will give back the state to the people: right-wing populism, nationalism and new political challenges, političke perspektive: časopis za istraživanje politike 9(1):37–66

Nussbaum MC (2012) The new religious intolerance overcoming the politics of fear in an anxious age. The Belknap Press of Harvard University Press, Cambridge

OSI (2010) Muslims in Europe, Budapest

OSI (2011) Un voile sur les Réalités, New York

OSI (2013) Somalis in Oslo, New York

Parent N (2018) Four voices of refugee solidarity along the Balkan route: an exploratory pilot study on motivations for mobilization. Migr Lett, July 15(3):423–436

Rainer Forst (2013) Toleration in conflict past and present, Cambridge University Press

Ramadan T (1999) To be a European Muslim: a study of Islamic sources in the European context. The Islamic Foundation, Leicester

Ramadan T (2004) Western Muslims and the future of Islam. Oxford University Press, Oxford

Raz J (1988/first issue 1986) The morality of freedom. Clarendon Press/Oxford University Press, Oxford

Sayer D (2018) Prejudice, hysteria and a failure of political leadership: of refugees and November 17 in Prague. New Perspect 26(2(S)):137–140

Scanlon TM (1996) The difficulty of tolerance. In: Heyd D (ed) Toleration: an elusive virtue. Princeton University Press, Princeton, pp 226–239

Schoenhuber MP (2018) The European union's refugee deal with Turkey: a risky alliance contrary to European laws and values. Houst J Int Law Spring:634–670

Stanley J (2018) How fascism works: the politics of us and them. Penguin, New York

The Marakesh global compact (2018) Global compact for safe, orderly and regular migration, UN

Urbinati N (2019) Me the people: how populism transforms democracy. Harvard University Press, Cambridge

Walzer M (1997a) The politics of difference: statehood and toleration in a multi-cultural world. Ratio Juris 10:165–176

Walzer M (1997b) On toleration. Yale University Press, New Haven

Williams B (1996) In: Heyd D (ed) Toleration: an impossible virtue? Princeton University Press, Princeton/Chichester, pp 18–27

Williams MS, Waldron J (eds) (2008) Toleration and its limits, Nomos; 48. Press, New York University

Yachouh R (2018) A qualitative investigation of the mental health needs of Syrian refugees and immigrants. Available at Pro Quest

Zolo D (1997) Positive tolerance: An Ethical Oxymoron. Ratio Juris 10(2):247–51

Fear and Toleration

34

Robert Paul Churchill

Contents

Introduction	674
The Causes and Consequences of Fear and In-group/Out-group Biases	675
The Neurosciences of Fear and Other Basic Emotions	675
Fear, Enmity, and Us/Theming	678
Liberal Democracy, Toleration, and Civility	680
Liberal Democracy	680
Toleration as a Duty of Civility	682
Recognition Respect and Second-Personal Agents	684
Fear, Empathy, and Toleration	686
Decreasing Fearfulness and Intolerance	688
Addressing Socioeconomic Inequalities That Generate Fear and Distress	689
Ensuring the Viability of Civility and Public Reasoning	690
Democratizing Knowledge of Fear and Intolerance	692
Contact Theory: Collaborative Problem-Solving and Nonviolent Interaction	693
Increasing Opportunities for Helping	695
Summary	696
References	697

Abstract

This chapter is an in-depth examination of the interconnections between fear and similar negative emotions and toleration. Given the resurgence of prejudice, racism, and xenophobia, toleration has renewed significance for the theory and politics of liberal democracies. When understood as a duty of civility that promotes public reasoning among citizens, toleration is necessary if liberal democracies are to thrive. Fear, anger, and disgust and other negative emotions have the effect of negating, blocking, and hindering tolerant attitudes and behaviors. Fear is also strongly associated with the inherent human proclivity to automatically distinguish "Us" versus "Them" with prejudice for members of one's own

R. P. Churchill (✉)
Department of Philosophy, George Washington University, Westminster, MD, USA

© The Author(s), under exclusive licence to Springer Nature Switzerland AG 2022
M. Sardoč (ed.), *The Palgrave Handbook of Toleration*,
https://doi.org/10.1007/978-3-030-42121-2_37

in-group and enmity for members of out-groups. This chapter develops the conception of toleration as a duty of civility and explains how toleration facilitates public reasoning. In addition, the chapter considers how our sensitivity to fear and pain, when it is awareness of other's fearfulness, often enhances capacities for empathy, altruism, and possibly toleration as well. To date, toleration has not been well studied in the sciences and further research is required on fear as promoting intolerance, on the connections between fearfulness and out-group prejudice, and on the possibly positive consequences of fear. Insofar as we presently know many of the ways fear undercuts toleration and threatens the stability of liberal democracies, the chapter ends with a review of a number of important ways to decrease the effects of fearfulness, resist intolerance, and strengthen toleration.

Keywords

Toleration · Fear · Altruism · Emotions · Empathy · Liberal democracy · Neuroscience · Prefrontal cortex · Public reason · Duty of civility · Second-personal agents · Recognition respect · Inequality · Contact theory · Complex emotions · Anger · Disgust · Neutrality · Democratizing knowledge · Deepfakes

Introduction

Studies of the effects of fearfulness (and cognates such as anxiety, enmity, distrust, and insecurity) on toleration could hardly be more important given the rise of prejudice, racism, and xenophobia, along with demagoguery and right-wing nationalism. Fortunately, recent research in psychology, the neurosciences, neuroeconomics, and evolutionary theory offer new insights into understanding the interconnections between fearfulness and toleration, as well as democratic theory and public policy. Yet, new research shows that some consequences of fear seem paradoxical, and might possibly contribute positively to increased toleration.

On the negative side of the ledger, so to speak, fear and other negative emotions operate to negate, block, or hinder tolerant attitudes and behaviors. These emotions also associate strongly with the inherent human proclivity to distinguish "Us" from "Them," with prejudice for one's own in-group and prejudice against out-groups. Yet, despite being "hardwired" for fear as a basic emotion, evolution has endowed humans with a highly complex prefrontal cortex (PFC) and complex, interactive nervous system. Hence, on the positive side, while managing Us/Theming, the PFC learns from experience and can modulate, inhibit, or even rewire and thus "rewrite" so-called "affect programs" for fear. More surprisingly, research on brain imaging (fMRI studies) demonstrates that fear, when it is the awareness of fearfulness in others, can enhance empathy, and may enhance toleration as well. Moreover, recent studies suggest that the capacity to feel the emotions deeply, including fear, is required to engage in sound reasoning and decision-making, just as it is for altruistic and helping behaviors, and so, may be connected to the role of toleration in upholding civility and public reasoning.

This chapter is divided into four sections. Section "The Causes and Consequences of Fear and In-group/Out-group Biases" surveys the neuroscience of fear as a basic emotion as well as the evolutionary adaptability of certain "affect programs" that trigger fearful actions and form dispositional states such as intolerance. The Section "The Causes and Consequences of Fear and In-group/Out-group Biases" also investigates possible connections between fear and the basic process of "enemy making," namely, the evolutionary basis for Us/Theming and corresponding prejudice and enmity.

As toleration occurs most readily and fully within liberal democracies, section "Liberal Democracy, Toleration, and Civility" illuminates the relationships between liberal democracy, neutrality, and toleration. Because each of these concepts is discussed elsewhere in this *Palgrave Handbook*, their treatment here is brief, and intended only to support a key conception of toleration presented as necessary for liberal democracy. Thus issues central to the literature on toleration, such as the principle of neutrality, the necessary and sufficient conditions for toleration, and the so-called paradoxes of toleration are summarized only insofar as needed to support the focus of the section "Liberal Democracy, Toleration, and Civility." Instead, greater efforts are made to explain how toleration relates to recognition respect and second-personal agency, as well as toleration as crucial for the duty of civility and the commitment to public reasoning.

Section "Fear, Empathy, and Toleration" examines how it is possible for fear to promote certain "better angels of our nature." Connections between perceptions of others' pain and fearfulness may be very important in discovering how persons can become more tolerant. Finally, section "Decreasing Fearfulness and Intolerance" returns to the significance of toleration in sustaining a flourishing liberal democracy along with the duty of civility and a commitment to public reasoning. However, This last section "Decreasing Fearfulness and Intolerance" focuses attention on important measures that can be taken to preserve the quality of public reasoning and to resist the corrupting effects of fearfulness and enmity toward out-groups while increasing civility and toleration.

The Causes and Consequences of Fear and In-group/Out-group Biases

For the sake of coherence and the logic of exposition, this section, and others as necessary, is divided into progressive subsections. Each subsection is identified by section number and a number designating its place in that section.

The Neurosciences of Fear and Other Basic Emotions

Identifying the possible expressive movements of the facial muscles, psychologists have demonstrated that, when combined, they yield six basic human emotional expressions: anger, disgust, fear, happiness, sadness, and surprise (Ekman and Friesen 1978). A meta-analysis of hundreds of studies conducted across dozens of cultural groups found that viewers reliably interpret the meaning of fearful, angry, happy, and other basic expressions, even when displayed by members of even distant cultures across the globe (Marsh 2017: 187). Hence, these basic emotions are not learned culturally or through socialization; instead, the basic emotions were evolutionarily adaptive for our remote ancestors. The basic emotions became "hardwired" in the sense that each one has a distinct and dedicated neurological circuit connecting the limbic system, and especially the amygdala, with the prefrontal cortex, the endocrine system, and the autonomic and sympathetic nervous systems (Burton 2015).

Basic emotions such as fear are innate, universal (and possessed by human infants and many animals), automatic, and expressed with lightening-like rapidity. Indeed, because of the high survival value associated with the basic emotions, they were hardwired as "affect programs" that trigger a panoply of associated states and emotions as well as bodily processes that prepare an individual for action (Burton 2015). Like the emotions of disgust and surprise, basic fear responses (e.g., glimpsing a snake near one's feet) are so automatic as to be virtually "cognitively impenetrable" (Burton 2015) as well as largely unconscious and uncontrollable.

Fear and fearfulness are named differently, depending on context, circumstances, strength, and duration as, for example, anxiety, insecurity, dread, panic, and terror. Consider, for instance, a college graduate's panic upon realizing she is going to be late for an important job interview, or a motorist's terror on suddenly discovering that he has lost control of his vehicle. It is not completely known how so-called "complex," or secondary emotions are related to those most basic. It may be that some are "built" as blends of others: perhaps contempt is a blend of anger and disgust, and kindness is a blend of happiness (or joy), trust, and surprise (or anticipation). It has also been suggested that more specific, "complex" emotions are "amalgams" of basic emotions and cognitions (Burton 2015). Thus, for instance, hopelessness might result from anger combined with beliefs such as "Nothing worthwhile can come of this" and "I'll never succeed however hard I try."

Such accounts suggest that forming complex emotions requires both recursion and interchangeability. Blending is recursive when new emotions or beliefs are mixed in, and the complex is characterized by interchangeability because some emotions or cognitions can be substituted for others. It is likely that the most commonly experienced or important combinations are those to have earned specific names. Although an argument for the claim cannot be made here, it is highly likely that there is a "fear suite" of complementary negative emotions; in other words, fear as basic is somehow causally related to a set of auxiliary complex emotions (some of which may also be related to other basic emotions), such as abandonment, agony, apprehension, aversion, despair, distress, insecurity, misery, upset vulnerability, upset, worry, and woe.

While fear and its inevitable fight-or-flight syndrome are often associated with physical threats, humans are also capable of responding in the same way to *social threats*; the amygdala reacts to social threats in exactly the same way it reacts to physical danger (Amodio 2019). Hence, the circumstances and objects that trigger fear are subject to learning and cultural conditioning, as well as the significance we attach to them. While humans are hardwired to fear only a small number of real objects and situations (e.g., spiders and predatory animals), in modern societies, humans have been conditioned to fear perceived threats to identity, status, and socioeconomic well-being. For instance, there is nothing remotely deadly about a course grade; a student's fears of failing an exam are in large part a result of the values his or her culture attaches to academic success. With complex emotions generally, the emotions as well as their objects are culturally shaped and context dependent. Some, for instance, schadenfreude, were not common to all peoples at all times, and some such as romantic love have had culturally specific origins.

As we shall see, however, we do have innate dispositions, or "event-related potentials" to the subliminal perception of differences, especially other-race faces, discussed below in connection with "Us versus Them." Nevertheless, most of what we fear we learn to fear by trial and error, although the central brain regions most involved in feeling afraid and anxious, the amygdala, is highly vigilant of and sensitive to uncertainty and unpredictability and thus predisposes us for "prepared learning" (Sapolsky 2017: 36). The more recently evolved basolateral amygdala (BLA) wraps around the ancient amygdala and learns fear that it then sends to the central amygdala (36). BLA neurons can be remapped into new circuitry, and the greater the activation of the amygdala in humans the greater the behavioral signs of fear (Ledoux 1990; Sapolsky 2017).

Because the amygdala is also highly activated when subjects are angry and aggressive (Sapolsky: 31), we can speculate that there is a likely connection between the basic emotions of fear and anger. Perhaps hatred, as a complex emotion, represents a blend of fear and anger plus cognitive elements, while loathing represents a blend of fear and disgust. In any case, it is difficult to imagine how the body is automatically prepared by fear for dramatic and often fierce fight-or-flight responses unless there is an intrinsic connection between fear and anger. Moreover, projections from the insular cortex, which processes gustatory disgust and repulsive smells, also activate the amygdala, and thus suggest that disgust too may be connected with fear and anger. The connections between all three may lie in an ancient, core brain structure known as the periaqueductal gray (PAG) that mediates projections of pain (Sapolsky: 41). After all, it is well known that pain and its anticipation trigger both fear and aggression.

Three additional points about the amygdala and fear are important for this discussion of tolerance. First, the amygdala reacts with lightning-like speed and wholly subconsciously when not mediated by the prefrontal cortex (PFC). Ordinarily, sensory information from various modalities courses into the brain where it is processed and sent to the BLA and the amygdala. However, sensory information entering the brain can bypass the cortex enabling the amygdala to react to frightening stimuli before there is awareness in the cortex. Regrettably, along with increased speed comes decreased accuracy; for instance, the amygdala may inform the PFC that one is seeing a handgun before fuller processing in the visual cortex can report that it's actually a cell phone.

Second, just as certain social threats will trigger unconscious negative emotions, fear, anger, and disgust can be activated symbolically in humans and some other mammals. For instance, experimenters can provoke anger, fear, and disgust in subjects by showing them pictures of, respectively, fearful, angry, and disgusting facial expressions. These emotions also can be provoked in subjects by having them think about appropriate ideas or scenes. Moreover, we have learned to attach these emotions to abstractions as well as social situations. For example, subjects will react with disgust when asked to think about something "morally disgusting" – such as a serious violation of a social norm (Sapolsky: 41).

Thirdly, our brains are not very good at calculating the actual state of the world with accuracy. Our brains evolved not to be accurate, but for the sake of survival. Consequently, our brains "are systematically biased toward perceiving, remembering, and predicting bad things" (Marsh: 209) that could threaten survival over good things that would at best incrementally improve it. This negativity bias is also prevalent in our social lives; for instance, negative comments from others have a stronger impact than positive comments, so much so that a psychologist has estimated that, to be successful, romantic relationships must be marked by at least a five-to-one ratio of kind and supportive comments to unkind comments (Gottman 2015). Likewise, the worse the action, the more likely it is to be remembered and used to estimate what an individual or group of persons is really like (Marsh: 210).

Fear is dampened down or inhibited in the prefrontal cortex (PFC). The left-side, or dorsolateral, PFC (diPFC) is the seat of executive function, and as such is the most "rational, cognitive, utilitarian, unsentimental" part of the PFC (Sapolsky: 54). The right side of the PFC, or ventromedial PFC (vmPFC), is the part directly connected to the limbic system and the amygdala. The vmPFC enables the emotions to bear on decision-making, sometimes aware to us only as intuitions or gut feelings. In fully functional and healthy adults, the diPFC and vmPFC typically collaborate in reasoning, planning, and making decisions (Sapolsky, 78). Research has demonstrated that Damasio's (2005) theory is correct; individuals whose vmPFC has been damaged not only have trouble making decisions but also show poor judgment.

These remarks about the PFC can be summed up by the claim that "the frontal cortex makes you do the harder thing when it is the right thing to do" (Sapolsky: 45). Combined with working memory, executive function, and action initiation, the PFC enables us to rein-in impulsivity, defer gratification, engage in long-term planning, and regulate our emotions. That said, it must be noted that there is greater interindividual variability among persons than average levels of whole-brain differences between humans and chimps (Sapolsky: 45). Moreover, resting metabolic rate in the PFC varies approximately 30-fold among people (Sapolsky: 63). While the causal effects of metabolic differences are not well understood, they might be a critical factor in considering why some people find it easier to be tolerant than do others.

Fear, Enmity, and Us/Theming

Our brains form dichotomies based on race, gender, and status, at an alarming speed. It takes only a 50-millisecond exposure to the face of someone of another race to activate the amygdala, 150 milliseconds to process the gender of a face, and 40 milliseconds to distinguish low-status from high-status presentations (Sapolsky: 88 and 388). The amygdala is notoriously averse to ambiguity and uncertainty and biased toward associating danger with difference (Olson et al. 2005). It is well confirmed that people shown facial images at a subliminal speed judge neutral other-race faces as angrier than neutral same-race faces. The same is true with perceptions of threat; White subjects rapidly shown pictures of people holding either a gun or a mobile phone were far more likely to "see" Black persons carrying guns than Whites, regardless of whether the image was of an armed person (Cornell et al. 2007). Moreover, the more racist someone is on an implicit bias (or association) test, the more activation there is of the amygdala.

While humans are hardwired to make these distinctions, we are not hardwired to fear the face of another race or to have gender- or status-related biases. We have been hardwired by evolution as social creatures to distinguish between in-group presentations in this way; in fact, because making such distinctions was so adaptively advantageous, Us/Theming will track even minimally significant, and even arbitrary markers of sameness and difference. We feel positive associations with people who share traits with us, even when they are meaningless, and often have negative feelings about those who differ from us.

In a classic experiment Sherif et al. (1961) and his associates were able to demonstrate how easy it is to provoke what can be called "marginal" Us versus Theming in a population and then to extinguish it. Sherif had boys at a summer camp divided into two groups (the Eagles and the Rattlers) and allowed them to select markers of in-group identity and difference. After members of the two groups engaged in hostilities, Sherif assigned the two groups of boys to work together on a project they regarded as important. Working together led to the extinction of Us/Theming among the boys.

Why, then, the proclivity for humans to be biased in favor of in-group members and against Them? We approach an answer by considering that pro-sociability is about group identification. Inclusive fitness required that resources, often scarce, be allocated preferentially among kin and tribe; when in-groups became larger and more anonymous, in-group markers were required (Sapolsky: 390). In addition, anticipations and expectations center on cooperation and on shared reciprocal obligations and expectations of mutuality (Sapolsky: 393). When everyone in a group follows the rules of reciprocal pro-sociality, then everyone prospers. However, this arrangement only works when it applies to those with whom you expect to keep interacting and who can therefore be reasonably expected to reciprocate (Marsh: 111).

From an evolutionary perspective, therefore, quickly recognizing a face or some other marker as signifying "not-one-of-us" must have had a very high adaptive value. However, evidence does not support the view that humans are hardwired to fear the faces of other races (Sapolsky: 87). Nor is there evidence of innate biases based on gender or social status. Still, if a group is suddenly threatened by another group, then the fight-or-flight response must be activated very quickly in order to be effective. Thus, while it seems highly unlikely that our ancient hunting and gathering ancestors had contact with peoples of widely divergent racial make-up, discerning a threatening difference, e.g., a face darkened by absence of light (at night), marked by war paint, or disfigured by blood, injury, or disease, must have been of adaptive value.

For present purposes, it is important to note that the ease and reliability with which Us/Theming occurs, even when differences are artificial, as well as its frequent recalcitrance may be obstacles for toleration. Just as it is difficult to tolerate what you fear, Us/Theming is basically antithetical to toleration, or so it seems. There is, in addition, a vicious circle at work: fear, anger, and disgust increase Us/Theming while, in turn, Us/Theming increases aversion to and avoidance of the markers borne by Them. (See section "Liberal Democracy, Toleration, and Civility" for the view that persons per se cannot be the objects of toleration.) Can this vicious circle be replaced by a virtuous circle? Research, as discussed in section "Decreasing Fearfulness and Intolerance," suggests the answer is yes, although the difficulties of doing so testify to how little progress we have made in getting the PFC to do what is harder but right and getting the diPFC and vmPFC to cooperate proficiently.

Liberal Democracy, Toleration, and Civility

The objective of this section is to establish a background understanding of liberal democracy and toleration. It is critical to review the major features of liberal democracy because, for the purposes of this chapter, toleration will be understood as occurring within such political entities. This section also makes brief comments about the duty of civility as necessary for a liberal democracy to flourish, a subject taken up in more detail in section "Decreasing Fearfulness and Intolerance."

Liberal Democracy

By *liberal democracy* we can understand a democratic political system that is a constitutional democracy, that is, one that is based on the rule of law, majoritarian decision-making, and institutionally organized restrictions on government and majoritarian power in order to protect all citizens' basic rights and liberties. This is so far necessary, for a liberal democracy, but not sufficient. A liberal democracy must also be characterized by fundamental principles of political equality and fairness, or justice, among its members, although not all of the fundamental principles ensuring basic equality and fairness are enshrined in its formal constitution or structure. At a minimum, a liberal democracy must ensure citizens equal respect as members.

Equal respect requires equality of political participation and of social, economic, and cultural opportunity. Moreover, equal respect entails treating citizens as autonomous and a condition often characterized as neutrality, namely, according equal respect to the diversity of its citizen's characteristics, as well as the diversity of their choices and plans in pursuit of their visions of the good and the right. Finally, liberal democracies require a social capital characterized, in part, by what Rawls called the duty of civility, and especially a willingness to engage in public reasoning (Rawls 1993, 1997). The principle of neutrality requires further discussion in this subsection, whereas further comment on the duty of civility and public reasoning will be made in the next subsection.

The principle of neutrality looms large in the literature on political liberalism because toleration as neutrality is the sine quo non for an effective, sustainable constitutional and democratic society. Many contemporary political philosophers equate toleration with the principle of neutrality and derive it from the respect owed to individuals as personally and ethically autonomous beings with the requisite capacities for planning and pursuing their individual objectives and projects (Kymlicka 1995; Simmons 2007). In part, neutrality is an institutional norm that is embedded in part in constitutional provisions, laws, and appellate court rulings imposing limits on government and majority power, and establishing legal rights or protecting freedoms.

Toleration is sometimes understood as neutrality and is regarded as necessary as a modus vivendi, or agreement that however strongly the visions and interests of persons or groups differ, certain limits must be respected and democratic processes and arrangements must prevail. Yet, toleration understood as neutrality is not sufficient on its own to sustain a viable liberal democracy. There are a number of reasons in support of this judgment. First, insofar as toleration as neutrality is required, it is not exercised voluntarily by public officials or citizens. As is well known, the term "toleration" is far from univocal (Churchill 1997); indeed, to tolerate derives from the Latin for "to bear," "to lift," or "to carry," so it is hardly surprising that toleration and tolerance are often used in connection with the ideas of enduring, or putting up with, or being indifferent to, what one cannot change, or one does not have power or the will to resist.

Of course, the notion of toleration as a modus vivendi is not inconsistent with a grudging consensus not to interfere with what one dislikes in order to pursue one's own objectives, however objectionable they are to others. In addition, there is no inconsistency between acting as required by a law or political duty and willing to do as a law requires. The example Kant offers of the dutiful shopkeeper is instructive here; the shopkeeper can return the correct change as required by law, or the shopkeeper can do so because it is willed as the right thing to do. The point is that toleration as neutrality ignores this difference. On the contrary we seek a notion of toleration that has moral resonance; it reflects the associations between toleration and respect for others as fellow citizens, and as a civic virtue it has many characteristics in common with virtues in general.

Toleration understood as neutrality can never be more than a commitment to formal principles, and procedures; it cannot answer questions about the scope or content of toleration; that is, what beliefs, acts, and practices actually must be tolerated and which, if any, fall beyond the bounds of toleration? These questions are to be resolved by citizens within a democratic governing structure committed to neutrality. To be sure, boundary lines may be established by law or mutual consent among members, but once some behavior or practice is recognized as "outside" or "inside" those boundaries, it ceases to be a matter of toleration understood as neutrality.

However, toleration as a modus vivendi alone is unstable, for the commitment it requires of citizens is too weak: as soon as a majority or partisan faction is powerful, it is likely to pursue its interests contrary to laws passed or policies previously established and repeal a boundary line, erect a new one, or set it in a different public "space." Moreover, many issues may be politically and morally fraught even within well-ordered constitutional democracies; there may be close divisions over highly contested matters, and it may take time to resolve issues that provoke strong emotions, including fear, anger, and disgust, among members. Hence, if liberal democracies are to thrive, the toleration as neutrality – as a formal principle and institutional arrangement – must be supplemented with toleration as a publicly recognized attitude and disposition among citizens to engage with one another on the basis of a duty of civility.

Toleration as a Duty of Civility

There are three necessary and jointly sufficient conditions for toleration as a civic virtue. These can be understood as the objection, forbearance, and rejection conditions (Forst 2004, 2012). First, what a tolerant person finds objectionable must be nontrivial, otherwise there is no real significance to forbearance and we ought to characterize the individual's attitude as indifference, rather than toleration. Second, to count as serious, the objection must be based on more than personal interest, prudence, preference, or taste; rather it reflects a considered judgment that one's objection is reasonable; that is, that the nature or consequences of something to which one objects are sufficiently serious to arouse concern. For example, a cis-woman is not tolerant if she has a preference for all-gender restrooms (her acceptance of gender fluidity supersedes her tolerance); but a cis-woman is tolerant if she believes it wrong that there are all-gender restrooms but forbears from attempting to have them prohibited.

In addition to an objection condition, there must be a forbearance component that, although in tension with the objection, prevails, or "trumps," the objection. The forbearance condition need not negate or cancel out the objection; civilly tolerant individuals can believe their objections are reasonably grounded, but they accept other, secondary, or higher-order reasons, to guide their attitudes and actions. Moreover, because disputes over drawing boundary lines arise in so many different context and involve so many different ideals and interests (e.g., whether to tolerate the desecration of a national symbol – e.g., the flag – but not public displays of the desecration of religious icons, such as a crucifix submerged in urine or the burning of the Qur'an), higher-order reasons for or against may be of many different kinds. Examples of such reasons include respect for others' efforts to seek the truth, for the importance of certain practices in other people's lives, an understanding of scientific research on gender or personal identity, an appreciation of one's own epistemic fallibility, and beliefs about the value of a reciprocal give-and-take in a pluralistic society. Such higher-order reasons provide the conscious explanations individuals give one another if they are asked about being tolerant.

Note that, because of the objection condition, we cannot regard one's forbearance as a genuine instance of toleration as a civic duty unless the forbearance is a matter of choice capable of being supported by reasons. As noted in the subsection "Liberal Democracy," if one grudgingly endures or puts up with something without having considered that being reasonable recommends forbearance, then one's attitude or behavior is not toleration or tolerance. Indeed, citizens who appear willing to "go along" but offer no plausible reasons for voluntarily doing so and express anger or annoyance for having to "put up" with a situation are subject to the suspicion that they would interfere with or obstruct what they object to if and when they have the ability to do so.

In keeping with toleration as voluntarily exercised, there no necessary connection between toleration as civic duty and having the power to prevent or to interfere with something they find seriously objectionable (Williams 1996). Certainly forbearing when one is powerful might be evidence of tolerance; nevertheless, there is no contradiction in conceiving of a powerless minority, religious fundamentalists, for instance, or a powerful majority, having serious moral objections to same-sex civil unions, unisex bathrooms, and same-sex partner adoptions but nevertheless tolerating these states of affairs. It is sufficient that members of a minority show that, even if they did have the requisite capacity (or do have it), they would (will) not interfere, and that others accept their objections as sincere as well as their forbearance as reasonable.

So far, two necessary conditions for toleration as a civic duty have been discussed: the objection and forbearance conditions. These conditions are jointly necessary and sufficient when joined with a third condition, the so-called rejection condition. Toleration requires drawing boundaries; if nothing can be conceived to be in the realm of the intolerable and to be rejected, then toleration becomes vacuous. Hence, happy-go-lucky souls who have an open-handed "live and let live" outlook, and cannot conceive themselves as being opposed to anything others want, cannot be virtuously tolerant in the sense understood here. Whatever the merits of such generous persons, their promiscuous "anything goes" outlook fails to meet the rejection condition. Toleration as a civic duty requires that one be willing to take a stand on important issues, and offer reasons for objection to what one regards as outside acceptable boundaries. The fact that there are free riders who do not care, come what may, thus cannot be regarded as a criticism of toleration.

A proper understanding of toleration as a civic duty enables us to set aside certain so-called "paradoxes of toleration." Some have been skeptical of the psychological possibility of being virtuously or civilly tolerant (Horton 1994; Mendus 1999). A paradox seems to arise when both the reasons for objection and the reasons for acceptance are held to be moral, because they appear to require individuals to entertain contradictory beliefs. A tolerant individual believes, as the objection condition, that something is morally wrong, and yet, simultaneously believes, as the forbearance condition, that it is morally right to tolerate the doing (by others) of what is regarded as immoral. Not all cases of toleration rise to the level of moral concern; however, even when they do the appearance of paradox is easily dissolved.

We need only to distinguish between various kinds of moral reasons, and then rank these different reasons by order, or priority. For instance, with respect to abortion, meat eating, gambling, pornography, handgun ownership, and spanking children, a person can consistently (both conceptually and psychologically) regard these activities as immoral and believe and act on the conviction that higher-order moral reasons justify their forbearance, and hence toleration. For instance, one tolerates decisions to seek licenses to carry a handgun when applicants have grounds for believing their personal safety requires being armed, although reject handgun ownership when such needs do not exist.

A second supposed paradox arises out of the apparent possibility of conceiving of an intolerant person as tolerant, which seems contradictory. The so-called "paradox of the tolerant racist" presumes it possible for a racists, an anti-Semites, a xenophobes, etc. to be tolerant of persons against whom they have an irrational hatred or prejudice. On this confounding view, racists or xenophobes are supposedly tolerant if they curb their desires to discriminate against persons they regard as inferior, and bizarrely, such racists or xenophobes supposedly become increasingly tolerant the stronger their hatred and prejudice, as long as they do not act on them.

The effort to formulate this puzzle reveals why such a "paradox" is fatuous. In the first place, because we must presuppose that a racist or xenophobe harbors irrational hatred for members of their target groups, it is, consequently, extremely unlikely that a racist's objections to the target group could be reasonable in the minimal sense required by the objection condition. Second, it makes no sense to regard someone as tolerant or intolerant of the characteristics of persons over which the latter have no control, such as age, ability or disability, place or conditions of birth, ethnicity, gender, race, and sexual orientation (Churchill 2007). As persons (generally) are not at liberty to change or alter such ascribed characteristics, it makes no sense to hold them to blame for possessing them.

Third, persons prejudiced against a group based on a shared group characteristic, such as being a Jew or a Muslim, cannot specify how members of the group could change or behave to be "tolerable," except, of course, to cease being members of the despised group (by conversion) or by being displaced or removed (by deportation or ethnic cleansing). This shows that what we suspected at the outset, namely, that in addition to their blind prejudice, racists, xenophobes, and other biased persons are really opposed to toleration itself, and, of course, to the ideals of inclusivity. The existence of racists and other bigots in no way demonstrates the incoherence of moral toleration, however.

Recognition Respect and Second-Personal Agents

As indicated in the subsection "Liberal Democracy," a thriving liberal democracy requires a viable civic culture (Almond and Verba 1989), or sufficient social capital that includes toleration along with trust, cooperation, and reciprocity (Putnam 2000).

Rawls (1993) claims that a liberal state retains its legitimacy only if citizens, in their public capacity, commit to the "ideal of public reason." Forst (2012) has a similar fundamental norm in mind when he speaks of the "discursive principle of justice," as does Habermas (1998) in speaking of "communicative ethics." Knowing that controversy can occur against the backdrop of deep, possibly intractable, disagreements, citizens must commit to arguing for any law or policy they advocate on the basis of public reasons. As indicated in the subsection "Toleration as a Duty of Civility," toleration as a duty of civility requires that we be reasonable, that is, that we be willing to engage with others by appealing to considerations we can expect them to regard as reasonable. Of course, different persons and factions make their cases based on different reasons. Nevertheless, reasons are "public" in the required sense when they are consistent with everyone else's status as a free, equal, and reasonable, and feeling fellow citizen.

Thus, no reasons are public unless they *could be* reciprocally acceptable among free and equal persons. Hence, members of a society must be able to accept or reject public reasons depending on their merits or demerits, and without appeal to proposers or detractors' race, ethnicity, religion, gender, socioeconomic status, or particular and unshared visions of the good life. For instance, claims that one should be allowed not to have her children vaccinated against common and dangerous diseases, or that it is permissible to subject homosexual, bisexual, or trans minors to so-called "conversion therapy," fail to be public reasons because they advert to ethnic, religious, or cultural commitments; they fail because only those who share their particular commitments and mistaken beliefs could find them plausible. Whatever plausibility they have as reasons derives from faith, ethnic practices, or cultural membership that other citizens can reasonably reject.

In addition, as the well-being of children and youth is an objective which we can expect all citizens to share – whatever their other commitments – public contestations about the best way to produce such well-being should be evidenced to all. With respect to issues such as non-vaccination, "conversion therapy," exorcism (where it might still be practiced), or refusing blood transfusions (by the Jehovah's Witnesses), these become more susceptible to public reasoning to the extent that potential victims voluntarily consent, rather than being subjected to coercion, and to the extent that allowing such practices does not result in harm to those outside the parochial (e.g., religious) group.

Ought certain practices be permitted within a religious or ethnic community to uphold the values of the community, and despite the disapproval of a majority? This question returns us to the very heart of toleration, for whereas reasons adverting to faith, ethnicity, or cultural traditions cannot by nature be public reasons in a pluralistic society, what is required in order to preserve a faith-based or cultural community about which its members care deeply *is* a concern that appeals to the public reasoning of us all, and thus *is* a subject for higher-order reasoning, and possible toleration.

In addition, higher-order and public reasons are derived from what, following the Darwell (1978), we call recognition respect and what Nagel (1970) refers to as the equivalency of persons. Others are recognized as agents or persons equivalent in the public sphere to oneself, so that the self is seen as just one person among others. Nagel represents this recognition of equivalency as the cognitive basis for a sense of fairness: "You see the present situation as a specimen of a more general scheme, in which the characters can be exchanged" (83). In addition, says Nagel, the most basic argument a victim can present to a perpetrator is "How would you like it if someone did that to you?" (82) – that is, if the roles were reversed.

To this "You and I" equivalency discussed by Nagel we can apply the conception of *second-personal agents* (Darwell 2006; Tomasello 2019). To regard others as second-personal agents is to recognize them as engaging capably and properly with you in joint, collaborative activities. Tomasello (2019) has argued that second-personal relationships arose in human evolution as a product of joint intentional collaboration – a joint agentic "we" requiring a cooperative spirit and respect for partners (during duration of the collaboration) as equivalent to the self.

Thus toleration as a civic duty can be characterized, in part, as a disposition or proclivity to regard others as second-personal agents, and intolerance as the failure to do so. Moreover, recognizing others in terms of second-personal agency requires a normative sense of joint commitment, and hence, at least some minimal trust, as well as equality and respect. As Tomasello points out (2019: 211), collaborators regarding each other as second–personal agents have the normative standing to commit "we" normatively to self-regulate both "you" and "I," which entitles us to have mutual expectations about the behavior of the other, and entitles either of us to call the other out for noncooperation. Of course, it may be rational on occasion not to trust another member of society and not to engage with them in collaboration. For this reason, it is more appropriate to say of toleration that it requires of democratic citizens that each recognizes every other as a *potential second-personal agent*, for the limited purposes of public engagement required within a well-ordered constitutional democracy.

Fear, Empathy, and Toleration

Given the extensive data about the close connections between fear and negative emotions as well as fear and Us/Theming, it seems paradoxical that there could be a connection between fear and empathy. And yet, the research of Marsh (2017) and others strongly suggests that the way our brains' respond to other's distress is intrinsic to our capacities for experiencing caring and concern for others (Marsh: 98). Of course, it is our perception of the pain and fear of others, and not our own experience of pain or fear that elicits empathetic feelings, and hence, once again, a paradox of toleration is only apparent and not real. Remarkably, however, perceiving the distress or danger of others can elicit empathy and altruistic behavior at the same time as it evokes fear in us. As Marsh stresses, "true selfless heroism emerges not from the absence of fear, but because of it. Their bravery lies in their ability to recognize and empathize with acute distress, while simultaneously overcoming or overriding their own fear in the face of danger. They are able to respond altruistically because even while they empathize with others' fear, they do not allow fear to flood their own system preventing them from acting to help" (154).

It is remarkable that the brain is capable of such complexity. Alongside the reptilian amygdala response to fear with the primitive fight-or-flight syndrome, the cascade of neural firing in the amygdala, and regions in the cortex such as the mid-cingulate gyrus and anterior insula enable us to internally recreate and hence understand another person's emotions (Marsh: 135–7). If this is "mirroring," then it is not a simple neuronal mirroring, but a complex product of conjoint processing throughout a whole matrix, that is, complex circuitry throughout whole brain systems. Of course, it is equally fascinating that the amygdala, with its starring role in amplifying one's own fear productions, is also on center stage in responding to others' fears. Visual information about human fearful facial expressions is conveyed from the retina to the superior colliculi atop the brain stem, to the thalamus, and then to the amygdala (Méndez-Bértolo et al. 2016). Marsh avers that "no other facial expression that we know about gets passed along this same speedy route to the amygdala" (132).

Fear expression in others plays a privileged role for us probably because it communicates vulnerability, submission, and appeasement, the traits that trigger the inhibition of violence (Blair et al. 1995). While not always as reliable and straightforward as it is in other mammals, humans do have a so-called integrated inhibition mechanism (VIM) (Marsh: 58). Perceptions of others' fear are most likely to trigger inhibitions against aggression when the face of a fearful person is seen, especially the eyes and the wide white sclera of fearful facial expressions (registered at a mere seventeenth of a millisecond) (Marsh: 132). In any case, the VIM is responsible for the development in children, after the age of two, of an increasing aversion to hurting others. Without a reliable VIM, children could not become trustworthy members of social groups; moreover, the VIM continues to work throughout life, unless it is impaired similar to the way psychopaths have defective amygdalae rendering them incapable of recognizing fearful expressions (Marsh: 88–91).

Of course, what has been said so far is about the connections between fear in others and empathic responses. There remain two lingering but linked questions: What happens when fearful persons are perceived as members of despised out-groups? Second, what about toleration? While perceptions of others suffering enhance empathy, do they also enhance tendencies to tolerate the differences we might associate with others? Researchers found that subjects were – by an almost two-to-one majority – willing to experience pain (electric shocks) rather than watch another student, "Elaine" continue to suffer (Batson et al. 1980). Even when offered a chance to escape, over half the volunteers offered to take "Elaine's" place.

Yet, Theming raises its ugly head when we learn that volunteers who perceived "Elaine" as similar to themselves were twice as likely to take Elaine's place as those who did not (Batson et al. 1980). The extent to which suffering enhances empathy for members of out-groups is highly controversial. Activation in the amygdala is less when one views the fearful faces of out-group members (Sapolsky: 395), and it is notorious that there is less inhibition when aggression is committed against Them, as in warfare or ethnic cleansing. Yet, disregarding the welfare of Them often appears to depend on Us – the impression that one has no choice, or the uniquely human ability to believe that the harm We cause can be justified by our superiority or ideology. Notably, however, Marsh argues that Stanley Milgram's (in)famous shock experiments actually demonstrate that "the pull of compassion is, on average, stronger than the pull of obedience" (Marsh: 37). When the proximity of "Mr. Wallace" – the individual being shocked – is as close to a naive subject as the authority figure, then obedience plummets (Marsh: 37). In any case, extreme altruism, the kind that involves being a universal kidney donor (willing to donate to anyone), is impossible without a capacity to respond to the distress of anyone regardless of group membership.

To date, toleration, in contrast to altruism, basic emotions, and empathy is not well defined in the sciences. Hence, there has been little research on connections between empathy and toleration. However, it stands to reason that empathy is closely related to toleration, both in terms of empathetic "warm" emotions and "cool" cognitions. Because empathy is closely associated with emotions underlying compassion and care, it seems likely that the enhanced ability to be empathetic would enhance toleration as well. To be sure, the objection condition must still be in play, but as toleration requires recognition respect and seeing others as second-person agents, increasing empathy likely also increases the "cooler" cognitions involved in understanding others as having an equal share in the fate of a common but important enterprise.

Decreasing Fearfulness and Intolerance

We cannot conclude this chapter on the effects of fearfulness on toleration without at least some brief comments on decreasing the causes of fearfulness and overcoming intolerance. Accepting the benefits liberal democracies make available imposes certain obligations on those who accept those benefits, and among these is a duty of civility to be tolerant. In addition, because toleration requires engaging in public reasoning and adopting the second-personal perspective, it follows that one cannot have an irrational "intolerance" of other persons, based on race, ethnicity, gender, place of origin, etc. Such objections do not constitute intolerance; rather, they are manifestations of prejudice, and a willingness to discriminate or exclude altogether. For this reason, it is quite right that liberal democracies should continue to recognize the "intolerance" of persons as hate crimes or violations of basic human rights, and contrary to fundamental norms. Nevertheless, there will always be fractious disagreements about boundary drawing, as well as over what does or does not cross the boundary. Moreover, as demonstrated in the section "The Causes and Consequences of Fear and In-group/Out-group Biases," human beings are innately given to responding fearfully to perceived threats and equally predisposed to forming in-groups and out-groups on the basis of perceived differences. Both are major causes of intolerance, and worse.

It follows that citizens of liberal democracies and their elected political leaders should invest significantly in public programs and new institutional arrangements that will diminish and mitigate the distresses that fuel intolerant attitudes and behaviors. Doing so will increase the welfare of all concerned, and provide long-term safeguards for democracy itself. Likewise, citizens, in discharging their duty of civility, ought to pursue and support a number of grassroots and "self-help" initiatives that have the effects of decreasing the odds that controversies will result in incivility and intolerance. Among possible programs, arrangements, and initiatives only a small number can be considered here. Certainly, though, the following can be considered as among the most important.

Addressing Socioeconomic Inequalities That Generate Fear and Distress

Surely the most urgent measure is to address the extreme and rampant socioeconomic inequality through reforms of taxation policies, redistribution programs, and increasing opportunities for those lower on the gradient of socioeconomic status (SES). Over 60 academic papers demonstrate strong correlations in developed countries between increases in inequality and increases in violence, as well as nine other key social problems, including life expectancy, infant mortality, obesity, and mental illness (Payne 2017: 48; Sapolsky: 438–441). Importantly, at most, only 20% of a person's self-evaluation is based on actual SES markers. What is most significant is not one's objective situation, but how one perceives one's status based on comparisons; that is, on *feeling poor* (Payne: 13–14).

Subjective perceptions of being left behind or having violated expectations about how one's life should be going are common. Of course one's feelings occur in the context of social meanings about the "status ladder" influenced by the media and especially the social groups with which one affiliates. For instance, Whites in American who harbor implicit biases and oppose immigration reform see themselves as being left behind in a social milieu saturated with White privilege, "affirmative action" in favor of Blacks, and nostalgia for White supremacy. Feeling one has fallen behind in this context often results in anger, frustration, fear, and resentment.

An important study of American men who felt the need to carry guns in public reports that having handguns with them helps these men "address social insecurities far beyond crime" (Carlson 2015: 10–15). Owning guns is about a crisis of confidence in American society, and, in carrying guns, men feel "a sense of duty, relevance, and even dignity" (Carlson: 29). The connections between rising inequality, dignity as honor, and the potential for violence are also emphasized by psychologists and neurologists (Daly 2017). Steep SES gradients close off recognized and accepted opportunities for personal advancement, as well as achieving status and self-esteem. Thus extreme inequalities make confrontations and threats more fraught; even slights and insults have a far greater effect when status is insecure (Daly 2017).

It stands to reason that the steeper the SES gradient, the greater the generation of a social dominance orientation (SDO) among the fearful and insecure. SOD is a measure of how much people value prestige, hierarchy, and power. Individuals with high SDO scores are characterized by automatically expressed prejudices when feeling threatened, greater acceptance of bias against low-status out-groups, and, when male, greater sexism (Sapolsky: 430). Moreover, persons with high SDO are less likely to experience activation of the insula and anterior cingulate when seeing others suffer, and hence, less likely to have empathy for the less fortunate.

It is hardly surprising that SOD correlates highly with another consequence of steep SES gradients: right-wing authoritarianism or RWA (Sapolsky: 475). RWA is a measure of how much a person values orderliness, submission to authorities, and domination of others. As an SES gradient becomes steeper and more people become increasingly socially anxious, RWA scores also rise. Individuals high in SDO and RWA are particularly prone to promote Theming (Sapolsky: 421). Moreover, because they find it deeply distressing when status relations are ambiguous, complex, and shifting – where they and others do not "know" or "keep to" their "proper places" – they are especially susceptible to demagogues who heap stereotypes onto the heads of designated "losers." Added to this, studies show that having lower ranking others on whom to displace aggression is one of the most reliable ways to relieve chronic stress (439).

Finally, both those who see themselves falling behind and those persistently subordinated and thwarted live with chronic, even toxic levels of stress. Excessive levels of stress hormones such as adrenaline and cortisol take a toll on virtually every organ system, especially the heart and cardiovascular system, the respiratory system, and immunological responses to diseases, including cancer (Sapolsky: 437–438; Payne: 121–131). Chronic and excessive stress also negatively affect the PFC, promoting a "fast living style" marked by a dramatic increase in risky behaviors, poor judgment, and a persistent failure to consider long-term consequences (Payne: 57–82). Despite steadily declining death rates throughout the developed world, chronic stress has resulted in an increasing death rate within certain American demographic groups "dying of violated expectations" (Payne: 121).

It has been well said that, "When humans invented material inequality, they came up with a way of subjugating the low ranking like nothing ever before seen" (Sapolsky: 445). Extreme inequality is indeed a scourge afflicting us all. Research shows that inequality does not just destroy meaningfulness for the poor, it affects "the whole range of people living in areas beset by it" (Payne: 54).

Ensuring the Viability of Civility and Public Reasoning

In addition to vigorously addressing SES inequalities, liberal democracies and their citizens must protect the civility and social capital that a flourishing democracy requires as well as supporting public reasoning. Careful balances must be found between civility and public reason, on the one hand, and free speech and other fundamental rights and liberties, on the other. A few important initiatives are considered here, however controversial they might be. First, we are well past the point at which elected demagogues such as Donald Trumps should be allowed to rely on falsehoods. Persons in positions of public trust commit "epistemic injustices" (Fricker 2007) when they withhold or distort truths that hinder equal participation by all in public reasoning, or when politicians intentionally degrade the quality of public reasoning for personal or partisan advantage.

Second, some measures must be found to curb the runaway chaotic and polluting effects of irresponsible Internet sites and platforms, as well as certain alleged "news" and "information" outlets. While it might be difficult to do so, distinctions must be made between newspapers and outlets committed to purveying unadulterated news, and other communicative products that the public and legislative bodies should recognize for what they are, namely, commodities and services offered to consumers either directly by media platforms or through second parties, such as bloggers on Reddit.

These communicative products and services could be subjected to standards of transparency and quality, while social media providers might be held accountable for falsified and distorted content and required to warn users of social media platforms, such as Facebook, that they could be held liable for posting false and libelous content. Why cannot citizens be permitted to expect at least the same level of transparency and critical evaluation for online sites exhibited by Wikipedia, which tags pages containing unverified material? Precedents for such expectations already exist with requirements that products in the food or drug industry be inspected and tested, and found "wholesome." It is time we have analogous standards for the "communicative industry."

A few proposals worth consideration are more far-reaching. One would be to rule that contents on publicly accessible media outlets such as You Tube, Twitter, and blogs like Reddit are "public discourse"; that is, rather than presumptively private and privileged, such discourse lies entirely within the public domain, analogous to advertisements and political campaign ads. As such, content in online platforms would be subject to the same standards of prohibited "hate speech" or coercive measures specifically designed to intimidate and silence certain individuals or groups from participating in public reasoning, or to promote hatred and possible violence against members or designated groups.

The need for imminent protections of public reasoning from threats in cyberspace has become more urgent because of the creation and circulation of apparently realistic "deepfake" videos – fabricating videos in which persons appear to say or do something that did not take place, or did not take place as presented. This was illustrated dramatically by the viral spread of a video of House Speaker Nancy Pelosi that was altered to make her speech slurred and stunted to appear as if she was inebriated. The video was viewed more than three million times on Facebook, while Facebook refused to take it down. Deepfakes such as this are especially worrisome because of their potential to undermine candidates and mislead voters. As psychologists and artificial intelligence (AI) experts note, after the fact exposés of fake news and deepfake videos do not diminish the effect of the delusion on most viewers.

Perhaps, the only reliable way to neutralize the potential effects of deepfakes is to require that all political campaigns submit any ads or videos in advance to an impartial team of forensic researchers for authentication. It is unlikely, of course, that authentication could ever work with Facebook videos "and things thrown around in WhatsApp" (q. in Harwell 2019) for deepfake creators can examine codes used by AI authenticators and find workarounds. Nevertheless, enforced regulations of political ads and videos would establish a benchmark for political honesty, and allowing media outlets to have access to deepfake detecting tools would enable them to assess allegedly newsworthy video when it arrives (Harwell 2019).

Finally, while focusing on institutional reforms to protect public reason, serious consideration should be given to limiting the terms of public servants, especially because too many of them seek to turn their positions into sinecures. Psychological research conducted over the last two decades has found that subjects who possess power over others act as if they are suffering from a traumatic brain injury (Keltner et al. 2003). Those accustomed to power became more impulsive, less risk-averse, and crucially less adept at taking the view of others. Aspects of this disorder of power, or "hubris syndrome," as it has been called, appear to have been corroborated by neuroscientists (Useem 2017). Using transcranial magnetic stimulation, researchers find that being powerful can impair specific circuitry that is typically initiated when one observes the suffering of others (Useem 2017). As noted in the section "Fear, Empathy, and Toleration," the cornerstone of empathy lies in neural processes that "mirror" what is occurring in the neurology of the person in pain. Yet it is precisely such "mirroring" that degrades in the brains of the powerful (Useem 2017). In addition, persons who enjoy power are less able to make out other people's individuating traits, rely more heavily on stereotypes, are less capable of taking the role of the other, and tend increasingly to rely on their own personal "vision" for social navigation (Useem 2017). If further research tends to confirm this creeping "political pathology," then this constitutes justifiable grounds for limiting terms of public service.

Hate speech intended to silence, fake news, and deepfake videos, like lying by public servants, represent additional forms of epistemic injustice, for they are harms committed against persons as knowers. Barring these forms of manipulation and corrosive disinformation protects the quality of public reasoning necessary for a liberal democracy, and hence, taking these measures benefits everyone equally, regardless of their own particular values or visions of good and right in life. Because liberal democracies require knowledgeable and informed citizens, all will be lost if too many citizens become indifferent, blasé, or too ignorant to engage in public reasoning. Active resistance to these damaging effects must be made throughout society.

Democratizing Knowledge of Fear and Intolerance

The term "democratizing knowledge" was coined to refer to new knowledge citizens must have in order to maintain a liberal democracy (Lakoff 2008: 19). Obviously, this must include increasing self-awareness of, and hence, individual control over the effects of innate and learned fear and related emotions, as well as a better understanding of the ways bias and intolerance undermine the quality of public reasoning and social capital. Democratizing must also reveal why our mind finds fallacious thinking and conspiracy thinking attractive, such as "patternicity" (Shermer 2011), the evolved tendency to seek meaning in patterns, even when meaningless "noise." Knowledge about the ways fake news, deepfake videos, demagoguery, and propaganda lead people astray must also be part of the "curriculum."

Democratizing knowledge begins as an educative enterprise, as illustrated by efforts to increase education on diversity in high schools and colleges and by organizations such as the Southern Poverty Law Center and its magazine, *Teaching Tolerance*, as well as computer sites where individuals can test themselves, without costs, to expose the extent of their own implicit biases (Haidt 2012) and exercise ways of improving their own mental "hygiene," and learning how to identify and overcome their particular fallacious, biased, and stereotyping tendencies. As formal education, training should include a truthful and unsparing examination of a people's history and politics; moreover, learning how to discover the truth needs to continue throughout the life course, beginning with instruction for children as soon as they are able to understand the content, continuing through high school, and to be complimented in college with at least a year of a study combining the elements of logic, scientific reasoning, and rhetoric.

Neurologists have emphasized that once humans become accustomed to rely on subconscious, unexamined thinking, engaging the PFC requires a higher metabolic cost and is thus harder work. However, the PFC must also engage in considerable "cognitive gymnastics" (Sapolsky: 400) in fabricating, rationalizing, and inventing ad hoc justifications to maintain falsehoods against truths inconsistent with one's intuitive, or gut, beliefs or feelings. However, engaging in these gymnastics over time has a much higher cost in terms of lower success, greater stress, and lower health. Moreover, once well trained to engage the diPFC and the vmPFC in conscious, collaborative reasoning, whatever resistance or pain was formerly associated with hard thinking becomes replaced by pleasure and contentment.

Contact Theory: Collaborative Problem-Solving and Nonviolent Interaction

"Contact theory" has been proposed by psychologists as a way of decreasing prejudice ever since Allport's groundbreaking study of prejudice in the 1950s (Allport 1979). Further research indicates that in order to effectively decrease hostility between members of Us versus Them rather than exacerbate enmity, additional conditions must be met. One is the presence of "superordinate" goals where everyone works together on a task they care about (Sherif et al. 1961). There must also be roughly equal numbers from each side; everyone should receive equal and unambiguous treatment; contact needs to be lengthy and occur on neutral, nonthreatening grounds (Sapolsky: 420). Contact is also more successful when combined with techniques for democratizing knowledge. For instance, priming individuals to engage in perspective taking, and having them think of an out-group member as an individual with a particular life story (Sapolsky: 418–20). Such techniques lessen "essentialism," the tendency to think of Them as all possessing the same unalterable traits. Whereas it is difficult to conceive proactively arranging for contact among antagonistic groups on a large and continuing scale, liberal democracies might institute 1-year or 2-year universal conscription programs for young men and women. Service might be incentivized by payment for higher education, or forgiveness of debt, for example. These service programs would be modeled on the example provided by the Peace Corps, Teach for America, Habitat for Humanity, and the Nature Conservancy.

We have long known from historical experience that persons find it much more difficult to harm others who are physically close to them, rather than remote or distant, and when they must do so using their own hands. Neurological studies using philosophy's (in)famous "runaway trolley problem" now show that even when subjects just *think* about taking (bodily) actions to harm one stranger in order to save a larger number, they are far more inhibited than they are when they can achieve the same outcome mechanically by pulling a lever. When required to choose between imaginary scenarios, one in which they could either push a person onto a track to bring a runaway trolley to a halt, or alternatively, divert the trolley onto a different track on which an individual standing on the track would be killed, 70–90% opted to pull the lever rather than push a person onto the track, although the same number of lives would be saved and lost in each scenario (Greene et al. 2001).

Because pulling the lever is more mechanical and more distant from the site of a death caused, it helps to foster the delusion that there is no personal involvement. Brain imaging studies show high activation of the diPFC in subjects asked to think about pulling the lever, but greater inhibition of the amygdala, and hence, less emotional repugnance attached to one's actions. By contrast, when subjects are asked to personally push a person onto a track to stop a runaway trolley, their vmPFCs activate along with their amygdalae and diPFCs. The more negative emotions subjects reported, the less likely they were to see themselves as harming others. By contrast, the greater the abstract conceptualizations about intentionally harming a person for the supposed benefit of others, the more the diPFC inhibits the amygdala. This evidence clearly reminds us that fear is not always bad or unwanted; sometimes it assists us in doing the right thing.

In certain situations, encounters between a charismatic or inspiring leader of an out-group and a dominant and repressive in-group can significantly affect the attitudes and feelings of members of the in-group. This has been demonstrated repeatedly by persons such as Mohandas K. Gandhi in India, Martin Luther king, Jr. in the USA, Abdul Ghaffar Khan in Afghanistan and Pakistan, and Nelson Mandela in South Africa. Their powerful effects on adversaries are the more remarkable as their civil disobedience and resistance can be expected to generate anxiety and fear, and usually does in staunch defenders of repressive regimes. These unique leaders succeed through remarkable courage, nonviolence, steadfastness of purpose, and respect for their adversaries. Thus, through a manifest magnanimity of character that enemies did not conceive possible of them and through minimally threatening behavior, these "great souls" have earned grudging respect, and even admiration, from former in-group enemies.

At present it is not well known why and when nonviolent civil disobedience and resistance is likely to succeed, hence further research is required. One interesting insight comes from psychological research with a "stereotype content model" (Fiske et al. 2002). According to this research, dominate in-groups form stereotypical models of out-groups with two primary axes: warmth (e.g., malevolent versus benevolent) and competence (e.g., ignorant and unable versus knowledgeable and able). Thus, the theory suggests that when minorities assert their rights in maximally respectful and minimally threatening ways, they can cause some of those rejecting them to recalibrate the "content" of their models of the out-group: upgrading both the warmth and the competency of those formerly suppressed.

Increasing Opportunities for Helping

Experimental and longitudinal studies consistently demonstrate a positive relationship between various forms of helping and well-being (Dunn et al. 2008). This relationship is bidirectional; that is, persons who are helpful and generous report higher levels of well-being, understood as being able to meet basic needs and having a sense of meaning and purpose, and likewise, those who experience higher well-being are inclined to be more helpful and generous. By contrast, decades of research on misanthropy find that this trait, which reflects cynical attitudes about human nature and lack of faith in other people, is inversely related to most indications of well-being (Marsh: 232–233).

The urge to respond with care for others is innate, and one often strong enough to override considerable risk to oneself (Marsh: 176–177, 183). Data supports the hypothesis that kindness toward strangers results from fast and intuitive processes while excessive rational deliberation in the diPFC suppresses it (Rand 2016). This is consistent with altruists' reports that their rescuing behaviors do not require deliberation; rather, their actions are "fast and intuitive" (Marsh: 224). Danger certainly causes fear, but it does not overwhelm benevolent actions. In addition, it appears that caring behavior can release neurotransmitters, particularly oxytocin, that induces the amygdala to reduce aversion to unfamiliar sights, smells, and sounds, and inhibit aggression and avoidance (Marsh: 192–193).

Finally, when individuals are willing to presume that they can trust strangers, this willingness can initiate an "upward spiral of cooperation and increasing trust" (Marsh: 215). Trust as a self-fulfilling prophecy has been demonstrated in neuroeconomic games like the Ultimatum Game. The roles are structured in this two-person game, so that one player is given a certain sum of money to allocate, offering some or none to the other player. The second player then decides whether to accept the offer or refuse it; if the second player accepts, then the players receive the amounts allocated by the first player, if the second player refuses, neither player receives anything. Thus, from the perspective of classical economics, it would be rational for the second player to accept whatever he or she is offered as long as it is more than zero, and rational for the first to selfishly offer as little as he or she can get away with.

However, when people play the Ultimatum Game they overwhelmingly allocate and accept offers that come to approach even divisions. This happens because humans are social animals typically expecting to be observed, to continue to interact with others, and to be complemented when their behavior is fair and criticized when it is not. As it happens, the Ultimatum Game typically involves an indeterminate number of multiple rounds, and so, the optimal strategy that emerges is known as "tit-for-tat:" start out offering what you would expect in return and then doing whatever your partner did in the last round. For our purposes, it is worth emphasizing that there are no appreciable differences in outcomes or strategies when players are strangers as compared with friends. This demonstrates that even perfect strangers can perceive each other as second-personal agents, and that regarding someone unknown as probably trustworthy is the most advantageous approach for everyone (Marsh: 215).

Summary

The relationship between fear, other emotions, and beliefs, attitudes, and behaviors is far more complex than is suggested by the simple notion of a fight-or-flight response. Obviously, fear contributes to aversion and avoidance of what is perceived as threatening, even different. Given that social fears produce effects very similar to physical threats, fear in the social domain has a deleterious effect on toleration – understood as the duty of civility and willingness to engage in public reasoning – necessary for a thriving liberal democracy. Hostility to out-groups, often attached to insignificant markers of difference, is also based on innate mechanisms that demonstrate some connections with fear. Enmity towards out-groups is also a threat to the toleration required by liberal democracy.

Further research is required to determine how much and when fear contributes to enmity toward out-groups. In addition, further research should clarify the contexts in which and the extent that fear contributes to pro-sociality. Studies demonstrate that awareness of fearfulness in others can produce a mirror-like effect in observers, and that some individuals – altruists – are able to overcome fear of harm to oneself and engage in rescuing behavior. Moreover, early research results suggest that sound reasoning requires that the cortex accesses the full range of emotions, thus fear when properly modulated and balanced by other cortical processes may have an important role in promoting the kind of regard for others that public reasoning and tolerant individuals require.

Given the significance of toleration for liberal democracy, greater research on the subject is required in the sciences as well as in political science and philosophy. Finally, it is past time for public officials and citizens to given concerted thought to how toleration supports liberal democracy and how toleration is to be preserved, even strengthened, against the resurgence of racism and xenophobia and the onslaught of fake news, hate speech, demagoguery, and propaganda.

References

Allport GW (1979) The nature of prejudice: The 75th anniversary edition. Perseus, New York
Almond GA, Verba S (1989) The civic culture. Sage, Thousand Oaks
Amodio DM (2019) The neuroscience of stereotyping and prejudice. http://ww8.gsb.columbia.edu/leadership/sites/leadership/files/David_Amadio_ColumbiaSept09.pdf. Accessed 11 Nov 2019
Batson CD et al (1980) Is empathic emotion a source of altruistic motivation. J Pers Soc Psychol 40:290–302
Blair RJ et al (1995) A cognitive developmental approach to morality: investigating the psychopath. Cognition 57:1–29
Burton N (2015) Heaven and hell: the psychology of the emotions. Acheron, London
Carlson J (2015) Citizen-protectors: the everyday politics of guns in an age of decline. New York, Oxford
Churchill RP (1997) On the difference between non-moral and moral conceptions of toleration: the case for toleration as a moral virtue. In: Ravazi M, Ambuel D (eds) Philosophy, religion, and the question of intolerance. SUNY Press, Albany, pp 189–211
Churchill RP (2007) Toleration and deep reconciliation. Philos Contemp World 14:99–113
Cornell J et al (2007) The role of stereotypes on decisions to shoot. Eur J Soc Psychol 37:1102–1117
Daly M (2017) Killing the competition: economic inequality and homicide. Routledge, New York
Damasio A (2005) Descartes' error: emotion, reason, and the human brain, Rep ed. Penguin, New York
Darwell S (1978) Two kinds of respect. Ethics 88:36–49
Darwell D (2006) The second-person standpoint: respect, morality, and accountability. Harvard, Cambridge, MA
Dunn EH et al (2008) Spending money on others promotes happiness. Science 319:1687–1688
Ekman P, Friesen W (1978) Pictures of facial affect. Consulting Psychologists, Palo Alto
Fiske SA et al (2002) A model of (often mixed) stereotype content: competence and warmth respectively follow from perceived status and competition. J Pers Soc Psychol 82:878–896
Forst R (2004) The limits of toleration. Constellations 11:312–325
Forst R (2012) Toleration. In: Zatta EN (ed) The Stanford encyclopedia of philosophy. http://plato.stanford.edu/archives/sum2012/entries/toleration. Accessed 10 Apr 2018
Fricker M (2007) Epistemic injustice: power and the ethics of knowing. New York, Oxford
Gottman JM (2015) Principia amore: the new science of love. Routledge, New York
Greene JD et al (2001) An fMRI investigation of emotional engagement in moral judgment. Science 293:2105–2108
Habermas J (1998) The inclusion of the other. Studies in political theory. MIT, Cambridge, MA
Haidt J (2012) The righteous mind: why good people are divided by politics and religion. Vintage, New York
Harwell D (2019) Top AI researchers race to detect deepfake videos: we are outgunned. washingtonpost.com/technology/2019/06/12/top-ai-researchers-race-detect-deepfake-videos-we-are-outgunned. Accessed 12 Jun 2019
Horton J (1994) Three (apparent) paradoxes of toleration. Synth Philos 9:16–18
Keltner D et al (2003) Power, approach and inhibition. Psychol Rev 111:265–284
Kymlicka B (1995) Multicultural citizenship. Oxford, UK, Oxford
Lakoff G (2008) The political mind: why you can't understand 21st-century politics with an 18th-century brain. Viking Penguin, New York
Ledoux J (1990) The emotional brain: the mysterious underpinnings of emotional life. Simon and Schuster, New York
Marsh A (2017) The fear factor: how one emotion connects altruists, psychopaths, and everyone in-between. Basic Books, New York
Méndez-Bértolo J et al (2016) A fast pathway for fear in human amygdalae. Nat Neuro 19:1041–1049
Mendus S (1999) The politics of toleration: Tolerance and intolerance in modern life. Edinburgh, Edinburgh

Nagel T (1970) The possibility of altruism. Princeton, Princeton

Olson A et al (2005) The role of social groups in the persistence of learned fear. Science 309:778–789

Payne K (2017) The broken ladder: how inequality affects the way we think, live, and die. Viking, New York

Putnam RD (2000) Bowling alone: the collapse and revival of American social capital. Simon and Schuster, New York

Rand DG (2016) Cooperation fast and slow: meta-analytic evidence for a theory of social heuristics and self-interested deliberation. Psychol Sci 27:1192–1206

Rawls J (1993) Political liberalism. Columbia, New York

Rawls J (1997) The idea of public reason revisited. Chicago Law Rev 64:765–807

Sapolsky RM (2017) Behave: the biology of humans at our best and worst. Penguin Random House, New York

Sherif M et al (1961) Intergroup conflict and cooperation: the robbers cave experiment. University Book Exchange, Norman

Shermer M (2011) The believing brain: from ghosts and gods to politics and conspiracies – how we construct beliefs and reinforce them as truths. St. Martin's, New York

Simmons AJ (2007) Political philosophy. New York, Oxford

Tomasello M (2019) Becoming human: a theory of ontogeny. Harvard, Cambridge, MA

Useem J (2017) Power causes brain damage: how leaders lose mental capacities – most notably for reading people – that were essential to their rise, The Atlantic. theatlantic.com/magazine/archive/2017/07/power-causes-brain-damage/52871/. Accessed 13 Sept 2018

Williams B (1996) Toleration: an impossible virtue? In: Heyd D (ed) Toleration: an elusive virtue. Princeton University Press, Princeton, pp 18–27

Toleration, "Mindsight" and the Epistemic Virtues

35

Colin Farrelly

Contents

Introduction	700
The Paradox, and Limits, of Toleration	702
Tolerant Parents	704
Toleration Among Groups	709
Epistemic Virtue and the Case of Tolerating Hate Speech	711
An Autonomy-Based Response	715
Conclusion	717
References	718

Abstract

In this chapter a *virtue epistemological* account of toleration is developed and defended that draws attention to a cluster of "epistemic virtues" (collectively referred to as "mindsight" (Siegel (2010) Mindsight: the new science of personal transformation. Bantam Books, New York)) that are integral to exercising toleration as both a personal and public virtue. Virtue epistemology applies a normative analysis to the cognitive lives of individuals and intellectual communities (e.g., democratic country). By bringing to the fore the potential virtues and vices of our cognitive lives, virtue epistemology can offer an account of toleration that is distinct from that provided by *autonomy-based* arguments. The latter ignores, or at least brackets, our cognitive lives. A virtue epistemological account of toleration can help resolve the so-called "paradox of toleration," as well as elaborate on the limits of toleration as a virtue.

C. Farrelly (✉)
Queen's University, Kingston, Canada
e-mail: farrelly@queensu.ca

© The Author(s), under exclusive licence to Springer Nature Switzerland AG 2022
M. Sardoč (ed.), *The Palgrave Handbook of Toleration*,
https://doi.org/10.1007/978-3-030-42121-2_27

Keywords

Autonomy · Epistemic Virtue · Hate speech · Mindsight · Psychology · Toleration · Virtue epistemology

Introduction

Toleration is both a personal and public *virtue*. As a personal virtue, it is something that an individual person – in their capacity as a parent, co-worker, partner, or friend – can display towards those whose beliefs, opinions, or practices they believe are wrong, false, or otherwise objectionable. A tolerant parent, for example, will be able to distinguish between those cases where they ought to tolerate the less than ideal decision-making judgments of their teenage child (e.g., concerning their choice of apparel, friends, and music) and those decisions that warrant parental intervention to protect the teen from significant harm (e.g., truancy and drug abuse). While a tolerant parent might express their disapproval to their teen, in hopes of dissuading their offspring from bad choices concerning their apparel, friends, or choice of music, such a parent does not aspire to *compel* (e.g., via threats of grounding the teen) compliance on such matters when there is no immediate danger or risk of harm to their teen. From Elvis Presley's gyrating hips to the sex, guns, and violence often glorified in hip hop music, many parents have had to endure the inner psychological struggle of finding the healthy balance between wanting to coddle and control their children's lives and choices and letting their teens assert some independence (and, along with that independence, some mistakes, and misjudgments).

A polity can exercise toleration as a *public* virtue, a virtue which we can ascribe to a legislature, judiciary, or the collectivity of citizens which constitute a liberal democracy. As a public virtue, toleration entails institutionalizing legal protections for freedom of speech and association, as well as cultivating cultural practices and norms of civility and deliberation (vs violence and repression). Constitutional rights provide legal protections to citizens to ensure that majorities cannot unjustifiably intervene to suppress the beliefs and cultural practices of those in the minority. And cultural norms of deliberation and civil contestation encourage disagreements to be resolved via an open and robust "marketplace of ideas" vs compelling compliance to some preordained conception of the good that is immune to scrutiny and criticism.

As John Horton (1996) and others (King 1976; Raphael 1988) have pointed out, the "core of the concept of toleration is the refusal, where one has the power to do so, to prohibit or seriously interfere with conduct one finds objectionable" (Horton 1996). There are thus three important elements of the tolerant mindset:

1. The judgment that some belief or practice is objectionable (e.g., wrong)
2. The capacity to suppress the objectionable belief or practice
3. The decision to not suppress, despite it being objectionable, the belief or practice in question

(1) and (3) address the *psychology of the virtue of toleration*. That is, (1) and (3) reveal a tension, even paradox, in the fact that someone has reasons for objecting to X (e.g., a particular belief or cultural practice) and yet they do not, and would not, support the suppression of X.

In this chapter a *virtue epistemological* account of toleration is developed and defended that draws attention to a cluster of "epistemic virtues" that are integral to exercising toleration as both a personal and political virtue. Virtue epistemology applies a normative analysis to the cognitive lives of individuals and intellectual communities (e.g., democratic country). Rather than placing the normative focus on the more traditional concerns of ethics, such as "how ought I to *act*?", virtue epistemology instead focuses on the question "what should I *believe*?". By bringing to the fore the potential virtues and vices of our cognitive lives, virtue epistemology can offer an account of toleration that is very distinct from that provided by *autonomy-based* arguments. The latter ignores, or at least brackets, our cognitive lives.

The epistemic virtues identified in this chapter – such as a sensitivity to the salient facts; intellectual humility; fairness in evaluating the arguments of others; insight into persons, problems, and theories; and the teaching virtues (Zagzebski 1996) – are grouped together as a cluster of the cognitive skills and flexibility needed to possess what the clinical psychiatrist Daniel Siegal (2010) has coined "mindsight." Siegal describes mindsight as follows:

> Mindsight is a kind of focused attention that allows us to see the internal workings of our own minds. It helps us to be aware of our mental processes without being swept away by them, enables us to get ourselves off the autopilot of ingrained behaviors and habituated responses, and moves us beyond the reactive emotional loops we all have a tendency to get trapped in. (Siegal 2010)

Mindsight involves much more than simply having introspection into (and emotional regulation of) one's own mental processes; it also involves having such insight into the minds of others (including a collectivity, such as a society or legislature). And this is what makes the skills of mindsight so integral to the virtue of toleration. Mindsight provides us with cognitive "maps" not only of our own mind but maps to comprehend the mental sea of other minds that exist in a pluralistic intellectual community. In the sections that follow, the epistemic virtues associated with mindsight will be invoked to resolve the so-called "paradox of toleration," as well as elaborate on the limits of toleration as a virtue. Two cases of mindsight are considered – the case of tolerant parents and the prohibition of hate speech. The latter case draws on the example of the Canadian Charter case of *R. v Keegstra* (1990), which involved the conviction of a high school teacher who taught his students that the holocaust was a hoax.

In the following section, two significant challenges to any conception of toleration as a virtue are detailed. These challenges are (1) the alleged *paradox of toleration* (that we should tolerate some beliefs and practices we object to) and

(2) delineating the *limits of toleration* (detailing when, and why, we should not tolerate some beliefs and practices we object to). The section titled "Tolerant Parents" explores how a *virtue epistemological* defense of toleration could be employed to address these two problems. This helps set the stage for applying the virtue epistemological account of toleration, in later sections of the chapter, to inter-group toleration and the design of hate speech legislation.

The Paradox, and Limits, of Toleration

The so-called paradox of toleration is most obvious when attention is given to the conflicting beliefs of the agent who displays the virtue of toleration. As already noted in the Introduction, toleration entails that we actually *object* to the belief or practice in question (otherwise, it is not truly toleration as you do not "tolerant" a belief or practice you actually endorse or are supportive of or indifferent to). Perhaps we believe the belief is wrong, or the cultural practice in question is offensive, superstitious, or antiquated. And yet we also believe that we ought not to intervene to suppress this belief or practice. Stated in this general way, it appears the tolerant agent holds conflicting beliefs – there are reasons to want X to be diminished (if not be eliminated), *and* there are reasons to want to protect the right to hold, express, or practice X. But once we delve into the *psychology* of toleration, in particular the importance of the ensemble of "epistemic virtues" constitutive of the capacity for, and flexibility of, *mindsight*, we can see that this so-called paradox of toleration is illusory. The devil is really in the details of understanding the beliefs behind holding premise (3) – the decision to not suppress, despite its being objectionable, the belief or practice in question.

One way to resolve this apparent paradox of toleration is to simply appeal to the primacy of the value of autonomy. Autonomy is a central value/principle in Western liberal thought. A standard argument for toleration is to begin with a commitment to respect for individual autonomy (Raz 1988) and argue that the rights to freedom of conscience, religion, and expression ought to be treated as (nearly) unassailable. Toleration is thus an expression, so the argument goes, of the commitment to the sanctity of autonomy and the legal and political rights that extend from that moral ideal.

This autonomy-based argument could be summarized as follows:

> *Autonomy-Based Resolution of the Paradox of Toleration:* While there may be good reasons for wanting to suppress X – X being some viewpoint, belief, or practice we find objectionable and/or believe to be wrong – we don't desire to suppress X because doing so would violate the autonomy of those who hold X. Respect for autonomy trumps the reasons for aspiring to suppress X.

A second major challenge facing an account of toleration is delineating the *limits of toleration*. Surely there are certain beliefs, expressions, and conceptions of the good that a tolerant society should not tolerate. For example, a tolerant society will not tolerate those who advocate the use of violence to bring about societal reform or change. Terrorists, for example, should clearly not be tolerated by a liberal democracy committed to the security of all persons and the nonviolent means of societal reform open via the democratic process. The strategy of an autonomy-based account of toleration is to limit the virtue to the toleration of those practices and beliefs that do not themselves pose a serious threat to the autonomy of others. Terrorists, militants, and revolutionaries that advocate the use of violence obviously threaten the stability, and thus individual autonomy, of a tolerant society. Such expressions should be constrained rather than tolerated. Otherwise toleration risks becoming a *vice* rather than a virtue as it would violate, rather than protect, autonomy.

Similarly, though it is a more complex and contentious case to consider (Farrelly 2003), the public expression of hate against identifiable groups potentially threatens the autonomy and equality of those who are the target of such expressions. This can make members of the identifiable group more susceptible to hate crimes and societal discrimination. Thus one could make an autonomy-based argument for limiting expressions that pose a legitimate threat to the autonomy and security of others.

In the Kantian ethics tradition, which ranges from the work of Immanuel Kant to John Rawls, autonomy entails living in accordance with those laws that we would "self-legislate" as rational beings. Moral agents, according to this tradition, make decisions about what is right or wrong by engaging in *introspection* and deducing what the demands of reason are. This entails stripping away our contingent desires or particular attributes (e.g., desires or conception of the good) by applying the "categorical imperative" ("act only in accordance with that maxim through which you can at the same time will that it become a universal law") or the Rawlsian (1971) "veil of ignorance" in a hypothetical original position. This is at the heart of the project of Kantian ethics, an ethic that critics have argued functions with an "unencumbered conception of the self" (Sandel 1982, 1996). A conception of the person that presumes it makes sense to talk about persons who can be "unbound" by the moral duties and responsibilities that constitute our identity as parents, siblings, and compatriots.

When transposed into the epistemic domain, this Kantian idea of moral autonomy gives rise to a conception of "epistemic autonomy," an account of epistemic capacities that envisions a kind of cognitively infallible Robinson Crusoe-type deliberator. Elizabeth Fricker describes this ideal of epistemic autonomy as follows:

> [A] superior being, with all the epistemic powers to find out everything she wanted to know for herself, could live up to this idea of complete epistemic autonomy without thereby circumscribing the extent of her knowledge. Given the risks involved in epistemic dependence on others ... , this superior being is, I suppose, epistemically better placed than humans are. That is, if she knew at first hand just as much as I myself know in large part through trust in others' testimony, she would be epistemically more secure, hence both practically more independent, and—in some abstract sense—more autonomous than I am. In the same way that I might regret that I cannot fly, or live to be 300 years old, I might regret that I am not such a being. (Fricker 2006)

This account of the moral and epistemic ideal of autonomy is flawed because it is fatally abstract. It ignores the basic truism that autonomy requires *interdependence* with many and distinct minds because the volitional aspects of autonomy cannot be disconnected from the cognitional aspects. No person exists as a Robinson Crusoe-type moral agent. We are social, embedded deliberators. "In the epistemic domain [autonomy] requires believing certain things because an authority tells me to do so. In the practical domain it no doubt requires doing certain things because an authority tells me to do so" (Zagzebski 2012). The virtue epistemologist Linda Zagzebski emphasizes the importance of *reflective self-consciousness*, a kind of "cognitive filter" that helps us demarcate what is worth believing and what ought to be challenged, modified, or rejected. And this "cognitive filter" is what I shall refer to in this chapter as "mindsight" (Siegal 2010), a skill that permits us to hold others cognitively present with our own mind and to appreciate the potential pros and cons of such interdependence. Mindsight is a constitutive element of tolerant persons and a tolerant polity.

Can virtue epistemology offer us a distinctive strategy for addressing the so-called paradox and limits of toleration? This chapter makes the case for answering that question in the affirmative. And by considering such a conception of toleration, we can better appreciate how important our cognitive lives are to the exercise of toleration as a virtue.

Tolerant Parents

To begin to piece together the distinctive appeal of a virtue epistemology-based account of toleration, let us consider the case of a tolerant parent and her somewhat rebellious teenager. This is an example that is harder for an autonomy-based argument to address because the status of the autonomy of the teen is somewhat precarious. A teen lays somewhere in the tenuous middle ground between a dependant child, who lacks the capacity to make informed decision-making and thus can (at least in many circumstances) be justifiably treated paternalistically, and an adult who we would consider autonomous.

Consider the following scenario (which shall be referred to later as the case of *healthy* (and *tolerant*) *parenting*). Over the past year, Beth and her 16-year-old son Davis have been experiencing higher-than-usual conflict in their mother-child relationship. When Davis was younger, he and his mother shared time together going to church every Sunday and discussing their mutual interest in dogs and reality TV shows. But as Davis developed into a teenager, and recently started at high school, Beth has noticed him pulling away from her and being influenced more by his peer group. It started with some of the clothes Davis wanted to wear, which included wearing T-shirts of heavy metal music bands his mother did not care for. Davis also stopped taking clarinet lessons and opted instead to teach himself the electric guitar. Most evenings after school, Davis hangs out at a friend's house playing music. Davis has also grown his hair long and has even expressed, to his mother's dismay, a desire to have his nose pierced!

Davis's mother Beth has expressed her objections to Davis. But despite his mother's disapproval, Davis continues to engage in these behaviors. Beth finds it challenging to navigate the space between being a *proactive caregiver* for Davis and giving him the space needed to permit him to grow and develop into an autonomous adult.

What would a tolerant parent do in such a predicament? Let us suppose that Beth actually does possess the ability to dissuade Davis from some of these activities by grounding him or even just threatening to ground him, for his choice of clothes, music, and friends. Davis is not so insolent as to refuse her efforts to intervene and stop him from expressing his new interests and time with friends. So Beth has the *capacity* to interfere with the expression and realization of Davis's preferences, *and* she objects to many of the decisions and behaviors her son is making and displaying. Should she seek to intervene, through threats of grounding Davis or confiscating his guitar, to help ensure Davis desists in engaging in the behavior she finds objectionable?

If we invoke an autonomy-based defense of the virtue of toleration in this case, there is little guidance that can be provided. Either Davis is considered as a fully autonomous agent, in which case his mother should tolerate his fashion and choice of friends and hobbies, or he is not considered an autonomous agent. In the latter case, Beth is thus justified in acting in a strongly paternalistic fashion, intervening in Davis's decisions to help improve the odds of her son flourishing.

By contrast, a virtue epistemological approach makes our *epistemic competence* (or incompetence) the focus of our normative analysis of tolerance as a virtue. Starting with the parent and child relationship is thus instructive because it is an example that clearly demonstrates a critical factor of our psychology – that we are psychologically *interdependent*. Contra the ideal of "intellectual autonomy" invoked earlier by Fricker (2006), which presupposes that the ideal is knowing everything we want to know for ourselves without relying on others, a virtue epistemological account of autonomy presumes autonomy requires *interdependence* with many and distinct minds. For Zagzebski, this requires *reflective self-consciousness*, a kind of "cognitive filter" that helps us demarcate what is worth believing and what ought to be challenged, modified, or rejected.

The potential this focus on our psychological interdependence has for the virtue of toleration will be developed by elaborating first on two distinctively parental virtues that take into consideration the "epistemic capacities" of a parent's offspring – the virtues of *acceptingness* and *committedness*. Rosalind McDougall argues that the virtue of acceptingness requires "a parent to acknowledge the reality that their child's characteristics will be unpredictable" (McDougall 2007). While Beth might have hoped her son would continue to excel playing the clarinet and spend his free time watching TV with his mom, Beth (when she possesses the virtue of acceptingness) understands that, as a teen, Davis's interests will evolve and change.

By contrast the virtue of committedness is the expectation that "parents will (and should) nurture their children to adulthood." Approvingly citing Onora O'Neill (2002), McDougall claims that committedness is the idea that children should be born to parents "who have reasonable expectations and intentions of being active and present to bring up the child" (McDougall 2007).

What the parental virtues of acceptingness and committedness track is a more fundamental intellectual virtue of understanding our internal worlds, what Daniel Siegal calls "mindsight." Siegal characterizes mindsight as follows:

> Mindsight is a kind of focused attention that allows us to see the internal workings of our own minds. It helps us to be aware of our mental processes without being swept away by them, enables us to get ourselves off the autopilot of ingrained behaviors and habituated responses, and moves us beyond the reactive emotional loops we all have a tendency to get trapped in. (Siegal 2010)

Expanding upon the multifaceted skill of mindsight, Siegal argues that we must be able to form a "me map," a "you map," and a "we map" if we are to perceive, and respond appropriately to, our own mind and the minds of others. Let us unpack these concepts by applying Siegal's argument to three parental examples of navigating parenting during the often tenuous teen years.

The following three cases will now be considered and contrasted: (1) *healthy parenting,* (2) *intolerant (or helicopter) parenting*, and (3) *neglectful parenting*. The first example emulates the virtues of acceptingness and committedness and as such helps reveal the importance of mindsight for the virtue of toleration. The *intolerant parent* possesses an excess of committedness and a deficiency of acceptingness. And this can be contrasted with a *neglectful parent* where a deficiency of "committedness" is present and there is an excess of acceptingness.

To ensure Beth and her son continue to have a healthy relationship, Beth must possess mindsight, for without this skill navigating the teen years with her son will prove precarious. When reflecting on her feelings about Davis's recent change in behavior, Beth invokes the following cognitive "maps" to explain the complex emotions she often feels about these developments:

Beth's "me map": "I love and care deeply for my son Davis. His health and wellbeing has been a central concern and priority in my life since he was born 16 years ago. I am not the perfect parent (who is?), but I genuinely do aspire to satisfy the demands of the parental virtue of committedness. I have made mistakes along the way, but I am learning and try my best. I am unhappy with many of the decisions Davis has been making concerning his fashion, friends and the amount of time he dedicates to his current hobbies. I worry that peer-pressure might lead him to make decisions that jeopardize his health and wellbeing. But I am also aware that my protective instinct sometimes leads me to over-react. I am conscious of this tendency of mine, and am learning to navigate my emotions more effectively."

Beth's "you map" of her son Davis: "Davis is a good son. He is no longer my 'little boy', he is growing up so quickly! Along the way he is learning to assert his independence, making decisions that I do not always agree with (sigh!). He wants to feel accepted by his peer group and feel some independence from his mother.

This has resulted in some new risk-taking behaviour of his part and a 'realignment' of his values. Some of his new values come into direct tension with the values he was raised to embrace."

Beth's "we map" of her mother-son relationship: "Davis and I enjoy a typical mother-child relationship. We genuinely care about each other, but sometimes struggle to adapt to the healthy boundaries of an evolving parent-child relationship. At times he really pushes my buttons, and no doubt sometimes I am overprotective and reactive and can make him feel smothered. But on the whole, we find a way to maintain peace and a measured compromise that permits him some independence (within limits!) and me the peace of mind that he is genuinely safe and ok."

Contrast these cognitive maps, which exemplify important elements of mindset, with the *intolerant parent* and *neglectful parent's* "inner maps" which are presented in stark terms to make the contrast vivid. An *intolerant* (or *helicopter*) *parent* has the following cognitive maps of their teen who is in the same situation as Davis:

Intolerant parent's **"me map" of the teen-parent relationship:** "I am the parent and know what is best for my teen. My parents were very stern and firm with me when I was growing up and that kept me out of trouble. I apply that same parenting style to my own teen."

Intolerant parent's **"you map" of their teen:** "My teen is easily swayed by peer pressure, evident by the fact that they frequently challenge authority (e.g. parents, teachers, pastor, etc.) and thus they need some stern guidance to stay on the right track in life! If I granted my teen some leeway in their choice of fashion, friends and hobbies they could mess up their life for good. So my teen needs me to always 'be on their case' (as my teen would describe it!)."

Intolerant parent's **"we map" of the teen-parent relationship:** "One day my teen will thank me for my 'tough love' approach. I have much more wisdom and life experience than my teen, so their judgement does not really count for much. With discipline and consistency I can keep my teen in line and engaging in the behaviors I want them to display, thus avoiding the behaviors I disapprove of."

And finally compare the opposite end of the spectrum, with the example of *a neglectful parent*. In this example the teen displays some seriously disturbing (even criminal) behavior. The teen of *the neglectful parent* has a track record of abusing drugs and skipping school and was recently arrested for theft. And yet despite these problematic behaviors, a *neglectful parent* takes a "hands-off approach" to parenting their teen because the parent lacks mindsight:

Neglectful parent's **"me map"**: "I'm a busy person, with two demanding jobs, a new partner, mounting debt and a busy social life. My kids, including my teen, will be fine with a 'hands-off' approach to parenting. Parents shouldn't coddle their offspring."

***Neglectful parent's* "you map" of their teen:** "Sure my kids will make mistakes, we all do. That's life. They will learn from their mistakes. Experience is the best teacher."

***Neglectful parent's* "we map" of the teen-parent relationship:** "I do my thing, and let my teen do their thing. End of story."

The three different parents– *healthy parent*, *helicopter parent*, and *neglectful parent* – display different degrees and types of psychological interdependence with their children which are all filtered through different epistemic virtues or vices. Virtue epistemology makes these belief systems a focus of *moral evaluation*. Of the three parenting attitudes, the healthy parent has the most accurate internal map of their teen's cognition. The healthy parent exemplifies "mindsight." Firstly, the healthy parent has *humility* – they recognize that parenting, especially a teen, is not always easy. And to help the parent navigate through these complex cognitive and emotional tasks, they seek *psychological connectedness* and *interdependence* (versus striving for some ideal of "epistemic autonomy") with their teen and others (e.g., other parents). The healthy parent acknowledges they will (inevitably) make mistakes and they have an openness to trying different styles of parenting (e.g., more lax or more stern) in light of the successes and failures they experience trying to navigate these often challenging years of parenting. This improvisational and adaptive cognitive and emotional state permit the parent-child relationship to possess more flexibility than the rigidity of either the *helicopter* or *neglectful parent*.

The *healthy (tolerant) parent* will permit their child to assert (with limits) some independence, indeed to even make mistakes. This is an important stage in the development from adolescence to adulthood, something the *healthy parent* actually understands about her teen's mind. Thus the *healthy parent* possesses the epistemic virtues of "sensitivity to details" (like a child's age and stage of cognitive development) and "insights into problems" (such as a teen's desire to "fit in" with their peers), as well as "fairness in evaluating the arguments of others." To the healthy parent, when their teen expresses a very strong desire for the clothes they want to wear and friends they associate with, the fact that it is a desire they have about their own life provides the parent with a compelling rationale for taking these wishes seriously (though not necessarily deferring to them, depending on how severe the consequences of possible misjudgments could be).

By contrast the *helicopter parent* is intolerant, because such a parent cannot interpret the cognitive state of their teen children so accurately. They still see their teen as a *completely dependent child*, and thus the *helicopter parent* adopts a very strong paternal stance with respect to influencing their teen's behavior. And the *neglectful parent* also fails to accurately internalize the inner workings of their teen's mind, treating them as one might an adult one has no special care-taking relationship with, or responsibility to.

Siegal's concept of "mindsight" incorporates at least the following "epistemic virtues" that are integral to toleration as a virtue:

1. The ability to recognize the salient facts; sensitivity to details
2. Fairness in evaluating the arguments of others

3. Intellectual humility
4. Insight into persons, problems, and theories
5. The teaching virtues: the social virtues of being communicative, including intellectual candor and knowing your audience and how they respond (Zagzebski 1996)

The tolerant parent, like the initial example of the mother, Beth, will possess each of these epistemic virtues. Beth is aware of the salient facts (i.e., her teen is not a young child), and she aspires to be fair in evaluating the arguments her son gives for wanting to dress the way he does and hang out with his choice of friends. Beth has the humility to recognize that she doesn't always know what is truly best for a teenager. She has important insight into the teen brain, understanding a teen's need for some independence and the intense pressure they can be under from peer pressure. And finally Beth possesses the teaching virtues, knowing that her teen son would not likely respond positively to threats for compliance with all her wishes. So she picks her "non-negotiables"– that homework be done, no drugs, and be home at the agreed-upon time, etc. Beth lets the issues of her son's fashion, choice of friends, and hobbies be decisions *he* makes, provided her non-negotiables are respected by him. She knows that, should she try to be more heavy-handed and control these other aspects of her teen's life, she risks him rebelling, thus pushing him even further away.

Mindsight, which is the culmination of the intellectual virtues Zagzebski (1996) identifies, help the healthy parent adopt a tolerant, but still committed, parental attitude to navigating the sometimes precarious parent-teen relationship.

Let us now consider cases of the virtue of toleration where the persons involved are adults (rather than teens) and the society must grapple with the issue of determining what the *limits* of toleration are.

Toleration Among Groups

The concept of "mindsight"– that we can hold in our mind, with focused attention, the internal workings of our own minds as well as those of others, without responding reactively – provides critical details into the *psychology of toleration*, details that help explain how the paradox of toleration can be resolved by a virtue epistemological conception of toleration. The virtue of toleration is composed of a number of distinct *epistemic* virtues, virtues which are integral to the exercise of toleration.

Recall that toleration entails that we have both (a) reasons for objecting to a belief or practice (let's call it "X") and yet we also have (b) reasons, indeed overriding reasons, for not suppressing X. Responding only to (a), by seeking to suppress practice X, would be to respond reactively, in a fashion that demonstrates a lack of mindsight (and hence toleration). What separates the tolerant agent (e.g., person or institution) from the intolerant agent is thus the internalization of (b). And when one probes behind the reasons for why we might tolerate something we find objectionable, one discovers some nuanced combination of "intellectual virtues," such as a recognition of the salient facts, fairness in evaluating the arguments of others, intellectual humility, insight into persons and problems, and the social virtues of being communicative.

To illustrate the explanatory and normative potential of a virtue epistemological conception of toleration, I will now consider a case of group tolerance and intolerance. The hypothetical example I consider reveals a generational divide between the interdependence of members of a religious group and citizens with a sexual orientation that contravenes the teachings of that religion.

A devoted religious family has run a family-owned business for the past few decades, since they first immigrated to the United States in the 1960s. The family's country of origin was a conservative theocracy, a country where homosexuality was (and still is) a criminal offense punishable by death. The small family business they established in the United States typically employs approximately 5–6 part-time employees to help cover shifts when the immediate family members are not available to work. The family business was originally created by the grandfather of the family, but he now only works a few hours a week as he is semiretired. His granddaughter now manages the family business, including the important decisions about the hiring and firing of part-time employees.

Both grandfather and granddaughter adhere to the same religion, a religion that strongly disapproves of homosexuality and considers such behavior sinful. But the grandfather and granddaughter differ in terms of how their religious beliefs impact their decisions about hiring workers for their family business. When the grandfather originally created the family company many decades earlier, he was adamantly opposed to hiring anyone who was openly LGBTQ, for he felt this would bring shame upon the family by giving the impression that they condoned sinful behavior. The granddaughter takes a very different perspective than the one her grandfather took many decades earlier. The granddaughter knows that her grandfather's attitude constitutes *discrimination* and that it is actually illegal and immoral to deny someone employment based on their sexual orientation.

The inner workings of the mind of the grandfather and granddaughter can be represented as follows:

The grandfather's "me/you/we map" of himself and members of the LGBTQ community when he first immigrated to the United States in the 1960s:

> Homosexuality is a sin, and those who engage in such acts are sinners. In my home country where I grew up such acts were subject to severe criminal punishment. Just because such behaviour is not illegal in the country I now live in does not mean I have to accept it. Our family business is an extension of my family and thus my religious values. These cannot be separated. Therefore, we cannot employ anyone who is openly gay as that would imply we condone such behaviour, which we do not. It would bring the family shame.

The granddaughter's "me/you/we map" many decades later:

> Like my grandfather, I also believe homosexuality is a sin. That is the traditional view of the religion I espouse. However, our family business is a place of *business*. As such it provides opportunities for employment to the broader public, in return for the financial

gains we receive from employing good workers. And members of the LGBTQ community can be good workers, and as such should have equal opportunity to work for us or any other place of employment. I would not want an employer discriminating against me based on my religion or gender (something that did occur within my grandfather's lifetime). It is not my prerogative to judge and unfairly discriminate against others in terms of their employment, wage or promotion. My responsibilities as an employer must trump my own personal sensibilities on issues unrelated to a person's suitability for the job. This is something my grandfather had a difficult time understanding.

The granddaughter possesses many epistemic virtues that her grandfather lacks. Significant societal progress, such as The Employment Non-Discrimination Act which prohibits discrimination in employment based on sexual orientation, was implemented and enforced during the formative years of the granddaughter's life. Such legislation helped ensure societal norms were more inclusive than the discriminatory culture in which her grandfather was raised decades earlier in an intolerant theocracy. The granddaughter has insight into the history of discrimination (the epistemic virtue of "insight into problems"), she is aware of the rationale behind the legislative initiatives to prevent such injustices, and she has a grasp of the distinction between the "personal" and the "public." And while she disapproves of homosexuality, she does not see members of the LGBTQ community as "subhuman," as persons to be deprived of equality of opportunity.

In this family business example, the grandfather is intolerant, and the granddaughter is tolerant. The former aspires to prevent members of the LGBTQ from enjoying their basic rights and liberties, whereas the granddaughter can separate her personal religious views from her moral and legal responsibilities as a citizen and employer. She does not seek to prevent LGBTQ persons from working in the family business because she believes the equality of all persons ought to trump her personal convictions on topics that ought not, by law, to be a factor in the hiring, promotion, pay, and firing of employees.

A strength of a virtue epistemological conception of toleration is the fact that it makes our *cognitive lives* an important *focus* of the virtue of toleration. What a person believes – about themselves ("me map"), others ("you map"), and a collectivity ("we map") – will determine how successful they are at exercising the epistemic virtues integral to toleration.

To illustrate how the epistemic virtues can inform legislative initiatives concerning the scope and limitations of toleration, I will now consider the case of Canada's hate speech legislation (Section 32 of the Canadian Criminal Code). The famous legal decision of *R v Keegstra* (1990), involving a high school teacher that taught his students the holocaust was a hoax, provides a fruitful example for teasing out the normative potential of a virtue epistemological account of toleration.

Epistemic Virtue and the Case of Tolerating Hate Speech

Since the rise of Donald Trump's Presidency in 2017, the United States has grappled with renewed concerns about toleration, racism, and violence. A few months after President Trump took office, an assortment of "alt-right" groups protested the removal of Confederate monuments in Charlottesville, Virginia. The "Unite the Right" event involved confrontations with counter-demonstrators, which culminated in the death of the counter-demonstrator Heather Heyer. Heyer was killed in a hit-and-run incident. James Field Jr. was later charged with first-degree murder and sentenced to life in prison plus 419 years.

Racial hatred poses a significant challenge for liberal democracies and their exercise of the virtue of toleration. To what extent, if any, should hate speech be tolerated in a society that espouses the freedom and equality of all its citizenry? The epistemic virtues of "mindsight" are, I shall now argue, essential in exercising toleration as a virtue rather than a vice. Toleration can be a vice when the society tolerates expressions that threaten the security and equality of its citizens, especially persons that are members of groups that have been historically discriminated against. Conversely, a society's effort to redress historical injustice and promote equality can be taken too far when it unreasonably intrudes upon the expressions and autonomy of citizens. The epistemic virtues can help a polity navigate the tenuous middle ground of finding a compromise between the aspirations of freedom and equality for all.

During the 1960s the prevalence of anti-Semitic sentiments motivated the Canadian Minister of Justice to appoint a special committee to report on hate propaganda in Canada. The Cohen Report (1966) noted that hate "is as old as man and doubtless as durable" and that the report would explore "what it is that a community can do to lessen some of man's intolerance and to proscribe its gross exploitation" (Plaut 1967). Creating a Parliamentary committee to assess the problem, and potential solutions, to hate propaganda demonstrated a commitment to exercise the epistemic virtue of having "insight into persons and problems." Had Canadian law-makers simply ignored (as they had historically, until the 1960s) the problems of racism and intolerance, by burying their heads in the sand and pretending such issues were not a problem, their ignorance would have perpetuated intolerance, and they would have exemplified intellectual vice rather than virtue.

Focusing on the problem of hate propaganda also displays the epistemic virtue of "recognizing the salient facts." Expressions of hate against identifiable members of a group can exacerbate the problems of violence and discrimination. Humans are *social* beings and as such are influenced by what they see on TV and read in newspapers and on social media. Many of the findings and recommendations of the Cohen Report eventually found their way into law in 1970 in the form of Section 319(2) of the Canadian Criminal Code, which states:

> 319(2) Every one who, by communicating statements, other than in private conversation, wilfully promotes hatred against any identifiable group is guilty of
> (a) an indictable offence and is liable to imprisonment for a term not exceeding two years; or
> (b) an offence punishable on summary conviction.

Various aspects of this legislation are illustrative of "collective mindset," an integral feature of healthy democratic lawmaking. These issues were explicitly addressed in the Supreme Court of Canada's landmark 1990 decision, *R v Keegstra*, in which Section 319 was upheld as a constitutional limitation on freedom of expression. The case involved the conviction of James Keegstra, a teacher who taught his students that the holocaust was a hoax.

A number of features of the legislation, and the judicial decision to uphold the legislation, are worth noting as exemplar examples of the epistemic virtues of "collective mindsight." Firstly, lawmakers decided to limit censorship to only *public*, not private, expressions of hate. Extending the scope of criminal law to penalize hate expressed in private conversation would be to impose intrusions that no free society should tolerate. While racism and discrimination are bad, and should be abated, doing so at the cost of policing the private conversations of citizens was deemed an even more repugnant outcome. Furthermore, it is the public dissemination of hate that is likely to have the most significant impact on harming identifiable members of vulnerable groups as they reach audiences many times larger than the audience in private communications.

Secondly, lawmakers added the phrase "willfully" promoted hatred as their goal was to curtail the expressions of those who consciously seek to undermine the equality and security of members of identifiable groups. This is a particularly vivid "mindsight" virtue. Legislators believed a *"mens rea"* (or guilty mind) was an integral component of hate propaganda. Thirdly, the law uses the strong term "hate" and not simply "offense to" or "dislike of." And fourthly the law only pertains to expressions that target an identifiable group (which means any section of the public distinguished by color, race, religion, national or ethnic origin, age, sex, sexual orientation, gender identity or expression, or mental or physical disability), but not hate against a specific person. This element of the law also tracks "collective mindsight" in that lawmakers aspired to limit the scope of the criminality of hate speech to communication that targeted groups. It is the groups (rather than specific persons) who are the victims of historical discrimination.

When elaborating on the harms of hate propaganda, in the Canadian Supreme Court decision to uphold Keegstra's conviction, Chief Justice Dickson remarked:

> First, there is harm done to members of the target group. It is indisputable that the emotional damage caused by words may be of grave psychological and social consequence....A second harmful effect of hate propaganda which is of pressing and substantial concern is its influence upon society at large.... It is... not inconceivable that the active dissemination of hate propaganda can attract individuals to its cause, and in the process create serious discord between various cultural groups in society. (R v *Keegstra* 1990)

Perhaps the most distinctive element of Canada's hate propaganda legislation that exemplifies the epistemic virtues of collective mindsight is the "special defenses" in Subsection 3 of Section 319, which states the following:

> No person shall be convicted of an offence under subsection (2)
> (a) if he establishes that the statements communicated were true;
> (b) if, in good faith, the person expressed or attempted to establish by an argument an opinion on a religious subject or an opinion based on a belief in a religious text;

(c) if the statements were relevant to any subject of public interest, the discussion of which was for the public benefit, and if on reasonable grounds he believed them to be true; or

(d) if, in good faith, he intended to point out, for the purpose of (their) removal, matters producing or tending to produce feelings of hatred toward an identifiable group in Canada.

An examination of these defenses will be limited to just the first two defenses – *truth* and *religion* – as they are (arguably) the most stark examples of the collective mindsight at play in the crafting of the law.

The first defense, truth, recognizes that Canadians have a primary interest in the truth, even if the truth expresses hate against an identifiable group. This special defense sought to protect the dissemination of the truth from the scope of the criminal provision against hate speech. This displays a fidelity to the epistemic virtues of humility and of being fair when evaluating the arguments of others. If what someone is communicating is true, then society has a vested interest in ensuring the person is free to express the truth. The goal of hate propaganda legislation is to reduce hate speech, not suppress the truth.

The second defense, the religion defense, appeals to the epistemic virtue of fairly evaluating the arguments of others. Religion is an integral aspect of identity for many Canadians. And while a law that criminalized religious hate propaganda would go further in terms of protecting the equality and security of identified groups, the Parliament decided that it would come at too heavy a cost if it threatened freedom of religious expression. Whether or not one agrees with this particular defense, I think it demonstrates how lawmakers aspired to balance many competing viewpoints and values when crafting the law.

When reflecting upon Section 319(2) of the Canadian Criminal Code, it is not implausible to construct the following "we map" which I believe accurately reflects the specific details of this legislation (which isn't to endorse it as the ideal law, only as a contender for being an illuminating example of the "epistemic virtues" in action):

Canadian "We Map": "As a free and democratic society we believe it is important to take seriously both the freedom and equality of all our citizens, and to pursue fair and reasonable measures which help mitigate the injustices and discrimination of the past. So we have criminalized those expressions that pose the greatest risk to identifiable groups- public, wilful expressions of hate against identifiable groups. These public expressions should not be tolerated. We do, however, have one further proviso we believe should be added. There can be a few, specific, exceptions to this law. When the interests in protecting certain expressions, even hateful expressions, are so significant (such as the truth) as to warrant protection of hate speech, then we should come down on the side of toleration vs intolerance. For example, in cases where the expression is true, or part of one's religion. This law takes seriously the reality that, at least in non-ideal societies, tradeoffs must take place between fundamental values. And we believe 319(2) finds a reasonable balance between freedom and equality."

The legal philosopher Wayne Sumner describes the balancing act Section 319 attempts to accomplish as follows:

The optimal trade-off, or balance, is that at which any further gains in one of the values would be outweighed by greater losses in the other. Freedom of expression would be better protected were there no legal constraints whatever on the circulation of hate propaganda, while the security of minority groups would be more effectively safeguarded by legislation a good deal more restrictive than s. 319(2). Somewhere between the two extremes we seek a balance point at which the greater protection for minorities afforded by stronger legislation would be outweighed by the chilling effect on political speech, while the greater protection for expression afforded by weaker legislation would be outweighed by the increase in racial hatred. (Sumner 1994)

Canadian society is a multicultural society of approximately 37 million people. The population is comprised of Indigenous Peoples (approximately 5% of the Canadian population) and immigrants and descendants of immigrants from Europe (e.g., France, Great Britain), Asia, and elsewhere. Collective "mindsight" is integral to the virtue of toleration as it brings together a host of distinct "epistemic virtues" – such as having intellectual humility (e.g., the truth should be protected), sensitivity to details (e.g., public expressions of hate are more harmful than private conversations), fairness in evaluating the arguments of others (e.g., religion is a fundamental value for many Canadians), and insight into problems and persons (e.g., racism and hate are perpetual problems in need of addressing). The Canadian example of regulating hate speech helps make concrete the work the epistemic virtues can do when exercising toleration as a public virtue.

Attention will now be given to a possible objection concerning the distinctiveness of the virtue epistemological conception of toleration advanced in this chapter. This objection comes from a defender of the *autonomy-based* defense of toleration. The objection is that an autonomy-based defense of toleration need not bracket the issue of the psychology of toleration. Indeed, when supplemented with the epistemic virtues of "mindsight," such an account of toleration seems compatible with the account that has been advanced so far.

An Autonomy-Based Response

A virtue epistemological articulation, and defense, of toleration as the exercise of distinct epistemic virtues (culminating in "mindsight") might face the following type of objection from a proponent of an *autonomy-based* account of toleration:

> *Autonomy-Based Defense of Mindsight:* Defending toleration on grounds of the importance of the moral value of autonomy is predicated on a psychology very similar to the skill of "mindsight" invoked in this chapter. That is, tolerant citizens will function with a "you map" that prioritizes the autonomy of other persons, and this is so because this map will be one in which they recognize that, whatever others want for their lives, they should be the authority on deciding what to pursue and how to pursue it. So the psychology of toleration is just as foundational to an autonomy-based defense of toleration as it is a virtue epistemological defense.

I have some sympathy with such a response, as it is certainly true that an autonomy-based argument could invoke an account of the psychology of toleration to make it sound both plausible and compelling. Consider the following example, which is invoked to help flesh out the force of this objection. Let us call this example the *intolerant neighborhood*.

Here are the pertinent details of the *intolerant neighborhood* example. David lives in a small suburban township where the vast majority of people share the same religious faith and ethnicity. David's new neighbors, a family of six that come from a different cultural and religious background than the majority of people living in David's town, just moved into the house beside him. The family has placed religious symbols (important to their minority culture) on display on their front lawn. This has upset some members of the township, so much so that a few have created a social media "protest petition" they hope will pressure David's neighbors to either remove the symbols or to consider moving out of the township.

The authors of the petition arrive on David's doorstep to see if they can add his name to the list of neighbors who support their campaign. But David refuses to support the petition. While it is true that David disagrees with the religious beliefs of his neighbor (and it does bother him to have to see their religious symbols on display everyday), he does not support efforts (coercive or noncoercive) to *compel* them to remove such symbols. David expresses his shock and disdain to the petitioners for their intolerance. He tells them that the petition is shameful. He provides the following justification for his stance:

> **David's Response to His Intolerant Township:** "My neighbours, like the rest of us, have an interest in living an *autonomous* life- this means they should decide for themselves what they will and will not display in their home and on their property. The local community and government should not put pressure (overtly or covertly) on them to remove their religious symbols from their personal property."

Implicit in David's reasoning are "me," "you," and "we" maps, maps that display a fidelity to autonomy in a manner compatible with the exercise of mindsight. In examples of this kind, an autonomy-based account of toleration could certainly be characterized in ways that make it indistinguishable from the virtue epistemological account of toleration. But this is only so because this scenario is one where the value of autonomy looms large. Such an account will be strained when addressing the more complex and nuanced cases addressed in the earlier sections of this chapter, such as the tolerant parent navigating the teen years where an adolescent is not fully rational and autonomous and the case of hate speech that risks undermining the equality of vulnerable groups. The psychology of toleration in those two cases involved grappling with nuances like the reality that teens are in a transition stage between being dependent upon their parents and being fully autonomous. And in the case of hate speech, the virtue of toleration requires grappling with the issue of the trade-offs that inevitably arise when tolerating expressions and cultural practices that might erode other significant societal values (such as equality).

The main constraint of a "psychologically-informed" appeal to an autonomy-based defense of toleration is that it unnecessarily limits itself by being committed to the primacy of autonomy. This rigidity is a limitation in circumstances where only *quasi-autonomous* concerns arise (e.g., a teen's desire for more independence) and when other significant values (like equality) directly conflict with autonomy. The rigidity of an autonomy-based defense presupposes that autonomy will trump other values, an inflexible attitude that is counter to intellectual humility. By emphasizing mindsight, and its constitutive "epistemic virtues" (e.g., intellectual humility, insight into problems), a virtue epistemological conception of toleration as a virtue does not prejudge the weight to be placed on autonomy or any other value (e.g., equality). In many circumstances, like David's intolerant neighborhood, autonomy should reign supreme. But in other circumstances, it ought not to reign supreme. A virtue epistemological account of tolerance helps elucidate when invoking the primacy of autonomy is appropriate, and when (and *why*) invoking its primacy is not appropriate.

Conclusion

Virtue epistemology shifts the traditional focus of ethics away from the question "how should I *act*?" towards the question "what should I *believe*?". Virtue epistemology makes our cognitive lives (e.g., beliefs, motivations, attitudes, thought processes, etc.) a subject of moral inquiry and scrutiny. As such virtue epistemology provides the foundations for an original and compelling account of toleration as a virtue, one which makes the *psychology of toleration* a central focus of normative analysis. The so-called paradox of toleration arises when an agent or polity holds the following two, apparently contradictory, beliefs: (1) the belief that some belief or practice is objectionable *and* (2) the belief that, despite its being objectionable, the belief or practice in question should not be suppressed.

The virtue epistemological account of toleration advanced in this chapter attempts to resolve this alleged tension by utilizing the "epistemic virtues" that help explain how the introspective and flexible mind can consistently hold these two, apparently contradictory, beliefs. Such a mind possesses a cluster of intellectual virtues that Siegel describes as "mindsight" – the ability to "be aware of our mental processes without being swept away by them, ... to get ourselves off the autopilot of ingrained behaviors and habituated responses, and moves us beyond the reactive emotional loops we all have a tendency to get trapped in" (Siegal 2010).

Mindsight requires having the ability to recognize the salient facts, intellectual humility, insight into problems, fairness in evaluating the arguments of others, etc. Unlike an autonomy-based account of toleration which makes respect for autonomy the central justification for exercising toleration, the virtue epistemological account advanced here emphasizes a number of distinct epistemic virtues. And the central cases of toleration examined in this chapter – the teen-parent relationship, tolerant employers and neighbors, and the censorship of hate speech – were utilized to reveal the importance, and provide some specific details, of how "mindsight" can help illuminate toleration as a virtue. Virtue epistemology can offer us an original and helpful normative lens for exploring the appeal and limits of toleration.

References

Farrelly C (2003) Neutrality, toleration and reasonable agreement. In: Castiglioni D, Mackinnon C (eds) Toleration, neutrality and democracy. Kluwer, Amsterdam

Fricker E (2006) Testimony and epistemic autonomy. In: Lackey J, Sosa E (eds) The epistemology of testimony. Oxford University Press, New York

Horton J (1996) Toleration as a virtue. In: Held D (ed) Toleration: an elusive virtue. Princeton University Press, Princeton

Keegstra Rv (1990) 3 S.C.R. 697

King P (1976) Toleration. Allen and Unwin, London

McDougall R (2007) Parental virtue: a new way of thinking about the morality of reproductive actions. Bioethics 21(4):181–190

O'Neill O (2002) Autonomy and trust in bioethics. Cambridge University Press, Cambridge

Plaut WG (1967) Book review: the report of the special committee on hate propaganda in Canada. Osgoode Hall Law J 5(2):313–317

Raphael DD (1988) The intolerable. In: Mendus S (ed) Justifying toleration: conceptual and historical perspectives. Cambridge University Press, Cambridge

Rawls J (1971) A theory of justice. The Belknap Press of Harvard University Press, Cambridge, MA

Raz J (1988) Autonomy, toleration, and the harm principle. In: Mendus S (ed) Justifying toleration: conceptual and historical perspectives. Cambridge University Press, Cambridge

Sandel M (1982) Liberalism and the limits of justice. Cambridge University Press, Cambridge

Sandel M (1996) Democracy's discontent. The Belknap Press of Harvard University Press, Cambridge, MA

Siegal D (2010) Mindsight: the new science of personal transformation. Bantam Books, New York

Sumner W (1994) Hate propaganda and charter rights. In: Waluchow WJ (ed) Free expression: essays in law and philosophy. Oxford University Press, Oxford

The report of the special committee on hate propaganda in Canada (Cohen Report) (1966) Queen's Printer and Controller of Stationery, Ottawa

Zagzebski L (1996) Virtues of the mind: an inquiry into the nature of virtue and the ethical foundations of knowledge. Cambridge University Press, Cambridge

Zagzebski L (2012) Epistemic authority: a theory of trust, authority, and autonomy in belief. Oxford University Press, Oxford

36 Tough on Tolerance: The Vice of Virtue

Thomas Nys and Bart Engelen

Contents

Introduction	720
Our Original Analysis: Why Tolerance Is Not a Virtue	721
Refining the Analysis	722
Two Ways Out of Another Paradox	726
Kant on Justice, Virtue, Respect, and Tolerance	729
Summary	733
References	734

Abstract

It is commonly accepted that tolerance is a virtue, a desirable character trait that should be fostered and cultivated, especially in liberal societies. In this chapter, we consider the plausibility of an alternative view, namely that tolerance is not necessarily a virtue. This view adopts a broad and normatively neutral definition of tolerance as simply meaning: deliberately refraining from intervening with conduct one finds objectionable. Moreover, if tolerance is to play an important role in the kind of liberal and pluralist democracies we are currently living in, then such a broad and neutral conception is much more suitable than a more narrow and normatively laden one. Tolerance can and should be something enforceable through law, which becomes difficult, if not impossible, when one understands it as a virtue.

T. Nys (✉)
University of Amsterdam, Amsterdam, The Netherlands
e-mail: T.R.V.Nys@uva.nl

B. Engelen
Tilburg University, Tilburg, The Netherlands
e-mail: B.Engelen@tilburguniversity.edu

© The Author(s), under exclusive licence to Springer Nature Switzerland AG 2022
M. Sardoč (ed.), *The Palgrave Handbook of Toleration*,
https://doi.org/10.1007/978-3-030-42121-2_30

Keywords

Tolerance · Intolerance · Virtue · Justice · Respect · Kant

When you were young and your heart was an open book
You used to say live and let live
(you know you did, you know you did, you know you did)
But if this ever changing world in which we're living
Makes you give in and cry
Say live and let die. (Paul and Linda McCartney, Live And Let Die (1973))

Introduction

Is tolerance a virtue? Is it a morally desirable character trait that is univocally good and that we should therefore foster and cultivate systematically, particularly in liberal societies (e.g., Byrne 2011, 287)? One way of being tough on the concept of tolerance is by claiming that it is not a virtue (Engelen and Nys 2008), thereby withholding it the precious label of something that is always good. But the reason for doing so could be emblematic for a different sense of toughness: the idea that we should be tough on tolerance because it should be something we can demand from others on grounds of *justice*. In this chapter, we will analyze why and how tolerance can indeed be considered a virtue, an approach that is quite lenient at the *conceptual* level. However, we will also stress the need for toughness in the second, *practical* sense. In a Kantian spirit, we show why tolerance can and should be enforced through law, which is arguably crucial if tolerance is to play a meaningful role in contemporary societies.

This chapter starts out by reconstructing a broad and normatively neutral conception of toleration that allows us to appropriately distinguish between cases of tolerance, nontolerance, and intolerance (Section "Our Original Analysis: Why Tolerance Is Not a Virtue"). Next, we show that such an understanding escapes the famous paradox of tolerance that the "virtue approach" (which understands tolerance as a virtue) seems particularly vulnerable to. Analyzing how the virtue approach can deal with this paradox will help us to understand the nature of virtue (Section "Refining the Analysis"). Next, we provide two additional arguments in favor of a broad and neutral understanding of tolerance (Section "Two Ways Out of Another Paradox"). First, it avoids the epistemological worries raised by the virtue approach: How exactly can we know who is and who is not virtuously tolerant? Second, a broad and neutral understanding of tolerance allows for its enforcement when urgently needed, enabling tolerance to play an important role in liberal democracies like ours. We further unpack this line of thought by investigating Immanuel Kant's thoughts on the relationship between tolerance, morality, virtue, and justice (Section "Kant on Justice, Virtue, Respect, and Tolerance"). In the end, we formulate our conclusions (Section "Summary").

Our Original Analysis: Why Tolerance Is Not a Virtue

Our original analysis (Engelen and Nys 2008) started from what we considered to be the best available definition of tolerance, namely that by John Horton: "the deliberate decision to refrain from prohibiting, hindering or otherwise coercively interfering with the conduct of which one disapproves, although one has the power to do so" (Horton 1998, 429–430). For someone to be tolerant, they need to satisfy three conditions: (1) disapprove of something, (2) be able to interfere, yet (3) deliberately refrain from interfering. This also implies that there are three paradigm categories of nontolerance, each one failing to meet one of these three conditions.

The first category concerns people who violate the "objection component" (Forst 2017; also Carter 2013) and do not feel any disapproval towards the conduct at hand (or broader: they lack any of the possible objectionable opinions, attitudes, practices, or even states of affairs). This may be due to utter indifference or because of positive attitudes such as acceptance or endorsement. Suppose one subscribes to someone's conduct or opinions, without any reservation. Homosexuals who endorse their homosexuality cannot be said to tolerate homosexuality, on Horton's definition, because they do not disapprove of it. Likewise, you do not tolerate people who kiss their children goodnight, because you probably believe it is a nice thing to do. This approach avoids normative background assumptions about what one *should disapprove* of or what *is objectionable* (cf. Avramenko and Promisel 2018, 849) and focuses exclusively on what people themselves *disapprove* of or *find objectionable* (cf. Scanlon 1996, 226). In order to be able to tolerate something, one needs to actually disapprove of or object to it, regardless whether it should be disapproved of or objected to. When slavery was largely accepted, slave-owners did not "tolerate" the conduct of fellow slave-owners because they felt no objection or disapproval. Even some slaves themselves could fall short of tolerating slavery, namely if they saw no problem with the practices of their slave-owners (for example, because of adaptive preferences). To tolerate means to bear a burden, and if there is no burden borne, the notion of tolerance stops making sense.

This "no burden" disqualifier also applies to people who are entirely indifferent toward the conduct at hand. Suppose, for instance, that you like peanut butter and jelly sandwiches. Of course, you do not "tolerate" fellow PB&J lovers, because you endorse their preference and think they make the right choice in opting for such a delicious kind of food. But you probably also do not "tolerate" people choosing another type of topping. After all, you typically do not care about what others eat. Again, there is no burden to bear here and hence no decision to refrain from interfering, as there is no reason to interfere from the start. To shift the example from the silly to the significant: Could we be said to "tolerate" smoking if we simply do not care how it affects the lives of those who smoke? Could we be said to "tolerate" the religious food prescriptions of Jews and Muslims (kosjer and halal) if we, quite frankly, could not be bothered? It seems not and Horton's definition captures that intuition.

Secondly, we get to the most obvious category of nontolerant people: those who are plainly intolerant. Here is an example.

> Consider a person who objects to homosexuality and who tries his very best to purify the world of such 'repulsive' or 'unnatural' behavior. He believes that homosexuals should be punished or that they should receive treatment for their 'illness'. When he sees homosexuals holding hands he will insult them or even use violence to put an end to such 'obscenities'. (Engelen and Nys 2008, 46)

Such a person is not tolerant because he makes a decision to interfere with the conduct he finds objectionable. Such a person violates not the "objection component" but the "acceptance component." Rather than say "live and let live," an intolerant person is fed up with this particular conduct and actively intervenes in the hope of ending all this wickedness and debauchery. Note that the plainly intolerant are remarkably consistent. Like those who agree and endorse the conduct and those who are utterly indifferent, there is no discrepancy between the thoughts and actions of intolerant people. They are not bearing a burden either, since they are simply translating their feelings of disapproval into actions and thus do not deliberately decide to refrain from interfering. There is no "split" between having objections and ultimately deciding not to act upon them. Again, putting normative issues aside, and focusing only on a person's attitudes and thoughts, one should say that people are also intolerant when they object to and actively prevent or protest practices of murder, rape, and theft.

And then there is a third category that falls short of tolerance: those who object and would like to be intolerant but somehow lack the power to act on their own objections. As Horton's definition points out, tolerance requires the deliberate decision not to use one's power to intervene. Suppose a group of Hell's Angels decides to give a party at my apartment (avoiding the cleanup in their own clubhouse). They kick in the door, lock me up in the closet, and start drinking my precious Belgian beer collection. I strongly object to this and would interfere if I could, but I simply cannot do anything about it. My inaction – me angrily sulking in the closet – does not amount to tolerance because it arises not out of a deliberate decision to refrain from intervening but out of the impossibility to intervene. Intervening is simply not one of my options. If I could, I would be intolerant, but I simply cannot. My intolerant mindset does not translate into actual intolerant behavior because of my lack of power.

Refining the Analysis

Horton's definition of tolerance plausibly differentiates between cases of tolerance, intolerance, and nontolerance. But note that it is normatively neutral: it says nothing about whether or when these attitudes of tolerance, intolerance, or nontolerance are appropriate. More importantly, it does not say anything about the reasons for tolerance. Many authors believe this is why we should move beyond it and adopt a more refined conception that captures what is distinctly desirable about tolerance. This is exactly what the *virtue approach* offers. Tolerance has been called an "elusive virtue" (Heyd 1996), an "impossible virtue" (Williams 1996), and a "paradoxical value" (Scheffler 2010, 312). The virtue approach typically focuses on the specific moral reasons for deciding not to intervene with whatever one finds objectionable. On this account, a virtuous person does not just act in some desirable way but acts out of a virtuous attitude or on the basis of a virtuous character, having "come to recognize the value of virtue and why it is the appropriate response. Virtue is chosen knowingly for its own sake" (Athanassoulis 2019).

One prominent idea here is that tolerance is necessarily based on respect for (or recognition of) other people's autonomy. When tolerant, we acknowledge that everyone has the right to act upon their own conceptions of the good, even though we find some of their behavior objectionable. Tolerance is a virtue, this approach argues, especially in our pluralist societies, because the alternative is that we either stop caring altogether (and become indifferent) or give up on liberal principles like liberty, autonomy, equality, and respect (and become intolerant).

It is, however, possible to resist this general move in the literature and stick to the broader and neutral conception of toleration. The main reason for this recalcitrance is that fear of (legal) punishment (or anticipation of some reward) should be able to count as a plausible motive for tolerance. On such an understanding, for example, people who do nothing to hinder gay marriage because they fear the scorn of their liberal-minded neighbors can rightly be said to tolerate gay marriage. They definitely bear a burden and willfully decide not to do anything about the conduct they find objectionable. Even if it is not respect that is motivating them, they can still be called tolerant.

Or think of an alternative, perhaps more plausible version of the Hell's Angels story. In this version, they do not lock me up but simply threaten me to the extent that I do not dare to intervene. Here, I *do* make a deliberate decision not to intervene, which suffices to call me tolerant, whereas, in the previous version, I wanted to be intolerant with every fiber of my body and soul but simply *could not* act it out. Now, however, I could intervene and put my foot down, but I *do not want* to because I am too scared and do not want to risk whatever negative consequences might ensue.

The value-laden virtue approach argues that being scared is not the same as being tolerant. Tolerance is a virtue, based not on prudential but on moral reasons (Carter 2013, 203). Take people who object to gay marriage (for example, because the thought of gay sex makes them feel "uneasy") but chooses not to intervene because the think that the sexual preferences and acts of consenting adults are a private matter that should be respected. Their reason not to intervene is a moral one and this is what makes them genuinely tolerant.

But let us return to our two Hell's Angels scenarios. In the first, one is not tolerant because one lacks the power to intervene. In the second, one could intervene but fear motivates one to forego any opportunity for intervention. One can rightly point out that this distinction is not as clear-cut as it may seem. In the second scenario, the costs involved can be so high that they basically amount to coercion or force. If the Hell's Angels manage to make me fear for my life (without locking me up in a closet), can one still plausibly claim that I could intervene if I wanted to and that it is thus my deliberate decision not to? When exactly does external influence become so powerful that the decision to intervene is no longer really an option?

Nevertheless, we believe that the difference between duress (and fear) and coercion is real, while at the same time admitting that it is matter of degree. The difference is the extent to which one's nonintervention is based on a "deliberate decision," as Horton puts it. When I am locked up in a closet (a clear-cut case of coercion), my circumstances do not allow me to act on my (intolerant) decision. Intervening is simply not an option available to me. If it were, I would definitely choose to do so. In contrast, if the Hell's Angels do not lock me up but I am simply afraid of them, I can still weigh my options (and intervening is one of those) and *decide* to refrain from interfering in what I disapprove of. The cost that is being imposed on me enters my decision-making process instead of thwarting it altogether.

So whenever not intervening is due to something else than a deliberate decision – being locked up, or in some other sense being incapacitated (cf. Laegaard 2013, 524) – there is no real toleration. Imagine that I object to homosexuality and that a gay couple has sex right next to me, while I am asleep. It seems clear that I am not tolerating this at all (while also not being intolerant; as I am not intervening). If I were awake and in the position to do something about it, I definitely would.

This issue is relevant because of its implications for the question whether tolerance can be enforced. On a nonvirtue view, if racists refrain from discriminating against people of color purely because it is illegal and because they want to avoid possible (legal) punishment, this counts as tolerance. In fact, the cost involved can be legal or financial but also, in case of more informal sanctions of intolerant behavior, social and emotional or even physical (as in the second Hell's Angels scenario). Instead of splitting hairs on what "coercion" or "compulsion" means exactly, the main point here is whether toleration can be enforced. Laws and fines can definitely enforce tolerance, even if they do not amount to outright coercion (putting people behind bars is a notable exception, of course). After all, citizens can genuinely *decide* to obey or violate the law.

Let us focus now on the other side of the spectrum: the difference between tolerance and indifference. As mentioned, the indifferent are *not* tolerant as they do not object and thus have no burden to bear. Imagine you care less and less about some conduct you previously found "intolerable," such as people being rude or making spelling mistakes. While you used to intervene on each occasion, you might start to wonder whether getting upset is worth the fuss. The previous point about the costs involved is also relevant here. After all, one could say that it is not that you do not want to intervene; it is just that, because of even a small cost (the little effort or hassle involved in intervening), you decide to let it go.

As with the "duress versus coercion" distinction, we can allow that there is a grey area due to the gradual difference between indifference (you do not intervene because you do not care) and tolerance (you do care but have weightier reasons not to intervene). Perhaps you do object to someone making a pastrami sandwich instead of using PB&J. But it is not worth fighting for, so you tolerate the silly and weird pastrami people.

Still, there are clear-cut cases. In an extreme case of indifference, you watch people making other than PB&J sandwiches and feel nothing. It just does not register; you do not think about it and you simply have no reason to intervene.

Sure, if some cost were involved, that would be an additional reason for keeping schtum and letting things pass; but no such reason is needed. At the other extreme, you could fiercely object and thus score high on the "objection component" but also be extremely lazy and thus perceive the costs of interfering as very high. Imagine you are a vegan and object to pastrami sandwiches on principled grounds (after all, as Mitch Hedberg put it, "it's like a cow with a cracker on either side"). However, you simply cannot bring yourself to say something when you see a friend ordering one of those horrible things. In our view, this means that you are tolerating your friend's conduct, since you (1) object, (2) have the power to intervene but (3) deliberately decide not to. Whether it is laziness motivating your inaction or something else (besides being incapacitated, which does not motivate but merely causes your inaction) does not matter. What matters is that there is a balance, with reasons to intervene (objection component) against reasons not to intervene (acceptance component), which in the case of tolerance tips over to nonintervention (Forst 2017). Reasons to intervene can be very small (close to indifference) or quite big but they exist and are outweighed by reasons not to intervene. You decide to let it go, because the costs involved are too big, relatively speaking. True indifference means that *regardless* of whether there is a cost, you let things pass. Even if there were no cost at all, an indifferent person would never intervene, as they lack any reason to do so.

Of course, on a broad understanding, moral reasons can motivate tolerance as well. When you refrain from intervening, because you think it is important not to impose your view of the good life on others and want to respect other people's rights, liberties, and autonomy, acknowledging that they have different values that inform their choices, you are also obviously being tolerant.

Note that both the neutral and the virtue approach to tolerance have demarcation issues. Whereas the first needs to distinguish "tolerance" from "impotence" and "indifference" (as we tried to do above), the virtue approach needs to ensure that tolerance does not collapse into full acceptance or endorsement. At first, this seems obvious enough. While there is a kind of "acceptance" at play in tolerance, this does not amount to wholehearted agreement. Tolerant people do not endorse the other's (reasons for their) conduct (first level) but only their right to make those decisions on the basis of their own reasons (second level). Disagreement persists at the level of underlying values (reasons, motives, beliefs, etc.), but one decides not to act on it. After all, so the value-laden virtue approach goes, one values people acting on their own values.

So which demarcation problem haunts the virtue approach? Well, if you refrain from interfering based on your moral conviction that others are allowed to "live their own life," the normative force of your objection seems to be overwritten. Your opposition becomes a crude psychological force that you consider morally illegitimate, something that *ought* not to motivate your actions. The difficulty then is to understand how a single person can both object while also, all-things-morally-considered, accept. Our moral reasons for acceptance threaten to evaporate the (necessary) "objection component." This is one of the paradoxical results that the virtue approach to toleration gives rise to (cf. Scheffler 2010, 312; also Carter 2013, 197).

In light of this paradox, it is extremely interesting that there is a strand in the literature that claims that tolerance as a virtue *should* involve such an evaporation. True tolerance, it is argued, means that one no longer objects and even that any trace of opposition is morally suspect (cf. Horton 2011).

> Instead toleration now demands more than resisting interference or condemnation; the tolerant citizen, it is argued, should avoid causing the pain associated with uncomfortable conversations, personal criticisms, or even difference of opinion (...). Toleration has become positive demand for recognition and respect. To deny such demands is construed as cruelty. (Avramenko and Promisel 2018, 850–851)

We agree with Promisel and Avramenko that this tolerance-as-sheer-respect approach is fundamentally flawed as it basically collapses into full acceptance. Tolerance as a meaningful notion necessarily requires a component of rejection and opposition. Our contemporary, super-diverse societies – in which values inevitably tend to conflict – requires proper tolerance, with people bearing the burden of value pluralism, insisting that people should eliminate their differences of opinion is unrealistic, overly demanding, and basically prescriptively useless. And, more importantly, it would belie the meta-ethical fact that our moral universe is characterized by genuine value pluralism.

Two Ways Out of Another Paradox

Before we go into the advantages of the broad understanding of tolerance, we want to recall how easily it can avoid another famous "paradox of tolerance." Here is how Karl Popper (1945 [2013], 581) described this "paradox of tolerance":

> Unlimited tolerance must lead to the disappearance of tolerance. If we extend unlimited tolerance even to those who are intolerant, if we are not prepared to defend a tolerant society against the onslaught of the intolerant, then the tolerant will be destroyed, and tolerance with them. [...] We should therefore claim, in the name of tolerance, the right not to tolerate the intolerant.

It is important to see how the virtue approach typically gives rise to this paradox. If tolerance is a virtue, then it is always desirable to be tolerant (P1). But this implies that it is good to tolerate the intolerable and the intolerant (P2). This then would undercut tolerance itself, since tolerating the intolerant will lead the intolerant to prevail. Hence, tolerance will be practically self-defeating (C).

One way to avoid this paradox is to drop the normative language altogether: tolerance is not a *virtue* and hence not necessarily *good* (against P1). Whether, what and whom we *should* tolerate (for example, the intolerant) is an issue completely separate from the conceptual issue whether we *actually* tolerate someone or something. The paradox does not arise in the neutral approach, which is perfectly compatible with the idea that we *should* only tolerate specific people (for example, whoever tolerates us or subscribes to liberal principles of respect for each other's rights and liberties). As such, it enables us to claim that we should not tolerate the intolerant at all (against P2).

This way out of the paradox focuses on the psychology of people (their feelings/reasons/motives for objection and whatever feelings/reasons/motives that lead them to put up with something) while sidestepping the issue whether these feelings and reasons are justified, desirable, or not. It allows for the straightforward claim that it is not always good to tolerate something. Some forms of intolerance, like bigotry or slavery, should simply *not* be tolerated.

This could be seen as a huge advantage over the virtue approach (Engelen and Nys 2008). Yet, an adequate understanding of virtue can help the virtue approach escape the paradox equally well. More precisely, P2 does not necessarily follow from P1. Take courage as a noncontroversial example of a virtue: it is always good to be courageous. Still, as Kant noted, such virtues could easily turn into vices, when accompanied by the wrong motives. In the opening pages of the *Groundwork*, Kant famously discusses the cold-bloodedness of the scoundrel ("Das kalte Bluteines Bösewichts"), arguing that such a noble character trait (cold-bloodedness) is not always good. However, it would be a mistake to conclude that it is not always good to be courageous. After all, we only call an act courageous when it is good. A terrorist who sacrifices his own life in committing atrocious crimes is not courageous but a coward. This shows that the judgment of goodness, its appropriateness, is *internal* to the concept of virtue. David Hume was very aware of this.

> The word virtue, with its equivalent in every tongue, implies praise, as that of vice does blame; and no one, without the most obvious and grossest impropriety, could affix reproach to a term, which in general acceptation is understood in a good sense: or bestow applause, where the idiom requires disapprobation. (Hume 1757 [1996], 135)

On a proper understanding of tolerance as a virtue, then, it is indeed always good to tolerate. But if "tolerating" the intolerant is wrong, then allowing them to be intolerant is not a matter of tolerance. Allowing the intolerable to persist is not what a virtuous person would do and hence does not count as tolerance. This value-laden conception of tolerance can indeed claim that tolerance is always good (i.e., a virtue; confirming P1) but that one can only tolerate 1) the kinds of conduct that *should* be allowed for (the tolerable; what to tolerate) and 2) on the basis *that* they should be allowed for (why to tolerate). This then is perfectly compatible with claiming that one should not tolerate the intolerant (denying P2) and escaping the paradox.

An example of this strategy can be found in the analysis of Richard Avramenko and Michael Promisel (2018). To avoid the objection that tolerance collapses into sheer acceptance or respect, they recast tolerance as an Aristotelean virtue in order to understand how tolerance can turn into a vice, both as a deficiency and as an excess. A person who is deficient in tolerance is "surly and quarrelsome" (2018, 855). Such people, whom we have called "intolerant" before, put their mouths and fists where their minds are, regardless of how this affects the well-being of others. Their obvious lack of concern for others' well-being is what makes them fall short of being virtuous. But there is also a vice at the other side of the spectrum: someone who suffers from an excess of tolerance and who is "obsequious" or a "flatterer" (2018, 855). Such a person is *overly* concerned with pleasing others, even when objecting to their conduct. A flatterer decides not to cause offense, even when "some speeches and deeds are so ethically objectionable that silence is not appropriate" (2018, 855).

Avramenko and Promisel's approach provides a way out of the paradox as they deny P2 and argue that intolerance (or, the intolerant) should not be tolerated. Thereby, they also qualify P1, stressing that tolerance is always good but that it is limited to those cases where the conduct at hand should be tolerated. If you put up with something genuinely intolerable, you are no longer tolerating it but are being obsequious and sucking up to the intolerant.

According to Avramenko and Promisel, the recent shift in the literature toward respect and recognition and the corresponding tendency to move beyond objection and opposition exposes the danger of tolerance collapsing into obsequiousness and flattering. In line with Aristotle, they stress that, sometimes, one needs to inflict pain and discomfort: "under certain circumstances, it is virtuous to disapprove and contest another's convictions or conduct in a way that may cause pain" (Avremenko and Promisel 2018, 857). On their view then, it can be virtuous to be "intolerant." Since "virtue is the appropriate response to different situations and different agents" (Athanassoulis 2019) and requires the practical wisdom to act appropriately, understanding tolerance as a virtue does not mean that one should always tolerate. Tolerance means letting live what deserves to live and letting die what deserves to die. Given that it is okay to act on one's objections to what is genuinely objectionable, flattering fails in this respect in that it lets live what deserves to die.

But it is possible to opt for a different strategy. Take an intolerant person A who objects to X, and does something, Y, about it. This person does not let things pass. Now another person B can either tolerate this (Y, the intolerant behavior toward X) or not. This person asks whether or not to let Y pass. Importantly, this story is purely descriptive and is compatible with whatever (one might think of) the moral desirability of X and Y and of A's and B's motives for doing X and Y. For example, X may be (believed to be) objectionable (for example, rape), which would make Y appropriate. Or X may be unobjectionable (eating a PB&J sandwich), which would make Y inappropriate. We should applaud intolerance in the first case but not in the second. Stripping the notion "tolerance" from any normative connotation prevents the paradox from getting off the ground because it no longer implies that tolerance is necessarily good or virtuous. The answer to the question when tolerance is morally appropriate should be settled on a case-by-case basis (and, of course, the virtue approach also needs to answer that question). In addition, and as stressed before, the reasons for tolerance could be much broader than what is assumed when understanding tolerance as a virtue.

While both approaches can escape the paradox, the neutral approach arguably has an edge over the virtue approach because of practical reasons. Central to this argument is the idea that when tolerance is desirable, we should *enforce* it and *make* people tolerate. The reason for this is *value pluralism*, which not only pervades contemporary societies as a practical reality (with which any meaningful notion of tolerance should be able to deal), but also as a meta-ethical truth about the nature of values. Pluralism is the background against which an attitude of tolerance makes sense: there is plurality of valuable ways of life that deserve to be lived, even though any individual might prefer another way of life. We will all need to put up with that plurality. While we cannot enforce the virtue of tolerance, we can enforce tolerance in its neutral understanding and make people refrain from interfering for other than moral reasons. Respect or recognition for other ways of life that one objects to is not something that can be extracted from people; we can only demand outward conformity with such (inner) respect. This is the Kantian aspect of the discussion that deserves closer inspection.

Kant on Justice, Virtue, Respect, and Tolerance

In his *Groundwork to the Metaphysics of Morals* (1785), Immanuel Kant famously argues that only actions that are motivated "from duty" have moral worth. A shopkeeper can be honest out of calculated self-interest or out of a concern for reputation. Although "in conformity with duty," his actions would nevertheless be performed from the wrong maxim, or so Kant argues (1785 [1999], 53; [4:397]). Although fine and recommendable, Kant stresses that such outward honesty does not exhibit a good will.

Apart from raising the bar for moral purity, this requirement also introduces an *epistemological problem*. After all, Kant (1785 [1999], 61; [4:407]) holds that it is very difficult, if not impossible, to know whether someone actually acted "from duty," that is, out of genuine respect for the moral law. Even our very own dutiful behavior could be motivated by covert impulses and desires hidden to ourselves. Kant pushes the point so far as to claim that, due to this epistemological uncertainty, there might not have been a single good deed in the whole history of mankind. Interestingly, however, this epistemological problem does not occur when it comes to actions *against* duty. If someone is dishonest, for example, when breaking a promise, then evidently there cannot be an underlying good will. So, while we have to ponder the depths of the human heart when it comes to identifying true goodness, evil is very much "in your face" and clearly manifests itself to the naked eye.

Now, when faced with gross manifestations of immorality, we can (and should) do something about them. According to Kant, we can use the means of justice in order to get people to act not *from* but at least *in conformity with* duty.

> After all, the Metaphysics of Morals is divided into two parts, and the difference between the Doctrine of Virtue and the Doctrine of Right is that in the former duties cannot be coerced (I cannot force you to love your fellow man, for example), whereas in the second (the Doctrine of Right) obeying duties can be coerced (for example, promises in contracts, laws of the state, etc.). (Schossberge 2006, 166)

What does this mean? If one believes that the moral law or categorical imperative disqualifies deceit as immoral (O'Neill 2002), then we can use the instruments of justice to coerce those who are inclined to deceive into compliance with the moral law (the Doctrine of Right). We simply enforce compliance and do so for good reasons. This does not present epistemological problems nor does it require near-impossible investigations into the human heart, because no maxim could ever make deceit (or other actions that violate the moral law) moral. Surely when we use coercion, people's reasons and motives to comply could (and, most likely, will) boil down to fear of legal punishment. This implies that the question of moral worth (the Doctrine of Virtue) is beyond the scope of the law. What is more, duties of virtue (what is morally desirable) by definition lie beyond the law's reach. People may act out of respect for the moral law but we can only enforce outward compliance through legal means. Nevertheless, and importantly, it is the moral law (the rational insight into the wrongness of deceit) that justifies the use of these legal, coercive means. While moral goodness cannot be enforced by legal measures, it provides the underlying moral justification for the practice of these legal measures.

Let us connect this to the topic of tolerance and intolerance. If the intolerance of bigots, racists, sexists, et cetera necessarily involves the violation of some people's rights and liberties and if this is what makes their intolerance morally wrong or inappropriate, then we are justified in using coercive means to combat intolerance and enforce tolerance (at least in a neutral sense of the word). On this view, it does not really matter *why* people choose to abstain from such interference. When we legally coerce them into tolerance and make them bear what they object to, they may do so out of fear of legal punishment. If this fear – or some other kind of self-interest – motivates their compliance, they will act in conformity with but not from moral duty. So while we cannot say that their tolerance results from a good will, we can say that they do what they should be doing, that is, tolerate what should be tolerated.

Of course, this raises the underlying but fundamental question: what should people tolerate and what not; when exactly is (in)tolerance appropriate? (Note that the virtue approach also needs to answer that important first-order question: "What ought to be the object of toleration?".) If we return to Kant, the answer is clear. People should tolerate whatever morally permissible ends others have, so all the acts that people are morally allowed to perform. They are allowed to make PB&J sandwiches, and kiss their children (or their gay lover) goodnight. If you object to any of these practices, you should nevertheless condone them and society can rightfully make you do exactly that. While it may be controversial to determine exactly which results the categorical imperative yields, the point here is that, to the extent that it does yield results, the distinction between the Doctrine of Right and that of Virtue holds and is applicable. There are permissible and impermissible actions – what Shelly Kagan (1989) calls "options" and "constraints" – and there is an extent to which allowing for the permissible and restraining the impermissible is both possible and required. In fact, this is what the realm of justice is all about.

To locate the importance of tolerance firmly within the realm of justice in no way denies the relevance of the realm of virtue. Kant does not take the Doctrine of Virtue to be somehow less important. Like that of Right, its importance comes from the unconditional requirements of the moral law. We ought to act from duty, not merely in correspondence with it. What this entails and how it can be achieved is the subject of the Doctrine of Virtue. The perfect duty of respect, for example, is something we owe to all persons (Fahmy 2013, 276) and we should figure out what this looks like and how to achieve it. Understandably, many authors with Kantian affinities who are concerned with toleration look for inspiration in this part of Kant's theory (for they believe toleration is a virtue). But that approach is rather unfortunate. For given Kant's pessimism about human nature and given the difficulty in attaining a good will (his tenacious "Hang zum Bösen"), there is an urgency to the demands of justice, or rather a practical feasibility to politics and law that is absent in the realm of virtue. Social and legal instruments and institutions should not overestimate people's ability to attain virtue and should thus befit a "community of Devils" (Kant 1795 [1996]). As such, taking the demand of tolerance as a demand of justice has pragmatic priority over taking it as a demand of virtue.

To illustrate the rather unfortunate attention that has paid to the Doctrine of Virtue in light of the problem of toleration, let us discuss Rainer Forst's (2007a, b, 2017) Kantian model of tolerance as respect. In his view, tolerance is and should be more than mere peaceful coexistence or modus vivendi, captured in the adagio "live and let live." According to Forst, tolerance is necessarily based on moral reasons. This understanding of toleration captures nicely the positive connotation that the notion "tolerance" has in ordinary language: not only is tolerance morally preferable over violence or coercion, its nonviolence is actually more robust (than nonviolence due to indifference, for example) because it is based on moral principles held by the agents. Sune Lægaard (2013, 523) summarizes Forst's views on the advantages of his "respect conception" as follows.

> Toleration out of respect promises to provide a way of handling conflicts and problems under conditions of pluralism in a way that is principled and might justify some of the accommodation and openness toward ethnic, cultural and religious minorities that proponents of multiculturalism as a normative position demand, while avoiding the problems of more demanding notions of 'recognition' or 'respect for difference'. So toleration out of respect seems very inviting, both in theory and practice.

The problem, however, is not that respect as the motivating moral reason for tolerance would not be *good* but that it would be *useless*. In Kant's taxonomy, the duty of respect is a perfect duty of virtue (Taylor 2005). Respect is a particular kind of attitude, something that we owe to others but that cannot be enforced. Imagine you are a racist but police presence prevents you from hitting a person of color in the face. In this scenario, there is no respect, as that would entail that your reason for restraint is your acknowledgment of the other person's equal worth as a moral being. On Forst's approach, your lack of respect means there is no (genuine, virtuous) tolerance on your behalf. As mentioned, the problem here is epistemic: in real life, we can never *know* whether or when someone is genuinely tolerant, since that would require having access to someone's true motives (which is something even introspection cannot provide us).

If one looks at what Kant himself has to say about the virtue of respect, the ill-fit with contemporary discussions of toleration as a virtue becomes clear. To understand what kind of attitude respect entails, one can analyze which *vices* are associated with not fulfilling the duties of respect. Understanding these vices will reveal that the Kantian duty of respect does not provide the best way of approaching tolerance.

Kant gives three clear examples of such vices of disrespect, violations of this particular duty of virtue: arrogance, defamation, and ridicule (Fahmy 2013, 733; MS 6:462–467). Now, we do not – at least not necessarily – call a person who is arrogant, spreads gossip, or ridicules another, intolerant. One could be arrogant or dismissive without "prohibiting, hindering or otherwise coercively interfering with the conduct of which one disapproves" (Horton 1998, 429–430). The disrespectfulness of arrogance, defamation, and ridicule does not (necessarily) consist in the active interference that is necessary for intolerance.

What this shows is that the virtue of respect goes *beyond* the mere "outwardly" doing what the duties of justice require. Kant himself gives the example of beneficence: we should (as a duty of justice) help the poor but when we do so, we should also (as a duty of virtue) make sure that this help is not condescending or degrading (cf. Fahmy 2013, 737). In the end, people should get what they are due, both in terms of justice and virtue. Likewise, we should tolerate the (tolerable) behavior of others (duty of justice), but that is not enough: we should also do that in a respectful way (duty of virtue). Arrogance, ridicule, or defamation can occur *in* instances of tolerance, and are not necessarily characteristic of intolerance.

Of course, it would be great if people not only tolerate others in the broad and neutral sense, but also show them the respect that they are due. But that is not something that the law can and should enforce. We cannot *demand* that people are not only tolerant but also respectful, simply because we can never know for sure when that occurs. Moreover, as a specific *ground* for toleration, Forst's respect approach might be too restrictive in that it presupposes what is actually contested (i.e., the different reasons *for* tolerance) and thereby ignores the pluralism that toleration should allow for. We therefore agree with Sune Lægaard (2013, 520) in his critical analysis of Forst's virtue approach.

> Forst's respect conception is problematic since it presupposes that answers to very substantial normative questions, which are precisely what people tend to disagree on under conditions of pluralism, are already at hand. The respect conception therefore seems to be at best a theoretical idea belonging in ideal-theory, not a useful practical solution to actual conflicts under conditions of pluralism.

It is helpful, therefore, to return to what Bernard Williams (1996) has to say on the subject. He argues that, while the *virtue* of tolerance is based on respect for autonomy, its *practice* "has to be sustained not so much by a pure principle resting on a value of autonomy as by a wider and more mixed range of resources. Those resources include (...) power, to provide Hobbesian reminders to the more extreme groups that they will have to settle for coexistence."

Note that Williams allows for two notions of tolerance: (1) a neutral, behavioral one where (the practice of) tolerance is about refraining from interference, even if that is motivated by fear of (Hobbesian) punishment, and (2) a value-laden, attitudinal one in which tolerance is a virtue. Though both notions are conceivable, valid, and important, there lies a danger in the preoccupation with the latter.

If tolerance is understood as a virtue, the lack of tolerance in our societies should then primarily be understood in terms of a lack of virtue. The problem, on this approach, lies with people's flawed and deficient characters and whatever cultural, social, educational, or, why not, genetic factors cause their disrespectful or "unvirtuous" attitudes. We think this worryingly misidentifies the problem. Intolerance is a social and political issue that first and foremost needs to be addressed through political and legal means. This is not to say that people's attitudes and educational issues are not important, but simply that tolerance as a matter of *justice* has priority over such moral qualms.

If tolerance is conceived as a virtue that requires doing the right thing for the right reasons (or with the right attitudes), we risk seeing it as an aspect of character improvement; something that is morally praiseworthy and that we should all (continue to) strive for. While this is obviously important and valuable, it also diverts attention from the demands of justice, which should have priority (cf. Lovibond 2015). If tolerance is to remain pivotal in contemporary societies, the question what needs to be tolerated and what not is central. The question what the (moral or other) reasons or motives for such tolerance are should take second stage in this respect.

Summary

In this chapter, we have discussed the advantages of a broad and neutral understanding of tolerance as noninterference, which can be motivated by moral reasons (such as principled respect for other people's liberties) but also by more prudential reasons (such as the desire to avoid legal sanctions). The alternative "virtue approach," which provides a narrower and value-laden definition of tolerance as morally motivated, raises both epistemological problems (how can we ever come to know whether someone is really tolerant or not?) and pragmatic or policy-related problems (how can we ever enforce tolerance of what should be tolerated if we cannot coerce people to be appropriately motivated?).

The neutral approach encourages one to not see tolerance as a virtue, but simply as putting up with something one deems objectionable. Depending on what that "something" is, putting up with it is morally desirable or not. The moral evaluation of one's (in)tolerance primarily depends on the moral evaluation of what one does (not) tolerate, and less so on why one does so (one's underlying attitudes and reasons). Tolerance is so crucial in our societies because of value pluralism, the simple fact that there often is no single best solution to moral problems. This is why we believe that people *should* tolerate the opinions and conduct that are compatible with such pluralism. People should put up with alternative lifestyles or choices; it is simply not up to them to interfere.

Such tolerance is valuable regardless of whatever reasons one might have for putting up with whatever should be put up with. Calling such plain tolerance a deficient type of tolerance that falls short of being virtuous painfully ignores the fact that, in a just but not ideal world, we can and should ensure that people get to live their own lives, according to their own conceptions of the good. Intolerance then is not a problem because it is vicious or disrespectful but because – or better: when – it inhibits people from living according to their own valid conceptions of the good. This then is a final advantage of the broad and neutral approach to tolerance: it puts priority on the fate of the should-be-tolerated (the appropriate objects of toleration) instead of the could-be-tolerant (the moral mindset of the subject engaged in toleration).

References

Athanassoulis N (2019) Virtue ethics. The Internet Encyclopedia of Philosophy, https://www.iep.utm.edu/virtue/. Accessed 25 Oct 2019

Avramenko R, Promisel M (2018) When toleration becomes a vice: naming Aristotle's third unnamed virtue. Am J Polit Sci 62(4):849–860

Byrne P (2011) Religious tolerance, diversity, and pluralism. R Inst Philos Suppl 68:287–309

Carter I (2013) Are toleration and respect compatible? J Appl Philos 30(3):195–208

Engelen B, Nys T (2008) Tolerance: a virtue? Towards a broad and descriptive definition of tolerance. Philos Contemp World 15(1):44–54

Fahmy MS (2013) Understanding Kant's duty of respect as a duty of virtue. J Moral Philos 10:723–740

Forst R (2007a) A critical theory of multicultural toleration. In: Laden AS, Owen D (eds) Multiculturalism and political theory. Cambridge University Press, Cambridge, pp 292–311

Forst R (2007b) To tolerate means to insult: toleration, recognition, and emancipation. In: van den Brink B, Owen D (eds) Recognition and power. Cambridge University Press, Cambridge, pp 215–237

Forst R (2017) Toleration. In: The Stanford encyclopedia of philosophy, Fall 2017 edition, edited by Edward N. Zalta. https://plato.stanford.edu/archives/fall2017/entries/toleration. Accessed 25 Oct 2019

Heyd D (ed) (1996) Toleration: an elusive virtue. Princeton University Press, Princeton

Horton J (1998) Toleration. In: Craig E (ed) The Routledge encyclopedia of philosophy, vol IX. Routledge, London, pp 429–433

Horton J (2011) Why the traditional conception of toleration still matters. Crit Rev Int Soc Pol Phil 14(3):289–305

Hume D (1757 [1996]) Of the standard of taste. In: Hume D (ed) Selected essays, edited with an introduction by Stephen Copley and Andrew Edgar. Oxford University Press, Oxford

Kagan S (1989) The limits of morality. Oxford University Press, Oxford

Kant I (1785 [1999]) The groundwork to the metaphysics of morals. In: Kant's practical philosophy, translated and edited by M. Gregor, with an introduction by C. M. Korsgaard. Cambridge University Press, Cambridge, pp 37–108

Kant I (1795 [1996]) Toward perpetual peace. In: Kant's practical philosophy, translated and edited by M. Gregor, with an introduction by C. M. Korsgaard. Cambridge University Press, Cambridge, pp 311–352

Lægaard S (2013) Toleration out of respect? Crit Rev Int Soc Pol Phil 16(4):520–536

Lovibond S (2015) Ethics in the media and in philosophy. In: Essays on ethics and feminism. Oxford University Press, Oxford

O'Neill O (2002) Autonomy and trust in bioethics. Cambridge University Press, Cambridge, MA

Popper K (1945 [2013]) The open society and its enemies: new one-volume edition. Princeton University Press, Princeton
Scanlon TM (1996) The difficulty of tolerance. In: Heyd D (ed) Toleration: an elusive virtue. Princeton University Press, Princeton, pp 226–239
Scheffler S (2010) The good of toleration. In: Scheffler S (ed) Equality and tradition: questions of value in moral and political theory. Oxford University Press, Oxford, pp 312–336
Schossberge C (2006) Raising a question: coercion and tolerance in Kant's politics. Ethic@: Int J Moral Philos 5(2):165–171
Taylor RS (2005) Kantian personal autonomy. Political Theory 33(5):602–628
Williams B (1996) Toleration: an impossible virtue? In: Heyd D (ed) Toleration: an elusive virtue. Princeton University Press, Princeton, pp 18–27

Toleration and Close Personal Relationships

Michael Kühler

Contents

Introduction	738
Close Personal Relationships	739
Toleration	742
Toleration in Close Personal Relationships	746
Summary and Future Directions	754
References	754

Abstract

Toleration – understood in the sense of being a personal virtue – is traditionally seen as a key element for enabling and maintaining peaceful relations among people with diverse and conflicting beliefs, values, or ways of life. In political and moral philosophy, toleration is thus mostly discussed as a relation between strangers, that is, between people who do not care about or even reject each other. Conversely, the idea of merely tolerating one's friends or loved ones apparently does not make much sense. However, tolerating certain traits of one's friends or loved ones, or tolerating (some of) the friends of one's friend or beloved, could very well be a reasonable option. Yet, what conceptual and practical consequences does such a possibility have for our understanding of love and friendship? And how may toleration be understood in such relationships? The general question for the chapter is thus: what conceptual and practical place may toleration reasonably have in close personal relationships?

Keywords

Toleration, Close personal relationships, Love, Friendship, Family, Kinds of reasons

---

M. Kühler (✉)
Department of Philosophy, University of Münster, Münster, Germany
e-mail: michael.kuehler@uni-muenster.de

© The Author(s), under exclusive licence to Springer Nature Switzerland AG 2022
M. Sardoĉ (ed.), *The Palgrave Handbook of Toleration*,
https://doi.org/10.1007/978-3-030-42121-2_24

Introduction

Without doubt, toleration is a crucial idea and practice when it comes to pursuing peaceful coexistence in society. Very roughly speaking, toleration amounts to an attitude or practice, according to which, despite not agreeing with others on their beliefs, values, or way of life, or even rejecting them altogether, one puts up with them, that is, one abstains from trying to impose one's own beliefs, values, or way of life on others by either political means or outright force. Simply put, toleration's motto is "live and let live."

Accordingly, toleration has been mostly discussed in political and moral philosophy, as it primarily pertains to relations among strangers as well as the stance the state may take toward some of its citizens' beliefs, values, cultural practices, or whole way of life (for the debate in recent decades, see King 1976; Horton and Mendus 1985, 1999; Mendus and Edwards 1987; Horton and Nicholson 1992; Heyd 1996; Castiglione and McKinnon 2003; McKinnon 2006; Williams and Waldron 2008; Edyvane and Matravers 2012). In so doing, moral and political debates on toleration have addressed questions such as: How should toleration be defined more precisely? Should toleration have its limits, and if so, where should the line be drawn and how could this be justified, especially from a moral or liberal point of view? Assuming that toleration is an attitude of merely grudgingly putting up with others, would toleration not fall short of what is actually morally required of citizens living in a pluralist society and a liberal state, namely equal respect or even recognition of everyone alike? If so, is there still conceptual and practical room left for toleration at all within a moral and liberal framework, be it in the sense of a personal virtue of citizens or in the sense of an institutional stance and practice of a liberal state that is conceived of as explicitly value-neutral?

Obviously, these are all highly important questions that need to be addressed and thoroughly discussed (cp. the corresponding entries in this handbook). However, when aiming at the phenomenon of toleration in connection to close personal relationships, that is, between family members, friends, or lovers, which are clearly not relationships among strangers, most of the above questions appear to be beside the point. To be sure, toleration plays the usual moral and political role and raises the accompanying questions when it comes to how family, friends, or lovers may treat strangers. The more interesting question is, however, if toleration may also play a part in these close personal relationships. After all, there seems to be something odd about the idea that family, friends, or lovers merely tolerate each other.

Yet, everyday wisdom undoubtedly has a place for the idea and practice of toleration when it comes to practical questions of how one may make close personal relationships work. Arguably, parents should – within certain limits – tolerate their child's questionable hobby in order to let the child develop his or her own identity. Being a good friend may require tolerating a friend's opposing political views – again within certain limits – because this may not be what the friendship is about. A lover may need to tolerate the beloved's obnoxious friends in order not to pressure the beloved into having to choose between lover and friends. In general, in being a parent, a friend, or a lover, we certainly often enough rather tolerate than respect or admire some more or less tiny quirks of the persons we care about. However, if so, what does this mean for our understanding of family, friendship, and (romantic) love? What place may toleration reasonably have in such close personal relationships, and what notion of toleration is involved more precisely?

The following sections aim at providing answers to these questions. Section "Close Personal Relationships" explains the notion of close personal relationships in more detail in order to lay the foundation based on which the role and understanding of toleration in such relationships can be discussed. Likewise, section "Toleration" explains the notion of toleration and its conceptual range in more detail in order to provide the flipside of the foundational discussion. Section "Toleration in Close Personal Relationships" then brings both discussions together and develops an answer to the question of toleration's understanding and place in close personal relationships. Finally, section "Summary and Future Directions" adds a brief conclusion.

Close Personal Relationships

Firstly, the notion of close personal relationships needs to be explained in more detail. How may it be defined for the topic at hand? What basic feature do family, friendship, and love have in common to be grouped together here?

At first glance, family appears to be a natural and prime candidate for close personal relationships (Peterson and Bush 2012; Brake 2016; Satz 2017; Halwani 2018). Yet, mere biological relatedness should not be equated with the idea of family consisting of a group of – although often but not necessarily biologically related – people who care about each other. Moreover, not all groups of people who are biologically related and considered a family actually do care about each other, as ample stories of cold-heartedness, neglect, or even abuse occurring within families sadly prove. Hence, for family to count as *close* personal relationship for the topic at hand, the notion of *caring about each other* is taken to be the crucial characteristic.

Aside from this necessary condition of caring about each other, close personal relationships among family members may differ in a number of aspects. For instance, the relationship may be asymmetrical and feature substantial inequality, as is typical between parents and their – especially young – children. Yet, other family members may have a more equal relationship, like siblings of roughly the same age or the parents among each other. To be sure, these differences and asymmetries need to be discussed in more detail when it comes to understanding the notion, institution, and accompanying normative ramifications of the family, including more concrete questions of who may show toleration toward whom in what respect and to what degree. However, for the topic at hand such questions can be characterized as role-specific and more or less casuistic follow-up questions to the underlying foundational question of what role, if any, toleration may play within family relations to begin with. It is only this latter question that is being discussed in this chapter. Consequently, the following discussion will focus on the central characteristic of *caring about each other*, not the least because of its significant implications for discussing the possible role of toleration in close personal relationships later on. Moreover, caring about each other is not only a central aspect of (good) family relations but also of friendship and most accounts of romantic love (Badhwar 1993; Helm 2017a, b).

In this regard, the explanation of friendship still owes much to Aristotle's seminal books VIII and IX in his *Nicomachean Ethics* (Aristotle EN). There, he distinguishes between three kinds of friendship (*philia*) based on their specific purpose: pleasure, utility, and virtue. Being friends because of pleasure or utility are nowadays hardly seen as genuine friendships because "friends" of these sorts primarily only care about what they want to get out of the "friendship," namely their own pleasure or utility. This is also the reason why already Aristotle thought of these friendships as deficient. Only the third kind of friendship, out of virtue, can be considered real friendship. Here, friends care about each other for the friend's own sake and in light of the friend being virtuous, that is, of good moral character. Moreover, friends to some degree share their lives, that is, share at least some important interests, engage in joint activities, and enjoy a degree of intimacy – not necessarily of a sexual nature but rather in terms of intimate knowledge of and affection for each other. Accordingly, *philia* may be translated not only as friendship but also as a friendship type of love, as it is featured prominently in the traditional threefold distinction of love: *eros* (love as desire), *philia* (love as friendship), and *agape* (unconditional godly or neighborly love) (Soble 1989).

From a more current point of view, it may be a matter of debate whether real friendship requires the friends to be of good moral character. However, practically everyone agrees that there is no friendship if there is no mutual caring about the other, no sharing of lives and activities, or no degree of intimacy (Helm 2017a). Moreover, the latter two apparently only gain their specific meaning on the basis of mutual caring. While a lot of people, for example, coworkers or professional athletes in team sports, engage to a substantial degree in joint activities and may even have intimate knowledge of each other, they may also not care about each other for the other's own sake and, therefore, cannot be considered friends. Hence, further discussion about these aspects notwithstanding, *caring about each other* can be considered to be central also for real friendship, in addition to (good) family relations.

However, what exactly does *caring about each other* amount to? Since *philia* should be understood as a kind of love, one might put it in terms of friends *loving* each other, thus at the same time adding the third kind of close personal relationships to the mix (Helm 2017b). In this regard, both Aristotle as well as current accounts describe it in terms of a well-meaning attitude toward the friend and being motivated to promote the friend's well-being and flourishing. As Harry G. Frankfurt puts it in his influential account of love as caring, lovers are "disinterestedly devoted to" the beloved's interests and ends (Frankfurt 1994, p. 135). Thus, friends and lovers alike want to see the beloved flourish for the beloved's own sake and in light of the beloved's own ends and values, and they want to help and support the beloved in this. Being a (loving) friend in terms of caring about the other, thus, includes that one does not try to impose one's own agenda, values, or preferences on one's friends but support them in flourishing according to what is important to them. Yet, this does not mean that as a friend one has to be completely uncritical, but that possible criticism or advice has to be based on the perspective of the other, not on one's own. However, it does mean that as a friend or lover, one cannot be indifferent about what is important to one's friends or loved ones because whatever they hold dear obviously has substantial impact on their flourishing and well-being (Kühler 2020, 2021).

To sum up, despite differences in a number of aspects, for family, friendship, and love alike, the idea of caring about each other in terms of being disinterestedly and actively engaged in supporting the other's flourishing and well-being is a shared and central aspect.

Still, one further influential account of romantic love should be mentioned that does not neatly fit this idea of mutual caring, namely the age-old idea of love as union. Starting at least with Plato's *Symposium*, the idea of lovers merging or forming a union has been of tremendous influence on our idea of romantic love. In the *Symposium*, Aristophanes tells the following myth (Sheffield and Howatson 2008, pp. 189c–193d). Once, we were all double-creatures with four legs, four arms, and two heads. We were even a threat to the gods themselves, which is why Zeus split us in two halves, that is, in our current appearance. Each of these halves then desperately searched for its other half and yearned for being reunited again. Love is then nothing but the desire for being reunited and, if fulfilled, the union itself.

Modern union accounts flesh out this ancient idea in terms of the lovers forming an emphatic *we* and sharing a we-identity (Fisher 1990, pp. 26–35; Nozick 1990, p. 82; Solomon 1994, p. 193). While it is a matter of contention what this might mean exactly (see, e.g., Friedman 1998; Merino 2004), the general idea is that the lovers no longer see themselves as independent individuals but as fundamentally belonging together, that is, as being a part of their shared *we*. Accordingly, their whole perspective is shaped by their shared we-identity. To give a trivial example, lovers would no longer consider separately what color they like for the new curtains in their apartment and then discuss on which color they can agree, but each lover would consider this question based on their shared we-identity to begin with, that is, based on the shared values and preferences of their *we*.

However, union accounts may come in weak or strong versions. While weak versions only claim that the shared we-identity is a supplement to or partial modification of the lovers' individual identities, strong versions claim that it completely redefines and replaces the lovers' prior individual identities. It is primarily this latter, strong version of the lovers' union that appears to be incompatible with the idea of caring about each other, simply because there would be no longer two persons with separate individual identities loving each other (Soble 1997). Likewise, strong union accounts seem to be incompatible with the very idea of toleration playing any role within love, for, apparently, the only option would be the lovers' shared *we* tolerating itself, which appears to be absurd.

However, it may be argued that toleration might still come into play, if only because there are still different physical beings involved but also because the we-identity needs to be established first. Accordingly, the way the lovers determine how their shared we-identity will be constituted and which values, preferences, etc. will be included may very well involve a (temporary) stance of toleration of one of the lovers. Moreover, assuming that the shared we-identity is not set in stone but may change over time, the lovers continuously contribute to how their shared we-identity evolves and changes. Arguably, assuming that the lovers still stay separate persons – albeit sharing a we-identity – this might involve, at least temporarily, a tolerating stance toward certain changing traits of the evolving shared we-identity, either from the perspective of the shared we-identity so far, following strong versions of love as union, or from each individual lover's take on their shared we-identity and how it would be preferred to evolve, following weak versions.

Toleration

While the central characteristic of close personal relationships, namely caring about each other, highlights what the persons in questions share or value in each other, toleration takes its starting point in what people disagree on and what divides them. Toleration is a peaceful reaction to such disagreements and differences (Forst 2013, 2017).

As mentioned in the introduction, toleration is primarily discussed in political and moral philosophy, namely as a virtue people may be required to exhibit toward strangers in light of deep disagreements about beliefs, values, or whole ways of life as well as in the sense of a state's practice, whereas the virtuous personal attitude is sometimes labeled *tolerance* to distinguish it from *toleration* as a state practice (Murphy 1997). However, how is toleration to be defined more precisely? For, obviously, only with a more precise definition can its potential role in close personal relationships be discussed.

Unsurprisingly, toleration's definition is already a matter of contention. The following concepts of toleration have been put forward. Firstly, the traditional concept (Horton 2011) defines toleration as an agent A (an individual, a group, or an institution) for some reason *objecting* to certain actions or practices of someone else B (likewise an individual, a group, or an institution), or even rejecting B as such, but having outweighing other reasons for accepting B or their actions or practices nonetheless. Thus, A *refrains* from interfering with or preventing B from acting accordingly, although A has the power to interfere (Horton 1996, p. 28; Cohen 2004, pp. 69, 78f.). The traditional concept of toleration, thus, features three ingredients:

1. *Objection*: What is tolerated must be regarded as objectionable, that is, as in some way bad or wrong. For, otherwise, one might as well be indifferent about it or even see it in a positive light.
2. *Acceptance*: Despite one's objection, one has outweighing reasons for accepting the object of toleration nonetheless or at least for not interfering with it. For, otherwise, one's reasons for objection would lead to such interference and to (attempts at) preventing or eliminating the action or practice in question.
3. *Power*: For toleration to be practically meaningful, one must have sufficient power to interfere and actively decide not to make use of it. If one did not have

such power, toleration becomes indistinguishable from merely putting up with matters one cannot change.

In political and moral philosophy, this traditional concept of toleration is taken to capture situations of peaceful coexistence even under conditions of grave disagreements about beliefs, values, or ways of life, including the rejection of individuals or communities as such.

However, it has been discussed whether power should be understood as actual power or if a hypothetical assumption of power may already be sufficient (Forst 2013, p. 25f.; Newey 2013, pp. 142–162; Balint 2017, pp. 28, 36–38). After all, although it may be hard to distinguish between a tolerant attitude and one of merely grudgingly putting up with what one cannot change, it is easily imaginable that a person, while not actually having the power to interfere, also would not do so if she had the power. Arguably, such a person may be reasonably considered being tolerant.

Furthermore, while emphasizing the power component in terms of actual power, Peter Balint has recently argued in favor of a broad concept of toleration that drops the objection component instead. According to this concept, one may already be regarded as tolerant if one has the power to interfere but intentionally abstains from doing so (Balint 2017, pp. 5f., 23f.). This concept is, indeed, useful when it comes to describing even a value-neutral liberal state as tolerant. However, when focusing on a personal attitude, the concept obviously makes it hard to distinguish between toleration and mere indifference. Hence, for the purpose of this chapter, sticking with the traditional concept of toleration is more useful because it allows to highlight and address the phenomenon of objection happening in close personal relationships.

The traditional concept of toleration has two more crucial conceptual characteristics, namely a lower and an upper limit. The lower limit is reached in case one does not have reasons for objection but maybe even reasons for appreciation. If so, one's attitude would be either indifference or appreciation but not toleration. The upper limit is reached if one's reasons for objection outweigh any reasons for acceptance and, thus, lead to interfering. This would denote matters one cannot tolerate, that is, one is intolerant about. Cases of toleration, therefore, only appear within the range of these two limits, that is, between being indifferent or even appreciative and being intolerant.

Naturally, this raises the question of which reasons may be considered plausible and convincing for drawing both lines. In this regard, the traditional approach to defining toleration leaves room for yet another important conceptual variation: toleration defined as a moral concept to begin with and as merely a descriptive one (Horton 1994; Forst 2013, pp. 18–23, 32; Balint 2014, p. 266f., 2017, pp. 78–88). While the descriptive concept of toleration accepts all kinds of reasons for drawing both lines, the moral concept of toleration only accepts moral reasons for doing so or at least reasons that may be considered morally acceptable. Toleration is then understood as a morally commendable or required attitude to begin with. The descriptive concept, on the other hand, leaves the moral evaluation of toleration an open question. For instance, from the perspective of the descriptive concept, a racist who does not act on his racism would have to be described as tolerant, which appears to be implausible and has been described as the paradox of the "tolerant racist" (Horton 1994, pp. 16–18; Forst 2013, p. 19). Yet, it may very well be argued that this result is only paradoxical if one presupposes toleration as a moral concept in the first place. If the question about the moral status of a person's tolerant attitude is left open, as the descriptive concept argues, the paradox disappears (Balint 2014, p. 277f.). Accordingly – the moral and political debates about toleration notwithstanding – the descriptive concept of toleration seems to be better suited to capture all facets of toleration in close personal relationships, as it allows for a maximum range of possible kinds of reasons for objection and acceptance. In any case, since the question of where to draw the limits of toleration only needs to be reflected against the background of close personal relationships for the purpose of this chapter, it can safely be assumed that at least the central element of such relationships, namely caring about each other, lies within the boundaries of what is morally allowed.

Yet, in general, following the descriptive concept, the following four kinds of reasons may be invoked for toleration's objection and acceptance components and for pinpointing both the lower and upper limits of toleration (Kühler 2019a, p. 237f., b, p. 8f.).

1. *Moral reasons* are derived from a perspective on morality that defines it in terms of universally and objectively valid claims about "what we owe to each other" (Scanlon 2000).
2. *Ethical reasons* are derived from a broader perspective on what may constitute a good life, including different, competing, and partially conflicting values and practices (Habermas 1991).
3. *Pragmatic reasons* are derived from merely instrumental, prudential reasoning about which means best support one's own ends and interests, whatever these may be (Habermas 1991).
4. *Political reasons* are derived from a liberal and value-neutral political perspective on how to live together peacefully and cooperate with each other despite, and independent of, a pluralism of values and ways of life (Rawls 1993, pp. 131–172, 2001, pp. 26–38).

    While the – contested – notion of independent political reasons obviously plays an important role in political debate on toleration, such reasons are clearly irrelevant in close personal relationships and for determining the corresponding limits of toleration. Instead, reasons that are derived from how family, friends, and lovers care about each other need to be added. They may be dubbed *reasons of love*.
5. *Reasons of love* are derived from people caring about each other and are directed at the other's flourishing and well-being for the other's own sake (Frankfurt 2004).

In addition to the question of how to define the general *concept* of toleration, Rainer Forst has suggested four different *conceptions* of toleration, which specify the traditional *concept* of toleration differently in some respects (Forst 2013, pp. 26–32).

Firstly, the *permission conception* is characterized by Forst as the social relation between an authority or majority and one or more minorities, with the former allowing the latter to live according to their own beliefs as long as the dominant position of the authority or majority is not questioned. Secondly, the *coexistence conception* is similar to the first with the exception of the affected groups being equally powerful, which is why toleration is granted reciprocally. Thirdly, the *respect conception* grounds toleration in equal moral respect, which is why others are taken to have a moral right to living according to their own beliefs and values, even though one disagrees with these. Finally, the *esteem conception* goes even a step further in that it consists of respecting others as moral equals but also having a sense of esteem or appreciation of their beliefs, values, or way of life, although one does not consider adopting them in one's own life.

While Forst's distinction between these four conceptions is certainly illuminating, it is also clear that it is so primarily against the background of political philosophy. Yet, Forst's further characterization of the four conceptions in terms of the possible kinds of reasons involved as well as the clarification of the object of toleration, that is, of what exactly is tolerated, is helpful for the topic at hand. In general, for both the permission and the coexistence conception the outweighing reasons for acceptance, that is, for toleration, can be merely pragmatic reasons. Essentially, the line of reasoning is that interfering with what one objects to would be more trouble than it is worth, while toleration allows one to avoid the costs of conflict or outright violence.

Importantly, this also means that both the permission and the coexistence conception are compatible with a lack of moral respect of others in that also persons or groups as such may be included in what one merely tolerates. It is mainly because of this aspect that these conceptions of toleration have traditionally been criticized as inadequate or even insulting, that is, as falling short of what is actually morally required, namely equal moral respect or recognition (Goethe 1981, p. 385; Galeotti 2002; Forst 2013, p. 3).

Conversely, both the respect and the esteem conception exclude mere pragmatic reasons, at least as primary reasons, and instead require outweighing moral reasons for acceptance, with the esteem conception even adding ethical reasons of appreciation for acceptance to the mix. Moreover, the condition of equal moral respect for persons also means that persons or groups can no longer be considered possible objects of mere toleration but only their beliefs, values, or way of life. In addition to Forst's considerations, it is then easy to see that one may also have outweighing reasons of love for acceptance in case one not only morally respects the other person but also cares about her.

Following this characterization of toleration based on the kind of outweighing reasons for acceptance, Forst's list of conceptions of toleration can be revised as follows in order to suit better the topic at hand (Kühler 2019a, pp. 242–244).

1. *Pragmatic conception*: This conception highlights the merely pragmatic outweighing reasons for acceptance. Accordingly, a tolerant stance is only considered the best or most cost-effective overall means, at least for the time being, to

pursue one's own ends. Moreover, the pragmatic conception is compatible with the object of toleration being persons or groups.

2. *Moral conception*: This conception highlights that toleration is granted out of moral respect. The outweighing reasons for acceptance are, therefore, moral reasons, which is why persons and groups are excluded as possible objects of toleration. "The person of the other is *respected*; her convictions and actions are *tolerated*" (Forst 2013, p. 30).

3. *Ethical conception*: This conception refers to one's own values or way of life, which is taken to include the possibility of allowing others to live according to their own beliefs and values. "For example, an agent's religious belief may include seeing others with a different religious belief or none at all as being gravely mistaken and fundamentally damned. However, the agent's religious belief may at the same time also include the claim that everyone has to find the true and right religious belief, i.e., of course, the agent's own, freely in order to find salvation. Tolerating others is, therefore, a vital part of the agent's religious (ethical) outlook" (Kühler 2019a, p. 243). Still, because the ethical conception of toleration, thus, fundamentally depends on the specific values of the agent in question, it may very well include persons or groups as objects of toleration once again. On the other hand, it may also include and even go beyond moral respect in that others and their values or way of life are not only respected but also appreciated due to one's own multicultural convictions. The concrete details of the ethical conception are, therefore, directly derived from the person's specific beliefs and values.

It could be argued that ethical considerations in the above sense may very well include reasons of love as a specific part of one's values and conception of a good life. Accordingly, the ethical conception of toleration would allow for outweighing reasons of love. However, for the purpose of this chapter, it is necessary to look more closely into the role that reasons of love can play for toleration in close personal relationships.

Toleration in Close Personal Relationships

Surprisingly, neither the philosophy of love nor the debate on toleration comprises much discussion of toleration in close personal relationships. While the notion of toleration is sometimes mentioned in contributions to the philosophy of love, it is usually not analyzed in further detail (see, e.g., Halwani 2018, pp. 32f., 75–85, 90). Notable recent exceptions are Bowlin (2016, Chap. 6) and Maurer (2021), who both discuss toleration in loving relationships in comparison to the closely related attitudes of forgiveness and forbearance. Both toleration and forbearance may be seen as patiently enduring certain aspects of one's beloved to which one objects, but while forbearance and forgiveness always need to be given freely, toleration may be required as a constant stance out of considerations of justice or of love.

The combined characterizations given above allow to follow up on these claims and discuss toleration's role in more detail. In a first step, a number of conceptual aspects of toleration can be excluded as inappropriate when it comes to close personal relationships. Most importantly, the possible objects of toleration can be narrowed down. Since close personal relationships are characterized by caring about the other person, this person cannot be the object of mere toleration. For, this would imply that one has reasons to reject the person altogether, which would obviously be inconsistent with the idea of caring about him or her. In slight variation of Forst's quote: "The person of the other is *[loved]*; [some of] her convictions and actions are *tolerated*" (Forst 2013, p. 30).

However, not even all personal characteristics, like beliefs, values, or preferences, among others, might be considered a proper object of toleration. Given that caring about a beloved includes caring about his or her well-being and being motivated to promote the beloved's flourishing for his or her own sake, this implies that one can neither be indifferent to nor reject those characteristics, values, preferences, etc. that the beloved cares about, that is, that have a crucial impact on the beloved's identity and his or her well-being and flourishing. Instead, one has at least prima facie reasons of love to appreciate and promote all of the beloved's beliefs, values, preferences, etc. that the beloved cares about and that are important for his or her identity and flourishing.

While being indifferent or having outweighing reasons for rejection concerning either the person of the beloved as such or that which he or she cares about is clearly inconsistent with the idea of caring about the beloved, merely having reasons for objection to what the beloved cares about but at the same time having outweighing reasons for acceptance may very well be considered consistent with caring about him or her. For instance, it seems to make perfect sense to say that I merely tolerate my beloved's – to my mind obnoxious – friends. First of all, due to my love I cannot have outweighing reasons for rejecting them altogether. Yet, secondly, I might very well have reasons for objection because I think that these friends do my beloved no good. Still, thirdly, I would have outweighing reasons for accepting them nonetheless, or at least for not interfering with my beloved spending time with them, because I think that everyone, including my beloved, should be allowed to choose their friends freely.

Yet, it seems that, in analogy to Goethe's seminal saying about mere toleration being insulting, it could likewise be argued that mere toleration of what the beloved cares about falls short of what love – either in terms of family, friendship, or romantic love – actually requires, namely appreciating and sharing what one cares about for the other's own sake. Consequently, if I were merely to tolerate my beloved's friends, I would fail to show the appreciation and sharing of what my beloved cares about, namely his or her friends. In this regard, the idea of sharing need not imply spending time with my beloved's friends myself but arguably only a supportive attitude whenever my beloved wants to share with me something in relation to his or her friends, for example, stories about their joint activities. Listening to these stories with a merely tolerating attitude could very well count as falling short of what love requires.

Be that as it may for the moment, there seems to be at least ample room for toleration in case of beliefs, preferences, etc. the beloved does *not* care about. For example, while my friend might prefer to watch a specific movie tonight with me, this is also not something that is especially important to him or her or will affect his or her flourishing. Accordingly, I can easily be indifferent about the movie or even have reasons for objecting to it (both to the movie itself and to watching a movie at all if my friend also does not care about whether we watch a movie or do something else instead) because I think the movie is horrible or because I would rather do something more meaningful together than watch a movie. Yet, I may very well have outweighing reasons for acceptance nonetheless, that is, for watching the movie with my friend, for instance because I like doing my friend a little favor, or because I want to spare us an argument about what to watch or do instead, or because I got to decide on the last movie we watched together. If so, it seems fair to say that I merely tolerate watching this specific movie with my friend without this having any relevant impact on our friendship – as my friend does not care about the movie, which is why our friendship is not at stake in the first place, and because we still certainly enjoy each other's company.

To sum up, there may be two possible objects of toleration in close personal relationships that need to be distinguished: firstly, characteristics, beliefs, preferences, or actions that the beloved cares about and that contribute to his or her flourishing, and, secondly, anything that the beloved does not care about or that does not contribute to his or her flourishing. While the latter easily allows for toleration, the former presents a challenge in that it raises the question of whether mere toleration may be considered compatible with caring about the beloved and his or her flourishing.

In order to shed further light on the matter, it is helpful to explore which kinds of reasons for objection and outweighing acceptance and which resulting conceptions of toleration may be considered appropriate in close personal relationships. This also helps to disentangle the apparent confusion about how to assess the abovementioned case of merely tolerating what the beloved cares about, like his or her friends. For, both scenarios may differ in terms of the kinds of reasons involved, which would explain the two different and apparently mutually exclusive assessments.

First and foremost, caring about the beloved implies that one has reasons of love for appreciating and supporting the beloved and his or her well-being and flourishing, which makes it impossible to have at the same time reasons for rejecting the beloved as a person or for harming him or her. Yet, it may be a matter of debate what *truly* contributes to the beloved's well-being and flourishing, which is why one's reasons of love might create a tension between appreciating and promoting what the beloved *in fact* cares about and what he or she *should* care about based on a critical reflection of what may be considered *truly* contributing to his or her well-being and flourishing (Kühler 2017). Hence, while one's reasons of love prima facie speak in favor of appreciating and promoting what the beloved cares about, it is also possible that they speak in favor of objection based on what may be considered truly contributing to the beloved's well-being and flourishing – assuming that it is not inconsistent to have both reasons of love for promotion and objection at the same time.

Moreover, if one's reasons of love for objection are outweighing, this would mark an upper limit of toleration in close personal relationships and lead to interfering with the beloved's life in this regard for the beloved's own sake, that is, in order to promote the beloved's true well-being and flourishing. Accordingly, crossing this upper limit of toleration and, thus, no longer being able to tolerate the matter in question would lead to acts of a loving paternalism in close personal relationships – whereas it is an open question, of course, if such a loving paternalism may be considered legitimate, even if only for the epistemic question of who might know better what truly contributes to someone's well-being and flourishing but also for the general moral requirement of respecting the beloved's autonomy.

Assuming, however, that one may still have outweighing reasons for acceptance nonetheless, while still treating the reasons for objection as valid, this would mark a case of toleration in close personal relationships – whereas Maurer would characterize such cases as examples of forbearance (Maurer 2021). The interesting question is now which kinds of reasons may be considered compatible with caring about the beloved and his or her flourishing, that is, not falling short of what love requires.

First of all, the combination of having reasons of love for objection in light of considerations of what truly contributes to the beloved's well-being and flourishing and at the same time having outweighing reasons of love for acceptance because respecting the beloved's autonomy contributes even more to his her flourishing, including the hope and trust that the beloved eventually sees that the matter in question does not truly contribute to his or her well-being and flourishing, is clearly compatible with caring about the beloved. More precisely, both objection and outweighing acceptance are directly based on one's caring about the beloved. This makes the abovementioned case of merely tolerating the beloved's friends intelligible in terms of not falling short of what love requires. It is precisely one's loving attitude that comprises both reasons of love for objection and outweighing reasons of love for acceptance because, on the one hand, arguably, the friends in question do not truly contribute to the beloved's well-being and flourishing, but, on the other hand, not interfering with the beloved's autonomy in choosing his or her friends and with whom to spend time contributes to his or her flourishing even more and may be considered a fundamental feature of loving someone to begin with. Hence, such *toleration out of love* – which may be considered an additional conception of toleration applicable *within* close personal relationships – can be considered not only compatible with but a direct expression of what love or caring about others may require of us. Moreover, this holds in general if one's outweighing reasons for acceptance are reasons of love, regardless of which kind one's reasons for objection are.

However, what about the other conceptions of toleration mentioned above and what if other kinds of reasons are involved as outweighing reasons for acceptance? While it should be stressed again that, due to caring about the other person, close personal relationships by definition involve reasons of love for appreciating and promoting what the beloved cares about and what contributes to his or her well-being and flourishing, it remains an open question what to make of cases in which these reasons have a considerably weaker impact on the person's reasoning and motivation to act than other kinds of reasons. Arguably, it might be concluded that this diminishes the person's caring about the beloved to the same degree – if caring about others can be assumed to be characterizable in varying strengths in the first place. For instance, what if, in the example of tolerating my beloved's friends, my reasons of love both for objection and outweighing acceptance do not play a decisive role? What if my reasoning and practical stance would be led more by pragmatic, moral, or ethical reasons instead?

Firstly, having primarily outweighing pragmatic reasons for acceptance implies considering the situation primarily from the perspective of one's own interests and preferences. Consequently, while caring about the beloved by definition still plays a role, it would always be accompanied and even downplayed by self-centered considerations. For example, accepting my beloved's friends could be based primarily on merely pragmatic outweighing reasons in the sense that not interfering with my beloved meeting them or listening to my beloved telling me stories about them would help me avoid an ugly argument with my beloved, which is what I prefer. While this may correctly be considered a tolerating stance, the primary influence of pragmatic, self-centered reasoning behind this stance may, arguably, be considered as the precise reason for criticizing the tolerating stance as lacking in what is required of caring about the beloved for his or her own sake. Moreover, this would explain the differing assessment of the case described above. Accordingly, it may be argued that the *pragmatic* conception of toleration, even if accompanied by – comparatively weaker – reasons of love falls short of what love or caring about the other requires, which is why it may be considered inappropriate within close personal relationships – even though it can be argued that one's own reasonable interests and preferences somehow need to be weighed against the ones of the beloved in general.

Much the same may hold, secondly, for ethical reasons. If I had primarily outweighing ethical reasons for acceptance, which rather reflect my own values and what I care about – besides my beloved – this could likewise be criticized as falling short of what love or caring about my beloved for his or her own sake requires. If so, the *ethical* conception of toleration, too, would have to be considered inappropriate within close personal relationships.

However, such criticism apparently relies on my ethical outlook being self-centered, just like the pragmatic perspective. If, on the other hand, what I value and care about may be characterized as a shared ethical outlook to begin with, my ethical reasons would already include my beloved's perspective. Hence, my ethical reasons would already reflect the idea of love as mutual care, intimacy, and a sharing of lives and activities. If so, the ethical conception of toleration would essentially be equivalent with toleration out of love and, thus, clearly be appropriate within close personal relationships. Still, it may, analogously, lead to the question of how to weigh one's own values and conception of a good life against what the beloved cares about, which may very well mark one's ethical upper limit of toleration.

Finally, consider I deeply cared about morality, so that I would consider myself having first and foremost outweighing moral reasons for accepting my beloved's friends or at least for not interfering with their friendship because morality requires respecting my beloved's autonomy, which includes respecting choices about friends and with whom to spend time. This may, again, be correctly characterized as a tolerating stance. Yet, it may likewise be criticized in lacking what love or caring about the other requires, for it would once again replace or downplay the role of outweighing reasons of love for appreciating and promoting what my beloved cares about, which in this case means accepting his or her friends or at least not interfering with these friendships out of love. To be sure, taking a moral stance on the matter is certainly correct in that I would meet the basic moral obligation of respecting my beloved's autonomy. However, if moral reasons are the decisive reasons, this raises the question of whether I miss out in treating my beloved as the special person he or she is supposed to be for me due to my love (Williams 1981; Wolf 2012; Fedock et al. 2021). Accordingly, the stance of taking the moral high ground could be regarded as at least underrepresenting what is of crucial importance when it comes to toleration within close personal relationships.

Yet, on the contrary, it may also be argued that toleration is a moral requirement within close personal relationships to begin with, which is why moral reasons should be the decisive reasons throughout (Velleman 1999; Maurer 2021). Moreover, moral reasons can and should be the decisive reasons to mark an upper limit of toleration, that is, if the matter in question is morally unacceptable. What if my beloved's friends tended to drag my beloved into harmful and morally questionable situations? Outweighing moral reasons would then speak in favor of interfering, thus characterizing the choice of friends and the resulting actions as not tolerable (anymore). Arguably, if these moral reasons would still be outweighed by reasons of love for accepting the friends and their actions nonetheless, my non-interfering and caring about my beloved could be criticized on moral grounds. In addition, it could be argued that my non-interfering is also misguided when it comes to promoting my beloved's true flourishing – if true flourishing would comprise a good moral character, just like Aristotle argued in the case of real friendship.

Given the above discussion, the conception of *toleration out love* appears to be the only appropriate conception *within* close personal relationships. However, the above clarifications on the kinds of reasons involved in toleration allow for a clearer demarcation of the lower and upper limits of toleration *concerning* close personal relationships, as these limits may also help to explain some of the limits of close personal relationships in general. Put in another way, if these limits are reached, the close personal relationship as such would be put into question.

The lower limit of toleration is reached, just like in the case of toleration in the political context, if the person is indifferent about the matter in question. This means that the person has neither particular reasons for objection nor for acceptance, whereas this lack of particular reasons simply leads to non-interference. Put differently, the person just does not care about the matter in question at all. In case of close personal relationships, this does not pose a problem as long as the beloved also does not care about the matter in question. For example, if I am indifferent about my beloved drinking coffee or tea in the morning and my beloved also does not care about choosing either one, this obviously does not put any strain on the relationship. However, being indifferent about something that the beloved *does* care about proves to be a problem in the context of close personal relationships. Given the above discussion, caring about the beloved implies that one *cannot* be indifferent about matters the beloved cares about but rather that one has reasons of love for appreciation and promotion. Hence, if one, indeed, remains indifferent about what the beloved cares about, this would put into question the very core of what having a close personal relationship means, namely caring about the other person and his or her (true) well-being and flourishing. Thus, the lower limit of toleration at the same time marks the limit of having a close personal relationship at all.

Still, in everyday practice this will likely not be much of a problem, as switching from being indifferent to a stance of appreciation and promotion because one cares about the other person does not pose a threat to one's own values and preferences. This is strengthened by the fact that this switch does not imply that one necessarily has to care about the matter in question oneself but rather only indirectly in light of the beloved caring about them (Kühler 2020, 2021). Consequently, if one still remained indifferent, this would have to be interpreted as a lack of caring about the other person to begin with.

Analyzing the upper end of toleration proves to be more complex and challenging, as different kinds of reasons for objection can come into play, which, when being outweighing, may put the close personal relationship into question in different ways. Firstly, as discussed above, if one has outweighing reasons of love for objection, this leads to the challenge of paternalism within close personal relationships. Accordingly, this does not necessarily put into question the relationship as such. Yet, it certainly poses a challenge, for it raises the question of how to justify paternalistic interferences with the beloved's autonomy. This depends to a large degree on the specific nature of the close personal relationship. For instance, if parents act paternalistically toward their – especially young – children, this may certainly be considered legitimate and even morally required. On the other hand, paternalistic actions within romantic relationships, in which the lovers are considered equals, are certainly harder to justify and may even put the relationship as a whole at risk. In any case, for the topic at hand, outweighing reasons of love for objection mark an upper limit of toleration and lead to the accompanying challenge of a loving paternalism within close personal relationships.

Secondly, one may have outweighing pragmatic reasons for objection in case the matter in question proves to be a serious obstacle to pursuing one's own ends and interests. While this may mark an upper limit to one's toleration, it raises doubts about the nature of the relationship to begin with. Following the discussion above, it would rather show a lack of caring about the beloved. Accordingly, having outweighing pragmatic reasons for objection would not be a case of toleration *within* close personal relationships but rather one *concerning* close personal relationships, as this *pragmatic* upper limit to toleration would at the same time mark the limit of having or maintaining a close personal relationship in the first place.

Thirdly, having outweighing ethical reasons for objection would depict cases in which what one cares about oneself – besides the beloved – conflicts with what the beloved cares about. Assuming, as mentioned above, that ethical reasons stem from what one cares about in an identity-forming sense, this upper limit of one's toleration concerning close personal relationships marks cases of conflicts between such identity-forming values (Kühler 2020, 2021). For instance, an atheist, who sees religious belief as mere superstition to be overcome, would apparently be at odds with him- or herself if he or she cared about a devoted religious believer and would now have reasons of love to appreciate and promote the beloved's religious belief – and vice versa. Consequently, this *ethical* upper limit of toleration marks the limit of one's own ability to engage in and maintain close personal relationships in light of conflicting identity-forming values, at least if neither of the persons involved is willing or capable of changing their own identity-forming values to resolve the conflict.

Aside from simply ignoring such conflicts between identity-forming values in everyday life – which usually only works as a temporary solution at best – changing one's identity based on changes in one's identity-forming values may very well be the result of a close personal relationship (Rorty 1987, p. 401; Krebs 2014, p. 22). Usually, family, friends, or lovers have a significant influence on who we are and how our identity and what we care about changes over time. Accordingly, both the pragmatic as well as the ethical upper limits of one's toleration concerning close personal relationships may over time be subject to change precisely because of these relationships or because one wants to pursue them in the first place and is, thus, open to a change in one's identity. Moreover, often enough only certain aspects of one's identity-forming values need to change to make the relationship work. For instance, the atheist may very well remain an atheist him- or herself and only lose his or her dismissive attitude toward religious persons to make the relationship work – or vice versa. Of course, this raises the question of who should change to which degree and whether this might be considered fair.

Finally, as mentioned above, having outweighing moral reasons for objection would characterize cases in which the matter in question cannot be tolerated on moral grounds. This *moral* upper limit of toleration concerning close personal relationships would, thus, create the well-known conflict between what one's particular love may (supposedly) require and what impersonal morality demands. Having outweighing moral reasons for objection and acting on them would then show a person's acknowledgment of impersonal and objective moral demands taking precedence over personal attachments. Accordingly, it might either be argued that morality creates certain limits of acceptable close personal relationships to begin with – morality would then be characterized as generally overriding (Gert and Gert 2017) – or that morality infringes on the very core of what caring about others requires (Williams 1981; Wolf 2012). Either way, the moral upper limit of toleration concerning close personal relationships would at the same time mark the limit of engaging in or maintaining a morally questionable relationship.

Of course, everyday practice knows a certain gray area when it comes to – at least temporarily – tolerating (potentially) morally dubious actions or dispositions of one's beloveds. This holds all the more due to the possibility of influencing the beloved in order to become a morally better person. Even Aristotle argued that, before ending a friendship in case the friend shows signs of lacking in virtue, one should try to help the friend in becoming virtuous again (Aristotle EN, IX, 3).

In sum, the above discussion allows to paint a more precise picture of how and in what sense toleration may play a role within or concerning close personal relationships. In so doing, it also sheds further light on how the limits of toleration based on different kinds of reasons may affect the practice and scope of engaging in and maintaining close personal relationships in general.

Summary and Future Directions

Toleration, as an attitude of "live and let live," is typically discussed within moral and political philosophy, where it is characterized as a personal virtue or state practice in order to facilitate peaceful coexistence among strangers. Close personal relationships, on the other hand, are characterized by people who mutually know and care about each other. Within such relationships, toleration may find a place in terms of a *toleration out of love*, that is, if one has outweighing reasons of love for appreciating and promoting, that is, accepting, what the beloved cares about despite having also reasons for objecting to the object of toleration. Defining the lower and upper limits of one's toleration based on the kind of outweighing reasons involved then adds to understanding how this affects and limits one's capability of engaging in or maintaining certain close personal relationships.

The discussion in this chapter has been confined to general conceptual questions of toleration's possible role *within* and *concerning* close personal relationships. Yet, intriguing questions arise when thinking about how toleration's specific role and content may be affected by the precise nature of the close personal relationship in question. For instance, while it has been shown that toleration may play a role in relations between family members, friends, or lovers alike, and how toleration may come into play in general, the specific scope and objects of toleration will certainly differ between these relationships. Accordingly, follow-up discussions based on the conceptual framework described in this chapter may add to understanding the specific relational dynamics in more detail.

References

Aristotle (EN) Nicomachean ethics. translated by WD Ross, The internet classics archive. http://classics.mit.edu/Aristotle/nicomachaen.html
Badhwar NK (ed) (1993) Friendship: a philosophical reader. Cornell University Press, Ithaca
Balint P (2014) Acts of tolerance: a political and descriptive account. Eur J Polit Theo 13:264–281
Balint P (2017) Respecting toleration. Traditional liberalism and contemporary diversity. Oxford University Press, Oxford
Bowlin JR (2016) Tolerance among the virtues. Princeton University Press, Princeton
Brake E (2016) Marriage and domestic partnership. In: Zalta EN (ed) The Stanford encyclopedia of philosophy, winter 2016. Stanford University, Metaphysics Research Lab
Castiglione D, McKinnon C (eds) (2003) Toleration, neutrality and democracy. Springer, Dordrecht
Cohen AJ (2004) What toleration is. Ethics 115:68–95
Edyvane D, Matravers M (eds) (2012) Toleration re-examined. Routledge, London
Fedock R, Kühler M, Rosenhagen R (eds) (2021) Love, justice, and autonomy. Philosophical Perspectives. Routledge, New York, forthcoming

Fisher M (1990) Personal love. Duckworth, London
Forst R (2013) Toleration in conflict: past and present. Cambridge University Press, Cambridge
Forst R (2017) Toleration. In: Zalta EN (ed) The Stanford encyclopedia of philosophy, Fall 2017. Stanford University, Metaphysics Research Lab
Frankfurt HG (1994) Autonomy, necessity, and love. In: Necessity, volition, and love, vol 1999. Cambridge University Press, Cambridge, pp 129–141
Frankfurt HG (2004) The reasons of love. Princeton University Press, Princeton
Friedman M (1998) Romantic love and personal autonomy. Midwest Stud Philos 22:162–181. https://doi.org/10.1111/j.1475-4975.1998.tb00336.x
Galeotti AE (2002) Toleration as recognition. Cambridge University Press, Cambridge
Gert B, Gert J (2017) The definition of morality. In: Zalta EN (ed) The Stanford encyclopedia of philosophy, fall 2017. Stanford University, Metaphysics Research Lab
Goethe JW von (1981) Werke. Hamburger Ausgabe in 14 Bänden. Beck, München
Habermas J (1991) Vom pragmatischen, ethischen und moralischen Gebrauch der praktischen Vernunft. In: Erläuterungen zur Diskursethik. Suhrkamp, Frankfurt am Main, pp 100–118
Halwani R (2018) Philosophy of love, sex, and marriage. An introduction, 2nd edn. Routledge, New York
Helm BW (2017a) Friendship. In: Zalta EN (ed) The Stanford encyclopedia of philosophy, fall 2017. Metaphysics Research Lab, Stanford University. https://plato.stanford.edu/archives/fall2017/entries/friendship/
Helm BW (2017b) Love. In: Zalta EN (ed) The Stanford encyclopedia of philosophy, fall 2017. Metaphysics Research Lab, Stanford University. https://plato.stanford.edu/archives/fall2017/entries/love/
Heyd D (ed) (1996) Toleration: an elusive virtue. Princeton University Press, Princeton
Horton J (1994) Three (apparent) paradoxes of toleration. Filozofska Istraživanja/Synth Philos 9:7–20
Horton J (1996) Toleration as a virtue. In: Heyd D (ed) Toleration: an elusive virtue. Princeton University Press, Princeton, pp 28–43
Horton J (2011) Why the traditional conception of toleration still matters. Crit Rev Int Soc Pol Phil 14:289–305. https://doi.org/10.1080/13698230.2011.571874
Horton J, Mendus S (eds) (1985) Aspects of toleration. Philosophical studies. Methuen, London
Horton J, Mendus S (eds) (1999) Toleration, identity and difference. Palgrave Macmillan, London
Horton J, Nicholson P (eds) (1992) Toleration: philosophy and practice. Ashgate, London
King P (1976) Toleration, 2nd edn. Allen & Unwin, London, 1998
Krebs A (2014) Between I and Thou – on the dialogical nature of love. In: Maurer C, Milligan T, Pacovská K (eds) Love and its objects. What can we care for? Palgrave Macmillan, Basingstoke, pp 7–24
Kühler M (2017) Toleranz und/oder Paternalismus im engeren sozialen Nahbereich? Z Prakt Philos 4:63–86. https://doi.org/10.22613/zfpp/4.2.3
Kühler M (2019a) Modus vivendi and toleration. In: Horton J, Westphal M, Willems U (eds) The political theory of modus vivendi. Springer, Dordrecht, pp 235–253
Kühler M (2019b) Can a value-neutral liberal state still be tolerant? Crit Rev Int Soc Pol Phil. https://doi.org/10.1080/13698230.2019.1616578
Kühler M (2020) Liebe und Konflikte zwischen identitätsstiftenden Werten. Philokles Zeitschrift für populäre Philosophie 24:36–62
Kühler M (2021) Love and conflicts between identity-forming values. In: Mayer C-H, Vanderheiden E (eds) International Handbook of Love: Transcultural and Transdisciplinary Perspectives. Springer, Dordrecht, forthcoming
Maurer C (2021) Tolerance, love and justice. In: Fedock R, Kühler M, Rosenhagen R (eds) Love, justice, and autonomy. Philosophical Perspectives. Routledge, New York, forthcoming
McKinnon C (2006) Toleration. A critical introduction. Routledge, London
Mendus S, Edwards D (eds) (1987) On toleration. Clarendon Press, Oxford
Merino N (2004) The problem with "we": rethinking joint identity in romantic love. J Soc Philos 35:123–132
Murphy AR (1997) Tolerance, toleration, and the liberal tradition. Polity 29:593–623

Newey G (2013) Toleration in political conflict. Cambridge University Press, Cambridge
Nozick R (1990) Love's bond. In: The examined life. Philosophical meditations. Simon & Schuster, New York, pp 68–86
Peterson GW, Bush KR (eds) (2012) Handbook of marriage and the family, 3rd edn. New York, Springer
Rawls J (1993) Political liberalism. Columbia University Press, New York
Rawls J (2001) Justice as fairness. A restatement. Belknap Press, Cambridge
Rorty AO (1987) The historicity of psychological attitudes: love is not love which alters not when it alteration finds. Midwest Stud Philos 10:399–412
Satz D (2017) Feminist perspectives on reproduction and the family. In: Zalta EN (ed) The Stanford encyclopedia of philosophy, summer 2017. Stanford University, Metaphysics Research Lab
Scanlon TM (2000) What we owe to each other. Belknap Press of Harvard University Press, Cambridge
Sheffield FCC, Howatson MC (eds) (2008) Plato: the symposium. Cambridge University Press, Cambridge
Soble A (ed) (1989) Eros, agape, and philia: readings in the philosophy of love. Paragon House, New York
Soble A (1997) Union, autonomy, and concern. In: Lamb RE (ed) Love analyzed. Westview Press, Boulder, pp 65–92
Solomon RC (1994) About love. Reinventing romance for our times. Hackett Publications Co., Reprint 2006, Indianapolis
Velleman JD (1999) Love as a moral emotion. Ethics 109:338–374
Williams B (1981) Persons, character and morality. In: Luck M (ed) Philosophical papers 1973–1980. Cambridge University Press, Cambridge, pp 1–19
Williams MS, Waldron J (eds) (2008) Toleration and its limits. New York University Press, New York
Wolf S (2012) "One thought too many": love, morality, and the ordering of commitment. In: Heuer U, Lang G (eds) Luck, value, and commitment. Themes from the ethics of Bernard Williams. Oxford University Press, Oxford, pp 71–92

Hospitality and Toleration

38

Andrew Fiala

Contents

Introduction	758
The Continuum of Toleration and Hospitality	759
Brute Tolerance, Brute Hospitality, and Moral Choice	761
Mere Toleration, The Modus Vivendi, and Liberal Toleration	764
Two Ways to Move from Toleration to Hospitality	767
A Moral Argument Based in Existential Need and Compassion	768
A Political Argument Based in a Cosmopolitan Political Ideal	769
Summary and Future Directions: The Task of Practical Wisdom and Enlightenment	773
References	773

Abstract

This chapter describes the continuum between toleration as a negative idea and hospitality as a more positive or affirmative concept. It locates this discussion in historical sources including: ancient Greek, Christian, and early modern thought, including Kant. It further considers contemporary discussions of mere toleration as a modus vivendi, liberal toleration, and sources for thinking about hospitality in cosmopolitanism and multiculturalism. It explains the difference between toleration and hospitality, while noting that those who claim that toleration includes acceptance and positive recognition of difference would do better to use the term hospitality than toleration. The chapter concludes by considering two arguments in favor of hospitality: an existential argument about compassion and a political claim focused on emerging cosmopolitan norms.

Keywords

Toleration · Tolerance · Hospitality · Liberalism · Modus vivendi · Golden Rule · Cosmopolitanism

A. Fiala (✉)
Department of Philosophy, California State University, Fresno, CA, USA
e-mail: afiala@csufresno.edu

© The Author(s), under exclusive licence to Springer Nature Switzerland AG 2022
M. Sardoč (ed.), *The Palgrave Handbook of Toleration*,
https://doi.org/10.1007/978-3-030-42121-2_35

Introduction

There is a continuum between the negative focus of toleration and the more positive focus of hospitality. Toleration tells us what not to do: it tells us not to oppress, fight against, or censor. Toleration focuses on what can be called negative rights or negative liberty: toleration encourages us not to violate people's rights or limit their liberty. It establishes a kind of negative peace, to borrow a concept from the literature on peace studies and pacifism, which prevents direct and overt violence or oppression (see Galtung 1964; Boersema 2017). Hospitality is positive: it tells us to welcome, support, and accept. Hospitality can be understood in terms of positive rights or positive liberty. It is part of the project of positive peace (see Fiala 2018). It encourages us to develop an affirmative and proactive kind of social interaction. However, hospitality remains at a distance from even more positive and affirmative values such as friendship, love, and the thick bonds of a homogeneous community.

This chapter provides a structural account of the relation between toleration and hospitality. By locating toleration and hospitality on a continuum, it shows their interrelation. Toleration and hospitality, as described here, are primarily connected to social and political structures. But the concepts can also be understood in terms of virtue. We can stipulate a distinction here between structural (political) *toleration* and *tolerance* as a virtue. Although our ordinary language does not use these terms with precision, it is useful to use the term *toleration* to describe a situation or a condition in which tolerating occurs, while using the term *tolerance* to describe a virtue, disposition, or habit of tolerating. Toleration is something that exists in social relations and systems of political life – when there is disapproval or difference without overt conflict, violence, proscription, condemnation, or prohibition. Toleration often involves restraint on power organized hierarchically – as in the case of the state tolerating dissent. But there can also be a condition of mutual toleration: when each party has the capacity to fight against the other but chooses not to. In distinction from *toleration* as a political condition, *tolerance* as a virtue of individuals is a general disposition to be tolerant or a habit of responding tolerantly. This virtue is located among vices that fall on either side of the virtue: there can be too much tolerance (we might call this a lack of self-respect or self-assertion) and there can be too little tolerance (this is what we usually mean by intolerance). This distinction between political toleration and the virtue of tolerance has been made elsewhere (see Murphy 1997; Fiala 2003, 2005; Nys and Engeln 2008), but ordinary usage allows for substantial slippage and overlap between toleration and tolerance. Hospitality can also be understood in terms of the distinction between a condition/situation of hospitality and a virtue/disposition toward hospitableness.

Understanding these ideas as virtues helps us see why we might locate them on a continuum. Virtues are interconnected. As Socrates suggested in *Protagoras*, "virtue is one": there is (or there ought to be) a unity of the virtues (see Penner 1973). Tolerance, then, is not a stand-alone virtue; nor is hospitality. These virtues are connected with other virtues as well, which are coordinated by practical wisdom. At the social and political level, we ought to seek a similar coherence and integration in linking toleration and hospitality with other social and political values.

Throughout the chapter, historical connections between toleration and hospitality will be discussed with reference to authors in the European tradition who developed these ideas as part of a more general view of political philosophy and the good life. In the ancient world, we see this in both Stoic and Christian sources. In the modern world, the link can be found in authors central to the liberal tradition, especially in the work of Kant, who links what he calls a "cosmopolitan right to hospitality" to a general concept of toleration.

The Continuum of Toleration and Hospitality

The toleration-hospitality continuum is described here in schematic fashion. This schema inevitably simplifies things. This simplification is useful for understanding the conceptual field. But we must note that this analysis does *not* suggest that there is a simple developmental schema running through the whole. Nor do these concepts occur discreetly and in separation. Nor are these the only values that matter in social and political life. The reality of life is more complicated than this schema allows. The conceptual foci are abstractions. Actual relationships and identities are more unstable than this representational schema allows. There are complex intersectional considerations that disrupt any simple representation of social and political life. And yet, we can gain clarity by considering such an abstract representational schema that looks like this.

	Mere toleration	Liberal toleration	Hospitality	Community
Primary conceptual framework	Modus vivendi	Negative rights	Positive rights	Friendship and love
Common values	Enmity remains	Shared political values	Shared social values	Shared moral values
Political framework	Minimal social contract	Liberalism	Inclusive multiculturalism	Communitarianism
Moral framework	Prudential self-interest	Human rights	Cosmopolitan humanity	Shared tradition and ideal of the good life

At one end of this continuum, we find "mere toleration." This can be understood as a practical acceptance of co-existence, which develops as a modus vivendi, which is the primary framework for understanding the concept. Here the parties do not interfere with one another – but without agreeing about fundamental political values, moral norms, or metaphysical postulates. Mere toleration is a condition that can exist between individuals, parties, or peoples who remain enemies but who refrain from fighting based upon self-interest and strategic concerns. In political philosophy, this would be understood in terms of a rudimentary social contract, where the contract develops in Hobbesian fashion from out of a state of war but only advances to the level of a very minimal agreement (a truce or a stalemate) aimed at avoiding war.

Beyond mere toleration is "liberal toleration." The primary conceptual focus of liberal toleration is the idea of negative rights. At this stage of the continuum, there is agreement in principle about basic values that establish the right to be tolerated. This basic political agreement includes some common understanding of liberty rights or rights that prevent interference. This agreement can be achieved through something like what Rawls describes as overlapping consensus or it can rest upon an even deeper common understanding of human nature, political normativity, or moral value. These shared moral values are understood in terms of something like basic/universal human rights. With liberal toleration, enmity is overcome through some appeal to shared public and political values. But the liberal social relation remains thin: the parties share a common set of negative political values but are not engaged in a more affirmative process of recognizing difference and accepting the other; and in the private sphere there remain substantial differences of value about what Rawls calls comprehensive schemes.

Beyond liberal toleration, we find "hospitality," which is thicker – moving from negative rights to something like positive duties. Hospitality is based upon some common agreement about more positive norms of interaction: an agreement between hosts and guests. This idea of hospitable social relations has a cosmopolitan focus insofar as it establishes an ethical relation for welcoming strangers – even those who are not a party to the original social contract or members of the polity community. But hospitality is not only for the radical other who comes from a distant land, it is also a shared social act that cements local relationships among those who are different. The function of hospitality is to broaden social solidarity among those who exist within a social setting and, in the cosmopolitan version of hospitality, with strangers and new arrivals. The limit of cosmopolitan or multicultural hospitality is that since it is understood as establishing social relations among parties who remain strangers, this relation falls short of genuine friendship. In political philosophy, hospitality might be understood in relation to what I call here "inclusive multiculturalism," which aims to welcome diversity in a positive and affirmative way but without requiring the homogeneity of a community of friends – say by setting up institutions in ways that provide for differential group rights and other ways that seek to include and affirm differences.

Beyond hospitality and the multicultural/cosmopolitan social and political relation, we find "community," which brings people together under a shared set of moral values and a common vision of the good life. This is what so-called communitarian philosophies aim at: a community of like-minded people who agree about morality and politics and who share a common tradition that gives meaning and purpose to life. This is an ideal of friendship and love, something like what Martin Luther King, Jr. called "the beloved community." This is an ideal of deep and thick interconnection, which we will not discuss much here, except to point out that this ideal seems unattainable in a world of strangers that emphasizes liberty and negative rights.

Brute Tolerance, Brute Hospitality, and Moral Choice

With this schematic continuum in place, let's consider the conceptual field in more detail. We began by noting that toleration is negative. It is about what we ought not do when we do not like something. To tolerate is to put up with something we find unpleasant or disapprove of. While toleration is sometimes thought of as a simple capacity to endure, toleration as a political concept and in virtue ethics includes a stipulation about the capacity of an agent to reject, condemn, prohibit, destroy, or avoid the thing tolerated (as we shall see in a moment). But in a very simple sense, toleration is a physical capacity – something like fortitude, understood as the strength to withstand and survive. In this sense, which we might call *brute tolerance*, we say that people tolerate pain. This was the sense in which the Latin term *tolerantia* was first employed by Cicero and Seneca (see Forst 2013). In *Letter 66*, for example, Seneca connects *tolerantia* with other virtues, providing a list of Stoic virtues (Seneca 1917–1925): tranquillity, simplicity, generosity, constancy, equanimity, endurance (*tranquillitas, simplicitas, liberalitas, constantia, aequanimitas, tolerantia*). In this standard English translation (by Gummere), *tolerantia* is translated as endurance. This sort of endurance can be called brute tolerance because it is something that animals can do: they can exhibit fortitude and suffer bravely. Brute tolerance has more to do with physical capacity than with moral choice: some people are born with a capacity to endure pain, a capacity for physical strength and psychological fortitude, which can be developed with training.

But brute tolerance is not yet tolerance as a moral virtue and political value. It is only when endurance is a matter of choice involving moral agency that toleration gains moral worth and political value. In the present chapter, we are only concerned with the virtue of tolerance as directed toward others: tolerance not as a strength of inner fortitude but tolerance in social relations. And in the political sense, brute tolerance is of little value, except perhaps as the capacity of a group or polity to endure crises, wars, and disruptions. In the ancient world, a source for understanding the virtue of tolerance as oriented toward others can be found in Aristotle and in the later Stoics. Aristotle appears to have something like this in mind in *Nicomachean Ethics*, where he describes the virtue of agreeing and disagreeing in appropriate ways and in relation to qualities such as friendship and gentleness (Aristotle 1934, Book IV; see Avramenko and Promisel 2018). As is well-known, Aristotelian virtues are associated with vices of excess and deficiency. The vices associated with tolerance are, on the one hand, bitterness, harsh-temperedness quarrelsomeness, and intolerance, and on the other hand, obsequiousness, flattery, and conformism. While tolerance is not a primary virtue for Aristotle, it comes to be more important in the later Stoics. Marcus Aurelius, for example, provides an account of a moral form of tolerance that is especially poignant given his role as emperor (and that remains somewhat puzzling given his role in oppressing Christians and making war). Perhaps Marcus only has in mind a kind of tolerance among citizens and within the social sphere of the ruling class. At any rate, Marcus says, "Remember that all rational beings are created for one another; that toleration (*anexesthai*) is a part of justice; and that men are not intentional evildoers" (Aurelius 1969, 4.3). Although Marcus shares the Stoic sense of the importance of developing the inner strength to bear and forbear (*anexesthai kai apexesthai*) pain and suffering, he also clearly links toleration to the need to endure and put up with the misdeeds of other people (see Aurelis 1969, 5.33).

It is in this social sense that the complexity of toleration as a political value begins to unfold, including the so-called paradox of toleration, which we will describe below. Social or moral toleration must be freely chosen – and it is directed toward something we would otherwise not choose to affirm. Three conditions must be present to say that some thing or some person is being tolerated in this more complicated moral and political sense.

1. There must be a judgment of disapproval of the thing in question.
2. The person or institution that tolerates must have the capacity to act upon their disapproval.
3. The tolerating person or institution must choose to refrain from acting upon that disapproval.

This means that it does not make much sense to say that powerless people or cowards are tolerant. An abused child does not tolerate her abusive parents: she has no choice but to submit to their abuse. But a loving parent may tolerate the misbehavior of a child: the parents could punish but choose not to. In the same way, it makes little sense to say that oppressed groups tolerate their oppression: they may have the brute fortitude to endure but they have no choice in the matter or capacity for resistance. In this regard, toleration is what those with the capacity for choice – and the power to act – do towards others, including those who lack that capacity. Toleration is in this sense hierarchical. The paradigm examples is what we mean when we say that the state tolerates dissent: the state has the power to quash dissent but it chooses not to exercise that power. This is what gives toleration a somewhat paradoxical appearance – called by some "the paradox of toleration" – and which is connected to the problem of whether we ought to tolerate the intolerant and in general why we should tolerate things we condemn (See: Williams 1996; Heyd 1996; Fiala 2005; Churchill 2007; Nys and Engeln 2008; Churchill 2015). One general response to this set of problems reminds us that there are a variety of values connected to toleration including the pragmatic desire to avoid violence, practical interest in positive relationship, general respect for liberty, or other sorts of affirmations of values such as of peace, kindness, civility, and so on.

Hospitality can also be subjected to the kinds of distinctions and clarifications made above. Hospitality is a positive idea that creates duties of various sorts. Hospitality does not primarily tell us what we should not do (although it does tell us not to be inhospitable); rather, it tells us what we ought to do. To be hospitable is to welcome, include, and reach out to others. Hospitality is oriented toward a positive, active, and supportive set of attitudes, institutions, and behaviors. Hospitableness can be understood in nonmoral ways – as a kind of brute hospitality (to parallel our discussion of brute tolerance above). An ecosystem can be called hospitable, for example, when it is able to support life (we say, for example, that a desert is inhospitable). There is a kind of passivity in such a description (of what we might call for symmetry's sake, brute hospitality): an ecosystem does not do anything to support life. But hospitality in the human realm is active and engaging. Symbols of hospitality include reaching out to shake a hand, bowing to honor and receive another, opening a door, setting a place at the table, passing a plate of food, and so on. As an activity of moral agency, hospitality as a moral or political value also involves freedom and choice in the same sense that toleration does. It would not make sense to say that a conquered people are genuinely hospitable, when they have no choice in the matter. But with hospitality, the choice is not negative (as it is with toleration, which chooses not to act on a negative judgment). Rather, the choice of hospitality is positive: to reach out, to offer, to give, to support, to welcome, and to include.

Hospitality can be understood in either a political or a moral (or virtue) sense. On the one hand, *hospitality* is used to describe a condition, structure, or institutional practice. A state, an institution (such as a school), or a person can show hospitality by helping to establish a condition in which people feel welcomed and included. Hotels and restaurants are said to be in the hospitality business, for example. On the other, *hospitable* names a virtue or a disposition (what we might call *hospitableness*). Hospitable people tend to be welcoming and inclusive. They choose to be this way; they think that it is good to be so; and they work to develop the habit of hospitality. The idea of hospitality as a moral and political value is found in many places in and in many traditions. A frequently cited source is the Old Testament book of Exodus. For example (Exodus 23:9): "You shall not oppress a stranger; you know the heart of a stranger, for you were strangers in the land of Egypt." The New Testament builds upon this and the command to love your neighbor as yourself to develop an ethic that includes the need to welcome strangers, care for the sick, feed the hungry, and so on. The parable of the Good Samaritan provides an exemplar (Luke Chap. 10): the Samaritan goes out of his way to help a stranger who is injured on the Jericho road, healing his wounds and providing for his care (see discussion in Fiala 2016).

The opposite of hospitality is hostility or enmity. It is worth noting that hospitality and hostility share a common root in the related Latin words *hostis* and *hospis* – which can mean host, guest, and enemy. Hospitality involves being a good host/guest while hostility occurs when the host-guest relation is broken (see Sheringham and Daruwalla 2007; Derrida 2001; Friese 2009; Shepherd 2014). The complexity of the relationship between guest-host-enemy is of fundamental importance to ethics and to political philosophy. Derrida once said that "ethics is hospitality: ethics is thoroughly coextensive with the experience of hospitality" (Derrida 2001, p. 17). There is substantial complexity behind this claim. But we might simplify this by suggesting that if ethics is about our relationship with "the other," then hospitality ought to be a guiding value. Or to simplify even further, we might say that the Golden Rule, which demands that we love others as ourselves, is fundamentally about hospitality. The Golden Rule does not merely demand that we leave each other alone. Rather, it demands that we actively work to support our neighbors.

Mere Toleration, The Modus Vivendi, and Liberal Toleration

Of course, this mention of the Golden Rule opens the question of who exactly counts as a neighbor. Hospitality and toleration have been extended in various ways to different groups of people in various relationships. Some people are hospitable to co-religionists, for example, while being intolerant of nonbelievers. This shows us that the concepts in question can be mixed in various ways in actual regimes. Repressive political regimes are generally both intolerant and inhospitable. But a regime can provide for legal toleration while still being inhospitable. Other regimes provide for official toleration, while also seeking to create conditions that are welcoming and inclusive. A person can be tolerant – in the sense that the person does not actively condemn others – but also inhospitable – insofar as the person does not actively welcome others. Ideally, a virtuous person would be both tolerant and hospitable.

This way of describing a range of possible combinations of these values helps us begin to understand the difference between "mere toleration" and something more inclusive. Mere toleration in the political realm is simply leaving each other alone. There are a variety of reasons to leave one another alone, often including merely pragmatic or strategic consideration. Mere toleration need not even affirm liberty, as a basic and shared value which permits everyone including the minority to have basic rights, such as freedom of speech, conscience, and assembly. Toleration that affirms liberty is a central consideration of liberal democratic theory. Following John Rawls, we might stipulate that liberty is (or ought to be) a primary and shared value, arrived at through a kind of overlapping consensus (Rawls 1971). But even Rawls recognizes that there will be problems for this ideal, acknowledging that a merely pragmatic modus vivendi is different from overlapping consensus (Rawls 2005). Rawls thinks that a mere modus vivendi is unstable, since it depends upon a balance of forces that can shift; but he holds out the hope that a pragmatic modus vivendi may develop over time into an overlapping consensus. Indeed, Rawls suggests in places (Rawls 1987, 2005) that there may even be a back and forth movement between a mere modus vivendi and a more stable overlapping consensus. For example, in examining the historical development of the idea of toleration, Rawls asks, "how might it happen that over generations the initial acquiescence in a liberal conception of justice as a modus vivendi develops into a stable and enduring overlapping consensus?" (Rawls 1987, p. 18). His explanation is that our actual commitment to comprehensive doctrines is "loose" and subject to "slippage." And over time, there is the possibility of development from modus vivendi to a more comprehensive liberal concept: "The conjecture, then, is that as citizens come to appreciate what a liberal conception does, they acquire an allegiance to it, an allegiance that becomes stronger over time" (Rawls 1987, p. 21).

There is a sort of developmental narrative in Rawls's theory, which might be rejected by critics who fail to see how or why we might develop beyond the kind of radical difference and residual enmity of the modus vivendi. While Rawls seeks something deeper than a merely pragmatic modus vivendi, scholars such as John Horton have suggested that this may be the best we can get in a world of division and difference. Horton describes his approach as a realist critique of liberal moralism.

His approach is grounded in self-interest and prudential concerns, and Horton admits that the modus vivendi is not a panacea for social conflict and that it will remain unstable (Horton 2010, 2011; see Jones 2017). Nonetheless Horton thinks the idea more accurately describes political reality. He says, "At the heart of the idea of a modus vivendi is the thought that the parties find the political order one that they are on the whole willing to work within, one that they are at least willing to put up with" (Horton 2019, p. 11). The point is that the parties can agree to get along, even if they do not agree about anything else. Horton notes that these parties will also likely disagree with the idea of value-pluralism (which we find in both liberalism and in inclusive multiculturalism): they can agree to disagree even if they think that they are right and that the other party is wrong and should properly either be converted or destroyed. That situation is basically one of mere toleration: we choose to leave alone that with which we disagree – and which we could continue to struggle against. In other words, enmity can remain even though parties grudgingly agree to tolerate one another. In such a situation, we are fairly far away from the idea of hospitality, which focuses on welcoming strangers who are not considered enemies.

While Horton has suggested that toleration can be established under a modus vivendi, Newey has pointed out that this seems problematic. Newey emphasizes the negative judgment and capacity for negation as part of toleration, noting that if there is a mere modus vivendi, what seems to be lacking is the capacity for negation: the parties would like to eliminate one another but lack to the capacity to do so. As Newey explains, "If modus vivendi simply amounts to a stalemate between two sets of people, each of whom would rather they were able to impose their will on the other, it is hard to square with toleration. Each would prefer to enforce a monoculture on the other, and given this stance, neither seems to count as tolerant" (Newey 2017, p. 426). Horton has explained further that, despite this objection, a fairly robust sort of toleration can develop from out of a modus vivendi (Horton 2019). There are a variety of pragmatic reasons that divergent people would seek a tolerant modus vivendi. Horton explains, "there are myriad pragmatic reasons for seeking a modus vivendi, some of which will be rooted in the costs of repression and others in the benefits of a more congenial and constructive relationship than one based on simple domination. But there are also likely to be moral reasons" (Horton 2019, p. 9). The point is that there is no one prevailing reason which the parties need to agree to. Horton concludes, "The actual motivational resources available to support a modus vivendi in any given context will always be contingent and circumstantial" (Horton 2019, p. 10).

There is more to be said about this fascinating and ongoing debate regarding liberal theory. If Horton is correct and a merely pragmatic modus vivendi is the best we can hope for, we have what I have called mere toleration: a grudging, realistic, or prudential recognition that toleration is useful for allowing for peaceful co-existence among persons and parties who expect not to be able to agree about much. It might be that this grudging acceptance is a result of a stalemate, as Newey suggests. In some actual cases, this is quite obvious: consider, for example, the set of "status quo" rules that govern access to holy sites in Jerusalem. Or it might be that the parties understand their own self-interest as involving something other than the pursuit of intolerant domination. Perhaps they would rather trade with one another than continue to fight – in some version of an economic or capitalist theory of peace (see Fiala 2021). But whatever the reason, the development of mere toleration is to be applauded, at least as an antidote to violence and a source for a temporary kind of stability. Mere toleration is better than intolerance, hatred, and violence.

But the begrudging and pragmatic nature of mere toleration helps to explain why mere toleration is often thought to be limited and negative. A merely pragmatic modus vivendi in which we agree to leave each other alone does not provide a source of hope for weaving together a tighter social fabric. This point is found in the first structural element of toleration that I mentioned at the outset: the negative judgment that leads to the choice of toleration. Mere toleration in a pragmatic modus vivendi begins with a negative judgment: we tolerate those things we do not approve of. Toleration occurs when we refrain from negating that thing. We allow it to exist. Newey points out that one of the reasons we allow the other to exist may be because of a stalemate or power dynamic. But this implies that if the power dynamic shifts, violent repression, and intolerance may reappear. And this way of describing things depends upon a remaining negative judgment. Thus, those who are merely tolerated will still feel the presence of a negative judgment and they may also feel the threat of potential violence, repression, and intolerance.

One way of describing this is to point out that mere toleration falls short of full-fledged recognition (see Oberdieck 2001; Galeotti 2002; Fiala 2005, 2013). Groups or individuals who are merely tolerated may thus continue to feel rejected, despised, or threatened. They will feel unwelcomed and unaccepted. What is often desired is something more than mere toleration that moves toward recognition, acceptance, and inclusion as full members of a polity. This is where liberal toleration comes in and beyond that hospitality. Liberal toleration rests upon an agreement about basic rights of respect and recognition. It allows for inclusion as citizens and respect for fundamental equality of rights. This agreement develops by way of overlapping consensus in Rawls's account and where each party shares a commitment to something like public reason. The parties no longer remain enemies. Instead they view each other as human persons with the right to be left alone and the right to pursue their own good in their own way. Liberal toleration represents a move beyond mere toleration. But a liberal polity can consist of individuals and groups who remain at a distance and thus a society that is not inclusive or accepting of difference. It is with the move to hospitality that we see the affirmation of something more positive: of welcoming and accepting the other in a way that goes beyond both mere toleration and liberal toleration.

It is important to pause here to point out a terminological dispute that confuses matters. Some accounts of tolerance and toleration define it in a way that does not include a negative judgment. In 1995, the United Nations declared a year of celebration for tolerance, establishing November 16 of subsequent years as the International Day of Tolerance. In the documentation for this, the United Nations explains that tolerance is "respect, acceptance, and appreciation" of diverse cultures and ways of life (United Nations 1995). The UN further states that "tolerance is harmony in difference." A wide range of popular discussions focus on the idea of "teaching tolerance," with the (incorrect) assumption that tolerance is the same as acceptance. And scholarship continues to equivocate between tolerance as mere allowance of difference and a more robust sense of tolerance as acceptance. For example, a 2016 report for the European Union says, "Tolerance, in its broadest sense, can be understood as accepting difference" (Van Driel et al. 2016, p. 18). Toleration and tolerance, as I have described them above do not require affirmation and acceptance: both mere toleration and liberal toleration remain more negative than that. Acceptance of difference is, using my terminology, a matter of hospitality – and is more closely associated with cosmopolitanism and multiculturalism than with liberalism or the minimal social contract of the modus vivendi.

One of the issues that creates this terminological problem is a kind of equivocation about what exactly is being accepted. On the one hand, the idea of acceptance might be focused on overcoming any negative judgment toward the other. But on the other hand, perhaps all that we are being asked to accept is difference itself and the tolerant situation in which there is a negative judgment and remaining difference. In the first case, the use of the world tolerance is not appropriate: pure acceptance that overcomes the negative judgment is simply not tolerance as we've defined it here. But in the second case, we have something like liberal tolerance: we accept the common idea of liberty and respect for human persons, while allowing for differences to continue to exist. But it is likely that what the United Nations and the European Union have in mind is something more like hospitality and inclusion under a framework of multiculturalism and cosmopolitanism.

Given this complexity and difficulty, we can understand why there are those who suggest that toleration is insulting. For those who want full acceptance, tolerance is inadequate because it still contains the negative judgment. This idea can be traced back to Goethe, who said in an oft-quoted aphorism, "Tolerance should only be a temporary attitude. But with time it has to lead to recognition. To tolerate means to insult" (quoted in Weber 2016). Forst has explained that we ought to be more subtle than Goethe allowed. He explains that it is possible to imagine a "non-hierarchial form of mutual toleration that is not an 'insult' but represents a specific form of recognition" (Forst 2013, p. 329). The issue, as Forst describes it, is a matter of structural relations. Toleration becomes insulting when there is a status hierarchy or political power differential, toleration is granted to some subordinate or minority group. But if the status hierarchy were changed, the insulting nature of toleration would also change. As Forst points out, the goal might be something like mutual toleration. In this case – in a condition of mutual toleration, we agree to leave each other alone, as equals who prefer to remain at a distance from one another. Again, this may fall short of what is desired in more interconnected social relations, which aim at mutual recognition instead of mutual toleration. Recognition implies that there is some kind of positive respect and affirmative evaluation that goes beyond the negative judgment that is the basis of toleration.

Two Ways to Move from Toleration to Hospitality

The way to move beyond mere begrudging co-existence is to supplement toleration with hospitality. In the real world, there are a variety of ways that this has been described and put into practice. Programs that emphasize acceptance, intercultural understanding, interfaith collaboration, and school inclusivity programs are ways of supplementing mere toleration. There is a complex cultural and pedagogical story to be told about how such efforts might be organized and whether and why such efforts are successful. But the focus of this chapter is conceptual, not empirical. At the conceptual level, the question is what justifies the move beyond toleration, what leads us to go beyond the negative disengagement of toleration toward the positive engagement of hospitality. I mentioned that the call for hospitality has roots in religious traditions: we see it in religious texts, in the idea of the Golden Rule, and in the parable of the Good Samaritan. But given our discussion above, about the kind of radical diversity and remaining enmity that exists in the condition of modus vivendi, it seems obvious that calls for hospitality that are grounded within religious or ethical worldviews (within what Rawls would call comprehensive schemes) will not work to push us beyond a grudging modus vivendi.

Perhaps calls for hospitality simply demand more than can be obtained in a world of strangers and enemies. Value pluralism and radical diversity may mean that toleration is the best we can hope for. But I will suggest an argument here that may be used to supplement toleration: a moral argument based in the existential needs of individuals and a political argument that aspires toward a kind of cosmopolitan humanity. These arguments would be rejected by a realist such as Horton; and they may demand more than is supportable by Rawlsian liberal theory which focuses on justification within the common norms of public reason within a polity. Such arguments thus move us beyond mere toleration and beyond Rawlsian liberalism.

A Moral Argument Based in Existential Need and Compassion

A moral argument for hospitality begins with the basic needs of common humanity, including the common human need to build and establish moral relations with other people. As one anthropological essay explains, "One of the principal functions of any act of hospitality is either (in the case of an existing relationship) to consolidate the recognition that hosts and guest already share the same moral universe or (in the case of a new relationship) to enable the construction of a moral universe to which both host and guest agree to belong" (Selwyn 2000, p. 19). Rituals and practices of hospitality reinforce shared social relations within social groups; they also help to welcome newcomers and build new social relations. This structural/functional analysis can be supplemented by an even more basic argument that is found in the ancient Hebrew texts (cited above) that point out that those who have been strangers will recognize the value of hospitality. Each of us has been a stranger and may be one again. We can imagine ourselves in the place of a stranger, a visitor, and a refugee. In the parable of the Good Samaritan, this is explained in terms of compassion and the ability to see the need of the other. In Luke 10:33, Jesus explains that the Samaritan had compassion (*splagchnizomai* – in Latin, *misercordia*) that is based on seeing (*oida* from *eido*) the need of the injured man on the side of the road. Hospitality emerges as a human response to need. Trudy Conway explains this as follows:

"hospitality is neither decreed and enforceable by law, nor formally codified in detailed rules of etiquette. The gracious welcoming of the stranger into one's community is simply the humane response to the social other that makes civil society possible and renders diverse communities more livable" (Conway 2009, p. 5; see Derrida 2000). Conway grounds this in numerous examples of how basic rules of hospitality form the background of social relations in most of the world's cultures. The basic rule of hospitality is a moral rule for individuals, a customary rule, that is not grounded in law. As I have argued elsewhere, it grows out of a kind of Golden Rule ethic (see Fiala 2016). The basic idea of loving your neighbor as yourself points to the idea of welcoming strangers in need, listening to their stories, and remaining open to their presence and personality. Not only is the host guided by the morality of compassion but the guest is also guided by a similar responsiveness. Hospitality also instructs guests not to be rude and obnoxious. The guest ought to be humble and grateful, just as the host ought to be generous and gracious.

The norms of hospitality are either moral, religious, or customary norms found throughout the world's traditions. As such they demand more than what the mere toleration of the modus vivendi allows and what the domestic liberalism of public reason allows. In the first case, enmity is presumed as a constant problem; in the second case, the liberal polity is understood as focused primarily on negative rights, equality, and procedural justice that is not amenable the project of need satisfaction, care ethics, or compassion. Despite these criticisms, the fact that the moral norm of hospitality tends to be found throughout the world's traditions points us toward a cosmopolitan extension of the idea of hospitality.

A Political Argument Based in a Cosmopolitan Political Ideal

Moral hospitality is focused on relations among individuals. But this can be extended in ways that help inform political philosophy, social structures, and the legal system. I have already mentioned that inclusive multiculturalism can be understood in relation to the idea of welcoming strangers. Cosmopolitan political philosophy develops along similar lines. Kwame Anthony Appiah explains his idea of cosmopolitanism, for example, as an ethical and political idea for a "world of strangers." He focuses our attention on the basic idea of kindness to strangers, which is one of the titles of one of the chapters in his book, *Cosmopolitanism: Ethics in a World of Strangers* (Appiah 2006). Martha Nussbaum has more recently pointed out that the Stoic/Cynic tradition that gives rise to cosmopolitanism in the ancient world wanted to establish norms of respect for common humanity that extends to the wide world beyond the circles of social relations in which we live. She says of this idea of expanded circles of concern: "in general we should think of nobody as a stranger... in the end, human beings have fully equal worth" (Nussbaum 2019, p. 78). This idea developed from its ancient roots in Stoic and Cynic philosophy, with additions from Christianity, toward further development in the idea of the law of peoples as found in the early modern period (see Baker 2013) and on toward discussions of global justice that push beyond liberalism toward the idea of a cosmopolitan redistributive system.

This idea of cosmopolitan justice holds that hospitality is not merely a matter of individual charity but also that it is a matter of justice and right. Seyla Benhabib explains this in an essay on Kant's idea of hospitality in relation to contemporary proponents of global justice:

> Hospitality is not to be understood as a virtue of sociability, as the kindness and generosity one may show to strangers who come to one's land or who become dependent upon one's act of kindness through circumstances of nature or history; hospitality is a right which belongs to all human beings insofar as we view them as potential participants in a world republic (Benhabib 2004b, p. 1783).

This idea of hospitality as a right helps make the move beyond domestically oriented liberalism toward cosmopolitanism and the idea of a law of peoples that limits and regulates the behavior of states. We see this in Kant's political philosophy.

Kant's discussion in *Perpetual Peace* occurs against the backdrop of European colonialism and in response to the problem of stateless persons and noncitizens. Kant points out that what he has in mind in discussing the right to hospitality is part of a positive argument for peace that goes beyond a mere cessation of hostility. The other two positive conditions for peace are the spread of republican government and the creation of an international federation of peace. Kant also brings in an oblique defense of the need for freedom of speech and a kind of toleration. What he calls a "secret" article of peace is that philosophers ought to be consulted (presumably so that the state can be enlightened about the morality of war). Kant explains that the state might secretly invite philosophers to comment but, "it will allow them to speak freely and publicly on the universal maxims of warfare and peacemaking" (Kant 1991b, p. 115). He continues, "the philosopher should be given a hearing." And he concludes, "It is not expected that kings will philosophize or that philosophers will become kings... Kings or sovereign peoples should not, however, force the class of philosophers to disappear or to remain silent, but should allow them to speak publicly" (Kant 1991b, p. 115). In other words, the public use of reason ought to be encouraged as part of the project of bringing about peace, which is another way of saying that toleration of critical reason is part of the project of creating perpetual peace. Kant made this point again in the essay "What is Enlightenment?" where he called for something more than mere toleration. He explained that an enlightened prince would decline to accept the "presumptuous title of tolerance" (or the arrogant name of tolerance, *hochmütigen Namen der Toleranz*) (Kant 1991a, p. 58). Kant seems to think that the state ought to seek out enlightenment and consult with experts including philosophers who provide critical insight into the conduct of war, foreign policy, and violations of hospitality that undermine peace.

With toleration in the background as an assumption let us turn to Kant's account of hospitality. Kant describes the third condition for peace as follows: "cosmopolitan right shall be limited to the conditions of universal hospitality" (Kant 1991b, p. 105). Kant explains that because the earth is finite, people will find themselves together with other people and must "necessarily tolerate (*dulden*) one another's company" (Kant 1991b, p. 106). But hospitality appears to go a step further than a mere strategy of avoidance. Kant further explains, "Hospitality means the right of a stranger not to be treated with hostility when he arrives on someone else's territory" (Kant 1991b, 105). But he also suggests that visitors and guests have an obligation not to invade, exploit, and enslave. Kant focuses on the bad behavior of Western colonial powers who have been behaving "inhospitably" and "unjustly" in far-flung places by invading, enslaving, and exploiting native populations (Kant 1991b, 105–107; see Fiala 2014). World peace will develop when visitors and guests behave hospitably, which means respecting one another's human rights broadly conceived – to be received with respect and to behave respectfully when welcomed.

At issue here is not toleration, as understood in terms of a negative relation in which we leave one another alone. The question of hospitality arises, for Kant, because of the fact that aggressive Western powers violated the spirit of hospitality and created conditions that are disruptive of peace. The point is that Kant is describing norms for a world that is already interconnected – and in ways that extend far beyond a basic, grudging modus vivendi. The cosmopolitan idea of hospitality asks us to consider an interconnected world in which we need universal moral norms to help regulate the behavior of guests, hosts, visitors, trading parties, embassies, messengers, refugees, and those who offer asylum. We move beyond basic toleration as we circulate and move between and across borders in a world that has become even more mixed and interconnected in the centuries since Kant was writing. Toleration is a basic guide for what may not be done. But beyond toleration is a more positive claim about the right to be welcomed and treated with humanity (along with a claim about the need of political authority to seek out enlightenment by consulting those who offer critical insight).

Kant's view represents a progressive stage in the development of thinking about international law and the law of peoples, building upon previous work by Vitoria, Vattel, Grotius, and Pufendorf. It is important to note in reference to this historical development that the earlier European accounts of hospitality were offered in support of European colonialism. Francisco Vitoria, for example, discussed hospitality in the 1530s with regard to the right of Spanish colonization, which he grounded in an account of hospitality that he found in the "law of nations" – as outlined in the Christian tradition. Vitoria argued that there was a basic right of strangers to be received hospitably that was grounded in Biblical scripture and in Natural Law with roots extending back to Virgil's *Aenid*. He concluded on this basis that "refusal to receive strangers and foreigners is wrong in itself" (Vitoria 1532, Third Section). Vitoria's claim that the Spanish had a right to be greeted hospitably by the native American was warped by rapacious colonial policy, his basic idea of hospitality as a principle of international law was taken up and developed further. The warping of this idea is seen in Vitoria's claim that when the natives refused hospitality – and refused to allow the Spanish to proselytize and trade with them – the Spanish had a right to respond aggressively. These ideas were debated further by Las Casas, who offered a less cynical account of Indian hospitality, and others, culminating in Kant's theory of hospitality.

Kant reinterpreted the idea of hospitality that Vitoria and others had used to justify colonialism. Robert Wai concludes, "Kant clearly rejected the expansive interpretation of a cosmopolitan right of hospitality as a right to trade or a right to occupation. Kant accepted that a host society could have ethical reasons for refusing to trade with a foreigner" (Wai 2011, 164; also see Brown 2010). Kant's discussion of hospitality could thus be read as an incipient critique or European colonialism (see Fiala 2014). While not denying that Kant remains a source of Eurocentrism and racism (see Park 2013), I mean that Kant seems to understand that nations, such as China and Japan, who behave inhospitably toward Western powers may be justified in doing so. He says that China and Japan have "wisely placed restrictions" on Europeans. And Kant criticizes the hypocrisy of colonial powers who "make endless ado about their piety, and who wish to be considered as chosen believers while they live on the fruits of iniquity." This discussion reminds us that hospitality can be employed for ideological purposes – and that a genuinely cosmopolitan development of hospitality must be careful to avoid using hospitality as a wedge or a cudgel.

Since Kant wrote, these ideas have developed further toward a more robust idea of international law, as embodied in treaties and in institutions such as the United Nations. There is a developed set of ideas about the importance of hospitality seen in ideas about the right to asylum, the rights of refugees, and underlying this, the question of a basic moral obligation to provide positive care and assistance for strangers in need (see Benhabib 2004a; Schott 2009; Meckstroth 2018). At a basic level, hospitality can be understood as a supplement to toleration which demands something more than merely leaving the other alone. It may also be thought of part of a continuum of development in which liberal ideas are extended in a cosmopolitan direction (we saw this above with regard to Rawls who seemed to imply a kind of developmental model that goes from modus vivendi to liberalism). This helps explain why contemporary theorists (mistakenly on my interpretation) describe toleration in more positive terms – as demanding positive recognition, affirmation, and acceptance: it is likely that what is being asked for is not merely toleration but rather hospitality and that the natural inclination of people who equivocate in this way is to simplify the continuum under the rubric of toleration. But Kant's claim that tolerance remains arrogant provides us with a clue: beyond toleration is hospitality as a universal right as well as active consultation of alternative points of view in search of enlightenment.

In subsequent discussions of cosmopolitanism, there is a remaining question of the scope of the idea: whether it is a moral ideal with thick universal roots or a merely a historical achievement developed through an empirical process of treaty formation, institution building, and so on (see Brown 2013). As I have discussed it here, cosmopolitan hospitality exists as an aspiration that aims to move beyond liberal political philosophy that is focused on the nation state. But it is possible that in the international arena we return to something like the modus vivendi approach. Perhaps it is possible for domestic political arrangements to move from modus vivendi to liberal polity. But when the international arena is understood as a further iteration of the Hobbesian struggle, realists such as Horton may argue that international law and universal ideas about cosmopolitan right are merely forms of a modus vivendi which do not rest upon any deeper moral or metaphysical foundation.

Summary and Future Directions: The Task of Practical Wisdom and Enlightenment

Let's return, in conclusion, to an Aristotlelian vantage point for understanding the continuum that connects toleration and hospitality. Aristotle reminds us that virtue is a mean. He also suggests that practical wisdom ought to lead to a unity of the virtues (see Telfer 1989). The virtue of tolerance falls, as a mean, between intolerant bitterness and obsequious flattery. Hospitality can also be analyzed in this way, with the virtue of hospitality located between inhospitable coldness and sycophantic deference. One can be entirely unwelcoming to strangers or too unctuous and submissive in welcoming everyone: one can refuse to welcome guests or one can allow guests to take advantage of welcoming kindness. When toleration and hospitality are understood in this Aristotelian way as virtues found in the mean, and in connection to the goal of finding a unity of the virtues, we can understand the difficult task of practical wisdom. We ought to aim to find a balance between tolerance and hospitality, while also seeking to integrate these virtues with other virtues including justice, self-control (sophrosyne), self-respect, courage, honesty, compassion, and wisdom itself.

In this chapter, I have shown how difficult this project is, given the complexity of both toleration and hospitality. We have seen that toleration and hospitality are interrelated and connected along a continuum. We have discussed how toleration is related to the idea of negative rights, while hospitality is related to the idea of positive rights. We have seen how hospitality and toleration are grounded in different theories of social and political philosophy and ethics. Different theories of politics, morality, and social life will integrate these values in different ways. Practical wisdom and enlightenment can be developed by thinking more carefully about how this integration ought to take place.

References

Appiah KA (2006) Cosmopolitanism: ethics in a world of strangers. Norton, New York

Aristotle (1934) Nicomachean ethics. In Aristotle in 23 Volumes, Vol. 19 (trans: Rackham H). Harvard University Press/William Heinemann Ltd., Cambridge, MA,/London. Greek text at http://www.perseus.tufts.edu/

Aurelius M (1969) Meditations, trans. by Maxwell Staniforth. (Baltimore: Penguin, 1969). Also see Marcus Aurelius, Meditations, trans. by A.S.L Farquharson with introduction by Andrew Fiala (New York: Barnes and Noble, 2003); and The Communings with Himself of Marcus Aurelius, Emperor of Rome, revised text and translation by C.R. Haines (Cambridge, MA: Harvard University Press, 1961)

Avramenko R, Promisel M (2018) When toleration becomes a vice: naming Aristotle's third unnamed virtue. Am J Polit Sci 62(4):849–860

Baker G (2013) Right of entry or right of refusal? Hospitality in the law of nature and nations. In: Baker G (ed) Hospitality and world politics. Palgrave Macmillan, London

Benhabib S (2004a) The rights of others: aliens, residents, and citizens. Cambridge University Press, Cambridge

Benhabib S (2004b) The law of peoples, distributive justice, and migrations. Fordham Law Rev 2004:1761–1787. Available at: http://ir.lawnet.fordham.edu/flr/vol72/iss5/19

Boersema D (2017) Peace: negative and positive. In: Fiala A (ed) The Routledge handbook of pacifism and nonviolence. Routledge, New York

Brown G (2010) The Laws of hospitality, asylum seekers, and cosmopolitan right: a Kantian response to Jacque Derrida. Eur J Polit Theo 9(3):308–327

Brown G (2013) Between naturalism and cosmopolitan law. In: Baker G (ed) Hospitality and world politics. Palgrave Macmillan, London

Churchill RP (2007) Moral toleration and deep reconciliation. Philos Contemp World 14(1 (Spring)):100–113

Churchill RP (2015) Liberal toleration. In: Fiala A (ed) The Bloomsbury companion to political philosophy. Bloomsbury, London

Conway T (2009) From tolerance to hospitality: problematic limits of a negative virtue. Philos Contemp World 16(1 (Spring)):1–13

Derrida J (2000) Hospitality. Stanford University Press, Stanford

Derrida J (2001) Cosmopolitanism and forgiveness. Routledge, New York

Fiala A (2003) Toleration. Internet encyclopedia of philosophy. http://www.utm.edu/research/iep/t/tolerati.htm. First published Spring 2003

Fiala A (2005) Tolerance and the ethical life. Continuum, London

Fiala A (2013) Religious liberty and the virtue of civility in democratic and religiously diverse communities. In: Fiala A, Biondo V (eds) Civility and education in a world of religious pluralism. Routledge, New York

Fiala A (2014) Eurocentrism, hospitality, and the long dialogue with China. In: Wang K, Demenchonok E (eds) Intercultural dialogue: in search of harmony in diversity. Cambridge Scholars Publishing, Cambridge

Fiala A (2016) Secular cosmopolitanism, hospitality, and religious pluralism. Routledge, New York

Fiala A (2018) Transformative pacifism. Bloomsbury, London

Fiala A (2021) The capitalist peace and pacific capitalism. In: Lal S (ed) Peaceful Approaches for a more Peaceful World. Brill, Leiden, forthcoming

Forst R (2013) Toleration in conflict: past and present. Cambridge University Press, Cambridge

Friese H (2009) The limits of hospitality. Paragraph 32(1):51–68. www.jstor.org/stable/43151905

Galeotti AE (2002) Toleration as recognition. Cambridge University Press, Cambridge

Galtung J (1964) An editorial: what is peace research? J Peace Res 1:1

Heyd D (1996) Toleration: an elusive virtue. Princeton University Press, Princeton

Horton J (2010) Realism, liberal moralism and a political theory of modus vivendi. Eur J Polit Theo 9(4):431–448. https://doi.org/10.1177/1474885110374004

Horton J (2011) Modus vivendi and religious conflict. In: Mookherjee M (ed) Democracy, religious pluralism and the Liberal dilemma of accommodation. Springer, Dordrecht

Horton J (2019) Toleration and modus vivendi. Crit Rev Int Soc Polit Phil 2019:1–19. https://doi.org/10.1080/13698230.2019.1616879

Jones P (2017) The political theory of modus vivendi. Philosophia 45:443. https://doi.org/10.1007/s11406-016-9800-1

Kant I (1991a) What is enlightenment? In: Kant's political writings. Cambridge University Press, Cambridge

Kant I (1991b) Perpetual peace in Kant's political writings. Cambridge University Press, Cambridge

Meckstroth C (2018) Hospitality, or Kant's critique of cosmopolitanism and human rights. Political Theory 46(4):537–559

Murphy AR (1997) Tolerance, toleration, and the liberal tradition. Polity 29(4 (Summer)):593–623

Newey G (2017) Modus vivendi, toleration and power. Philosophia 45:425–442. https://doi.org/10.1007/s11406-016-9798-4

Nussbaum M (2019) The cosmopolitan tradition: a flawed but Noble idea. Harvard University Press, Cambridge, MA

Nys T, Engeln B (2008) Tolerance: a virtue? Towards a broad and descriptive definition of tolerance. Philos Contemp World 15(1 (Spring)):44–53

Oberdieck H (2001) Tolerance: between forbearance and acceptance. Rowman and Littlefield, Lanham

Park PKJ (2013) Africa, Asia and the history of philosophy: racism in the formation of the philosophical canon. SUNY Press, Albany

Penner T (1973) The unity of virtue. Philos Rev 82(1):35–68

Rawls J (1971) A theory of justice. Harvard University Press, Cambridge, MA

Rawls J (1987) The idea of an overlapping consensus. Oxford J Leg Stud 7(1 (Spring)):1–25

Rawls J (2005) Political liberalism, Expanded Edition. Columbia University Press, New York

Schott RM (2009) Kant and Arendt on hospitality. Jahrbuch für Recht und Ethik/Annu Rev Law Ethics 17:183–194

Selwyn T (2000) An anthropology of hospitality. In: Lashley C, Morrison A (eds) Search of hospitality: theoretical perspectives and debates. Butterworth/Heineman, Oxford

Seneca (1917–1925) Ad Lucilium Epistulae Morales, volume 1–3 (trans: Gummere RM). Harvard University Press/William Heinemann, Ltd.; Cambridge, MA/London. (at perseus.tufts.edu)

Shepherd A (2014) The gift of the other: levinas, derrida, and a theology of hospitality. James Clarke & Co., Cambridge

Sheringham C, Daruwalla P (2007) Transgressing hospitality. In: Morrison AJ, Lynch P, Lashley C (eds) Hospitality: a social lens. Elsevier, Amsterdam

Telfer E (1989) The Unity of the moral virtues in Aristotle's 'Nicomachean ethics'. Proc Aristot Soc 90:35–48

United Nations (1995) Declaration of day of tolerance (1995) at: http://portal.unesco.org/en/ev.php-URL_ID=13175&URL_DO=DO_TOPIC&URL_SECTION=201.html

Van Driel B, Darmody M, Kerzil J (2016) "Education policies and practices to foster tolerance, respect for diversity and civic responsibility in children and young people in the EU" NESET II report. Publications Office of the European Union, Luxembourg. https://doi.org/10.2766/46172

Vitoria F (1532) De Indis (On the Indians). In: Scott JB, Nys E (eds) De Jure Belli (1532). Oceana Publications Inc./Wiley, New York/London. (1964) Wikisource: https://en.wikisource.org/wiki/De_Indis_De_Jure_Belli/Part_2

Wai R (2011) The cosmopolitanism of transnational economic law. In: Bailliet C, Aas KF (eds) Cosmopolitan justice and its discontents. Routledge, London

Weber B (2016) To tolerate means to insult: towards a social practice of recognition. In: Zirk-Sadowski M, Wojciechowski B, Cern KM (eds) Towards recognition of minority groups. Routledge, London

Williams B (1996) Toleration: an impossible virtue? In: Heyd D (ed) Toleration: an elusive virtue. Princeton University Press, Princeton

Toleration and Compassion: A Conceptual Comparison

39

Yossi Nehushtan and Emily Prince

Contents

Introduction	778
Toleration and Compassion: Definition	778
Reasons for Toleration and Compassion	781
Toleration and Compassion, Acts and Omissions	786
Toleration, Compassion, and Power	787
Are Toleration and Compassion Moral Virtues?	790
Summary and Future Directions	794
References	795

Abstract

This chapter aims to explore a currently underdeveloped conceptual comparison between toleration and compassion. The chapter clarifies the meaning of toleration and compassion, highlights a few misconceptions regarding both concepts, and describes the often overlooked differences and similarities between them. As to toleration, it entails making adverse judgment about another, having reasons to harm another, and not acting on those reasons. As to compassion, it entails witnessing the suffering of another and acting in order to alleviate this suffering. Building on these definitions, we find that both toleration and compassion can result from the same state of mind and be justified behind the "veil of ignorance"; both can result in the same behavior – and be expressed simultaneously; both can be expressed by either acts or omissions; both can be exercised by the powerless; and both may be desirable under certain circumstances – yet both are not moral virtues, that is, they are not inherently morally valuable.

Y. Nehushtan (✉)
Keele University, Newcastle-Under-Lyme, UK
e-mail: y.nehushtan@keele.ac.uk

E. Prince
University of Sheffield, Sheffield, UK

© The Author(s), under exclusive licence to Springer Nature Switzerland AG 2022
M. Sardoč (ed.), *The Palgrave Handbook of Toleration*,
https://doi.org/10.1007/978-3-030-42121-2_38

Keywords

Toleration · Compassion · Harm · Power · Moral virtue · Empathy · Sympathy · Pity

Introduction

This chapter aims to clarify the meaning of toleration and compassion, to highlight a few misconceptions regarding both concepts, and to describe the often overlooked differences and similarities between them. Both toleration and compassion are complex concepts. Both entail a complex state of mind and a nonintuitive behavior toward others. And both are often misunderstood – and being wrongly equated with other concepts.

The chapter starts with a brief definition of toleration and compassion, asserting that toleration entails making adverse judgment about another, having reasons to harm another, and not acting on those reasons; whereas compassion entails witnessing the suffering of another and acting in order to alleviate this suffering. Section "Reasons for Toleration and Compassion" explains why despite the clear differences between toleration and compassion, both can result from the same feelings (e.g., sympathy, empathy, and pity) – and both can be justified by using the intellectual exercise of being behind the "veil of ignorance." Section "Toleration and Compassion, Acts and Omissions" describes why the common view, according to which toleration entails an omission (not acting) while compassion entails positive acts, is misguided, as both toleration and compassion can be expressed by both acts and omissions. Section "Toleration, Compassion, and Power" explores the relation between toleration, compassion, and power, and concludes that even though having absolutely no power prevents one from being either tolerant or compassionate, these cases are quite rare, which means that the powerless can normally also be tolerant or compassionate after all. Section "Are Toleration and Compassion Moral Virtues?" concludes the conceptual analysis and clarifies why both toleration and compassion are not moral virtues, that is, why they are not inherently morally valuable.

Toleration and Compassion: Definition

There are many different, and often conflicting, formulations of toleration and compassion to be found in academic writings, with little consensus on definite features of the concepts. Here we will offer our definitions of both concepts and will build on these definitions to illustrate the often overlooked differences and similarities between the meaning and practice of both toleration and compassion.

As to toleration, Nehushtan suggests that at its essence it means refraining from harming others, although the tolerant person has good reasons (in her opinion) to harm them (Nehushtan 2015). More specifically, the tolerant person makes an adverse judgment about another person, the adverse judgment provides the tolerant person with reasons to harm the other, but the tolerant person restrains herself and avoids harming the other. Balint offers a similar definition according to which toleration entails "an objection, the power to negatively act on this objection, and intentionally not acting in this way" (Balint 2017). The relation between being tolerant and having the power to not tolerate will be discussed below. Here we focus on the elements of adverse judgment, having reasons to harm the other, and intentionally deciding to not act on these reasons.

The objection or the adverse judgment about the other can be aimed toward both other people as such and their behavior or views. It may be limited to the moral values of the other person – or extend to mere dislike or disapproval for any reason. There is wide agreement that "the objection component" is part of the definition of toleration (Forst 2003), and that it refers to something one would prefer did not exist (Tailche 2017). That "something" can range from a slightly disruptive neighbor up to one's ethnicity or sexual identity. Toleration and its "objection component" do not require a moral element, appealing to the belief system of the one who is being tolerated. As Cohen rightly argues, "one can tolerate another's behaviour... that one dislikes, though one recognises that there is nothing morally wrong with it" (Cohen 2004).

The tolerant person has a specific kind of objection towards another or makes an adverse judgment of a certain kind about them. This objection or adverse judgment is of a kind that gives the tolerant person reasons to harm the other person. X may morally object to Y's behavior (e.g., Y cheating on their partner), yet that objection may not provide X any reasons to harm Y. Not harming Y, therefore, will not be an act of toleration. In all the cases where the need to harm the other person is not evoked, the element of restraint does not exist. It is important to distinguish between cases in which a person or the state has no reason to harm the other and cases in which such reasons do exist. The principle of toleration reflects the second category. The first category may involve other terms such as recognition, acceptance, understanding, indifference, approval, and apathy, among others. Although these terms might be combined in the discourse of toleration in certain contexts, they do not explain the core meaning of the concept. It is therefore misguided to argue, for example, that most people are tolerant out of indifference (Balint 2017). Those who do not care about the behavior of the other person, those who are indifferent toward it, do not have reasons to harm that person, do not have to restrain themselves, and are therefore indeed indifferent, but not tolerant.

The first two elements of toleration are objection and reasons to harm the "thing" to which we object. The third element is that of restraint, whereby the tolerant person decides not to act on the reasons to harm the other. The element of restraint suggests that an intentional decision to not harm the other must be made. Although toleration involves the lack of a negative interference (an omission to act) mere inaction is not enough, it must be chosen (Cohen 2004). The reasons for intentionally deciding to avoid harming the other could be of any kind, as will be elaborated below.

Toleration, therefore, includes elements that may be perceived as "negative," such as making adverse judgments about others, as well as elements that are normally seen as desirable, such as not harming others. It is this combination of an attitude that may cause discomfort (as no one desires being merely tolerated) and an attitude that is normally encouraged (not harming others) that causes the confusion between toleration and other related concepts.

As with toleration, the concept of compassion has often been misunderstood and at times disregarded. And much like toleration, the outlook on compassion has often been negative, but for different reasons. Describing compassion as an emotion has frequently put it at odds with principles such as rationality and objectivity, with feminist scholars also arguing that women are further disadvantaged due to the use of "derogatory terms" such as "emotional beings" (Wilkinson 2017). Additionally, and similarly to toleration, compassion – despite being perceived as "negative" in a certain, limited way – is generally perceived as positive, perhaps even as a moral virtue. Reilly, for example, views it as a "primitive responsiveness" (Reilly 2008), suggesting we all have it within us to innately act toward fellow human beings in a compassionate manner.

It is rare that scholars settle easily on a definition of compassion, with most leaning to defining it in the form of a multilayered process rather than as a single term. Some, such as Feenan (2017), do not decide on a definition at all, preferring to discuss compassion in terms of its object. This does not seem a helpful approach as, in order to discuss and implement the concept with any consistency, some form of objectivity and conceptual clarity is necessary. Here, compassion will be taken as a three-stage process, instead of as one fixed emotion. This appears to be the generally acceptable approach, incorporating the main principles whilst also conveniently aligning with the Oxford English Dictionary definition (Gerdy 2008). The first part of compassion involves witnessing suffering, the second states that the suffering is of another being, and the third step is a desire to alleviate this suffering. The Latin roots of the word compassion are "compati" meaning "to bear or suffer" (Jazaieri 2018) and so it seems only natural that this would be the object of a compassionate response. Suffering may be defined as undergoing "an impact that is too much... subjected to what is too intense for it to be objectified by the suffering self as a coherent experience" (Diamantides 2017). This, by all accounts extreme feeling of the sufferer, is witnessed by the observer at a distance, separated from them (Nussbaum 1996), to assess the seriousness of the suffering. This then leads to the final step: a "call to action" (Bandes 2017), whereby the observer tries to relieve the condition of the sufferer. As discussed below, it is this final step which is perhaps the most important in defining compassion.

Common understandings of compassion conflate it with concepts such as sympathy, empathy, and pity. Emotion terminology is always slippery (Bandes 2017) and with the terms being used interchangeably in everyday speech, it is easy to see why this confusion occurs. The exact differences between the concepts will not be discussed at length here; however, it is important for clarity, and to foster a better understanding of the practical importance of compassion, to note the main distinctions. The third part of the process of compassion takes it one step further than both empathy and sympathy; instead of simply feeling with or for the sufferer, the compassionate observer is moved to try to help alleviate the suffering they see. It elicits a practical response.

Neuroscientific research has documented distinctions between responses in feelings of empathy and compassion (Gu et al. 2017), confirming the need to keep the terms separate in order to effectively nurture this pragmatic reaction. A scientific study defined compassion as "a feeling of concern for the suffering of others that is associated with the motivation to help" and empathy as shared emotion (Klimecki et al. 2014). They found "distinct patterns of functional brain plasticity" (how the brain modified itself) and concluded that "training two seemingly similar social emotions altered brain activation… and changed affective responses of opposing valence." Although this does not prove that the defining feature of compassion is the desire to stop the suffering witnessed, it does provide evidence that there is a neurological difference between empathic and compassionate responses. This suggests that it is correct to view the two terms as distinct from one another and that it is important to find a way in which to do this, as for example here with the differentiation based on motivation to alleviate suffering.

At the definition level, the differences between toleration and compassion are quite clear. Toleration entails making adverse judgment about others – whereas compassion entails feeling empathy, sympathy, or pity toward others. Toleration entails having reasons to harm the other – whereas compassion entails no such thing. Toleration entails "not harming" which is typically the result of not acting – whereas compassion entails alleviating the other's suffering which normally requires a positive act. Yet these two clearly distinct concepts do have surprising similarities. They also interact in ways that justify rethinking the relation between them. These are the two themes that guide the following discussion.

Reasons for Toleration and Compassion

Tolerant behaviors could result from several reasons or motives. They can be identical in their outcome but the reasons underlying these behaviors may vary. Two main reasons for toleration or two types of toleration can be noted: toleration as a right, and utilitarian-pragmatic toleration (Nehushtan 2015).

Toleration as a right means that one has the right to be tolerated while others are under a duty to tolerate. If the tolerant person acknowledges this right, she refrains from harming what she considers negative, since she acknowledges the fact that the other person has a right to err or to behave negatively. Alternatively, she acknowledges that the other person has a right not to be harmed despite the tolerant person's adverse judgment of the other's behavior, opinions, or identity.

The other kind of toleration is utilitarian-pragmatic toleration. Here, the tolerant person tolerates the other – although the tolerant person has reasons to harm them – because she thinks that under the current circumstances, it is preferable for her or for society in general to tolerate the other person. Here, toleration has no inherent moral value. The main characteristic of this type of toleration is its temporariness. The tolerant person opts for toleration not out of acknowledgment of the other's right, but rather as the outcome of a risk assessment at a given time and place.

But toleration may also result from the same reasons that could lead to a compassionate approach, and in fact – may exist alongside compassion. A convict, for example, may be granted a pardon due to his bad health, despite the authorities having reasons not to grant a pardon – reasons that are derived from the adverse judgment that they make about the convict or his deeds. The prisoner does not have a right to be granted a pardon and there are not necessarily pragmatic reasons to justify it. Granting the pardon in this case may be perceived as an act of both toleration and compassion. Generally, a compassionate behavior is the result of witnessing the suffering of others and wishing to alleviate this suffering. But in certain cases where we make an adverse judgment about the sufferer or their deeds, this adverse judgment may give us reasons to not make the sufferer better-off, even though we could easily help them. We may, however, decide to not act on these reasons and improve the situation of the sufferer after all, as we either recognize, understand, or share the sufferer's distress. In these special cases, compassion exists alongside toleration. We may also say that the reason for toleration in such cases is either sympathy, empathy, or pity, and that the act of alleviating the suffering of the sufferer is an act of both toleration and compassion at the same time. It would have been an act of compassion only, and not that of toleration as well, if we made no adverse judgment about the sufferer, and if the only sentiments we had toward them were those of sympathy, empathy, or pity.

In other cases, we may sympathize or empathize with the sufferer, yet decide not to make them better-off even though we could easily help them. If our decision results from an adverse judgment we make about the sufferer or their deeds, then we still sympathize or empathize with the sufferer but at the same time act with intolerance toward them. In that specific case, the refusal to be compassionate is in fact an act of intolerance. That would be the case, for example, when we genuinely sympathize or empathize with a convict who asks for a pardon due to his bad health, yet we decline the convict's plea for a pardon because we accord more weight to the convict's victims' suffering or distress, should the convict get the pardon. Here, we act on the reasons to harm the convict – by preventing his early release – and are therefore being intolerant towards him. Accordingly, we do not act on our feelings of empathy or sympathy and are therefore not being compassionate toward him.

Toleration, therefore, can result from acknowledging the other's right to be tolerated; from pragmatic-utilitarian reasons; or from sympathy, empathy, or pity – thus being an act of compassion as well.

Compassion, much like toleration, is a combination of acts (or omissions), state of mind, and having certain reasons for these acts or omissions. We noted earlier that compassion may result from sympathy, empathy, or pity. That begs two questions regarding the reasons for compassion. The first is whether compassion can also result from pragmatic-utilitarian reasons. The second is why one would or should act on their feelings of sympathy, empathy, or pity, or put differently – what could morally justify a compassionate act.

As to the first question: one can witness the suffering of another and act in order to alleviate this suffering, without feeling any sympathy, empathy, or pity towards the sufferer. The reasons for alleviating the suffering of the other can be purely utilitarian, even selfish, for example, being praised for one's generosity, gaining social status or social acceptance or forgiveness, impressing others who may then benefit the "compassionate" in return, or gaining political power. However, while toleration can result from utilitarian reasons – compassion cannot. A tolerant attitude starts with making an adverse judgment about another. Even when the tolerant person decides to not harm the other, that adverse judgment does not disappear. The core of toleration is not acting on the reasons one has for harming another. The core of toleration is the element of restraint. The reasons for this restraint are irrelevant so far as we ask whether a certain behavior is tolerant. The reasons are only relevant for deciding which type of toleration is being exercised: toleration as a right, toleration out of utilitarian reasons or toleration out of empathy, sympathy, or pity. Compassion, however, entails a certain positive attitude toward the sufferer. It requires sincerity or good will. Unlike toleration, compassion cannot be exercised with grudge or with lack of good faith. A compassionate act does not have to be a pure altruistic act (if such acts exist at all) – but its dominant motive must result from feelings such as empathy, sympathy, or pity – that will in turn trigger one to act in order to alleviate the suffering of another.

As to the second question: we know that compassion may result from sympathy, empathy, or pity. But it is not always clear what would move people to act on these feelings and to therefore be compassionate. It is not therefore clear what the reasons for compassion could be. Unlike the reasons for toleration, we would normally not argue that others have a right to be treated with compassion, or that compassion is warranted for pragmatic-utilitarian reasons. The reasons for compassion lie, therefore, elsewhere.

According to Nussbaum (1996), compassion partly involves a realization that the observer may end up in the situation of the sufferer and so, due to this sense of community, we want to improve the situation of suffering for everyone. We may all be subject to the same levels of suffering and would not want to be in as bad a situation where the tables turned. This approach is very close to the Rawlsian intellectual exercise of making decisions behind a veil of ignorance (Rawls 1971). Generally speaking, and behind that hypothetical veil of ignorance, we are required to decide about the principles of justice that will exist in a certain society, without knowing who we will be in that society. We do not know our fortune in the distribution of natural assets and abilities, our intelligence, strengths, and weaknesses. We do not know our conceptions of the good or our special psychological propensities nor our place in society, our class position, or social status. All we know is that we will find ourselves in a certain society that will be governed by the principles of justice that are decided by us behind that veil of ignorance. In that position, we are rational persons concerned to further our own interests, but without knowing in full what these specific interests may be.

Being inspired by the idea of the veil of ignorance, it can be argued that we need to put ourselves in that position in order to decide which moral principles should guide our behavior. Each and every time a specific moral question arises, a question of a kind of "how should we treat others," we should distance ourselves from the specific case and imagine ourselves in a position where we need to provide a moral answer to the moral question, without knowing which "player" we are or end up being within that specific case. And within the context of compassion, we do not know if we end up being the sufferer, the observer, or an interested third party. We do know that after providing the moral answer to the moral question regarding that specific case, we could find ourselves as any of the "players" in the case. This will allow us to make moral decisions that will be universal, coherent, and consistent – rather than affected by our known position in a certain case.

It is often noted that compassion requires an aspect of the imagination (Del Mar 2017). We have to imagine the suffering that the other person is going through in order to try to alleviate it, necessitating some degree of creativity to know what the sufferer's personal situation might be. Putting ourselves in the shoes of another requires practice, particularly due to personal experiences and biases influencing our perceptions of others. Putting ourselves behind a veil of ignorance may help us in overcoming natural tendencies that may in turn lead us to refuse being compassionate toward others. We may view the suffering as a deserved consequence of the sufferer's behavior, which we deem as deviant, and will not feel sympathy, empathy, or pity toward the sufferer nor have a desire to stop the suffering. We may have "imaginative resistance" (Del Mar 2017) that results in reluctance to imagine the suffering of a convicted murderer, for example, in order to treat them compassionately. We may also believe we are unlikely to find ourselves in the situation of a convicted murderer and so do not see it as necessary to prevent their suffering. Putting ourselves behind a veil of ignorance may help us to avoid these natural tendencies. This is necessary in cases where there is no close relationship between the sufferer and the observer. But compassion (much like toleration) can also be the attitude between people who have close relationship.

Indeed, an obvious reason for compassion would be having a close relationship with the sufferer. There is an obvious positive correlation between the salience of the sufferer and levels of compassion shown. Where an individual is more important to us, we are more likely to react with higher levels of compassion. The task of putting ourselves in the sufferer's shoes is made easier when a loved one is concerned, as one naturally knows more about their life as a whole and the degree to which they may be suffering. This may also be the case when an individual is merely similar to someone important to us, for example, to a child or spouse as we are predisposed to care more for certain individuals. This can be reflected in our professional work (Diamantides 2017) and other aspects of life. When we see a sufferer who reminds us of ourselves or a salient person, similarity bias leads to higher levels of compassion. We are more likely to treat them almost as if they were a loved one and are inclined to do more to lighten their suffering.

It seems that putting ourselves behind a veil of ignorance, as rational, selfish, and risk-hating human-beings, will result in us being more compassionate toward others. It is easier to do it when the sufferer is a loved one, but the "veil of ignorance rationale" does not lose its strength when the sufferer is a stranger. The veil of ignorance rationale becomes in fact more important and meaningful when the sufferer is a stranger. This insight takes us back to the principle of toleration.

Unlike compassion, toleration does not have to result from feelings such as empathy, sympathy, or pity. Unlike compassion, toleration is a burden and is often perceived as a negative attitude. Toleration is almost always accompanied by disapproval and exercised grudgingly. A tolerant behavior might in fact offend the one who is being tolerated (Green 2008) as it is unpleasant to be tolerated. People and groups wish to be recognized as equals. They wish or demand that their values and ways of life are recognized as equal and worthy of respect – rather than just being tolerated. The tolerated person is a burden that lies on the tolerant person's shoulders. The tolerant person may even clarify this point to the tolerated person who indeed would have preferred that the equal treatment they receive would derive from recognition or respect rather than toleration. Compassion does not entail any of the above. However, the same veil of ignorance that provides a moral justification for compassion may also provide a moral justification for toleration. This is the case whether we perceive toleration as a right or as a behavior that can be justified by pragmatic-utilitarian reasons.

If the tolerant person believes that the other has a right to be tolerated, then the tolerant person acknowledges the right of the other to err or to behave badly, or she acknowledges the right of the other not to be harmed despite the adverse judgment that she makes about the other's behavior, opinions, or identity. The primary justification for the existence of the right to be tolerated lies in the importance attached to an individual's autonomy (Raz 1987). Autonomy, in this context, is the freedom granted to individuals to be "the authors of their own life" and thus make decisions that seem to others meaningless, wrong, or even damaging. Williams emphasizes that in order to acknowledge toleration as a right, we should acknowledge a certain "good" that justifies toleration as such and accept that that "good," in the liberal view, is the individual's autonomy (Williams 1999). But why should we perceive autonomy as valuable? Why should we allow people to be "the author of their own life," including allowing them to make wrongful and even harmful decisions? One possible answer is that behind a veil of ignorance, we would always prefer to live in a world where autonomy is perceived as valuable. Behind the veil of ignorance, and subject to a few possible exceptions, no rational, selfish, and risk-hating human being would prefer having less autonomy rather than more of it.

As to pragmatic-utilitarian toleration, it can be found in cases in which someone is tolerant because not tolerating the other would be too costly; or because they are not powerful enough to act intolerantly; or the damage to society as a whole resulting from not tolerating the other would outweigh the damage caused by that other person; or giving the power and the authority to the state not to tolerate the other person might lead to an exploitation of this power in unjustified cases; and so on. These paradigmatic cases explain the value of pragmatic-utilitarian toleration. They also explain why pragmatic-utilitarian toleration can be justified behind a veil of ignorance. Without knowing whether we end up as the ones who will be forced to tolerate others for utilitarian reasons – or as the ones that will not be harmed because they will be tolerated, and if we are rational, selfish, and risk-hating people, we would want to live in a society where toleration is being exercised also for pragmatic-utilitarian reasons.

It is therefore the intellectual exercise of putting ourselves behind a veil of ignorance that provides the moral justification for seeing toleration as a right, seeing toleration as an outcome of utilitarian calculation, and showing compassion toward people who we may not know.

Toleration and Compassion, Acts and Omissions

The common view is that toleration entails not harming the other whereas compassion entails acting in order to help the other. Toleration and compassion (and also intolerance and lack of compassion), however, may entail both positive acts – and omissions. Put differently, we can tolerate others by positively making them better-off; not tolerating them by not helping them; be compassionate toward others by not harming them or not making them worse-off; and showing lack of compassion by actively harming others.

Omissions in general pose an interesting case within the discourse of toleration, since an omission can be an expression of intolerance and toleration alike. An omission is an expression of intolerance toward others if they are worse-off (or not better off) as a result and if the omission results from an adverse judgment about them. This is passive intolerance as opposed to active intolerance, which finds its expression in acting in a way that harms someone.

Toleration normally means not harming others or not making them worse-off, even though the tolerant person thinks there are good reasons for harming others or making them worse-off. Normally we harm others by acts. But harm can also be caused by omission. A person's condition can be worsened in cases where we abstain from protecting them or helping them when either (a) others prevent them from doing something or force them to do it or (b) when they need help for any other reason. Therefore, if we do not prevent Y from harming X and if our sole or main motivation is an adverse judgment we make about X, we are being intolerant toward X (and perhaps, but not necessarily, tolerant toward Y).

Moreover, and regardless of the existence of Y who wishes to harm X, X's condition can be worsened simply because we avoid helping them (e.g., we refrain from donating money to them). If we avoid helping X only or mainly because we make an adverse judgment about them (or about their values, characteristics, or behavior), we are being intolerant toward them. Accordingly, if we choose to help X despite our adverse judgment, we are being tolerant toward them.

An omission will be an expression of toleration if the tolerant person avoids harming the other person despite the adverse judgment that they make about the other. That would be a case of passive toleration, as opposed to active toleration, which means acting in order to benefit someone despite the adverse judgment that is made about them. If we prevent Y from harming X, even though we make an adverse judgment about X, we may be intolerant toward Y (depending on the causes for our action) but in any case, we are being tolerant toward X – and we do that by actively helping them.

Compassion normally entails acting in order to help the sufferer, yet it can also entail refraining from harming others or from making them worse-off. To take one example: a policymaker who works for a commercial company may have to decide on a certain policy that will indirectly affect the well-being of others in a meaningful way. Let us assume that some of those who will be affected by this policy are currently experiencing suffering, and that the policymaker has only two options: they can decide on a policy that will financially benefit the commercial company but, as a side effect, will make the sufferers worse-off; or they can do nothing and leave the sufferers in their current position. Choosing the second option may well be an act of compassion. The policymaker identifies the suffering of those who will be affected by their new policy. The policymaker has good reason to decide on a policy that will make the sufferers worse-off; however, they may have feelings of sympathy, empathy, or pity toward the sufferers. By choosing to do nothing, to not apply the new policy, the policymaker acts on the feelings of sympathy, empathy, or pity, thus showing compassion toward the sufferers, yet without alleviating their suffering.

The attitude of the policymaker in this case cannot be described as toleration, because even though the policymaker had reasons to harm the sufferers (financially benefiting the commercial company) and even though the policymaker did not act on those reasons, the policymaker did not make any adverse judgment about the sufferers. The attitude of the policymaker can also not be described as sympathy, empathy, or pity, because they did not just have these feelings but in fact acted on them. Compassion better describes that attitude in this case, even though no suffering was alleviated.

Toleration, Compassion, and Power

The common view is that toleration can only be exercised by the powerful toward the powerless (Derrida 2003; Raphael 1988; Nicholson 1985). The "power" aspect of toleration, so it is argued, connotes a hierarchy between the person tolerating and the object of this toleration. It entails an idea of a "superior status" (Edyvane 2017). Forst goes further than that by arguing that the party tolerating must be in a "socially dominant position" (Forst 2003) with the power over the person being tolerated to negatively act toward their behavior if they wished. Negatively acting on this objection may be defined as prohibiting or suppressing the behavior one disapproves of (Edyvane 2017).

It is true that in order to be able to tolerate others, the tolerant person must necessarily have some control over the situation; that is, they must possess the ability to act on their objection or adverse judgment, should they so decide. Without the potential means to follow through with such an aversion, one cannot be said to be tolerant. This, however, should not be confused with being the powerful side or being in a socially dominant position. A person (or a group) can be normally and continuously powerless but also tolerant toward the powerful, as long as they are not completely powerless – and most people and groups are not. In cases of total lack of power, the powerless clearly cannot be tolerant since the element of restraint from harming the other or from acting on the adverse judgment that is made about the other does not exist. One who cannot harm the other or cannot act on their objection to the other, in any way or to any extent, cannot be perceived as someone who restrains herself and therefore cannot be perceived as tolerant. In these cases, it can be said that not harming the powerful or not acting on the objection to the powerful other is not an expression of toleration but merely an act of surrender or acquiescence (Augenstein 2010). However, such cases are extremely rare, and it seems that the academic writing does not refer to these kinds of cases when the link between toleration and power is discussed. The lack of power that is discussed here, and in the literature, refers to situations where one side is significantly more powerful than the other. It refers to a situation where the powerless can harm the powerful, but the harm caused will be relatively marginal, will not achieve its goal (at all or only marginally) and most importantly – might bring about a harsh counter-reaction of the harmed powerful or of a third party. Accordingly, the powerful are those who can harm another while taking the risk of suffering a marginal reaction, if any.

In these circumstances, there are several cases in which the behavior of the powerless can still be classified as tolerant. The powerless may make an adverse judgment about someone powerful. This adverse judgment may provide reasons to harm that powerful person. If the powerless refrains from acting upon these reasons – that is, refrains from harming the powerful – the powerless are being tolerant. If the powerless would have refrained from harming the powerful even if they had the power to harm them without suffering a non-marginal response, then the powerless are not only tolerant but also recognize the other's right to be tolerated. If the powerless refrain from harming the powerful only because currently they do not have enough power to harm them without suffering an undesirable counter-reaction, the powerless are still tolerant but for utilitarian reasons only.

In another example, two parties in a dispute could refrain from harming each other, although each of them has good reasons to harm the other. In such a case, they are mutually tolerant. The reason might stem from the fact that they are equally powerful and have an equal ability to harm each other. In this case, their equal ability to harm each other makes them powerless against each other. Their mutual toleration is not generated from the acknowledgment that the other has a right to be tolerated. It relies on utilitarian reasons, and as such it is temporary and subject to varying circumstances.

As noted above, it seems that the academic writing according to which the powerless cannot be tolerant does not relate to the rare and unimportant cases where the powerless cannot harm the other in any way. It seems that the situations at hand are those that depict substantial, at times ongoing, differences between the power possessed by the powerful and that of the powerless. This is the case, for example, in a relationship between a parent and child, the king and his subjects, and the majority group and minority groups. However, in all of these cases, the powerless can still harm or offend the powerful – or act on the objection to the powerful. A child who thinks she has good reasons to harm one of her parents can act upon these reasons and insult the parent, refuse to speak to him or cause damage to the parent's possessions. A subject who thinks he has good reasons to harm or offend the king can act upon these reasons and publicly ridicule the king. Members of a minority group who think they have good reasons to harm or offend the majority can condemn the majority's conduct, avoid the presence of members of the majority group, avoid trading with them, or ask a third party to intervene and harm the majority. More often than not, the intolerant act of the powerless will not be effective and will not achieve its goals. Their intolerant acts might be followed by a counter-reaction of the powerful which would make the powerless even worse-off. Nevertheless, as long as the powerless acts in order to harm the powerful because the powerless makes an adverse judgment about the powerful, the powerless is intolerant of the powerful. Accordingly, if the powerless refrains from taking these actions because of any reason whatsoever, then the powerless restrains themselves and are in fact tolerant.

All the above cases and examples do not contradict the common view that the tolerant must be in a position to voluntarily decide not to use their power to harm another despite their capacity to do so (Augenstein 2010). According to this view, without the capacity to harm someone and without making a voluntary decision not to harm them, we are facing, yet again, not an expression of toleration but merely an act of surrender or acquiescence. In all the above examples and cases, the powerless do have the ability to harm the powerful, yet the powerless may voluntarily decide to avoid harming the powerful because of various possible reasons.

The ability of the powerless to be intolerant toward the powerful and thus also to be tolerant towards them stems from the fact that intolerance, as well as toleration, can be exercised to various degrees. Classifying a certain behavior as intolerant does not depend upon the kind of negative attitude shown toward others or the extent of the harm inflicted on them. Any negative attitude toward the other is an expression of intolerance (if it results from an adverse judgment that was made about the other). The negative attitude toward the other can be expressed in relatively mild ways such as condemning the other, avoiding their presence or avoiding helping them. It could also be expressed in not such a mild way, by, for example, discriminating against someone, humiliating them or torturing them. All of these are expressions of intolerance to various extents. It is hard to imagine situations in the private sphere or in the public sphere in which the powerless cannot take even one action that expresses intolerance toward the powerful. When it is established that the powerless have the ability not to tolerate the powerful, it becomes clear that they could also tolerate the powerful.

Thus far it has been argued that toleration does not connote a hierarchy between the person tolerating and the object of this toleration, does not assume that the tolerant has "superior status," and does not require that the party tolerating must be in a socially dominant position. But even in cases where the tolerant is normally the powerful one, for example, when the tolerant side is the state itself, it may find itself powerless under certain circumstances. That temporary or context-specific lack of power may in fact be the reason for the normally powerful but now powerless' toleration. This would be a case of utilitarian-pragmatic toleration, where the normally powerful cannot achieve their goals at all or effectively through an intolerant behavior or cannot achieve their goals through an intolerant behavior without suffering a meaningful and harmful counter-reaction. To take one example, the state, which is normally the powerful party, may make an adverse judgment about the practice of religious-ritual circumcision that, let us assume, is being observed by religious minorities in that state. This adverse judgment may provide the state with reasons to interfere and harm the powerless minority by, for example, criminalizing ritual circumcision, thus being intolerant toward that practice and the religious people who wish to follow it. The state, however, may decide to refrain from criminalizing this practice, and by that to tolerate it. The state's toleration may result from acknowledging the importance of freedom of religion – but it may also result from its lack of power. The state may believe that an intolerant reaction toward ritual circumcision will be futile or that the harm that will be caused to society as a whole or to important public interests as a result of the state's intolerant response will outweigh the expected benefits. The state may tolerate the normally powerless minority due to lack of power to achieve its goals through an intolerant approach. Under these circumstances, the state is in fact the weaker party – and its weakness is the reason for its toleration. Toleration, therefore, can be exercised by both the powerful and the powerless. Things are slightly different, however, regarding compassion.

Compassion entails witnessing suffering of another being and acting in order to alleviate this suffering. A compassionate response does not have to involve hierarchy or element of condescension. The compassionate observer may be at a distance from the sufferer but not above them. There is not necessarily a power balance at play. The compassionate, however, must have the ability to act in order to alleviate the suffering of the other. Mere wish to alleviate the suffering of the other, without acting on that intention, would mean that the observer feels pity, sympathy, or empathy toward the sufferer, but is not being compassionate toward them. Regarding toleration – if one completely lacks the power to not tolerate others, then not acting on the reasons for not tolerating them cannot be perceived as toleration. Regarding compassion – if the observer completely lacks the power to act on their reasons for showing compassion toward others, they simply cannot be compassionate toward them. But much like the case regarding toleration, it is hard to think of cases where one is completely powerless – to the extent that it prevents them from being compassionate. This is so because, much like toleration (and intolerance), compassion can be exercised to various extents. Compassionate acts do not have to require great effort, time, or indeed – power. They can be trivial, perhaps even ineffective, precisely because the compassionate lacks the power or ability to do more than that, but as long as one acts on their feelings of sympathy, empathy, or pity, with an intention to alleviate the suffering of another, then that attitude can be perceived as compassion, regardless of its efficacy.

Are Toleration and Compassion Moral Virtues?

When we ask whether toleration and compassion are moral virtues, we ask whether they are valuable *as such*; whether they have intrinsic value, in the sense that their desirability is not contingent and does not hinge on the prospects on them leading to desirable results. For our purposes, we can think about two possible meanings of being "valuable as such" or for having "intrinsic value."

Intrinsic value type 1 can be expressed as: "X is always good regardless of the consequences." For example, "toleration is always valuable regardless of the circumstances or its consequences." This is probably the strongest, "purest" claim for something being valuable "as such." Some may claim that this is the only possible meaning of being "valuable as such."

Intrinsic value type 2 can be expressed as: "X always brings about better consequences than the alternatives." For example, "toleration always brings about better consequences than intolerance." This is a mixed argument with both instrumentalist and non-instrumentalist foundations (with the former being more dominant).

Toleration is often perceived as a mixture of an inherently good act and a morally dubious state of mind: inherently good act or result – as toleration results in "not harming"; morally dubious state of mind – because of the grudge that accompanies the tolerant behavior, as, after all, the tolerant person makes adverse judgment about others and restrains herself from acting on that judgment. But perhaps we should perceive both elements of toleration (not harming – and grudge) as neither good nor bad in themselves. Perhaps toleration itself (much like intolerance) is neither good nor bad. Toleration might be unjustified and even morally wrong if things that should not be tolerated are tolerated. Accordingly, intolerance might be justified and even morally necessary regarding things that should not be tolerated. The argument that toleration is a moral virtue and that one must always be tolerant is therefore misguided. If toleration is indeed always good and if to be tolerant is a moral duty, then intolerance is always bad. Even then, and if one must always be tolerant, it will never be justifiable to take measures to confront intolerance. But this categorical conclusion is clearly mistaken. All agree that sometimes we need not tolerate the intolerant (Nicholson 1985). But one surely cannot claim that because toleration is always good and intolerance always wrong, it is sometimes permissible not to tolerate the intolerant. This is simply self-contradictory.

Thus, the notion that toleration is a moral virtue is either misguided or does not mean that one should always be tolerant. All it may mean is that one should be tolerant unless compelling reasons allow or demand an intolerant response to something that is rightly perceived as wrong or "negative." Perhaps it would be better to give up entirely an attempt to describe or to justify toleration as good and simply to argue that toleration and intolerance are not end-points on a spectrum of good and bad but can be either good or bad according to the circumstances.

Therefore, classifying toleration as a moral virtue, as an interim virtue or as a lesser evil, cannot be part of the concept of toleration itself. At most, we can classify certain tolerant behaviors as morally necessary, morally allowed, lesser evils, or morally wrong. The question of how we should decide which tolerant behavior falls into which category is a normative and complex question that will not be discussed in more detail here. Suffice it to say that if the primary justification for the existence of the right for toleration lies in the importance attached to the individual's autonomy (Raz 1987); if toleration is a means to protect and promote an individual's autonomy;

and if the state has an obligation to protect and promote an individual's autonomy; then the state has to be tolerant. On the other hand, since intolerance means, inter alia, harming the other, then the same harm principle that allows the state to interfere with someone's liberty (or to harm him) in order to prevent him from unjustly harming another allows the state – and sometimes requires the state – to be intolerant toward those who are unjustly intolerant toward others.

Be that as it may, the one point that should not be overlooked is the all-important necessity of making a distinction between the concept of toleration and the practice or the value of toleration. As to the concept of toleration, it describes a behavior and a state of mind that are neither inherently morally good nor morally dubious. The concept of toleration is morally neutral in the sense that it does not describe a behavior that has any intrinsic value. Toleration, therefore, does not have any intrinsic value, as it is not always valuable regardless of the circumstances or its consequences, nor does it always bring about better consequences than intolerance.

Same can be said about the concept of compassion. The "starting point" regarding compassion is different to that of toleration. Whereas toleration is often described as a mix of positive and negative elements, compassion seems to entail nothing but positive elements: being aware of the suffering of another person – and acting, or at least trying to act to alleviate this suffering, acting on emotions such as sympathy, empathy, or pity. But compassion, much like toleration, is not a moral virtue. It does not have intrinsic value and it is not valuable as such regardless of the circumstance or its consequences. Being compassionate is morally warranted only toward those who deserve it.

If toleration and compassion are moral virtues, if they have intrinsic value and are always valuable, it may mean that we have a general moral duty to either tolerate others or be compassionate toward them. But that is not the case. We can think of four possible cases: (1) cases where we do have a duty to tolerate others or be compassionate toward them; (2) cases where we have an imperfect duty to tolerate others or be compassionate toward them; (3) having no such duty yet still being morally allowed to tolerate others or be compassionate toward them; and (4) having a moral duty to not tolerate others or be compassionate toward them. We will briefly discuss these cases in turn.

First, there are cases where we have a moral duty to tolerate others. In these cases, others have a right to be tolerated that is normally justified by the principle of autonomy, as discussed above. We may have a moral duty not to harm those who act in a way that we perceive as misguided, because being autonomous means having a right to do wrong without being subjected to sanctions. We may also have a moral duty to be compassionate toward others, to act in order to alleviate their suffering. This duty may arise within specific contexts, for example, when we are under a duty of care, which may include a duty to alleviate the suffering of those who are under our professional or personal care. We may also have a moral duty to be compassionate toward others, if, for example, they deserve compassion; we are better positioned to alleviate their suffering; doing so will require minimal effort of us; and we have no compelling reasons to not be compassionate toward them. "Good Samaritan" laws may entrench that moral duty as a legal one.

Second, there are cases where we have an imperfect duty to tolerate others or be compassionate toward them. Imperfect duties, for our purposes, are duties we should not ignore but at the same time we may be morally allowed to not act on them. As opposed to perfect duties – and even though we should always consider whether and how to follow them – they do not always dictate our behavior. Duties may be imperfect because perceiving them as perfect duties would be "asking for too much" of people. Donating money for charity or directly to those who are in need, for example, can be perceived as an act of compassion, if we accept that people can be compassionate from afar, without creating any direct contact with the sufferer. If we observe the suffering of those who are in need; feel sympathy, empathy, or pity toward them; and act on these feelings by donating money – and with an intention to alleviate the suffering of others – we can be perceived as compassionate. The duty to donate money to charity – or the duty to be compassionate toward those who are in need – is normally an imperfect duty. Its extent and even existence depend on changeable circumstances regarding both the observer and the sufferer. Even though donating money to charity and by doing so being compassionate toward those in need is almost always morally admirable, we do not always have a moral duty to take positive acts that are morally admirable. More specifically, it would be "too much" expecting people to take positive actions to alleviate the suffering of others, all others, each and every time they become aware of this suffering. It is easier to justify a moral duty to be compassionate when it entails not harming others rather than positively helping them, but even though compassion can be manifested by both acts and omissions, it is normally the positive act of helping that is part of a compassionate behavior. Therefore, the duty to be compassionate is generally an imperfect duty. Things are slightly different regarding toleration.

It is hard to think about the duty to tolerate others, in cases where this duty exists at all, as an imperfect duty, precisely because toleration normally entails not harming others rather than positively helping them. Put differently, the duty to tolerate asks less from us than the duty to be compassionate. When a duty to tolerate exists – and requires an omission (refraining from actively harming others) – it will almost never "ask too much of us" and will therefore normally be a perfect duty. The cases where toleration entails a positive act are quite rare. These are cases where one makes an adverse judgment about another; this adverse judgment gives the tolerant person reasons to harm the other, yet the tolerant person refrains from acting on these reasons – by not only by refraining from harming the other, but actually by actively helping the other or making them better-off. It seems that only very rarely will we have a moral duty to be tolerant by actively helping others. And when such a duty exists – it will be a perfect duty only within very specific contexts, presumably mostly in cases where the tolerant is the state itself or a professional that provides a certain service (e.g., medical staff).

The third case raises no special difficulties. There is nothing unusual about a situation where we are morally allowed to act in a certain way – without having a duty to do so.

The fourth case is where we have a moral duty to not tolerate others or be compassionate toward them. We already noted above that intolerance might be justified and even morally necessary regarding things that should not be tolerated – and that all agree that sometimes we need not to tolerate the intolerant. Nehushtan, for example, suggests that unjustified illiberal intolerance should not be tolerated by a liberal state (Nehushtan 2015). According to this approach, the tolerant liberal state, as a starting point, should not tolerate anything that denies the justifications of toleration and toleration itself. More specifically, if toleration enables autonomy and if the state has a duty to ensure and promote autonomy, then the state has a duty to ensure and promote toleration. Since unjust intolerance is by definition unjustly harming others, then the state is under a moral duty to not tolerate the intolerant in order to defend autonomy and toleration itself.

Compassion, much like toleration, should be shown only toward those who deserve it. Being compassionate toward those who do not deserve it may unjustly harm either rights or interests of third parties and will therefore be morally wrong. If state's officials are compassionate toward convicted sex-offenders, for example, who show no regret or willingness to be rehabilitated, that will unjustly harm or negatively affect the victims of these crimes. There is in fact a moral duty to not show compassion in such cases.

Both toleration and compassion are therefore not moral virtues. They do not have intrinsic value and they are not valuable as such. Their value depends on the circumstances and their practice should be justified rather than being accepted as always desirable.

Summary and Future Directions

This chapter aimed to explore a currently underdeveloped conceptual comparison between toleration and compassion. The common and accurate understanding of toleration is that it is, at its essence, a "negative" attitude that entails making adverse judgment about others and exercising restraint thus eventually not harming them. Compassion, on the other hand, has a much more positive connotation, being entangled with feelings such as sympathy and empathy. It is much more pleasant to be at the receiving end of a compassionate attitude than at that of a tolerant attitude. It is these clear differences between these two concepts and attitudes that probably led to seeing them as indeed different, perhaps even unrelated. But there are similarities and links between toleration and compassion after all. Both can result from the same feelings and be justified behind the "veil of ignorance"; both can result in the same behavior – and be expressed simultaneously; both can be expressed by either acts or omissions; both can be exercised by the powerless; and both may be desirable under certain circumstances – yet both are not moral virtues, that is, they are not inherently morally valuable.

This conceptual analysis of these two complex, related concepts lays the ground for a normative evaluation of the practice of toleration and compassion, exploring the cases in which they may be morally justified, allowed, or prohibited.

References

Augenstein D (2010) Tolerance and liberal justice. Ratio Juris 23:437
Balint P (2017) Respecting toleration: traditional liberalism & contemporary diversity. Oxford University Press, Oxford
Bandes SA (2017) Compassion and the rule of law. Int J Law Context 13(2):184
Cohen AJ (2004) What toleration is. Ethics 115(1):68
Del Mar M (2017) Imagining by feeling: a case for compassion in legal reasoning. Int J Law Context 13(2):143
Derrida J (2003) Autoimmunity: real and symbolic suicides. In: Borradori G (ed) Philosophy in a time of terror, vol 127. The University of Chicago Press, Chicago
Diamantides M (2017) Law and compassion: between ethics and economy, philosophical speculation and archeology. Int J Law Context 13(2):197
Edyvane D (2017) Toleration and civility. Soc Theory Pract 43(3):449
Feenan D (2017) Law and compassion. Int J Law Context 13(2):121
Forst R (2003) Toleration, justice and reason. In: Castiglione D, Mckinnon C (eds) The culture of toleration in diverse societies: reasonable toleration. Manchester University Press, Manchester
Gerdy K (2008) Clients, empathy, and compassion: introducing first-year students to the "Heart" of lawyering. Nebraska Law Rev 87(1):1
Green L (2008) On being tolerated. In: Kramer M, Grant C, Colborn B, Hatzistavrou A (eds) The legacy of HLA Hart: legal, political, and moral philosophy, vol 277. Oxford University Press, Oxford
Gu J, Cavanagh K et al (2017) An empirical examination of the factor structure of compassion. PLoS One 12(2):3
Jazaieri H (2018) Compassionate education from preschool to graduate school: bringing a culture of compassion into the classroom. J Res Innov Teach Learn 11(1):22
Klimecki OM, Leiberg S, Ricard M, Singer T (2014) Differential pattern of functional brain plasticity after compassion and empathy training. Soc Cogn Affect Neurosci 9(6):873
Nehushtan Y (2015) Intolerant religion in a tolerant-liberal democracy. Hart, Oxford
Nicholson PP (1985) Toleration as a moral idea. In: Horton J, Mendus S (eds) Aspects of toleration, vol 169. Routledge, London
Nussbaum M (1996) Compassion: the basic social emotion. Soc Philos Policy 13(1):27
Raphael DD (1988) The intolerable. In: Mendus S (ed) Justifying toleration: conceptual and historical perspectives. Cambridge University Press, Cambridge, MA
Rawls J (1971) A theory of justice. Harvard University Press, Cambridge, MA
Raz J (1987) Autonomy, toleration and the harm principle. In: Gavison R (ed) Issues in contemporary legal philosophy, vol 313. Clarendon Press, Oxford
Reilly R (2008) Ethics of compassion: bridging ethical theory and religious moral discourse: studies in comparative philosophy and religion. Lexington Books, Lanham, p 41
Tailche K (2017) Toleration beyond superiority in the formation of non-violent identities: reflections from the Andalusian League (1933–1954). In: Kalliokoski T, Huisjen D Jr, Paivansalo PV (eds) Tolerance, LIT Verlag Münster, p 29
Wilkinson I (2017) The controversy of compassion as an awakening to our conflicted social condition. Int J Law Context 13(2):212
Williams B (1999) Tolerating the intolerable. In: Mendus S (ed) The politics of toleration, vol 65. Edinburgh University Press, Edinburgh

Toleration and Religion

John William Tate

Contents

Introduction	798
Conditions of Toleration	799
Toleration and Religion	803
Medieval Persecution	804
Protestant Persecution	806
The Moral Challenge of Toleration	808
Toleration and Pragmatism	809
Reformation "Success"	812
The Limits of Toleration	813
"Things Indifferent"	814
The Ascendancy of Toleration	817
The Possibility of Political Toleration	818
The Desirability of Toleration	820
The Continuing Relevance of Toleration	821
Conclusion	823
Summary and Future Directions	823
References	824

Abstract

Toleration and religion are intimately related, not least because toleration first arose in Europe as one means of avoiding conflict arising from religious differences. This chapter discusses these historical origins of toleration and its association with religion. In particular, it focuses on the development of ideas of toleration as these emerged amidst the religious conflict ushered in by the Protestant Reformation of the sixteenth century. It considers obstacles, existing at that time, to the widespread acceptance of religious toleration, centered, not least, on the "moral challenge" to which toleration gives rise among the

J. W. Tate (✉)
Discipline of Politics and International Relations, Newcastle Business School, College of Human and Social Futures, University of Newcastle, Newcastle, NSW, Australia
e-mail: John.Tate@newcastle.edu.au

© The Author(s), under exclusive licence to Springer Nature Switzerland AG 2022
M. Sardoĉ (ed.), *The Palgrave Handbook of Toleration*,
https://doi.org/10.1007/978-3-030-42121-2_41

religiously devout. It considers how pragmatic arguments for toleration, adopted by political authorities seeking to avoid conflict among rival religious denominations within their jurisdiction, circumvented this "moral challenge." It then considers debates concerning not only the "possibility" of toleration but its "desirability" – such reservations arising as a result of the clear inequalities that toleration is perceived to involve. Finally, the chapter seeks to address the question of whether toleration remains a relevant policy within contemporary liberal democracies, the plurality and diversity of whose populations have only increased over time, and within which conflicts such as those centered on religion have not entirely abated.

Keywords

Toleration · Religion · Catholicism · Protestantism · Persecution · Reformation · Pragmatism · Realpolitik · St. Augustine · St. Thomas Aquinas · John Locke · John Stuart Mill

Introduction

This chapter looks at the relationship between toleration and religion. It points out that the relationship is an intimate one, toleration first arising as a practical political matter within European polities due to the reality of religious conflict. It identifies how religious differences are capable of giving rise to circumstances in which toleration is a reasonable response, but also makes clear how such circumstances can equally give rise to opposite outcomes, resulting in religious persecution.

The chapter begins by considering toleration in conceptual terms and identifies five conditions of toleration. It then briefly considers the circumstances in which religious differences were likely to give rise to demands for toleration. It then focuses on the absence of religious toleration for dissident Christians at odds with the Catholic Church within the medieval world and the persistence of persecution among both Catholics and Protestants in the Reformation era that came after. It seeks to explain why it was so difficult for individuals and institutions at this time to affirm an ideal of toleration, as an alternative to such persecution, and does so by considering the "moral challenge" to which toleration gives rise among the religiously devout. It then identifies how pragmatic, as distinct from normative, reasons for toleration were able to circumvent this "moral challenge" and render toleration, as state policy, a possibility.

The chapter looks at the sixteenth-century Reformation – a period of enormous religious upheaval in Europe, inaugurated when the Augustinian monk, Martin Luther, nailed his 95 theses criticizing the Catholic Church to the castle church door at Wittenberg, on October 31, 1517 (Elton 1988: 15; Chadwick 1976: 43). Unlike previous revolts against the authority of the Catholic Church, the Reformation was a "success" in that the Pope, and his secular allies among ruling princes, was not able to eradicate and extirpate this rebellion. This "success" therefore confronted secular rulers in Europe with the reality of deep religious differences within their borders, and the chapter explains how in this context toleration of such differences became one policy option, among others, for secular political authorities to avoid religious conflict and violence within their territories.

The chapter then considers not only the *possibility* but also the *desirability* of toleration as public policy. Against those who insist that toleration is no longer a *desirable* policy, given the inequalities inherent in some of its premises, the chapter considers those who insist on the continuing *relevance* of toleration, given the persistence of the animosities and conflicts, not least those centered on religion, which gave rise to demands for toleration in the first place.

Conditions of Toleration

At a conceptual and practical level, toleration is widely seen, within the literature, to be only possible when a set of *five* specific conditions are in play. *Firstly*, the demand for toleration is initiated when individuals seek an entitlement to publicly express, exercise, or manifest some aspect of themselves, their beliefs, or their practices, free from the interference of others. For convenience sake, let us describe this as a demand to exercise a "liberty." The conditions of toleration are initiated when individuals seek an entitlement to exercise this "liberty" free from the interference of others (Condition 1).

Secondly, such a specific demand, under Condition 1, is only necessary if there is a possibility that such liberties might be interfered with by others with the result that individuals might not be able to exercise them freely. Condition 2 therefore arises when whoever has the disposition to interfere with these liberties is willing to do so in ways that limit or expunge such liberties. Such a disposition arises from some sort of opposition, hostility, or aversion to these liberties or the individuals seeking to exercise them. Without this disposition, and this aversion, there would be no need for an individual or group to seek toleration under Condition 1 since there would be no propensity on the part of others to interfere with the liberties they seek to exercise. As Andrew Jason Cohen puts it:

> Toleration is not indifference.....[W]e think of ourselves as tolerating only when we recognize something and disapprove or, at least, dislike it......Some negative response is necessary for our lack of interference to count as toleration. (Cohen 2004: 71. See also Jones 2007a: 384–85, 2012: 266–67; Scanlon 2003: 187; Vernon 1997: 53, 71; Waldron 1997: 351; Horton 1994: 8; Coffey 2000: 10)

We see, therefore, that a second basic condition of toleration (Condition 2) is the presence of those with a disposition to interfere with the "liberty" for which toleration is sought, seeking to limit or expunge that liberty, due to their aversion to that liberty or those seeking to exercise it. A basic question has arisen in the literature concerning this aversion. This question is whether this aversion ought to be of the "morally right kind" (Balint 2014: 264) – arising on the basis of some sort of moral judgment impugning those seeking toleration or that for which toleration is sought – or whether it can simply be an affective or emotive aversion towards the same without any explicit moral foundation at all (see Horton 1996: 29–30; Cohen 2004: 88–90; Balint 2014: 266–67; Raz 1986: 401–02; Raphael 1988: 139). Moral disapproval is usually the result of some sort of intellectual judgment, arising from normative commitments. Such disapproval can give rise to "aversion." "Aversion," however, may at times involve no self-consciously moral element at all but instead be a negative reaction arising from affective or emotive dispositions. An example of this contrast might be a moral disapproval of pornography versus an aversion to loud conversations in a library. The ordinary language meaning of "toleration" allows us to speak of tolerating loud conversations in a library, just as much as it allows us to speak of tolerating pornography, even if our aversion to these loud conversations is not premised on a moral (as distinct from an emotive) opposition. Consequently, it seems that the aversion necessary under Condition 2 can arise from an affective or emotive disposition, as well as from a moral judgment, and that either is therefore a sufficient condition for toleration under the terms of Condition 2 (see Cohen 2004: 88; Balint 2014: 264, 266–67).

The third condition of toleration (condition 3) concerns the reasons capable of convincing those with a disposition to interfere *not* to act on their aversion (be that aversion of a moral or emotive kind). Toleration is only possible if those with a disposition to interfere with the liberties advanced under Condition 1 can find "reasons" not to act on their aversion and, on this basis, recognize the entitlements of individuals to exercise such liberties. As Jeremy Waldron puts it:

> An argument for toleration is an argument which gives a reason for not interfering with a person's beliefs or practices even when we have reason to hold that those beliefs or practices are mistaken, heretical or depraved. (Waldron 1997: 351)

Such "reasons" are important because only non-interference arising from certain types of "reasons," amount to acts of toleration. A fortiori, it is possible for non-interference, in certain circumstances, not to amount to an act of "toleration" at all. For instance, if we chose not to interfere with a person's liberties because we were indifferent to the exercise of these liberties, and so did not care whether they were exercised or not, the noninterference that arises from this indifference would not amount to an act of toleration. One explanation why is that the aversion to those liberties necessary for toleration (Condition 2), which the reasons for toleration (Condition 3) are meant to override, would be absent in the case of such "indifference". The "reasons" for toleration, arising under Condition 3, which underwrite our decision not to interfere, must therefore be of the type that ensure that our non-interference amounts to an act of "toleration." Glenn Newey makes this point when he states that, when it comes to "reasons" for toleration, "[n]ot just any reason will do. It is not sufficient for my tolerating a practice, for example, if my reason for notintervening is that someone has bribed me to do so, or that someone else will beat me into insensibility if I do intervene" (Newey 2001: 317. See also Horton 1996: 38–39).

There are a number of such "reasons" for toleration capable of arising under Condition 3. As we shall see, these include reasons premised on the normative entitlements of individuals to exercise their liberties under Condition 1. But these "reasons" for toleration can also include pragmatic considerations concerning the negative material consequences that might arise if such toleration is not granted.

Needless to say, therefore, the "reasons" for toleration arising under Condition 3 must be reasons that those with a disposition to interfere recognize as having some genuine import or legitimacy – with the result that they are genuinely capable of convincing them not to act on their aversion (Condition 2) to the liberties sought under Condition 1.

Having said that, it might be thought that the pragmatic reasons for toleration identified above – where toleration is granted because of the adverse consequences associated with its alternative – is an instance of that coercion to which Newey refers above, which in forcibly compelling non-inteference, does not enable an act of toleration at all. It is at this point, therefore, that Newey's proposition must be qualified, because there is a venerable tradition of toleration being endorsed, as a pragmatic policy, so as to avoid the civil and political upheaval that might arise in its absence. Such a tradition includes those sixteenth century French Catholic thinkers, known as the "Politiques," who "were in favour of subordinating religion to the political interests of the state and hence willing to concede coexistence with Protestants when necessary to preserve or restore civil unity and peace" (Zagorin 2003: 146. See also Sabine 1963: 399–400). Certainly, Newey is correct that toleration would *not* arise if the coercion compelling noninterference allowed for no alternative, for then there would be no freedom of agency making a choice to engage in toleration possible. But if individuals are capable of interfering, and possess the aversion motivating them to do so, but consider refraining on the basis of the adverse reactions they believe might arise as a consequence, such pragmatic considerations do amount to a "reason" for toleration arising under Condition 3 and, if given priority over the aversion arising under Condition 2, make an act of toleration possible.

Fourthly, toleration is possible only when those with the disposition to interfere decide to *act* on the "reasons" for toleration, arising under Condition 3, and refrain from interfering with the liberties sought under Condition 1, their continuing aversion to these liberties or those seeking to exercise them (Condition 2) notwithstanding. Such a situation only arises when those with the disposition to interfere have comparatively evaluated the competing imperatives for interference (arising under Condition 2) and non-interference (arising under Condition 3). If, in the minds of those with the disposition to interfere, the reasons arising under Condition 3 outweigh those arising under Condition 2, then noninterference (and so toleration) will (ceteris paribus) be the result (Condition 4).

In the context of Condition 4, "non-interference " must be understood broadly. It may be the case that literal "non-interference" is all that is required to achieve toleration. At other points, "non-interference" (and therefore toleration) may be partial, qualified by various restrictions or reservations. For instance, it might be that a particular municipality tolerates "loud music" in public but only at certain times of the day, or smoking in public but only in certain designated spaces. Further, as Peter Jones points out, sometimes toleration, when engaged in by governments, requires more than non-interference, such as establishing the legal conditions to ensure individuals do not suffer such "interference," in the form of discrimination and other disadvantages (Jones 2006: 125–126, 2007a: 386–388).

A *fifth* condition of toleration concerns the capacity of those with the disposition to interfere to actually act on that disposition and impede or expunge the liberties sought under Condition 1. As we shall see below, many toleration theorists argue that unless a person or an institution has the capacity to materially impede the liberties sought under Condition 1, but choose not to, they are not engaging in toleration. This is because, in the absence of such capacity, not interfering with these liberties is not really a case of toleration at all, because the agent in question is impotent to act otherwise. In other words, unless noninterference is a genuine choice, wherein the alternative is possible, toleration has not taken place. Glenn Newey made this point with his reference to coercion above. Peter Jones does so as follows:

> [W]e can tolerate only what we are able to prevent. If we object to x, but are powerless to prevent it, we cannot tolerate x. Toleration exists only when intolerance is an option. We can adopt a tolerant stance or possess a tolerant disposition even though we are powerless; that is, we might resolve not to prevent x even if we could. But, strictly, we actually tolerate x only if we are actually able to prevent x but opt not to do so. (Jones 2007a: 384–85. See also Jones 2007b: 10)

Concerning Condition 5, questions arise in the literature concerning how effective must be the capacity of those with the disposition to interfere to impede or expunge the liberties for which toleration is sought under Condition 1. Must such capacity extend to a full efficacy, so that a person or institution can be said to be only engaging in toleration when they have the full capacity to reverse this toleration and completely expunge the liberties in question? Or can this "capacity" for intolerance extend only to a partial ability to achieve this end, interfering with or impeding these liberties rather than expunging them altogether? Or must a person only *believe* that they have this capacity to be capable of toleration?

Toleration theorists differ on these points, but in each case, their concern is to determine how far must our capacity for "intolerance" extend before our alternative choice to engage in "toleration" can be said to be meaningful (see Raphael 1988: 139; Jones 2007a: 384–85, 395n; Galeotti 2002: 22, 89; Cohen 2004: 72–73, 93–94; Horton 1996: 28; Balint 2014: 267–268; Mendus 1989: 9; Newey 2001: 317–18; Williams 1996: 19). Further, it is surely the case, as Peter Jones points out, that behavior that seeks to reverse the process of toleration but fails to do so (thereby demonstrating the "impotence" identified above) can still, nevertheless, be described as "intolerant" behaviour even though it did not achieve its ends (Jones 2011: 446). A choice, therefore, not to engage in such behavior would, ipso facto, be an act of "toleration" (so long as the person exercising such choice believed, at the time, that they possessed the capacity to reverse and therefore deny toleration, and so were not aware of their incapacity).

Certainly some capacity, or at least a belief in a capacity, to reverse the process of toleration is widely perceived to be a necessary condition of any act of toleration itself (Condition 5). This is because only in such circumstances can "toleration" be perceived as a discretionary choice on the part of an individual or institution, given that they have the full, partial, or presumed capacity to (effectively) act otherwise.

None of the conditions above guarantee that, in any particular circumstance, toleration will be an inevitable outcome. Often, in the minds of those with a disposition to interfere, the reasons for interference arising under condition 2 may outweigh the reasons for toleration arising under Condition 3, so that Condition 4 does not take place at all. But in those circumstances where those with the disposition to interfere affirm the "reasons" for toleration arising under Condition 3, their continuing aversion to that which is seeking toleration (Condition 2) notwithstanding, toleration (Condition 4) is (ceteris paribus) likely to take place.

Toleration and Religion

Within Europe, it was religion that animated the first widespread practices of toleration. Of course, there had been clear demands among religious minorities for noninterference (and therefore for what we would understand as "liberty") for as long as there have been religious and political authorities with the power, disposition, and discretion to deny this. But such demands for "liberty" do not give rise to "toleration" unless the latter is a conceivable policy which those in authority wish to apply in response. As Herbert Butterfield tells us, "[l]ong before the sixteenth century, the Church had been ready to grant an exceptional toleration to Jews and to those who had been brought up in paganism" (Butterfield 1977: 578). Equally, the Middle Ages saw significant disputes between the Catholic Church and various secular state institutions concerning the respective limits of either church or state authority, the extent to which one ought to "tolerate" the jurisdiction of the other, and therefore the respective "liberties" of each (Hughes 1960: 37–39). However toleration as a policy, applied by state authorities to individual Christians, emerged in the sixteenth and seventeenth centuries, in the wake of the European Reformation. The Reformation arose as a revolt against the authority of the Catholic Church, and spread to wide areas of Europe, the dissidents engaging in this revolt eventually coming to be known as "Protestants" (Crankshaw 1971: 75).

One reason why the religious differences, made possible by the Reformation, ultimately gave rise to a policy of toleration among some political authorities within Europe was due, in part, to a series of features specific to the religions that sought such toleration. Firstly, for the dissidently devout, their religious faith was often the most important element within their life and the source upon which they governed both their own actions and their relations with those around them. Secondly, there was a widespread belief among some Protestants that such faith was ultimately a personal matter, between the individual and God, and not something that ought to be governed by authoritative institutions of church or state (Elton 1988: 16–19). Some, but not all Protestants, therefore came to the conclusion that if faith was the most important element of a person's life, and if it was a personal matter between the individual and God, then wider institutions, such as church or state, or wider elements of society, should not interfere with this but instead should "tolerate" a person's entitlement to make their own choices concerning such matters, so long as those choices did not result in any material harm to society or the state. The seventeenth-century English philosopher, John Locke, gave expression to this point of view in 1667:

> [W]hatsoever the magistrate enjoined in the worship of God, men must in this necessarily follow what they themselves thought best, since no consideration could be sufficient to force a man from or to that which he was fully persuaded was the way to infinite happiness or infinite misery. Religious worship being that homage which I pay to that God I adore in a way I judge acceptable to him, and so being an action or commerce passing only between God and myself, hath in its own nature no reference at all to my governor, or to my neighbour, and so necessarily produces no action which disturbs the community. (Locke 1993a: 189)

If individuals or institutions adopted this particular perspective, affirming that however averse they were to particular religious beliefs or practices (Condition 2), religion was nevertheless a personal matter, concerning the relationship of an individual with their God, and so not a matter with which wider institutions or elements of society should interfere, then this constituted one reason (arising under Condition 3) why toleration should occur. Locke advanced such a position as follows:

> I say that....speculative opinions and divine worship.....are those things alone which have an absolute and universal right to toleration....and that in these every man hath his unlimited freedom appears because bare speculations....cannot by any means either disturb the state or inconvenience my neighbour, and so come not within the magistrate's cognizance.....The other thing that hath just claim to an unlimited toleration is the place, time, and manner of worshipping my God. Because this is a thing wholly between God and me and of an *eternal concernment*, above the reach and extent of polities and governments which are but for my well-being in this world. (Locke 1993a: 187–88. Emphasis added)

Medieval Persecution

But as we shall see, such a process of reasoning, leading to such conclusions, was somewhat rare in the Europe of the sixteenth and seventeenth centuries. It was even less common in the European centuries preceding the Reformation, encompassed by what we now know as the Middle Ages. Within medieval Europe there was little acknowledgment among ruling authorities that any reasons for toleration (Condition 3), as applied to Christians at odds with the established Church, had legitimacy. It was the African Church father, Augustine of Hippo, active in the fourth and fifth centuries A.D., who was often cited by medieval authorities as espousing the relevant biblical justification for persecution, rather than toleration, of those Christians at odds with church orthodoxy. As Mark Goldie states:

Scripturally, it was claimed that Christ himself had authorized religious coercion of the wayward, for, as St Augustine had explained, Jesus' injunction in St. Luke's Gospel to 'compel them to come in' must be understood in relation to the church (Luke 14:23). *Compelle intrare* became the cardinal text for Christian brutality and remained a pulpit staple. The Christian magistrate, guided by the Christian pastor, was duty bound to suppress error, for 'he beareth not the sword in vain: he is the minister of God, a revenger to execute wrath upon him that doeth evil.' (Romans 13:4) (Goldie 2010: x)

Perez Zagorin provides an expanded explanation of the key biblical doctrine of "compelle intrare," referred to by Goldie in the passage above, and relied upon by Augustine and his successors as justification for using force against those at odds with church orthodoxy. Such force, Augustine insisted, was justifiable if used as a means to convince the wayward of the "truth":

Maintaining that people could be changed for the better through the influence of fear, [Augustine] concluded that 'when the saving doctrine is added to useful fear', then 'the light of truth' can drive out 'the darkness of error'. To reinforce his view, he quoted the parable of the feast in the Gospel of Luke (Luke 14:21–23), another of the texts that was to figure prominently in future tolerationist controversy. In this parable, a man prepared a great feast to which he invited many guests who failed to appear. After summoning from the city the poor, the blind, and the lame to come and eat, he found that room still remained, so he ordered his servants to 'go out into the highways and hedges, and compel them to come in [*compelle intrare* in the Latin vulgate], that my house may be filled'. 'Do you think', Augustine asked in a comment on this passage, 'that no one should be forced to do right, when you read that the master of the house said to his servants, 'Whomever you find, compel them to come in'? [Augustine] referred also to the example of the conversion of the apostle Paul, who 'was forced by the great violence of Christ's compulsion to acknowledge and hold the truth' (Acts 9:3–18). The main point, he claimed, was not whether anyone was being forced to do something, but whether the purpose of doing so was right or wrong. While no one could be made good against his will, the fear of punishment could persuade a person to repudiate a false doctrine and embrace the truth he had previously denied...Augustine was convinced that the coercion of heretics was therefore a greater mercy because it rescued them from lying demons so that they could be healed in the Catholic fold. (Zagorin 2003: 29–30)

John Coffey, however, warns against laying at Augustine's door the responsibility for the bloody persecution and public executions that often accompanied the attempts of church and state to stamp out heresy in the Middle Ages. Coffey points out (as does Zagorin) that Augustine always drew the line at the death penalty for those refusing to conform to established church doctrine or authority:

Augustine's notoriety as the 'father of the Inquisition' is not entirely deserved; according to Henry Chadwick, 'Augustine would have been horrified by the burning of heretics'. Fines, imprisonment, banishment and moderate floggings were one thing, but the death penalty was an illegitimate weapon for Christians to wield in their war against error. To use early modern terminology, Augustinian persecution was 'medicinal' rather than 'exterminative'; it treated the heretic as a patient to be healed, rather than a cancer to be excised. (Coffey 2000: 23. See also Zagorin 2003: 31–32)

According to Coffey, no such reservations characterized the dominant Catholic theologian of the Middle Ages, St. Thomas Aquinas. He perceived heretics not only as lost souls in need of salvation, but, if they refused to recant, a canker on the face of Christendom that ought to be forcibly removed. The death penalty for heretics was therefore something that Aquinas countenanced (Coffey 2000: 23; Zagorin 2003: 43). The existence of large-scale revolts against Catholic orthodoxy during the medieval period, among Waldensians, Cathars, Hussites and others, galvanized the willingness of the Church to countenance the death penalty for those it perceived as "heretics":

> The medieval Inquisition was established to counter the threat of these groups, and the fourth Lateran Council of 1215 codified the theory and practice of persecution. The greatest medieval theologian, Thomas Aquinas, summed up the standard medieval position when he declared that obstinate heretics deserved 'not only to be separated from the Church, but to be eliminated from the world by death.' (Coffey 2000: 23)

Of course, "heresy," just like "blasphemy," has no meaning in the absence of an established and authoritative institution capable of defining "orthodoxy," since without "orthodoxy" as an authoritative norm, there is no basis for stigmatizing perspectives at odds with it as "blasphemous" or "heretical." Concepts like "heresy," "blasphemy," and "orthodoxy," therefore, are entirely the by-products of relationships of power – this being the power of entrenched institutions of church and state to (a) define "orthodoxy"; (b) define as "heretical" or "blasphemous" that which is perceived to be at odds with such "orthodoxy"; and (c) enforce such "orthodoxy" as an authoritative norm (not least by persecuting "blasphemy" and "heresy" as heterodox) with the material means at their disposal. Only in this context is "orthodoxy" given the semblance of legitimacy which, ipso facto, renders "heresy" and "blasphemy" illegitimate. "Orthodoxy," "heresy," and "blasphemy" are therefore contested and contentious terms, being very much the product of relationships of power within the religious and political world and the capacity of some groups, rather than others, to ascribe to their position the legitimacy of one, thereby stigmatizing their opponents with the opprobrium of the other.

Consequently, persecution and, if necessary, extirpation of what was designated as "heresy" and "blasphemy" were possible during the Middle Ages because of the material power (and religious supremacy) of the Catholic Church, and the alliances it established with those secular ruling authorities willing to uphold, within their territories, its authority and doctrine as "orthodox":

> Thus throughout the Middle Ages, in spite of significant manifestations of opposition, the Catholic Church preserved its institutional and doctrinal supremacy in Europe as the one religious body of Western Christendom, maintaining its dominance both by teaching and evangelistic preaching and by force. Not until the Protestant Reformation of the sixteenth century was its supremacy overthrown by heresies that successfully resisted all efforts at repression. (Zagorin 2003: 36)

Protestant Persecution

Lord Acton states that "[t]he most violent and prolonged conflicts for religious freedom occurred in the Middle Ages between a Church which was not threatened by rivals and States which were most attentive to preserve her exclusive predominance" (Acton 1962: 115). He therefore concludes that "[r]eligious liberty [is] therefore......possible only where the coexistence of different religions is admitted, with an equal right to govern themselves according to their own several principles" (Acton 1962: 115).

But the Protestant Reformation, which produced these different religions, did not put an end to religious persecution. Not only Catholic but Protestant authorities engaged in wide varieties of religious intolerance and persecution. In England under the Tudors, toleration was denied to those considered Catholics, heretics, or blasphemers, while, by the time of Elizabeth I, the English state and Church of England were engaged in an internal struggle with a "Puritan" opposition (Bindoff 1958: 225–46; Kamen 1972: 161–62). These "Puritans" (after the Restoration of Charles II known as "Dissenters" because of their inability to outwardly conform to the doctrines of the Church of England) were denied toleration by a resurgent Church of England and an Anglican-dominated English Parliament from 1660 to the Revolution of 1688 (Cranston 1952: 620). Even so "judicious" a sixteenth-century Church of England divine as Richard Hooker declared in *Of the Lawes of Ecclesiastical Politie*:

> Will any man deny that the Church doth need the rod of corporal punishment to keep her children in obedience? (Hooker 2000)

One alternative to toleration considered by a number of institutions, including the Church of England at key points in its history, was "comprehension," wherein established (state-endorsed) ecclesiastical institutions, like the Church of England, would widen their doctrinal orthodoxy (by minimizing its essential conditions) to encompass those other faiths with whom they had sufficient theological affinity, but would leave outside of "comprehension" those more radical faiths whose alterity rendered them incapable of such incorporation. The Church of England ultimately rejected such a policy as a means of responding to the religious diversity in its midst. But "comprehension" was nevertheless widely acknowledged as a possible alternative to toleration. As Herbert Butterfield states:

> A neater way of disposing of the divisions in religious belief was the policy of "comprehension" which, while envisaging a broader kind of Church that would embrace both parties, involved some negotiation for a kind of compromise. This way of recovering unity was the one most congenial to the heads of great monarchies. Some of the supporters of toleration were anxious that the established Catholic system should not be too severe in the case of differences about minor points; and some would have liked to see Christianity reduced to a restricted number of inescapable doctrines – something like the Apostles' Creed, perhaps. All this involved the hope that, by finding a lowest common factor, and regarding the rest as nonessential, they might pacify Christendom and achieve a system tolerable for all. (Butterfield 1977: 578. See also Bejan 2017: 32–33).

Protestants might believe that religious faith was ultimately a matter between the individual and God, but for many Protestant authorities, this did not mean that they ought to tolerate those religious beliefs and practices that they believed to fall outside the pale of all acceptable religion or those which they believed were a threat to civil peace or the security of the state (see Plamenatz 1972: 62–65, 66, 69). Once more, the path to "toleration" was a path less traveled.

The Moral Challenge of Toleration

One reason why toleration was a path less travelled was because there were clear obstructions in the way of religiously devout individuals (and therefore political or church authorities when populated by such individuals) engaging in the process of reasoning, identified above, that led to toleration. These obstructions resided in the fact that, for many such individuals, toleration constituted an insurmountable moral challenge (see Tate 2016a: 233–334, 2016b: 668–669). After all, in the minds of the religiously devout in these centuries, when it came to matters of religion, what John Locke describes above as matters of "eternal concernment" were often at stake. For many, the fate of one's immortal soul depended on affirming the "one true religion," the religion acceptable to God, and so there were deep disputes between Catholics and Protestants concerning "the proper standard of religious knowledge, or what was called 'the rule of faith'" capable of identifying this "one true religion" (Popkin 1979: 1). Such differences emerged not only between Catholics and Protestants but between Protestants themselves. Almost all agreed, however, that adherence to the "one true religion" was an essential condition of eternal salvation. As Locke put it in 1689:

> Every man has an immortal soul, capable of eternal happiness or misery; whose happiness depending upon his believing and doing those things in this life which are necessary to the obtaining of God's favour, and are prescribed by God to that end, it follows from thence, first, that the observance of these things is the highest obligation that lies upon mankind, and that our utmost care, application, and diligence ought to be exercised in the search and performance of them, because there is nothing in this world that is of any consideration in comparison with eternity. (Locke 1993b: 421)

Locke, in his later years, was an advocate of toleration. But to many among the religiously devout, to tolerate those one believed to be in grave error concerning religion, allowing them the liberty not only to live by their erroneous faith but to propagate it to others, was putting the immortal souls of others at risk. From this perspective, to affirm reasons under Condition 3 to "tolerate" such error appeared as a gross and negligent act, one which any political or religious authority which had the genuine spiritual interests of its subjects in mind would never countenance:

> To grant 'the publique freedome of heresies', suggested [Thomas] Bilson, was to countenance the 'murder of souls'. [Saint] Augustine, Thomas Case noted, had declared that those who called for liberty of conscience only gained '"Libertatem perditionis", liberty to destroy themselves'. Instead of shepherding their subjects along the path to heaven, towards true freedom, irresponsible magistrates allowed them the liberty to choose hell. In contrast, the godly ruler should compel the lost to come in to the banquet. 'Mercy is cruel', said [Edwin] Sandys, 'and why should not the church compel her abandoned children to return, if her abandoned children compel others to perish?'. (Coffey 2000: 35. My addition)

Such perspectives, perceiving toleration less as a source of liberty for minority dissidents and more as a threat to the immortal souls of others, explain why both individuals and institutions found it difficult to find reasons, under Condition 3, why they should overcome their aversion to religious heterodoxy and tolerate it instead. The perspective of "eternity" – the belief that immortal souls were at stake in most questions concerning religion – therefore produced the "moral challenge" which made toleration such a difficult option for many of the religiously devout to affirm.

Certainly, there were some, by the seventeenth century, who affirmed freedom of religious conscience as a matter of principle (see Plamenatz 1972: 70). But these were likely to be radical intellectuals or minority sects, well outside the mainstream. Those within the mainstream who did affirm toleration often did so with deep reluctance, as a purely interim measure, until more favorable conditions could be achieved: "Wherever it was established, it became clear that toleration, as a working system, was subject to serious limitations. Its own upholders tended to regard it as only a temporary expedient – a thing necessary perhaps until a General Council of the Church had met and established a new order. Alternatively, there was an assumption that after a period of generous treatment, the heretics would voluntarily return to the fold" (Butterfield 1977: 578).

Consequently, the "moral challenge" to which toleration gave rise certainly ascribed a very bad name, among the religiously devout, to toleration itself. Herbert Butterfield provides an indication of this, quoting Elisabeth Labrousse in what he calls the *Dictionary of the History of Ideas* (but without any further reference) as follows:

> Lexicology tells us…that up to the beginning of the eighteenth century, the word *'tolérance'* had, in French, a pejorative meaning [it signifying] a lax complacency towards evil. In 1691, in his admonition to Protestants (*VIe avertissement aux protestants, III, ix*), Bossuet still proudly described Catholicism as the least tolerant of all religions and, as if to compete with this proud boast, the Walloon Synod of Leden (an overwhelming majority of whose members were Huguenot refugees) firmly condemned religious toleration as a heresy (Butterfield 1977: 573).

Toleration and Pragmatism

Yet toleration did eventually become prevalent in Europe, despite the "moral challenge" it presented. One reason for this is because other reasons for toleration could arise under Condition 3 which effectively circumvented this "moral challenge." These were often pragmatic reasons, focusing not on the entitlement of individuals to exercise their liberties, free from interference, but on the conduciveness of toleration to achieving secular ends such as civil peace and state security. Such pragmatic reasons for toleration were often affirmed by state institutions, and their political leaders, when it was apparent that denying toleration would produce greater upheavals, undermining civil peace, than such denial would avoid. In such contexts, political rulers could make a pragmatic decision to engage in toleration, even if, as individuals, they were thoroughly opposed to the religious practices for which toleration was sought, and otherwise had no inclination to support the religious liberties of those individuals engaging in them. As Perez Zagorin states:

> If elsewhere in Europe Catholic governments sometimes consented to the compromise of coexistence with Protestantism, it was to avoid the still greater evil of civil conflict, not because they accepted the principle of tolerance..... Since hardly anyone considered religious pluralism other than an evil, this pragmatic policy was generally regarded as a *temporary expedient*, not a lasting solution to religious division. (Zagorin 2003: 146. Emphasis added)

John Locke gave expression to precisely such pragmatic reasons for toleration in *An Essay Concerning Toleration*, written in 1667 but not published until 1876. However he did not present such reasons as a "temporary expedient" (such as Zagorin describes in the passage above). Rather, within Locke's text, such pragmatism was coupled with normative (i.e., non-pragmatic) reasons for toleration centered (as in the passages from Locke quoted above) on the entitlement of individuals to exercise their liberties free from interference. Locke's pragmatic reasons for toleration were as follows. Addressing himself directly to the political rulers in England at the time, Locke declared that any attempt by the English state to deny toleration to "dissenters" (whom elsewhere he calls "fanatics"), and engage in persecution instead, was a "hazardous" policy because (a) these dissident sects were at present divided and of no threat to the state, but (b) any persecution by the state was likely to lead them to unite against it and, in their resistance, produce more upheaval than persecution of them would quell:

> For the fanatics taken all together being numerous, and possibly more than the hearty friends to the state religion, are yet crumbled into different parties amongst themselves, and are at as much distance one from another as from you, if you drive them not further off by the ill-treatment they receive from you, for their bare opinions are as inconsistent one with another as with the Church of England. People, therefore, that are so shattered into different factions are best secured by toleration, since being in as good a condition under you as they can hope for under any, 'tis not likely they should join to set up any other, whom they cannot be certain will use them so well. But if you persecute them you make them all of one party and interest against you, tempt them to shake off your yoke and venture for new government, wherein everyone has hopes to get the dominion themselves or better usage under others. (Locke 1993a: 207. See also Locke 1993a: 192–193, 197–98, 200, 204–205, 206–207; see also ► Chap. 51, "John Locke and Religious Toleration")

Such pragmatic arguments for toleration avoid the "moral challenge" to which toleration gives rise by entirely circumventing the spiritual considerations that underwrite this "moral challenge." The "moral challenge" arose only for those who placed the spiritual salvation of others ahead of other imperatives. Because toleration, in their minds, could endanger the salvation of others, by allowing "heresy" to proliferate, they were likely to oppose toleration.

But the pragmatic argument for toleration, identified by Locke and Zagorin above, refers solely to the secular interests of state authorities in securing civil peace and state security within their borders. It does not refer to the spiritual interests of those seeking toleration or those affected by their doctrines, because such matters are irrelevant to such secular concerns. When toleration is justified in these pragmatic terms (as a practical means of securing secular ends), the "moral challenge" to which toleration gives rise is no longer relevant because spiritual interests are no longer at stake at all.

The other significant feature of such pragmatic arguments for toleration is that they are entirely distinct from normative arguments. The latter, in making their case for toleration, are likely to make reference to the entitlement of individuals to the liberties advanced under Condition 1, or the "autonomy" such liberty will make possible for them, or some other distinctly normative consideration (all of which constitute "reasons" for toleration arising under Condition 3). In contrast, pragmatic arguments for toleration (if directed to the wider secular ends identified above) do not focus on such individual concerns, since such concerns are not the primary goal in question, even if the achievement of that primary goal (civil peace or state security) does secure these individual considerations as an incidental outcome.

Both pragmatic and normative arguments for toleration, therefore, each resort to "reasons," arising under Condition 3, as justification for such a policy. But only normative arguments seek to justify toleration in terms of the entitlements of individuals seeking toleration under Condition 1.

Needless to say, once we shift from justifying toleration in normative terms, and instead seek to employ pragmatic reasons for toleration, the dynamic surrounding the justification of toleration entirely alters. Normative reasons, centered, for instance, on the entitlement of individuals to religious liberty or a belief that religion is solely a matter between the individual and God, allow for toleration as the only reasonable policy outcome to achieve such ends. This is because it is only the noninterference endorsed by toleration which allows such liberties or such a one-to-one spiritual relationship between the individual and God to proceed unimpeded. There is, therefore, in the context of such normative reasons, a *necessary* relationship between toleration as a policy and the ends it seeks to achieve. Given the need to achieve these ends, no substitute for toleration is plausible.

However once toleration is employed by political rulers as a *pragmatic* means of achieving aggregate outcomes, such as civil peace or state security, this *necessary* relationship disappears, and toleration becomes a *contingent* means of achieving such ends. This is because such ends may also be achieved by means other than toleration. After all, if civil peace is the primary end desired by government, and if government believes that religious differences are undermining this peace, then, if the government has no necessary commitment to the religious liberties of individuals, it is possible that, with a change in empirical circumstances, religious persecution and the forcible imposition of outward religious conformity, rather than toleration, might be considered by government the best means to achieve civil peace or at least be perceived as being so. In such circumstances, having relied entirely on pragmatic arguments for the validity of toleration, proponents of toleration have no basis upon which to repudiate such a shift in policy, other than an empirical claim that state authorities are mistaken that more effective means than toleration exist to achieve these ends.

Consequently, in relation to Condition 3, it is only normative reasons for toleration which ensure an unconditional argument for toleration itself. This is because they presuppose a *necessary* relationship between toleration and the ends it seeks to achieve, with the result that no substitution for toleration as a policy is plausible if such ends are to be attained. Pragmatic reasons for toleration, by contrast, establish no such unconditional argument for toleration because they establish no such necessary relationship between toleration and its ends.

Reformation "Success"

It was the "success" of the sixteenth-century Reformation, inaugurated by an Augustinian monk, Martin Luther, which imposed upon European state rulers the practical problem of ensuring civil peace between rival religious denominations within their borders, and therefore impelled them to consider both the normative and pragmatic arguments for toleration identified above. Of course, Luther's protests against the "worldly" practices of the Papacy and the Church it governed were not new. Protest movements had arisen on this basis before, but all had been suppressed by the Papacy in alliance with European political authorities. As John Stuart Mill states:

> [T]he Reformation broke out at least twenty times before Luther, and was put down. Arnold of Brescia was put down. Fra Dolcino was put down. Savonarola was put down. The Albigeois were put down. The Vaudois were put down. The Lollards were put down. The Hussites were put down. Even after the era of Luther, wherever persecution was persisted in, it was successful. In Spain, Italy, Flanders, the Austrian empire, Protestantism was rooted out; and, most likely, would have been so in England, had Queen Mary lived, or Queen Elizabeth died. Persecution has always succeeded, save where the heretics were too strong a party to be effectually persecuted. (Mill 1971: 89)

According to Mill, therefore, the reason for the "success" of the Reformation that Luther inaugurated was centered on *realpolitik*. Some European rulers took up arms to defend the Lutheran rebellion against the Pope that occurred in their territories. Within German states, for instance, Catholic and Protestant princes came to blows until a truce was ultimately achieved with the Peace of Augsburg (1555). This allowed for the ongoing coexistence of Catholic and Lutheran states within the territories of the Holy Roman Empire but fell well short of "toleration" for individual Christians – the population of each principality being required (under the principle of "cuius regio, eius religio") to conform to the religion of their prince (be this Catholic or Lutheran), though they were allowed unimpeded emigration if they could not (Hughes 1960: 247; Green 1961: 150; Butterfield 1977: 581). Such arrangements under the Peace of Augsburg extended only to Catholics and Lutherans. A rival Protestant denomination, Calvinism, had no such entitlements and could be persecuted by princes of either denomination (Hughes 1960: 247).

Nevertheless, what such political agreements between states meant was that the Reformation, unlike its predecessors, was not to be reversed, with the result that a permanent religious division existed within Western and Central Europe, replacing what was once (with some periodic exceptions) a spiritual monopoly of the Catholic Church under a single Pope. But the Peace of Augsburg did not end the violence or bloodshed between Catholic and Protestant. This continued for more than a century elsewhere in Europe:

> During the 130 years between 1559 and 1689, Europe passed through a tumultuous and anarchic period of civil wars and rebellions. Each upheaval had its own distinct character; each had multiple causes. The one common denominator, which constantly recurred, was Protestant-Catholic religious strife. Luther had inaugurated the ideological controversy in 1517, but it spread with heightened intensity after the Habsburg-Valois dynastic wars came to a close in 1559. The French civil wars of 1562–1598, the Dutch revolt against Philip II, the Scottish rebellion against Mary Stuart, the Spanish attack on England in 1588, the Thirty Years' War in Germany between 1618 and 1648, the Puritan Revolution of 1640–1660 and the Glorious Revolution of 1688–89 in England were all religious conflicts, though of course they had other causes as well......Both sides eventually lost their crusading zeal. But by the time the ideological conflict burned out during the seventeenth century, it had left a permanent impress on nearly every aspect of European life: on concepts of liberty and toleration, on party politics, business enterprise, social structure, science, philosophy, and the arts. (Dunn 1970: ix)

Consequently, it was the Reformation and its aftermath, and the religious divisions and conflicts this entrenched, that forced sixteenth and seventeenth-century European state authorities to at least consider the possibility of toleration as a means of securing civil peace within their borders. In other words, it was the "success" of the Reformation that placed toleration firmly upon the political agenda in Europe. As J.W. Allen states:

> It was absolutely impossible in the sixteenth century that the question of how governments should, or had best, deal with religious contumacy, or with 'heresy', should not be widely debated and from many different points of view. It was a question which, however put, directly and acutely affected the lives of multitudes of men and women all over Western Europe. Every government had to make up its mind at least as to practical action; and that in face of all manner of difficulties and complications. To the question as a practical one put in general terms, every possible answer, as had already been stated, was given. It was maintained that under some circumstances it was expedient, under others inexpedient, to 'persecute', and that the ruler had a right to judge and to act at his discretion. It was also maintained that he had no choice about the matter. It was asserted that he was bound to endeavour to stamp out false religion by force, if force were necessary; it was maintained, on the contrary, that he was bound, morally, to allow people to preach and worship as they pleased, so long as they did not break the peace or incite to breach of it...... 'Toleration' as a practical solution of intolerable difficulties and 'toleration' as a general principle of action in relation to religious differences, both appear quite early in the sixteenth century. (Allen 1960: 73–74)

The Limits of Toleration

Of course, when considered as a government policy, as distinct from a means of private engagement between individuals, "toleration" only arose at the discretion of established political authorities. It was they who decided whose liberties, sought under Condition 1, would be accorded toleration under Condition 4. Noninterference by these authorities was what enabled the liberties sought under Condition 1 to be exercised unimpeded, and therefore for toleration to occur. As John Locke stated:

> Force, you allow, is improper to convert men to any religion. Toleration is but the removing that force. (Locke 1963: 62)

But "noninterference" was always understood by political authorities to have limits. Irrespective of the reasons – normative or pragmatic – by which political authorities (under Condition 3) chose to justify toleration, they always placed limits on the "noninterference" that made such toleration possible, thereby placing limits on toleration itself, ensuring some of the "liberties" sought under condition 1 fell *inside* these limits and others fell outside their scope. Such limits were often (as we shall see in the following paragraphs) imposed for pragmatic reasons, centered on the same concerns for civil peace or state security which (as we saw above) sometimes provided reasons for the policy of toleration itself.

Religious practices that violated civil peace, for instance, were likely to fall outside the limits of toleration, and therefore be proscribed. John Locke, for example, argued that although religious groups within a territory ought to have the liberty to proselytize and seek to convert others to their faith, *none should use force to achieve these ends*, with the result that those who did so should be denied toleration (Locke 1993b: 395, 399, 405, 421–22). Here is an example of a liberty (Condition 1) which, Locke argued, state authorities ought to tolerate, so long as it did not overstep the civil boundaries or limits which these same authorities set for it – limits which were imposed in the interests of maintaining civil peace by ensuring (at the very least) that liberties exercised by an individual under Condition 1 were consistent with a similar liberty exercisable by others.

Such limits on toleration could also be more comprehensive. Locke, for instance, was insistent that there are some religious or nonreligious doctrines which should be denied toleration altogether within Protestant societies. These included Catholicism, "Mahometism" and atheism (Locke 1993a: 188, 197, 202–03, 1993b: 426. See other ▶ Chap. 51, "John Locke and Religious Toleration"). But he also believed a range of more specific religious doctrines should be denied toleration, including doctrines that taught that "dominion is founded in grace" or "faith is not to be kept with heretics" (Locke 1993b: 425).

"Things Indifferent"

But in order to better understand the limits imposed on toleration, it is important to consider the specific basis upon which a figure such as Locke sought to impose such limits, in order to perceive how such limits could be justified upon either religious or non-religious grounds. Whereas some sixteenth and seventeenth century toleration theorists sought to impose *religious* limits on toleration, refusing to tolerate that which was perceived to fall too far outside the pale of acceptable religious opinion

(Plamenatz 1972: 62–66, 69), Locke insisted that the basis for such limits must be grounded solely in "civil" (non-religious) interests, centered on the secular ends of state authority, such as civil peace or state security, in which all individuals subject to state authority have a common interest (Locke 1993a: 191–193, 195). Such limits should not be based on religious considerations, Locke insisted, because (a) it is only civil concerns rather than religious ones, in which all individuals subject to state jurisdiction have a common and commensurate interest, and therefore it is only on the basis of reasons articulated in such terms that they are likely to agree (individuals being irrevocably divided on matters of religion) (Locke 1963: 119, 121, 419, 420, 1993b: 407, 431), and (b) it is only in relation to civil interests that states (in Locke's view) ought to exercise authority because it was only for the protection of such civil interests that (Locke believed) individuals consented to state authority and established it in the first place (Locke 1993a: 186, 192–193, 195, 1993b: 393, 394–396, 1963: 119, 121, 1965: II § 83, 123, 124, 131, 134, 135, 149, 171, 222). Consequently, as the above and the following makes clear, Locke was of the view that any limits imposed by states upon toleration, and therefore any interdiction imposed upon that which fell outside these limits, should be justified solely in terms of reasons articulated in "civil" (as distinct from religious) terms because only then would the imposition of such limits, and the exercise of such interdiction, be (a) likely to elicit the agreement of those subject to them and (b) fall within the rightful jurisdiction of state authority.

To this end, Locke argued that Protestant political authorities ought to deny toleration to Catholics and Mahometans not because they believe their religious doctrines to be in error (which would be a religious reason for imposing a limit on toleration) but rather for the purely "civil" reason that they owe their allegiance to a foreign prince – this being the Pope in Rome or the Mufti in Constantinople – with the result that they are a threat to state security (Locke 1993a: 197, 202–03, 1993b: 426). Equally, atheists are to be denied toleration, not because of the sacrilege involved in denying the existence of God but rather because of the civil danger arising from the fact that they cannot be trusted to abide by their "[p]romises, covenants, and oaths" (Locke 1993b: 426. See also Locke 1993a: 188; see other ▶ Chap. 51, "John Locke and Religious Toleration"). Those who insist that "dominion is founded in grace" or "faith is not to be kept with heretics" are to be denied toleration because, Locke points out, they are seeking, on the basis of their personal religious convictions, an exemption to the general rule of law, and yet such exemptions render the law unworkable, they being available to all, given that "everyone is orthodox to himself" (Locke 1993b: 390). The result, Locke insists, is that "the private judgement of any person concerning a law.....for the pubic good, does not take away the obligation of that law, nor deserve a dispensation" (Locke 1993b: 423. See also Locke 1993a: 191. See also Locke 1993a: 201, 1993b: 403).

But while such "civil" concerns inform the limits of Locke's toleration, justifying the exclusion of those doctrines and practices which fall outside these limits, they also assist in determining what falls *within* these limits, and so is entitled to toleration. For instance, "idolators," or those engaging in "animal sacrifice" – practices which Locke, as a devout Protestant, would have believed to be at odds with the will of God – were to be tolerated, firstly, because of Locke's commitment to the ideal of individual religious liberty, but secondly, because these practices, however sacrilegious, had no detrimental "civil" effects, being "not prejudicial to other men's rights, nor do they break the public peace of societies" (Locke 1993b: 415, 417. See ▶ Chap. 51, "John Locke and Religious Toleration"). However, should these practices become "prejudicial" to such secular concerns – such as when animal sacrifice interferes with public food supplies – Locke insists they may be denied toleration (Locke 1993b: 415). But again, Locke is careful to articulate such prohibitions in "civil" as distinct from religious terms, insisting that when animal sacrifice is denied toleration so as to preserve public food supplies, a "law is not made about a religious but a political matter; nor is the sacrifice but the slaughter of calves thereby prohibited" (Locke 1993b: 415).

We see, therefore, that Locke repudiates religious or theological considerations as a means of determining what falls inside or outside the limits of toleration (see Locke 1993b: 420), instead appealing solely to secular "civil" concerns. In this way, Locke argued, political authorities could treat religious matters as "things indifferent," and so subject to their jurisdiction solely for their civil and not their religious or spiritual significance (Locke 1993a: 190–91, 193. See ▶ Chap. 51, "John Locke and Religious Toleration"). As Locke put it, even religious doctrines that appear "false and absurd," but which have no adverse "civil" effects, ought to be tolerated, because "the business of laws is not to provide for the truth of opinions, but for the safety and security of the commonwealth, and of every particular man's goods and person" (Locke 1993b: 420).

Here, it seems, we have a very nascent version of that phenomena which Rawlsian liberals call "public reason, in which, Rawls tells us, citizens should be "ready to explain the basis of their actions to one another in terms each could reasonably expect that others might endorse" (Rawls 2005: 218). Locke knew that "in this great variety of ways that men follow, it is still doubted which is this right one" (Locke 1993b: 407), with the result that, in matters of religion, "diversity of opinions.....cannot be avoided" (Locke 1993b: 431). He therefore knew that any attempt to justify the public exercise of state authority on religious grounds would not give rise to propositions that "each could reasonably expect that others might endorse," and so would create far more divisions than it resolved. Further, any attempt to justify state authority on religious grounds would be at odds with his insistence that the state treat all matters of religion as a "thing indifferent", as well as being at odds with his Protestant belief that religion is a matter which (in the absence of any "civil" consequences) falls outside the jurisdiction of political authorities, instead residing ultimately in the consciences of individuals alone (Locke 1993a: 189, 191, 193, 1993b: 393, 394, 396, 403, 405, 405–06, 411, 412, 421–22, 422, 422–23, 423). Locke's insistence, therefore, that the exercise of state authority, including the limits it imposed on toleration, be justified solely in terms of "civil" interests, in which all subject to state authority had a commensurate interest, was a deliberate attempt to ensure political agreement between individuals invidiously divided on religion, thereby avoiding the religious conflicts that he knew were inherent in the English society of his time.

The Ascendancy of Toleration

We saw that in the Middle Ages, toleration for dissident Christians was not on the agenda of either the Catholic Church or secular rulers. On the contrary, many perceived virtue in stamping out what was designated by the Church as "heresy." As Perez Zagorin states:

> Religious intolerance and persecution, therefore, were seen not as evils but as necessary and salutary for the preservation of religious truth and orthodoxy and all that was believed to depend on them. (Zagorin 2003: 16)

We saw that normative arguments for toleration, arising under Condition 3, were often precluded by the "moral challenge" to which religious toleration could give rise among the religiously devout. We also saw that pragmatic arguments for religious toleration circumvented this "moral challenge," but at the cost of any *necessary* connection between toleration and the ends it sought to achieve.

So why, in the wake of the sixteenth and seventeenth century wars of religion, did religious toleration come increasingly to prevail, at least in Western Europe and its colonial offshoots? One reason was a combination of lived human experience and, perhaps, increasing secularization. Inhabitants within these societies arguably got used to the presence of religious diversity, and, as time passed and individuals no longer worried as much about the eternal fate of human souls (one symptom of increasing secularization) the "moral challenge" of toleration declined. When religious diversity did not produce deleterious results, individuals and governments were increasingly willing to affirm toleration as a positive norm (and not merely as a *fait accompli* arising from their incapacity to engage in effective persecution) and to do so precisely because of the individual religious liberty toleration made possible. Such an affirmation of religious liberty as an end in itself was reinforced by the increasing presence within these cultures (from the eighteenth century onwards) of liberal ideals affirming these ends and Enlightenment ideals espousing freedom of thought and inquiry. As these ideals became more widely disseminated and entrenched throughout Europe and elsewhere, the normative entitlement of individuals to affirm their own religious beliefs (and the freedom from interference, upheld by toleration, that made this possible) were more likely to be positively endorsed. This meant that, although an aversion to rival religious faiths might remain (Condition 2), such positive recognition of these entitlements, on the basis of liberal, Enlightenment, or some other set of ideals, provided normative reasons for toleration under Condition 3.

However, according to John Stuart Mill and Herbert Butterfield, there is another set of reasons that explain the increasing prevalence of toleration in the wake of the religious conflict of the sixteenth and seventeenth centuries. These reasons reside in the pragmatic realities of *realpolitik* discussed earlier. When, in the wake of the Reformation, neither Catholics or Protestants could, after more than a century of struggle, eradicate the presence of the other, then (as explained above) the presence of both within a single polity made mutual toleration a practical necessity if such upheaval was not to continue. Mill, in a passage quoted earlier, declares that toleration arose in those instances where "the heretics were too strong a party to be effectually persecuted." Herbert Butterfield provides a similar explanation for the proliferation of toleration, centered in the same *realpolitik*:

> [Toleration] was not so much an ideal, a positive end, that people wanted to establish for its own sake; but, rather, a *pis aller*, a retreat to the next best thing, a last resort for those who often still hated one another, but found it impossible to go on fighting any more. It was hardly even an 'idea' for the most part – just a happening – the sort of thing that happens when no choice is left and there is no hope of further struggle being worthwhile. (Butterfield 1977: 573. My addition)

Some asked of what worth was the forcible imposition of outward religious uniformity by state authorities if, in some circumstances, due to the resistance it elicited, such forcible imposition resulted in the physical extermination of the heterodox religious minorities upon whom it was applied? In this respect, John Locke refers to "the extreme absurdity they are guilty of, who, under pretence of zeal for the salvation of souls, proceed to the taking away their lives" (Locke 1963: 72. See also Locke 1993b: 392).

Consequently, one argument for toleration, arising under Condition 3, was the unacceptable human cost which, it was increasingly recognized, was associated with its alternative. Of course, such an argument for toleration assumes that state authorities are imposing religious uniformity for normative reasons – "under pretence of zeal for the salvation of souls." If they are imposing such uniformity for pragmatic reasons, centered on civil peace or state security, the "extreme absurdity" to which Locke refers may not arise. We see, therefore, how, in the case of state authorities, reasons for toleration (arising under Condition 3) are dependent, for their cogency, on the purposes state authorities are seeking to achieve.

The Possibility of Political Toleration

As we move further away, historically, from the agonistic animosities generated by the Reformation, and more towards contemporary political cultures informed by liberal or Enlightenment values, state authorities, arriving at reasons for toleration under Condition 3, are less likely to concede such toleration for the pragmatic or *realpolitik* reasons identified above and more likely to advance toleration for the normative reasons mentioned, centered on the entitlements of individuals to exercise the liberties they seek. Yet if such state authorities, in endorsing these normative reasons for toleration, are fully convinced that individuals deserve the liberties they seek under Condition 1, it may be that their affirmation of this entitlement (Condition 3) expunges the aversion to these liberties which, under the terms of condition 2, is also a necessary feature of toleration. Further, if state authorities endorse, as a general principle, a liberal ideal of "neutrality," wherein "[t]he state should not seek to promote any particular conception of the good life because of its presumed *intrinsic* superiority – that is, because it is supposedly a *truer* conception" (Larmore

1987: 43), then this is presumably a further reason why any aversion, arising under Condition 2, cannot be sustained by state authorities, since such aversion would be premised on the sort of evaluative distinctions, based on "truth" or "superiority," ruled out by the principle of "neutrality."

However, if state authorities do not retain their aversion towards that which they tolerate, some have questioned whether (as a result of the absence of Condition 2) they are engaging in toleration at all. Rather, are they perhaps more likely to be engaging in a positive endorsement of the liberties advanced under Condition 1, without the reservation (Condition 2) that characterizes toleration?

If such a criticism has cogency, then it is a criticism that applies not just to recent liberal democratic states, upholding such principles as a liberal ideal of "neutrality," but also to much earlier periods. We saw above that a late seventeenth-century figure like John Locke argued that state authorities should approach all matters of religion as "things indifferent," and of relevance to state policy solely insofar as such matters affected those "civil" interests which fell within the state's jurisdiction, thereby refusing to premise state action on any judgments centered on the "truth" or "superiority" of religion itself. If states adopt such an "indifferent" perspective concerning the religious beliefs or practices they choose to tolerate, then (as with "neutrality") such "indifference" means there is no room for the aversion identified under Condition 2 as a necessary feature of toleration. We reach, therefore, the ironic conclusion that if we rigorously apply Condition 2 as a necessary feature of toleration, then the type of toleration engaged in by Lockean or (later) liberal state authorities does not (as a result of the "things indifferent" or "neutrality" principle) amount to toleration at all.

Peter Jones has sought to avoid such a conclusion by insisting it is possible for modern state authorities to engage in policies of toleration even though such authorities do not exhibit an aversion to that which is tolerated, and therefore do not fulfill what we have called Condition 2. He refers to such toleration as "political toleration," because it is undertaken by states, in the exercise of their authority, rather than by individuals in their private relationships. He insists that the aversion which we have identified under Condition 2 is not a necessary condition of such "political toleration" since "political toleration" refers to the broad conditions that states put in place to allow tolerant outcomes to occur, and so is not entirely analogous with the specific practice of toleration identified by our five conditions above:

> [W]e need to rethink our understanding of political toleration – toleration secured by or through the state – to suit the changed political circumstances in which we now live. In the past, political toleration has been intelligible as toleration extended by a ruler to his or her subjects. But that ruler-subject model of toleration is inappropriate to liberal democratic regimes. We should now think of a tolerant political order not as one in which a government tolerates its subjects but as one that upholds an ideal of toleration among its citizens. It might do that by, for example, maintaining an order of things in which citizens are prevented from using political power to impose their favoured form of life upon other citizens who are committed to other forms of life. (Jones 2007b: 12. See also Jones 2007a: 383–87; Balint 2017: 23–24)

Consequently, Jones states that "we should conceive [of] political toleration not as toleration extended by a society's rules and institutions to the population they regulate. Rather rules and institutions can be adjudged tolerant because and in so far as they uphold an ideal of toleration. They secure an order of things in which people can live their lives as they see fit, unprevented by disapproving others who might otherwise impede them" (Jones 2007a: 387). In this way, Jones seeks to retain the ideal of toleration, at an aggregate political level, in political circumstances where state authorities no longer possess the aversion to that seeking toleration which had once characterized religiously minded monarchs in premodern regimes.

The Desirability of Toleration

We saw above that political toleration is, according to scholars such as Peter Jones, still possible in the absence of Condition 2. But in cases of toleration where Condition 2 is present, some scholars have questioned not the *possibility*, but rather the *desirability* of toleration, castigating it as an outmoded ideal.

Those who adopt this point of view conceive toleration to be *undesirable* because they perceive it to be an inherently unequal practice, and therefore a poor alternative to more egalitarian means of granting people an entitlement to specific liberties. This undesirability arises from two inequalities which are said to be inextricably associated with toleration itself. One entails an asymmetry of evaluation and the other an asymmetry of power.

The inequality involving an asymmetry of power is generally assumed to arise between those who engage in toleration and those subject to it. This asymmetry refers to the presumed capacity, on the part of those engaging in toleration, to reverse this practice and engage in prohibition and proscription instead (Condition 5). This presumes an unequal power between those with the capacity to engage in toleration and those subject to it, because the former can override the liberties of the latter without the latter possessing the capacity to successfully defend these liberties (or override the liberties of the former) in turn.

The second inequality refers to an asymmetry of evaluation and concerns the aversion (Condition 2) which, it is believed, those who engage in toleration necessarily feel for the object of toleration – that is, for the opinions, beliefs, values, or practices for which a liberty is sought under Condition 1, or for the persons seeking to exercise this liberty. Such a process involves an asymmetry of evaluation because the evaluative perspective of those engaging in toleration, involving disapproval, distaste, or disdain for the object of toleration, is the only evaluative perspective considered relevant to the practice of toleration itself (under Condition 2). The evaluative perspective of those subject to toleration is not a condition of toleration at all.

In the view of some, it is both of these asymmetries, and the inequalities to which they give rise, which render toleration an outmoded ideal in contemporary liberal democratic polities, since it is assumed that, within such polities, the differences between individuals, and the diversity to which these give rise, ought to be regulated by more egalitarian arrangements and commitments (see Jones 2007a: 386). As David Heyd states:

> The successful career of the idea of toleration paradoxically led to its own decline, or at least made it superfluous in its traditional political form. In the second half of the twentieth-century religious, ethnic, and sexual minorities have become more and more impatient with the status of being tolerated. In a multicultural society, the demand for recognition supersedes that of toleration. (Heyd 2008: 175)

From this perspective, toleration appears as a second-best (and highly unequal) alternative to the recognition of equal liberties, articulated perhaps in terms of a discourse of equal "rights." Such a rejection of toleration is not new. It was advanced as long ago as the late eighteenth century by George Washington. Writing as US President to the Hebrew Congregation of Newport, Rhode Island, in 1790, and referring to the individual rights upheld by the new American Republic, he declared:

> All possess alike liberty of conscience and immunities of citizenship. It is now no more that toleration is spoken of, as if it was by the indulgence of one class of people, that another enjoyed the exercise of their inherent natural rights. (Washington 2020)

The French philosopher, Jacques Derrida, is far removed from George Washington in time and perspective, but he too expresses similar sentiments regarding the doctrine of toleration, viewing it as a relationship of inequality that falls short of contemporary egalitarian standards:

> Though I clearly prefer shows of tolerance to shows of intolerance, I nonetheless still have certain reservations about the word 'tolerance' and the discourse it organizes. It is a discourse with religious roots; it is most often used on the side of those with power, always as a kind of condescending concession.…Indeed, tolerance is first of all a form of charity.….Tolerance is always on the side of the 'reason of the strongest', where 'might is right'; it is a supplementary mark of sovereignty, the good face of sovereignty, which says to the other from its elevated position, I am letting you be, you are not insufferable, I am leaving you a place in my home, but do not forget that this is my home. (Derrida 2003: 127–28).

The Continuing Relevance of Toleration

Yet irrespective of the *desirability* of toleration when measured against more egalitarian and reciprocal arrangements, there are those who still insist on the *relevance* of toleration, at least as a means of ensuring peaceful interpersonal relations between individuals whose relationship is characterized by aversion. Such a reality is underwritten by the persistence of hostility between different groups within contemporary societies, and therefore the possibility of conflict between them. John Horton, for instance, has declared that "in so far as individuals or groups are genuinely and deeply committed to beliefs and practices that are mutually antagonistic, particularly when they are bound up with ideas of right and wrong, the sacred, or fundamental values," then "a measure of disparagement, condescension or even hostility may be a normal concomitant of such commitments" (Horton 2012: 23). Such individuals or groups may not even be able to grant to each other the purely "symbolic" recognition (such as Anna Elisabetta Galeotti advocates) in which they do not concede any intrinsic worth to each other's differences but accord to those differences their place among the "viable and normal alternatives" present in a plural society (Galeotti 2002: 104, 108).

Such deep aversion and animosity can arise in many circumstances, but it is particularly likely to arise in circumstances of religious antagonism where matters of "eternal concernment" are perceived to be at stake. As the following statement by Stanley Fish suggests, some of the religiously devout, in such situations, may not be amenable to reasons for toleration (such as arise under Condition 3) when such "reasons" are not fully in accord with their religious perspective:

> [A] reason persuasive to the devout would have to be a reason compatible with the content of their devotion, and . . . a reason which instead trumps, or claims to trump, that content will be seen as no reason at all but as a wolf in reason's clothing. (Fish 1997: 2299; see also Fish 1997: 2288, 2291)

Further, when matters of "eternal concernment" are perceived to be at stake, some among the religiously devout may place little worth on secular constraints, embodied in laws upholding the rights of others, particularly if they believe that divine imperatives demand otherwise. Recent violent responses to blasphemy, among a small minority of the religiously devout, elicited by Andres Serrano's *Piss Christ*, Salman Rushdie's *Satanic Verses*, or the Muhammad cartoons appearing in the newspapers *Jyllands-Posten* and *Charlie Hebdo,* are evidence of this (see ▶ Chap. 30, "Toleration and Respect"). Jeremy Waldron points to the reason for this absence of constraint among the minority of the religiously devout engaging in such violence as follows:

> Faith treats of eternal life and eternal suffering, prospects in comparison with which earthly laws and earthly sanctions pale into insignificance. (Waldron 1993: 136)

Given such circumstances, to ask the religiously devout to "extend *more* than toleration" towards those to whom they are hostile, in a way that requires them to give up their aversion and affirm the equal entitlements of those whom they believe have impugned their God, or engaged in some other form of sacrilege, may "begin to intrude in a significant way on the integrity of their beliefs" (Horton 2012: 21). In the absence of these possibilities, a toleration which occurs in the context of a persistent aversion is perhaps the best we might hope for, and one means whereby peaceful coexistence between those fundamentally at odds with each other might be maintained. Concerning how we might convince the religiously devout to affirm such toleration, I have argued elsewhere that a skepticism towards the scriptural claims of revealed religion – but a skepticism that allows the devout to retain the full plenitude of their religious faith intact – is the only reason for toleration (Condition 3), outside of their own religion, likely to convince the devout to tolerate that which, on the basis of their faith, they find abhorrent (Tate 2016a: 240–42, 2016b: 667–674).

Consequently, even though state laws may endorse equal "rights" for citizens, and other egalitarian arrangements, individuals in their interpersonal relations may still possess aversion and animosity towards each other, irrespective of the "rights" each legally bear. To convince such individuals to treat those with whom they are at odds in ways that accord with such "rights" and the equal entitlements to which they give rise (when they do not perceive these others as deserving of such equality) may require convincing them to "tolerate" these others when they are not able to accord them such "equality" on more egalitarian terms. Only then are they most likely to act, in their daily practice, in accord with the legal obligations that such "rights" impose, because such toleration allows them to retain their aversion to the recipient of such "rights" even as they treat them in ways that formally accord with these legal obligations. In such contexts, Horton says, "toleration in the traditional sense, rather than something more demanding, may be the most that can reasonably be required when such convictions are at stake, if we do want to permit deep differences" (Horton 2012: 20. See also Jones 2006: 142–43).

Conclusion

This chapter has considered how, historically, it was religion, within Western and Central Europe, which first gave rise to widespread demands for toleration. It has sought to explain why religious toleration was not, initially, a widespread policy adopted in response to religious conflict and division but how, over time, it became an increasingly prevalent ideal. It has distinguished different "reasons" for toleration, centered on normative and pragmatic concerns, and has looked not only at the *possibility* and *desirability* of toleration but also at its continuing *relevance* over time.

Summary and Future Directions

Toleration among Christians is a policy and a practice with a history that extends back to the sixteenth century. It remains a relevant policy, applying to much wider sections of contemporary communities, beyond the realm of religion, because the aversion, presupposed by toleration, often persists within societal relations and therefore within contemporary polities, with rival and highly diverse groups often finding it difficult to affirm the equal worth of each other. This is often particularly the case in relation to religious conflict, where, in the view of some of the religiously devout, matters of "eternal concernment" are at stake. Such tensions render toleration a relevant policy in these circumstances, since more egalitarian demands, requiring such individuals to overcome their aversion as a means of according to others their equal entitlements, may evoke resistance or refusal. Toleration allows such individuals to accord such equal entitlements to others but still retain their aversion. Future developments will determine just how relevant the policy and practice of toleration remains.

References

Acton L (1962) Essays on freedom and power. Meridian Books, Cleveland
Allen JW (1960) A history of political thought in the sixteenth century. Methuen, London
Balint P (2014) Acts of tolerance: a political and descriptive account. Eur J Polit Theo 13(3):264–281
Balint P (2017) Respecting toleration. Traditional liberalism and contemporary diversity. Oxford University Press, Oxford
Bejan TM (2017) Mere civility: Disagreement and the limits of toleration. Harvard University Press, Cambridge MA
Bindoff ST (1958) Tudor England. Penguin, Harmondsworth
Butterfield H (1977) Toleration in early modern times. J Hist Ideas 38(4):573–584
Chadwick O (1976) The reformation. Penguin, Harmondsworth
Coffey J (2000) Persecution and toleration in Protestant England, 1558–1689. Pearson Education Ltd., Edinburgh Gate
Cohen AJ (2004) What toleration is. Ethics 115(1):68–95
Crankshaw E (1971) The Habsburgs. Weidenfeld and Nicolson, London
Cranston M (1952) The politics of John Locke. Hist Today 2(9):619–622
Cranston M (1957) John Locke. A biography. Longmans, Green and Co., London
Derrida J (2003) Autoimmunity: real and symbolic suicides – a dialogue with Jacques Derrida. In: Borradori G (ed) Philosophy in a time of terror. Dialogues with Jűrgen Habermas and Jacques Derrida. University of Chicago Press, Chicago, pp 85–136
Dunn RS (1970) The age of religious wars 1559–1689. W.W. Norton & Company, New York
Elton GR (1988) Reformation Europe 1517–1559. Fontana Press, London
Fish S (1997) Mission impossible: settling the just bounds between church and state. Columbia Law Rev 97(8):2255–2333
Galeotti AE (2002) Toleration as recognition. Cambridge University Press, Cambridge
Goldie M (2010) Introduction. In: Goldie M (ed) John Locke: a letter concerning toleration and other writings. Liberty Fund, Indianapolis, pp ix–xxiii
Green VHH (1961) Renaissance and reformation. Edward Arnold, London
Heyd D (2008) Is toleration a political virtue? In: Williams MS, Waldron J (eds) Toleration and its limits. New York University Press, New York, pp 171–194
Hooker R (2000) The laws of ecclesiastical polity, vol. VIII, iii, 4. In: R Hooker, The works of Richard Hooker, Oxford: 1885, cited in J. Coffey, Persecution and toleration in Protestant England, 1558–1689. Pearson Education Ltd., Edinburgh Gate: 21
Horton J (1994) Three (apparent) paradoxes of toleration. Synth Philos 9(1):7–20
Horton J (1996) Toleration as a virtue. In: Heyd D (ed) Toleration. An elusive virtue. Princeton University Press, Princeton, pp 28–43
Horton J (2012) Why the traditional conception of toleration still matters. In: Edyvane D, Matravers M (eds) Toleration re-examined. Routledge, London, pp 9–26
Hughes P (1960) The reformation. Burns & Oates, London
Jones P (2006) Toleration, recognition and identity. J Polit Philos 14(2):123–143
Jones P (2007a) Making sense of political toleration. Br J Polit Sci 37(3):383–402
Jones P (2007b) Can speech be intolerant? In: Newey G (ed) Freedom of expression. Counting the cost. Cambridge Scholars Publishing, Cambridge, pp 9–29
Jones P (2011) Political toleration: a reply to Newey. Br J Polit Sci 41(2):445–447
Jones P (2012) Legalising toleration: a reply to Balint. Res Publica 18(3):265–270
Kamen H (1972) The rise of toleration. McGraw-Hill, Toronto
Larmore CE (1987) Patterns of moral complexity. Cambridge University Press, Cambridge
Locke J (1963) A second letter concerning toleration. In: John Locke, The works of John Locke, VI. Scientia Verlag, Aalen, pp 61–137
Locke J (1965) In: Laslett P (ed) Two treatises of government. New American Library, New York

Locke J (1993a) An essay concerning toleration. In: Wootton D (ed) J Locke, Political writings. Penguin, London, pp 186–210

Locke J (1993b) A letter concerning toleration. In: Wootton D (ed) J Locke, Political writings. Penguin, London, pp 390–436

Mendus S (1989) Toleration and the limits of liberalism. Macmillan, London

Mill JS (1971) On liberty, in JS Mill, utilitarianism, liberty, representative government. Everyman's Library, London, pp 61–170

Newey G (2001) Is democratic toleration a rubber duck? Res Publica 7(3):315–336

Plamenatz J (1972) Man and society. A critical examination of some important social and politial theories from Machaivelli to Marx. Longman, London

Popkin RH (1979) The history of skepticism from Erasmus to Spinoza. University of California Press, Berkeley

Raphael DD (1988) The intolerable. In: Mendus S (ed) Justifying toleration. Conceptual and historical perspectives. Cambridge University Press, Cambridge, pp 137–154

Rawls J (2005) Political liberalism, rev. edn. Columbia University Press, New York

Raz J (1986) The morality of freedom. Clarendon Press, Oxford

Sabine GH (1963) A history of political theory. 3rd ed. George G Harrap & Co., London

Scanlon TM (2003) The difficulty of tolerance. Essays in political philosophy. Cambridge University Press, Cambridge

Tate JW (2016a) Liberty, toleration and equality. John Locke, Jonas Proast and the letters concerning toleration. Routledge, New York

Tate JW (2016b) Toleration, skepticism and blasphemy: John Locke, Jonas Proast and Charlie Hebdo. Am J Polit Sci 60(3):664–675

Vernon R (1997) The career of toleration. John Locke, Jonas Proast, and after. McGill-Queen's University Press, Montreal

Waldron J (1993) Rushdie and religion. In: J Waldron, Liberal rights. Collected papers 1981–1991. Cambridge University Press, Cambridge, pp 134–142

Waldron J (1997) Locke: toleration and the rationality of persecution. In: Dunn J, Harris I (eds) Locke, vol II. Edward Elgar Publishing, Cheltenham, pp 349–374

Washington G (2020) From George Washington to the Hebrew congregation in Newport, Rhode Island, 18 Aug 1790. Founders Online, https://founders.archives.gov/documents/Washington/05-06-02-0135

Williams B (1996) Toleration: an impossible virtue? In: Heyd D (ed) Toleration: An elusive virtue. Princeton University Press, Prinston, pp 18–27

Zagorin P (2003) How the idea of religious toleration came to the West. Princeton University Press, Princeton

Toleration and Religious Discrimination

41

Andrew Shorten

Contents

Introduction	828
Toleration, Neutrality, and Religious Accommodation	829
Religion, Discrimination, and Collective Exemptions	833
Justifying Collective Exemptions	836
Objections to Collective Exemptions	838
Weighing Burdens	840
Basic Interests	841
Material Burdens	842
Communicative Injuries	843
Domination	844
Severity and the "Baseline Puzzle"	846
Summary and Future Directions	848
References	849

Abstract

Toleration plays a central role in debates about the accommodation of religious beliefs and practices in liberal democracies. This chapter addresses one such debate, which concerns whether liberal societies ought to tolerate discriminatory practices when, or even because, they are performed by religious associations and institutions. After briefly discussing some recently canvassed arguments in support of tolerating discrimination by religious associations, it turns to the question of how political communities might establish the limits to this form of toleration, a question so far neglected by philosophers. One reason why a tolerant state might refuse to allow religious associations to discriminate is to avoid injuring third-parties, a long-established basis for restricting toleration. This "third-party injuries" objection is carefully unpacked, and it is suggested that third-parties might be injured by particular religious accommodations in at least four different ways.

A. Shorten (✉)
Department of Politics and Public Administration, University of Limerick, Limerick, Ireland
e-mail: andrew.shorten@ul.ie

© The Author(s), under exclusive licence to Springer Nature Switzerland AG 2022
M. Sardoč (ed.), *The Palgrave Handbook of Toleration*,
https://doi.org/10.1007/978-3-030-42121-2_1

Some tentative suggestions are then made about how to establish the significance and relevance of these injuries.

Keywords

Religion · Religious Accommodation · Discrimination · Collective Exemptions · Domination · Toleration

Introduction

Toleration plays a central role in debates about the accommodation of religious beliefs and practices in liberal democracies. This chapter focuses on one such debate, namely, whether liberal societies ought to tolerate discriminatory practices when, or even because, they are performed by religious associations and institutions. For example, ought schools with a religious ethos be permitted to consider religious beliefs when appointing teachers or selecting students? Should religious employers be allowed to opt out of antidiscrimination laws? Should firms with religious owners, or religious charities, be permitted to deny services to someone because of their sexuality or gender identity? Not only are these questions, and others like them, pressing for many societies today, but they also raise some difficult philosophical challenges concerning how political communities should establish the limits to toleration.

The first parts of the chapter are conceptual. The first section, "Toleration, Neutrality and Religious Accommodation," situates the debate over religious accommodation within the wider context of philosophical debates about the nature of toleration. Here it is argued that religious accommodations, including exemptions from antidiscrimination laws, are manifestations of toleration but are not tied to any particular conception of toleration, such as the traditional conception of toleration as forbearance or more recent theories of toleration as recognition. The next section, "Religion, Discrimination and Collective Exemptions," discusses religious discrimination in general and suggests that accommodations to permit discrimination by religious associations can be characterized, following Cécile Laborde (2017), as "collective exemptions." Some examples are then presented to illustrate the surprising range of public policy domains in which this variety of religious accommodation can be found.

The remainder of the chapter addresses some related normative issues. The general impetus behind collective exemptions is to alleviate burdens that would be experienced by religious firms, schools, charities, hospitals (etc.) if they were required to structure themselves, or provide services, on terms they regard incompatible with their ethos (Shorten 2015, 244–249). But why should political communities remove these burdens? The next section, "Justifying Collective Exemptions," sketches some different possible answers to this and argues that any plausible theory will supply, at most, a pro tanto case for collective exemptions. Attention then turns to the other side of the coin, as it were, and the remainder of the chapter focuses on the question of when liberal states might be justified in refusing to tolerate discrimination by religious associations, even in the face of compelling reasons in support of toleration. The section "Objections to Collective Exemptions" thus identifies three different objections to collective exemptions and discusses one of these in detail.

This is the third-party injuries objection, which says that we have grounds to reject an otherwise justified religious accommodation if accepting it would have the effect of (unfairly or unjustly) transferring costs or burdens onto people who themselves do not benefit from the accommodation in question. This objection has been directed against religious accommodations in general, and not only collective exemptions. For example, workplace accommodations have been criticized for burdening the employers or colleagues of beneficiaries (Jones 1994), and exemptions from mandatory vaccination schemes and compulsory military service have been criticized for undermining attempts to advance general welfare or achieve a collective good (Leiter 2013, 100). Meanwhile, when it comes to collective exemptions, injured third-parties include people as various as teachers unable to apply for posts in religious schools, LGBTQ+ people refused goods or services, and employees denied comprehensive medical insurance.

Although there are reasons to think that the third-party injuries objection bites especially hard against collective – as opposed to individual – exemptions, it is not invariably decisive. One could accept that an accommodation is burdensome for, or even harmful to, third-parties but deny that the burden is of sufficient weight, or of the right kind, to override the original claim for an accommodation. To assess how powerful third-party injuries objections are in particular cases requires a mechanism to establish their normative significance. The final section, "Weighing Burdens," takes up this challenge, distinguishing between four different kinds of injuries and introducing a difficult puzzle about how the severity of those injuries might be established. The upshot of the discussion is that there remains considerable indeterminacy when it comes to establishing the appropriate limits to toleration, at least when it comes to permitting religiously inspired discrimination.

Toleration, Neutrality, and Religious Accommodation

The traditional conception of toleration is one of forbearance: one agent tolerates another by refraining from negatively interfering with a practice they object to and which they could prevent, if they chose to (see, e.g., Mendus (1989), Shorten (2005), Horton (2011), and Cohen (2014)). This view has recently come under pressure. For instance, Peter Balint (2017) recommends dropping the objection condition and instead proposes a permissiveness conception of toleration. This merely requires that someone intentionally refrain from negative interference when they have the power to prevent a practice. Even more radically, Anna Elisabetta Galeotti (2002) has argued that the forbearance model ought to be replaced by something she calls toleration as recognition. According to her reinterpretation, toleration today is best understood not in terms of intentional restraint but rather as the requirement to take positive action to address the marginalization or stigmatization of minority identities and practices.

Both Balint and Galeotti's revisions are responses to the idea that neutrality has made toleration redundant. The concept of neutrality, like toleration, is both lauded by many political theorists, especially liberals, and fiercely contested. The basic idea is that a neutral state ought to be studiously indifferent about the merits, or demerits, of its members' ways of life. Meanwhile, toleration as forbearance comes into conflict with this because it involves the negative appraisal of whatever practices are being considered for toleration. Accordingly, if a state is neutral, then it seemingly cannot engage in forbearance toleration.

One way to characterize this predicament, from the perspective of forbearance toleration, is to say that toleration in a neutral state is restricted to "horizontal" citizen–citizen relations and plays no role in "vertical" state–citizen relations (these terms come from Jones 2015). However, dispensing with the idea of a tolerant state seems peculiar to many, and Balint and Galeotti's proposals represent different attempts to rescue toleration as an ideal for state–citizen relations. Balint does this by making toleration compatible with neutrality. On his account, a state can be tolerant and remain neutral by following a policy of indifferent permissiveness, allowing people a wide sphere of liberty without judging the merits of their different practices and ways of life. This is because, as we have seen, he thinks that toleration does not presuppose disapproval on the part of the tolerator. Meanwhile, Galeotti's model moves in the opposite direction and is intended to surpass neutrality, which she regards as at least partially responsible for the marginalization and stigmatization of minority ways of life. On her account, liberal democratic societies already have majority biases built into them. For example, some social differences are perceived as being broadly acceptable, such as vegetarianism, and others are markers of inferiority or an outsider-status, such as (updating one of her examples) being trans or Muslim. State neutrality does nothing to address these dynamics and arguably exacerbates them. Accordingly, it must be replaced with forms of recognition in which the state positively affirms the value of different ways of life for the sake of social equality.

Interestingly, practices of religious accommodation, including collective exemptions, are compatible with each of these different conceptions. Religious accommodation involves giving religious people a "break" (Nussbaum 2008, 21), for instance, by sensitively applying rules or adjusting procedures to avoid burdening people of faith. So, accommodation might take the form of a workplace revising its uniform code, meal plans or holiday arrangements to meet the distinctive needs of its religious employees. Or, a local authority could adjust its procedures to improve access to public services for religious citizens. Among legal and political theorists, probably the most widely discussed form of religious accommodation is the rule-and-exemption strategy. Typically, this involves exempting religious individuals from otherwise generally applicable rules, as when Muslims and Jews are permitted to consume Halal and Kosher meat, in which the animal is not stunned prior to slaughter, as would normally be required, or when Sikhs are permitted to work on building sites while wearing a turban and not protective headgear, as would otherwise be required. As will be demonstrated in the next section, the cases with which this chapter is concerned are best understood as exemptions exercised by associations or institutions, as opposed to individuals. These "collective exemptions" raise many of the same issues as their individually exercised counterparts, and some others too.

According to Aurelia Bardon and Emanuela Ceva, religious accommodation represents "a sort of middle ground" between toleration as forbearance and toleration as recognition (Bardon and Ceva 2018, 438). This is because accommodation takes the form of differential or special treatment, and because its justification typically proceeds from an acknowledged shortcoming of the ideal of neutrality, both of which are characteristics Bardon and Ceva associate with toleration as recognition. Meanwhile, they believe that accommodation does not usually amount to full blown toleration as recognition, since it does not necessarily involve positively affirming the value of different ways of life, because it often does little (or nothing) to address the stigmatization or marginalization of religious minorities, and because religious groups that are not stigmatized or marginalized at all can be justified beneficiaries of it.

Although Bardon and Ceva are careful to hedge their claim that accommodation moves us in the direction of recognition, their claim is still too strong. For one thing, at least some forms of accommodation do not take the form of special treatment, despite what Bardon and Ceva suggest. Consider, for instance, accommodations that have arisen from human rights law in Europe or First Amendment law in the USA. These do not pick out particular groups for special treatment. The same goes for at least some statutory exemptions. For instance, although it is often claimed that Sikhs have an exemption in British law to allow them to carry a kirpan, the relevant legislation does not contain an exemption specifically for Sikhs but instead provides for knives to be carried for occupational reasons, for reasons of national dress, and for religious reasons (Jones 2020, 208).

Notwithstanding this, it is true, as Bardon and Ceva say, that many accommodations, and especially exemptions, are intended to remove or mitigate the adverse effects of neutrally justified laws. For example, consider the requirements that people wear hardhats on building sites or refrain from carrying knives in public. These laws are neutrally justified, serving important public purposes, despite giving rise to a special and distinctive burden for Sikh men. However, to say that accommodations often arise from the shortcomings of neutrality falls well short of saying that they move us in the direction of toleration as recognition, as Bardon and Ceva seem to assume. For instance, the purpose of the exemption to hard hat laws is (merely) to restore options or negative liberties, to enable Sikh men, like others, to work on building sites, and it has nothing to do with affirming the value of a group identity or correcting social marginalization or stigmatization. Further, this is all that most exemptions do.

A different basis for claiming that accommodations are incompatible with neutrality has been suggested by Balint, who believes that their justification depends on a non-neutral distinction between conscientious beliefs, on the one hand, and mere preferences, on the other. Advocates deem only the former to be a protection worthy characteristic, but according to Balint there is no satisfactory reason for prioritizing "conscientious beliefs over preferences" (2017, 73). So, for example, when it comes to claims for accommodations regarding police (or other) uniforms, Balint thinks that neutrality disallows any principled distinction between turban-wearing Sikhs and the fashion-conscious. Their respective claims may be of different weights, but not different types.

Balint is right to note that proponents of religious accommodations must draw some kind of distinction between characteristics that deserve protection and those which do not. Moreover, it is also the case that there are some decidedly non-neutral ways of drawing this distinction. For example, some proponents of exemptions believe that only religious beliefs and/or practices deserve protection (e.g., McConnell 1985; Laycock 1990). Nevertheless, there are other ways to draw the required distinction that do satisfy the requirements of neutrality, such as, arguably at least, Laborde's appeal to "integrity-protecting commitments" (2017), Martha Nussbaum's (2008) appeal to both secular and religious claims of conscience, and Jocelyn Maclure and Charles Taylor's (2011) distinction between "meaning giving" and "trivial" beliefs and practices. These political theorists, albeit in different ways, identify something that is valuable to everyone, such as living with integrity or according to one's conscience, in order to provide a neutrally justified basis for religious accommodations.

So, then, accommodations, including exemptions, are compatible with neutrality, properly understood, and are therefore also compatible with the permissiveness conception of toleration. Further, religious accommodations need not necessarily take one down the path toward toleration as recognition, and it is neither the case that a theory of recognition is required to justify accommodations nor that the practice of religious accommodation implies a form of recognition. Notwithstanding this, one can of course justify at least some accommodations by appealing to recognition, and so the theory of toleration as recognition, like the theory of toleration as permissiveness, is certainly compatible with religious accommodation. Finally, what about the theory of toleration as forbearance?

Recall, what makes forbearance toleration distinctive is the inclusion of the objection condition – there must be disapproval of whatever is being tolerated. As noted earlier, the objection condition seemingly comes at the cost of state neutrality, therefore implying that only political theorists who reject neutrality can support religious accommodations as manifestations of forbearance toleration. One such thinker is Bhikhu Parekh (2000, 279), who during a discussion of laws concerning female genital mutilation recommends the rule-and-exemption strategy on the basis that it involves conveying a (desirable) message that society disapproves of the practice, while nevertheless permitting it in a restricted form and on an exceptional basis. Since he is sharply critical of neutrality, Parekh is not troubled by the possibility of a state negatively appraising its citizens' practices.

Meanwhile, Jones has argued for the same conclusion – that religious accommodations manifest forbearance toleration – but without giving up on the idea of state neutrality (Jones 2015, 550–551). To illustrate, consider his argument about the rule-and-exemption approach. Here, Jones emphasizes that it is usually the case that when an exemption is sought, the relevant rule is justified by reasons that apply to everyone, including those seeking an exemption. Consider, for example, the reasons that might be invoked to justify a law to prohibit people from carrying knives in public, or to require construction workers or motorcyclists to wear protective headgear, or to require animals to be stunned prior to slaughter. These bear upon Sikhs, Muslims, and Jews as much as anyone else, meaning that any exemptions are granted in spite of the powerful reasons in favor of banning the practices. Consequently, the objection condition is satisfied by exemptions because there is always a reason to object to anyone not complying with the rule in question. As such, exemptions manifest forbearance toleration, since they combine objection with permission. What distinguishes his theory from Parekh's, however, is that Jones does not regard exemptions as sending a (disapproving) message, since he resists the construal of toleration as a relationship, in which one person tolerates another, or in which the state tolerates some of its citizens. Instead, he thinks it better to see exemptions "as representing a society's public stance on what should and should not be tolerated" (Jones 2015, 551). Thus, he concludes that "[t]oleration is a feature of the exemptions themselves rather than an expression of any particular person's or party's toleration" (Jones 2015, 551).

Religion, Discrimination, and Collective Exemptions

So far it has been demonstrated that the question of whether religious accommodations qualify as a form of toleration does not turn on the particular conception of toleration one subscribes to. This section discusses religious discrimination in general, introduces a distinction between discrimination against religion and religiously inspired discrimination, and then discusses some illustrative examples of the latter. As will become clear, collective exemptions are, at least for the most part, exemptions to permit religious associations to engage in religiously inspired discrimination. The question of whether associations should be permitted to engage in such discrimination, then, is a question about what practices ought to be tolerated and about where the limits of toleration should be drawn. These are taken up directly in sections entitled "Justifying Collective Exemptions," "Objections to Collective Exemptions," and "Weighing Burdens."

According to Benjamin Eidelson, an act or a practice is discriminatory when it treats someone less favorably than some real or counterfactual other, in some particular respect, and when this differential treatment is explained by reference to a particular property or trait (Eidelson 2015, 17). Discrimination, according to this view, is not a moralized concept, and is not wrong as such. In the case of religious discrimination, the properties or traits that Eidelson refers to are religious in character, and religious discrimination comes in two basic forms – discrimination against religious believers and discrimination that is religiously inspired (or, as Laegaard's (2018) instructive discussion has it, religious beliefs and practices can either be the object or the subject of discrimination).

Religious discrimination in the form of disfavoring people because of their religious beliefs or practices is widespread, but only of tangential relevance to the aims of this chapter. Sometimes such discrimination is readily apparent, as when employers refuse to hire workers from a particular group, while in other instances it may be difficult to discern. For instance, consider *Noah v. Desrosiers* (2008), a UK employment tribunal. This case arose after Sarah Desrosiers, owner of a hairdressing salon in London specializing in "funky, spunky and urban" hairdressing, declined to offer a position to Bushra Noah, because Noah was unwilling to remove her Islamic headscarf, and because Desrosiers insisted that her staff showcase the salon's styling by making their own hair visible (Jones 2015, 553). The tribunal found that although Desrosiers had not directly discriminated against Noah, her policy of requiring staff to make their own hair visible was indirectly discriminatory.

The other form of religious discrimination, which is the subject of this chapter, is religiously inspired discrimination. Many examples of this have also arisen in employment tribunals. For example, consider Lillian Ladele, who worked as a registrar of births, deaths, and marriages for the public authorities in London (*Lillian Ladele v. London Borough of Islington*, 2008). After the Civil Partnerships Act (2004) permitted gays and lesbians to establish legally recognized partnerships, Ladele requested that she not be required to officiate at such ceremonies, which she regarded as contrary to her Christian faith. In other words, she sought a workplace accommodation to facilitate religiously inspired discrimination.

Not all cases of religiously inspired discrimination involve workers seeking accommodations from their employers. For example, consider Ashers Baking Company in Northern Ireland, whose owners – Daniel and Amy McArthur – refused to make a cake for Gareth Lee bearing a message to promote same-sex marriage, because they regarded it as contrary to their Christian faith (*Lee v. Ashers Baking Company*, 2018). Here it was the bakery itself, or perhaps its owners, who sought permission, from the state, to discriminate in an otherwise unlawful way. At around the same time a strikingly similar case was heard in the USA (*Masterpiece Cakeshop v. Colorado Civil Rights Commission*, 2018), although here it was a wedding cake for a gay couple that the owner of the shop, Jack Phillips, refused to bake.

An interesting feature of the bakery cases, which distinguish them from *Ladele*, was that permission to discriminate was sought by commercial firms, or by the owners of those firms. Perhaps the most infamous – and widely discussed – example of this phenomenon is *Burwell* vs. *Hobby Lobby Stores, Inc* (2014), in which a "closely-held" American chain of arts and crafts stores, employing more than 13,000 people, sought – and was granted – an exemption from the requirement to provide health plans including emergency contraception to their employees, as would otherwise have been required by the Affordable Care Act (2010).

Sometimes cases like these are discussed as if they directly comparable to Ladele's situation, on the grounds that in each of them an individual (or family) requests an accommodation for the sake of their conscientious convictions. This is perhaps why the McArthurs themselves, like Phillips and – in the case of Hobby Lobby – the Green family, featured so prominently in public discussions about these cases, where it was often implied that the conflict at stake was between the rights of these individuals and those of their customers or employees. However, cases like *Hobby Lobby*, and perhaps *Ashers* and *Masterpiece* too, are better characterized as examples of what Laborde (2017) calls "collective exemptions" (also referred to as "institutional exemptions" (Shorten 2015), arguably a more accurate label (Shorten 2019, 710–711)). These religious accommodations are characterized by two things. First, they take the form of exemptions from generally applicable rules (usually antidiscrimination or civil rights laws). Second, they are exercised by institutions, such as churches, schools, hospitals, or firms, as opposed to individuals.

Such exemptions are widespread and come in a variety of forms, and as the following three indicative examples illustrate. First, schools with a religious character are sometimes exempted from antidiscrimination laws to allow them to select pupils on religious grounds. This was referred to as the "baptism barrier" in Ireland, where it was expressly provided for in section 7 of the Equal Status Act (2000) and was recently eliminated in the Education (Admission to Schools) Act (2018). A slightly different version of religiously selective admissions is also permitted in schools in England and Wales, where the recent trend has been toward facilitating religious selection in faith schools rather than discouraging it (Clayton et al. forthcoming). Similarly, admissions policies in religious universities and higher education institutions have also attracted controversy. For instance, in *Trinity Western University v British Columbia College of Teachers* (2001) the Canadian Supreme Court allowed a religious teacher training college to (effectively) exclude (noncelibate) homosexuals, though in a later case, *Trinity Western University v. Law Society of Upper Canada* (2018), the court reached the opposite conclusion regarding a proposed law school at the same university.

Second, publicly funded schools with a religious ethos have also been granted exemptions from employment discrimination laws. For example, legislation in Ireland permits schools with a religious ethos to take "action which is reasonably necessary to prevent an employee or a prospective employee from undermining the religious ethos of the institution" (Employment Equality Act, 1998, s. 37). Thus, schools may consider the beliefs and conduct of prospective employees, and ethos-undermining conduct outside of the workplace is potentially grounds for dismissal. Although the extent of this provision has not been tested in the courts, empirical evidence suggests that it has discouraged many lesbian, gay, and bisexual teachers from disclosing their sexuality (Gowran 2004, 42; see also Gray 2013; Neary 2013).

Indeed, there have been a number of cases, in Ireland and elsewhere, in which teachers have been removed from their posts in religious schools, for reasons that would not be lawfully available to other employers. Probably the most infamous example of this in Ireland was Eileen Flynn, who taught Irish and History in a convent school from 1978 to 1982 in County Wexford and who was sacked after giving birth outside of marriage and deciding to raise her child with her partner, who himself was separated from his spouse (divorce was not available at the time in Ireland) (*Eileen Flynn v. Sister Mary Anna Power and The Sisters of the Holy Faith* 1985). In a similar and contemporaneous case in the USA, Susan Little was removed from her post in a Catholic elementary school after entering a second marriage because, although being legally valid, it did not satisfy the requirements of Canon

Law (*Little v. Wuerl*, 1991). In a more recent case the European Court of Human Rights supported the decision to terminate the employment of Fernández Martínez, a priest who taught religion and ethics in a public school and whose salary was paid by the Spanish state, after it became public knowledge that he was married with three children (*Martinez v. Spain*, 2014).

Third, and outside of schools, religious accommodations have also been granted to charities and publicly funded bodies to enable them to refrain from providing services that are odds with their religious mission. For instance, in the USA a number of states permit religious hospitals to refuse to provide abortions. Similarly, religious adoption agencies have also been granted accommodations to allow them to lawfully refuse to place children with LGBTQ+ parents. For instance, this was expressly facilitated on a temporary basis in the UK in the 2007 Equality Act (Sexual Orientation) Regulations, in an accommodation that has long since expired (Shorten 2015, 247–248). Although now seemingly settled in the UK, this issue remains fiercely contested in the USA (see, e.g., Corvino et al. (2017, 113–114) and Tebbe (2017, 193–194)).

So, then, political communities will often face the issue of deciding whether to extend collective exemptions to permit religiously inspired discrimination. The remainder of the chapter will focus on arguments that might be given for either permitting or prohibiting such discrimination. It is worth noting that there is an additional option, which I do not consider in this chapter, and which has been suggested in different ways by Stephen Macedo (1998) and Corey Brettschneider (2012). This is to permit religiously motivated discrimination while also using the expressive or educative capacities of the state to criticise it and encourage reform. Some of what is said later may be indirectly relevant for determining when such "transformative" projects ought to be launched.

Justifying Collective Exemptions

To date, legal and political theorists have devoted more attention to formulating arguments in support of collective exemptions than to asking when these might justifiably be overridden, including by the interests of third-parties. This second issue is addressed in sections "Objections to Collective Exemptions," and "Weighing Burdens." This section briefly discusses the justification of collective exemptions and, in particular, suggests that any argument in support of them can deliver, at most, pro tanto grounds for collective exemptions. These grounds might be overridden by, among other things, the interests of third-parties or the goal of protecting freedom and equality for all.

This framework conflicts with a claim that some critics (e.g., Schragger and Schwartzman 2013; Cohen 2015; Laborde 2017; Baumeister 2019) have attributed to a theory that has come to be known as "religious institutionalism." According to this, churches and other religious institutions have rights akin to those of sovereign states, an idea captured by Paul Horwitz's description of religious bodies as "sovereign within their own spheres" (2009, 83) and by Richard Garnett's claim that the state should respect the autonomy of the church as an "organized society with its own laws and jurisdiction" (Garnett 2016, 50; see also Smith 2016). If this theory is true, then the third-party injuries objection is redundant, since the rights of religious associations cannot be "balanced against the rights of others or measured against important state interests" (Schragger and Schwartzman 2013, 919).

A number of different grounds – legal and normative – have been proposed to justify religious institutionalism, but according to Jean Cohen the "heart" of the case in its favor is a controversial interpretation of state neutrality (Cohen 2015, 188). According to this, a neutral state cannot consistently affirm its own supremacy because it cannot authoritatively deny the claims of religious believers to be subject to a higher authority (McConnell 1985, 15). Given this, secular authorities cannot simply presume to have a right to govern the affairs of religious associations, and it is religious bodies themselves which "must have the authority to determine the scope of their own competence" (Laborde 2017, 167). Accordingly, the fact that collective exemptions happen to almost always be exemptions from antidiscrimination laws is in a sense contingent, since in other areas of law too the liberal democratic state lacks the authority to trespass on the sovereignty of religious associations.

However, at least when interpreted as a strict thesis about jurisdictional autonomy, religious institutionalism entails an implausibly austere conception of sovereignty. This assumes that sovereign bodies have no duties to people either within or outside their jurisdiction, since if they did then their authority would be limited. But hardly anyone still believes this about the state, and it stretches credibility to insist upon it for religious institutions, not least because it undermines whatever grounds we have for criticizing tyranny and oppression within them.

So then, any plausible argument for collective exemptions must fall short of the "sphere sovereignty" view. A number of such arguments have been canvassed by liberals in recent writings, including ones appealing to freedom of conscience (Schragger and Schwartzman 2013), a right to "close association" (Sagar 2017), and a combination of freedom of religion and freedom of association (Shorten 2017). Perhaps the most complete is Laborde's recent adaption of the "integrity" argument for individual religious accommodations to the special case of collective exemptions. The integrity argument is usually employed to explain why individuals are entitled to religious exemptions (see, e.g., Bou-Habib (2006), Vallier (2015), Lenta (2016), and Seglow (2017)). Laborde argues that collective exemptions can be justified on broadly similar grounds, by reference to the morally weighty interests that the members of (religious and other) associations have in being able to preserve their collective integrity, which could be frustrated by the strict (exemptionless) application of antidiscrimination rules. The protection of collective integrity, to be clear, is not valuable in itself, but only insofar as it allows individual members of associations to live with integrity (Laborde 2017, 174). In any case, one thing it requires, according to Laborde, is that people be able to maintain the "coherence" of their associations, and this means ensuring that the activities which they engage in and the rules governing their internal affairs are consistent with the ethos or beliefs of the association (Laborde 2017, 160–196; see also Shorten 2015, 249–252). Applied strictly, antidiscrimination laws may therefore jeopardize the "coherence" of an association if, for instance, adoption charities are required to provide services to gays and lesbians or religious employers are required to consider hiring nonbelievers.

Laborde's argument is based on an appeal to freedom of association, already long identified by liberal political theorists as playing a crucial role in justifying and limiting group rights (see, e.g., Barry (2001) and White (1997)). Like other liberal egalitarian approaches to religious accommodation (e.g., Maclure and Taylor 2011; Eisgruber and Sager 2007), her argument does not single out religious associations in particular for special treatment, but instead says that a wide range of voluntary and identificatory groups are eligible for accommodations. Crucially, at least for my purposes, Laborde acknowledges that however powerful people's coherence interests are, they can be overridden by other imperatives, including an obligation on the part of the state to protect "equal access to key opportunities such as housing, education, and employment" (Laborde 2017, 186).

Objections to Collective Exemptions

If Laborde's argument or another to the same effect holds, then some religious associations are entitled to exemptions from antidiscrimination laws, at least on a pro tanto basis. Nevertheless, liberal democratic states will also sometimes be justified in refusing (otherwise justifiable) exemption claims, if there are weighty and countervailing considerations on the other side of the ledger. Philosophers have not written much about these and the remainder of this chapter makes a start on rectifying this.

At least three different kinds of reasons could be given in opposition to a collective exemption claim. First is the exemption proliferation worry, which as Nick Martin (2019) has observed, is essentially a slippery slope objection. As he construes it, this objection is that "if we grant some exemptions, then to be consistent we will have to grant so many exemptions that cumulatively they undermine, for example, social cohesion, the purpose and effectiveness of the law, legal obligation, and political authority" (Martin 2019, 81). So far, the exemption proliferation objection has mostly been directed against individual exemption claims. However, its force might in fact be compounded in the case of collective exemptions, if it is true that an extensive regime of collective exemptions could become a de facto regime of legal pluralism.

Second are worries that collective exemptions could frustrate legitimate state goals. An interesting example of this are the exemptions extended to publicly funded schools with a religious ethos, which might undermine attempts to cultivate civic virtues. Indeed, the connection between pupil composition and the ability of children to learn the virtues of civility and tolerance already features in public and academic discussions of school admissions policies (see, e.g., Clayton et al. forthcoming). For related but different reasons one might also worry about the effects of collective exemptions to allow firms or public bodies to discriminate on grounds of sexual orientation or gender identity, for instance, if one believes that these are likely to undermine social cohesion.

Third are concerns about third-party injuries, since collective exemptions will often have the effect of transferring costs or burdens onto non-beneficiaries. For instance, permitting religious selection during school admissions will diminish the range and quality of educational opportunities to some children. Similarly, religious exemptions for adoption agencies, hospitals, and firms like Hobby Lobby make it difficult, and sometimes impossible, for people to access basic or essential services.

By comparison with individual exemptions, the third-party injuries objection bites especially hard against collective exemptions. One reason for this is that these are nearly always exemptions from antidiscrimination or civil rights laws. Another is that the burdens they generate usually fall on particular people, such as employees or people with protected characteristics. Meanwhile, individual exemptions, if they burden anyone at all, often do so indiscriminately. For instance, an exemption to allow Sikh men to carry a kirpan is costly for everyone, since it exposes each of us to modestly increased risks, but it does not pick out the members of any group for negative treatment. By contrast, an exemption to allow a firm to discriminate on grounds of sexuality or gender identity does precisely this.

It should not be surprising that individual and collective religious exemptions tend to generate different kinds of injuries to third-parties, since the two terms refer to different kinds of legal incident (the analysis here is based on Shorten (2015, 250) and Shorten (2017, 245–246); for a similar account see Laegaard (2015, 224)). On the one hand, an individual who has a legal right to an exemption, such as a Sikh who is permitted to carry a kirpan or someone who has obtained a religious exemption from vaccination requirements, has a Hohfeldian liberty (or privilege). As such, they have no duty to refrain from doing something that everyone else has a duty to refrain from doing, or they have no duty to do something that everyone else has a duty to do (Hohfeld 1919). On the other hand, institutions benefitting from collective exemptions acquire Hohfeldian powers and immunities (a power is the ability to alter legal relations, while an immunity refers to being protected against, or not liable to, someone else's power). By virtue of enhancing the powers of particular institutions, collective exemptions have the effect of creating vulnerabilities, since someone (or some group) must be liable to the powers they establish. This can be illustrated by considering the collective exemption for religious schools permitting them to discriminate on otherwise unlawful grounds when appointing teaching staff. In short, this exemption has three aspects: first, it equips the school with a power to select and enforce a particular recruitment policy; second, it disables the state from enforcing its preferred policy within the school; third, it makes employees (and potential employees) vulnerable to what would otherwise be unlawful discrimination. These employees and potential employees are the third-parties who are injured by this particular exemption.

What makes someone a third-party to an exemption is not that they do not belong to the religious community who ostensibly benefit from the exemption in question, but rather that they themselves do not benefit from it. Indeed, the third-parties injured by a particular collective exemption might include people who regard themselves as members of the exemption-seeking association, people who are unambiguous outsiders, and all of the shades of gray in between. For example, exemptions to permit the use of religious criteria when hiring staff primarily set back the interests of people who are firmly outside of the association, with neither a contractual nor religious connection to it. By contrast, the exemption for Hobby Lobby undermined the interests of its employees, each of whom were insiders in the contractual sense, and some of whom may also have been insiders in the religious sense.

Some of the most difficult collective exemption cases are ones in which membership is at stake, and for which the key question is whether the association should have the final say over its own membership rules. For the most part, it is uncontroversial that the freedom of association also entails a freedom to disassociate, such that churches – like other voluntary associations – ought to be free to refuse membership according to their own standards. However, exclusion may sometimes seem to be wrongfully discriminatory. For instance, the UK Supreme Court was faced with this issue in 2009, in a case involving the Jewish Free School, which at that time selected pupils on grounds of matrilineal descent, and therefore excluded children whose mothers had converted to Judaism. Ultimately the court ruled that this was incompatible with the UK's race equality laws (*R(E) v. Governing Body of JFS*, 2009). So while the school was permitted to give Jewish applicants preference over non-Jews, it was not permitted to decide for itself which applicants qualified as Jewish and which did not.

Weighing Burdens

This section sketches some of the issues a political community will confront when attempting to establish when religiously.inspired discrimination falls beyond the limits of toleration. It does so by discussing the third-party injuries objection in greater detail and by identifying some different ways in which a third-party might be injured by a collective exemption. Specifically, it is suggested that a collective exemption might be objectionable because it (a) threatens the basic interests of a third-party, (b) materially burdens them, (c) communicates a dignity-undermining message, or (d) increases their vulnerability to domination. The same exemption might injure the same third-parties in more than one of these ways, or it might injure different third-parties in different ways.

Different normative theories might acknowledge only some of these injuries, or they might emphasize some to a greater extent than others. Further, they will conceptualize some of these injuries in different ways to one another. Accordingly, this chapter only proposes a provisional and ecumenical outline of a normative theory of third-party injuries, and this sketch makes no pretensions to being either comprehensive or complete. In addition to distinguishing among some of the different ways in which third-parties might be injured by religious accommodations, this section also draws attention to some difficult philosophical puzzles that any complete normative theory of these injuries must answer. In particular, it is argued that establishing the significance of a particular third-party injury objection will require an explanation of the *severity* of the injury in question, which is a surprisingly difficult task.

Basic Interests

The first way in which a collective exemption might injure a third-party is by threatening their basic interests. For example, consider *Cannata v. Catholic Diocese of Austin* (2012), which found that a church pianist was not protected by disability discrimination laws because he was covered by the "ministerial exception." Or consider again *Hobby Lobby*, which permitted contraception insurance coverage to be withheld on grounds of conscience. In both cases, at least according to some critics, the basic interests of workers were set back because their employer benefitted from a religious accommodation. Similar cases have also arisen outside the workplace. For instance, one of the key objections to the so-called "baptism barrier" in Ireland was that it sometimes made it highly difficult for some parents in rural areas to find school places for their children, and that this compromised either their, or their children's, basic interests.

Since philosophers endorse different theories about the nature and significance of basic interests, they are likely to disagree about when and whether a religious accommodation really does injure the basic interests of third-parties. For instance, someone might believe that *Hobby Lobby* did indeed negatively affect the firm's female employees without accepting that their basic interests were compromised. Or, consider the injuries that arise when a third-party is excluded from a particular association, as in *JFS*. According to Stuart White (1997), an exclusion rule like this is "presumptively unjust" only if it threatens people's basic interests, which understands to include (certain) economic opportunities, opportunities for community or civic participation, and dignity or self-worth. This is a plausible interpretation of the kinds of interests that people might have which might be sufficient to override free association rights, but it is only one view among others.

Another reason why there might be disagreement about whether a particular accommodation really does jeopardize the basic interests of a third-party is because the effects of an accommodation can be characterized in different ways. For example, consider John Devaney, who claimed that an exemption from noise pollution laws to permit the ringing of church bells had interrupted his peace, alienated him from his children, and caused his marriage to fail (*Devaney v. Kilmartin*, 2015). Presumably Devaney really did have basic interests in peace and in maintaining good relationships with his family, and these interests were indeed set back, but one might doubt that the religious accommodation itself was directly responsible for the harms he suffered.

As indicated above, no particular normative theory about basic interests and religious accommodations will be defended here. Nevertheless, it is worth noting something distinctive about basic interests, which is arguably not the case for the other kinds of injuries discussed later, namely, that the size of an injured group is irrelevant when it comes to establishing the normative significance of a third-party injuries objection. For example, consider an exemption that would compromise the exit rights of female group members. It hardly matters whether the affected group in question is large or small. Or consider the recent extensions to the doctrine of the "ministerial exception" in the USA, such as the decision in *Cannata*. If these decisions were objectionable because they injured the basic interests of third-parties, then it hardly seems to matter how many people's basic interests were jeopardized. Indeed, one might object to including an exemption clause in primary legislation on the grounds that it might potentially compromise the basic interests of a single person, and even if one thought that to be unlikely. (Notice that one might believe this either because one thinks that basic interests justify rights in Dworkin's sense (i. e., as "trumps") or because one believes that basic interests cannot be aggregated.)

Material Burdens

The second way in which a collective exemption might injure third-parties is by materially burdening them, such as by depriving them of opportunities or by making options more costly. Courts and legislators have generally been quite willing to recognize material burdens to third-parties, even when those burdens are quite modest. For example, in 1982 the American courts ruled that although Amish employers might have powerful religious objections to making social security contributions for their workers, an exemption to facilitate this ought not to be granted because, among other things, doing so would put their tax-paying competitors at a disadvantage (*United States v. Lee*, 1982). In a subsequent case the US Supreme Court also rejected a religiously based claim to an exemption from minimum wage laws, despite its being apparently supported by the employees themselves, on the grounds that it might depress the wages of other workers employed in the same labor market but by different firms (*Tony and Susan Alamo Foundation v. Secretary of Labor*, 1985).

Material burdens have two distinctive aspects. First, a third-party might be burdened simply in the sense that someone else's exemption leaves them with less than they otherwise would (or should) have had. For instance, if a religiously owned pharmacy is permitted to refuse requests for emergency contraception, then women who need emergency contraception will be materially burdened in the sense of incurring additional travel costs, assuming other pharmacies are accessible. Second, and in addition to this, a material burden might also have the effect of requiring a third-party to subsidize someone else's religion. For instance, had Amish employers been exempted from paying social security contributions, this would arguably have resulted in their competitors subsidizing Amish religious beliefs and practices.

Some material burdens may be significant enough to qualify as an injury to basic interests, depending one's theory of basic interests. For material burdens that do not pass this threshold, then the number of people injured by an accommodation is likely to be relevant when calculating the significance of the objection. For example, an exemption that is likely to depress the wages of workers in a particular sector of the economy will be more objectionable the more people it burdens. At the same time, however, recall that some material burdens might be objectionable because they require third-parties to subsidize the religious preferences of others. In cases like these what seems to be objectionable is the fact that some (and not all) are required to subsidize another religion, and not the number of people paying the subsidy. One might try to explain away this difference by saying that people have basic interests in not subsidizing other people's (different) religious beliefs. Perhaps this is true but notice that many people do not take themselves to have this interest.

Communicative Injuries

Another way in which a collective exemption might injure a third-party is by communicating a message that compromises their dignity or their standing as an equal. This definition is deliberately tentative, since different normative theories will fill in the details in different ways. There are at least two mechanisms by which a collective exemption might impose a communicative injury. First, an exemption might allow a beneficiary themselves to directly convey a stigmatizing or humiliating message to a third-party, such as when a pharmacist – intentionally or otherwise - stigmatizes a customer as "sinful" by refusing to provide the person with emergency contraception. Second, providing an exemption might also convey, albeit indirectly, a message from the state itself about the relative worth of an affected group. For instance, when a liberal state permits religious adoption agencies, hotels, or other service providers to discriminate on grounds of sexual orientation or gender identity, it arguably conveys a signal, both to the public at large as well as to LGBTQ+ people in particular, about how seriously it takes their interests and rights.

By comparison with material burdens, courts and legislators have been rather reluctant to recognize purely communicative harms. One reason for this is that identifying whether a message is genuinely harmful will require accounting for various contextual considerations. For instance, is the injured group already socially marginalized? Does the injury caused by the exemption fit into a wider pattern of discrimination? And so on. Another reason is that communicative injuries might be thought to fall under the principle of free expression, and so denying an exemption *because* of the message it communicates would unjustly prevent the group in question from expressing itself. Whatever the merits of this view, notice that it is often exaggerated. Even if communicative injuries ought not to be considered when establishing how weighty a third-party injury is, the other injuries I discuss cannot be set aside for the same reason.

The logic of communicative injuries seems to be quite different to that of material burdens, since these are often more objectionable when fewer people are affected. Of course, as was the case for material burdens, sometimes a communicative injury may be so severe as to jeopardize a person's basic interests, perhaps by undermining their standing as an equal or compromising their fundamental interests in dignity. In such cases, as with threats to basic interests in general, the number of third-parties injured by an accommodation is irrelevant. Meanwhile, when a communicative injury falls short of threatening basic interests, the size of the injured group may matter, and this raises the question of whether a third-party injury is worse *because* it falls on a small group.

Caution is required here. The fact that communicative injuries seem to be of greater significance when they injure smaller groups will often reflect the fact that such injuries are often more severe because small groups often already have low social status and are socially vulnerable. If this is right, then a communicative injury is not more objectionable *because* it is experienced by a small group. Rather, group size tends to inversely affect the *severity* of a communicative injury, and more severe injuries are more objectionable than less severe ones. Recall that our question is whether the size of a group injured by an accommodation matters, independently of the severity of that injury. The answer to this is probably yes, but as with material burdens, it is that a (non-basic interest threatening) communicative injury is more objectionable if it falls on more people, rather than fewer. So, if two groups experience different communicative injuries, and the injuries experienced by each member of the smaller group is more severe because their group is small, then a third-party injuries objection to the respective accommodations would be stronger in the case of accommodation that injures the larger group, simply because it affects more people, and even though each person who was injured experienced a less severe communicative injury.

Domination

The final way in which a collective exemption might injure a third-party is by rendering them vulnerable to domination, or by enhancing their vulnerability to domination. Characteristically, this happens when an exemption has the effect of equipping religious authorities with arbitrary powers over things like access to membership, the provision of services, or the allocation of roles, positions, and associated responsibilities within an institution. For example, recall the teachers mentioned earlier, such as Susan Little, the teacher from Pennsylvania whose contract was not renewed because her second marriage did not satisfy the demands of Canon Law. Like Martinez and Flynn, she experienced at least two immediate injuries: she was materially burdened because she lost her income and she experienced a communicative injury because she was publicly stigmatized as being unfit for her job. In addition, her experience also made it readily apparent that she and other similarly situated teachers had long been, and remained, vulnerable to domination in a way that was not true for other workers, whose employers did not benefit from religious accommodations. In other words, she was injured not only by being sacked, but also beforehand, by virtue of a religious accommodation that left her exposed to disciplinary sanctions which could be applied with a significant degree of arbitrariness.

In the sense that the term is used here, domination refers to an asymmetric social relationship characterized by both dependency and arbitrary power (Lovett 2010). A person depends on a relationship when it is too costly for them to exit it. This might be because the alternatives are unattractive or because they anticipate reprisals or sanctions. This kind of dependency is a ubiquitous feature of associational life, and is often a welcome one, as in the case of successful marriages and friendships. Further, it is perhaps inevitable within religious associations, both because of their powerful psychological and emotional ties and because religious authorities often have monopolistic control over valued options (consider, say, Eucharistic rites for Catholics).

While collective exemptions neither create nor exacerbate the dependency of members of religious associations, they often do have significant effects on the other ingredient of domination – arbitrary power. On Lovett's account, power is arbitrary insofar as "its exercise is not reliably constrained by effective [and commonly known] rules, procedures, or goals" (2012, 139). In religious associations the most egregious examples of arbitrary power include things like the abilities to enforce secret rules, to flout publicly known ones, to enforce them selectively, or even invent them at whim. Exemptions have the effect of facilitating all of these things because they make members liable to particular interferences whose justification need not be publicly justified and which can be exercised without public scrutiny and at the discretion of the religious authorities. For instance, consider workers who may be sacked for conduct that is at odds with the religious ethos of their employer, such as teachers seeking IVF treatment. What makes them dominated is the fact that establishing whether their conduct is grounds for termination is at the discretion of their employers.

So, then, exempting a religious institution from a generally applicable rule will often provide additional opportunities for power to be exercised arbitrarily and it is in this "scope enhancing" sense that exemptions exacerbate domination within religious associations. It is true, of course, that much can be done to reduce this scope, including carefully crafting legislation to reduce the possibility of powers being used on a discretionary basis or reducing dependency by providing employees of religious associations with alternative options (Shorten 2017, 251–253). Nevertheless, it is difficult to imagine how domination can be entirely eliminated in religious associations, not least because religious rules often cover many different and significant parts of their members' lives, including intimate conduct, and because they are nearly always difficult, and often impossible, for members to challenge.

It may seem as if the injury of domination is essentially communicative, having more to do with subject-formation than vulnerability to arbitrary power. For instance, consider the message sent to people who are vulnerable to dismissal on the basis of their sexuality or gender orientation, and as a result of an accommodation that has been granted by their state to their employer. Simply being in this position and knowing that others are aware that you are in this position may cause one to internalize a message of inferiority. However, there is a distinctive injury that people suffer when they are vulnerable to the arbitrary power of another, even without them being aware of it, or suffering a communicative injury. For example, when Susan Little decided to remarry she may have been unaware of the effect that doing so would have on her employment status. Nevertheless, the fact that her employer held the discretionary power to terminate her employment was enough to confirm her status as dominated.

It is worth noting one way in which domination differs from the other three kinds of injury. Earlier, a third-party was defined as someone who does not benefit from a particular exemption. One possible implication of this is that a member of an association who endorses an internally discriminatory rule is not a third-party to any collective exemptions to that rule, but rather is a beneficiary of them. In the absence of a theory of false consciousness, this is the case even if the exemption in question threatens their basic interests or worsens their material situation. However, when it comes to domination, an exemption which has the effect of exacerbating someone's vulnerability to domination potentially injures them *even when* they endorse the exemption in question. So, for instance, a teacher who agrees that schools ought to be able to dismiss teachers for their personal conduct is nonetheless injured if an exemption further empowers their employer to exercise this power over them arbitrarily.

Severity and the "Baseline Puzzle"

Suppose a political community knows how and how many third-parties are injured by a particular exemption. This still leaves the question of establishing the severity of those injuries, and this will require addressing the "baseline puzzle." Very roughly, this is that if a third-party has been injured by a religious accommodation then they must be worse-off, but worse-off by comparison with what? There are two plausible ways to answer this question, each suggesting a different "baseline" for establishing the severity of a burden. Ultimately, the appropriate baseline will depend on one's normative theory of the injury in question.

To begin, notice that there is an implausible way to answer the baseline puzzle, which is to compare people according to their situation immediately prior to the exemption in question being granted. The problem with this is that it will sometimes deliver counterintuitive results when exemptions are built into primary legislation. For example, Utah recently prohibited discrimination on grounds of sexual orientation and gender identity but exempted religious employers and landlords. Since LGBTQ+ citizens lacked protections before this law was passed, this exemption did not burden them by the standards of this answer – one cannot lose something one never had.

Meanwhile, the first of the two plausible ways to establish the severity of a third-party injury is to compare people according to what they would have had if the relevant law were applied on an exemptionless basis. This is the "counterfactual test," and by its standards, LGBTQ+ citizens in Utah were indeed made worse off by the exemption for religious employers and landlords.

The standard objection to the counterfactual baseline is that it assumes that people have an entitlement to whatever it is that the exemption denies them, but this is sometimes unsettled. For example, consider *Hobby Lobby*. It is true that female employees were made worse-off by the exemption in at least one important sense, since without it their insurance would have included emergency contraception coverage. However, it is much more controversial to say, as the counterfactual baseline implies, that female employees were *injured* by the exemption. This is because, for at least some supporters of the exemption, Hobby Lobby had a (corporate) right to not be complicit in the provision of emergency contraception.

For them it is unfair to say that female employees of Hobby Lobby were injured by the exemption, since the workers are worse-off only by comparison with a scenario in which the rights of Hobby Lobby were not respected.

The alternative is to employ a moralized baseline, which avoids the objection just described by expressly comparing third-parties according to what they *should* have. Strictly speaking, there are a cluster of such baselines, which depend on one's underlying theory of moral rights. For instance, libertarians have defended a minimal moralized baseline, in order to argue that the female employees of Hobby Lobby were not injured when they were denied insurance coverage for emergency contraception, since they had no (moral) right to this in the first place. A less frugal approach, suggested by Tebbe, Schwartzman, and Schragger (2017), is to set a moralized baseline according to the substantive values that the regulation or law in question is seeking to advance. By this standard, *Hobby Lobby* did indeed injure female employees, since providing emergency contraception insurance coverage was one of the aims of the relevant legislation. Likewise, the Utah exemption also burdened LGBTQ+ people, since protecting them from discrimination was the explicit aim of the law in question.

Moralized baselines face two difficult issues. First is the problem of establishing what the baseline itself ought to consist in and how its authority is established. For instance, the libertarian baseline consists in a fixed set of moral rights, whose authority is established independently. By contrast, a baseline might instead derive its authority form popular consent and be established by reference to values implicit in the surrounding political culture or constitution. The second issue, meanwhile, arises from value pluralism. Most of the cases discussed in this chapter involve conflicts between equality of opportunity and either freedom of religion or freedom of association. It would seem that any substantive moralized baseline must endorse a particular way of trading those different values off against one another. For some pluralists, however, there is no possibility of settling on a definitive ordering.

So, then, both counterfactual and moralized baselines are vulnerable to objections. Notwithstanding these, some kinds of third-party injuries seem to lend themselves toward one baseline or the other. For instance, when it comes to establishing the severity of a communicative injury, a moralized baseline is arguably appropriate, since establishing how badly someone has been injured by a humiliating message requires some theory about the level or kind of dignity to which a person is entitled, and only a moralized baseline can supply this. Indeed, a counterfactual baseline might underestimate the severity of a burden imposed on an already disfavored group. This can be grasped by considering a society in which gays and lesbians are already regularly exposed to dignity-undermining speech, and where an exemption further added to this.

Meanwhile, when it comes to establishing the extent to which a third-party is made vulnerable to domination by an exemption, there are good reasons to prefer a counterfactual baseline. Recall, accommodations exacerbate the domination of third-parties by exposing them to further arbitrary powers. A moralized baseline will sometimes mischaracterize the severity of a burden generated by accommodations for employers, since some firms who do not benefit from religious accommodations nevertheless have a greater capacity to exercise arbitrary powers over their employees than do some institutions who benefit from them. For example, teachers in religious schools are made more vulnerable to domination when their employers benefit from (certain) religious accommodations, but may overall be less vulnerable to arbitrary powers than other workers in other employment sectors. It might be thought that this is actually a reason to prefer a moralized baseline, since domination in nonreligious firms matters to. However, the advantage of a counterfactual baseline, when it comes to assessing a third-party injuries objection, is that only it draws attention to domination that is specifically caused by the exemption in question.

Summary and Future Directions

This chapter has demonstrated that the question as to whether to permit religiously inspired discrimination is a paradigmatic case of toleration. After describing some different arguments to have been given in favor of tolerating this kind of discrimination, and suggesting that any such argument can deliver, at most, pro tanto grounds for "collective exemptions," some powerful considerations on the other side of the ledger were considered. Establishing the normative weight of these is complex, a point illustrated by focusing on the third-party injuries objection. Third-party injuries, it was suggested, come in at least four different varieties, and different normative theories will interpret them differently and make space for more or less of them.

Overall, this chapter identified some of the difficult challenges that political communities must confront when attempting to establish whether to tolerate discrimination by religious associations. Although philosophers have long discussed accommodations for religious individuals, they have only recently turned their attentions toward the issues raised by the widespread practice of accommodating religious associations and institutions. Nevertheless, a number of dividing lines are starting to become apparent. For instance, must accommodations for associations take the form of corporate rights or are they reducible to individual rights? Are these accommodations fundamentally a matter of religious freedom, freedom of association, or something else? Are these accommodations compatible with prevailing conceptions of state sovereignty, or do they herald a return to premodern forms legal pluralism?

Meanwhile, philosophers have not made much progress when it comes to understanding the reasons to not tolerate religiously motivated discrimination, and the preliminary sketch of this issue in this chapter indicates at least three broad lines of inquiry that require further investigation.

First, do the purposes of institutions seeking accommodations make a difference? For instance, does it matter if it is a school or a charity or a profit-making firm? When it comes to establishing the case in favor of toleration, it is arguably the form of association, rather than its purposes, that is significant (Laborde 2017, 181). However, the significance of a third-party injury objection may perhaps depend on the kinds of activities the relevant association engages in and also whether it is profit making.

Second, to what extent should contextual considerations inform judgments about the normative significance of third-party injuries? For instance, consider accommodations that have the effect of reducing the availability of abortion services, or ones that allow schools to discriminate when appointing staff or selecting pupils. Whether these jeopardize the basic interests of third-parties will often have to do with the availability of alternatives. Is it fair to deny an accommodation for factors beyond the control of the relevant association?

Third, to what extent can philosophical analysis settle the question of what kinds of religiously motivated discrimination ought to be tolerated? This chapter has suggested that in addition to proposing arguments in favor of tolerating religiously motivated discrimination, philosophers should also be concerned to identify the limits to this kind of toleration. However, establishing the existence, or even the normative weight, of reasons against toleration does not settle anything in practice, since a framework to integrate the considerations from each side is still required. For instance, should we employ some kind of balancing test? Do some considerations trump others? Can these issues be resolved philosophically, or are they ultimately a matter of political judgment?

Acknowledgments Earlier versions of this chapter benefitted from helpful comments from fellow participants at workshops in Konstanz, Leuven, and Irvine, including François Boucher, Nina Hagel, Kathryn Heard, Eszter Kollar, Haimo Li, Nick Martin, Nathaniel Mull, Nashon Perez, Colin Rowe, Micah Schwartzman, Jonathan Seglow, Aristel Skrbic, Antoon Vandevelde, Jens Van 'T Klooster, Bouke de Vries, and Alexa Zellentin.

References

Balint P (2017) Respecting toleration: traditional liberalism and contemporary diversity. Oxford University Press, New York
Bardon A, Ceva E (2018) The ethics of toleration and religious accommodation. In: Lever A, Poama A (eds) The Routledge handbook of ethics and public policy. Abingdon, Routledge
Barry B (2001) Culture and equality: an egalitarian critique of multiculturalism. Polity, Cambridge
Baumeister A (2019) Religion and the claims of citizenship: the dangers of institutional accommodation. In: Seglow J, Shorten A (eds) Religion and political theory. Rowman and Littlefield, New York, pp 99–118
Bou-Habib P (2006) A theory of religious accommodation. J Appl Philos 23(1):109–126
Brettschneider C (2012) When the state speaks, what should it say? Princeton University Press, Princeton
Clayton M, Mason A, Swift A, Wareham R (forthcoming) The political morality of school composition: the case of religious selection. Br J Polit Sci. https://doi.org/10.1017/S0007123418000649
Cohen AJ (2014) Toleration. Polity, Cambridge
Cohen J (2015) Freedom of religion, Inc: whose sovereignty. Neth J Legal Philos 3:169–210
Corvino J, Anderson RT, Girgis S (2017) Debating religious liberty and discrimination. Oxford University Press, New York
Eidelson B (2015) Discrimination and disrespect. Oxford University Press, New York

Eisgruber CL, Sager LG (2007) Religious freedom and the constitution. Harvard University Press, Cambridge, MA
Galeotti AE (2002) Toleration as recognition. Cambridge University Press, Cambridge
Garnett R (2016) The freedom of the church (toward) an exposition, translation and defence. In: Schwartzman M, Flanders C, Robinson Z (eds) The rise of corporate religious liberty. Oxford University Press, Oxford, pp 39–62
Gowran S (2004) 'See no evil, speak no evil, hear no evil?' The experiences of lesbian and gay teachers in Irish schools. In: Deegan J, Devine D, Lodge A (eds) Primary voices: equality, diversity and childhood in Irish primary schools. Institute of Public Administration, Dublin
Gray EM (2013) Coming out as a lesbian, gay or bisexual teacher: negotiating private and professional worlds. Sex Educ 13(6):702–714
Hohfeld W (1919) Fundamental legal conceptions. Yale University Press, New Haven
Horton J (2011) Why the traditional conception of toleration still matters. Crit Rev Int Soc Pol Phil 14(3):289–305
Horwitz P (2009) Churches as first amendment institutions: of sovereignty and spheres. Harv Civil Rights-Civil Liberties Law Rev 44:79–131
Jones P (1994) Bearing the consequences of belief. J Polit Philos 2(1):24–43
Jones P (2015) Toleration, religion, and accommodation. Eur J Philos 23(3):542–563
Jones P (2020) Toleration, neutrality and exemption. Crit Rev Int Soc Pol Philos 23(2):203–210 https://doi.org/10.1080/13698230.2019.1609397
Laborde C (2017) Liberalism's religion. Harvard University Press, Cambridge, MA
Laegaard S (2015) Disaggregating corporate freedom of religion. Neth J Legal Philos 44(3):221–230
Laegaard S (2018) Discrimination and religion. In: Lippert-Rasmussen K (ed) The Routledge handbook of the ethics of discrimination. Routledge, Abingdon, pp 207–217
Laycock D (1990) The remnants of free exercise. Supreme Court Rev:1–68
Leiter B (2013) Why tolerate religion? Princeton University Press, Princeton
Lenta P (2016) Freedom of conscience and the value of personal integrity. Ratio Juris 29(2):246–263
Lovett F (2010) A general theory of domination and justice. Oxford University Press, Oxford
Lovett F (2012) What counts as arbitrary power? J Polit Power 5(1):137–152
Macedo S (1998) Transformative constitutionalism and the case of religion: defending the moderate hegemony of liberalism. Political Theory 26(1):56–80
Maclure J, Taylor C (2011) Secularism and Freedom of Conscience. Cambridge, MA.: Harvard University Press
Martin N (2019) Exemption proliferation. In: Seglow J, Shorten A (eds) Religion and political theory. Rowman and Littlefield, New York, pp 81–98
McConnell M (1985) Accommodation of religion. Supreme Court Rev:1–59
Mendus S (1989) Toleration and the limits of liberalism. Palgrave, London
Neary A (2013) Lesbian and gay teachers' experiences of 'coming out' in Irish schools. Br J Sociol Educ 34(4):583–602
Nussbaum M (2008) Liberty of conscience. Basic Books, New York
Parekh B (2000) Rethinking multiculturalism. Palgrave, London
Sagar LG (2017) The puzzle of the Catholic Church. In: Batnitzky L, Dagan H (eds) Institutionalising rights and religion. Cambridge University Press, Cambridge
Schragger R, Schwartzman M (2013) Against religious institutionalism. Va Law Rev 99(5):917–985
Seglow J (2017) Religious accommodation: responsibility, integrity, and self-respect. In: Bardon A, Laborde C (eds) Religion in liberal political philosophy. Oxford University Press, Oxford, pp 177–190
Shorten A (2005) Toleration and cultural controversies. Res Publia 11(3):275–299
Shorten A (2015) Are there rights to institutional exemptions? J Soc Philos 46(2):242–263
Shorten A (2017) Accommodating religious institutions: freedom v. domination. Ethnicities 17(2):242–258
Shorten A (2019) May churches discriminate? J Appl Philos 36(5):709–717

Smith SD (2016) The jurisdictional conception of church autonomy. In: Schwartzman M, Flanders C, Robinson Z (eds) The rise of corporate religious liberty. Oxford University Press, Oxford, pp 19–37

Tebbe N (2017) Religious freedom in an egalitarian age. Harvard University Press, Cambridge, MA

Tebbe N, Schwartzman M, Schragger R (2017) How much may religious accommodations burden others? In: Lynch HF et al (eds) Law, religion and health in the United States. Cambridge University Press, Cambridge

Vallier K (2015) The moral basis of religious exemptions. Law Philos 35(1):1–28

White S (1997) Freedom of association and the right to exclude. J Polit Philos 5(4):373–391

Religious Toleration and Social Contract Theories of Justice

42

Phillip J. Donnelly

Contents

Introduction	854
The Challenges of Definition	855
Rethinking Religion	859
The Possibility of Religious Toleration	861
Contractarian Traditions	863
Lockean Nature and Toleration Traditions	866
Summary and Future Directions	869
References	871

Abstract

Because "religious toleration" is a concept with a particular (and controverted) history, its very usage foregrounds the challenges in navigating between historical particularities and conceptual generalizations. This chapter begins by considering the antinomy that arises from the mutually challenging claims of historical positivism and conceptual positivism. Using an alternative to both of these approaches that may be designated "traditionary inquiry," this chapter considers whether not only "religion" but specifically "religious toleration" can be conceptualized apart from the self-legitimating narrative offered by the modern nation state. Given the central place of John Locke among early modern conceptions of the state and religious toleration, the chapter culminates in an account of how Locke negotiates between competing traditions of contractarianism, even as he presumes a crucially Protestant conception of faith. The issues raised by Locke's attempt to hold together conflicting species of contractarianism provide the occasion for reflection on how debates regarding religious toleration may be helpfully framed in the present.

P. J. Donnelly (✉)
Baylor University, Waco, TX, USA
e-mail: Phillip_Donnelly@baylor.edu

© The Author(s), under exclusive licence to Springer Nature Switzerland AG 2022
M. Sardoč (ed.), *The Palgrave Handbook of Toleration*,
https://doi.org/10.1007/978-3-030-42121-2_51

Keywords

Toleration · Religion · Tradition · Historical positivism · Religious violence · Contractarianism · John Locke · Thomas Hobbes · John Milton · Roger Williams

Introduction

"Religious Toleration" is a concept with a particular history. When citizens in modern nation-states rely on this concept, it is often attended by a specific narrative regarding how the past has shaped the present and therefore justifies present circumstance – whether that circumstance involves a cultural practice, a legal precedent, or a political principle. A crude summary of that narrative might go something like this: "In the past, most people favored some version of state-sanctioned religious uniformity, but because of the violence that resulted most famously from the seventeenth-century 'Wars of Religion,' Europeans (and now much of the world) have learned to tolerate religious difference for the sake of civic peace." This narrative is what leads Alan Levine, for example, to characterize "toleration" as being among "the most attractive and widespread ideals of our day. It is a cornerstone of liberalism, a key protection for both individual citizens and minority groups, and in general is the predominant ethos of all moral civilizations in the modern world" (Levin 1999, 1; cf. Rawls 1996a, b, 1–13, 140–75). A variety of historical investigations (including other chapters in the present volume) have complicated this narrative at multiple levels (e.g., Murphy 2001; Wilken 2019). Nevertheless, the story remains powerfully influential across much of the Western world and beyond it. One central difficulty in speaking about the topic of religious toleration today arises from the fact of its status *as* a historical concept. Even the most modest attempts to define, for example, "religion" or "toleration" must navigate between offering either a strictly conceptual (stipulative) or strictly historical (usage-based) definition. As a result, the first section of this chapter provides an account of the apparent impossibility of definition. Because of the antinomy between what may be designated "historical positivism" and "conceptual positivism," this first section culminates in proposing a species of "traditionary inquiry." Such an approach makes it possible to understand how the modern concept of religion has been historically constructed and ultimately to venture an account of religious toleration that is genuinely postmodern. The final two sections of the chapter consider the traditions of reflection regarding the civil order and religious devotion that were inherited by John Locke (1632–1704). Without duplicating the more detailed historical treatments of early modern figures available in other chapters of the present volume (i.e., ▶ Chap. 49, "Early Modern Arguments for Toleration"; ▶ Chaps. 51, "John Locke and Religious Toleration," and ▶ 40, "Toleration and Religion"; ▶ Chap. 50, "Thomas Hobbes and the Conditionality of Toleration"), this account ultimately focuses on the role of what might be called the "social contract theory of justice" in relation to the arguments for religious toleration by Locke and others. Clarity on this point will require a distinction between social contract theory in general ("contractarianism") and a species of such contract theory which makes the very notion of justice dependent upon intrahuman agreement. Ultimately, the tensions at work in these philosophical and theological traditions illuminate a variety of issues that continue to animate debates regarding religious toleration.

The Challenges of Definition

The difficulties attending the definition of "religious toleration" arise not only from the fact that "religion" and "toleration" are contested categories but also from the manner in which those definitional contests are conducted. The underlying issue is a disagreement regarding the character of linguistic meaning and the function of definitions in different sorts of argumentation. This is not simply to observe that, for example, historians and philosophers have different purposes (and hence different modes of argument and canons of evidence); rather, the difficulty arises also from the inseparability of these discourses amid their disagreements. Historical inquiry is oriented toward the understanding of individual particulars (whether events, actions, persons, or things); philosophical inquiry is oriented toward understanding the realities that are shared in common by such particulars. Both kinds of inquiry arguably serve genuine human goods; however, each discourse involves characteristic contrasting difficulties. The typical historian's risk might be called "historical positivism." This approach would ban all recourse to definitions that are not based on historical usage, ostensibly disowning any reliance on stipulative definition. In such a view, any attempt at conceptual clarification, for example, could be viewed with suspicion as an unwarranted anachronistic projection (by the present onto the past). On the other hand, the risk for those oriented toward philosophical inquiry might be called, "conceptual positivism." In this contrasting view, explicit stipulative definitions would tend to be the only sort of definitions admissible as argument – given the inconsistency and imprecision of much historical usage. This approach takes as axiomatic the belief that the history of a given word's usage may be irrelevant to its present operative meanings and assumes that a new definition may be posited at any time. At root here is a disagreement regarding the capacity for explicit definitions to reveal the character of reality and the degree to which reality may (or may not) be faithfully rendered by such generalizations. This disagreement, it should be noted, is not so much between the disciplines of history and philosophy per se but between two extreme versions of each respective discipline. Nevertheless, these two approaches are indeed often at work within more moderate formulations in each respective domain of inquiry; more importantly, each tendency raises an issue for the other discipline – resulting in a pair of challenges that need to be addressed together in considering religious toleration. The resulting tension from these mutual challenges might run as follows. If one starts an account of religious toleration with either historical narration or clarifying stipulative definitions, in either case, the very decision regarding how to begin could imply a presumption regarding which is most basic to human inquiry. The difficulty with a thorough-going historical positivism is that, as a result of presuming that the past is reducible to discrete individual particulars (atelic and formless historical motion), it could be taken to imply a disowning of all common nouns – to the extent that common nouns require generalizing beyond individuals. By contrast, an orientation toward conceptual positivism runs the opposite risk of merely projecting the value judgments of the present (whether of an individual or a group) onto the past. These mutual challenges arise specifically because debates about religious toleration so manifestly foreground both the historically conditioned character of concepts and the role of stipulative general definitions in historic debates.

The difficulties that can arise in historical treatments of religious toleration are well illustrated by Evan Haefeli whose overview of the topic culminates with the claim that:

> In our treatment of toleration as a single idea, a perfectible quality, we have missed out on its fundamentally partisan and relational character. That is, toleration exists in the relationship between the tolerated and the tolerator. It is advocated and implemented by different groups in different ways for different, often partisan, reasons. Exactly what that is and how that is done is in a constant state of flux. And it does not end. Toleration is not a transcendent category. One cannot achieve a perfect form of toleration, for toleration cannot exist outside of a particular dynamic. It depends entirely on its context. (Haefeli 2010, 258)

Haefeli rightly discerns that public toleration (of anything) is necessarily related to differences in political power (depending on who does the tolerating and who is tolerated); however, such a general claim cannot be sustained if Haefeli's final sentence is given full force. Recognizing that toleration is not a transcendent category does not mean that it cannot function as a category at all. If Haefeli's initial generalization is correct, then "toleration" can indeed be understood as a species of political and legal practice, that is, as a conceptual generalization that can be intelligible across more than one historical context. To the extent that the "it" in the first sentence quoted above refers to anything, Haefeli presumes there is a general kind of action called "toleration," which has a "fundamentally partisan and relational character." To imply that there is no possible concept of toleration that might extend across a variety of contexts, however, goes too far; if that were the case, toleration would not be "fundamentally" anything. This is not to fault Haefeli but to point out that even the most detailed and careful historical attention to individual particulars depends to some extent on transhistorical concepts, even if only to the degree that any given historical account relies on common nouns (which may indicate general categories that are not necessarily transcendent). In this sense, although the extreme formulations that result from what I call "historical positivism" might make a definition of religious toleration seem impossible, the actual practice of historians suggests that a definition might indeed be possible. What might not be possible, however, is an historical account or definition that avoids altogether relying on some philosophical assumptions.

The contrasting challenge, designated here as "conceptual positivism," arises from recognizing that some reliance on conceptual categories is inevitable, even in the most finely grained historical account. The difficulty, however, is that, if general concepts are assumed to be the most basic element of human inquiry, then there may be a tendency simply to multiply stipulated definitions, leaving only abstractions with no relation to lived experience – or an abstraction that is only an arbitrary imposition on any lived experience that is not the speaker's. This problem is famously dramatized in a comic mode by Lewis Carroll's *Through the Looking-Glass*:

> "When I use a word," Humpty Dumpty said in rather a scornful tone, "it means just what I choose it to mean—neither more nor less"
> "The question is," said Alice, "whether you can make words mean so many different things."
> "The question is," said Humpty Dumpty, "which is to be master—that's all." (Carroll [1865] 2003, 219)

If Humpty Dumpty is correct, and the meanings of words are reducible to the arbitrary judgments of those who happen to hold power, then the use of stipulative definitions, especially when applied to the reading of historically distant texts, risks becoming mere self-projection. If, however, we consider the careful philosophical use of stipulative definitions in a more charitable manner, we can recognize that such an approach merely presumes that language can name, or at least gesture in some manner toward, aspects of reality – which may include general concepts or individual particulars. In effect, such a practice assumes that a well-crafted stipulative definition may lead to insight regarding the character of that to which the words gesture. Nevertheless, because "religious toleration" is a concept with a particular history, the challenge for any stipulative definition is how to offer genuine insight regarding the realities that it names while allowing for the historically conditioned character of both the actions designated by that name and those (in the past and the present) who seek to understand such actions.

In short, the root difficulty is that the past usage of terms and our present stipulated meanings may be distinguished, but they also seem to be never entirely detachable. Even those who object most stridently to ways that abstraction and generalization can misconstrue individual realities (e.g., Acadia 2021) nevertheless persist in using common nouns. On the other hand, even those who insist that the past usage of a given term need not determine a present definition are themselves individual particular speakers who have inherited a set of cultural, linguistic, and politico-mythic assumptions. In the postindustrial West, and especially (but not exclusively) in the English-speaking world, the category of "religious toleration" is intrinsic to contemporary self-understanding of a liberal political order. In this sense, no matter how much a given philosopher, for example, aims to use a stipulative definition, the very use of the designation, "religious toleration," evokes a governing metanarrative regarding the growth of "liberty" (typically construed as the absence of bodily compulsion or threat). Is it possible to offer a definition of "religious toleration" that could be intelligible across historical contexts and yet could also enable rather than disable understanding of historical particulars (including the present)? One such definition is offered by Andrew Murphy who defines it as "a governmental response to religious dissent or diversity in a society, a response that eschews coercion and extends legal protections to non-mainstream religious groups" (Murphy 2001, x). In this sense, the focus of this chapter is not "tolerance" understood as a personal quality or even as a virtue (Cf. Murphy 1997; Bowlin 2016). At the same time, the question at issue is not whether particular people are tolerant or even whether a given regime practices religious toleration. What Murphy's definition also makes clear is that the object of inquiry is a political doctrine – something that includes but is not reducible to either the merely personal or merely practical – regarding the character and extent of state regulation of religious practice. This definition is uniquely helpful in the way that it unites an appreciation of two things: the inherited character of public discourse and the philosophical orientation of that inherited discourse which continues to shape understanding and action in the present.

In offering an alternative to both historical and conceptual positivism, Murphy's definition exemplifies an approach that may be called "traditionary inquiry" (Cf. Gadamer 1989; MacIntyre 1988, 1990, 2007; Stout 2004). The term, "tradition," comes from the Latin word, *traditio*, which refers to the action of handing something over. In this sense, a tradition is simply "what one has been given" by other people – most notably the testimony that one has been given about either particular events or the way things are generally. Even in domains of knowledge that modern and postmodern Western culture typically sets in opposition to tradition, such as the natural sciences, the limits of time require a reliance on testimony. Given those limitations on time, no one is able to reperform every experiment in the history of a given discipline or domain of inquiry. Instead, scholars do what is called "a review of the literature." Such a review is, in effect, the recounting of testimony regarding past experiments or investigations that explains the occasion and basis for the present inquiry. The existence of such literature reviews in the physical sciences reveals that these disciplines are traditions of inquiry. "Traditions," in this sense of "what one has been given" (in the form of testimony) is intrinsic to many daily activities, and not only to specialized inquiry. Traditionary inquiry (so understood) is not simply a blind reliance on gossip or "the dead hand of the past" because there are ways of evaluating the reliability of various kinds of testimony and its sources – whether in the marketplace, the workplace, or the laboratory. Such traditionary inquiry includes at least three elements: a reliance on testimony to some degree, a consensus regarding the content of that testimony, and a further consensus regarding how to evaluate new testimonies or discoveries in a given domain. Alasdair MacIntyre famously defined a living intellectual tradition as, "an historically extended, socially embodied argument and an argument precisely in part about the goods which constitute that tradition" (MacIntyre 2007, 222). The customary modern perception that "reason" and "tradition" are detachable from each other is mistaken because in practice they are mutually constituting (Cf. Gadamer 1989, 281–282) (Not all traditions are, of course, intellectual traditions; although any given tradition may include intellectual content, its primary operation may be oriented toward any number of practical ends.). The feature of testimony ensures that traditionary inquiry is not simply a narrative about the past but should include the dramatic mode, in the sense that there is some attempt to let the voice of the historical other resound and be heard. The key point to appreciate is that human action, speech, and reflection persistently rely on and respond to (whether by negation or affirmation) what has been given by means of testimony. Although this sense of "traditionary inquiry" resembles Hans-Georg Gadamer's notion of "historical horizons" in some important ways (Gadamer 1989, 302–307), it differs from Gadamer's account in its emphases. In addition to appreciating the necessity of interpretive assumptions in any act of understanding, the kind of traditionary inquiry described here also emphasizes that such enabling assumptions may be normally articulated and publicly contested in a given community of practice. In this way, traditionary inquiry allows for both the inherited character of public discourse (amid the vagaries of particularity) and the necessary role for individual agency in the receptive action of understanding (an act that involves some generalization).

Rethinking Religion

Given this characterization of "religious toleration" and "traditionary inquiry," there still remains the vexed question of how (or whether) to define "religion." Whether one considers the definition of "religion" offered by Thomas Hobbes (2000 [1651], 42) or John Milton (1998b [1673], 1151) in the seventeenth century, or by more recent authors such as John Hick (1989, 3–17) or Charles Taylor (2007, 16–20), what they all share in common is a reliance on stipulative definitions which are vulnerable to the objections identified above. Philosophers giving stipulative definitions in the last century have tended to favor the designation "transcendent" to distinguish the orientation that makes a given set of practices, ideas, or institutions qualify as "religious." One conceptual difficulty is that the qualifier "transcendent" is equivocal, depending on what exactly is being transcended. The thing being transcended could be the tangible cosmos as a whole, but it could also be only the human aspects of daily existence or human power, whether of an individual, a community, or humanity in general. On the one hand, most things in the cosmos, including humans, arguably transcend something else; at the same time, the human experience of the quotidian may not be reducible to the merely tangible. Such difficulties explain why attempts to establish a merely functional definition of religion that eschews any specific belief content have not proven widely persuasive.

Rather than either multiplying arbitrary distinctions endlessly or using the term, "religion," so broadly that it excludes nothing, a traditionary mode of inquiry considers how present usage functions in relation to the stories that it presumes about past and future action. In *The Myth of Religious Violence*, William Cavanaugh offers just such an account of the shifting concepts that attach to the term "religion":

> In the medieval application of the term, *religio* was primarily used to differentiate clergy who were members of [religious] orders from diocesan clergy. Secondarily, *religio* named one relatively minor virtue in a complex of practices that assumed the particular context of the Christian church and the Christian social order. With the dawn of modernity, however, a new

concept with a much wider and different significance came to operate under the term religion. Religion in modernity indicates a universal genus of which the various religions are species; each religion comes to be demarcated by a system of propositions; religion is identified with an essentially interior, private impulse: and religion comes to be seen as essentially distinct from secular pursuits such as politics, economics, and the like. (Cavanaugh 2009, 69)

In contrast to this understanding of religion that has predominated in European culture since the end of the seventeenth century, Cavanaugh contends that the premodern concept of "religion": (1) was synonymous with worship and did not identify a genus that contained species; (2) indicated a moral virtue (analogous to devotion or piety) rather than only a list of doctrines; (3) named a set of embodied worship practices that were not merely interior, and (4) was not construed as a kind of institutional force that could be differentiated from nonreligious institutional forces (2009, 65–69).

Cavanaugh's account is distinguished by its careful treatment of historical evidence that also keeps in view the present function of "religion" as a category. Through a detailed consideration of the various factions involved in the Thirty Years War (1618–1648), Cavanaugh shows that the historical debates regarding the degree to which the conflicts were caused by religious, economic, or political forces (among others) are doomed to fail because of the essentialism and anachronism involved in the very categories (Cavanaugh 2009, 141–180). Ultimately, he identifies four component beliefs that are central to what he calls the "myth of religious violence": (1) that combatants were divided by religious differences; (2) that religion was the primary cause of the wars (rather than political, economic, or social causes); (3) that "religious causes must be at least analytically separable from political, economic, or social causes"; and (4) that the rise of the modern nation-state brought peace rather than causing the wars (2009, 141–42). Cavanaugh goes on to show the untenability of each of these key elements. He demonstrates, for example, that there was no correlation between warring factions and confessional identities (2009, 142–151), and that there has been no successful attempt by scholars to identify (either in the historical record or analytically) any predominantly religious cause or motivation for the particular conflicts (2009, 151–60). Ultimately, once doubt is cast on the very notion that something essentially "religious" can be abstracted from the various aspects of shared human living, a different historical reality becomes apparent: The function of the category of "religion" (in the modern sense outlined above) is precisely to legitimate the sovereignty of the nation-state. "The rise of the modern state did not usher in a more peaceful Europe, but the rise of the state did accompany a shift in what people were willing to kill and die for" (2009, 10). Cavanaugh is careful to emphasize that his account involves no nostalgia for "medieval forms of government" any more than, for example, the argument of Michel Foucault in *Discipline and Punish* (1977) "implies a nostalgia for corporal punishment" (2009, 179); rather, the point is to reveal something about the present. Nor does Cavanaugh's account cast doubt on the important human goods served by the separation of church and state. By showing the untenability of the myth of religious violence that continues to legitimate the modern liberal state, we are better able to perceive the continued operation of the state's use of violence in the present. By understanding that the early modern shift in political power from the church to the state was not simply the "victory of peaceable reason over irrational religion" (2009, 179), we are in a position to recognize how the modern liberal state continues to conceal its reliance on violence.

In this sense, the very recourse to the concept of "religion," understood as a genus for sets of beliefs that are held privately and can be distinguished clearly from public institutional realities, is to presume the truth of the self-legitimating narrative of the modern nation-state. To be clear, in this account, the term, "religion," does indeed refer to a concept (involving at least the four elements noted above); however, that concept proves to be a misleading account whose effect is to justify the state's exclusive claim to regulate the motion of bodies and to wield lethal force. The modern concept of religion is therefore "ideological" in the sense that it serves to conceal and legitimate the operation of interpersonal forces that might otherwise be recognized as unjust. In contrast to the customary sociological characterization of religious discourse generally as a source of ideological delusion, Cavanaugh's account shows that the typical sociological reliance on the modern concept of religion is itself a source of ideological misperception. To rely on the modern concept of religion – namely, as a species of internal belief system that can be distinguished from public institutional forces – ensures that we misunderstand those actions so characterized as "religious" and ensures that we accept the modern state's justification of itself as the only legitimate protection from religious violence.

The Possibility of Religious Toleration

Does this imply that the very concept of "religion," and therefore "religious toleration," should be abandoned? Not necessarily. To reject the specifically modern concept of religion is not necessarily to abandon all use of the term or even of similar concepts. A genuinely postmodern account of religion, which attempts to get beyond the presumed categories of modern discourse, could offer a corrective to the customary ideological operation of the concept. Such an account would need to allow for the fact that, although liberal political regimes have not necessarily appeared around the world, the social consequences of global information technology have reinforced the worldwide presumption of what Charles Taylor calls the "immanent frame," that is, the tendency to construe the tangible cosmos as sufficient to itself and not as something in need (ontically or epistemically) of any reality beyond itself (Taylor 2007, 539–593). In other words, although some questions regarding the existence or nonexistence of "God" are of specifically modern Western origin and formulation, the globalization of industrial and postindustrial forms of life has presented other cultures with analogous questions regarding the presumed sufficiency of the material world for the fullness of human flourishing. Without presuming that everyone is subject to the logic of global information technology, the question of religious toleration can therefore reasonably be asked together by those of us who do indeed share (to varying degrees) in the paradoxes of that subjection, for whom at least analogous questions regarding the sufficiency of the immanent frame may be posed (or ignored).

The underlying issue is agency: Who is speaking when the term "religion" is used in a given instance? Even if one speaks from the position of a fictive character or a historical figure (including one's past self), there is usually some way in which a given speaker can be implicitly located to some degree. Thus, for example, Paul Griffiths, in *Religious Reading* (1999), offers a general definition of "religion," but he does so in the voice of a confessing Christian who is in dialogue with Buddhist friends, rather than as one who presumes religion is a purely private set of interior beliefs from which the state must protect the public. Griffiths is also working specifically in the context of comparative reading practices. As a result, he defines religion as a species of "an account" (which may be verbal or performative in some other way), an account that has the three requisite qualities of being "comprehensive," "unsurpassable," and "central" (Griffiths 1999, 3–13). The notion of an "account" is important because, in contrast to the typical modern understanding of religion, an account may include doctrines but is not necessarily reducible to them. Likewise, an account may embodied or narrated, rather than being either merely internal in character or propositional in form. This is not to imply that Griffiths' particular definition is the best one; by his own account, it is intended only for very specific purposes (1999, 7). Because Griffiths effectively recovers a premodern understanding of religion as a virtue, his account could be difficult to incorporate, for example, into a political doctrine of "religious toleration," to the extent that a modern nation-state presumes to disconnect moral virtue from law. Rather, his manner of using both a term and conception of religion at all shows that such usage need not be captive to modern assumptions.

What should also be noted, however, is that Griffiths is able to avoid the modern ideological use of religion because he speaks as the inheritor of a specific tradition of inquiry who is in direct conversation with other faith traditions. When he suggests that both Christian and Buddhist reading practices can be characterized as "religious," he does so on the basis of his explicitly located agency in receiving a given faith tradition. The point of this example is to show that conceptions of religion (whether assumed or stated) are inseparable from not only the purposes embedded in a given discourse (such as the myth of religious violence, or the story of interfaith dialogue) but also the agents involved (the identity and social location of speakers and addressees). By recovering a concept of religion that is not necessarily captive to modern assumptions, the example of Griffiths also suggests that the difficulty with the concept may be a function of life in a modern nation-state, an issue that becomes acute whenever English-speakers refer to "religious toleration" as a political or legal principle (Cf. Smith 1995, 63–127). Thus, even if one settles on a plausible definition of both "religion" and "toleration," a definition of "religious toleration" might remain inaccessible. One may, for example, define "religion" in a formal and phenomenal sense, as Griffiths does, as a habit (virtue) of embodied speech and action that is a comprehensive, unsurpassable, and central account. At the same time, one may follow Murphy in construing "toleration" as a political doctrine regarding action that avoids coercion and extends protection to adherents of nonmainstream groups. However, as soon as these categories are combined and the "groups" are specified as "religious groups," the self-understanding of the modern nation-state presumes to disconnect politics and law from virtue formation. Curiously, the now widely presumed disconnection between politics, law, and moral formation is not shared by early modern theorists of the nation-state, such as John Locke (Di Biase 2017). Nevertheless, there is one basic assumption that is shared by Cavanaugh, Griffiths, Locke, and many other early modern defenders of religious toleration: Even when religion is understood as an embodied interpersonal virtue (like devotion, or worship), it is not something that the state can use its authority to induce by coercion (whether by direct compulsion or threat). This suggests that some account of religious toleration, understood as a political doctrine, may be possible that does not depend on the myth of religious violence.

Contractarian Traditions

In order to appreciate what such an account might involve, we shall focus here on an early modern figure who played a central role in articulating the very notion of "religion" that Cavanaugh brings into question: John Locke. Without repeating here the account of Locke's writing provided in the chapter of the present volume that is devoted to his writing (▶ Chap. 51, "John Locke and Religious Toleration"), the rest of this chapter shows the importance of the fact that Locke is the inheritor of multiple traditions of argument regarding the nature of civil authority (most notably its origins) and of religious devotion. Locke's attempt to hold together elements from these various traditions illuminates similar tensions that continue to animate contemporary discourse.

Although historical accounts of religious toleration arguably too often focus exclusively on John Locke's *Letter Concerning Toleration* (▶ Chap. 49, "Early Modern Arguments for Toleration"), the preoccupation with Locke is not only a social reality that needs to be accounted for but also a legal reality that needs to be addressed. Thus, for example, when a pair of contemporary American legal scholars attempt to make a case against "religious institutionalism," their argument ultimately rests on an explicit and direct appeal to Locke: "the sanctity of individual conscience is at the heart of the Lockean justification for free exercise and disestablishment" (Schragger and Schwartzman 2013, 920). The authors also clearly signal their concern about the church as an "enemy of toleration and of religious liberty." The issues at stake are not merely historical; the arguments advanced by these legal scholars address pressing legal questions in the present regarding how courts should weigh the competing claims of institutions and individuals. Quite apart from the explicit point in question, the article illustrates the authoritative role of Lockean political discourse in contemporary American legal argumentation: By means of the Locke citation, the principle of the primacy of individual conscience is posited as a premise. This claim then provides the basis for the ensuing argument that all rights granted to institutions are ultimately reducible to the rights of individuals (Schragger and Schwartzman 2013, 931). In light of the account of "religion" outlined above, however, we can now recognize that this particular manner of privileging interiority and the presumed peace that results from the authority of the state are distinctive features of the concept of "religion" that was forged in the early modern period. What is the presumed source of individual rights? The Lockean answer, of course, is "nature."

One important difficulty in Locke's conception of the human "state of nature" (as outlined in his *Second Treatise of Government*) is that it involves a fundamental tension that results from trying to hold together two conflicting versions of social contract theory. At the same time, as Andrew Murphy notes, there is no historical correlation or necessary relationship between "contractarianism" per se and arguments for religious toleration in the early modern period (Murphy 1997). There is, however, an important distinction to make between two species of "contractarianism": One might be called a "social contract theory of political sovereignty"; the other might be designated a "social contract theory of justice." According to the first kind of contractarianism, the legitimacy of any given political authority derives from an agreement, or contract, between the rulers and those who are governed. Such a view of political rule was held by figures as different as William Penn, John Winthrop, and Roger Williams (Murphy 1997, 371–80). The crucial point to appreciate is that such a view presumes that there is a moral order that transcends the civil order (a so-called "natural law") and that individuals may appeal to the authority of that natural moral law in public deliberation. The belief in a natural law, by which subsequent laws of the state may be judged, provides the crucial framework in which any agreement between the ruler and those ruled is established and regulated (in Locke's case, the appeal to natural law in the *Second Treatise* is part of his justification for the Glorious Revolution of 1688). The belief in such a moral order could be and was historically used to argue for either religious conformity or religious toleration (Murphy 1997). There is, however, another species of "contractarianism." A "social contract theory of *justice*" (rather than sovereignty) presumes not only that political authority derives from an agreement between parties but also that there is no inter-subjective moral order that exists apart from the agreement (contract) among individuals that constitutes the inception of civil society. In short, one version of contractarianism presumes that there is a moral order that transcends civil society (a natural law) while the other version of contractarianism presumes that there is no moral order in nature that is greater than the (constructed) agreements among individuals – including the most basic agreement that constitutes civil society. Michael Lessnoff suggests that the latter kind of "contractarianism" is not strictly a "social contract theory," precisely because it does not rely on a notion of natural law (Lessnoff 1986, 20–25); such a stipulation, however, does not account for the fact that the notion of agreement, or contract, is better understood as the distinguishing feature of such accounts (cf. Guthrie 1969, 141–47). This other species of contractarianism might be designated "constructivist contractarianism." This view was not only widely held among ancient sophists (in fifth Century BCE) (Lessnoff 1986, 20–21), but also by moderns such as Niccolo Machiavelli (1996, 1.2.3) and Thomas Hobbes (2000 [1651], 1.6, 1.13–15). Most notably, the social contract theory of justice was presented by (and would have been accessible to early modern readers through) the character of Glaucon in Plato's *Republic* (1992, 358b–359c). Glaucon's speech (considered further below) is, in some sense, only a recapitulation of the view that arguably predominated among the popular ancient Greek sophists; its larger significance, however, is that it provides a subtle formulation of the particular account to which Socrates' central argument in the *Republic* is ultimately a response. In effect, the social contract theory of justice is like a shadow tradition to which the Aristotelian and Platonic accounts of political origins, and their ensuing traditions, are responding.

There are three points to appreciate in light of the distinction between these two kinds of contractarianism. First, it is important to appreciate that the constructivist contractarian position is indeed an ancient and recurring tradition, despite appearing modern, or even postmodern. Second, a distinctive feature of Locke's account is that he attempts to hold together elements from both kinds of contractarianism (both natural law contractarianism and constructivist contractarianism). This explains the tension at work in the way that Locke characterizes "nature" as a source of both moral law and strife. Third, although natural law contractarianism may or may not be used to argue for religious toleration, there remains an open question whether the constructivist contractarian account can provide any warrant for religious toleration at all. By appreciating the continued vitality and currency of this tradition of constructivist contractarianism, we can appreciate more clearly the persuasive challenges at work in present debates regarding religious toleration. Each of these three points requires some explanation.

The social contract theory of justice ("constructivist contractarianism") was arguably a popular tradition in Greek antiquity, but it tends to appear novel in the early modern period, given the intervening predominance of the Platonic and Aristotelian traditions. In the second book of Plato's *Republic*, Glaucon challenges Socrates to present an account of justice – understood in terms of how a person lives practically among others – and to show why justice should be chosen for its own sake, rather than as a means to some other end. In recounting what many people ("they") say, he recounts the customary sophist account of the origins of civil society:

> They say that do to injustice is naturally good and to suffer injustice bad, but that the badness of suffering it so far exceeds the goodness of doing it that those who have done and suffered injustice and tasted both, but who lacked the power to do it and avoid suffering it, decide that it is profitable to come to an agreement with each other neither to do injustice nor to suffer it. As a result, they begin to make laws and covenants, and what the law commands they call lawful and just. This, they say, is the origin and essence of justice. (Plato 1992, 358e–359a)

Is there a moral order that transcends human political arrangements, or does justice derive ultimately and only from agreements among human beings? As the context of the dialogue makes clear, the answer to this question is of immediate practical importance: If Socrates cannot answer this widely held view, then there is no reason not to become a tyrant if one can do so with impunity (Plato 1992, 342e–355, 359c–367e). A similarly hypothetical story is recounted by Machiavelli in his *Discourses on Livy*, but with a concrete historical orientation:

> For since the inhabitants were sparse in the beginning of the world, they lived dispersed for a time like wild beasts; then as generations multiplied, they gathered together, and to be able to defend themselves better, they began to look to whoever among them was more robust and of greater heart, and they made him head, as it were, and obeyed him. From this arose the knowledge of things honest and good, differing from the pernicious and bad. For, seeing that if one individual hurt his benefactor, hatred and compassion among men came from it, and as they blamed the ungrateful and honored those who were grateful, and thought too that those same injuries could be done to them, [in order] to escape like evil they were reduced to making laws and ordering punishments for whoever acted against them: hence came the knowledge of justice. (Machiavelli 1996, 1.2.3)

Although there is no explicit reference to a "contract," it is clearly implied in the act of "making" some man a "head" who is to be obeyed. As in Glaucon's recapitulation of the sophist founding myth, Machiavelli's story suggests that moral order arises only on the basis of humans entering into such civil society. Only after the constitution of the bond between ruler and ruled do other human fabrications such as the laws or justice arise.

In a similar vein, Thomas Hobbes maintains that there is no conception of justice outside the social contract. A semantic confusion in *Leviathan* arises from the fact that Hobbes uses the term "Law of Nature," but what he means is not a moral order in the cosmos, but rather the operative facts concerning desires and aversions that constitute a merely subjective sense of "good" or "evil," understood as respective synonyms for "pleasure" and "pain" (2000 [1651], 1.6). On this basis, he later explains "justice":

> And in this Law of Nature, consisteth the Foundation and Originall of Justice. For where no Covenant hath preceded, there hath no Right been transferred, and every man has right to every thing; and consequently, no action can be Unjust. [...]. Injustice is no other than *the not Performance of Covenant*. And whatsoever is not Unjust, is *Just*. (2000 [1651], 1.15)

This conception of justice, as dependent on the civil order that is constituted by intrahuman agreement, follows necessarily from what Hobbes has already established regarding the "natural condition" of mankind in which "nothing can be unjust" (2000 [1651], 1.13). There is a common misperception that the Hobbesian account of the "state of nature" is somehow equivalent to a Christian understanding of the doctrine of human corruption due to sin. What Hobbes presents, however, is actually the opposite of the Christian doctrine of original sin: In contrast to the view that sin is a humanly chosen corruption of an initially good created order, Hobbes posits that violence is, in fact, ontologically necessary (Cf. Donnelly 2009, 14). At issue is whether one assumes that violence is a temporary corruption of a peaceful social reality or whether peace is merely a temporary order imposed (by coercion) on a more primal and inevitable violence.

Lockean Nature and Toleration Traditions

What then distinguishes Locke's account of the "state of nature" (and the ensuing origins of civil society) is that he attempts to hold together elements from both of these two traditions, both the "natural law contractarian" and the "constructivist contractarian" traditions. There is an obvious sense in which Locke seems to appeal only to the notion of natural law in order to argue for a contractarian account of the origins of political authority. In his account, civil society emerges out of the state of nature when people, in order to preserve life, liberty, and property, consent to form a government. Even in the state of nature, however, Locke maintains that there are moral norms dictated by the Law of Nature (Locke 1988 [1689], 271, 351). In this sense, Locke seems to follow the tradition that posits a moral standard that transcends political regimes and by which they may be judged (Cf. Harrison 2003, 169–89). The difficulty, however, is that, in arguing for the importance of the ongoing consent of the governed, he posits a "state of nature" that is more like the constructivist contractarian account. On the one hand, he describes the original human condition as "a State of Peace, Good Will, Mutual Assistance, and Preservation" (1988 [1689], 280), on the other, however, the state of nature is also violent:

> [T]he Enjoyment of [the freedom in the state of nature] is very uncertain, and constantly exposed to the Invasion of others. For all being Kings as much as he, every Man his Equal, and the greater part no strict Observers of Equity and Justice, the enjoyment of the property he has in this state is very unsafe, very unsecure. This makes him willing to quit this Condition, which however free, is full of fears and continual dangers. (1988 [1689], 350)

This is not a merely momentary lapse in consistency; the tension here goes to the heart of Locke's account because, although he attempts to make the state of nature less harsh than Hobbes, it is nevertheless sufficiently fraught with violence and pain to induce the creation of the social contract that legitimates political authority. Although Locke seems (in contrast to Hobbes) to insist that humans are naturally social rather than merely violent, his account of the origins of civil society compels him to assume that the state of nature is, in some sense, always already corrupted – hence a state from which people desire to escape by entering civil society. In the most profound sense, the Lockean "state of nature" not only fails to be Edenic, but it is also not even genuinely "good" by Locke's own account; it is (as with Hobbes) a necessary condition for the creation of a subsequent good – the civic order forged by humans. Thus, although Locke attempts to posit a natural law that would transcend political regimes, his account of the origins of civil society (and the subsequent warrant for political legitimacy) requires that there is no ultimate human good in nature. In effect, despite Locke's claims to the contrary, his account seems to remove any warrant for discerning a moral law in nature because the human social good must be added to the violent state of nature. This would seem to be a result of his decision to replace the Christian doctrine of creation (as an original peaceful good social condition) with the constructivist contractarian state of nature (as a condition of strife). This is what is at stake in recognizing that "Locke follows Hobbes in substituting the state of nature for the createdness of nature as the primal truth" (Grant 1998, 16).

Although Locke's *Letter concerning Toleration* relies indirectly on his contractarian account of the origins of civil society, it also joins that account with a specifically Protestant theological understanding of Christian faith. Locke gives three reasons that civil authority does not extend to religious matters: First, "it appears not that God has ever given any such Authority to one Man over another, as to compel any one to his Religion" (Locke 2010 [1689], 13); second, the magistrate's "Power consists only in outward force: But true and saving Religion consists in the inward perswasion of the Mind" (2010 [1689], 13); third, "though the rigour of Laws and the force of Penalties were capable to convince and change Mens minds, yet would not that help at all to the Salvation of their Souls" (2010 [1689], 14). At one level, Locke's arguments are based on his definition of a commonwealth, which he defines as "a Society of Men constituted only for the procuring, preserving, and advancing of their own *Civil Interests*," which interests he defines as "Life, Liberty, Health, and Indolency of Body; and the Possession of outward things, such as Money, Lands, Houses, Furniture, and the like" (2010 [1689], 12). To the extent that the practice of religion does not infringe on the right to life, liberty, and property, it should not be regulated by the state (2010 [1689], 44). In the *Letter*, Locke does not explicitly refer to the state of nature, but it is clearly assumed in his account of how the purposes of the civil order are distinct from religion's focus on the salvation of souls:

> These things being thus explain'd, it is easie to understand to what end the Legislative Power ought to be directed, and by what Measures regulated; and that is the Temporal Good and outward Prosperity of the Society; which is the sole Reason of Mens entering into Society, and the only thing they seek and aim at in it. And it is also evident what Liberty remains to Men in reference to their eternal Salvation; and that is, that every one should do what he in his Conscience is perswaded to be acceptable to the Almighty, on whose good pleasure and acceptance depends his eternal Happiness. (2010 [1689], 47–48)

In this way, Locke seems to reinforce many of the key points that Cavanaugh sees at work in early modern definitions of "religion": He construes religion as something concerned with inward persuasion regarding propositional doctrines that are clearly distinguishable from those activities governed by civil authorities. However, there is a deeper tension at work here: On the one hand, Locke maintains that civil authority – the reason for entering into civil society – is limited to the external matters of "temporal good and prosperity"; on the other hand, Locke maintains that there is a moral order that is not merely concerned with material goods but which humans are nevertheless obligated to obey (Di Biase 2017). In this way, the tensions between the two forms of contractarianism continue to operate as a tension within Locke's argument for religious toleration. When he insists that civil authority is utterly different from religious authority, he relies on the social contract theory of justice, to the extent that his notion of civil society is limited to merely immanent concerns of "nature" that may be addressed by human agreement. When, however, he maintains that there is a natural law that transcends the state (and which citizens, as political actors, are bound to obey) (Di Biase 2017), he risks reintroducing a transcendent order that is both moral and religious (because he connects religious faith with a moral order that goes beyond the civil order of merely temporal goods). The irony here is that, to the extent that Locke fails to be consistent on this point, he arguably preserves some alternative to the reduction of "religion" to an internalized set of doctrines.

Beyond his basic distinction between civil authority and religion, Locke maintains that "[t]he *Prinicipal Consideration*" "which absolutely determines this controversy" is the fact that coercion cannot produce genuine faith (2010 [1689], 31). In making this second point, Locke is recapitulating traditional arguments regarding the nature of faith, arguments like those of Milton in his *Treatise of Civil Power in Ecclesiastical Causes* ([1659]) and Roger Williams in his *Bloudy Tenent of Persecution* (2001 [1644]). Such arguments draw upon the specifically Protestant account of the relationship between saving faith (justification) and good works (sanctification). The key point to appreciate is that this distinction was not simply a disjunction: Although works could not cause salvation in the Protestant account, genuinely sanctified good works did indeed nevertheless result from saving faith (Donnelly 2009, 58). In this sense, although such Protestants insisted that external conditions could not determine one's saving faith (understood as a kind of knowledge), such faith did indeed result in embodied public consequences in the form of both rites and virtues. A second crucial point is that the sanctified works that resulted from faith were also designated by the term "worship." Thus, when Milton refers to "true Religion," he defines religion as precisely this twofold unity that operates in this particular direction – going from saving faith ("knowledge of God") to the living action of sanctified works ("service of God") (Milton 1998c [1659], 1121–1124; cf. 1998a [1644], 980–981; 1998b [1673], 1151–1152). As an inheritor of this tradition, Locke simply invokes the category of "faith" with the understanding that it cannot be compelled by external means. For none of these writers, however, including Locke, was it presumed that a genuine living faith was entirely subjective or even private, to the extent that such faith necessarily resulted in an embodied life of public actions that could be observed. Thus, to the extent that Locke relies on this Protestant understanding of faith as the crux of his defense of religious toleration, there is a twofold tension within his argument. On the one hand, there is the tension between the two species of contractarianism that shapes his conflicted concept of "nature" which is the precondition for the social contract – nature is both a source of moral law and yet also a source of violence. On the other hand, the Protestant conception of faith that provides content for his notion of "Religion" is essential to the logic of his political claim that compulsion cannot induce faith, even as he thereby appeals to a moral order that both transcends the civil order and seems to be necessarily religious.

Summary and Future Directions

Despite the historically conditioned character of religious toleration as a concept, there is an alternative to both historical positivism or conceptual positivism. The use of traditionary inquiry to consider the concepts of religion and religious toleration allows for both the generalizing quality of concepts and the individual particularities involved in the use of concepts. It addition to presuming that religion is uniquely liable to become the source of dangerous actions, modern accounts of religion tend to emphasize its internal and doctrinal character, as well as its institutional distinction from other aspects of life. Even when traditionary inquiry establishes the possibility that "religion" could be understood apart from the self-legitimating story of the modern nation-state, there remains the question whether those who live in such regimes can successfully combine "toleration" (as a political doctrine) with such a reconfigured account of "religion." Locke's arguments illustrate the difficulties in such an attempt – difficulties that persist to the extent that citizens in modern nation-states still appeal to both species of contractarianism and still inhabit Locke's ambivalence about religion and moral order.

This account raises a variety of issues that warrant further investigation, including questions that are (1) historical, (2) philosophical, (3) theological, and (4) political in orientation:

1. Historical: Although Locke's influence on American constitutional history is well known and although Lockean empiricist epistemology is central to the history of American Evangelicalism (Noll 1994, 59–108), there remains an important historical question regarding Locke's reception that falls between these two discourses: Given Locke's combined influence in these two domains, what role did Locke's *Second Treatise* have in persuading American Christians that they could hold both a Christian doctrine of creation and a constructivist contractarian conception of nature? Such an account could explain why so many American Christians assume a political ontology that is arguably more Hobbesian than Christian.
2. Philosophical: Can a social contract theory of justice (constructivist contractarianism) explain on its own terms why religious devotion to anything greater than the state should be tolerated? If that question cannot be answered positively, how could constructivist contractarianism provide an alternative to civil war in resolving fundamental moral disagreements?
3. Theological: Paul Griffiths' project on interfaith dialogue deserves to be taken up by a new generation of scholars who can extend and test his account of religious reading in contexts that are oriented toward the formation of communities that may exist inside nation-states without assuming that devotion to the civil order must replace religious devotion.
4. Political: Citizens in modern states who do not identify with any particular faith tradition may consider what they assume to be the warrant for the civil order that governs communities. Whether political regimes are assumed to be the source of moral order or to be subject to some moral order beyond themselves, in either case, there will be consequences for fellow citizens who do not share the same view regarding the warrant for civil authority – consequences regarding both the persuasive condition of those fellow citizens and their relative political status.

Acknowledgments The author is grateful for the research assistance of Ryan Sinni and Sydney Nicholson.

References

Acadia L (2021) 'Only your label splits me': epistemic privilege, boundaries, and pretexts of 'religion'. Intertexts 25(1–2): forthcoming (ms)
Bowlin J (2016) Tolerance among the virtues. Princeton University Press, Princeton
Carroll L (2003 [1871]) Alice through the looking-glass. Barnes and Noble, New York
Cavanaugh WT (2009) The myth of religious violence. Oxford University Press, Oxford
Di Biase G (2017) Locke's coercive morality. Historia Philosophica 15:11–30
Donnelly PJ (2009) Milton's scriptural reasoning: narrative and protestant toleration. Cambridge University Press, Cambridge
Foucault M (1977) Discipline and punish: the birth of the prison (trans: Sheridan A). Vintage, New York
Gadamer HG (1989) Truth and method, 2nd rev. ed. (trans: Weinsheimer J, Marshall G). Crossroad, New York
Grant GP (1998) English-speaking justice. Anansi, Toronto
Griffiths PJ (1999) Religious reading: the place of reading in the practice of religion. Oxford University Press, Oxford
Guthrie WKC (1969) History of Greek philosophy, vol 3. Cambridge University Press, Cambridge
Haefeli E (2010) Toleration. Relig Compass 4(4):253–262
Harrison R (2003) Hobbes, Locke, and confusion's masterpiece: an examination of seventeenth-century political philosophy. Cambridge University Press, Cambridge
Hick J (1989) An interpretation of religion: human responses to the transcendent. Yale University Press, New Haven
Hobbes T (2000 [1651]) In: Tuck R (ed) Leviathan. Cambridge University Press, Cambridge
Lessnoff M (1986) Social contract. Humanities Press International, Atlantic Highlands
Levin A (1999) Early modern skepticism and the origins of toleration. Lexington Books, Lanham
Locke J (1988 [1689]) Second treatise of government. In: Laslett P (ed) Two treatises of government. Cambridge University Press, Cambridge
Locke J (2010 [1689]) A letter concerning toleration. In: Goldie M (ed) John Locke: a letter concerning toleration and other writings. Liberty Fund, Indianapolis
Machiavelli N (1996) In: Mansfield H, Tracov N (trans): Discourses on Livy. University of Chicago Press, Chicago
MacIntyre A (1988) Whose justice? Which rationality? University of Notre Dame Press, Notre Dame
MacIntyre A (1990) Three rival version of moral enquiry: encyclopaedia, genealogy, and tradition. University of Notre Dame Press, Notre Dame
MacIntyre A (2007) After virtue: a study in moral theory, 3rd edn. University of Notre Dame Press, Notre Dame
Milton J (1998a [1644]) Areopagitica. In: Flannagan R (ed) The Riverside Milton. Houghton Mifflin, Boston
Milton J (1998b [1673]) Of true religion. In: Flannagan R (ed) The Riverside Milton. Houghton Mifflin, Boston
Milton J (1998c [1659]) A treatise of civil power. In: Flannagan R (ed) The Riverside Milton. Houghton Mifflin, Boston
Murphy A (1997) The uneasy relationship between social contract theory and religious toleration. J Polit 59(2):368–392
Murphy A (2001) Conscience and community: revisiting toleration and religious dissent in early modern England and America. Pennsylvania State University Press, University Park
Noll M (1994) The scandal of the evangelical mind. Eerdmans, Grand Rapids
Plato (1992) Republic (trans: Grube GMA, Reeve CDC). Hackett, Indianapolis
Rawls J (1996a) Introduction to the paperback edition. In: Political liberalism. Columbia University Press, New York, pp xxxvii–lxii
Rawls J (1996b) Political liberalism. Columbia University Press, New York

Schragger R, Schwartzman M (2013) Against religious institutionalism. Va Law Rev 99(5): 917–985
Smith SD (1995) Foreordained failure: the quest for a constitutional principle of religious freedom. Oxford University Press, Oxford
Stout J (2004) Democracy and tradition. Princeton University Press, Princeton
Taylor C (2007) A secular age. Harvard University Press, Cambridge
Wilken RL (2019) Liberty in the things of God: the Christian origins of religious freedom. Yale University Press, New Haven
Williams R (2001 [1644]) In: Groves R (ed) The bloody tenent of persecution for cause of conscience, discussed in a conference between truth and peace: who, in all tender affection, present to the high court of parliament, (as the result of their discourse) these, (among other passages) of highest consideration. Mercer University Press, Macon

Toleration and the Protestant Tradition

43

Manfred Svensson

Contents

Introduction	874
The Reformation and the Fact of Pluralism	875
From Castellio to Locke. A More Promising Protestant Tradition?	877
Toleration and Nineteenth-Century Models of Religious Thought	879
Summary and Future Directions	883
References	884

Abstract

The division of Europe along confessional lines plays an important part in the history of toleration, shaping both standard narratives about the past and the apparent tension between strong confessional commitments and the possibility of toleration today. The present chapter offers a survey of this debate in the post-Reformation period, including the tradition running from Castellio to Locke. After considering the problems that can be found both in confessional Protestantism and in this parallel humanist tradition, the chapter turns to several nineteenth-century thinkers (Vinet, Kierkegaard, and Kuyper), who reflect reception of and resistance to certain modern transformations of the concept. While nothing like a uniquely Protestant framework for toleration emerges from this survey, the chapter points to sources that are significant both for understanding this ambivalent historical trajectory and for furthering contemporary reflection.

M. Svensson (✉)
Department of Philosophy, Universidad de los Andes, Santiago, Chile
e-mail: msvensson@uandes.cl

© The Author(s), under exclusive licence to Springer Nature Switzerland AG 2022
M. Sardoĉ (ed.), *The Palgrave Handbook of Toleration*,
https://doi.org/10.1007/978-3-030-42121-2_59

Keywords

Toleration · Tolerance · Reformation · Protestantism · John Calvin · Sebastian Castellio · John Locke · Alexandre Vinet · Søren Kierkegaard · Abraham Kuyper

Introduction

What is the place of toleration in the Protestant tradition? And conversely, what is the place of Protestantism in the tradition of toleration? These questions can be raised out of sheer historical interest, as part of the search for the origins of toleration. But they are also contemporary questions: not only because the arguments uncovered may have enduring relevance but also because Protestantism is still a living tradition. Broadly defined, Protestants today comprise 37% of the world's Christians, who in turn represent a third of the world population (Liu 2011). The history of Protestant reflection on tolerance may have something to say to the various facets of this tradition. If the Protestant view of toleration is a consistent one, it may also be part of that faith's message to the rest of the world.

Considering toleration alongside the Protestant tradition, in other words, is one way of thinking about the intersection between systematic and historical reflection on toleration. This may in fact be one of the most fruitful areas of research open to scholars interested in that intersection. Such a claim must, however, be distinguished from the "Whig interpretation" of history that dominated much of the scholarship on toleration from the Enlightenment until the 1980s (for a typical example, see Jordan 1932). According to that view, the past is divided between forces of light and forces of darkness, and toleration naturally emerges as progress makes it possible to leave behind these backward forces. When Herbert Butterfield published his indictment of this interpretation of history, his key example was the Reformation, presented this way (Butterfield 1931). Today the Whig interpretation has rightly been set aside, and the Protestant contribution to toleration is much less clearly defined. But this hardly makes the place of the Reformation and later Protestant thought a secondary matter in the history of toleration. A more nuanced understanding of Protestantism's role in the history of toleration still has much to add to the discussion.

This chapter will first consider the relationship between the Reformation and the fact of pluralism and toleration before then moving onto the nonconfessional Protestantism represented by Castellio. His vision is often presented as a more promising starting point for toleration, but there are reasons to consider it deficient both as a variant of Protestantism and as an understanding of toleration. A final step will bridge the gap between the post-Reformation era to three nineteenth-century thinkers seldom thought of as involved in these discussions: Alexandre Vinet, Søren Kierkegaard, and Abraham Kuyper. These authors mark both the progress and the tensions and confusions of the modern discussion on toleration as internalized by Protestant thought. Considering these various stages of the discussion, one can obviously conclude that this is a history with significant failures and shortcomings. The compatibility between toleration and strong confessional allegiance, however, is not only an occasional historical reality but a concept that finds strong support in the deepest intellectual sources of this tradition.

The Reformation and the Fact of Pluralism

There are at least two sides to the Reformation's relationship with toleration. One question is what the Reformers and their successors thought about toleration. But whatever the magisterial Reformers may have believed about the ideal of toleration and however they may have acted on that belief, the Reformation undeniably set off a process of pluralization. The first step is considering the issue at this factual level. In the aftermath of the Reformation, the religiously unified political community largely remained in place as an ideal, but it would quickly cease to be a reality in fact. This is the case at least on the pan-European level: Europe ceased to be the religious and political unity that it had been. Individual political societies of course continued to exhibit such internal unity, but they now bordered other societies of a different confession. Internally, within a single commonwealth, the fact of pluralism had not yet become a common phenomenon. But neither was it nonexistent. This is a fact that looking beyond the southern and northern regions where confessionally uniform nations were the norm makes all the more apparent. The Netherlands, like the Holy Roman Empire and much of Eastern Europe, became societies inhabited by more than one religious group. As Diarmaid MacCulloch notes, "It is sad that we remember Transylvania for Count Dracula, who never existed, rather than as the first Christian polity officially to declare that everyone ought to be able to worship God in their own way without interference." MacCulloch has in mind a 1568 Declaration of the Transylvanian Diet, which affirmed that "no one is permitted to threaten to imprison or banish anyone because of their teaching, because faith is a gift from God" (MacCulloch 2016, 7–8). Analogous declarations, edicts of toleration, and other forms of acceptance of religious pluralism became a reality throughout the European continent.

Although interconfessional conflict certainly played a significant role in the post-Reformation period, what emerges from recent historiography is a process that utilized different strategies of accommodation. In order to recognize these strategies, though, it is important to acknowledge the many forms of toleration that have existed in the past, instead of searching for policies that resemble those of today (Kaplan 2007). As Alexandra Walsham has noted, research into local conditions contradicts the common assumption that strong religious beliefs drove a wedge between neighbors and rather highlights "the extent to which dissenting groups were assimilated and integrated into wider society in this period, the capacity that people exhibited to absorb difference and tolerate heterodoxy in their midst" (Walsham 2006, 11). This is, as mentioned, one way to approach the question. It starts not from a principle but rather from the simple fact of toleration as one possible response to pluralization. In his summary of this scholarship, Scott Dixon states that tolerance arose from "both principle and pragmatism, but it was the latter that contributed most to shaping confessional relations" (Dixon 2012, 149). Considering the debates on toleration in the wake of the English Civil Wars, Blair Worden comes to a similar conclusion regarding the subordinate place of the arguments for religious toleration: disorder had simply "made religious pluralism a fact of life, which advocates of tolerance now judged likelier than intolerance to reconcile with society's requirements of peace and prosperity" (Worden 2009, 163).

In the context of the views put forward by the magisterial reformers, this emphasis on the pragmatic origins of toleration sounds plausible. Luther had opposed the use of secular means in religious matters in his treatise *On secular authority* (1523), but he abandoned this conviction less than a decade later in a turn analogous to the one experienced by Augustine a millennium before. In Luther's *House Postil* of 1544 on Matthew 13 (WA 52, 130–5), for instance, one can find practically the complete set of Augustinian arguments for coercion, and Luther also quotes the same texts Aquinas cited in his exposition of Matthew (*Super Mt.*, cap. 13 lect. 2). Augustine's texts called for more toleration within the Church but also for the intervention of secular force when it comes to those who break the bond of charity, dividing the Church (see, among other studies, Bowlin 1997). When faced with this patristic and medieval legacy in writings of the Reformation, it is tempting to say that there is nothing new under the sun: pre-Reformation approaches to dissent remained firmly in place. That impression can be confirmed through looking at episodes like Servetus' execution in Geneva. This is a tragic event but one that hardly corroborates the popular image of Calvin as a singularly intolerant tyrant. It rather confirms that the standard approach to persecution of heresy prevailed in Geneva as it did in the rest of Europe. Until the end of the seventeenth century, a broadly recognizable family of arguments in defense of coercion continued to dominate in various regional and confessional settings (for the English case see Goldie 1991).

But is the contrast between principled and pragmatic approaches to toleration the adequate lens for evaluating this evidence? Principled and pragmatic approaches are perhaps better seen as significantly integrated: Confronted with the fact of pluralism, people discover not only that they have to live together but also that the capacity for living together is something that their own traditions can view as an intrinsic (and not merely pragmatic) good. If this is the case, it is not simply a rejection of those traditions that will lead to tolerant dispositions, but a discerning reappropriation. This is particularly true in the case of the broadly Augustinian tradition assumed by the Reformation. There were, after all, two sides to Augustine's critique of the Donatists: They were rightly coerced, he argued, because they had broken the bond of unity and love of the Church; but they broke that bond precisely because they ignored the mixed nature of the Church, a body in which wheat and tares grow together. In other words, Augustine's position entailed both intolerance *ad extra* and a call for more tolerance within the Church. Changing pragmatic circumstances can obviously lead towards a recovery of the resources for toleration present in this side of Augustine's legacy.

The Reformation, moreover, did more than sustain and develop different aspects of the Augustinian reflection on toleration. An important example of this is an element of Calvin's teaching that has been neglected by scholarship on the Reformation and toleration: the recurring presence in his writings of a "toleration of the cross" (*tolerantia crucis*) as one of the ingredients of the Christian life. Calvin's discussion of this toleration of the cross draws from his Biblical exegesis and from the Stoic and Augustinian legacy, and it shows with peculiar intensity the way in which elements of the Christian and philosophical tradition can unite in calls to forbearance. And as a matter of fact, the concept was tremendously influential: This was the first section of Calvin's *Institutes* translated into English and several other languages, and it continued to be published as a stand-alone text well into the nineteenth century. In the global Calvinist world, a devotional call to tolerance was thus often the first acquaintance readers would make with Calvin (See Calvin's *Institutes* III, 7–8 and Jones 2009).

From Castellio to Locke. A More Promising Protestant Tradition?

This Calvinian theme may nevertheless seem to be too mild an approach to offer guidance today and too insignificant to counterbalance the image of the intolerant Calvin that developed in the wake of the Servetus case. If anything, many conclude, it would be better to seek orientation and inspiration from one of Calvin's opponents, Sebastian Castellio, whose *On Heretics* and *Advice to a Desolate France* offer something like a first principled critique of the theology of religious coercion (for a biographical introduction, see Guggisberg 2003). As a matter of fact, Castellio now has a place in histories of toleration which he did not have a century ago (see, for instance, Zagorin 2003, 93–144). He also plays an important role for those who search for distinctively Protestant approaches to toleration. The example of Christ and the apostles, the sanctity of conscience and faith commitments, and the need for peace in approximating knowledge of God through productive dialogue – David Fergusson rightly stresses the presence of these themes in Castellio's writings in defense of tolerance (Fergusson 2004, 113–116). Castellio furthermore presents these arguments in a way that clears the air of much moral obfuscation: "To kill a man is not to defend a doctrine, but to kill a man," he writes (Castellio 1965, 271). It is not surprising that contemporary Protestants view his work as a more "usable past" than that of the magisterial reformers.

But the issue is arguably more complex. In the work of Castellio one does indeed find the arguments summarized by Fergusson and others, but there are other aspects of his approach that are more problematic to the very notion of toleration. Consider, first, his claim that Catholics wrongly persecute Protestants because they do not believe "in the Pope, or mass, or purgatory, and such other things, all of which so completely lack any foundation in the Scriptures, that even their names are nowhere to be found in them" (Castellio 2016, 7). Here Castellio is not merely telling

Catholics how they should act vis-à-vis Protestants, but how they should recalibrate the importance of their own beliefs. Only if they submit their faith to a radical sort of revisionism – one which will turn these disputed doctrines into things indifferent (*adiaphora*) – will they be counted as tolerant. And this is not a disproportionately anti-Catholic argument. He criticizes Protestants too for not being "satisfied with the fact that there is agreement on the main points of religion which are clear and evident from the Holy Scriptures" (Castellio 2016, 11). As these portions of Castellio's *Advice* illustrate, his work has a strong tendency towards *concordia* rather than *tolerantia* (though the presence of the latter must be acknowledged as well). Instead of admitting that there may be something important in the issues at hand and calling the contending parties to come to grips with them through appropriate means, Castellio presses doctrinal minimalism on both sides of the conflict. His advice is to focus on the evident principles on which they already agree. Should they follow this advice, however, tolerance as traditionally understood would actually become superfluous. Tolerance is needed in the face of conflict, but this is instead a theology of conflict avoidance.

Edwin Curley has labeled this position "Erasmian liberalism," and he correctly identifies some further problems in this approach. Castellio's emphasis on moral uprightness and on the difficulty of establishing theological truth, for instance, were hardly the best way to persuade those who took a high view of theological doctrine of the need for toleration (Curley 2003). Curley moreover rightly identifies this Erasmian background as the pattern upon which John Locke formed his own approach to toleration. This is a point worth stressing when it comes to questions about the theological origins of liberalism. Jonathan Israel is one among many scholars who have described Locke's approach to toleration as "inherently theological, and Christian in a distinctly Protestant sense" (Israel 1999, 103). This is clearly a misleading description. Locke's vision does indeed have theological elements, but they are of decidedly Erasmian ancestry; instead of merely defending the equal political rights of heretics, for instance, both Castellio and Locke engage in redefining the very notion of heresy (Castellio 2016, 38; Locke 1968, 149–155). Locke's view of toleration rests not only on a minimalist view of doctrine but also on a contractualist conception of the Church, one that collides with Protestantism as strongly as it does with Roman Catholicism (for a more detailed version of this admittedly controversial characterization of Locke, see Svensson 2019). Both with regard to doctrine and to church membership, the assumption is that when it comes to doctrine and to church membership, strong religious commitments and tolerance have a strained relationship. Though it is still possible to admire the exhortation to toleration found in the Erasmian tradition from Castellio to Locke for its moral earnestness, to state the problem as frankly as possible, this is a tradition that fails both as a Protestant tradition and as a coherent account of toleration.

This is, in fact, the great drama of the sixteenth and seventeenth centuries: Those who held to robust confessional agendas and to a traditional conception of toleration typically had very restrictive views on the limits of toleration; those who favored more reasonable limits, however, often ascribed to an inadequate view of toleration, one that takes disagreement itself as a step on the road to intolerance. Are there exceptions to this rule? Certainly. One might refer to the writings of John Williams for the compatibility between tolerance and mission (Bejan 2017), to John Owen for toleration's consistency with finely grained Christian dogmatics (Svensson 2016), and to William Penn – stretching the Protestant tradition to include the Society of Friends – for a toleration that goes hand in hand with a robust public morality (Murphy 2016). These three men, moreover, were actively involved not only in writing on toleration but in the practical shaping of different societies. But these names do not represent the mainstream of Protestant thought in their times. In turning to the nineteenth century, the post-Reformation era must be left with obviously mixed results.

Toleration and Nineteenth-Century Models of Religious Thought

This section will briefly consider three very different contexts and authors. The work of Vinet, which we will consider first, offers a glimpse into the way Protestants alternately reflected and resisted certain Enlightenment approaches to toleration. A brief consideration of Kierkegaard will, next, suggest that some of the transformations discussed in the previous section gradually rendered the concept of toleration useless for thinkers like him. Finally, it becomes evident that some of the most productive thought on these issues can therefore be found in authors who scarcely use the traditional terminology of toleration (a matter we will illustrate with Kuyper, though a similar point could be made about the Anglican John Neville Figgis).

First is the Swiss critic and theologian Alexandre Vinet, a largely forgotten ecumenical Huguenot, whose career was as distinguished in theology as in the study of French literature. From the 1820s to the 1840s he published a series of works defending freedom of worship and the convergence of Christianity with a kind of liberalism. In one revealing presentation of his vision, he discusses two kinds of liberalism in terms that clearly echo Augustine's discussion of the two cities. Like Augustine's cities, these types of liberalism are created by two types of love: "the one selfish and savage, of which all the world is capable; [...] the other, intellectual, generous, truly social, is the fundamental idea of Western civilization and the condition of all true progress" (Vinet 1877, 258; for the parallel in Augustine, see *Gn litt* XI, 15, 20.). Two important elements of Vinet's approach to toleration emerge from this religious philosophy. The first of these is Vinet's distinctive approach to the question of tolerating the intolerant. The idea of excluding the "intolerant" from tolerance was already in the air. Writing in 1763, Voltaire had stated that "men must avoid fanaticism in order to deserve toleration" (Voltaire 1912, 73). There is, of course, a defensible version of this idea, namely when "fanaticism" or "intolerance" refer with precision to those who actively seek the exclusion of others. When Karl Popper, for instance, wrote about the self-destructive nature of a limitless tolerance and of the need to keep the intolerant at bay, he was writing in a post-war context in which everybody knew who the "intolerant" were and of what actions they were capable (Popper 2013, 581, n. 4.). But today such language is often abused, to the point of labeling any strong commitments held by a foreign or unpopular party fanatical. Here Vinet offers an approach that differs from Voltaire and later versions of this argument, instead claiming that "if ever toleration can find a noble opportunity for exerting itself, it is toward the intolerant" (Vinet 1877, 275). Vinet captures the notion that as a virtue tolerance must entail a sacrifice, "since its effect is to leave in existence what we would fain see destroyed" (Vinet 1877, 275). As he writes, "this virtue is beautiful as the sacrifice is great" (Vinet 1877, 275). This view in fact led him to believe that ultimately tolerance would become a virtue especially characteristic of those with strong religious convictions.

But this view collides with the second distinctive feature of Vinet's approach to toleration. As Vinet's is a progressive religious philosophy, he cannot but expect toleration to play a merely transitional role. It is an "insufficient palliative" for "times of fanaticism and oppression," and so it is ultimately an "insult to the rights of humanity" (Vinet 1877, 276). Upon reading these words, one cannot but recall Goethe's "to tolerate is to insult" (Goethe 1981, 507). Published around the same time, these words reveal the common aspiration that progress would make reciprocal judgment, and thus the need for toleration, superfluous. Thus, while Vinet resists one modern discourse on toleration, the one that is satisfied with the intolerance of "fanaticism," he embraces another modern tradition of toleration: One that expects a future in which all toleration, not only that of fanaticism, has been rendered superfluous. The problems with such a view are perhaps more evident centuries later: In the absence of the hoped-for progress, conflicting judgments appear to be a permanent feature of the human condition, and it is not particularly helpful to have dispensed with toleration in the name of a higher ideal.

The next author, Kierkegaard, did not fall for any such illusions regarding progress. But before turning to him it may be helpful to consider his slightly less famous fellow countryman, NFS Grundtvig, whose original position – for an orthodox church of the people, against the rationalist clerics – had taken a special turn after he spent much of the years 1830–1832 in England. His experience of a "broad Church" in England led him to the conviction that this was the model that would make his defense of old-fashioned believers in Denmark viable. In other words, instead of seeking to expel liberals from the Church, Grundtvig campaigned for a "broad-Church" model, with implications for the freedom of all those involved: The State would lose its power to enforce doctrine and mattes of conscience, more liturgical and doctrinal freedom would be left to individual pastors, and each congregation would have greater freedom in the choice of its pastor. Together with the "loosening of parish bonds" – permission to worship in the parish of one's choice – as Bruce Kirmmse explains, these measures were above all directed at protecting the freedom of orthodox peasants to avoid rationalist priests. But instead of pursuing that goal through the American model of disestablishment, this proposal consisted rather in a people's Church of the widest possible theological margins, since only thus could the nexus between popular culture and orthodoxy – a nexus that was Grundtvig's chief concern – be preserved (Kirmmse 1990, 214–217). What is of interest here is of course the identification of this ideal with toleration. In its own peculiar way, it shows to what degree a quite Erasmian understanding of toleration had come to prevail not only in liberal discourse but in more traditional circles as well.

What then about Søren Kierkegaard, the most important religious thinker of Denmark's Golden Age? One finds in Kierkegaard a deep religious thinker who was far more radical than Grundtvig in his critique of Christendom and in his willingness to disrupt the establishment. But at the same time, he had an eye for the vacuous discourse of toleration that he found in the accommodations of his contemporaries. Confronted with a tolerance that has been turned into indifference, some will try to restore it to its traditional form of forbearance or permission (for this "traditional" conception see Horton 2011); but some, like Kierkegaard, will rather be inclined to do away with the concept altogether. "It is a kind of disloyalty to Christianity to keep it to oneself. And their talk of tolerance is nonsense. Xnty has never been tolerant in such a way that it allows other ppl. to remain pagan, [to] be damned. No, it has been intolerant in such a way that the apostle would rather lose his life proclaiming Xnty to them" (Kierkegaard 2011, 337 (NB4:106)). As this chapter in his notebooks reveals, it is the loss of missionary zeal, dignified with the mantle of tolerance, that Kierkegaard most conspicuously protests against. If these words are directed against the Grundtvigians, Kierkegaard's complaint against other circles of the Danish Church strikes a similar tone (Kierkegaard 2012, 314 (NB13: 64)). Loss of zeal, compromise with the world, fear of martyrdom, these are the traits that Kierkegaard sees in contemporary tolerance-talk, one in which tolerance and indifference are more or less identified with one another. "But those who want to attain the emancipation of the Church in this way – sparing themselves from martyrdom – have introduced a concept of tolerance that is in complete conformity with worldliness (namely, tolerance = indifferentism), and this is the most frightful insult to Xnty" (Kierkegaard 2015, 214 (NB23:22)). Should we, then, consider Kierkegaard a champion of intolerance? As his few scattered remarks indicate, nothing of the sort seems to follow: "it certainly isn't intolerance to be willing to suffer in order to help others," he writes (Kierkegaard 2011, 338 (NB4:106)). But even when no apologies for intolerance are forthcoming, there is a price to be paid for rendering tolerance equal with indifference. Kierkegaard's attack on Christendom might have turned him into a significant apologist of religious freedom. His long concern with patience – "To Gain One's Soul in Patience" was a favorite subject in his *Discourses* – might have led him to profound reflection on the ethical and spiritual dimension of tolerance. But this did not happen. He could not find any positive use for the concept. The transformation that the concept of tolerance had gone through had simply ruined it for him.

This section comes to a close by turning to Abraham Kuyper. His case is different from Vinet and Kierkegaard in two important senses. First, Kuyper was not only a thinker and writer but a theologian who was also an institutional architect. He founded a political party, a university, and a newspaper and served as the Netherlands' Prime Minister between 1901 and 1905 (Bratt 2013). In this regard he resembles Williams, Owen, and Penn, all mentioned above. Second, Kuyper is a person who makes no special use, positive or negative, of the specific concept of toleration. But his approach to pluralism makes for a consistent framework into which the insights into toleration discussed thus far can be integrated and made fruitful for contemporary debate. If that is the case, this survey suggests an important difference between the post-Reformation phase and these selected nineteenth-century writers. As noted above, in the early phase it was among the confessionally minimalist positions that one found pleas for toleration. The more precise and useful understanding of toleration of the three nineteenth-century authors is instead found to be closer to orthodox positions.

Though the chronological distance between them is a relatively short one, the Christendom attacked by Kierkegaard lies in the distant past for Kuyper. The effects of liberalism, secularization, and of the French Revolution were already visible in his religious and political landscape. Kuyper's was thus a Christian vision for a post-revolutionary Europe. His response to the conditions in which he found himself was a pluralistic program that opposed the prophets of secularization and intolerance equally (Harinck 2020). Central to his approach was the notion of "sphere sovereignty," which played a role similar to the one held by subsidiarity in the simultaneously developing modern Catholic social teaching. Over against the unqualified sovereignty of the modern State, Kuyper stressed that "the family, the business, science, art and so forth are all social spheres, which do not owe their existence to the state." (Kuyper 1943, 90) But he set forth this view not only to stress the possibilities of harmonious interaction between each sphere and the state – the social pluralism that was being developed by contemporary Roman Catholicism (Hittinger 2002) – but also in order to highlight the idea that a plural social system was the way in which plural and conflicting visions would have to find their place in the modern world. Rather than pointing to some contemporary form of Erasmian *concordia*, he saw different "life systems" that were "wrestling which one another, in mortal combat" (Kuyper 1943, 11), and (here agreeing with Kierkegaard) he believed that these "principal *credos*" were "worth people risking their own lives for and disturbing the lives of others" (Kuyper 1998, 469). If this was going to foster something other than crude polarization, each "life system" needed substantive freedom to develop the institutions in which its view of the world would come to full visible expression.

In one sense, such rival visions of the world would relate to each other with "mere" tolerance, since they would be putting up with erroneous views rather than respecting an indifferent difference. This is not a sovereign granting an arbitrary edict of toleration, however, but distinct social groups reciprocally recognizing that they owe each other that tolerance. Contemporary Kuyperians have, moreover, developed this distinction between a plurality of worldviews and a plural social system into a threefold classification of diversity. There are diverse social structures and diverse worldviews, but there are also diverse cultures (for this threefold approach to pluralism see Mouw and Griffioen 1993; Chaplin 2006). If there is a modern tendency to see cultural difference and difference in worldview as roughly equivalent (often reducing the latter to the former), a distinctive feature of Kuyperian thinking has been the upholding of this difference. "Mexican" does not contrast with "Iranian" in the same way that "Catholic" contrasts with "Muslim." As mentioned above, the specific terminology of toleration is hardly present in Kuyper and only partially present in later Kuyperian debates (see, however, Chaplin 1993). But taking these distinctions into account makes it easier to navigate contemporary discussion on the respective merits of toleration and recognition. If cultural difference is an aspect of the goodness of creation, it is certainly not mere toleration that is called for. But in that case worldviews ought not be reduced to subproducts of cultural difference. Taking cultures and visions seriously makes space for both recognition and toleration in dealing with diversity.

Summary and Future Directions

Several competing narratives attempt to account for the relationship between toleration and the emergence of Protestantism. One such narrative presents Protestantism itself as a religion of freedom, which thus gives rise to toleration as a matter of course. A second narrative has held that, on the contrary, it is religious passion of the type seen in the post-Reformation wars of religion that must be tamed in order for toleration to emerge. These narratives not only shape today's understanding of the past, they also play a decisive role in conceptions of the relation between toleration and religion today. For both these reasons they must be revised: The record must be set straight, and the spell of such narratives over contemporary reflection must be broken. But this is easier said than done, and it is important to avoid replacing these narratives with other equally simplistic ones.

Protestantism obviously has a share in both the darker and the brighter sides of the modern history of toleration. Does it have a privileged place in the brighter side? Religious coercion, as John Coffey has written, was also condemned by some Roman Catholics, "but Protestants found it easier to repudiate the traditional position and denounce the church's historical record" (Coffey 2000, 211). That a profound transformation of the Christian tradition was necessary for toleration to become widely accepted is indeed a fact. This chapter has argued, however, that the key question is the precise nature of that transformation. One modern approach has held that a revisionist disposition with regard to one's own beliefs is an essential condition for toleration. That tradition can take many different forms. It can encourage believers to a minimalist conception of their doctrine, as seen with Castellio and Locke, or it can suggest that the absence of such revisionism unmasks the fanaticism and potential intolerance of the believer. It is crucial, then, to recognize that another approach to this required transformation has been present throughout Protestant history. Rejecting the legacy of religious coercion necessarily implied revising the ideal of a religiously homogeneous society, and above all it meant recognizing that not all means in pursuit of that ideal are licit. But this revision is compatible with holding to a traditional understanding of one's respective faith and seeking reasons for toleration within that tradition in all its comprehensiveness. Such reasons, which can be both philosophical and religious in nature, are not limited to the sanctity of conscience. They extend to conceptions of God, of self-control and bearing of the cross, and to views of the mixed nature of the church and of other communities. The post-Reformation world brought with it both these kinds of reinterpretation of

Christianity, and these two centuries of Christian reflection on toleration must be evaluated in the light of this ambivalence.

As mentioned in the introduction, there is more than historical interest to these questions. The alternatives that have emerged over the course of this discussion are still very much alive in the discussion of toleration and religion today. Once the compatibility of strong ecclesial or doctrinal commitments and toleration has been called into doubt, the question of whether it can be reconciled with mission, conversion, public confession, and the like also arises. But these are hardly marginal phenomena in religious life, and it is not helpful to conceive of toleration in terms that render it incompatible with such practices. Imagining some kind of minimalism or revisionism as a precondition for toleration has, moreover, become common outside the religious sphere. If in the seventeenth century doctrinal minimalism was often conceived of as a condition for toleration, during the last few decades something similar has happened with minimal ethics. But there is nothing inherently intolerant in comprehensive and strongly held moral visions. Familiarity with the historical alternatives to minimalism in the religious sphere enables more imaginative thinking about the compatibility between toleration and robust ethical views.

From the preceding considerations it does not follow, however, that a simple choice must be made between the traditions discussed here. Castellio's brushing aside of rationalizations, his view that "To kill a man is not to defend a doctrine, but to kill a man," can be appropriated by any sound understanding of tolerance and also by those who would reject his doctrinal minimalism. The same goes for Vinet's insight into the relation between toleration and sacrifice as a reason for tolerating the intolerant. To continue to be relevant today, orthodox positions must be as capable of integrating the best insights of the likes of Castellio and Vinet as they are of integrating the best results of the secular discussion on toleration.

Acknowledgments The author wishes to thank Rebecca West for her revision of this chapter's English version, and Matías Tapia for bringing Kierkegaard's relevant texts to my attention.

References

Aquinas (1980) Opera omnia. Frommann-holzbook, Stuttgart-Bad Cannstatt
Augustine (2004) On Genesis. New City Press, Hyde Park
Bejan T (2017) Mere civility. Disagreement and the limits of toleration. Cambridge, MA, Belknap
Bowlin J (1997) Augustine on justifying coercion. Annu Soc Christ Ethics 17:49–70
Bratt JD (2013) Abraham Kuyper: modern Calvinist, Christian democrat. Wm B Eerdmans, Grand Rapids
Butterfield H (1931) The Whig interpretation of history. G Bell, London
Castellio S (1965) Concerning heretics. Octagon Books, New York
Castellio S (2016) Advice to a desolate France. Acton Institute, Grand Rapids
Chaplin J (1993) How much cultural and religious pluralism can liberalism tolerate? In: Horton J (ed) Liberalism, multiculturalism and toleration. Palgrave, New York
Chaplin J (2006) Rejecting neutrality, respecting diversity: from "liberal pluralism" to "christian pluralism". Christ Sch Rev 35:143–176

Coffey J (2000) Persecution and toleration in protestant England 1558–1689. Pearson Education, Essex
Curley E (2003) Sebastian Castellio's Erasmian liberalism. Philos Top 31:47–73
Dixon CS (2012) Contesting the reformation. Wiley-Blackwell, Oxford
Fergusson D (2004) The reformed tradition and the virtue of tolerance. In: Storrar WF, Morton AR (eds) Public theology for the 21st century. Essays on honour of Duncan B. Forrester. T&T Clark, London, pp 107–122
Goethe W (1981) Maximen und Reflexionen, Werke. Insel, Frankfurt
Goldie M (1991) The theory of religious intolerance in restoration England. In: Grell OP, Israel J, Tyacke N (eds) From persecution to toleration: the glorious revolution and religion in England. Clarendon Press, Oxford
Guggisberg HR (2003) Sebastian Castellio, 1515–1563: humanist and defender of religious toleration in a confessional age. Ashgate, Aldershot
Harinck G (2020) Abraham Kuyper's vision of a plural society as a Christian answer to secularization and intolerance. In: Karpov V, Svensson M (eds) Secularization, desecularization, and toleration: cross-disciplinary challenges to a modern myth. Palgrave Macmillan, Cham
Hittinger R (2002) Social pluralism and subsidiarity in Catholic social doctrine. Ann Theol 16:385–408
Horton J (2011) Why the traditional conception of toleration still matters. Crit Rev Int Soc Polit Philos 14:289–305
Israel J (1999) Spinoza, locke and the enlightenment battle for toleration. In: Grell OP, Porter R (eds) Toleration in enlightenment Europe. Cambridge University Press, Cambridge
Jones DC (2009) The curious history of John Calvin's Golden booklet of the Christian life. Presbyterion 35:82–86
Jordan WK (1932) The development of religious toleration in England, vol 4 vols. Allen & Unwin, London
Kaplan B (2007) Divided by faith: religious conflict and the practice of toleration in early modern Europe. The Belknap Press of Harvard University Press, Cambridge, MA
Kierkegaard S (2011) Kierkegaard's journals and notebooks. Princeton University Press, Princeton and Oxford
Kierkegaard S (2012) Kierkegaard's journals and notebooks. Princeton University Press, Princeton and Oxford
Kierkegaard S (2015) Kierkegaard's journals and notebooks. Princeton University Press, Princeton and Oxford
Kirmmse BH (1990) Kierkegaard in golden age Denmark. Indiana University Press, Bloomington and Indianapolis
Kuyper A (1943) Lectures on Calvinism. Eerdmans, Grand Rapids
Kuyper A (1998) Sphere Sovereignity. In: Bratt JD (ed) Abraham Kuyper: a centennial reader. Eerdmans, Grand Rapids
Liu J (2011) Global Christianity – a report on the size and distribution of the World's Christian population
Locke J (1968) *Epistola de Tolerantia*/A Letter on Toleration. Oxford University Press, Oxford
MacCulloch D (2016) All things made new: the reformation and its legacy. Oxford University Press, Oxford
Mouw RJ, Griffioen S (1993) Pluralisms and horizons: an essay in Christian public philosophy. WB Eerdmans, Grand Rapids
Murphy AR (2016) Liberty, conscience, and toleration: the political thought of William Penn. Oxford University Press, New York
Popper K (2013) The open society and its enemies. Princeton University Press, Princeton
Svensson M (2016) The alms of authority? John Owen's understanding of toleration. J Church State 58:690–709
Svensson M (2019) John Locke, liberal theology, and toleration. In: Lauster J, Schmiedel U, Schüz P (eds) Liberale Theologie Heute – Liberal theology today. Mohr Siebeck, Tübingen
Vinet A (1877) Outlines of philosophy and literature. Daldy, Isbister & Co, London

Voltaire (1912) Toleration and other essays. GP Putnam's Sons, New York/London
Walsham A (2006) Charitable hatred: tolerance and intolerance in England 1500–1700. Manchester University Press, Manchester
Worden B (2009) The English civil wars 1640–1660. Orion, London
Zagorin P (2003) How the idea of religious toleration came to the west. Princeton University Press, Princeton

Atheist Toleration

44

Charles Devellennes

Contents

Introduction	888
Negative Atheism	888
Positive Atheism	892
Revolution Against Religion	896
Atheism Today	898
Summary and Future Directions	901
References	902

Abstract

Atheism has gone through several stages in history. From the ancient Greeks to the modern period, the term was largely used in a pejorative manner, to denigrate those with unorthodox beliefs about (the) god(s). This negative atheism was supplanted in the seventeenth century by a new conception of the atheist: as one capable of moral behavior. This positive atheism, as it emerged in the thought of Bayle, Meslier, and d'Holbach in particular, quickly became accepted even by nonatheists. As atheists advocated for a universal model of tolerance, they also became increasingly tolerated by their contemporaries. As atheism grew in importance, it is said to have played a role in the revolutions that rocked Europe from the eighteenth to the twentieth centuries. By looking at the French and Russian revolutions, this chapter argues that the link between atheism and revolution is more complex than it seems. Finally, this chapter looks at the rise of New Atheism in the twenty-first century to show how the movement has evolved in the recent past. It then analyses the thought of William Connolly, and proposes to widen the scope of atheism to include a movement past itself: turning positive atheism into a metatheism.

C. Devellennes (✉)
University of Kent, Canterbury, UK
e-mail: C.Devellennes@kent.ac.uk

© The Author(s), under exclusive licence to Springer Nature Switzerland AG 2022
M. Sardoč (ed.), *The Palgrave Handbook of Toleration*,
https://doi.org/10.1007/978-3-030-42121-2_34

Keywords

Agonistic respect · Atheism · French Revolution · Metatheism · Modernity · Negative atheism · Positive atheism · Respect · Secularism · Soviet atheism · Tolerance

Introduction

Atheism and toleration have a long common history, and this chapter shows that the two concepts emerged together in the modern period and have since had an important symbiotic development. This is not surprising given that atheists have been, and in many cases remain, some of the least-tolerated people in their own countries. Not only does antiatheist prejudice go as far back as ancient Greece, Rome, and early modern Europe, but there is also long-lasting evidence that atheists remain one of the least-liked groups in contemporary liberal democratic countries such as the United States. By providing an overview of two and a half millennia of atheist history, atheism is first seen to be conceived as a crime and therefore not as something worthy of toleration, a view that remained prevalent for much of written history. Only in the modern period, and particularly in the seventeenth century, is there a reversal of this trend. Atheists first become seen as moral beings in their own right during that period, and the extension of religious toleration to freedom from religion has been an essential contribution of the Enlightenment to modern discourses on toleration. By the time of the French and Soviet revolutions, atheism had grown into a position in its own right, capable of articulating a program for social change. These two revolutionary trends were seen to be atheistic, a view not entirely backed up by historical facts. Finally, by looking at the rise of New Atheism and the push for a more self-assertive form of irreligion, the challenges to contemporary atheism can be assessed against their historical background. There are still novel and innovative theories of atheist toleration being put together, and atheism is not only a thing of the past, but rather also a theory expanding to new horizons.

Negative Atheism

What is atheism and who are the atheists in our history? This question is surprisingly difficult to answer, not least because atheism has had a variety of different meanings in writings since the early days of philosophy in ancient Greece. The word itself, deriving from the Greek *átheos*, is a negative concept. The private prefix *a* is a negation of the word *theos*, meaning God, or gods. Literally meaning nongods, the atheist was seen by the ancients as the one who denies the gods of the city. As such, the term itself is negative: It is an accusation toward those who do not have sufficient piety, who believe in gods that may be harmful to the city, and was often invoked in times of wars or natural disaster to point the finger at those thought responsible for angering the gods. This is the first hurdle in the definition of atheism, in that everyone is an atheist of the gods they do not accept. When not faced with one's own religion, everyone denies the existence of others' gods to a degree. The Christian denies the gods of the ancient Greeks and Romans, the Muslim denies the gods of the Hindus, and the philosopher often denies the gods of his own people for a more nuanced and complex understanding of divinity. A definition that encompasses so many different beliefs and practices is problematic in its own right – what defines everything defines nothing. But in each context, the label was used to exclude and punish, with the penalty for atheism being death.

This is precisely the dilemma of the most famous of the ancient clashes between one of the earliest philosophers, Socrates, and the people of his city – Athens. Socrates had been teaching for all of his life that the gods were fundamentally different from those worshipped in the temples of the Acropolis, that divinity was a spark in all human beings that could not be the same as the material gods whose statues adorned the ancient sites of worship. For the authorities in Athens, this was pushing the freedom to philosophize too far, and Socrates was accused on two counts by a court of his fellow citizens: of impiety against the gods and of corrupting the youth. Plato (1970) tells us of the trial faced by his mentor, where Socrates is facing his accuser Meletus in open court – with 501 Athenians as judges. Against the accusation that he has shown impiety against the gods of the city, Socrates demands clarification from his accuser. After cross-examination, Meletus admits that what he means by the accusation of impiety is that Socrates is actually a "complete atheist" (*to parapan atheos*). The accusation is serious, for the penalty for such a crime as denying the gods is death. But it was music to Socrates' ears, for he knew he had a strong grasp of his own conception of divinity and could beat back this accusation without too much difficulty. Socrates' argument is simple: He claims to have received a divine mission during a visit to the oracle at Delphi, which required him to question the wisdom of all around him, and in particular of those who claim to be the wisest in society. This divine mission of doubt and challenge to those in authority was given to him by a divine entity, *daimonia*, or spirits that guide him toward constant ethical behavior – no matter what the risks of challenging authority mean for his personal safety. Socrates thus easily dispelled Meletus' accusation that he was a complete atheist in open court – how could he believe in supernatural forces and at the same time deny their very existence? On the other hand, he handed a clear victory to Meletus on both counts he was facing at his trial. Not only did he admit to having a conception of gods fundamentally different from his fellow-citizens, but also he defended his corruption of the youth and admitted he will never stop questioning those in power in his legal defense. Winning the philosophical argument, Socrates lost the trial and was sentenced to death by his fellow Athenians. It was enough, it turned out, to have a rather unconventional vision of the gods (rather than deny their existence altogether) to fall to the accusation of atheism. Socrates was thus not an atheist, but the accusation of atheism he faced tells us an important story about the early conception of the atheist. The atheist is someone whose unorthodox conception of divinity challenges the social order – itself based on an official religion, cult, and practices that are put at risk by this new religious thinking.

Whenever unconventional beliefs about the gods emerged, they faced the potential accusation of atheism. The early Christians living in the Roman Empire, Justin Martyr tells us, were accused of atheism and of hostility to Rome. And he admits that this accusation is true in respect to the gods of Rome and Greece – but they were not atheists with regard to the one true God (Roberts 1867). The early Christians were thus well aware that, to their pagan contemporaries, they seemed like they were denying the very nature of divinity. The Christian God was so different from the Greek and Roman deities that to the ancients it seemed like there were no gods as such in Christianity. Much later, during the Reformation, when the Catholic Church faced challenge from heretics of the Lutheran or Calvinist persuasion, the accusation of atheism was widespread on all sides of the debate. For a counter-Reformation Catholic, a Protestant was just a bad as an atheist for questioning the authority of the Pope and Church, and for a Protestant the worship of Christ in bread and wine was desecrating the very idea of a spiritual God. If one is to believe the literature of the sixteenth century, there were atheists everywhere as the accusation was flying across the theological debates of the time. It is around this time that the word atheist makes its way into modern languages, with the first use of the term in French in 1566 and in English in 1587, replacing the Latin term used prior to that. Atheism was exclusively used as an epithet of accusation toward those with whom one disagreed about the nature of God. But in that sense, it did not vary much from the ancient uses of the term. The atheist was still the one who denied the existence of a particular conception of God, rather than denied the existence of God altogether. The atheist remains the *bête noire* of Renaissance Europe – the one who denies the God of one's own Church, and the one who challenges the worldly power of the said Church. The accusation is in many ways more political than it is religious. Together with the Reformation came widespread secularizations – confiscations of Church property by newly converted Protestant rulers. In the city of Canterbury in the United Kingdom, where these words are being written, ruins of monasteries still bear witness to that bloody struggle of the sixteenth century. Saint Augustine's Abbey, once the pride of the city's religious orders and a strong local rival to the Cathedral priory, is an open-air museum rather than a place of worship. The theological struggle thus had strong political and revolutionary connotations: All of western Christian Europe was affected to some degree, with Kings and rulers having to pick sides and wars of religion disturbing the peace. The atheist was a convenient shorthand for the one who cannot be trusted or tolerated, and who can be condemned without hesitation. It was as politically expedient as it was theologically unsound as a definition. Everyone who denies the correct conception of God could be accused of atheism, and since the penalty was death (and confiscation of one's property), it was a convenient way to punish political opponents.

The apotheosis of the intolerance toward atheists can be seen in the trial of Luciano Vanini, an Italian doctor living in France in the seventeenth century. Vanini, who always denied the charge of atheism, was an avid reader of ancient philosophical texts which gave him a very unorthodox conception of divinity. While he was being questioned and tortured, as was the custom at the time, Vanini is famed to have picked up a piece of straw lying on the ground and said that it was enough proof of the existence of God. What Vanini meant was that God and Nature were the same, that the very existence of the universe was enough proof to belief in God (Vanini 2011). But this denied the power of revelation, the truth of the Bible, and, most importantly, the primacy of the Catholic Church in deciding on theological matters. Found guilty of atheism and blasphemy, he was condemned by the *parlement* of Toulouse, had his tongue cut out, was strangled to death, and his body burned at the stake. His fate acted as a powerful reminder to all those who dared have unorthodox beliefs in theological matters and that the potential consequences for being accused of atheism were real indeed. For the century and a half that followed, until at least the French revolution, it deterred many from airing their thoughts openly and sharing their views. Intolerance of dissent was strong and potentially lethal. The atheists, if they even existed at that time, could fear a similar fate to Vanini's if caught. If even a pantheist like Vanini could face death for his beliefs, one could fear the worst for anyone who actually claimed there is no God. Nor was Vanini a unique case. Many were condemned for much lesser offenses, such as selling books that had irreligious connotations, or failing to take off their hats while a religious procession was passing by. The Chevalier de La Barre, in 1766, a century and a half after Vanini, suffered a similar fate for impiety: His tongue was cut out, his head chopped off, and the remains burned at the stake. His crime had been to damage a crucifix and say some anti-Christian things (Onfray 2007). Once again, the atheist was someone being pursued for challenging the power of the church, rather than someone who actually denied the existence of the gods.

Negative atheism is an accusation brought about by one's enemies (Buckley 1990). By showing that someone does not believe in the right gods, or in the right interpretation of the one true God, accusers could easily discredit a person entirely. The presumption was that without the gods to hold someone to account, without a religious conscience and a belief in divine retribution, human beings could not be contained and their desires will lead them to the worst of crimes. If one does not even believe in God, how can one be expected to act morally and not take advantage of others? Without the threat of eternal damnation for one's crimes, what is holding back atheists and unorthodox believers from acting out on their deepest impulses? The accusation, in other words, was never only about belief and theology, but about morality and politics. Atheists are a threat to moral order, and they are a threat to political order. If they were to spread their beliefs, society would collapse altogether. Against the rising calls for tolerance coming during the Renaissance and Enlightenment periods, a powerful coalition of intolerance was holding its ground. One simply cannot tolerate such threats to peace and order. Instead, the emphasis was on conversions (forced conversions if needed), repression, and a call for unity. For much of the early modern period, tolerance was a dirty word, leading to accusations of *tolerantism* – often in combination with accusations of atheism. Tolerance of atheists, or of other faiths, was seen as an abdication of the duties to spread the faith in the one true God. The alternative, as defenders of the religious unity and the prevailing social order would have it, was total collapse of the *ancien régime*, the decline of the role of the monarchy, the aristocracy, and the clergy in favor of a ruleless and vengeful mob.

Even for early advocates of toleration, such as John Locke who was writing at the end of the seventeenth century, there was little doubt that atheists could not be part of the toleration contract. Locke argued that toleration was a worthy virtue, going against those who argued for conversion of unbelievers. But his defense of toleration was framed in exclusionary terms. Those who recognize an external power, such as Catholics who believe in the Pope's authority, or those who do not believe in a higher power, cannot be trusted to keep their word (Locke 2013). For all the progressiveness of their arguments, the moderates of the Enlightenment of whom Locke is a good example refused to extend religious toleration to the "atheists." In this, they were in full accordance with the counter-Enlightenment in finding the challenge to social order posed by atheists worthy of condemnation. It would take a wholly more radical version of toleration to push for atheists to be fully integrated members of society.

Positive Atheism

It took a particularly unorthodox thinker to make the very first argument in favor of tolerating atheists. It was Pierre Bayle, an exiled French Huguenot living in the Dutch town of Rotterdam who first took the plunge (Bayle 2000). Writing before Locke had denied atheists toleration, he argued that it is not any stranger for atheists to be good persons than for devoted Christians to be bad people. His argument was precisely that moral behavior is quite divorced from religious belief, because one's observance of morality is more linked to one's passions than to one's intellectual speculation. In other words, when a Christian acts immorally, it is not because they have a defective sense of faith or that they do not understand they are acting in an immoral fashion, but because they have other passions that compel them to act in the way they do. They may be driven by a quest for power, by greed, or other such passions, and they may then feel guilt for having betrayed their own faith, but at the moment of action the passions were stronger than belief. The same applies to atheists. A particularly vicious atheist would not be able to hold back their passions, but one that has a tempered character and a sense of virtue would be just as capable as a good Christian to obey the rules of morality. This type of moral argument is today quite widespread and accepted by most, but in the late seventeenth century it was a revolutionary idea. Bayle was sticking his neck out to argue this and was ferociously attacked by some of his contemporaries for having even suggested that atheists could be moral persons. Pierre Jurieu, Bayle's former mentor-turned-mortal-enemy, launched a personal crusade against Bayle that saw the latter lose his teaching position in Rotterdam. But the cat was out of the bag, and the argument proved convincing to many. It had the merit of isolating moral reasoning from theological speculation. Nor was Bayle alone in making this point, as Spinoza had made a passionate defense of the independence of morality a few decades before. From then on, it became more convincing to judge moral worthiness of persons not based on their religious beliefs, but rather on their actions. Bayle himself was not a complete atheist, in that he kept attending Church and professing his faith throughout his life, but he certainly thought he could live very well with atheists.

Who were the atheists of the seventeenth century? No one had actually claimed to be an atheist themselves at that stage in history, as all mentions of atheism were accusations against others. While Bayle had painted a picture of positive atheism, that atheists could be virtuous persons and therefore could be tolerated, he maintained on numerous occasions that they were still wrong about their lack of belief in God. One such "atheist," at least in the mind of Bayle, was the Dutch Jewish philosopher Baruch Spinoza, who had died a few years before Bayle emigrated to the Netherlands. What made Spinoza an atheist, according to Bayle, was his lack of belief in Divine Providence. According to Spinoza, there was no plan, by God or any other entity, to unfold human events in accordance with good or justice. These values were important, but they were human constructs, and human beings could not depend on a God to bring them about. But equally, Spinoza held a pantheist line similar to that found in Vanini and in ancient philosophers: that God is Nature: *deus sive natura* (De Spinoza 2018). Nature, or God, has no plan for moral behavior. Humans need to bring about good and justice themselves, otherwise they will be left with evil and injustice. Toleration, for Spinoza, was the worthiest of virtues precisely because it allowed each to make up their minds without undue interference from others. Nor was toleration a threat to social order. The politicians, Spinoza argued, had enough tools at their disposal to punish vice in this life without need for hypothetical punishment in the next life (De Spinoza 2007). But Bayle's definition of the atheist is still unsatisfactory. If the atheist is the one who does not believe in Divine Providence, what about all of those who equally do not believe in a divine plan but nonetheless believe that God exists? What about those who do not believe in God but think there is necessity in the universe? Atheists cannot be defined strictly along those lines, and it took someone to actually claim their own atheism to bring about a theory of what atheism is.

Ironically perhaps, it was a Catholic priest who was the first self-avowed atheist. Bayle knew that positive atheists were possible – and thought that someone such as Spinoza was one of them – but no one before Meslier had claimed to be an atheist themselves. The word was so fraught with negative connotations, and with threats to one's personal safety, that it was not until the memoirs of a countryside priest were found after his death in 1729 that it became clear there were people who thought of themselves as atheists out there. Meslier's work was revolutionary in more ways than one. It confirmed the worst fears of the opponents of atheism that it was a challenge to social and political order beyond theological beliefs. The alliance of priests and nobles came under particularly strong criticism by Meslier, who argued for the creation of a republic without King or God (Meslier 2009). Calling for expropriation of the rich landlords of the *ancien régime,* Meslier was using atheism to attack the social structures of his time. He did so after reading Bayle, showing that indeed moral restructuring was necessary, and that some of the worst excesses to morality had been done in the name of God, with the backing of both religious and secular authorities. The manuscript was well-known and popular, it circulated in clandestine book networks as early as the 1730s, and it was widely read and reedited even decades later, with Voltaire publishing two abridged editions of the work in the 1760s. But Voltaire was much more moderate and he was no atheist, and he used Meslier's critique of religion and nobility while cutting the atheism out of the text. Tolerance of atheists was still an issue with many members of a more moderate Enlightenment, and Voltaire thought atheism too dangerous to be spread to the masses. He was willing to tolerate Meslier's radical ideas about religion, but atheism was just one step too far. Meslier advocated for a complete change to the structure of society, taking the village as the central unit of production and distribution of wealth; his radical republic was taken as a model for all those who argued for redistribution of wealth and the abolition of privileges. An obelisk with him name was erected in Moscow in 1918, during the Russian revolution, commemorating him as a member of the workers' liberation movement – it still stands to this day in the Alexander Garden near the Kremlin.

Meslier's rather crude version of atheism was radicalized and systematized further by the work of a German-born aristocrat who naturalized as a French subject: the baron d'Holbach. In 1770 under a pseudonym, d'Holbach published his *System of Nature,* providing a full philosophical defense of atheism as a positive doctrine (d'Holbach 2016). Not only did he show that atheism was consistent with an understanding of natural phenomena, but also he defended a moral code based on a conception of utility that allowed for all to contribute to the public good. d'Holbach's system was the culmination of the arguments for positive atheism found in Bayle and Meslier and pushed them to their logical conclusion. If virtue is possible for atheists, maybe they have good foundations for their moral behavior. This foundation he found in the concept of utility, which all rational beings could follow. Studying atheists, d'Holbach found that they could actually propose a morality for all – including nonatheists. One could be a good atheist, a good Christian, or a good pagan if one followed the principles of public usefulness and moral behavior. It became all-the-more important, thus, to guarantee one's right to belief in God or not to believe in God, as personal behavior trumped personal belief. Toleration was fully universalized by d'Holbach, for whom personal belief was an absolute right – whatever that belief might be. Only laws concerning harmful behavior are useful in a public setting, what who one chooses to worship – or whether one chooses to worship – is irrelevant for the public servant. It took a systematic atheist, in other words, to put together the first universal theory of toleration, which actively forbade imposing one's religious belief on others. d'Holbach then elaborated on this model morality in his later work, placing toleration of beliefs as one of the cornerstones of his ethical system.

What did toleration look like, on the eve of the French revolution? Bayle's argument, by then accepted by many, was that morality is independent of theological thinking. This implied that you can be not only a good atheist, but also a good Jew, a good Muslim, or a good Hindu, while living in a majority Christian country. This was not only speculative either. By then, European powers had come to control many areas where people of different religions lived, through colonial and imperial expansion. There were the peoples of the Americas, with their varied beliefs in different gods, spirits, and natural forces, the slaving cities and trade posts of Africa, contact with India, China, and Japan, and many more interactions as they were told in numerous volumes of travel literature available at the time. In those books, the various beliefs and traditions of people unknown to Europeans were being described in great detail, diversifying the world and showing its complexity and variety. The city of Batavia alone, renamed Jakarta after Indonesian independence from the Dutch, had around 100,000 people living there, including European settlers, Chinese and Arabian merchants, as well as a majority of the nearby indigenous islanders. It was a world entrepot, storing goods from throughout Asia to be shipped back to Europe on large *fluytschepen,* the proud merchantmen of the Dutch navy. It was perhaps this exposure to numerous new cultures, great civilizations, and complex socio-political systems that convinced the philosophers that a fulfilling life was possible outside the Church. Medieval Europe had of course known the other religions of the book, but its interactions with other religions beyond Judaism and Islam were few and far between. The age of colonialism created cracks in the religious consensus in Europe, that religious belief and piety were necessary for a good communal and political life. It is not a surprise that some of the earliest debates on toleration happened in the Kingdom of Castile in the sixteenth century, with Bartolomé de las Casas advocating for the protection of the inhabitants of the new world. Some of the peoples encountered by Europeans could even be said to have no gods at all, and their practices did not resemble the religions the explorers and colonizers were accustomed to. The atheist, in other words, might actually exist out there on the fringes of the known world.

In those days, it was the Dutch republic that best symbolized the spirit of tolerance the philosophers were advocating for. In Amsterdam as in Batavia, an atmosphere of openness was prevalent. Spinoza and Bayle were free to write and publish what they wanted there, but they still had to face the consequences of their actions. Spinoza was excommunicated from his Jewish community, and Bayle lost his job at the *École Illustre* of Rotterdam because of his writings. Tolerance did not imply that others needed to help you, accept you within their religious community, or give you a job. It merely implied that you would not get arrested, tortured, and executed for your beliefs. Life for tolerated persons could still be difficult, they could still be attacked in public for their lack of piety, and they might lead solitary lives exiled from their families and loved ones. But they could write and say what they wanted, without fear of consequences from the state. Though this remained largely true, it could still be dangerous for atheists to live in the open, even in the Dutch system of tolerance. The political struggle between the Orangist and Republican factions was rife and saw scenes of violent retribution happen in the country – two of the republican leaders, the de Witt brothers, were killed and supposedly eaten by a mob in 1672. The Netherlands was the exception that confirmed the rule in the early modern period: Nowhere else were atheists really safe to admit their own beliefs. Even when other European countries eventually adopted acts of toleration, such as England in 1688 or France in 1787, they only covered specific Christian beliefs and never openly accepted atheism as a belief worthy of toleration. It would take an outright restructuring of the entire legal and political system to establish a legal code that would tolerate the atheists.

Atheists were thus uniquely placed to advocate for universal toleration. Since they were tolerated almost nowhere and were in small numbers, they wanted to put together a framework where they could be accepted everywhere by the majority religion. They also championed the rights of others to hold their own religious beliefs. Whereas Huguenots could find refuge in the reformed countries of Europe, and Protestants could move to the Americas in their quest for salvation, atheists had no refuge from persecution. Their answer to their dilemma was thus a truly universalist one, not a specifically atheist one. Everyone must be free to follow the dictates of their conscience, must be free to philosophize, must be free to worship or not worship, and must have their rights protected to believe what they will under the law. The only limit to tolerance, in other words, needs to be based not on philosophical or religious speculation, but on concrete reference to the common good, enshrined in law. Human sacrifices, for example, could be banned on the grounds that they deny the rights of those being sacrificed, forbidding the preaching of hate toward others could be banned on grounds of public safety, or preventing zealous crimes from being committed could be legislated, but these must be framed in terms that are not specific to any belief, but apply to all equally. In other words, atheist toleration argued that religion, as much as lack of religion, is a right for all. The only limits to be placed on that right must be with reference to common utility, rather than orthodoxy or reference to a God.

Revolution Against Religion

Though atheist philosophers prior to the French revolution had argued for universal tolerance, it is often assumed that revolution brought about antireligious feeling and widespread violence in the name of atheism. This picture is inaccurate, however, as it is not clear that atheism was driving the French revolution at all – though perhaps a form of secularism was. The revolutionary Camille Desmoulins is perhaps the best to understand this important distinction between atheism and secularism. While Desmoulins accepted that the nobility and clergy, as social orders, had to be abolished and their privileges withdrawn, he was also under the impression that atheism was madness and that belief in God was the only possible defensible theological position. He, however, argued that signs of revelation from the divine cannot be expected, and that all must be left to their own devices when it comes to belief in God (Israel 2015: 22). What needed to be fought against, in other words, was not God or belief, but rather the institutional dimensions of religion that had secured special rights and privileges under the *ancien régime*. But under such a revolutionary scheme, atheism was not the answer. Together with Robespierre, Desmoulins accepted that a new Cult to the Supreme Being needed to be established, responsible to the French republic rather than the Catholic Church. The land that was owned by the Church at the time needed to be confiscated, or rather secularized to borrow a term from the Protestant reformation, and made available for public use. Priests, bishops, archbishops, and cardinals were expropriated, their lands confiscated, and their revenues used to fight the revolutionary wars. What was at stake, in other words, was the rise of the state establishing itself as the guarantor of religious belief rather than an atheist state per se. The French revolutionary state was less of a haven of tolerance than a besieged republic, surrounded by hostile monarchies and reactionary armies backed by the moral support of the Catholic Church. Total war is hardly conducive to the value of toleration.

What the French revolution did achieve, however, was to break the claim by churches to have a monopoly on theological thinking. After the revolution, it was increasingly less believable, not only in France but also throughout Europe and beyond that churches could dictate their terms on all citizens. Though Napoleon had reconciled the French revolutionary state with the Catholic Church, he never restored the old order and kept the land that had been confiscated by his predecessors. Even with the restoration of the monarchy in France after the Napoleonic wars, the Catholic Church could not recover its power, and the changes to the legal structures imposed by Napoleon and his armies had freed many from the feudal ties that bound them closely to their parishes and restricted the rights of minorities, not least of all Jews who were now free from the society of orders that had limited them so much in medieval and early modern times (Sperber 2013). Putting all citizens under a similar legal background broke the back of the old aristocracy and clergy, for their claims to superiority had been shattered by the new legal structure. Though the old structure still existed in many places throughout the world, its days were numbered for it was never to return under its previous form. On the eve of the Russian revolution, only the Russian Empire still had a form of government reminiscent of the old feudal regime – and even the Tsars had abolished serfdom by then. Germany, the Austro-Hungarian Empire, and the Ottoman Empire were by no means democratic states then, but they all had legal measures in place to tolerate minorities and had established their dominance over their respective churches and mosques. Only Russia remained committed to a form of unity between Church and state as absolute as had been seen in prerevolutionary France.

It is perhaps not surprising then that the second example of revolutionary atheism is the Soviet Union and its state atheism. Unlike during the French revolution, it is much clearer that the state was openly trying to promote atheism during the Russian civil war and the socialist state that emerged at the end of it. Doubtless there could be no reconciliation between the Orthodox Church and the new regime, as the Church had provided support both for the Tsar and the counterrevolutionary forces during the war. But Lenin, a master politician, understood that open hostility with the Church in times of war was not in the interest of the new state. Instructions from the center were to avoid clashes, but revolutionary violence against priests was rife under local Soviet leadership – more than a 1000 of them died among the millions the conflict claimed. Religious property was also confiscated, as had been the case during the Protestant reformation and the French revolution. The extent to which the Church was targeted was largely based on this ownership of wealth in the country, with other owners equally targeted by state appropriations and nationalizations of private enterprise. All those who resisted these forced appropriations were treated ruthlessly, some summarily executed and many imprisoned.

After the war, antireligious propaganda escalated, led in particular by the communist youth (*Komsomol*). Anti-Christmases and Komsomol Easters were organized, but the senior leadership was still keen to avoid open conflict. "Scientific atheist education," based on voluntary groups was established, while simultaneously the new regime recruited priests to provide education in the villages. Lenin believed religion to be backward and representative of the old regime, but he thought it would wither away with education rather than through confrontation (Kenez 2006). The goal of the new state was to provide mass literacy, which it could then use for its own propaganda purposes. Later, when the Soviet Union was fighting Nazi Germany in the Great Patriotic War, antireligious propaganda was relaxed by Stalin and churches were once again integrated into the state for the war effort. Many of the antireligious attempts of the Soviet regime had found deep hostility from the people, for whom religious belief was an important part of their lives. The relaxing of restrictions on religion was thus possible, even under Soviet totalitarianism. Such a revival only happened where it was politically convenient, however. In places where the local church was associated with nationalist sentiment, such as Lithuania, the Soviet state remained as ruthless as it had always been (Kenez 2006: 153, 232).

State atheism has more to do with Marxism-Leninism than with atheism per se. Even at the worst of its history, it was never entirely intolerant of religion. There were persecutions and restrictions of privileges characteristic of authoritarian regimes, and even murders and summary executions especially in times of civil war. The mass arrests of the 1930s affected the remaining clergy alongside the rest of the population. The Stalin constitution of 1936 guaranteed religious freedom precisely at the time that the regime was committing its worst exactions against its own people. In a state where all are persecuted, it is difficult to draw the line between tolerance and intolerance. From the 1950s onward, the situation had stabilized, and after Stalin's death the policy of tolerance of religion was the norm. The fact that the Russian Orthodox Church could still claim 50 million members in the late 1980s shows that toleration was in effect, and persecutions by then a real and painful memory rather than a state policy.

Atheism Today

Atheism has come a long way from its inception; it is no longer merely an epithet of accusation against the unorthodox, nor are atheists forced into hiding in modern liberal democracies. In China, they may well be the largest group when it comes to religious belief, and in the majority if one includes the nonreligious in the count: 72% are either nonreligious or follow traditional Chinese folk religion. It is particularly difficult in the Chinese context, where Confucian, Taoist, and Buddhist teachings are not always considered religious to isolate atheism per se. It may well be that the concept of atheism, as it developed in Europe, is not entirely applicable in other contexts. In other countries, they are in a minority, but often a significant one. Some estimates put atheists at around or above 20% of the population in the Czech Republic, France, Sweden, and the Netherlands, and between 10% and 20% in many other European and other Western countries, including the United Kingdom, Australia, and Germany. In the United States, however, the number of self-identified atheists is much lower: perhaps as low as 3% of the population. But counting atheists poses an immediate problem of definition. Is a nonreligious person the same as an atheist? If you refuse a religious label, but nonetheless believe in spiritual energy, a nonanthropocentric God, or have had a falling out with your church, mosque, or temple while maintaining your faith in God – you might answer a survey question saying you are not religious – but a believer nonetheless. Equally, some religions do not require professions of faith and accommodate those who do not believe in a personal deity into their ranks. It is easy enough to be Jewish or a Buddhist without believing in a god – to be a religious atheist. An atheist might well answer that they belong to a religious community, in other words, while consistently denying a belief in God. Though they are often grouped together for counting purposes, the atheists and the nonreligious may well differ significantly from one another on that basis (Alexander 2019). It is likely, however, that atheism is at its peak today, and even if there has been a trend downward in some places, notably the former Soviet Union and eastern European countries since the end of communism there, overall there are more atheists in the world today than there have ever been.

This rise of atheism has come together with a self-assertion of atheists, notably through the work of the New Atheists in the early 2000s. Sam Harris, Richard Dawkins, Daniel Dennett, and Christopher Hitchens were the four horsemen of the atheist revival, at least in the English-speaking world (Harris 2004; Dawkins 2006; Dennett 2006; Hitchens 2007). Their collective work was widely read, they had an important media presence, and they made quite a sensation through their self-assertive claims about the superiority of atheism over religion. Overall, their arguments differed little from those one could find in the middle of the eighteenth century in France: Religion has played a negative role in human affairs and can be seen as detrimental to well-being, religious texts are historical artifacts and not revelation, it is possible to live a good life while being an atheist, and the more education you spread, the less likely religion is to play a significant part in people's lives. As Enlightenment philosophers had done before them, the New Atheists argued that natural phenomena are best explained by science, not religious texts, and life is better without God than it is with God. For all of their inflammatory posturing, the message remained one of fundamental tolerance of others with different beliefs. None of these four thinkers called for the use of public power and authority to close down churches, temples, or mosques. They all made appeals to human reason to let go of what they perceived to be the worst aspects of religion in contemporary life, notably its role in providing justification for fundamentalism, and its claims to be able to surpass scientific knowledge. Though they were portrayed as aggressive atheists by their opponents, one would be at pains to find calls for violence, curtailing of religious freedom, or intolerance in their work. What one finds, however, is a complete lack of respect for what some religious people hold sacred.

This leads us to an important distinction between tolerance and respect. Tolerance is a disposition toward others, but it is also an active virtue in the sense that it requires one to exercise restraint, to accept criticism, and to let others do what one believes is wrong. For Spinoza, Lars Tønder explains, it is precisely this active virtue that is so important to defend in political life (Tønder 2013). Once one has political power, the temptation to make others do what one believes is right is overpowering. Toleration, on the other hand, applies certain principles above that consideration. Toleration asserts that others must be let free to make their own choices, to have their own beliefs, and to be responsible for their own actions rather than be told what to choose, what to believe, or what to do. Respect, on the other hand, is something that one demands from others, due to one's superiority. In the Old Testament, it is respect of one's parents and elders that is placed above one's self. Respect is based on a type of superiority, justified in a variety of different ways, such as age, wisdom, or power. If one respects one's elders, it is a superiority based on age; if one respects the wise, irrespective of their age, it is a respect based on knowledge; if one respects figures of authority, it is because they hold positions of power and represent particular institutions. Respect is an important aspect of social life – basic levels of respect are expected in loving relationships, at work, and among friends. But at the political level, respect may be demanding too much. If you demand respect for your view that a particular policy should be based on your reading of the Bible, you are demanding too much from those who do not share your views on that reading. You may, however, still demand tolerance of this particular view. You may demand that your right to have such a view be upheld, that you be protected from others trying to impose a different view on you, and ultimately that you be tolerated by those who disagree with you. If respect is a virtue of social situations, toleration is the virtue of political institutions. Political institutions cannot shield you from the views of others, but they can protect your fundamental right to have your own views (and to discuss them, argue for them, and attempt to convince others of their truth).

The New Atheists showed little to no respect for religious views. That particular line of argument rendered them odious to many, for whom their own religious views called for very different conclusions than those of Dawkins, Harris, or Hitchens. But that did not make these thinkers intolerant. In fact, it was a rather apt example of what tolerance entails. It demands the ability of those who are offended by others' views to argue back, fight back with arguments, articles, interventions on television channels, pamphlets, and words rather than trying to get them banned or silenced. A tolerant society is not one without open disagreement or in perfect harmony. Quite the contrary, toleration implies disagreement and diversity. It comes about because of a pluralism of beliefs and practices. In a world where all believe more of less the same things, toleration is unnecessary. But in a world where there is fundamental disagreement about how to lead the good life, what is to be done, and how to do it, toleration is the most important of the political virtues. Without it, disagreements about ideas quickly turn into disagreements with rifles. When tolerance fails, the powerful can impose their will on the weak.

There is growing evidence that, even today, tolerance is still an important virtue for atheists (Doyle 2019). There are still many contexts where atheism is forbidden, such as in countries with laws against apostasy, where leaving your religion is outlawed and sometimes punishable by death. These are predominantly Muslim countries, but Christian and other religious countries also often break their own laws against blasphemy. In the UK, these laws were on the statute books until 2008, and they still exist in one form or another in Germany, Poland, Italy, Brazil, India, Finland, and Russia, among many others. Even in countries with no laws that disproportionately affect those who criticize religion, such as in the United States, atheists are often characterized as one of the least-liked groups in society. It would be unthinkable, for many Americans, to vote for an atheist for President of the United States. It is often speculated that a famous politician or business person is planning to run for office when they start to openly display signs of religiosity, making it the political canary of American elections. It is not surprising that atheists in this context have continued to push for increased tolerance as both legal and social structures are still biased against them in a number of contexts.

William Connolly, an American professor of political theory, has made that argument in perhaps the subtlest way in the recent past. Preferring to self-identity as a nontheist, rather than as an atheist – he perceives the label to have too many negative connotations – Connolly has argued for a middle ground between the demands of toleration and the demands of respect. Advocating for what he calls *agonistic* respect, he wishes for a world where the atheist, nonreligious, and the religious, are free to challenge each other's' beliefs in an atmosphere of friendship and fundamental engagement with others' being (Connolly 2005). Based on the ancient Greek concept of the *agon,* the struggle or the competition characteristic of sports events, the concept of agonistic respect, is thus one where all can not only openly compete with each other for the attention of their fellow-citizens, but also respect each other as participants in the same sport: the difficult game of talking about God and the universe. Just like in sports there can be no overall truth but merely a winner in a particular context, there is perhaps no answer to the question of God but only more or less convincing arguments. But unlike an agnostic, who will conclude that one cannot know, Connolly argues that he can make reasoned arguments in favor of particular positions that are more likely than others. It is unlikely, for him, that a God such as that defended by theists (those who belief in a personal God whom they can have a relationship with) exists. But that is not to exclude all conceptions of God, or gods, from the picture. A God as nature, which was Spinoza's position, is entirely reasonable, as is a God of absence, an initial mover of the universe, or a vision of God as love. Besides, a vision of a personal God as depicted on numerous medieval and Renaissance paintings, is not the vision most often advocated by theologians and religious figures today. Connolly's point is precisely that the subtlest of theologians, and the most convinced of nontheists, may well be closer than they think when they argue about God. Whether God is ineffable or inexistent may only be a matter of personal preference rather than fundamental disagreement about the issue. The question remains: Which position is the most convincing, in a contest where these are agonistically respectful of each other?

Summary and Future Directions

The future of atheism will be a lively debate not only between atheists and the religious, but also among atheists themselves to convincingly argue for a position that encapsulates the evolving reality of atheism in contemporary social and political life. In places where atheism is still outlawed or restricted, a more traditional conception of atheism is still appropriate, which challenges the hold that religious life still has on those who do not share others' beliefs. But in places where atheism is a significant and influential position, with large minorities – and in the case of China, perhaps even a majority – defending the position, the evolution of atheistic tolerance will be all the more fascinating. Perhaps there, a further form of atheism might emerge which, to follow Connolly's speculations, will be more generous and respectful of religious views that are close to its own formulation. Debates between atheists and theologians may well prove to be more constructive in this context than they have been in the past, where the common roots of thinking are guaranteed by a strong sense of mutual acceptance of the legitimacy and validity of one another's views. In this context, maybe atheism needs to move past itself and reformulate as less antagonistic of religion, and more constructive of a social and political worldview that extends beyond its denial of God. Precisely because atheism has called for universal toleration over the past 300 years, it is a philosophy in a unique position to further this spirit of intellectual challenge and furthering of human knowledge in nonexclusionary terms. Such an atheism that has moved past itself, which I have called elsewhere a *metatheism* (Devellennes 2021), moves past both theism and atheism and widens its philosophical scope by moving past its current historical formulation. Perhaps the most important development here would be to extend this metatheism beyond its western context, to include studies in China, Japan, and India notably where religion (or to put it in more accurate terms: a spiritual-philosophical worldview) and the lack of gods have existed for millennia. Such a global history of atheism remains to be written and would form the basis for a fully fledged articulation of a philosophy without god(s).

References

Alexander NG (2019) Rethinking histories of atheism, unbelief, and nonreligion: an interdisciplinary perspective. Glob Intellect Hist. https://doi.org/10.1080/23801883.2019.1657640
Bayle P (2000) Political writings. Cambridge University Press, Cambridge
Buckley MJ (1990) At the origins of modern atheism. Yale University Press, New Haven
Connolly W (2005) Pluralism. Duke University Press, Durham/London
d'Holbach PHT (2016) The system of nature. HardPress Publishing, Chicago
Dawkins R (2006) The god delusion. Bantam Books, New York
De Spinoza B (2007) Theological–political treatise. Cambridge University Press, Cambridge
De Spinoza B (2018) Ethics. Proved in geometrical order. Cambridge University Press, Cambridge
Dennett D (2006) Breaking the spell: religion as a natural phenomenon. Viking, New York
Devellennes C (2021) Positive atheism. Bayle, Meslier, d'Holbach, Diderot. Edinburgh University Press, Edinburgh. (In press)
Doyle J (2019) Group identity among atheist and Christian student clubs. Secularism and Nonreligion 8(10):1–11
Harris, S (2004) The end of faith: religion, terror, and the future of reason. W. W. Norton & Co., New York
Hitchens C (2007) God is not great. How religion poisons everything. Twelve, New York
Israel JI (2015) Revolutionary ideas. An intellectual history of the French Revolution from the rights of man to Robespierre. Princeton University Press, Princeton

Kenez P (2006) A history of the Soviet Union from the beginning to the end. Cambridge University Press, Cambridge
Locke J (2013) A letter concerning toleration. Broadview Editions, Peterborough
Meslier J (2009) Testament. Memoir of the thoughts and sentiments of Jean Meslier (trans: Shreve M). Prometheus Books, Amherst
Onfray M (2007) Contre-histoire de la philosophie 4. Les ultras des Lumières. Grasset, Paris
Plato (1970) The apology. The dialogues of Plato. Volume I. The apology and other dialogues (trans: Jowett B). Sphere Books, Aylesbury
Roberts A (1867) Justin Martyr and Athenagoras (trans: Donaldson J). T. & T. Clark, Edinburgh
Sperber J (2013) Karl Marx: a nineteenth-century life. W. W. Norton & Co., New York
Tønder L (2013) Spinoza and the theory of active tolerance. Political Theory 41(5):687–709
Vanini L (2011) Eight philosophical dialogues of Giulio Cesare Vanini. Philos Forum. https://doi.org/10.1111/j.1467-9191.2011.00397.x

Toleration and the Right to Freedom of Religion in Education

45

Zdenko Kodelja

Contents

Introduction	906
Why Should We Be Tolerant?	908
The Paradox of Tolerance	909
Toleration and Human Rights	910
Should the State Allow Students in Public School to Be Excused from Specific Parts of the Instruction that Are Contrary to Their or Their Parents' Religious Beliefs?	911
Should the Members of Some Religious Sects Be Exempted from Laws Regarding the Mandatory Education of Children?	912
Should Wearing Islamic Headscarves in Public School Be Tolerated?	915
Summary and Future Directions	921
References	922

Abstract

It is often claimed that tolerance – as a moral virtue and political ideal and principle – is an essential element of a liberal and democratic society, especially one marked by moral, religious, and cultural pluralism. For this reason, tolerance is also declared to be one of the most important political, cultural, and ethical values on which the so-called "European dimension of education" is based. If we add the widely spread agreement, expressed in some international human rights documents, that education must cultivate and promote tolerance as a virtue, then it seems that tolerance is an obvious and unquestionable good in education. But, on the other hand, there is also very broad agreement that some phenomena (violence, intolerance, indoctrination, as well as religious, racial, or sex discrimination) in schools are so bad or wrong that they must not be tolerated. Therefore, all intolerance is not something bad, nor is all tolerance something good. But if the tolerance of the intolerable is morally not acceptable, then we are faced with the

Z. Kodelja (✉)
Educational Research Institute, Ljubljana, Slovenia
e-mail: zdenko.kodelja@guest.arnes.si

© The Author(s), under exclusive licence to Springer Nature Switzerland AG 2022
M. Sardoč (ed.), *The Palgrave Handbook of Toleration*,
https://doi.org/10.1007/978-3-030-42121-2_53

paradox of tolerance, because we can, according to some definitions of tolerance, tolerate only that to which we object. In this chapter some theoretical and practical problems related to tolerance in education will be discussed in the context of human rights. Considering parents' right to ensure their children's religious and moral education in accordance with their own religious and philosophical convictions and recognizing the importance of religious liberty and freedom of conscience, the liberal democratic state is, among others, faced with the following crucial questions. First, should the state allow students in public school to be excused from specific parts of instruction that are contrary to their or their parents' religious beliefs? Secondly, should the members of some religious sects be exempted from laws regarding the mandatory education of children? Thirdly, should the wearing of Islamic headscarves in public school be tolerated?

Keywords

Toleration · Paradox of tolerance · Human rights · Education · Public schools · Secularity · Religious symbols

Introduction

The terms "tolerance" and "toleration" are usually understood as synonyms. In such a way they will be used also in this chapter. (which is a revised and significantly expanded text, which was first published in a book of selected papers presented in 2003 at the World Congress of Philosophy in Istanbul (Kodelja 2006).) However, according to some authors, they have – in certain contexts – different meanings and, therefore, refer to two distinctive concepts. Tolerance, for instance, is defined as a moral, social, or political virtue, while toleration, on the contrary, is not conceived as a virtue but rather as a political principle or, more precisely, as "a principle of justice" (Lukes 1997, p. 214). Although there is no agreement about a variety of issues regarding tolerance, it is undisputable that in contemporary philosophical and political discourses, tolerance has been discussed "as one of the fundamental ethical and political values" (Heyd 1996, p. 3).

Indeed, it is often claimed that tolerance is an essential element of a liberal and democratic society, especially one marked by moral, religious, and cultural pluralism. As such, tolerance has been declared to be one of the most important political, cultural, and ethical values on which the European Union and, consequently, the "European dimension of education" are based (Résolution sur la dimension européenne de l'éducation 1989, pp. 3, 5). In another political document it is also stated that tolerance should be promoted through education (Declaration on promoting citizenship and the common values of freedom, tolerance, and nondiscrimination through education 2015). However, these European documents are not unique in this respect. We can find similar formulations in the *Universal Declaration of Human Rights* (1948) ("Education should promote understanding, tolerance and friendship among all nations, racial or religious groups" (art. 26)), and in the UNESCO

Declaration of Principles on Tolerance ("Education policies and programmes should contribute to development of understanding, solidarity and tolerance among individuals as well as among ethnic, social, cultural, religious and linguistic groups and nations" (1995, art. 4.2)). Seen from this perspective, it seems that tolerance in education is an obvious and unquestionable value.

On the other hand, there is a broad consensus that some phenomena such as violence, drugs, intolerance, and indoctrination, as well as religious, racial, or sex discrimination in schools are so bad or wrong that they must not be tolerated. The requirement to oppose the intolerable phenomena has also been expressed in many documents. Discrimination, for example, is prohibited by the *Convention against Discrimination in Education*; intolerance, by the mentioned *Declaration of Principles on Tolerance*; indoctrination, by the *Protocol to the Convention for the protection of Human Rights and Fundamental Freedoms*; and so on. The USA and some other states have also enacted laws labeled "zero tolerance" about drugs, weapons, and violence in schools. As long as the object of intolerance in schools is violence and the possession of weapons, intolerance is seen as totally acceptable. But if the possession of all kinds of arms is prohibited on school property, should wearing the kirpan (a ceremonial knife which orthodox Sikhs hold as required by their faith) be forbidden too? The answer to this question is not unambiguous. In Canada, for instance, many schools have prohibited Sikh students from wearing their kirpans to school as a violation of schools' codes of conduct, which prohibit the carrying of weapons. However, since then, many courts have ruled to allow Sikh students to wear kirpans, recognizing the practice as their right based on freedom of religion, on condition that safety in school is not at risk (Barnett 2006, pp. 12–14).

Therefore, the conclusion that follows from the notion of tolerance in the previously mentioned documents should be that not all intolerance is something bad, nor is all tolerance something good. On the contrary, absolute tolerance may degenerate into a vice, whereas intolerance under certain circumstances might be a virtue. Consequently, the intolerance shown by a teacher towards students' violent behavior in school, for instance, could be understood as a virtue and as their moral obligation and legal duty, although, if it were carried to the extreme of cruelty, it degenerates into a vice. On the other hand, extreme toleration towards an evil like violence becomes, under certain circumstances, a vice, for example when a teacher permits an innocent student to become a victim of other students' physical or verbal abuse. In this case the teacher's extreme toleration of students' violence appears as a vice similar to "weakness of will," "weakness of character," or "moral weakness," and the teacher himself appears as one who "does something that he knows or believes he should (ought) not do, or fails to do something that he knows or believes he should do, when the occasion and the opportunity for acting or refraining is present, and when it is in his power, in some significant sense, to act in accordance with his knowledge or belief" (Santas 1966, p. 3).

We can see, then, that in this context, not only tolerance, but also intolerance, if it is under certain circumstances kept within just limits, can be in conformity with Aristotle's definition that moral virtue is "the right mean between two extremes which are as such both vices" (Pohle 1913, p. 2): "the one involving excess, the other deficiency" (Aristotle 1990, p. 45). Intolerance as a moral virtue is here understood in opposition to the conventional definition of tolerance, which can be formulated as not permitting something what we judge to be so morally wrong that it should not be allowed. I see no good reason to reject the statement that intolerance understood in this way is a moral virtue; even more, that what needs justification as a moral virtue is tolerance. Indeed, as Susan Mendus said, "it is difficult to explain why toleration should be considered a moral ideal where the thing tolerated is believed to be morally wrong, for thinking something morally wrong implies thinking it right to prevent it. And how can it be right to tolerate, or allow, something, which is believed to be morally wrong?" (Mendus 1992, p. 1251). In her opinion, "Enmity, hostility and antagonism are the necessary preconditions of toleration, but it is difficult to see why we should tolerate things which we find repellent or abhorrent, much less why we should count it a virtue so to do" (Mendus 1999, p. 3).

Why Should We Be Tolerant?

A lot of the philosophical discussion of toleration has tried to give a satisfactory answer to this question. But what all of this discussion so far suggests is that neither pragmatic nor utilitarian nor sceptical or relativistic arguments can offer such an answer. The most persuasive among them seems to be the argument derived from moral skepticism and relativism. According to it, we are not justified in imposing on others our own beliefs, because we can have no guarantee that we possess moral truth. But although such an argument can be used as a reason for tolerance "there are many reasons why one can be tolerant without being sceptical" (Bobbio 1994, p. 55). Even more, "sometimes one can be both sceptical and intolerant. Those who do not believe in truth will be tempted to submit every decision and every choice to force. This would be based on the principle that since one cannot command what is just, the just is what is commanded" (ibid., p. 65). Tolerance in matters of morality, therefore, is not necessarily the expression of moral skepticism and moral relativism or indifferentism. Moreover, if the principle of tolerance is based on the need for doubt, then we are, according to Joshua Halberstam, dealing with rational discourse rather than tolerance. But, for him, the other intrinsic arguments – those that either treat tolerance itself as a value (manifested in various forms: moral obligation, virtue, or recognition of rights) to which it is necessary to strive for its own sake or as a moral principle that is independent of circumstances and other value – are also not successful in justifying tolerance. In his view, the extrinsic arguments fail to give a consistent and convincing justification for tolerance as well. These arguments are teleological, that is, those who use them understand tolerance as a means to achieve some other goals: social stability, equality, truth, and so on. The problem is that, in this case, the thing that is tolerated is, on the one hand, allowed as long as it serves an external goal better than if it were prevented (given that this is less about tolerance and more about utilitarian computability or manipulation), but on the other hand, it is suppressed if it is perceived as a serious threat to achieve this external goal (which implies the recognition of intolerance as justified). In short, true tolerance is not possible under any circumstances. But even if it were possible, it could, in principle, always be eliminated as something unnecessary at the moment when the external goal that justifies its existence is achieved (Halberstam 1982).

The Paradox of Tolerance

The reason why it is so difficult to give a good answer to the question of why we are or should be tolerant lies in the paradoxical nature of tolerance. The problem, therefore, is that tolerance itself is something paradoxical (Halberstam 1982). If tolerance is unlimited, it is paradoxical in the sense that it necessarily leads to self-elimination, because it includes also the toleration of the intolerant, the fervent opponents of tolerance, who will abuse this unlimited tolerance of the tolerant, eliminate the tolerant, and with them the principle of tolerance. Precisely because tolerance of intolerance is self-destructive, the only solution to this paradox seems to be that toleration of the intolerant is not possible. But tolerance, which is merely tolerance of those who accept the principle of tolerance, is also paradoxical, as it is merely tolerance of like-minded people, while the *condition* sine qua non of tolerance is the tolerance of those who think differently. It is absurd to say that someone is tolerant of another if he allows him something with which he himself agrees or is indifferent to it. He is truly tolerant only if he disagrees with something and opposes it but nevertheless allows it, and if he does not prevent something that he believes is dangerous and harmful to himself and others. But this is true only on condition that he does not prevent it, even though he could have done so. This is so because for one who "allows" something just because he cannot have influence on it, we cannot yet say that he is tolerant. Therefore, we have a paradigmatic example of tolerance when someone allows something that evidently threatens his or her firm beliefs. The more he is convinced that another's views on an important issue are wrong and dangerous, the more tolerant he is if he allows the other to express them freely.

However, if "we need to tolerate other people and their ways of life only in situations that make it very difficult to do so," because "toleration is required only for intolerable" (Williams 1999, p. 65), then an important question arises, namely, whether teachers in school should and could be tolerant or not. The problem is that the teacher who wants to be tolerant should allow what is for him intolerable. If he does so, he is tolerant; if he does not, he is intolerant. But, if he, for example, permits students' violent behavior in school, he abdicates his role of an educator (Reboul 1995, p. 103). For this reason, we can agree with the claim that intolerance in education is sometimes necessary and unavoidable. The argument that justifies this claim is, according to Bruce Suttle, the following: "If education's goal is the development of a particular kind of person, and if tolerance involves respecting people as they are, then succeeding in our educational goals requires being intolerant of certain ways of thinking, valuing, and acting. As education is impossible without change, so change is irresponsible without a goal. To educate for a particular kind of person is to discourage the maintenance or development of certain types of persons. Therefore, educational intolerance is as necessary as it is unavoidable" (Suttle 1995,

p. 7). This means that a teacher cannot always be tolerant if he acts as an educator as well. But his position is paradoxical. On the one hand, he cannot, because of educational reasons, tolerate what is intolerable, and on the other hand, he can, according to the definition of tolerance, tolerate only what is intolerable. For, what is acceptable or indifferent for him, he cannot tolerate simply because "we are tolerant of others only when we disapprove of them, or of their actions and beliefs, but nonetheless refrain from imposing our own view" (Mendus 1999, p. 3). Since the presence of disapproval or hostility is the necessary condition of tolerance, "people with no convictions are not being tolerant if they allow others their way, or if they acquiesce with the opinions of others. They are simply 'indifferent'. Indifference is not toleration" (Carey 1999, p. 46). The paradigmatic example of toleration is, therefore, "the deliberate decision to refrain from prohibiting, hindering or otherwise coercively interfering with conduct of which one disapproves, although one has the power to do so. The moral ideal of toleration can be seen as a mean between intolerance, or the refusal to permit that which should be permitted, and indulgence or laxity, the permitting of that which should not be permitted, without lapsing into indifference, the refusal to judge that which should be judged" (Horton 1998).

The question of tolerance is therefore strongly connected with the question of its limits. Among the well-known examples of the limits of toleration is Locke's *A Letter Concerning Toleration*, in which he argues that persons who would not tolerate others in matters of religion should not themselves be tolerated. Locke also thought that Roman Catholics (because they serve a pope as a foreign prince) and atheists (because they cannot be trusted to keep their promises) must be excluded from tolerance. Today, when religious tolerance (at least in liberal democratic or nonconfessional states) is extended to atheists (religious liberty, protected by constitutions and international documents on human rights, also includes the freedom not to profess any religion), it seems that the thesis that atheists should not be tolerated is simply implausible and that only few are still prepared to maintain it. But in the USA, for example, where "religious tolerance is a part of the national history and mythology," a survey from 1994 shows that "barely half the population would allow an atheist to teach in college" (Vogt 1997, p. 92).

Toleration and Human Rights

Education is supposed to be an effective means of preventing intolerance and promoting tolerance. According to the previously mentioned *Declaration of Principles on Tolerance*, "the first step in tolerance education is to teach people what their shared rights and freedoms are, so that they may be respected, and to promote the will to protect those of others" (1995, art. 4.1). In this context, tolerance is declared as "consistent with respect for human rights" (art. 1.4), which are usually understood both as moral and internationally recognized legal norms that all states should respect and protect. In various international documents on human rights, tolerance is included as a principle and refers to different rights, including the right to freedom of religion. However, the problem is that "there is no general agreement on its content and limits: It is easier to invoke or proclaim the principle than to define it" (Broglio 1997, p. 252). In what follows, we will confine ourselves to addressing only some of the issues related to tolerance and the right to freedom of religion in education. Considering the right of parents to ensure their children teaching and education in accordance with their own religious and philosophical convictions on the one hand, and recognizing the importance of religious liberty and freedom of conscience on the other hand, the liberal democratic state is, among others, faced with the following crucial questions. First, should the state allow students in public schools to be excused from specific parts of the instruction that are contrary to their or their parents' religious beliefs? Secondly, should the members of some religious sects be exempted from laws regarding the mandatory education of children? Thirdly, should the wearing of Islamic headscarves in public schools be tolerated?

Should the State Allow Students in Public School to Be Excused from Specific Parts of the Instruction that Are Contrary to Their or Their Parents' Religious Beliefs?

The answer to the first question is ambiguous. In Europe, for example, the exemption from specific parts of the instruction is, according to the opinion of the *European Court of Human Rights*, allowed as "the only appropriate method for denominational education in one religion. Compulsory education in one religion without possibility of exemption would violate" (Digest of Strasbourg Case-Law relating to the European Convention on Human Rights 1985, p. 815) the parents' right to ensure their children teaching and education in accordance with their own religious and philosophical convictions, which is guaranteed by the *Protocol to the European Convention on Human Rights* (1952). In this document, it is clearly stated that "No person shall be denied the right to education. In the exercise of any function which it assumes in relation to education and teaching, the State shall respect the right of parents to ensure such education and teaching in conformity with their own religious and philosophical conviction" (Article 2). But this article "neither expressly nor implicitly grants a general right of exemption from all subjects where religious and philosophical convictions may be involved. Otherwise the State could not guarantee the right to education of all children" (Digest of Strasbourg Case-Law relating to the European Convention on Human Rights 1985, p. 815), which is also guaranteed by the same article. However, the state must have, according to the court's opinion, a "good reason for introduction of a subject in the public school, which may interfere with the religious or philosophical convictions of some parents," and it "must show respect for these convictions in the way in which the subject is taught. Respect must mean tolerance towards the different religious and philosophical convictions, which are involved in a particular subject" (ibid.). For this reason, the state "must take care that information or knowledge included in the curriculum is conveyed in an objective, critical, and pluralistic manner. The state is forbidden to pursue an aim of indoctrination that might be considered as not respecting parents' religious and philosophical convictions. That is the limit that," according to the court's opinion, "must not be exceeded" (ibid., pp. 810–811). Since indoctrination in public schools must not be tolerated, religious parents can accept such schools if they are, for example, persuaded that exposure of their children to other influences is compatible with religious education of their children and that it might help them to form their life ideals and also to make autonomous choices as to whether to accept or reject religious faith (cf. McLaughlin 1984, pp. 75–83). If they think that such exposure of their children to other influences is intolerable, they can choose confessional schools in which the education will be in accordance with their religious convictions. But protection of religious liberty and freedom of conscience in school are not limited only to the students and their parents. In Italy, for instance, where catholic religious instruction is an obligatory subject in public schools, the teachers in primary schools, who are obligated to teach all school subjects, also have the right to the "conscientious objection," which allows them to be excused from the obligation to teach catholic religion. (Pajer 1991, p. 452). Such a right should be recognized for all teachers who are required to teach a particular religion in public schools, provided that they are atheists, agnostics, or belong to another religion. We can find a similar conclusion in Peters' book *Ethics and Education*, in which he discusses the problem of the freedom of the teacher, and asserts that if a teacher who is an atheist or an agnostic is required to teach "Religious Instruction," he can refuse to teach it on conscientious grounds (Peters 1980, p. 203). In the USA, on the contrary, the "schools enjoy substantial discretion to excuse individual students from lessons that are objectionable to the student or the students' parents on religious or other conscientious grounds. However, students generally do not have a Federal right to be excused from lessons that may be inconsistent with their religious beliefs or practices" (Religious Expression in Public School 1998). Schools should also excuse students who do not wish to participate in the school celebration of the secular aspect of the religious holidays (Religion in the Public Schools: A Joint Statement of Current Law 1995, p. 4).

Should the Members of Some Religious Sects Be Exempted from Laws Regarding the Mandatory Education of Children?

The answer to the second question, whether the members of some religious sects in a liberal democratic society should be exempted from laws regarding the mandatory education of children, is also unclear. That it is actually so, at least on the philosophical level, demonstrates the opposing arguments about this particular "group right," which is legally recognized in the USA and Canada. Members of some religious sects there are permitted to "withdraw their children from schools before the legal age of sixteen and are not required to teach the usual school curriculum" (Kymlicka 1996, p. 85).

On the one hand, we have, among others, the arguments given by the communitarian philosopher Michael Sandel, who has defended the right of the Amish to withdraw their children from schools, because they can, in this way, ensure that their children will not learn about the outside world, and so they will not be tempted to stray from their true identity. In his opinion, people's religious affiliation is so profoundly constitutive of their identity that their principal interest is in protecting that identity, and not in being able to stand back and assess that identity. He has also argued "that freedom of conscience should be understood as freedom to pursue one's constitutive ends, not as freedom to choose one's religion" (Sandel 1990; Kymlicka 1996, p. 99).

On the other hand, we have, for example, the arguments given by the liberal political philosopher Will Kymlicka, which are based on the liberal model of religious tolerance. According to him, "Liberal tolerance protects the rights of individuals to dissent from their group, as well as the right of groups not to be persecuted by the state. It limits the power of illiberal groups to restrict the liberty of their own members, as well as the power of illiberal states to restrict the liberty of collective worship" (Kymlicka 1995, p. 158). Contrary to the communitarian model, which is based on group rights, the liberal model is based on individual liberty. Although both "models recognize the need for different religious communities to coexist, and hence are consistent with the fact of religious pluralism in modern societies," they "disagree fundamentally on the role of individual freedom within religious communities. The group-right model allows each group to limit the religious liberties of its own members so as to protect the constitutive ends and practices of the community from internal dissent." The liberal model of tolerance "insists that each individual has a right to freedom of conscience," including the right to dissent from his or her group as well as "to question and revise her religious beliefs" (Kymlicka 1996, pp. 96–97).

Since the liberal model of "mandatory education ensures that children acquire the capacity to envisage alternative ways of life and rationally assess them" (ibid., p. 87), it is understandable why such education, which is "aimed at presenting options and producing a chooser, that is, a person who has the skills to make informed and rational judgments about different goals and forms of life" (Harbertal 1996, p. 111), is not acceptable for the Amish. It is unacceptable also for some other religious groups, such as the Mennonites and Hutterites in Canada, who have also objected to the official model of education which aims to prepare "children for the rights and duties of citizenship" because they saw "a different purpose of education to prepare their children for life in their community" (Kymlicka 1996, p. 102). For, these religious groups want a totally different type of education, education that should ensure the transmission of "a particular tradition and development of a strong commitment to that particular way of life" (Harbertal 1996, p. 111). Moreover, education that encourages in children "sceptical reflection on the ways of life inherited from their parents or local communities, might be," according to Harbertal, "accompanied by deliberately attempting to negate certain alternative ways of life, either by teaching them and claiming that they are false or by excluding them altogether from the curriculum" (ibid.). William Galston also thinks that such education could mislead children into moral relativism, or even toward nihilism (1991, p. 253). But, as Brighouse showed, just the opposite is possible. Not the autonomy-facilitating education but the education limited to teaching only the virtues that, like civic tolerance, "support stability of the liberal state" can lead to relativism. Namely, "those in whom civic tolerance is inculcated, but who are not led to reflect critically about tolerance, are often deeply confused about why they should be tolerant, inferring that it has to do with the equal status of the beliefs of those whom they tolerate, rather than the equal status of the persons whose beliefs they are expected to tolerate. Since their own views are true and their fellows' views have equal status, they conclude that their fellows' views are true. Since their views and their fellows' views conflict, they conclude that truth can apply equally to conflicting views, and hence that some form of relativism must be true" (Brighouse 2000, p. 96).

The practice of education among the Amish and in some other such communities is, therefore, in conflict with the liberal concept of education and, according to the autonomy argument for toleration, is intolerant. However, Harbertal is convinced that there is nothing intolerant in the educational practice of the communities such as the Orthodox and kibbutz communities in Israel, whose aims are not "to produce a chooser in the name of value of autonomy," but to "foster loyalty to particular ways of life with stronger commitments" and "ensuring a continuation of the Jewish religious tradition" (ibid., p. 112). Nevertheless, if we judge such a sort of education on the basis of the previously mentioned autonomy argument for toleration, it is certainly seen as intolerant. As intolerant, it should be prohibited (Harbertal 1996, pp. 111–112). But here a new question arises: Does the liberal model of mandatory education, promoting individual freedom and personal autonomy, not entail intolerance to the groups which do not share these liberal values? The answer to this question is affirmative. Both the proponents of the communitarian model and the supporters of the opposite liberal model of toleration agree on that. Despite this, they evaluate such intolerance in a totally different manner. For the proponents of the group rights, such intolerance is unacceptable, and it should be replaced by the tolerance of the right of communities "to shape their own form of education as long as they do not violate the principle of toleration in its harm justification," therefore, on condition that communities do not "force or penalize individuals who actually choose an alternative way of life" (ibid., p. 112). Harbertal emphasizes that "the value of toleration does not obligate a community to pose that alternative to students and present it as a legitimate option for choice" (ibid.).

For the proponents of individual rights, who emphasize the strong connection between liberal tolerance and personal autonomy understood as freedom of individuals to assess and potentially revise their existing ends, such intolerance is necessary. As Kymlicka stated in his reply to Sandel's defence of the right of the Amish to withdraw their children from school: "If we wish to defend individual freedom of conscience, and not just group tolerance, we must reject the communitarian idea that people's ends are fixed and beyond rational revision. We must endorse the traditional liberal belief in personal autonomy" (Kymlicka 1995, p. 163). If we do not agree with this because we think that there are good reasons both for tolerating intolerant educational practices in such communities and not tolerating them, then the paradox of tolerance seems to be unsolvable.

Should Wearing Islamic Headscarves in Public School Be Tolerated?

According to international conventions on human rights, everyone has the right to freedom of religion, which includes freedom to manifest one's religion. One way to do this is to wear religious symbols such as the Islamic headscarf, Jewish yarmulkes, Sikh turbans, and Christian crosses. But the problem is that Muslim women (both students and teachers), despite this, do not have the same freedom to manifest their religion when they are in school. For, in some states they are forbidden to manifest their religion by wearing specific religious symbols, while in others they are either permitted or required.

France, for instance, is a secular state where a special law forbids teachers and students from wearing traditional Islamic headscarves in public schools, while teachers and students in Turkey, another secular state, were bound by a similar law until 2013. Turkey adopted the *Dress Regulations Act* which forbids wearing religious dress "other than in places of worship or at religious ceremonies, irrespective of the religion or belief concerned" in 1934 (Saxsena 2007). However, in October 2013 Turkey lifted its ban on women wearing the Islamic headscarf in state institutions (including universities and schools); but the new rules do not apply to the judiciary or the military. Despite this it is not clear if this decision by the government is in accordance with the constitution, since in a similar situation – in 2008 when the Assembly passed an amendment to the constitution which would have allowed women to wear the headscarf in universities – the constitutional court held that the wearing of headscarves in universities was unconstitutional. In 2004 the French parliament approved a law which prohibits religious symbols – including Islamic headscarves – that "ostensibly" manifest a particular religious belief in public schools. Among the forbidden conspicuous religious symbols are also Jewish yarmulkes, Sikh turbans, and large Christian crosses.

In schools in Germany, wearing Islamic headscarves is forbidden only for teachers (Gallala 2006, p. 593). According to Germany's Federal Constitutional Court, individual states (*Länder*) have a right to make legal provisions to prevent teachers from wearing Islamic headscarves. "The parliament of the *Land* of Baden-Wurttemberg brought in, on 1 April 2004, an amendment to Article 38 of the law on school education stipulating that teachers in public schools were not authorised to show religious, political, or philosophical convictions that might imperil the neutrality of the *Land* with regard to pupils, their parents or the stability of the school. In the preamble to this law, it was made clear that the ban concerned the Islamic headscarf. (...) The text of the law underlined, in contrast, that the ban did not concern the representation of Christian or Western values and traditions. (...) It can therefore be seen that the law of Baden-Wurttemberg does not respect the condition of non-discrimination between the members of different religious communities, as required by the Federal Constitutional Court decision. (...) The *Länder* of Saarland, Bavaria, and Hessen have passed laws similar to that of Baden-Wurttemberg, banning the Islamic veil and privileging the symbols of the Judeo-Christian tradition. (...) Berlin and Lower Saxony have banned religious symbols without granting any special privilege to Christian symbols" (ibid., pp. 599–600).

Just the opposite case is in Singapore, where students are not allowed to wear Islamic headscarves in public schools, while Muslim teachers are permitted to wear them (Asian Political News 2002).

On the other hand, there are two Islamic countries, postrevolutionary Iran and Saudi Arabia, where female Muslim teachers and students must wear Islamic headscarves in schools because all Muslim women are legally obliged to wear the *hijab* outside of their homes. In Iran the *hijab* (a scarf on the head and a long dress) became obligatory for all adolescent girls and women in 1981, 2 years after the Islamic Revolution. In 2005 Iran's Judiciary spokesman called "for taking legal action against women who do not observe *hijab* (the Islamic dress code), stressing that women who reveal part of their hair have breached the law and must be prosecuted" (Iran News). In 2006 in Saudi Arabia the law made it mandatory also for foreign schools to observe the Islamic teachings such as adoption of a dress code, not teaching any subject contradictory to Islam, etc. (Saudi Gazette 2006).

At first glance two things seem to be obvious. First, that the right to freedom of religion is necessarily violated in the first group of countries, because in each of them the laws prohibit wearing Islamic headscarves in public schools. Second, that this human right is not violated in the previously mentioned Islamic countries simply because in these countries wearing the *hijab* in public schools is not prohibited. This conclusion can be described in the following way: If it is true that whatever is not explicitly prohibited by the law is permitted, as Hobbes claims, and if it is also true that something that is legally permitted to be done – to manifest one's religion – cannot violate the right of someone to manifest his or her religion, it seems to be obvious that such a right is not violated. But both of these conclusions are false.

The first one is false because the right to manifest one's religious convictions can be limited without being also violated. The reason for being so is the fact that this right is recognized as a limited right and not as an absolute one. "A right is *absolute* when it cannot be overridden in any circumstances, so that it can never be justifiably infringed, and it must be fulfilled without any exceptions" (Gewirth 1984, p. 92).

According to the European Court of Human Rights, for instance, the right to manifest one's religion (as it is defined in the European *Convention for the Protection of Human Rights and Fundamental Freedoms,* as well as in other international documents on human rights) can be restricted in democratic societies, but only on condition that such restrictions are necessary for protecting the rights and freedoms of others, public order or morals, and public safety. If this condition is satisfied, the state is entitled to impose restrictions also on wearing the Islamic headscarf in schools. In the court's view, such restrictions were justified and in accordance with the European Convention when some secular universities in Turkey took measures which forbade wearing Islamic headscarves in universities (*Karaduman v. Turkey*; *Leyla Sahin v. Turkey*), and also when in Switzerland Geneva authorities prohibited a primary school teacher from wearing the Islamic headscarf in the performance of her teaching duties in school (*Dahlab v. Switzerland*). Therefore, it is not true that all laws which forbid wearing the Islamic headscarf in public schools violate the right to freedom of religion. However, this does not mean that it is impossible for any of the previously indicated laws to violate it. Some opponents of the French law which prohibits wearing the Islamic headscarves and other conspicuous religious symbols, such as Jewish yarmulkes, Sikh turbans, and large Christian crosses in public schools, are persuaded that it violates this right because these religious symbols "do not pose a threat to public health, order or morals; they have no effect on the fundamental rights and freedoms of other students; and they do not undermine a school's educational function" (Human Rights Watch 2004). On the other hand not only the supporters of the law are convinced that wearing the Islamic headscarf undermines the school's educational function since "the students who insisted on wearing it, also refused to attend physical education and biology lessons for religious reasons" (Galeotti 2002, p. 125). Since the instruction in public schools is free from any religious reference, there is, in their opinion, no reason for allowing the exemption of students from learning all school subjects, including life sciences and physical education (Canto-Sperber and Ricœur 2003). Nevertheless, despite all the differences between advocates and the opponents of this law, they share a common conviction that this law is an affirmation of the principle of secularity (*la laïcité*) in the French republic. Secularism is the normal translation of *la laïcité*, but many authors agree that this English term is inadequate in conveying its meaning. According to Cécile Laborde, "it would be a mistake to reduce *laïcité* to a conception of the proper relationship between state and religion," since it "is a broader moral and social philosophy, a complex set of ideals and commitments which constitute" in France some kind of alternative "to the liberal doctrine of toleration" (Laborde 2008, p. 7). As such, *laïcité* "encompasses a comprehensive theory of republican citizenship, articulated around three ideals: equality (religious neutrality of public sphere or secularism *strictu sensu*), liberty (individual autonomy and emancipation from religious oppression), and fraternity (civic loyalty to community of citizens)" (ibid., pp. 7–8). But this principle of secularity or, more precisely, *laïcité*, which was primarily based on the humanist and universalist principles of enlightenment thinkers, has for them a very different value. For the first ones it is something that should be defended because it assures freedom of conscience (understood as allowing "free adhesion to a religion and the rejection of any religion") and the equality of all citizens, whether believers, atheists, or agnostics, and it is as such a necessary condition for achieving the unity of the people over and above differences in beliefs (cf. Pena-Ruiz 1999). For the second ones it is just the opposite, something that should be changed. Among them is also Alain Renaut who speaks in favor of rethinking the republican principle of secularity (as it is understood and applied in practice at the moment in France), because he believes that it leads to the intolerance for cultural diversity. The law which prohibits the wearing of Islamic headscarves in public schools is an example of this intolerance for visible diversity. Since public schools should be, as he stresses, the places for learning tolerance and not intolerance for cultural diversity, they must permit that such differences find a form of presence and visibility in schools. And schools would fulfill this task, he thinks, much better in the context of the liberal model, which tolerates differences for allowing persons to recognize themselves as equals in their host countries. In fact, not only the schools but the whole society would, in his opinion, succeed better to establish equality on the grounds of a value of tolerance than on the principle of secularity, which shows more and more that it is unable to accept a difference (Renaut and Touraine 2005, pp. 29–30, 160, 162–163). For this reason, he prefers the model of liberal tolerance to the one of republican secularity, which involves intolerance for cultural diversity. Since this kind of intolerance has created a lot of tension in French society, he thinks that it would be better if it were replaced with the model of liberal tolerance. While Renaut sees in liberal tolerance the very framework through which recognition of cultural differences takes place, Anna Galeotti thinks just the opposite. She is persuaded that the existing liberal concept of toleration as freedom from the government's interference in certain areas is unsatisfactory in a context of contemporary pluralism. It is appropriate, she says, "if pluralism is conceived as a plurality of conflicting conceptions of the good. By contrast, if pluralism is understood as the plurality of groups and cultures, asymmetrically situated in democratic society, then the issues underlying toleration are seen as the contested claim of minorities for asserting their different identity in the public space" (Galeotti 1997, p. 223). On the other hand, defenders of the principles of *laïcité*, like Kintzler and Pena-Ruiz, argue that the principles of toleration do not apply with full force for students in public schools (Laborde 2008, p. 53). In their opinion, Islamic headscarves "infringe on the neutrality and civic purpose of schools in five different but interconnected ways," because they: "introduce signs of private and religious divisiveness into the public sphere"; "symbolize the primacy of the believer over the citizen"; "infringe on equality between pupils"; "undermine the civic mission of schools"; and "undermine the overall scheme of religious freedom" (ibid., pp. 53–54).

However, the French government and the Stasi Commission (the Commission for Consideration on the Application of the Principle of Secularity (laïcité) in the Republic whose main task was to give advice on whether wearing religious symbols in public schools should be allowed or forbidden), that is, the institutions that prepared the law, also believe that the forbiddance of wearing the Islamic headscarf and other conspicuous religious symbols in public schools is necessary for protecting the secular state. According to the commission, the two previously mentioned decisions of the European Court of Human Rights in the Turkish cases justify the imposition of limits by the state on religious freedom, if the manifestation of religion threatens the principle of secularity. Since this principle of secularity (*laïcité*) means in France the same as the principle of the neutrality of the state, it "implies the strict neutrality of the public service" as well. This means that public servants – including the teachers in public schools – "must not give the impression of favouring any religion or religious belief," because all users of public services – including students in public schools – "must receive equal treatment, regardless of their religion or beliefs" (Gallala 2006, p. 596; Schwartz 2005, pp. 88–89). It follows that teachers in public schools, like all other "public officials, must show the strictest neutrality. Therefore, it is forbidden for them" either to "express their religious beliefs or to manifest them by the wearing of certain religious symbols" (Gallala 2006, pp. 596–597).

This is the reason why teachers in France are not permitted to wear the Islamic headscarf in public schools. Even some known French philosophers who have defended the right of students to wear religious symbols in public schools have agreed that teachers should not be allowed to wear them in public schools (Canto-Sperber and Ricœur 2003).

A similar model of school, based on the principle of strict neutrality, was proposed by the German Federal Constitutional Court when it proposed two models of schools that *Länder* can choose without violating the right to religious freedom (manifestation of one's religion by displaying religious symbols). "The first model would be founded on open neutrality, according to which the school would be an open space for different religious and philosophical beliefs, and where tolerance and living in harmony with different cultures and religions would be learned. (...) In this model, the teacher could wear symbols showing his or her religious affiliation, unless it is proven by his behaviour that he is not fulfilling the obligation of tolerance and neutrality. In the second model, the *Land* would opt for a strict neutrality, according to which teachers would be required not to display in any way their religious affiliation. (...) This model would be chosen when the wearing of religious symbols by teachers had already led to conflicts and tensions in the *Land* schools" (Gallala, p. 599).

Therefore, teachers in public schools which are based on the principle of strict neutrality are forbidden from wearing religious symbols such as Islamic headscarves. However, in France (where schools must respect the legal framework based on the principle of secularity and strict neutrality of the state), not only teachers but also students are forbidden to wear them. But "it should be stressed," says Galeotti, "that the banning of the veil is not perceived as intolerance within this framework, but, rather, as the legitimate limit to liberal tolerance in order to preserve the neutrality of the public school and the equality of the students as would-be citizens, beside and beyond any particular memberships. The aim for ensuring equality for all students is not simply an instance of stubborn unwillingness to recognize diversity so long as it is not discriminatory; teachers should disregard any difference which has no effect on merit, but should be helped in this by a minimization of visible differences" (Galeotti 2002, pp.123–124). If we want to understand why the French law which prohibits wearing Islamic headscarves in public schools is within the republican framework seen not only as acceptable but also necessary, and within the liberal framework as unacceptable, we have to take into consideration the fundamental difference between republicanism and liberalism. Habermas describes this difference in the following way: "Republicanism, which goes back to Aristotle and the political humanism of the Renaissance, has always given the public autonomy of citizens priority over the pre-political liberties of private persons. Liberalism, which goes back to John Locke, has invoked (at least since the nineteenth century) the danger of tyrannical majorities and postulated the priority of human rights. According to republicanism, human rights owed their legitimacy to the ethical self-understanding and sovereign self-determination achieved by a political community; in liberalism, such rights were supposed to provide inherently legitimate barriers that prevented the sovereign will of the people from encroaching on inviolable spheres of individual freedom" (Habermas 2001, p. 116).

Despite the totally different answers to the question of whether the discussed French law violates the right to religious freedom or only limits it in order to protect basic republican values, there is no doubt that this right is not violated in all countries where wearing Islamic headscarves is prohibited by law.

If we now return to the aforementioned conclusion that the right to freedom of religion is not violated in Iran and Saudi Arabia simply because in these countries wearing the *hijab* in public schools is not prohibited, we have to say that this conclusion is false. It is false because the right to freedom to manifest one's religion or beliefs cannot remain a right – which presupposes freedom of choice – when it becomes a duty. And it is often argued that "for many Muslims, wearing a headscarf is not only about religious expression, it is about religious obligation" (Roth 2004). The eminent Muslim scholar Ali Jum'ah, Mufti of Egypt, also states: "A Muslim woman is obliged to wear hijab as soon as she reaches puberty, as indicated in the Qur'an, the Sunnah of the Prophet (...) and the consensus of Muslim scholars from early ages of Islam up till now. Hijab is known to be essential and necessary in religion; it is not merely a symbol that distinguishes Muslims from non-Muslims. It is an obligation that forms part and parcel of the Islamic religion" (Hijab: Religious Symbol or Obligation? 2012). However, although this seems to be a dominant interpretation, there are many other Muslim scholars like Mohamed Arkoun, Jammal al Bama, Tariq Ramadan, and so on, who claim that the wearing of a hijab is not a real Quranic obligation, but rather an Islamic prescription.

Regardless of who is right, it is true that whenever a woman has a duty to wear a headscarf, she has no right not to wear it. For this reason, the argument used in the French case that Muslim girls should be permitted to wear traditional Islamic headscarves in secular public schools not only because they have the right to publicly express their religion but rather because they have a religious duty to wear the headscarves reveals the aim of this requirement. It was not the right of Muslim girls to wear or not to wear Islamic headscarves but their right against the secular state, that is, the right to fulfill their religious duty by wearing Islamic headscarves in public schools. This means, then, that the right to manifest their religious convictions is here only a means for achieving something else: the right to do their religious duty.

Therefore, Muslim women do not have a right to manifest their religion by wearing the Islamic headscarves in either case: when it is forbidden by law and also when it is required by law as their religious duty. However, the question which arises here is whether or not the fact that laws in Iran and Saudi Arabia require women to wear the *hijab* means also that their right to freedom of religion is violated.

The answer to this question depends on how this human right is understood. If it is understood as a right that everyone has simply by virtue of being human, that is, as a natural right which as such exists "prior to and independently of any given political society" and, therefore, also independently of "formal recognition in a legal system" (Hayden 2001, pp. 5–6), then the right to freedom of religion is violated in Iran and Saudi Arabia because women are obliged by law to wear the *hijab*. In this context of natural rights theory, the right to freedom of religion is seen also as a moral right that "all humans *ought* to have recognized," and as liberty, or "freedom to choose one's own way of life" (ibid., p. 6). Since a free choice presupposes an ability to act according to the choice one has made, the legal obligation to wear the *hijab* means the same as preventing women from choosing not to wear it. In other words, this obligation means a violation of their right to freedom of religion. However, if the right to freedom of religion is not understood in such a way, but rather as a legal right guaranteed by international human rights law, then this right seems not to be violated in Iran and Saudi Arabia because of the fact that the governments of these countries either did not sign those international conventions on human rights that we cited before, or they signed them but reserve the right not to apply any provisions or articles that are in conflict with Islamic law (*Shari'a*).

This means that these states – like some other Islamic countries – are not legally bound by the articles of conventions which affirm the right to freedom of religion – including freedom to manifest one's religion or belief, if these articles are understood as incompatible with Islamic law. Since the obligation to wear the *hijab* is in both countries required by legislations founded on Islamic law, it is obvious that these articles, or more precisely, the paragraphs of these articles which affirm freedom to manifest one's religion, are seen as incompatible with Islamic law if this freedom is interpreted as freedom of choice, that is, as freedom to manifest or not to manifest one's religion or belief. In such a case the obligation to wear the *hijab* cannot be treated as a violation of human rights protected by international human rights law.

Therefore, the answer to the question of whether the laws in Iran and Saudi Arabia which require wearing the *hijab* violate the right to religious freedom is yes and no. It is so because human rights, as Habermas emphasizes, have at the same time moral content and "the form of legal rights. Like moral norms, they refer to every" human being, "but as legal norms they protect individual persons only insofar as the latter belong to a particular legal community – normally the citizens of a nation state. Thus, a peculiar tension arises between the universal meaning of human rights and the local conditions of their realizations: they should have unlimited validity for all persons" (Habermas 2001, p. 118), but until now this ideal has not yet been achieved. At the moment it is still so that nobody can attain the "effective enjoyment of human rights immediately, as a world citizen," because an "actually institutionalized cosmopolitan legal order" has not yet been established, although "Article 28 of the United Nations Declaration of Human Rights refers to a global order 'in which the rights and freedoms set in this Declaration can be fully realized'" (ibid., pp. 118–119). On the other hand, the national laws protect particular individual rights of their citizens "only in so far as they acquire the artificial status of bearers of individual rights" (ibid., p. 114). Since in Iran and Saudi Arabia their citizens are not recognized as bearers of the right to freedom of religion as it is understood in international documents on human rights, that is, as a right which includes also freedom to change one's religion, and freedom to manifest or not to manifest one's religion, they can enjoy this right neither as citizens of Iran or Saudi Arabia nor as world citizens.

Summary and Future Directions

The essence of tolerance is not in allowing something but in permitting what we firmly believe to be bad, dangerous, harmful, or erroneous. If we allow what we ourselves agree with or what we believe is good or irrelevant, we are not tolerant but at best indifferent. The second necessary condition for tolerance, however, is that we allow something we disagree with, even though we could have prevented it. For, if someone "allows" something just because he cannot influence it, we cannot yet say that he is tolerant.

An example of tolerance understood in this way was the permission of religious instruction in public schools by the communist Slovene government during the first few years after the Second World War, that is, before it was banned in 1952. In that interim period, despite the separation of church and state, religious instruction was tolerated in public schools. It is important to emphasize that the communist party and the government at the time was firmly convinced that religious instruction was harmful to students and dangerous to the secular state, but nevertheless did not abolish it although it could have.

But such a notion of tolerance seems to be in decline in contemporary society, and is increasingly being replaced or supplemented by some rather different concepts: tolerance as recognition, as harmony in difference, as open-mindedness, and so on. In the US and EU educational context, "tolerance is often assumed to be an attitude that is more or less interchangeable with open-mindedness" (Furedi 2011, p. 83), or "non-judgmentalism" (ibid., p. 80). Tolerance as recognition is understood as a revision of the liberal concept of toleration as freedom from governmental interference, which involves a "semantic extension from the negative meaning of non-interference to the positive sense of acceptance and recognition" (Galeotti 2002, p. 10). A similar revision of the traditional conception of tolerance is reflected in the idea of tolerance as "harmony in difference," which indicates that "tolerance is respect, acceptance and appreciation of the rich diversity of our world's cultures, our forms of expression and ways of being human" (Declaration of Principles on Tolerance 1995, art. 1.1).

However, the crucial question here is: How can we tolerate these differences and diversities, which have a positive value (since otherwise they could not be respected and appreciated), if we can tolerate only what is disapproved of? The answer is that we (individuals, groups, or states) cannot tolerate them as long as we attribute a positive value to them. We can recognize, accept, and appreciate them, but not tolerate. The same applies to human rights, including the previously discussed right to freedom of religion. The different answers to the raised questions (Should the state allow students in public school to be excused from specific parts of instruction that are contrary to their or their parents' religious beliefs?; Should the members of some religious sects be exempted from laws regarding the mandatory education of children?; and Should the wearing of Islamic headscarves in public schools be tolerated?), which, as we have seen, are country specific, do not seem to be due so much to the state's tolerance or intolerance but more to the different legal regulations of the relationship between the state and religious communities in specific countries on the one hand, and to the different interpretations of the right to freedom of religion on the other.

References

Aristotle (1990) The Nicomachean ethics. Oxford University Press, Oxford
Asian Political News (2002), Feb 4. http://findarticles.com/p/articles/mi_m0WDQ/is_2002_Feb_4/ai_84235891

Barnett L (2006) Signes religieux dans la sphère publique et liberté de religion. Bibliothèque du Parlement 14:3
Bobbio N (1994) Elogio della mitezza e altri scritti morali. Linea d'ombra, Milano
Brighouse H (2000) School choice and social justice. Oxford University Press, Oxford
Broglio FM (1997) Tolerance and the law. Ratio Juris 10(2):252–265
Canto-Sperber M, Ricœur P (2003) Une laïcité d'exclusion est le meilleur ennemi de l'égalité. Le Monde 10:12
Carey G (1999) Tolerating religion. In: Mendus S (ed) The politics of toleration. Edinburg University Press
Declaration of Principles on Tolerance (1995). UNESCO. http://portal.unesco.org/en/ev.php-URL_ID=13175&URL_DO=DO_TOPIC&URL_SECTION=201.html
Declaration on promoting citizenship and the common values of freedom, tolerance and non-discrimination through education (2015). Paris. https://op.europa.eu/en/publication-detail/-/publication/ebbab0bb-ef2f-11e5-8529-01aa75ed71a1/language-en
Digest of Strasbourg Case-Law relating to the European Convention on Human Rights, vol 5 (1985). C. Heymanns Verlag KG Köln, Berlin/Bonn/München
European Convention on Human Rights (1950) European convention on human rights – Official texts, Convention and Protocols (coe.int)
European Court of Human Rights, *Dahlab v. Switzerland*, Appl. 42393/98
European Court of Human Rights, *Karaduman v. Turkey*, Appl. 16278/90
European Court of Human Rights, *Leyla Sahin v. Turkey*, Appl. 44774/98
Furedi F (2011) On tolerance. Continuum, London
Galeotti A (1997) Contemporary pluralism and toleration. Ratio Juris 10(2):223–235
Galeotti A (2002) Toleration as recognition. Cambridge University Press, Cambridge
Gallala I (2006) The Islamic Headscarf: an example of surmountable conflict between *Shari'a* and the Fundamental Principles of Europe. Eur Law J 12(5):593–612
Galston W (1991) Liberal purposes. Cambridge University Press, Cambridge
Gewirth A (1984) Are there any absolute rights. In: Waldron J (ed) Theories of rights. Oxford University Press, Oxford
Habermas J (2001) The postnational constellation. Polity Press, Cambridge
Halberstam J (1982) The paradox of tolerance. Philos Forum 14(3):190–206
Harbertal M (1996) Autonomy, tolerance, and group rights: a response to will Kymlicka. In: Heyd D (ed) Toleration. An elusive virtue. Princeton University Press, Princeton
Hayden P (2001) The introduction to par one: history and theories of human rights. In: Hayden P (ed) The philosophy of human rights. Paragon House, St. Paul
Heyd D (1996) Introduction. In: Heyd D (ed) Toleration. An elusive virtue. Princeton University Press, Princeton
Hijab: Religious Symbol or Obligation? (2012). http://www.onislam.net/english/ask-the-scholar/morals-and-manners/dress-and-adornment/169874-hijab-religious-symbol-or-obligation.html?Adornment=
Horton J (1998) Toleration. In: Routledge encyclopedia of philosophy (electronic version). Routledge
Human Rights Watch (2004) France: Headscarf ban violates religious freedom, release, Feb. 27
Iran News. http://www.*iranian*.ws/cgi-bin/iran_news/exec/view.cgi/13/9073
Kodelja Z (2006) The limits of tolerance in education: some examples. In: Evans D (ed) The proceedings of the twenty-first World Congress of Philosophy: philosophy of education. Philosophical Society of Turkey, Ankara, pp 85–92
Kymlicka W (1995) Multicultural citizenship. Clarendon Press, Oxford
Kymlicka W (1996) Two models of pluralism and tolerance. In: Heyd D (ed) Toleration. An elusive virtue. Princeton University Press, Princeton
Laborde C (2008) Critical republicanism. The Hijab controversy and political philosophy. Oxford University Press, Oxford
Lukes S (1997) Toleration and Recognition. Ratio Juris 10(2):213–222
McLaughlin TH (1984) Parental rights and the religious upbringing of children. J Philos Educ 18:75–83

Mendus S (1992) Toleration. In: The encyclopedia of ethics, vol 2. Garland Publishing, New York
Mendus S (1999) My brother's keeper: the politics of intolerance. In: Mendus S (ed) The politics of toleration. Edinburgh University Press, Edinburgh
Pajer F (1991) L'insegnamento della religione in Europa all'inizio degli anni 90. In: Pajer F (ed) L'insegnamento scolastico della religione nella nuova Europa. Elle Di Ci, Leumann
Pena-Ruiz H (1999) Dieu et Marianne. Philosophie de la laïcité. Presses Universitaires de France, Paris
Peters RS (1980) Ethics and Education. George Allen and Unwin, London
Pohle J (1913) Religious toleration. In: The catholic encyclopedia, vol XIV, Charles G. Herbermann: catholic encyclopedia, volume 14: Simony-Tournon – Christian Classics Ethereal Library (ccel.org)
Protocol to the Convention for the protection of Human Rights and Fundamental Freedoms, as amended by Protocol No. 11 (1952). Paris
Reboul O (1995) La philosophie de l'éducation. Presses Universitaires de France, Paris
Religion in the Public Schools: A Joint Statement of Current Law (1995) https://onlinebooks.library.upenn.edu/webbin/book/lookupid?key=olbp26974
Religious Expression in Public School, U. S. Department of Education (1998) ED416591.pdf
Renaut A, Touraine A (2005) Un débat sur la laïcité. Stock, Paris
Résolution de la Conférence permanente des Ministres européen de l'Education sur 'la dimension européenne de l'éducation: pratique de l'enseignement et contenu des programmes' (1989) Newsletter/Faits nouveaux. Council of Europe, Strasbourg
Roth K (2004) France: headscarf ban violates religious freedom, Human Rights Watch, press release, Feb. 27.
Sandel M (1990) Freedom of conscience or freedom of choice. In: Hunter J, Guinness O (eds) Articles of faith, articles of peace. Brookings Institute, Washington
Santas G (1966) Plato's Protagoras and explanations of weakness. Philos Rev 75:3–33
Saudi Gazette (2006), Sept 9. https://saudigazette.com.sa
Saxsena M (2007) The French headscarf law and the right to manifest religious belief. The selected works. http://works.bepress.com/mukul_saxena/2
Schwartz R (2005) La jurisprudence de la loi de 1905. Archives de philosophie du droit 48:85–94
Suttle BB (1995) The need for and inevitability of educational intolerance, (electronic version)
UN Universal Declaration of Human Rights (1948) Universal declaration of human rights | United nations
Vogt WP (1997) Tolerance and education: learning to live with diversity and difference. Sage, London
Williams B (1999) Tolerating the intolerable. In: Mendus S (ed) The politics of toleration. Edinburg University Press

Education and Toleration

46

Johannes Drerup

Contents

Introduction	926
Toleration in Educational Contexts	927
Toleration as a Democratic Virtue and Aim of Education	932
Empirical Tolerance Research and the Possibility of Education for Tolerance	934
Education for Tolerance as Education of the Emotions	935
Education for Tolerance and Epistemic Virtues	941
Justifying Education for Democratic Tolerance	944
Conclusion	948
References	948

Abstract

Liberal democracies are characterized by a diversity of conceptions of the good life as well as by deep political, ethical, and religious disagreements and conflicts. Toleration is typically regarded as a central principle and virtue which is necessary to cope with these unavoidable conflicts and disagreements in a peaceful and civilized way. This chapter provides an overview on contemporary debates about the intricate nexus between education and toleration in the context of liberal democracies. While toleration is a central aim of democratic education, the educational systems of liberal democracies are also among the most fiercely contested "battle grounds" of contemporary conflicts of toleration (e.g., between the liberal state and parents). Education for tolerance thus is considered as a central educational means to cope with social and political conflicts and at the same time is a recurrent *object* and *theme* in these conflicts and controversies.

J. Drerup (✉)
Technische Universität Dortmund, Dortmund, Germany
e-mail: johannes.drerup@tu-dortmund.de

© The Author(s), under exclusive licence to Springer Nature Switzerland AG 2022
M. Sardoč (ed.), *The Palgrave Handbook of Toleration*,
https://doi.org/10.1007/978-3-030-42121-2_48

This chapter focuses on three basic and general questions and problems of the theory and practice of educating for tolerance. These include, first: How can education for tolerance be adequately conceptualized theoretically? Second: How is education for tolerance possible? And third: How should education for tolerance be justified? All three of these (partly related and overlapping) questions and problems are, at least to a certain extent, hotly disputed and controversial. In what follows it will be argued that despite these differing theoretical interpretations of the concept and of the positive (or negative) role and value of tolerance, tolerance constitutes a coherent, legitimate aim of democratic education.

Keywords

Toleration · Tolerance, Education · Democratic education · Democracy · Liberalism · Justice · Personal autonomy · Political autonomy · Pluralism

Introduction

Liberal democracies are characterized by a diversity of conceptions of the good life as well as by deep political, ethical, cultural, and religious disagreements and conflicts. Toleration is typically regarded as a central principle and virtue which is necessary to cope with these unavoidable conflicts and disagreements in a peaceful and civilized way. Toleration also plays a prominent role in contemporary debates about education and the educational systems of liberal democracies. While the latter are among the most fiercely contested "battle grounds" of contemporary conflicts of toleration, for instance, between the liberal state and parents or different communities (e.g., curricular debates about sex education or religious education), toleration is also a central aim of democratic education. Education for tolerance thus is considered as a central educational means to cope with social and political conflicts and at the same time a recurrent *object* and *theme* in these conflicts and controversies.

This chapter provides an overview on contemporary debates about the intricate nexus between education and toleration in the context of liberal democracies. Instead of focusing on detailed reconstructions of specific conflicts of toleration, it focuses on more basic and general questions and problems of the theory and practice of educating for tolerance. These include: first: How can education for tolerance be adequately conceptualized theoretically? Second: How is education for tolerance possible? and third: How should education for tolerance be justified? All three of these (partly related and overlapping) questions and problems are, at least to a certain extent, hotly disputed and controversial. In what follows it will be argued that despite these differing theoretical interpretations of the concept and of the positive (or negative) role and value of tolerance, tolerance constitutes a coherent, legitimate aim of democratic education. A plausible reconstruction of this aim, however, has to be conscious not only of the limits of toleration, but also of the limited possibilities of education and the educational system to foster toleration.

Toleration in Educational Contexts

Toleration or tolerance – in the following both terms are used interchangeably – is usually regarded as a central aim of education and education is likewise regarded as a central means to counteract intolerance. Before providing a reconstruction of the potential, the legitimacy, and also the ambivalences of education for tolerance and against intolerance, it will be necessary to clarify the meaning of the relevant concepts, such as toleration, intolerance, and education for tolerance.

Toleration is a hotly disputed concept. Rainer Forst (2013) has made a useful proposal to structure the debate about the conceptual characterization of toleration, by distinguishing a core concept and different normative conceptions of toleration that each claim to provide the most plausible interpretation of this core concept. The core concept of toleration, according to Forst, is constituted by the interplay of, among others, two different components:

(a) Objection component: The tolerated believes, practices, etc., are objected to for some reason.
(b) Acceptance component: The reasons for objection can, in principle, be trumped by reasons for acceptance, without, however, removing the negative judgment.

According to this schema – which will be complemented with a broader notion of toleration below (section "Toleration as a Democratic Virtue and Aim of Education") – if the reasons for acceptance are weightier (or of a higher order) than the reasons for objection, the agent tolerates X, if the reasons for objection are stronger, the agent does not tolerate X anymore. Depending on the conception of toleration, this basic conceptual structure will be filled in different ways, that is differing answers will be provided to the paradoxes of toleration (such as the paradox of drawing the limits) as well as conflicts of toleration will be interpreted and evaluated in different way. According to a permission conception of toleration, for instance, the relation between the two parties involved in a conflict is asymmetrical and the more powerful agent tolerates the weaker agent only on the condition that the latter does accept its inferior status and does not demands equal political rights. A neo-Baylean respect conception, which is the one defended by Forst (2013), assumes that just relations of toleration should be structured according to the principles of reciprocity and generality. According to this conception, it would, for instance, be unjust to accept the presence of a particular religious symbol in public schools, such as a cross, but not to tolerate other religious symbols such as a hijab worn by a teacher, because such a policy could not be reciprocally justified with respect to all the relevant individuals as free and equal citizens.

One can, moreover, distinguish between more demanding "maximalist" conceptions of toleration and more "minimalist" conceptions of toleration. A maximalist conception will be based, for instance, on more demanding preconditions of toleration in terms of capacities and attitudes of toleration as well as concerning the attitudes which tolerant agents ideally should cultivate (see, for instance, the notion of toleration as recognition by: Galeotti 2002). According to a more minimalist conception, in contrast, it may suffice, if an agent abstains from clear forms of intolerance, such as political violence or racism, without, however, presupposing that he or she has developed more complex cognitive and emotional self-, world-, and other-relations (for instance, in terms of an understanding of the "objects" of toleration). While a more demanding conception ideally should provide useful guiding principles and criteria to evaluate differing conflicts of toleration, it risks becoming irrelevant for the adequate interpretation of real-world politics, where things are usually more "messy" and complex than is assumed in ideal theoretical conceptions. This may hold, for instance, when tolerance is supposed to imply not just respect for persons, but respect for (cultural, religious, etc.) differences (see the critique of: Balint 2017), which is arguably a rather demanding ideal that may be interpreted as disrespectful by some agents. A more minimalist notion certainly has the advantage of not operating with high expectations concerning the capacities and orientations of agents and their education, which may be unrealistic and overly demanding. A conception of toleration that assumes, for instance, that most people most of the time are incapable of toleration, because their view on the political and social world is not sophisticated enough, is arguably rather implausible. By focusing on concrete minimal conditions of what counts as a sufficiently tolerant person or system, it can provide a minimal baseline that may be realistically achievable and capable of consensus in pluralistic societies. This is perhaps all we can hope for and expect, given the conflicts that pervade liberal democracies. "Aiming low," however, can have its downsides, especially if one aims too low, and thereby implicitly justifies relations of toleration, which may be interpreted, if confronted with the perspective provided by an alternative conception, as not entirely just, or even straightforward unjust.

Thus, each conception, to put it differently, is embedded in broader considerations and debates concerning what counts as a just, democratic and liberal social and political order and hence also develops different answers to the question of the instrumental or intrinsic value of tolerance (*why toleration?*), to the legitimate objects of toleration (*toleration with respect to what?*) and to the way of how toleration should be practiced in a specific sociopolitical constellation (*How does toleration express itself?*). Especially the last question, concerning the concrete practices of toleration (such as practices of civility; Peterson 2019) as well as of intolerance, is undertheorized in the contemporary debate. This also holds for the concept (or different conceptions) of intolerance (see: König 2019). Clear cases of intolerance, such as violence, can be distinguished from more controversial, boundary cases (for instance, if an agent X does not take another agent Y seriously due to his or her "cultural background") as well intolerance as an attitude (e.g., an agent X may *believe* that the freedom of speech of Y should be limited) and its expression in concrete practices or actions (X actually hinders Y from expressing her views or votes for a political party that promises to realize such a policy). Gandhi, for instance, certainly was a very tolerant person, when it comes to his concrete actions and practices (in line to the ideal of ahimsa), he was, however, certainly intolerant with respect to his views concerning the British Raj. This example already indicates that it makes little sense to use the term in- or nontolerance as a *thick, essentially negatively charged* concept, because we usually would not ascribe toleration as a virtue to a person who would tolerate grave social injustices. Tolerance (and intolerance) as a "normatively dependent concept" (Forst 2013) *in itself* does not provide the normative resources to delineate legitimate from illegitimate relations of toleration, understood as self-, world-, and other-relations. Likewise, the application of different conceptions and associated principles of toleration to a particular case is usually no simple exercise in deduction, which allows simple 1-to-1 assignments from general principle to particular practice. It is not always clear, for instance, what follows from a respect conception of toleration for the concrete, empirically informed design of practices and arrangements of toleration (see sections "Empirical Tolerance Research and the Possibility of Education for Tolerance" and "Justifying Education for Democratic Tolerance").

The distinctions between concept and conception and between maximalist and minimalist notions of toleration, as well as the methodological problems involved in applying principles to particular cases, are of relevance for an adequate reconstruction of the notion of education for tolerance.

Education is, like toleration, a hotly disputed if not even an essentially contested concept, which allows for differing normative interpretations that provide substantive answers to the three normative questions mentioned above (Why education for tolerance? Education for tolerance with respect to what? How should tolerance as an educational aim express itself in concrete practices?). For the purposes of conceptual clarification, it will suffice for the present moment to reconstruct the basic conceptual structure of education for tolerance.

Education for tolerance, understood as a formal conceptual notion, is an umbrella term which covers (more or less) intentional and conscious attempts to cultivate the *educational preconditions* (such as dispositions, capacities, attitudes) of toleration (for instance, as a democratic virtue) in asymmetrical interaction orders. It involves individual actions, collective practices, as well as educational arrangements that structure the interactions between agents (e.g., by formulating rules for appropriate interaction, or by promoting a specific school ethos). Since the concrete capacities and dispositions that are facilitative or even constitutive of tolerance as well as the educational means to bring them about are, to a certain extent, controversial, tolerance education can take a diversity of different forms (such as education of the emotions, etc.). This diversity of approaches is, moreover, rooted in the fact that also the reasons and causes of different forms of *intolerance* are highly diverse (see section "Empirical Tolerance Research and the Possibility of Education for Tolerance").

How the educational preconditions of tolerance as an educational aim should be interpreted depends on the results of theoretically guided empirical research as well as on the specific conception of tolerance. Based on a more minimalist conception of education for tolerance, one may, for instance, argue that there is widespread consensus that the avoidance of clear forms of *in*tolerance is among the most central aims which the school systems of liberal democracies can and should achieve. Tolerance education, on this reading, thus, is – both with respect to its central practices and means as well as with respect to its value and educational role – best understood ex negativo, as an aim of education, which should ensure a *minimum of civility*, for instance, understood in terms of negative liberty. Maximalist notions of education for tolerance will make stronger assumptions concerning the education of tolerant agents, for instance, in terms of knowledge about the objects of toleration or concerning the capacities for self-reflection which are assumed to be constitutive of the ability to be a tolerant agent.

Apart from these differing interpretation, it is one of the defining features of tolerance that the agent has to be "free" in a minimal sense, to be able to develop tolerant self-, world-, and other-relations (otherwise his or her attitude would be qualified as a form of unfree endurance, not as genuine tolerance; see: Forst 2013). Education for tolerance therefore cannot simply *produce* tolerant citizens, but only attempt to develop the educational preconditions that are assumed to make the development of tolerant attitudes possible or more likely. While indoctrination should not be tolerated from a liberal standpoint, it cannot be ruled out in principle that certain forms of coercion can be justified in order to ensure that basic forms of civility and toleration are adhered to in schools. Schools, for instance, are "compulsory spheres of pluralistic interaction" (Macleod 2010, 11), and children – compared to adults, who may choose to insulate themselves from certain aspects of diversity, which they object to – cannot simply choose to stay away from these influences. These problems already indicate that one cannot adequately reconstruct the educational dimension of toleration as a political principle and ideal without taking into account basic features of educational interaction orders, in which tolerance not just plays the role of an aim of education, but also is a constitutive element of educational attitudes and practices. Teachers, for instance, will under certain conditions have to intervene in the practices of students, and hence not tolerate these practices anymore (for instance, in the case of discriminatory statements; see for these types of cases: Callan 2011).

Furthermore, a sound conception of education for tolerance has to be conscious of the fact that children in many cases are only locally and not globally autonomous agents and are epistemically and emotionally more vulnerable than adults (Macleod 2010). Children are arguably – in most cases – also more susceptible to different forms of politically motivated manipulation and indoctrination, which are geared towards the propagation of intolerant agendas. To protect children against these kinds of attempts and influences therefore is one of the major aims of tolerance education. In line with this, it is important to take into account that children usually do not yet have developed a stable conception of the good and as a consequence also not stable reasons for objection or acceptance (Macleod 2010). In many cases, therefore, the major aim of education for tolerance is *indirect*. Educators, for instance, should not cultivate problematic objections (e.g., based on questionable prejudices as well as essentialist notions of the "other") in their students and then, in a second step, help them to overcome them in light of higher order principles as reasons for acceptance (see section "Toleration as a Democratic Virtue and Aim of Education"). This would obviously be problematic, because it may perpetuate or create the very conflicts which make tolerance necessary and hence in some cases may even count as an instance of an education for intolerance (Diehm 2010; Brown

2006; Witenberg 2019). This is one of the reasons why "education for tolerance" has a much more limited role to play in educational institutions than usually assumed. In many, if not most cases, the primary aim of democratic (and moral) education will be to ensure that tolerance does not become necessary in the first place and that illegitimate forms of intolerance are prevented. As long, however, dissent and disagreement are central features of life in pluralistic societies and given that no one can realistically be expected to accept or appreciate everything, we cannot do without tolerance, also in educational contexts. Thus, while it is correct that we can "oppose intolerance without advocating toleration" (Jones 2010, 41) and that a "diversity we can celebrate is not a diversity we need tolerate" (ibid.), it remains also true that toleration "makes difference possible; difference makes toleration necessary" (Walzer 1997, xii). The historical variability of conflicts and relations of toleration, which is also rooted in the changeability of typical objects of toleration and associated identity formations in differing sociopolitical contexts (for instance, the role, that being protestant and catholic, until quite recently played in Western countries in conflicts of toleration and nowadays has become almost irrelevant), may indicate that tolerance may be only an "interim value" (Williams 1996), which in the long run may be replaced by acceptance or appreciation of difference. While this will probably not hold for diversity tout court and in all respects, it is certainly true at least with respect to certain contexts and domains, such as sexual orientation, where in the last decades legal and ethical developments point into the direction beyond mere tolerance.

In light of these developments, it is of crucial importance to note that toleration is certainly only *one* educational aim and *one* potential response to diversity, among others. The legitimacy of toleration as an aim of education not only depends on the legitimate scope of the objects of toleration (2.2), but also on the ideal of social, political, and educational interaction that is aspired too (e.g., interactions based on notions of recognition or respect; Jones 2010; Sardoc 2010). Tolerance can in principle be combined (or complemented) with other normative attitudes and relations, such as different forms of recognition or respect that are addressed towards different aspects of the normative status and/or identity of the tolerated agent (Forst 2013; respect for the person – tolerance for practices, attitudes, etc.). A degree "of particularized recognition," for instance, "can aid the case for toleration. Hostility and condemnation are often accompanied by ignorance, misunderstanding and a lack of empathy. A better understanding of another's position can result in the recognition of something of value in it, even though it remains a position that we reject all things considered" (Jones 2010, 53).

A last point that needs to be mentioned is the *multidimensional* nature of conflicts of toleration (Macleod 2010) in educational constellations, where typically vertical toleration (between state and citizens/parents) intersects with horizontal toleration (between future citizens) in a variety of ways. The pedagogical realization of tolerance as an aim of democratic education may, for instance, conflict in various ways with the conceptions of the good of parents (e.g., debates about personal or political autonomy as aims of education; debates about the content of the curriculum). How these conflicts may be resolved in a reasonable way is a question that – to a certain extent – can only be answered dependent on the specific empirical context (see section "Justifying Education for Democratic Tolerance").

In short: Education for tolerance describes an empirically, normatively, and conceptually complex set of actions, practices, and arrangements. Some of these complexities are rooted in controversies over the normative status of the objection component in conceptions of toleration more generally and toleration as a democratic virtue in particular.

Toleration as a Democratic Virtue and Aim of Education

After the short outline of the different roles of toleration in educational contexts, we will now turn to the basic structure of tolerance as a democratic virtue, that is, as an aim of democratic education. A tolerant person can be descriptively characterized as able and willing to deliberate on her first-order reasons for objection (objection component) in the light of second-order reasons, principles, or values (acceptance component). A normative conception of toleration as a democratic virtue and educational aim has to provide a substantive account of the legitimate objects of toleration (objection component), the rationales and values provided to justify toleration (acceptance component), the limits of toleration and the epistemic quality of self-, world-, and other-relations (see sections "Empirical Tolerance Research and the Possibility of Education for Tolerance" and "Justifying Education for Democratic Tolerance"), which manifests itself in the interplay between the objection and acceptance component.

The democratic virtue of toleration marks a mean between two extremes: illegitimate political intolerance (such as political violence) or illegitimate political tolerance (such as the toleration of grave political injustices) (the following paragraphs are adopted from: Drerup 2019). Citizens that have cultivated the virtue of democratic toleration in its most basic sense accept elementary rules of democratic coexistence, such as the toleration of majority votes and opposing political views. They accept the basic fact that disagreement and a plurality of political views and conceptions of the good is a basic feature of democratic life. Political toleration is based on an "understanding that competing parties accept one another as legitimate rivals" (Levitsky and Ziblatt 2018, 8) and holders of individual rights – political opponents are not enemies who are undeserving of basic political respect. Respect for individual rights, including the right to democratic self-determination and the value of basic political equality, thus serve as a normative basis and justification of democratic toleration and its limits (a critique of toleration as a political concept, principle, and virtue is provided by: Heyd 2008; a defense on the basis of the respect conception can be found in: Forst 2013). Moreover, in what follows it will be emphasized that democratic toleration, as a virtue and as an educational aim as well as a central aspect of democratic forms of life and ingredient of tolerant societies, is both normatively and substantially dependent on the development of a variety of interrelated capacities and dispositions, such as epistemic virtues (e.g., accuracy, open-mindedness), which enable citizens to adequately regulate, moderate, and reflect on their cognitive and emotional responses to their own objections and to others in the public sphere (section "Empirical Tolerance Research and the Possibility of Education for Tolerance"). As a democratic and political virtue toleration can be analytically distinguished from toleration that refers to the moral, ethical, and/or private domain. The "political," however, intersects and overlaps normatively and empirically with these other domains (Mather and Tranby 2014) and a lack toleration in one's more private relationships certainly in many cases will have effects on other domains as well (and vice versa).

It is the content and scope of the *objection component* that exposes one of the crucial theoretical problems of a conception of democratic toleration as a virtue and as an educational aim (for the analogous debate concerning the notion of a "tolerant" liberal state: Balint 2017). It is prima facie difficult to make sense of a virtue or an educational aim that is essentially based on the fact that a person holds certain objections. The more objections such a person holds, the more virtuous she seems to become in case she finds higher-order reasons to nevertheless tolerate incriminated groups, practices, or traits. This view contradicts the folk-psychological intuition that a tolerant person is usually less judgmental and has fewer problematic prejudices (Horton 1996, p. 38). There are three theoretical strategies to deal with this problem, each of which provides one aspect of an acceptable solution.

According to the *first* strategy, it is necessary to operate with normative and epistemic restrictions that limit the acceptable scope of the objection component (Forst 2013), which implies that some prejudices are per se incompatible with toleration. A tolerant racist, in this sense, may be regarded as an oxymoron. The precise characterization of these restrictions is itself an object of controversy (cf. Bessone 2013). Depending on how demanding they are defined, this approach can be criticized either as an elitist conception of a tolerant person, which provides the basis for a problematic form of second-order intolerance towards those who do not conform to these rather demanding requirements, or as irrelevant to an understanding of real-world political conflicts of toleration (Balint 2017). To arbitrate in this debate, it is necessary to clearly distinguish between a normative approach to toleration as a virtue and a descriptive reconstruction of the relevant phenomena. From a purely descriptive perspective, racists certainly can be qualified as tolerant, but not, however, in terms of the virtue of toleration. Nevertheless, epistemic and normative constraints on the objection component are necessary for the justification of toleration as a virtue. These have to be sufficiently demanding enough in their formulation as to rule out prejudices that are themselves definitively expressive of intolerance and, at the same time, as moderate as possible in order to avoid unrealistic demands, according to which most people would be epistemically incapable of toleration.

The *second* strategy assumes that a person can also be qualified as tolerant when she does not object to certain groups, practices, or traits, which are commonly objected to in the societal and cultural environment in which she grew up (Gardner 2001). By expanding the scope of the concept of toleration in this way, it is possible to do justice to the expectation that a person is usually more tolerant when she is less judgmental. Based on such a broad notion of toleration, indifference (Balint 2017) – either in the sense of "I do not care about X" or in the sense of "X *should* not be relevant" – can then be qualified as an aspect of democratic toleration.

The *third* strategy stresses the importance of habituation in educational processes and acknowledges that toleration as a virtue does not *necessarily* have to go along with strong willpower and forms of self-conquest and -control. In contrast to the classical model, which is based on the premise that toleration consists of *balancing* different reasons, a neo-Aristotelian conception assumes that potential reasons for objecting to X are *silenced* by the way in which a tolerant agent is disposed to perceive a particular situation. According to this "perceptual approach", reasons for objection or acceptance do not have to be deliberately balanced in the first place, for instance, because the agent perceives X as a private matter (Owen 2011, 110). All three of these strategies should be taken into consideration in order to make theoretical sense of the virtue of democratic toleration as a coherent aim of education.

After having reconstructed basic conceptual issues concerning the notions of toleration, education for tolerance and tolerance as an aim of (democratic) toleration and before discussing basic normative and justificatory issues (section "Justifying Education for Democratic Tolerance"), the next section will deal with the question how education for tolerance is possible.

Empirical Tolerance Research and the Possibility of Education for Tolerance

Questions concerning the possibility and feasibility of education for tolerance can only be answered on the basis of the results of empirical social research. Drawing on the results of empirical tolerance research, in this section two types of educating in tolerance will be outlined that are constituting different ways of addressing the various sources and reasons for (in) tolerance. These include tolerance education as a form of education of the emotions and as a cultivation of epistemic virtues. Both forms of educating in tolerance can analytically be separated but overlap in practical and empirical terms. Together they constitute two central dimensions of a theory of educating for democratic tolerance.

As a point of departure, it is worth noting that the reasons, motivations, and normative resources for tolerance and intolerance can be found in all traditions and cultures (Nederman 2012) and that it would be empirically wrong and perhaps even intolerant to assume that tolerance both in its vertical (state – citizen) and in its horizontal (citizen – citizen) dimension would be a practice and value that is solely reserved for "Western" traditions and liberal societies. Nevertheless, this general observation does not rule out that some political systems, cultural patterns, and societal environments can count as more tolerant in important respects than others (for instance, with respect to the inclusion of minorities as holders of equal rights; Forst 2015; Drerup 2019). Furthermore, three important caveats are in order, when discussing the specific empirical relations between tolerance and education as well as practices and principles of tolerance education.

First, there is no straightforward *necessary* connection between being educated in certain respects and tolerance or intolerance. There are ample historical examples of highly educated individuals, who were at the same time highly intolerant and committed all types of atrocities. Likewise, one can obviously lack education in important dimensions, without automatically becoming intolerant. In accordance with this, it remains a matter of controversy in empirical research on tolerance to what extent there is a clear empirical connection between educational background and (in)tolerance (Rapp 2014; Vogt 1997). This is also one of the reasons why "educational" arguments can be highly problematic in political controversies about the roots of intolerance. Ascribing a lack of education to a political opponent can arguably in some cases be perceived as intolerant and as a rather questionable *political* argument (even though in some cases it is certainly true). Or, as Forsts puts it, empirical tolerance research "involves dangers of imprecise concepts and of over-generalised causal explanations. The latter can lead not only to the pathologisation of intolerant attitudes in general, and to setting the tolerant personality apart as the only strong one, but also to the tendency to make too strong inferences back to factors relating to the family, social conditions, the role of religion, etc. Viewed from the perspectives of individual and social psychology, the paths leading to intolerance are as diverse as those leading to tolerance. To be sure, the danger of inadmissibly generalising certain 'character types of tolerance' also exists at the philosophical level" (2013, 515–516).

Second, also due to the many methodological complexities involved in reconstructing reasons and explanations for intolerance in individuals or groups, it will usually be not simply possible to *deduce* practical recommendations for the design of educational institutions from the results of empirical social research on tolerance in a 1-to-1 manner. The theoretical and practical question of effectively educating for tolerance should certainly be empirically *informed* and different approaches should be *revised* in light of the results of empirical social research (for instance, when a particular educational program has counter-intentional effects), they can, however, only guide educational practice in limited way. In other words: There is a difference between the logic of research and the logic of educational practices and arrangements, which also has to be acknowledged with respect to the relation between education and toleration. Third, public schools are only one factor that influences the political education and socialization of children. Many sociopsychological reasons for developing intolerant attitudes and practices are rooted in factors beyond the school, such as social pathologies within the family or economic factors (see: Rapp 2014). Thus, one should be careful not to assume that all kinds of societal and political problems can be solved by educational means.

Education for Tolerance as Education of the Emotions

There is now a broad consensus in philosophical research on the emotions that the classical dichotomy between emotions and rationality is neither theoretically nor empirically tenable (Reichenbach 2018; the following paragraphs are adopted from:

Drerup 2020). Emotions, it is assumed, are constitutive for our relationship to the social and political world and to ourselves. The fact that forms of self-detachment, self-reflection, and self-control are also associated with feelings or express higher-order feelings (i.e., feelings that refer to feelings) already speaks against the supposed opposition between rationality and emotion. Moreover, whether and to what extent we wish to follow a feeling or not can also be a matter for rational decision (Hastedt 2005). In what follows, the concept of emotion or feeling stands for *"diverse forms of psychosomatic involvement in virtue of which one can have qualitative experiences of particularity and thus invest things with importance"* (Hastedt 2005, p. 21; emphasis in the original). What appears important and significant to someone, and how, depends on different forms of first- and second-order feelings (i.e., also moods, passions, etc.). At the same time, this form of involvement, as Hastedt points out with reference to the work of Agnes Heller, is generally bound up with one's particular, individual experience, and the associated relationships to the world, self, and society.

Cognitivist approaches in the theory of emotions assume that emotions are based on valuations, assessments, and judgments, and hence that they have cognitive and evaluative content and fulfill epistemic functions, for example, by opening up action-guiding perspectives on the world and what is important in it. They constitute a central foundation of moral coexistence and are intrinsically bound up with our identity and character. In this way, they found motivations to act, connect us with the world, and express what appears desirable and important or intolerable and contemptible to us (Reichenbach 2018). They can be more or less conscious and organized or more unconscious (Hastedt 2005), but are at least in principle accessible to reflection. They are socioculturally mediated (even if they can take direct hold of us; consider, for example, the "mediated immediacy" of fear, which grips us directly, but is nevertheless culturally mediated); their forms of expression and objects are historically contingent. However, emotions, their occasions, and their manifestations are not arbitrary. Depending on the context, they can be criticized as more or less correct, appropriate, and rational by appeal to epistemic, ethical, and political standards. This means in addition that it is not especially plausible to attribute *absolute or even infallible* epistemic authority to the individual when it comes to classifying and interpreting feelings, which are always socially constructed and at least in part intersubjectively accessible and open to discussion (see Hastedt 2005). At the same time, feelings have decided epistemic functions. However, probably only in the rarest cases will the reference to feelings alone constitute a plausible epistemic justification, because "arguments must ultimately demonstrate the legitimacy of feelings" (see Heidenreich 2019, p. 41).

As a constitutive aspect of our relationships to the world, self, and society, emotions are at the same time an unavoidable part of politics, and every political ideal is inevitably based on emotions (Nussbaum 2015). A central ambivalence, especially in political contexts, is that political emotions and their evocation or instrumentalization can be accompanied by unreflected behavior, political polarization, and a lack of differentiation, but also by solidarity and respect among equals.

Hence, it makes little sense to view emotions in politics or democratic education per se as desirable or worthy of rejection. This is also shown by the relationship between (in)tolerance and various political emotions, which can be schematized as follows. By influencing the objection or acceptance component, emotions can, for example,

1. Trigger or promote (in)tolerance
2. Go hand in hand with (in-)tolerant attitudes and practices, or
3. Express (in)tolerance

On a general level and simplifying somewhat, we can surmise that "negative emotions" (irrational fears, rage, envy, contempt for facts, etc.) *have a tendency* to trigger or promote intolerance, to be associated with intolerant attitudes, or can be seen as expressions of intolerance. Conversely, "positive emotions" (love, solidarity, respect, hope, etc.) *tend* to go hand in hand with tolerance. However, there can, of course, be cases for which this correlation does not hold. At any rate, the findings of empirical research on tolerance seem to confirm that *certain* emotions are associated with intolerance or trigger it especially frequently. More or less (rational or irrational) feelings of being under threat and fear of the loss of socio-economic status and of (more or less imagined) cultural homogeneity and identity are among the most important causal explanations offered for political intolerance, alongside dogmatism and authoritarianism (Rapp 2014). Individual factors (e.g., personality), group-based factors (e.g., tribalist thinking, the search for scapegoats), sociostructural factors (e.g., the economic system, social policy), or social-discursive factors (e.g., political instrumentalization) tend to contribute to the genesis and stabilization of these fears. Fear can therefore be regarded as an especially problematic politically relevant emotion because it can make people susceptible to political polarization, simple solutions and "felt" truths. It often goes hand in hand with a narrowing of the actor's cognitively and emotionally structured value horizon and can lead to a demonization of others, aggression, violence, etc. Furthermore, fear is often "contagious" (Sunstein 2005, 101) in the context of social groups and forms a "toxic combination" with other emotions (such as anger and contempt) (Nussbaum 2018, 151) – that is, the intensity and form of expression of other emotions change when they are accompanied by fear.

If we follow contemporary diagnoses in philosophy, political science, and sociology then we are currently living in an era of increasing political instrumentalization and production of fear and hatred of certain groups (Baumann 2016; Nussbaum 2018) by, among others, right-wing populist parties and their partly intolerant agendas. Historically speaking, however, these forms of emotional politics are, of course, nothing new and certainly are not a "fate" to be accepted. There are many different possible political and pedagogical ways of dealing with these developments. A particularly strong argument against emotionally deterministic positions is that fear and how actors deal with it and other reasons for intolerance are generally *also* shaped by early childhood experiences (Nussbaum 2018; Brumlik 2018) and by subsequent social and pedagogical experiences (Warnock 2001). In view of this state of affairs and of the present mood, it may come as a surprise that feelings play scarcely any role in the current philosophical debate over toleration and how it can be facilitated through education.

Emotional education as a form of democratic education in tolerance can be understood in general as involving the cultivation of the ability and disposition, which is based on and mediated by autonomy, to develop higher-order desires, motives, emotions, and reasons (acceptance component) that refer to first-order desires, motives, emotions, and reasons (objection component). In other words, it is primarily a matter of dealing as reflectively, autonomously, and appropriately as possible with "negative" and "positive" emotions and one's emotional involvement. Here the notion of "appropriateness" refers to the fact that the quality of the emotion and the object at which it is directed can indeed be subjects of discussion and allow intersubjectively intelligible evaluations not only in epistemic, but also in moral, ethical, political, and pedagogical respects. This is inseparable from the assumption that, even if our emotional reactions and their genesis are at least in part subconscious, we are still ultimately responsible for how we deal with our emotional reactions and conditioning (Warnock 2001). It goes without saying that this applies only to a limited extent to children. Among the assumptions and desiderata of the conception advocated here is that children should and can learn such responsibility.

There are no doubt good reasons to be skeptical about the possibility of teaching tolerance by educating the emotions, for example, when it comes to dealing with fears. One need only think of the many factors that can give rise to fears and of the classic technological deficiency of education, which in the final analysis always has to do with more or less "free" actors who can reject the pedagogically ambitious requirements. Therefore, it is always possible that educational efforts will fail in this area, as they can in any pedagogical practice. This is why, in pedagogical constellations and in the context of a liberal conception of the education of feelings, one cannot dispense with technologies in the broad sense (rules, techniques, established modes of dealing, etc.; see Tenorth 2002) and their effects, which are on the whole foreseeable, even if not always unambiguous. The fundamental justification for the possibility of the education of the emotions as a form of tolerance education is not only that intolerance is often associated with or triggered by specific emotions and that every form of education has emotional elements, but also that, as is empirically and historically sufficiently well documented, rational insight and education do not automatically lead to tolerance. For this reason, too, education in tolerance must strive to combat the emotional foundations of intolerance, even if it goes without saying that success cannot be guaranteed here any more than in other aspects of education in democracy (Brumlik 2018).

The following can be regarded as central *goals* of a democratic conception of education in tolerance as emotional education. A first fundamental goal consists in an emotional-cognitive sensitization, differentiation, and opening up of emotional-cognitive horizons of comparison and reference (e.g., different forms of life and conceptions of the good), which is inseparable from shared forms of rational deliberation. Politically problematic emotions such as hatred are usually associated with a certain loss of differentiation: "Hatred is fuzzy. It is difficult to hate with precision" (Emcke 2019, xii; see also Reichenbach 2018). At the same time, hatred and fear and the associated intolerance go hand in hand with a narrowing of reality that is generally a result of stereotypes (Emcke 2019, 27) and must be confronted with the *real* political and social heterogeneity of groups, ways of life, opinions, and practices. The confrontation with plurality and otherness in oneself and in conflicts with other human beings often triggers ambivalence and rejection that children must learn to deal with reflectively. Tolerance therefore calls for the formation of a "strong self" (Forst 2013) which learns to endure ambiguities and ambivalences in dealing with its emotions, instead of taking refuge in the overly simplistic, emotionally mediated myths of a homogeneous community, as this is imagined by right-wing populist ideologies.

A second goal is a well-founded emotional-cognitive identification with and loyalty toward fundamental values (*qua* basic and human rights) of liberal democracy (Nussbaum 2015). Tolerance education in liberal democracy must make clear the normative foundations on which it is based and, according to the limited justificatory pluralism cited above, cannot be tolerant of every conceivable emotionally grounded position. Teaching tolerance cannot be a matter of the imposition of "value priorities, interpretations and evaluations" by the teacher. Rather, it should turn primarily on "the only seemingly illegitimate question of *who*—i.e., what kind of person—this child should become" (Reichenbach 2018, 145). On the one hand, children should cultivate the ability and disposition to question and examine the desirability of their own (political and personal) cognitive-emotional evaluative commitments, and the associated attitudes of rejection and acceptance, in the light of higher-order principles. On the other hand, the concrete ways in which these reasons for tolerance are spelled out are not arbitrarily negotiable (e.g., and above all, the recognition of basic and human rights and value pluralism is not negotiable). In other words, a liberal-democratic emotional education is not viable without a certain affirmative component, which, of course, does not exclude well-founded criticism of democratic institutions. Moreover, in some cases it can fall to the teacher as a pedagogical and political authority to defend these fundamental values, and ideally also to impose them (Callan 2011).

A third goal consists in the regular practice of civilized and respectful forms of interaction with others and in enduring dissent and ambivalence. In other words, an essential feature of such education is also the epistemic and communicative containment of "strong" emotions that are potentially conducive to intolerance (fear, anger, hatred, etc.). In some cases, this may also involve creating strong "counter-emotions." No democracy can survive without affective attachment to basic democratic values and a certain justified anger when they are violated On the other hand, however, this must not translate into a pedagogical instrumentalization of and incitement to anger, as propagated by contemporary proponents of an agonistic democratic pedagogy. By contrast, Yacek and Hehemann argue with reference to Gandhi and Martin Luther King and the work of Martha Nussbaum that "anger can only become a political force for change if it is transformed into an affirmative, philanthropic disposition that strives to dissolve political fronts through solidarity" (Yacek and Hehemann 2019, 4). The associated educational and transformation process should be a reflective and directed one which examines the sources and justification of anger also with pedagogical support, while at the same time trying to transform them into positive feelings that foster tolerance (or render it superfluous), such as solidarity, confidence, and hope.

Reichenbach and Maxwell (2007) have reconstructed common social *practices* of emotional education. They can be interpreted as exhortations aimed at "stimulating the internalization of certain moral insights and evaluations, understood as the education of dispositions to express emotions appropriate to the situation" (see Reichenbach 2018, 144). These include, first, *imaginative* practices which can involve calling upon X to imagine the emotional reactions of Y in a certain situation, which can and should promote the ability to empathize and adopt the social perspectives of others; second, practices of *imitation*, such as inviting X to change or moderate how she expresses her emotions; and third, practices of *reappraisal* in which X is encouraged to critically reevaluate the appropriateness of her emotional reactions in a certain context in order to foster the ability to form moral and political judgments and to rationally correct and monitor her emotional reactions (Maxwell and Reichenbach 2007).

These three forms of exhortation, which are correlated with different traditions of emotional education (e.g., imitation with the Aristotelian tradition), are already implicit in practical pedagogical ways of dealing with emotions. Applied to the challenges outlined above, this can mean, for example, that we should help children to rationally question and problematize their fears (*reappraisal*) or, in some cases, to articulate them in the first place. Empirical research on tolerance also suggests that intolerance is often based on emotionally grounded misjudgments of the social world – induced, for example, by fears – and associated stereotypes, which can be countered by cultivating epistemic virtues (such as exactness and objectivity) (see below). The examination and correction of the justification of feelings in the light of public standards of rationality (Reichenbach 2018) can ideally contribute to breaking down irrational emotions (e.g., irrational forms of fear and guilty feelings) and associated epistemic vices (e.g., ignoring or contemptuously disregarding facts and evidence). This is all the more important given the manifestly irrational agendas of resolute enemies of liberal democracy (Leggewie 2017), who try to evoke and exploit political emotions for their political advantage.

In order to overcome intolerance, moreover, it is often sufficient if children develop even a minimum of empathy for the situation of refugees, for example, by imagining how they would feel if corresponding things happened to them and their family (*imagination*) (see Witenberg 2019). After all, intolerance goes hand in hand with a narrowing of the space of imagination and fantasy and thus with a view of reality that is passed through an extremely one-sided filter (Emcke 2019, 28). On this Emcke observes: "When the imagination is so restricted, the capacity for empathy with a given person also shrinks. A person who can no longer *imagine* how unique, how individual, every single Muslimah, every single migrant, every transgender person or every Black person is, who cannot imagine how similar they are in their fundamental pursuit of happiness and dignity, is also unable to recognize their vulnerability as human beings, and instead sees only the prefabricated image. And this image, this narrative, provides 'reasons' why an injury to Muslims (or Jews or feminists or intellectuals or Roma) is justifiable" (ibid., 30). This is supported by the reflections of Nussbaum, who observes in her plea for imaginative empathy: "Disgust denies fundamental human dignity to groups of people, portraying them instead as animals. Consequently respect grounded in the idea of human dignity will prove impotent to include all citizens on terms of equality unless it is nourished by imaginative engagement with the lives of others and by an inner grasp of their full and equal humanity" (Nussbaum 2013, 380).

Among the important pedagogical *means* and *techniques* of emotional education are – without making any claim to completeness – certain media, such as literature (e.g., Nussbaum 2013), but also films, pictures, etc. The central idea here is, among other things, that the use of media can enable children to think and feel their way into situations and individuals they would otherwise in many cases never or only very rarely encounter. How would it feel, for example, to come to Germany as a migrant, to leave one's home country, etc.? Another tried and tested means in the history of pedagogy since Locke and Rousseau at the latest is based on the socializing effects of pedagogically structured interactions and situations (e.g., international youth exchanges or initiating forms of group discussion under pedagogical guidance, thereby ideally facilitating democratic experience) or on the effects of what is known in research on social psychology as the "contact hypothesis" (Rapp 2014). The hope is that, through increased interaction, children and adults will overcome prejudices and if necessary exercise tolerance (Gardner 2001). Aside from the use of media and the effects of pedagogical techniques, we must not, of course, ignore forms of direct (knowledge-based) instruction, a central element of which can be to draw attention to and discuss the role of emotions in politics and society (Witenberg 2019). So much for the basic aims, practices, means, and techniques of education in tolerance as emotional education, which afford a variety of ways of dealing productively with political emotions.

Education for Tolerance and Epistemic Virtues

A second approach to tolerance education is less focused on the emotional basis and causes of intolerance, but has a more cognitive orientation (the following paragraphs are partly adopted from: Drerup 2019). It is based on the idea that the cultivation of epistemic virtues is a central means to counteract political intolerance and to enable and facilitate the development of toleration as a democratic virtue. Virtue epistemologists, such as Cassam (2019), assume that many contemporary political disagreements and the resulting social conflicts can be interpreted as consequences of epistemic vices. In line with this, empirical social research provides ample reasons for the assumption that cognitive deficits and epistemic vices are, in many cases, correlated with and contributed to political intolerance. Among these factors are:

- A readiness to adopt undifferentiated and uncritically reflected constructions, imaginations, stereotypes, and biases, which are, in many cases, expressions of or go along with political intolerance ("the people," the Muslims, etc.; for research on prejudices and implicit biases, see, e.g., Baumann 2016; Brownstein 2015)
- A disposition to uncritically adopt intolerant doctrines (such as certain conspiracy theories; for research on the relation between the belief in conspiracy theories, education and political intolerance, see, e.g., Van Prooijen 2017)

- Dogmatism, authoritarianism, and irrational feelings of threat as the most important general explanations for political intolerance in empirical tolerance research (e.g., Rapp 2014; see, for new research on the authoritarian personality: Brumlik 2018)
- A lack of political knowledge and cognitive skills (and a lack of positive evaluation of political knowledge and cognitive skills) as a contributory factor in political intolerance (see, for instance: Witenberg 2019)

Since all of these factors have a strong epistemic dimension, tolerance education in public schools should, among other factors, be based on the premise that, in order to counteract political intolerance, we have to strengthen and develop epistemic virtues among students. Especially from an educational perspective, we cannot make sense of toleration irrespective of a variety of other capacities and character traits. Toleration as a democratic virtue is essentially dependent on and embedded in a network of epistemic virtues, such as accuracy, objectivity, and impartiality, an orientation towards the truth, open-mindedness, a certain epistemic humility, critical thinking, and an epistemic deference towards trustworthy epistemic authorities. These interdependent virtues are all constituted by both normative and epistemic elements, without, however, being straightforward moral virtues. Simply put, the telos of moral virtues is doing the right thing and having the right moral attitude in the right situation, while the telos of epistemic virtues is, among others, getting things right epistemically, for instance, by forming true beliefs. Since both aims can conflict and epistemic virtues (and vices) do not always have politically or morally beneficial (or harmful effects) (Cassam 2019), also the relation between epistemic virtues and the virtue of democratic toleration is more indirect and complex. The educational and political rationale of cultivating epistemic virtues is not to resolve political conflicts of toleration, but rather to civilize and refine them intellectually by facilitating the development of more democratically tolerant inter-citizen relations and debates. As in the case of the education of the emotions, there is no guarantee that either particular educational arrangements will lead to the cultivation of epistemic virtues among particular students or that epistemic virtues will actually result in a more adequate perspective on social reality or in more political tolerance. Nevertheless, there is no reason for educational skepticism or pessimism here: Even though a person who is dogmatic, judgmental, and prone to uncritically follow the commands of idealized leaders will not necessarily be politically intolerant, she will almost certainly be more likely to be intolerant. A person who is less judgmental and perhaps also indifferent towards differences, which are commonly objected to in her social environment, is usually also more tolerant. The connection between epistemic virtues and toleration thus holds for both second-order reflective capacities and dispositions facilitative of toleration as a virtue (e.g., the capacity for responsible believe formation) and the way in which the objection component is structured in the first place (e.g., the possession of less problematic prejudices). Like in the case of education of the emotions, it is possible to provide some examples for major educational strategies, which could foster the acquisition and transmission of epistemic virtues and thereby counteract political intolerance.

The epistemic virtue of accuracy is crucial to the ability to adequately access and question the epistemic and normative quality of the content of the objection component. The disposition to think thoroughly and precisely about the categories and frames one employs, when making sense of the political world, can be cultivated by the critical discussion and deconstruction of abstract constructions of groups and collective orientations, which, in many cases, can lay the ground for political intolerance. A basic understanding of social psychological mechanisms (us vs. them), teachers who exemplify the virtue of accuracy in their own practice (Baehr 2013), the provision of fact-based knowledge about different conceptions of the good, and concrete practical knowledge based on lived experiences in interaction with relevant groups are often sufficient to at least irritate dogmatic and prejudiced forms of individually or socially established forms of perception. Accuracy as an epistemic aim of education does not make much sense without the assumption that we can differentiate between fact and fiction and between true and false claims, in the first place. A commitment towards the truth (or what one has good reasons to believe to be the truth) is constitutive of the ethos of teaching and the ethos of democratic debate. Therefore, it is important to note that political intolerance is often not just the product of the enforcement of absolutist epistemic and normative validity claims, but also of thoughtlessness with respect to what is actually the case, and carelessness with respect to the truth.

The virtues of objectivity and impartiality can be fostered by the provision of knowledge about the historical genesis and political contexts of conflicts of toleration. By developing a differentiated and knowledge-based view on these conflicts, taking multiple perspectives into account, students are less likely to adopt simplified constructions of conflicts of toleration, which, in some cases, prevent their peaceful resolution. Objectivity as a virtue is geared towards the acknowledgement of the existence of a shared and objective political and social reality. It can counteract subjective emotional projections and irrational feelings of threat, which are among the major sources of political intolerance and serve as a corrective to the more or less complete loss of reality, often exemplified by entirely delusional intolerant ideologies (Leggewie 2017). Moreover, the virtue of impartiality is vital for the ability to detect unjust relations of toleration, in which basic norms of political equality are violated (such as laws that are intolerant towards particular religions). Acknowledgment of the fact that complete objectivity and impartiality are only regulative ideals which can contribute to the principled acceptance that dissent and disagreement, with respect to epistemological, factual, as well as ethical and political issues, are permanent and normal features of democratic life.

Epistemic humility is of political and ethical importance when it comes to both an understanding of the limits of one's knowledge about the other and an acceptance of one's (partly) inevitable ignorance of many of the complexities of democratic processes. The acceptance of the inevitable complexities, difficulties, and protracted nature of democratic processes can counteract the belief in simple and often intolerant solutions, as proposed by populist politicians. It can also serve as a remedy to the overestimation of one's own knowledge about political matters, which can prevent the acceptance of the necessity of tradeoffs, compromises, and sacrifices in democracies (Allen 2004). A more realistic estimation of one's knowledge should not necessarily result in political paralysis, as it can foster a moderate form of skepticism towards the epistemic grounds of one's own judgments of toleration.

The virtue of critical thinking, among other factors, requires the ability to distinguish empirical and normative claims and to evaluate the soundness of arguments and evidence for a political position. It relies on a capacity for critical self-reflection and a certain independence of mind, as well as on a positive evaluation of the value of responsible belief formation and a "readiness to accept discursive responsibility in normative conflicts" (Forst 2013, 503–504). In contrast, the epistemic vice of an unfounded and highly selective radical epistemic skepticism (typically found among conspiracy theorists, which is hypercritical concerning all epistemic sources, except those that confirm one's own viewpoint) tends to undermine the very epistemic basis of minimally reasonable democratic debates, while being especially prone to epistemically induced intolerance.

The educational cultivation of these and other epistemic virtues, on the one hand, concerns processes of habituation, which dispose agents to perceive the other and conflicts of toleration in the right way. On the other hand, it is also a matter of more direct instruction, as well as deliberation, with regard to complex concrete cases, which is essentially dependent on the development of individuals' power of judgment. The acquisition and possession of these individual virtues are heavily dependent on the epistemic and social environment in which they are (or not) practiced and supported (Baehr 2013). Successful discursive initiation into relevant epistemic norms and practices, for instance, in the context of teaching and discussing controversial issues (Hess and McAvoy 2015), is moreover dependent on a positive second-order evaluation of their intrinsic and instrumental value by teachers and students.

To conclude: education of the emotions as well as the cultivation of epistemic virtues constitute two important dimensions of a theory of education for democratic tolerance.

Justifying Education for Democratic Tolerance

As was mentioned before, we can find reasons and resources for tolerance and intolerance in all traditions. This pluralism of sources of (in-)tolerance also expresses itself in a plurality of different possibilities to justify toleration (see, for instance: Nederman 2012). Especially in the context of a pluralistic society, we are facing a plurality of different, partly overlapping, partly conflicting notions of toleration and its value. Thus, one may argue that its "very pluralism seems to require pluralism of the ways to toleration" (Khomyakov 2013, 237). At the same time, however, it is argued that a justification of toleration based on, for instance, a conception of moral pluralism, which assumes that a plurality of incommensurable objective values exists, is only one view of the normative and social world among others, which may itself not be compatible with other notions of pluralism (Forst 2013) and therefore may be reasonably rejected. The same criticism, however, is also developed with respect to universalist justifications of toleration that claim to provide a universally shared (or shareable) normative basis, such as the right to justification, for dealing with toleration conflicts (Galeotti 2015). The systematic background problem of this debate is that the way tolerance is justified and conceptualized (e.g., with respect to notion of the tolerant person) may be interpreted as an intolerant imposition of a particular world view on individuals or groups that do not share the relevant values and norms. While the theoretical debate about a "tolerant" theory and justification of toleration (Rawls 2005) is ongoing, it can be assumed that on a most basic and minimal level, there is a broad consensus that toleration is a pivotal instrumental (or even intrinsic) value, because it ensures a peaceful coexistence (Walzer 1997) and therefore is a minimal precondition of leading a good life (or even: being alive at all).

This is one of the reasons why the pluralism of different sources and theoretical as well as lived justifications of toleration should be taken seriously in the context of a justification of democratic tolerance. One should be rather skeptical when it comes to either justifications of toleration that are based on a single principle (such as the harm principle: Cohen 2018) or claim to be applicable to all contexts in an equal manner irrespective of the particular normative and empirical features of a particular constellation. While the former tends to result in a form of stretching of principles which deduces normative claims from a master value, which arguably rests on differing normative foundations, the latter can result in a form of justificatory essentialism, which does not sufficiently take the lived plurality of practices and justifications of toleration into account. The respect conception defended by Forst (2013), for instance, provides a reasonable standard of justification for relations between adults as citizens of a liberal state. This does not necessarily hold for educational contexts of toleration, where we are dealing with children, who are not yet globally autonomous agents.

In this section, my aim is to briefly outline the general contours of a domain-specific justification of education for democratic tolerance, which is based on the moderately contextualist assumption that general principles and justifications cannot and should not be equally applied in the same way to all contexts of toleration. The tensions that result from an application of neo-Kantian, neo-Baylian, or political liberal justifications of toleration to educational contexts result from conflicting normative expectations concerning a normatively sound conception of democratic education and the standards of justification, which reasonably may be employed when it comes to conflicts of toleration between adults. While it may be plausible to assume, for instance, that a political liberal notion of respect should be devoid of epistemic criteria that limit who still counts as reasonable (Nussbaum 2011), in educational contexts, we certainly have to draw the limits of toleration also based on epistemic considerations. Likewise, it is certainly a central aim of democratic education to learn to participate as political equals in the public sphere. This does not imply, however, that educational policies or practices could or should entirely be justified democratically, without recourse to substantive educational as well as scientific expertise (for instance, when it comes to the contents of the curriculum). Otherwise, it would, for instance, be open to democratic – and not scientific – debate whether evolutionary theory should be taught in schools. Thus, even though a democratic and an educational justification of education for democratic tolerance are interlinked, they are not identical. Parents as citizens, for instance, certainly should have a say when it comes to decisions concerning educational policies that concern the upbringing of their children in public schools. This, however, does not imply that they have total authority over their children when it comes to decisions concerning the curriculum (e.g., in debates about sex education).

An educational *and* democratic justification of education for tolerance is based on a combination of elements of a *deliberative* conception of democratic justification (Culp 2019) and a *liberal perfectionist* justification (Drerup 2018) of democratic education, which is – *on a basic level* – geared towards

- Enabling all children to participate in collective processes of political deliberation and democratic self-determination (political autonomy)
- To critically reflect on the conditions of their upbringing and their inherited life forms (personal autonomy)
- The cultivation and affirmation of democratic values, virtues and life forms (among others, acceptance of universal human rights, respect, civility, solidarity, and justice)

The justification is liberal perfectionist in the sense that it assumes that the cultivation of *personal* autonomy, for instance, by fostering epistemic virtues, as well as the acceptance of the validity of basic human rights, is central not just for a flourishing collective democratic life, but also for a flourishing *individual* life. A liberal perfectionist justification thus is based on a liberal conception of the good individual life and a good collective democratic life. The justification is democratic (or: deliberative), because it is based on the idea of a reciprocal justificatory interconnection between a critical public sphere as an arena of collective democratic will-formation and self-determination, the institutional infrastructure of a liberal democracy, and a corresponding conception of democratic education. Thus, children (and adults), for instance, should learn to resolve their political and moral disagreements by deliberation, for instance, by discussing controversial issues concerning toleration and its limits in a civil manner. Moreover, they have to learn to accept that validity claims and opinions which do *not* conform to basic scientific as well as epistemic criteria (Hand 2008) do not and cannot have the same – *controversial* – status in educational settings as positions which do conform to these criteria and thus have to be tolerated as instances of reasonable disagreement.

Apart from these normative core ideas, criteria, and values (human rights; personal and political autonomy etc.), this dual justification relies on what may be called a limited justificatory pluralism, that accepts and integrates all those theoretical and lived justifications as well as practices of democratic toleration as political as well as educational resources, that are *not in conflict* with the basic values of liberal democracies.

The idea of a combination of a democratic and a liberal perfectionist justification is certainly not without internal tensions, especially with respect to conflicts of toleration between parents, communities, and the liberal state. It is, however, the only justificatory option that is both educationally *and* politically sound. One of the reasons for this is that these tensions to a certain extent are internal to a purely procedural notion of democracy itself. The success of contemporary right-wing parties, for instance, cannot plausibly be described as per se *anti*democratic, at least as long it is based on purely democratic strategies. The agendas put forward by these parties, however, are in many cases both illiberal and intolerant. It is one of the central tasks of the educational system in liberal democracies to counteract these intolerant tendencies, also in those cases when they are still in line with basic procedural features of the democratic game. A plausible notion of educating for tolerance in liberal democracies therefore needs a firm normative – liberal-perfectionist *and* democratic – foundation not only in order to define where the limits of political, moral, and educational pluralism are to be drawn, but also to help provide the educational and sociopolitical preconditions necessary to effectively defend liberal democracies against its intolerant and illiberal enemies.

In the remainder of this section, neither the concrete educational implications of a democratic and liberal perfectionist justification of education for tolerance will be spelled out (for instance, with respect to parents' rights or teaching controversial issues) nor will there be a reconstruction of the complex debate between liberal perfectionists and political liberals about the legitimacy of particular aims of education (Drerup 2018). Instead the focus will be placed on one of the central challenges for a theory of education for tolerance in nonideal circumstances and conditions: This challenge is rooted in the sometimes rather scholastic and also naive tendencies in the debate about toleration in political philosophy and political philosophy of education. While this in many cases primarily normative debate often assumes ideal conditions of toleration, including ideal political persons as well as ideal educators and students, it seldom takes into account how democratic education for tolerance is actually practiced in the first place (Diehm 2010) and the discrepancy between the sometimes rather lofty discourse about the ideal educational aims of democratic education and the empirical realities and its effects (see, for instance: Brennan 2016). Thus, not only the dark sides of tolerance discourses – such as exclusion and the reproduction of stereotypes as well as power hierarchies (Brown 2006; Drerup 2019) are largely ignored, but also the problem that – in real political and educational life – democratic and citizenship education in many cases itself is the problem in the sense that it reproduces intolerance, discrimination, and inequality (Merry 2020). The simple linear formula: more and better liberal democratic education = more and better liberal democratic capacities, dispositions, and virtues = more and better liberal democracies, in some cases just does not work out. In order to adequately reconstruct the many problems associated with education for tolerance, we need to cultivate a more realistic and not just normative take on the relevant issues as well as certain openness to differing methodological paradigms (such as poststructuralist power-theoretical critiques and systematic normative approaches). Each of these paradigms has its particular strengths and weaknesses – for instance, with respect to issues concerning normative justification or to the reconstruction of power dynamics, together they may help us to better us to develop a better, more realistic and fine-grained understanding of the different facets and dimensions of educating for tolerance in the liberal democracies we live in.

Conclusion

This chapter attempted to provide theoretical and practical answers and solutions to three general questions and problems of the theory and practice of educating for tolerance. These included: How can education for tolerance be adequately conceptualized theoretically? How is education for tolerance possible? How should education for tolerance be justified? My answers to these questions raised some of the major topics and factors which are of relevance in interpreting the differing and often ambivalent roles of toleration in educational contexts.

In conclusion, three general desiderata for philosophical research on tolerance education can be mentioned: The first desideratum is a closer collaboration and dialogue between theoretical approaches to tolerance education and practical programs of educating for tolerance. In some cases, the latter, for instance, operate with notions and "objects" of toleration, that are – from perspective of the philosophical debate – highly problematic. At the same time, it often remains rather unclear what exactly may follow from ideal-theoretical notions of toleration in practical terms. Second, theoretical approaches to toleration and empirical tolerance research need to be integrated in a better and more fine-grained way. To better understand the reasons and mechanisms which cause intolerance and enable tolerance in and beyond educational contexts is a challenge and task that can only be successfully dealt with based on interdisciplinary cooperation (e.g., between psychology, educational science and theory, political philosophy and sociology). Last but not least, more generalist approaches to education for tolerance should be complemented with empirically informed case studies on conflicts of toleration, which can help us to understand the sociopolitical dynamics of education for tolerance under real world and not just ideal-theoretical conditions.

References

Allen D (2004) Talking to strangers. The University of Chicago Press, Chicago/London
Baehr J (2013) Educating for intellectual virtues: from theory to practice. J Philos Educ 47(2): 248–262
Balint P (2017) Respecting toleration. Oxford University Press, Oxford
Baumann Z (2016) Strangers at our door. Polity, Cambridge
Bessone M (2013) Will the real tolerant racist please stand up? J Appl Philos 30(3):209–223
Brennan J (2016) Against democracy. Princeton University Press, Princeton
Brown W (2006) Regulating aversion. Tolerance in the age of identity and empire. Princeton University Press, Princeton
Brownstein M (2015) Implicit bias. In: Zalta E (ed) The Stanford encyclopedia of philosophy. https://plato.stanford.edu/entries/implicit-bias/. Accessed 28 May 2017
Brumlik M (2018) Demokratie und Bildung. Neofelis Verlag, Berlin

Callan E (2011) When to shut students up: civility, silencing, and free speech. Theory Res Educ 9:3–22
Cassam Q (2019) Vices of the mind. Oxford University Press, Oxford
Cohen AJ (2018) Toleration and freedom from harm: liberalism reconceived. Routledge, New York/Oxon
Culp J (2019) Democratic education in a globalized world. Routledge, New York
Diehm I (2010) Anerkennung ist nicht Toleranz. In: Schäfer A, Thompson C (eds) Anerkennung. Schöningh, Paderborn, pp 119–139
Drerup J (2018) Education for democratic tolerance, respect and the limits of political liberalism. J Philos Educ 52(3):515–532
Drerup J (2019) Education, epistemic virtues, and the power of toleration. Crit Rev Int Soc Pol Phil. https://doi.org/10.1080/13698230.2019.1616883
Drerup J (2020) Erziehung, Intoleranz und die Politik der Angst. Zum pädagogischen Umgang mit politischen Emotionen. In: Fischer C, Platzbecker P (eds) Erziehung – Werte – Haltungen. Schule als Lernort für eine offene Gesellschaft. Waxmann, Münster, pp 39–58
Emcke C (2019) Against hate (trans: Crawford T). Polity, Cambridge
Forst R (2013) Toleration in conflict. Cambridge University Press, Cambridge
Forst R (2015) Toleranz und Fortschritt. Franz Steiner Verlag, Stuttgart
Galeotti E (2002) Toleration as recognition. Cambridge University Press, Cambridge
Galeotti E (2015) Toleration out of conflicts. Review of Rainer Forst's 'toleration in conflict'. Eur J Polit Theo 14:246–255
Gardner P (2001) Tolerance and education. In: Horton J (ed) Liberalism, multi-culturalism and toleration. Palgrave, Houndmills/Basingstoke, pp 83–103
Hand M (2008) What should we teach as controversial? A defense of the epistemic criterion. Educ Theory 58(2):213–228
Hastedt H (2005) Gefühle: Philosophische Bemerkungen. Reclam, Stuttgart
Heidenreich F (2019) Die emotionalen Wirkungen politischer Entscheidungen – Von der naiven zur reflektierten Gefühlspolitik. In: Besand A et al (eds) Politische Bildung mit Gefühl. bpb, Bonn, pp 26–42
Hess D, McAvoy P (2015) The political classroom. Routledge, New York/London
Heyd D (2008) Is toleration a political virtue? In: Williams M, Waldron J (eds) Toleration and its limits. New York University Press, New York, pp 171–194
Horton J (1996) Toleration as a virtue. In: Heyd D (ed) Toleration. An elusive virtue. Princeton University Press, Princeton, pp 28–24
Jones PN (2010) Toleration and recognition: what should we teach? Educ Philos Theory 42(1):38–56
Khomyakov M (2013) Toleration and respect: historical instances and current problems. Eur J Polit Theo 12(3):223–239
König P (2019) The simplicity of toleration. Crit Rev Int Soc Pol Phil. https://doi.org/10.1080/13698230.2019.1616877
Leggewie C (2017) Anti-Europäer. Bundeszentrale für politische Bildung, Bonn
Levitsky S, Ziblatt D (2018) How democracies die. Crown, New York
Macleod C (2010) Toleration, children and education. Educ Philos Theory 42(1):9–21
Mather D, Tranby E (2014) New dimensions of tolerance: a case for a broader, categorical approach. Sociol Sci 1:512–531
Maxwell B, Reichenbach R (2007) Educating moral emotions: a praxeological analysis. Stud Philos Educ 26(2):147–163
Merry M (2020) Can schools teach citizenship? Discourse: Studies in the Cultural Politics of Education 41:124–138
Nederman C (2012) Toleration in a new key: historical and global perspectives. In: Edyvane D, Matravers M (eds) Toleration re-examined. Routledge, New York, pp 69–82
Nussbaum M (2011) Perfectionist liberalism and political liberalism. Philos Public Aff 39(1):3–45
Nussbaum M (2013) The new religious intolerance. Harvard University Press, Cambridge
Nussbaum M (2015) Political emotions. Harvard University Press, Cambridge
Nussbaum M (2018) The monarchy of fear. Simson & Schuster, New York

Owen D (2011) Must the tolerant person have a sense of humour? On the structure of tolerance as a virtue. Crit Rev Int Soc Pol Phil 14:385–403
Peterson A (2019) Civility and democratic education. Springer, Singapore
Rapp V (2014) Toleranz gegenuber Immigranten in der Schweiz und in Europa. Springer VS, Wiesbaden
Rawls J (2005) Political liberalism. Columbia University Press, New York
Reichenbach R (2018) Ethik der Bildung und Erziehung. utb, Leiden
Sardoc M (ed) (2010) Toleration, respect and recognition in education. Wiley-Blackwell, Chichester
Sunstein C (2005) Laws of fear: beyond the precautionary principle. Cambridge University Press, Cambridge
Tenorth HE (2002) Apologie einer paradoxen Technologie – über Status und Funktion von 'Pädagogik. In: Böhm W (ed) Pädagogik- Wozu und für wen? Cotta, Stuttgart, pp 70–99
Van Prooijen JW (2017) Why education predicts decreased belief in conspiracy theory. Appl Cogn Psychol 31:50–58
Vogt P (1997) Tolerance and education. Sage, Thousand Oaks/London/New Delhi
Walzer M (1997) On toleration. Yale University Press, New Haven/London
Warnock M (2001) The education of the emotions. In: Hirst P, White P (Hrsg.): Philosophy of Education, Vol. II, Education and Human Being (p. 211–223). London & New York
Williams B (1996) Toleration: an impossible virtue? In: Heyd D (ed) Toleration. An elusive virtue. Princeton University Press, Princeton, pp 18–27
Witenberg R (2019) The psychology of tolerance. Springer, Singapore
Yacek D, Hehemann Y (2019) Erziehung zum Wutbürger. https://www.praefaktisch.de/bildung/erziehung-zum-wutbuerger/. Accessed 23 Oct 2019

Toleration, Liberal Education, and the Accommodation of Diversity

Ole Henrik Borchgrevink Hansen

Contents

Introduction	952
Promoting Classical Toleration in Liberal Education	954
Is Classical Toleration Viable?	955
Promoting Modern Toleration in Liberal Education	960
Modern Toleration and Assimilative Pressure	962
Pedagogical Toleration: Combining Classical and Modern Toleration in Liberal Education	964
References	967

Abstract

Toleration is a central value in liberalism, and it is widely regarded as important for the accommodation of diversity. For these reasons, promoting toleration is also an integral part of liberal education. What such promotion should entail, however, is not entirely clear. A distinction is made between *classical toleration*, which requires that someone puts up with or endures what one disagrees with, and *modern toleration*, which conceives toleration more in terms of being open-minded, unprejudiced, or appreciative towards diversity. As objectives for liberal education, both classical and modern toleration face challenges with respect to the accommodation of diversity: promoting classical toleration is an insufficient strategy for the purpose of accommodating diversity, because it falls short when it comes to changing pupil's attitudes. Promoting modern toleration is a possible answer that challenge, but has also problems of its own, mainly related to the risk of exercising assimilative pressure on individuals and groups who do not fit a liberal mold. This chapter discusses whether a careful and dynamic *combination* of these strategies – a *pedagogical toleration* – could be more conducive to the liberal goal of accommodating diversity. This dual strategy may help to change

O. H. B. Hansen (✉)
Ostfold University College, School of Education, Ostfold, Norway
e-mail: ohh@hiof.no

© The Author(s), under exclusive licence to Springer Nature Switzerland AG 2022
M. Sardoč (ed.), *The Palgrave Handbook of Toleration*,
https://doi.org/10.1007/978-3-030-42121-2_3

pupils' attitudes towards different kinds of diversity while also being attentive to those pupils and parents, who remain skeptical towards a liberal agenda, whether they are multiculturalism skeptics or autonomy skeptics. The crucial issue is how to *balance* this combination of the promotion of classical and modern toleration in order to achieve that.

Keywords

Classical toleration · Modern toleration · Pedagogical toleration · Liberal education · Liberalism · Diversity

Introduction

Liberal democracies are diverse in a multitude of ways. Citizens hold a variety of conceptions of the good, both religious and secular. They have different ethnic, cultural, and linguistic origins and identities. They subscribe to different value systems, have different sexual orientations, and possess varied political or ideological preferences. These distinctions are the background for the important question of how liberal democracies can best accommodate diversity. This question is not in any way new but rather one that has occupied sociologists and political philosophers for generations, from Alexis de Tocqueville to Alfred Tönnies, John Rawls, and Charles Taylor. It is the core of the multiculturalism debate, and it remains highly topical within the liberal tradition today. The ambition of accommodating diversity is a constitutive element of liberalism and liberal theory because diversity is a consequence of freedom of thought and the value given to autonomous choice. Although diversity is a long-lasting and permanent feature of a liberal democracy, it is fair to say that the issue of accommodating diversity has seen increased public attention in Western liberal societies as a result of immigration.

One could argue that toleration (I do not distinguish between "tolerance" and "toleration." Although some scholars make such a distinction, there is no consensus on its substance) plays an important role in accommodating all kinds of diversity in the sense that a tolerant society can be seen as an accommodating one, in other words, a society in which people in general are (relatively) free to live the life of their choosing. This accommodative characteristic or attribute of toleration is a central commitment and fundamental value in liberal theory, and it is why toleration has been called the "substantial heart of liberalism" (Hampton 1989: 802). The concept of toleration initially came into play in the aftermath of the wars of religion waged between Catholics and Protestants in Europe during the sixteenth and seventeenth centuries, and it is in many ways part of the historical DNA of liberalism. Toleration was then a *state strategy* for coping with a conflict between these religious groups. Pierre Bayle's *Commentaire Philosophique* (1686), Locke's *A Letter Concerning Toleration* (1689), and later Mill's *On Liberty* (1859) offer universal arguments for toleration and are important contributions to the history of liberal toleration. The immense importance of the birth of this idea in modern history and as an important value in response to diversity, not only in relation to different Christian denominations but for other forms of diversity, should not be underestimated.

A tolerant, accommodative society requires not only a tolerant liberal state – in which state institutions and policies accept a wide variety of beliefs, practices, and ways of life – but also tolerant citizens who contribute to a culture of toleration in attitude and behavior. The liberal state has several strategies available for fostering citizens' toleration, but probably the most important one is education. Education plays a fundamental role in upholding democracy. This may be referred to as a *liberal education* in the sense that it promotes liberal values as one of its main objectives. Even if there is disagreement within the liberal tradition about how core liberal values should be interpreted, ordered, and balanced and regarding how far they should reach, liberally minded educational scholars all include freedom or individual liberty, autonomy, equal respect, basic civil and political rights, rationality, critical thinking skills, and toleration for diversity in the definition of a liberal education (Gutmann 1995; Rawls 1996; Galston 2002). That the promotion of toleration is considered an important and integral part of liberal education is reflected not only in scholarly writings (Castiglione and McKinnon 2001; Galston 2002) but also in national curriculum plans and international educational policy documents (Advisory Group to the Secretary of State for Education and Employment 1998; Parliamentary Assembly of the Council of Europe 2005; ODIHR Advisory Council of Experts on Freedom of Religion or Belief 2007; Council of Europe 2014), in central human rights documents (UNESCO 1995), and in empirical surveys of pupils (Bertram-Troost and Miedema 2009).

Given this prominent place of toleration in liberal education, an interesting question is how liberal education should go about promoting it. The answer is not so straightforward. Recall that historically – and in the seminal writings mentioned above – the focus has been primarily on the *political dimension* of toleration, which pertains to what degree the state accepts or restrains citizens' ways of life, an aspect which is often associated with negative freedom. However, when the promotion of toleration in liberal education is the issue, it is rather the *personal dimension* (i.e., toleration as an individual virtue) that is the focus. These dimensions are in many contexts merged, although it would be more expedient to keep them apart. The political and personal dimensions of toleration are admittedly similar in the sense that toleration in both cases concerns how an agent should relate to and act in situations of difference or disagreement. As mentioned above, they are also connected in the sense that they are both needed for a tolerant, accommodative society. The relevant difference, however, is that the agent of toleration is either an individual – the pupil – or a collective entity, such as the state, government, or school. This difference is important because the aspect of virtue associated with personal toleration is a less central attribute to political toleration. Even if a liberal democratic state is also based upon a set of values, the state or the school does not psychologically embody views, sympathies, and antipathies; likes and dislikes; or agreements and disagreements in the same way that individuals do. Personal toleration is very much centered on how individuals, including pupils, deal with such emotions, attitudes, and opinions, whereas the tolerant liberal state is preoccupied with policy making and the effect of such policies, whether these aim for either some kind of neutrality towards different views and practices or different kinds of politics of recognition.

Despite the status of toleration as a prominent educational objective, what it means to promote it is far from clear. This is partly related to the fact that there are several different understandings of toleration, not only among scholars but also in everyday understanding and definitely within the educational realm and among teachers. It could be argued that *classical toleration*, which at least until recently has enjoyed academic consensus and which requires only that someone puts up with or endures what one disagrees with, is problematic in an educational context, partly because it makes it difficult to uphold toleration as a virtue and partly because it is not the appropriate educational response in light of the objective to accommodate diversity. An alternative that has gained ground lately, which I call *modern toleration*, argues that toleration should be conceived more in terms of being open-minded, unprejudiced, or appreciative towards diversity (Hansen 2013). However, this understanding of toleration also faces challenges as a liberal educational objective. This chapter therefore aims to discuss which understanding of toleration should be promoted in liberal education in light of the accommodation of diversity.

This chapter first presents a plausible operationalization of classical toleration as a goal for an accommodative liberal education as well as three challenges to this operationalization. Second follows a discussion of these challenges, which shows that only one of them can be supported, namely, that the promotion of classical toleration is an insufficient strategy for liberal education in terms of accommodating diversity. Third, the promotion of modern toleration is presented as a potential answer to this challenge. Fourth, a critical discussion of modern toleration in light of the liberal goal of accommodating diversity demonstrates that it only partially counters the insufficiency challenge and has problems of its own, mainly related to the risk of exercising assimilative pressure on individuals and groups who are skeptical of a liberal agenda. Finally, a careful and dynamic combination of both classical and modern toleration – a *pedagogical toleration* – is suggested as a viable, although challenging, promotion of toleration in liberal education. The main reason is that liberal education is not only concerned with the formation of the individual pupil but also, as a representative of the liberal state, with the accommodation of real diversity in society as a whole, which includes concerns for societal stability. With this political perspective in mind, a liberal education mindful of its legacy should promote toleration in a way that strikes a balance between promoting attitudes of open-mindedness, non-prejudice, and appreciation for diversity while at the same time respecting and including the autonomy of those pupils and parents who do not fit a progressive liberal mold.

Promoting Classical Toleration in Liberal Education

In order to discuss whether the promotion of classical toleration is suited to accommodate diversity in liberal education, we must come to terms with what it means to *promote* this particular virtue. A classical liberal conceptualization of toleration implies that toleration should be regarded as reasoned acceptance of or noninterference with what is found objectionable (Horton 1996: 28). This understanding identifies two conditions, sometimes referred to as the double condition: the *objection condition*, expressing dislike or disapproval, and the *condition of noninterference* or *acceptance*, requiring the tolerator to not interfere with the object of toleration (King 1976: 37). This does not mean that the reasons for objection are eliminated but that they are trumped in a given context because the reasons for noninterference are considered stronger (Forst 2008: 79). Toleration is thus both an *attitude* and a requirement for a certain *behavior*. The object of toleration may refer to, for instance, a person's or group's behavior, values, opinions, religious, or cultural practices or the like. Accordingly, one could say that a person is tolerant if he or she disapproves of pornography being sold in stores but does not think it should be banned. Likewise, a person who disapproves of the practice by some Muslim women of wearing hijab but who does not think it right to interfere – either personally or through state restrictions – would be considered tolerant. Tolerance has special value because these acts of toleration are based upon reasons which, for the tolerator, trump his or her own objections. This classical understanding preserves the original linguistic meaning of toleration as a burden, which is how it has historically been viewed in the liberal tradition (Nehushtan 2007: 231–232). There seemed to be, at least until recently, widespread academic orthodoxy about this understanding (King 1976: 44–54; Horton 1991: 521; Raphael 1988: 139). Based on this classical understanding of toleration, a plausible operationalization of the concept in liberal education implies the following: schools teach pupils that in some cases, there are cogent reasons for leaving others alone or not trying to prevent them from behaving in a certain manner or from holding a certain opinion, even if one objects, that is, disapproves of or dislikes that behavior or opinion. This is a deliberately minimal operationalization but sufficient as a starting point.

Is Classical Toleration Viable?

When operationalized as an educational objective, classical toleration faces both conceptual and substantial challenges, which, in sum, question whether the promotion of classical toleration is in fact the pertinent response given the fact of diversity. These challenges concern *agency*, *scope*, and *appropriateness*.

The *agency challenge* is conceptual and relates to the nature of the tolerator: how does liberal education understand pupils (who are encouraged to be tolerant)? Since classical toleration requires a personal objection, the classroom situation is problematic simply because pupils do not share the same dislikes or disapprovals. From a strict definition of classical toleration, it follows that there is also a practical problem of operationalizing the promotion of classical toleration, namely, how to identify the objections pupils may or may not have on different issues. A reasonable solution is to acknowledge that proper toleration only takes place if pupils object to what public education promotes toleration for, but not requiring liberal education to identify a personal objection in each pupil in order to engage in the promotion of classical toleration. It is, in other words, sufficient for promoting classical toleration that some of the pupils find the object of toleration disagreeable.

The second challenge is substantial and concerns the *scope* of classical toleration. One could argue that promoting in pupils the disposition to not interfere with the object that they disagree with implies that liberal education implicitly accepts that pupils have objections that are not conducive to the accommodation of diversity, such as racist or discriminatory attitudes. Even though most would argue that not interfering is better than interfering given a racist person's disposition, it nevertheless seems paradoxical to call this person tolerant and to call the promotion of restraint in such a person for promoting toleration. This problem is often referred to as the paradox of the *tolerant racist* (Horton 1996; McKinnon 2006). In order to deal with this paradox, one needs to take a closer look at the scope of the promotion of toleration. In the above suggestion for the operationalization of classical toleration, it was proposed that such promotion meant that liberal education should teach pupils that in *some cases* it is better to leave others alone. The qualification "in some cases," however, begs the question of which cases and what distinguishes these cases from *other cases* where toleration is not required or should not be promoted. In order to delineate the scope of toleration, these "other cases" should be divided into two groups.

First, there are cases where toleration is not required because pupils should not object at all. Forst (2008: 79) is right in pointing out that toleration is a "normatively dependent concept [...] in need of other independent resources in order to gain a certain content and substance – and in order to be something good at all." How the objection more specifically should be understood is contested, and coming to grips with the objection condition is particularly important in an educational context. This means that liberal education needs to justify and specify what is permissible for pupils to object to by restricting the objection condition, that is, by restricting what types of objections pupils may permissibly have while still being considered tolerant. Such restriction is unavoidable in liberal education, as "any inculcation of the virtue of toleration [...] must attend to the questions about what it is reasonable to object to" (Horton 1996: 37). The hard question is where the limit of such restriction should be placed. It seems that the main dilemma for liberalism and the accommodation of diversity is to what extent liberal education should accept pupils' objections when these display illiberal attitudes that may be counterproductive for the accommodation of diversity, without attempting to change these attitudes. This issue will be revisited in the final chapter.

Second, there are cases where toleration is not required because the potential object of toleration should in fact not be tolerated (i.e., it is beyond the limits of toleration). In other words, some things cannot be tolerated because they should not be permitted (Horton 1996: 33). It is generally agreed that if the promotion of toleration is considered a valuable objective for liberal education, the *limits of toleration* also need to be identified. Theoretically, as Forst (2007: 1) points out, the limits of tolerance are to be found when the reasons for rejection are stronger than the reasons for acceptance or noninterference. Liberal education should, for instance, neither accept nor promote toleration for activities or opinions which are either clearly hateful and disrespectful, such as racism, or which threaten the security and stability of the democratic order, such as offensive illiberal groups (terror organizations) or individuals that encourage violence as a means to resolve conflict. Most cases, however, are not that clear-cut but rather belong in a gray area, for instance, including persons and groups fiercely opposed to religion (either in general or one in particular), who take issue with immigration from non-Western countries or who think that same-sex marriages should be prohibited. Although any attempt to identify the limits of toleration is bound to be controversial within a liberal framework, it is clear that liberal education nevertheless *must* place some limits on toleration if it is to be considered an ideal. Negotiating these limits is not only inherent to the public discourse in a liberal democracy but also relevant for a liberal education classroom. It is important, however, that the limits should not be understood with excessive touchiness that would lead to core liberal values, such as freedom of speech or religion, being threatened.

The third challenge concerns *inappropriateness*. Even though the operationalization of classical toleration in liberal education involves both restricting permissible objections and identifying certain limits of toleration, one could still argue that this is not what is needed in order to accommodate diversity – and thus that it is an inappropriate response. Two versions of this argument can be articulated: one claiming classical toleration is inappropriate because it is condescending and the other that it is inappropriate because it is insufficient.

The *condescending argument*, as described by Creppell (2003: 5) and Forst (2013), regards classical toleration as representing an attitude in which what is tolerated is considered to be something of lesser value. This is perhaps why no one really wants to be tolerated (Oberdiek 2001: 19), and it fits with Tariq Ramadan's (2010: 46–47) point that toleration is "charity on the part of the powerful." A related perspective is also expressed by Michael Walzer (1997: 52), who claims that "to tolerate someone is an act of power; to be tolerated is an acceptance of weakness." From this perspective, classical toleration contradicts and undermines the liberal value of equal respect and recognition. The condescending argument gains strength and is especially problematic if combined with asymmetrical power relations between the majority and minorities. If it is the majority – backed by a liberal-oriented value basis – who as tolerators assume a hegemonic position and who set the premise for what should be tolerated or not, minorities assume the unattractive and submissive position of being receivers. Promoting classical toleration in this context thus becomes a prerogative of the powerful majority and may reinforce an asymmetry of powers between majority and minority (Creppell 2003: 5).

The *insufficiency argument* shares the view with the condescending argument that classical toleration is an inappropriate response to diversity because it does not offer a path to increased understanding of others (Oberdiek 2001; Afdal 2010: 11) and hence does not contribute to an inclusive and accommodative society. Unlike the condescending argument, this argument concedes that classical toleration may manage to observe and practice certain limits of toleration and restrict the objection condition so as to uphold toleration as a virtue but that it nevertheless would be inclined to accept and indirectly condone disapproval or dislike for other people's opinions or attitudes that an accommodating society would be better off without. In diverse societies, mere *forbearance* is not enough, and liberal education therefore requires a more ambitious strategy. If liberal education is to contribute to accommodating diversity, classical toleration would be insufficient and only of limited assistance (Creppell 2003: 5; Brown 2001).

The condescending argument, although addressing an important issue, cannot be sustained because it relies upon both a simplistic operationalization of classical toleration and a too restricted or static understanding of the power relations in the classroom.

First, it is *simplistic* because it overlooks that the promotion of classical toleration is in fact a particular value-based activity and not a hands-off call for the mere endurance of others. Recall that classical toleration was characterized by reasoned restraint against what you find to be objectionable, and the reasoned restraint implied that the objections were trumped in a given context because the reasons for non-interference were considered stronger (Forst 2008: 79). Such reasons do not automatically neutralize the condescending argument. That depends on the nature of the reasons. According to Castiglione and McKinnon (2001: 224–225), there seems to be a consensus in the technical literature on toleration that respect for persons – and not skeptical, pragmatic, or instrumental modus vivendi forms of justification – is the appropriate reason for toleration. According to this view, which is solidly grounded in liberalism, only reasons that are associated with respect can make toleration a moral virtue, and it is this justification based on respect which sets classical toleration apart from condescending. There is, in other words, a kind of "higher principle" (Galeotti 2001: 275) involved. This does not mean that all views or beliefs are equally worthy of respect. It does mean, however, that our fellow citizens, through their capacity of working out a coherent view of the world (Larmore 1987: 64), have a moral right to choose their own conception of the good that, as long as they do not harm others, should be respected. In an educational context, this means that teachers both provide the pupils with reasons for why, in these cases, acceptance is more meritorious than interference and encourage discussion and reflection upon the legitimacy of these reasons. This is the most plausible operationalization of classical toleration in liberal education.

Second, and in prolongation of the first point, the condescending argument is simplistic because a plausible operationalization of the virtue of classical toleration *restricts* what types of objections pupils may permissibly have while still being considered tolerant. Finally, it is simplistic because promoting the virtue of classical toleration also observes limits, in the sense that there are certain values, views, and behaviors that liberal education cannot promote a toleration of. In line with the preferred liberal justification for toleration, it seems reasonable that the qualifications for the promotion of classical toleration – concerning both acceptable disagreements and the limits of toleration – should be connected to *respect for others' autonomy*. This implies that as long as someone's objections do not disrespect others, they may be considered tolerant if they refrain from interfering; objections which do not disrespect persons are, in other words, compatible with the virtue of toleration. This also implies that public education *may* promote toleration for people's opinions, values, and religious or cultural practices as long as these are not disrespectful, thus going beyond the limits of toleration. What is considered disrespectful or not is something liberal education needs to deal with. Pinpointing this limit and fleshing out all practical implications of it are beyond the scope of this chapter, since that would assume the existence of some form of universal or timeless (liberal) principle or weighing scale. This is rather an issue liberal education needs to revisit on a regular basis. A reasonable suggestion, however, is that the determining factor should involve a requirement of *psychological compatibility*. This means that in order to be not disrespectful, one's opinions or practices need to be psychologically compatible with respect for others' autonomy. In light of this, it follows that those who object to other races, even if these objections are tentatively backed by a set of arguments, however flawed (for instance, of an evolutionary nature), cannot be said to properly respect others, as they are not psychologically compatible with respect. Persons who, on the other hand, object to the view that living autonomous lives is necessary for human well-being or those who have objections towards religion (for instance, specific religious clothing restrictions) *can* be candidates for being tolerant. This is a deliberately wide qualification mainly geared towards establishing criteria for excluding disrespectful opinions or practices but a necessary one if classical toleration is to remain a viable educational objective for liberal education. This qualification nevertheless defuses the condescending argument, since condescension is not compatible with respect.

Finally, the condescending argument rests upon a too restricted or static understanding of the power relations in liberal classrooms. It seems to rely on the view that there is a clear vertical relation between the tolerating powerful majority and the minority being tolerated. This is, however, an inaccurate and unconvincing description in many liberal classrooms today. The power relations in the classroom are not simply a well-defined hegemonic majority tolerating inferior minority groups; they are complex, differentiated, ambiguous, and shifting. For instance, the majority of pupils in a public school classroom in a liberal democracy may formally belong to a Christian community. The value basis may also have some sort of Christian anchoring or in other ways favor a particular religious tradition in the legislation. This is the case in many European countries. At the same time, classrooms in these very same countries may be dominated by liberal, progressive values, and research suggests that in several countries, there is a dominating and hegemonic anti-Christian secularistic discourse in such classrooms (Flensner 2015; Lidh 2016). This is not to say that the power relations do not exist but that they play out in a more complex fashion than what is assumed, which does not automatically underpin the condescending argument.

The *insufficiency argument*, on the other hand, is more convincing. It seems as if classical toleration alone is not able to provide sufficient educational resources to accommodate diversity. It also seems intuitively true that if liberal education is able to change pupils' attitudes to make them more open-minded, unprejudiced, and appreciative of diversity, this must be conducive to the accommodation of such diversity. It would therefore be a disproportionately defensive strategy if liberal education were prohibited from using its pedagogical and persuasive powers in this direction. The question, as discussed later, is of course how far these coercive powers should reach.

Promoting Modern Toleration in Liberal Education

In light of this shortcoming and the aspiration to accommodate diversity, one could argue that toleration proper should be about having the right attitude to recognize and appreciate diversity rather than merely enduring it. Therefore, a liberal education should seek to foster these attitudes in pupils. This understanding of toleration, referred to as modern toleration, requires a reinterpretation of the classical understanding. The proponents of this understanding find the objection condition to be too restrictive in conditions of diversity and instead advocate a broader and more inclusive concept of toleration, wherein an objection condition is not required. Creppell (2003: 3), for instance, thinks there is no need for strong disapproval in order to talk about toleration. Afdal (2006, 2010) similarly claims that in public education, the conditions of dislike or disapproval are too strong and defend the weaker claim that the basic condition of toleration should be conceived of as one of difference. By removing the core of the classical concept of toleration – as a virtue of reasoned restraint towards what one finds objectionable – toleration is described along the lines of being open-minded, unprejudiced, or even appreciative of what is different, whether this concerns other religions, cultures, practices, ethnicities, values, beliefs, or sexual orientations. This understanding corresponds roughly with Michael Waltzer's (1997: 11) fourth definition of toleration as "openness to others; curiosity; perhaps even respect, a willingness to listen and learn," and it is implied in both Scanlon (2003: 192) and Gardner (1993: 88).

This simple construction of toleration in fact contains a *spectrum* of somewhat different characteristics that share the same distinctive feature of not requiring an objection condition. Modern toleration has no lack of support in temporary discourse. In common usage, both in the field of human rights and in an educational context, this understanding often seems to be the one that is implied. In common usage, for instance, the claim that young people in general are more tolerant than old people would not be understood by most people as "young people object to more, but manage to restraint themselves" but rather that "young people object to less than older people in terms of religious, cultural or other differences." Similarly, the description of a tolerant community or society in general parlance refers to a community wherein people have few objections (Balint 2017: 5). In Article 1 of the UNESCO Declaration of Principles of Tolerance (1995), for instance, tolerance is explained as "respect, acceptance, and appreciation of the rich diversity of our world's cultures." This understanding identifies toleration with multiculturalism in a normative sense, containing a clear resource-oriented and positive evaluation of plurality. In an educational context, this modern understanding of toleration is often implicit when describing schools' active encouragement of pupils to become open-minded towards and even to gain positive regard for other peoples, opinions, values, behaviors, or other differences, as we have seen. This is supported by empirical findings; for instance, Afdal (2006) shows that even if toleration among teachers contains a multitude of meanings and is conceptualized as a plastic concept (i.e., changing meaning with context). This means that the concept is used both thin and thick, negative and positive, and interestingly, as a double and single construct, that is, both with the objection condition and without it. There is, however, a development towards a thicker, more positive, and single constructed conception, where toleration goes from being a last resort to a key method of handling differences (Afdal 2006: 241–242). Afdal's material also suggests that a tolerant teacher is largely synonymous with excellence, professionalism, and a caring attitude.

Modern toleration, understood as an attitude of open-mindedness, being unprejudiced, and appreciating different forms of diversity, reflects highly important liberal values in the sense that these attitudes contribute to a culture of toleration and the accommodation of diversity. More specifically, promoting toleration by stimulating these attitudes can facilitate the identification of different minority groups who may be victims of prejudice, whether they be Muslims, Jehovah's Witnesses, people of African descent, or LGBT people. It also helps to improve mutual understanding, thus contributing to a culture of toleration. This argument can be seen as an extension of the condescending argument in the sense that it is based on the view that classical toleration stands in the way of developing the vital attitudes of respect and recognition because it somehow sees the tolerated ones as inferior. Instead, as Waltzer (1997: 52) expresses, "we should aim at something better that this combination, something beyond toleration, something like mutual respect." Or, from a critical multicultural perspective: "the demand for recognition goes far beyond the familiar plea for toleration" (Parekh 2000: 1). By recognizing that not one single religion or culture holds the truth, we may come to recognize the value of different cultures as vehicles for living meaningful lives. Amy Gutmann (1995: 561) has a similar point when she argues that toleration is not enough to accommodate diversity but that mutual respect among citizens is also a fundamental prerequisite for a just liberal order. Several proponents of modern toleration also apply a historical perspective, and a prevailing opinion seems to be that while classical tolerance has undoubtedly been of vital importance for the development of a democratic society in early modern Europe, in modern pluralistic societies, the demand for toleration in the classical sense is no longer called for, since many of those who previously needed to be defended from persecution are now protected by rights and the rule of law. Classical toleration is therefore best characterized as an "interim value" (Williams 1996: 26) and in a modern pluralist society, "the demand for recognition supersedes that of toleration" (Heyd 2008: 175).

In pedagogical practices, promoting toleration in this modern sense means that the focus of the teacher and the school shifts from the issue of *what the pupil should do* when he or she disapproves of something or someone to *what attitudes/dispositions pupils should have* when facing different types of diversity. Instead of merely promoting restraint, the main task for teachers becomes teaching pupils to be more open, unprejudiced, and appreciative. This shift can be described as a transition from deliberation to disposition, in Gardner's (1993: 90) terminology. It also goes hand in hand with a core idea of pedagogics – that of transformation – in the sense that it allows for and encourages the use of a number of pedagogical tools and strategies to change pupils' attitudes towards what is different, which may be beneficial for the accommodation of diversity. A part of this involves exposure to and teaching about different cultures, religions, worldviews, and ways of life in an adequate and non-stereotyped manner and with regard to internal diversity and individual differences. That toleration is gained through understanding of others is emphasized in Signposts (2014: 15), which is the Council of Europe's recommendations for policy and practice for teaching about religions and nonreligious worldviews in intercultural education. This form of toleration also resonates with the general social-psychological idea that increased contact between different cultural groups reduces tension, which is very much in line with the *intergroup contact theory* (Pettigrew et al. 2011).

Modern Toleration and Assimilative Pressure

Despite these advantages of promoting modern toleration, the critical question is whether this reinterpretation of toleration alone is sufficient for liberal education to accommodate *real* diversity, thus making classical toleration obsolete. It cannot be denied that there are challenges with respect to the accommodation of diversity, the main one being the potentially assimilative effects such promotion can have. When liberal education promotes toleration as open-mindedness, being unprejudiced, and appreciating diversity, toleration inevitably assumes substantial and normative status because it implies that pupils *should* have these positive attitudes towards particular cultural practices, religions, or people with other sexual orientations. There is no denying that this conveys the view that having these attitudes is synonymous with what it means to be a progressive liberal citizen. In fact, it could be argued that because of its attitude-changing ambitions, a concept of toleration without an objection condition is more restricted in terms of what kinds of diversity it can promote toleration for than the classical version, and hence it is more susceptible to or inclined to having an assimilative effect. When operationalized, the promotion of modern toleration may become too "narrowly liberal," standing in danger of developing liberal orthodoxy, becoming a dogma itself, and thereby alienating pupils and parents who are critical to a liberal agenda/orthodoxy. Such promotion is often also anchored in and justified by the value basis of liberal education, which contains very general formulations about the importance of being unprejudiced, open-minded, and appreciative of different forms of diversity. In addition, liberal education highlights a recourse-oriented attitude towards diversity as essential to a liberal, democratic, and accommodative society.

The main issue seems to be whether liberal education, through the promotion of modern toleration and its ambitious strategy, is capable of accommodating real diversity, which also includes those skeptical to a liberal agenda. Such skeptics come in many shapes and sizes, but two main groups are particularly relevant here. The first is pupils and parents who do not embrace or appreciate cultural or religious diversity. These can be called *multiculturalism skeptics*. Second is those who reject or remain opposed to progressive, autonomy-based liberal values in which critical and independent reflection is the ideal. These can be called *autonomy skeptics*.

Multiculturalism skeptics do not consider a religiously and culturally diverse society to be enriching, and they feel that at least some forms of immigration threaten national culture, identity, and way of life. Therefore, they do not want to be open-minded or appreciative of different religions or cultures. Even if such feelings of national identity often represent constructions that, when subject to historical scrutiny, are quite easily deconstructed, these feelings are nevertheless real and persistent. It follows from the ambitions of promoting modern toleration that if someone does not keep a sufficiently open mind or come to appreciate diversity, the preferred course of action by liberal education would be to change this attitude. Some teachers, backed by the general aspiration of accommodating diversity anchored in liberal education's value basis, may be tempted to view the promotion of open-mindedness and appreciation for diversity as legitimizing a slide towards *indoctrinating* open-mindedness. From this view, these attitudes are uncritically inculcated, and opposing opinions and critical voices are actively discouraged, censured, or stifled. This can easily be perceived as a push. Flensner and von der Lippe (2019: 283) show that pupils in Scandinavia who were critical about immigration policies and the presence of Islam felt that their opinions were unwelcome in the classroom and that there was a general culture of silence for what they called nonpolitically correct opinions. This suggests that there is a chance that the ambitions of promoting modern toleration are achieved at the expense of accommodating *real diversity*, and it can instead create mistrust/animosity towards liberal education from those pupils and parents who fail to comply.

A liberal education, however, is not only required to promote toleration as open-mindedness and appreciation for cultural and religious diversity but also for people with different sexual orientations, same-sex marriages, gay rights, and LGBT emancipation. These are examples of values-based attitudes that in today's liberal society are grounded in respect for individual autonomy and autonomous choice and the idea that a person should be free from religious and cultural prejudice and not limited by the weight of tradition. However, modern diversity also includes *autonomy skeptics*, who are represented in the classroom. Autonomy skeptics do not appreciate a society in which these progressive liberal virtues and the underlying ideal of individual autonomy assume a hegemonic position. Often, the reason is that they perceive the underlying autonomy ideal as threatening to more collective-oriented traditional values and practices. Interestingly, it is not uncommon for these reasons to be justified by reference to religious beliefs (Pew 2014). Promoting modern toleration towards, for instance, LGBT emancipation means trying to convince those who are critical to change their attitudes accordingly. Of course, this again runs the risk of assimilative pressure and mistrust towards liberal education.

On closer inspection, there may also be certain tacit tensions between these two liberal objectives: *multicultural ideals*, on the one hand, and *autonomy ideals*, on the other. Promoting open-mindedness and appreciation for different LGBT people may be in conflict with the views of many religious people, who also largely constitute or make up the religious and cultural diversity of liberal democracies. A liberal education promoting modern toleration is faced with the challenge of balancing or coordinating such potential tensions. In order to do so, the promotion of modern toleration may slide towards *avoiding* potentially autonomy-critical interpretations and elements in different religions and cultures and instead favoring a more harmonizing perspective of diversity (Andreassen 2016). Although it is understandable to create a safe space for pupils and to prevent hate speech, the problem with such avoidance is that promoting modern toleration becomes limited to those positions, groups, or representatives of different religions or cultures who largely share core liberal values. As a way of accommodating diversity, promoting toleration then implies a *narrowing of the scope* of real diversity by focusing on the liberal Muslim, liberal Christian, or liberal foreigner or groups and individuals that are generally well-integrated while leaving out both more conservative, tradition-oriented groups, and large, silent majorities of religious people who do not subscribe to the liberal ideal (Bowen 2010) but nevertheless represent the diversity of modern classrooms.

These challenges do not in any way suggest that the promotion of modern toleration has no place in liberal education. It shows, however, that it has certain problems, and therefore, the strategy of relying *solely* on the promotion of modern toleration needs to be reconsidered.

Pedagogical Toleration: Combining Classical and Modern Toleration in Liberal Education

Given that toleration is a core liberal value, an integral and important part of liberal education and paramount for accommodating diversity, what kind of toleration should be promoted? The previous discussions show that the accommodation of diversity through liberal education may benefit from promoting both classical and modern toleration. Therefore, the view that classical toleration is an interim value (Williams 1996: 26) that is now outdated is based upon wishful thinking and highly uncertain empirical assumptions, since the argument seems to imply the belief that a society will become so homogeneous that classical toleration, as in objection and restraint, is no longer called for. If we take prevailing disagreements and sound prediction about these disagreements in pluralistic societies into consideration, a more likely scenario is that there will continue to be a significant number of cases wherein pupils have objections that are not necessarily unreasonable, but nevertheless do not harmonize with a liberal value basis. This more realistic scenario is supported by a current rise in nationalism in Europe in particular, increasing polarization of politics and media as well as a wave of populism against liberal "elites" in many Western democracies (Müller 2016; Galston 2018).

At first sight, classical and modern toleration may seem to be mutually exclusive strategies, but this is an inaccurate description. In fact, promoting classical toleration alone is insufficient to accommodate diversity, but it does allow for interacting with modern toleration in liberal education. A careful *combination* of these strategies may be more conducive to the liberal goal of accommodating diversity. The reason is that this dual strategy may help to change pupils' attitudes towards different kinds of diversity while also being attentive to pupils and parents who remain skeptical towards a liberal agenda, whether they are multiculturalism skeptics or autonomy skeptics. The crucial question is how to *balance* this combination of the promotion of classical and modern toleration in order to achieve that. This is no easy task, but the answer to the question of when to promote classical vs modern toleration depends to a large extent on *how far* education pushes the promotion of open-mindedness and appreciation for diversity and how those who disagree or somehow do not come to appreciate different ways of life are met by liberal education as an institution. More specifically, this comes down to what teachers in the classroom should do when encountering pupils with attitudes that somehow fall outside what a liberal education value basis aims for and how to avoid putting undue assimilative pressure on these pupils and their parents by extent. Promoting what could be called *pedagogical toleration* may be a response to this. Pedagogical toleration implies that schools and teachers should be prepared to use different strategies for promoting toleration – hence differentiating between different pupils – depending on the particular context, the issue at hand, and the specific viewpoint or perspective (and the justification thereof) that these pupils and parents have. As long as the objections pupils and parents have are compatible with respect for other people's beliefs and practices, it might just be that liberal education should accept these objections even if promoting modern toleration would be the preferred educational strategy.

This may for some liberals seem like an evasive strategy, but pedagogical toleration should not be taken to mean that the skeptical attitude towards liberal values by *some* parents alone makes promoting open-mindedness or appreciation for different religions, cultures, or sexual orientations impermissible. That would undermine the pursuit of all educational goals unable to achieve full consensus, including the promotion of modern toleration, and such a stance would hold public education hostage to any kind of critical attitude on the part of parents, including those who reject basic liberal values. Parents have rights and interests in raising their children in accordance with their deepest commitments, but that does not include the right to prevent their children from being exposed to democratic persuasion, as Brettschneider (2012: 99) correctly points out. It *is* permissible for liberal democracies to foster basic liberal values and virtues, including a certain open-mindedness and appreciation for different ways of life, as this can – as argued previously – facilitate the identification of groups that in contemporary society may be victims of prejudice or negative publicity and help to improve cross-cultural relations as well as integration. Promoting open-mindedness and recognition for people with different sexual orientations is also a part of such democratic persuasion. This is in the interest of both the liberal democratic state and the individual pupil as a preparation for growing up in a diverse society, even if parents disagree. The point of pedagogical toleration is not therefore to refrain from shaping pupils' attitudes but rather that when liberal education engages in such activities, it cannot afford to be negligent about parents' religious or cultural values or ethical outlooks – and that this favors a certain restraint. The challenge and the pitfall are not being able to separate the state's and liberal education's persuasive powers from its coercive powers (Brettschneider 2012), even if there may be a fine line between them in pedagogical practice. Liberal education cannot be inattentive about this line, however fine. This restraint implies that at some point, for some of the pupils, liberal education should move from promoting modern toleration to classical toleration. As a teacher, you are in a position to explain both attitudes – open-mindedness and being unprejudiced and appreciative towards diversity, on the one hand, and classical toleration as reasoned restraint, on the other – and to engage in deliberation with both pupils and parents about the differences between them. In interaction with pupils, you *will* come to know which pupils have which types of objections and whether they will change their minds or not. Moreover, if school-parent relations are good, you should have a fair idea about their parents' position, thus being able to promote classical toleration when it is called for, even if this means assuming a position of a second-best strategy from a liberal education perspective.

The main reason for this dual strategy is related to *trust*. Trust is important for social stability and progress because it makes cooperation easier. People who trust each other do not need to control each other. Trust thus conserves time and resources, which can be used to move forward (Grimen 2009: 75). This is relevant to liberal education and school-parent relations as well. The problem with pushing pupils and parents to becoming more open-minded or appreciative of what is different is that it may be perceived as coercion. Such coercion jeopardizes *trust* between education and those parents who remain skeptical and may therefore be counterproductive to accommodating diversity. It is reasonable to assume that if parents feel that liberal education pushes a liberal agenda against their wishes, whether they are skeptical of multiculturalism or autonomy, they are more likely to mistrust education, which may jeopardize home-school cooperation. Moreover, a legitimate concern is whether this approach can generate unnecessary and undesirable conflicts or tensions between parents and their children.

If pupils and parents *mistrust* liberal education and feel marginalized and alienated as a result of assimilative pressure, this could result in *group polarization*. Group polarization is a theory proposed and discussed by Cass Sunstein (2003). According to Sunstein (2003: 11), *group polarization* occurs when like-minded people (e.g., members of a given religious group) who are engaged in deliberation with one another end up taking a more extreme position in line with their pre-deliberative views or tendencies. In other words, after discussions with their like-minded peers, they end up accepting or thinking a more extreme version of what they thought before these discussions. In order to avoid this and instead accommodate as much diversity as possible without jeopardizing stability, liberal education needs to include and find a place for illiberal individuals and groups. If liberal education includes the promotion of classical toleration as an educational strategy and is capable of a flexible application of it, this may make those liberal-critical parents more trusting and willing to cooperate. They may be more inclined to engage in productive discussions concerning what a liberal education should be about and be more receptive to arguments about how the promotion of toleration should be carried out.

This dynamic application of the promotion of toleration suggested here is demanding, but possible. It requires, however, a professional and knowledgeable teaching staff, which has developed an "understanding of the limits of rational discussion and a recognition of the affective or emotional dimension in significant choices" (Winch 2006: 11). More specifically, it requires teachers to have both multicultural competence and insight into general diversity: possessing in-depth knowledge about different religions and life stances (including their internal diversity), understanding the complexity of the multitude of ways people choose to live their lives, and maintaining the basic values of a liberal education as well as highly developed deliberative skills.

References

Advisory Group to the Secretary of State for Education and Employment (1998) Citizenship for 16–19 year olds in education and training. Further Education Funding Council Publications, Conventry

Afdal G (2006) Tolerance and curriculum: conceptions of tolerance in the multicultural unitary Norwegian compulsory school. Waxmann, Münster

Afdal G (2010) The maze of tolerance. In: Engebretson K, de Souza M, Durka G, Gearon L (eds) International handbook of religious education. Springer, Dordrecht, pp 597–615

Andreassen BA (2016) Religionsdidaktikk. Universitetsforlaget, Oslo

Balint P (2017) Respecting toleration: traditional liberalism and contemporary diversity. Oxford University Press, Oxford

Bertram-Troost G, Miedema S (2009) Semantic differences in European research cooperation from a methodological and theoretical perspective – translation and terminology. In: Valk P, Bertram-Troost G, Friederici M, Bérault C (eds) Teenagers' perspectives on the role of religion in their lives, schools and societies. Waxmann Verlag, Münster, pp 29–39

Bowen JR (2010) Can Islam be French? Pluralism and pragmatism in a secular state. Princeton University Press, Princeton

Brettschneider C (2012) When the state speaks, what should it say? Princeton University Press, Princeton

Brown W (2001) Reflections on tolerance in the age of identity. In: Botwinick A, Connolly WE (eds) Democracy and vision. Princeton University Press, Princeton, pp 99–117

Castiglione D, McKinnon K (2001) Introduction: beyond toleration? Res Publica 7:223–230

Council of Europe (2014) Signposts – policy and practice for teaching about religions and non-religious world views in intercultural education. Strasbourg, ISNB: 978-92-871-7914-2

Creppell I (2003) Toleration and identity – foundations in early modern thought. Routledge, New York

Flensner KK (2015) Religious education in contemporary pluralistic Sweden. Dissertation, University of Gothenburg

Flensner KK, von der Lippe M (2019) Being safe from what and safe for whom? A critical discussion of the conceptual metaphor of 'safe space'. Intercult Educ 30:275–288. https://doi.org/10.1080/14675986.2019.1540102

Forst R (2007) Toleration. In: Zalta EN (ed) The Stanford encyclopedia of philosophy. http://plato.stanford.edu/archives/fall2008/entries/toleration/

Forst R (2008) Pierre Bayle's reflexive theory of toleration. In: Williams JS, Waldron J (eds) Toleration and its limits. New York University Press, New York, pp 78–113

Forst R (2013) Toleration in conflict: past and present. Cambridge University Press, Cambridge

Galeotti AE (2001) Do we need tolerance as a moral virtue? Res Publica 7:273–292

Galston W (2002) Liberal pluralism. Cambridge University Press, Cambridge

Galston W (2018) Anti-pluralism. The populist threat to Liberal democracy. Yale University Press, New Haven/London

Gardner P (1993) Tolerance and education. In: Horton J (ed) Liberalism, multiculturalism and toleration. Macmillan Press, London, pp 83–103

Grimen H (2009) Hva er tillit? Universitetsforlaget, Oslo

Gutmann A (1995) Civic education and social diversity. Ethics 105:557–579

Hampton J (1989) Should political philosophy be done without metaphysics? Ethics 99(4):791–814

Hansen OHB (2013) Promotion classical tolerance in public education: what should we do with the objection condition? Ethics Educ 8(1):65–76

Heyd D (2008) Is toleration a political virtue. In: Williams JS, Waldron J (eds) Toleration and its limits. New York University Press, New York, pp 171–194

Horton J (1991) Toleration. In: Miller D, Coleman L (eds) Blackwell encyclopedia of political thought. Blackwell, Oxford, pp 521–523

Horton J (1996) Toleration as a virtue. In: Heyd D (ed) Toleration – an elusive virtue. Princeton University Press, Ewing, pp 28–43

King P (1976) Toleration. Allen & Unwin, London

Larmore C (1987) Patterns of moral complexity. Cambridge University Press, Cambridge

Lidh CH (2016) Representera och bli representerad: Elever med religiös positionering talar om skolans religionskunskapsundervisning (To represent and be represented: pupils who position themselves within a religious tradition talk about religious education in schools). Karlstad Universitet, Karlstad

McKinnon K (2006) Toleration – a critical introduction. Routledge, New York

Müller JW (2016) What is populism? Penguin, London

Nehushtan Y (2007) The limits of tolerance: a substantive-liberal perspective. Ratio Juris 20:230–257

Oberdiek H (2001) Tolerance – between forbearance and acceptance. Rowman and Littlefield, Oxford

ODIHR Advisory Council of Experts on Freedom of Religion or Belief (2007) Toledo guiding principles on teaching about religions and beliefs in public schools. Sungarf, OSCE Office for Democratic Institutions and Human Rights (ODIHR)

Parekh B (2000) Rethinking multiculturalism: cultural diversity and political theory. Harvard University Press, Cambridge

Parliamentary Assembly of the Council of Europe (2005) Recommendation 1720, Education and religion, adopted on 4 October 2005

Pettigrew TF, Tropp LR, Wagner U, Christ O (2011) Recent advances in intergroup contact theory. Int J Intercult Relat 35(3):271–280

Pew Research Center (2014) Views about homosexuality. https://www.pewforum.org/religious-landscape-study/views-about-homosexuality/

Ramadan T (2010) The quest for meaning: developing a philosophy of pluralism. Penguin Books, London

Raphael DD (1988) The intolerable. In: Mendus S (ed) Justifying toleration: conceptual and historical perspectives. Cambridge University Press, Cambridge, pp 137–154

Rawls J (1996) Political liberalism. Columbia University Press, New York

Scanlon TM (2003) The difficulty of tolerance: essays in political philosophy. Cambridge University Press, Cambridge

Sunstein C (2003) Why societies need dissent. Harvard University Press, Cambridge

UNESCO (1995) Declaration of principles of tolerance. Proclaimed and signed by the Member States of UNESCO on 16 November 1995. Retrieved from http://www.un.org/en/events/toleranceday/pdf/tolerance.pdf

Walzer M (1997) On toleration. Yale University Press, New Haven

Williams B (1996) Toleration: an impossible virtue. In: Heyd D (ed) Toleration – an elusive virtue. Princeton University Press, Ewing, pp 18–27

Winch C (2006) Education, autonomy and critical thinking. Routledge, London

> # Toleration Before Toleration

Cary J. Nederman

Contents

Introduction	970
Faith and Persecution in Imperial Rome	971
Reform and Heresy	973
Academic Dispute	976
Medieval Christianity and Non-Christians	978
From Practice to Theory	979
Skepticism	980
Functionalism	982
Nationalism	984
Dialogue	986
Mysticism	988
Summary and Future Directions	989
References	990

Abstracts

Although the idea of toleration (understood as forbearance of beliefs and practices different from one's own) is often supposed to be of modern invention, there were many medieval practices of tolerance involving religious, cultural, intellectual, and economic coexistence that may be found throughout the Latin Middle Ages. Even as the church spurred on persecutorial activities, its own traditions that militated against repression and violence could not be forgotten entirely. Moreover, it was often difficult to discern the demarcation between enthusiasm for reform and heretical zeal. Nor could ecclesiastical authority stem the effect of the flood of non-Christian writings that were pouring into Western Europe starting in the twelfth century. And the continued presence of and coexistence with unbelieving groups, especially the Jews, in the Latin West suggests that Christians were willing and able in everyday life to tolerate non-Christian communities. In

---

C. J. Nederman (✉)
Department of Political Science, Texas A&M University, College Station, TX, USA
e-mail: cary-j-nederman@tamu.edu

© The Author(s), under exclusive licence to Springer Nature Switzerland AG 2022
M. Sardoč (ed.), *The Palgrave Handbook of Toleration*,
https://doi.org/10.1007/978-3-030-42121-2_28

turn, recognition of these pockets of tolerant attitudes and behavior provides a crucial context for understanding the emergence of medieval criticisms of intolerance and of concomitant defenses of toleration. Various authors proposed quite disparate philosophical grounds for defending tolerance against those who would suppress otherness. Broadly speaking, medieval doctrines of tolerance may be classified according to a fivefold scheme, encompassing skeptical, functional, nationalistic, dialogical, and mystical frameworks. Each of the medieval paths to toleration depended upon distinct theoretical principles, but all of them led to the conclusion that differing views about theological and religious truths could be permitted and discussed.

Keywords

Middle Ages · Christianity · Persecution · Inquisition · Jews · Muslims · Marsiglio of Padua · John of Salisbury · Ramon Llull · Mysticism · Nicholas of Cusa · Heresy · *Respublica Christiana* · St. Augustine · Dialogue · Skepticism · Nationalism · Functionalism · Liberalism

Introduction

Toleration has seldom been taken as a hallmark of Christian thought or practice in Europe prior to the seventeenth century. The common impression is perhaps best summarized by the title of R.I. Moore's influential 1987 study of religious dissent and conformity during the Middle Ages: *The Formation of a Persecuting Society*. His main thesis – that a decided and growing trend toward the enforcement of orthodoxy against a range of medieval dissenters can be detected during the High Middle Ages – has become the hegemonic view, a position only reinforced by his latest book (Moore 2012). In Moore's own words, "The eleventh and twelfth centuries saw ... deliberate and socially sanctioned violence... directed, *through established governmental, judicial, and social institutions*, against groups of people defined by general characteristics such as race, religion, or way of life" (Moore 1987, 2007, 4; italics in text). From the late 1000s onward, the Roman church, generally in collaboration with secular powers, certainly pursued a systematic policy of imposing a unified set of Christian beliefs upon the inhabitants of Europe – and beyond. Heresies were stamped out, infidels were attacked, and dissonant voices were quieted (Bruschi and Biller 2003; Waugh and Diehl 1997; Frassetto 2006; Nirenberg 1996; Richards 1990). This tendency may be said to culminate in the Fourth Lateran Council of 1215, at which the institutional church took direct aim at the suppression of expressions of religious and intellectual difference, ranging from heresy to Judaism to intellectual dispute (Kelly 2019). The overarching goal was the realization in practice of the *Respublica Christiana*, the universal community of the faithful, which had been posited in theory by generations of clerics. No statement of this view could be more succinct than that of Mario Turchetti (1991, 5): "Christianity in medieval times simply reinforced the bond of religious concord, extending it to all aspects of communal life, in its construction of the monolithic *Respublica Christiana*." Similar assertions are so common that the list of them is nearly endless. (For references to a sampling of recent scholarship that incline in this direction, see Nederman 2013, nts 8–15.)

Yet, the picture sketched by Moore and his acolytes traverses only part of the terrain. Even as the church spurred on persecutorial activities, its own traditions that militated against repression and violence could not be forgotten entirely. Moreover, it was often difficult to discern the demarcation between enthusiasm for reform and heretical zeal. Nor could ecclesiastical authority stem the effect of the flood of non-Christian writings that were pouring into Western Europe starting in the twelfth century. And the continued presence of and coexistence with unbelieving groups, especially the Jews, in the Latin West suggests that Christians were willing and able in everyday life to tolerate non-Christian communities. In sum, careful investigation of the historical record suggests that forms of religious diversity, at an intellectual as well as a practical level, subsisted throughout medieval Europe, even when the institutional church made concerted attempts to eliminate them. In turn, recognition of these pockets of tolerant attitudes and behavior provides a crucial context for understanding the emergence of medieval criticisms of intolerance and of concomitant defenses of toleration. The present chapter investigates two distinct yet related countervailing aspects of the dominant narrative. First, it examines on-the-ground historical factors that opened up opportunities for tolerant practices in the period before the dawn of modernity. Second, it identifies and elaborates on writings that articulated and endorsed various principled defenses of toleration. The story of tolerance in the pre-modern West proves to be far more complex and murkier than one might suppose. It begins in the era of the Roman Empire.

Faith and Persecution in Imperial Rome

The Christianity of Roman antiquity is said to be a religion both persecuted and persecuting. But this statement requires some qualification. While the persecution of Christians occurred prior to the Christianization of the Roman Empire, it was seldom conducted on a systematic basis coordinated by imperial authorities. The Great Persecution of 303–312 was exceptional in this regard (see Ste Croix 1974a, b; Frend 1965; Sherwin-White 1974; Garnsey 1984; Moss 2013). Rather, persecution of Christians happened in a sporadic and localized manner and was sometimes even discouraged by imperial officials who sympathized with persons accused of holding Christian beliefs. To the modern mind, perhaps the most horrifying aspect of Roman persecutions was the nature of the charge: Merely to be "Christian," rather than to commit some definite offense, was sufficient to be prosecuted for a capital crime. It must be recognized, however, that this harshness stemmed from the very odd character of Christian belief when judged by pantheistic and indifferent Roman standards: It was universalistic and exclusivist. That is, Christians claimed the unquestioned validity of their faith for all people at all times and in all places and were unwilling to accommodate other deities or the public rites associated with the

Roman cults. Indeed, Roman society regarded Christianity to be atheistic, in precisely the sense that its adherents refused to "pay cult to the gods."

The Roman reaction to Christianity may usefully be contrasted with that of Judaism. The Jews had a long history of living and even thriving within non-Jewish civilizations in both the Eastern and Western worlds, while nonetheless maintaining their own cultural and religious identity (Schaefer 1997). Although it would be difficult to argue that Judaism was warmly welcomed, Louis Feldman's analysis of a census of ancient Greek and Latin texts (including Christian works) reveals a nearly balanced split between negative and positive opinions about the Jews (1993, 124). It is thus apt, according to Peter Garnsey (1984, 10), to "use the term 'toleration' in good conscience with respect to the Jews" when discussing their treatment under pagan Rome. In general, when Rome conquered the people, it stipulated that the new provincials make a sacrifice to the approved Roman deities in addition to their own Gods – a relatively unproblematic request to pantheist or pluralistic religions. In the case of the Jews, however, Rome even tolerated nonworship of its cult, provided that the unbelievers were prepared to pray to their own God for the sake of the emperor and empire. Although the Roman establishment was by no means fond of the peculiar beliefs and rites of Judaism, the antiquity of that religion earned its adherents the respect and forbearance of authorities.

The religious landscape changed dramatically in the fourth century, as Christianity moved rapidly from a proscribed faith to an officially protected and subsidized sect. Yet, the public privileging of the Christian religion cannot be equated with the state-sanctioned imposition of strict orthodoxy upon the lands under the control of the Roman Empire. Beyond the myriad practical problems involved with eliminating paganism and heretical Christian movements, Christianity's universalistic and exclusivist elements were tempered by biblical teachings about charity, patience, nonviolence, and the like. Jesus had advocated preaching and teaching by example as the appropriate techniques for disseminating his message. The employment of Church-endorsed state compulsion in order to enforce Christian conformity fit uncomfortably with scriptural lessons that advocated personal free choice and commended turning the other cheek in response to one's enemies.

At the end of the fourth century, St. Augustine grappled with the issue of whether he should call upon the resources of the Roman state to assist him in suppressing the Donatist heresy. Although Augustine ultimately embraced persecution and intolerance as the only practicable solution to the persistence and strength of Donatism, he did so only as a last resort, after nearly a decade of promoting less extreme measures. As he later explained in one of his letters:

> It seemed to certain of the brethren, of whom I was one, that although the madness of the Donatists was raging in every direction, yet we should not ask of the emperors to ordain that heresy should absolutely cease to be, by sanctioning a punishment on all who wished to live in it; but that they should rather content themselves with ordaining that those who either preached the Catholic truth with their voice, or established it by their study, should no longer be exposed to the furious violence of the heretics. (Augustine 1962, 2129–220)

These are hardly the words of a man to whom intolerance came easily. In his initial view, at least, the role of the state should be strictly limited to the protection of peaceful persons from religiously motivated attacks, in other words, a function essentially consistent with publicly approved toleration. In an open debate with Donatists, Augustine even attacked those among his own church who sought to persecute heretics, citing scripture in support of a policy of patient correction, forbearance, and prayer. Persecution, he says, is "the work of evil men" who do not comprehend the nature of the faith to which they pretend (Augustine 1962, 184–189).

A similar approach was adopted to the question of the appropriate relationship between Christianity and the writings of non-Christians, especially the pagan classics (For the following, see Cochrane 1957). In patristic times, considerable discussion occurred about whether the words and ideas of unbelievers could possibly contribute anything to the deepening of the Christian faith. Were such uninspired texts not corrupt and useless for salvation? St. Jerome cautioned against the unbridled use of pagan writings on the grounds that they were tainted with the stain of worldliness. St. Jerome echoed a concern that Tertullian had articulated (albeit more dramatically) two centuries earlier: "What is there in common between the philosopher and the Christian, between the pupil of Hellas and the pupil of Heaven?"

But the lack of forbearance toward pagan thought professed by Tertullian and Jerome did not ultimately prevail. Rather, St. Augustine's position, stated in his widely influential treatise, *De doctrina Christiana* (*On Christian Doctrine*), guided Christian scholars. Augustine, who possessed an excellent classical education, drew an analogy between pagan learning and the Egyptian gold taken by the Israelites in their flight as described in Exodus. Just as the Hebrews were justified in removing the gold from an "unjust possessor" and converting it to righteous uses, so the Christian intellectual may rightfully seize upon those elements of non-Christian teaching that are of assistance to him in the work of spreading the gospel (Augustine 1958, 2.4). Thus, Augustine counseled the study of a range of pagan philosophical, literary, historical, and rhetorical texts in order to improve the pedagogical and evangelical skills of Christian preachers and authors.

On the whole, the impression of early Christianity as a religion whose traditions were uniformly persecutorial – both as victim and as agent – demands modification. Even at the apex of their influence under the late empire, Christian leaders showed consistent ambivalence toward the use of their authority to achieve doctrinal purity. Heresy was always a concern, and proper reaction to religious deviation (whether popular or intellectual) stood as one of the central issues of the patristic age. Yet, the lessons of scripture, along with respect for the many important accomplishments of the pagan past, exercised powerful effects on the minds of the Fathers, leading them to resist the impulse to suppress all forms of religious dissent.

Reform and Heresy

Once Latin Christianity achieved official status in imperial Rome, and especially following the collapse of Roman dominion in its Western half, the interests of the church and secular authority intersected more closely into the medieval period.

Despite increasing efforts during the course of the Middle Ages to impose and extend control over Europeans both as political subjects and as faithful Christians, these were by no means uniformly successful. Indeed, evidence suggests that persecution did not halt dissent and, in some instances, may have only hardened the resolve of dissidents. This is true at all levels of medieval society: Theologians and philosophers did not forego the reading of Aristotle (and his Muslim commentators) because the church proscribed many of his teachings and texts; peasant Cathar heretics did not surrender their beliefs even when a Crusade was preached against them; kings and princes did not renounce their claims to political autonomy in secular (and even some spiritual) matters simply because the pope anathematized them. The centralized authority of the *Respublica Christiana* whose rhetoric has been documented above was often too frail in practice to realize the claims made by and for it. It is easy to be so dazzled by tales of the Crusades and stories of inquisitorial procedures (formal or informal) that one neglects the mundane realities of Christian Europe during the Middle Ages (see Prudlo 2019).

Chief among these realities was the sheer diversity of religious life which simmered near the surface of sanctioned Roman Christendom. Most important perhaps were the regional and even local differences of belief arising from the imposition of a literate, text-based religion upon an illiterate, custom-bound population. In order to make Christian doctrine comprehensible, it was often imbued or admixed with elements of traditional pagan superstition. (One might plausibly question whether it is even possible to speak of the vast mass of the medieval European populace as recognizably Christian at all in the substance of their faith.) Except in rare instances where such popular belief broke out into full-fledged heresy – as in the case of the Cathars – we know far too little about the content of the versions of Christianity practiced in the parish to form hard and fast judgments (Ladurie 1974). But one of the greatest frustrations of the ecclesiastical hierarchy remained the difficulty of ensuring that orthodoxy was disseminated to and adopted by the body of the Christian faithful (Murray 1971, 1974).

The fractured condition of religious life within medieval Europe thus rendered possible the wide airing of dissonant voices within Christianity. It is a crude caricature to depict the Roman church as a ceaseless fount of monolithic faith and guidance until Martin Luther and his fellow reformers tumbled the structure. This is to overlook, for instance, the unwavering medieval desire for reform, expressed in any number of movements, from the Gregorian renovation of the church to the Cluniac call for reform in "head and members" to the Franciscan glorification of evangelical poverty as a clerical ideal to the conciliarist agenda pursued by ecclesiological reformers in the age of the councils (Ozment 1980). The condition of the church at almost any moment in European history formed a source of dissatisfaction for a large number of faithful Christians, among them leading theologians and scholars, who saw it was their duty to edify the reprobates – clerics as well as laity – toward the end of restoring ecclesial purity. This reforming zeal was assuredly respectful of and deferential to authority, but it stubbornly opposed "real or apparent corruption and decline" (Ladner 1982). Indeed, if Giles Constable (1982, 62–66; 1996) is correct, the medieval mania for reform changed perspective sometime during the twelfth century from a conservative, backward-looking phenomenon to a progressive, perfectionist orientation. "Renovation" and even "innovation" became bywords of reform movements. The religious reformers of the High Middle Ages generally made every effort to remain within the pale. But, as scholarship has revealed, the mainstream reform movement associated with the rise of scholastic thought shared many important preconditions and characteristics with the more fanatical of the popular heresies (Fichtenau 1998). Indeed, medieval heresy might sometimes be properly characterized as reforming – a sentiment that has found itself in political disfavor with institutional church authorities. The official response to outright heresy was by no means a simple and settled matter. Suspected heretics always retained the option of publicly disavowing their opinions and recanting. This permitted them some leeway in returning to their former views or evolving new ones (one thinks in this connection of Peter Abelard, who maintained his intellectual independence in the face of repeated actions against him).

Excommunication and anathematization were the approved responses to the obdurate heretic (Vodola 1986, 14). Yet, the fact that the body of canon law regarding excommunication grew significantly during the twelfth and thirteenth centuries may not be a sign that the church was clamping down on heresy and dissent so much as an indication that excommunication itself had become a tool in coping with civil matters such as indebtedness and violence (Vodola 1986). Even in cases of heresy, however, excommunication was based on standards that were ambiguous and difficult to enforce. Alexander Murray (2015, 16–17) has pointed out that the very principle of excommunication stood in "an inevitable tension" with Christian teachings "that enemies had to be loved" and that the sacraments had a "medicinal" effect upon the sick soul of the heretic. Moreover, the social realities of medieval Europe "corroded" the impact of proclamations of excommunication: growing mobility and commercial intercourse rendered the ostracizing implications of excommunication increasingly obsolete, while the continued fragmentation and pluralization of ecclesiastical (and secular) jurisdictions made it difficult to ascertain where authority for declaration of excommunication lay (Murray 2015, 26–33).

In the most extreme instances of heresy, excommunication was unlikely to carry much weight with religious dissidents in any case, since such heretics were relatively unconcerned about the conditions of life in the present world. Rather, they believed that the church itself had become utterly corrupt and that their mission was to restore the faithful to some higher or more primal purity away from which the degraded priesthood had led them. Heretical sects generally claimed to enjoy privileged access to the revealed word of God, setting their followers in direct opposition to the established church. Hence, they did not even acknowledge the legitimate authority of the church to deny to them sacraments and salvation (Hamilton 1981, 19–20). This may help to explain the "increasing lay apathy towards excommunication" and its diminishing force in the secular sphere. Elisabeth Vodola (1986, 101) detected these developments, for example, in recurrent popular demands for the "guarantee of the civil rights of excommunicates" evident in the High Middle Ages. It may not be too far-fetched to conclude that the expansion of the law of excommunication during the twelfth and thirteenth centuries actually reflects a decline in its effectiveness as a method of ecclesiastical control of dissent.

In sum, the conflation of the church's war on heresy with its success in stifling all religious dissent is manifestly inaccurate. The urge to reform enjoyed a venerable lineage within ecclesiastical circles, and criticism of the practices of churchmen was widely regarded as worthy of forbearance. In general, the line between calling for reform of ecclesiastical practices and questioning central articles of faith was sufficiently blurred to permit a wider band of debate than is often supposed.

Academic Dispute

The Roman church had only slightly more success in regulating open differences of opinion among Christian teachers and scholars, theologians prominent among them. The medieval intelligentsia was in fact permitted reasonably wide latitude in debating fundamental issues concerning the faith, whatever our uninformed impressions may be. This becomes especially apparent after about 1100, when the pace of academic dispute picks up rapidly. By the turn of the twelfth century, one can find profound disagreements among Christian theologians about important metaphysical questions which touched upon both the divine nature and the nature of God's creations (Mews 1995a). Only the most obdurate thinkers and the most extreme positions were threatened with official condemnation, and then the decision to proscribe certain doctrines seems to have been as much the result of petty academic and ecclesiastical rivalries and jealousies as of any intrinsic danger posed by the ideas themselves (Mews 1995b). If never quite formally institutionalized, freedom of intellectual inquiry into matters of central concern to orthodoxy seems to have been remarkably well preserved in medieval Christendom.

Intellectual independence was in some measure legitimated by the predominance of the Augustinian attitude toward classical learning throughout the Latin Middle Ages. Even those medieval churchmen such as St. Bonaventure who were deeply suspicious of extensive reliance on the ideas of the pagan classics never proposed prohibition of their circulation entirely. No one questioned that a Plato or an Aristotle, a Cicero or a Seneca, or a Virgil or even an Ovid could teach the Christian scholar a great deal. Indeed, it was deemed senseless to shun pagans simply because they had the misfortune to be born prior to the Christian era and thus to have missed the opportunity to receive the word of Jesus (although it was sometimes suspected that Plato's thought must have enjoyed at least a little direct divine inspiration) (Bolgar 1954, 202–207). Ecclesiastical authorities generally moved to proscribe pagan doctrines only in cases where they directly conflicted with such established and fundamental tenets of Christian faith as the finite nature of creation or the eternity of the soul. And even then, there was no concerted attempt to suppress the classical texts harboring such ideas (Haren 1992, 194–211).

Two institutional factors perhaps helped to reinforce the intellectual autonomy of Christian scholars. First, the rise of universities throughout Europe after circa 1200 provided a measure of protection against the intrusion of the church into the dissemination of ideas. Prior to the formation of university communities, teachers were usually subject directly to the authority and regulation of ecclesiastical superiors, whose judgments of intellectual innovation could be harsh. As relatively orthodox theologians such as Gilbert de la Porrée – not to mention genuine freethinkers such as Peter Abelard – discovered, even the slightest perceived misstep could render their teachings susceptible to inquisitional procedures and clerical condemnation (Bollermann and Nederman 2014). The university, as a free and self-governing community of scholars, was better prepared to resist ecclesiastical incursions into the classroom, since it exercised its own discipline over its masters and students. Attempts on the part of churchmen to intrude into the daily operations of the university tended to be rebuffed or ignored: witness the general ineffectiveness of various ecclesiastical condemnations of Aristotelian learning. Indeed, the organization of university instruction on the basis of a scholastic curriculum necessarily encouraged open debate and discussion of nearly every topic in theology as well as the liberal arts (Leff 1968, 167–193). Of course, schoolmen might still be called before papal or episcopal authorities to defend themselves against the most serious charges of doctrinal errancy. But, as the case of William of Ockham in the early fourteenth century illustrates, these accusations were often as much a function of political intrigue – whether of the academic or the ecclesiastical sort – as of forthright concern about breaches of orthodoxy (Shogimen 2007, 36–74). Throughout the Late Middle Ages, many authors and teachers who were openly critical of the established powers continued to propound their views without ever undergoing formal inquisition or censure.

The other institutional development conducive to intellectual freedom in the Middle Ages was the growth in the authority and size of secular governments. Throughout Europe, kings and other lay rulers and communities increasingly required literate servants to perform the everyday tasks of administration, adjudication, and diplomacy. These offices were commonly filled by university-educated men – often, but not exclusively, lawyers – who, regardless of their clerical status, owed their careers to their temporal masters and who served them unfailingly. In many cases, such persons were behind plots to enhance the political or financial power of lay rulers at the expense of the church: For example, the Paris-trained counselors to the French King Philip IV ("The Fair") largely precipitated and guided his conflict with Pope Boniface VIII (Strayer 1980). The protection afforded by temporal lords also permitted authors to engage in hearty public debate about the foundations and legitimacy of ecclesiastical power and to propound with aplomb doctrines that may have been heretical as well as damaging to the church. At the most extreme, a ruler such as the German King Ludwig of Bavaria might gather around him a large retinue of infamous schoolmen to employ as an arsenal in a war of words with the papacy (Godthardt 2011). The Latin Middle Ages, then, produced a vital intellectual culture that proved capable of accommodating disagreement and dispute over questions that concerned not merely arcane scholastic topics but extended to matters of deep and immediate religious and political significance. Educated individuals in medieval Europe may not always have been happy about the cacophony of opinions expressed, but they seem to have accorded sufficient respect to their opponents that they responded with reasoned treatises, rather than seeking direct suppression of ideas with which they took exception.

Medieval Christianity and Non-Christians

Another token of forbearance during the Latin Middle Ages stems from the open dissemination of Islamic learning. Islam posed a challenge to Christianity different from that of pagan antiquity. Islam was a vital religious force with which the Christian West had repeatedly clashed over the salvation of souls. But the Crusades and religious violence in the Middle East formed only one side of the story. The Western presence in the Holy Lands also produced fruitful contact and growing familiarity with Islamic culture (Frassetto and Blanks 1999). Moreover, the Muslim presence came to be felt at least at the southern fringes of the Latin world. That Christians and Muslims were capable of coexisting in relative proximity is demonstrated by the circumstances of Spain, where so-called "convivencia" was the watchword for adherents to the various sects residing there (Mann et al. 1992). It may be largely true that medieval Christians would not have imagined living in complete equality with Muslims in the heart of Europe. Yet, the church did countenance scholars who studied the writings of their Islamic counterparts, especially commentaries on the pagan classics. Unlike Christianity, Islam had maintained a vigorous intellectual life during the Middle Ages, stimulated by the ancient Greek philosophers as well as its own doctrines. Islamic scholars read Greek and Hebrew, translated classical texts into Arabic, and produced voluminous commentaries and original studies. Largely through contact with Muslim sources, in turn, the Latin West renewed its acquaintance with the learning of the ancient Greek world (Rubenstein 2003). In this process, not only were original texts of philosophy, medicine, history, and the like translated into Latin (sometimes from an Arabic or Hebrew intermediary rather than directly from Greek), but also a large body of related Islamic writings became available. In certain cases, such books were mistakenly thought to be genuine work from Greek antiquity (as the case with the pseudo-Aristotelian *Secreta Secretorum* [Williams 2004]). But more often, Latin readers were fully cognizant of the Islamic provenance of the manuscripts before them, as in the instance of the writings of Avicenna (Ibn Sina) and Averroes (Ibn Rushd), both of whom were revered in the West (Jolivet 1988). Indeed, Averroes earned the title of The Commentator for his authoritative textual analysis of the corpus of The Philosopher, Aristotle. Without too great exaggeration, one might say that Islam played a major role in shaping the way in which Latin Christendom assimilated and embraced the wisdom of the ancients from the twelfth century onward. The intellectual importance of Islam in the Latin West is hardly compatible with an attitude of intransigence and indiscriminate intolerance toward all infidels.

Of course, one might say that the toleration accorded to Islam was "merely theoretical," since the ideas promoted by Arabic texts were just as disembodied in the Christian West (at least outside of southern Europe, where Muslims were visibly present) as the teachings of the long-dead Greek and Roman pagans. That is, one might suspect that an important distinction ought to be made between permitting a few Christian scholars to read non-Christian writings and an officially Christian society's ability to live on a daily basis with people who practiced a non-Christian faith. But we must remember that Christianity throughout the Middle Ages did coexist in just such fashion with another prominent religion, Judaism. The Jews were as much an anomaly in medieval Europe as they had been during the period of Roman ascendency. Jewish communities existed in many European cities, and though their members lacked rights identical to Christians, the common image of medieval Jews as under constant threat of pogrom or expulsion is now regarded as overdrawn (Elukin 2007). While never integrated into the mainstream of Latin society, Jews would not be entirely expunged from it either. Consequently, canon lawyers commonly defended a range of fundamental rights for Jews living under Christian jurisdiction in the West. They formed a stable presence in the West, their numbers fluctuating at about the same rate as the general European population (Stow 1992). Medieval Jewry may have been publicly reviled and despised, but it played a vital and ineliminable role in the social, economic, and intellectual life of the Middle Ages. Much of the explanation for this must be referred to the historical resilience displayed by Jewish communities, their ability to persevere in difficult circumstances. But some of the reasons for the perpetuation of Judaism in Western Europe also rest with Christianity itself. The Jews enjoyed a special place in the history of the Christian religion, inasmuch as Christianity styled itself as the fulfillment of traditional Hebrew prophesies (Pakter 1988). From the patristic era onward, the forbearance of Jewish communities by Christianity was often justified by their function as witnesses to the law of the Old Testament as well as by the scriptural promise of Jewish conversion at the end of the world (Cohen 1994, 20–21). Although hardly sufficient to halt popular expressions of anti-Semitism, it did afford to the Jewish faith a sort of formal (albeit limited) status worthy of toleration, the significance of which should not be disparaged.

From Practice to Theory

Thus far, practices of tolerance that existed and were pursued in pre-Reformation and pre-Enlightenment Europe have been surveyed. This chapter now turns to an analysis of medieval toleration from the perspective of intellectual history. As scholarship has already copiously documented, numerous writings beginning in the twelfth century yielded an array of defenses of conceptually coherent and philosophically well-grounded principles of religious, social, and cultural toleration (Nederman and Laursen 1996; Bejczy 1997; Patschovasky and Zimmermann 1998; Laursen and Nederman 1998; Nederman 2000; Lutz-Bachmann and Fidora 2004; Svensson 2011; Solari 2013; Nederman 2013). Included in this panoply are works by some of the best-known figures in the theology and philosophy of the Western Middle Ages, including (but by no means confined to) Peter Abelard, John of Salisbury, Ramon Llull, William of Ockham, Marsiglio of Padua, and Nicholas of Cusa. Some of these thinkers were considered to be unorthodox in their ideas, but many were solidly grounded on the accepted doctrines of the Roman church. None of them, however, may properly be classified as "precursors" to typically modern, liberal theories of tolerance, such as those found in the writings of John Locke, John Stuart Mill, or (more recently) John Rawls (Nederman 2016). The latter theories supposedly share several key properties:

1. They are secular, in the sense of removing conflicts concerning the diversity of religious beliefs and comprehensive doctrines from the realm of public reason.
2. They rest on some doctrine of the individual as a sovereign, autonomous, and inviolable being, possessing a fundamental "liberty of conscience" or "freedom of expression."
3. They regard as arbitrary many of the "limits" to tolerance typical of the Middle Ages, such as the denigration of alternate belief systems or the denial of certain foundational Christian dogmas about the nature of God (Richards 1996).

By contrast, the argument presented here proposes that the Western Middle Ages originated multiple theoretical approaches that offer alternatives to the rights-laden, modern, Western discourse of liberalism that has been taken as coextensive with the essence of principled tolerance. Specifically, one may identify five nonliberal approaches dating to the Latin Middle Ages that generated robust accounts of toleration. For the sake of analytical clarity, these frameworks may be termed: skeptical, functional, nationalistic, dialogical, and mystical. There is certainly some overlap between them as they were articulated historically, so the categories should be regarded as heuristic. For analytic purposes, however, each approach forms a logically distinct and intellectually coherent way of defending and advocating tolerant behavior and attitudes in the context of the general contours of the medieval worldview. Moreover, the theories proposed and investigated here should not be regarded as definitive. The aim, instead, is to provide a few exemplary illustrations of strands of thought that rise above the threshold of principled toleration.

Skepticism

Given the ordinary impression of Roman Christianity as rigid and confessionally absolute, the presence of skepticism in medieval thought may seem historically implausible. Yet, a number of important Latin thinkers self-consciously embraced versions of a skeptical doctrine (Denry et al. 2014). Throughout his writings, but especially in the *Policraticus*, the twelfth-century churchman John of Salisbury depicted himself as a proponent of the Ciceronian "New Academy," which had promoted a moderately skeptical methodology of probabilism in matters of the truth-seeking (Grellard 2013). John's moderate skepticism accepts that there are three reliable foundations for knowledge: faith, reason, and the senses (John of Salisbury 1990, 7.7). Thus, it does not behoove the philosopher to question his faith in the existence of God, nor the certitude of some postulates of mathematics, nor a number of other first principles which "one is not permitted to doubt, except for those who are occupied by the labors of not knowing anything" (John of Salisbury 1990, 7.7). Although John might seem willing to countenance as certain numerous knowledge claims, this turns out not to be the case. John in fact generates an extremely lengthy list of "doubtful matters about which the wise person is not convinced by the authority of either faith or his senses or manifest reason, and in which contrary claims rest on the support of some evidence" (John of Salisbury 1990, 7.2). The topics subject to doubt that John enumerates include major issues of metaphysics and cosmology (such as the nature of the soul and of body, time and place, and the status of universals), ethics (the unity of the virtues, the nature of virtue and vice, and legal and moral duties and punishments), natural science (magnitude, friction, the humors, and geography), and even theology (free will and providence, punishment of sin, angels, and what can be asked of God by human beings) (John of Salisbury 1990, 7. prologue, 7.2). This list is clearly meant to be illustrative rather than inclusive. In sum, John opens up to doubt and dispute an extraordinarily broad array of topics which for him are by no means settled and are thus appropriate for philosophical discourse.

In confronting all such debatable subjects, John counsels adherence to the academic method, since "the Academics have doubts regarding these matters with so much modesty that I perceive them to have guarded diligently against the danger of rashness" (John of Salisbury 1990, 7.3). Unique among all schools of philosophy, the Academy resists the temptation to replace open discussion of uncertain matters with prematurely closed dogma. In John's view, the moderate skepticism of the New Academy alone defends the liberty of inquiry that he requires for the quest for truth. Given the fallibility of the human intellect, we cannot be certain about many matters connected with human goodness and earthly well-being, as well as speculative knowledge. Hence, we must extend tolerance to persons who think and behave differently from us. Because wisdom and goodness are inevitably difficult to ascertain and are hence subject to debate, due to the nature of the human mind itself, John requires the exercise of forbearance.

John is clearly aware of the connection between his Academy-influenced skepticism and the necessity for a wide band of free judgment and expression: "... the spirit of investigation corresponds to Academic practices rather than to the plan of a stubborn combatant, so that each is to reserve to oneself freedom of judgment in the examination of truth, and the authority of writers is to be considered useless whenever it is subdued by a better argument" (John of Salisbury 1990, 7.prologue). The approach of the Academy requires that in all matters not settled beyond reasonable doubt, the force of the evidence alone should prevail. In turn, the determination of what position seems most plausible or defensible lies with the individual. In view of his skeptical predilections, John raises the priority of individual judgment to a universal principle, not susceptible to revocation in the manner of a privilege conceded by some external authority. John recognized this implication is signaled by his statement on more than one occasion in the *Policraticus* that freedom of judgment is a *ius*, a right that pertains to human beings. John insists upon the right of free inquiry and determination: "The Academy of the ancients bestows upon the human race the leave that each person by his right (*suo iure*) may defend whatever presents itself to him as most probable" (John of Salisbury 1990, 2.22; also 7.6). The source of this right is surely neither political nor (except indirectly) divine; it is not granted from above and therefore subject to limitation or removal. Rather, one's right to assert one's freedom to form one's own judgments derives from the fallibility of the human mind and the uncertain character of many knowledge claims. This is underscored in the *Policraticus* by John's remark that, regarding unsettled issues, "one is free to question and doubt, up to the point where, from a comparison of views, truth shines through as though from the clash of ideas" (John of Salisbury 1990, 7.8). Such a statement suggests that John understood very well the implications of his skeptical philosophy: The quest for truth in matters of practical as well as philosophical import demands the maintenance of openness and dissent. It is the responsibility of the wise person to uphold and defend the grounds of public debate. The realization of truth is hampered, not aided, by the suppression of divergent positions and the persecution of their adherents.

Functionalism

A second strand of toleration theory arises from the emergence during the European Middle Ages of greater acceptance among theorists of the worthiness of guarding the bodily welfare of human beings than one usually finds in either ancient pagan or early Christian society. The dignity of labor, the morality of commerce, and the protection of the poor from extreme deprivation formed key themes of political, economic, and theological writings after about 1100. In turn, these ideas support the claim that respect must be accorded to all parts of society that contribute to the temporal maintenance of the community, a teaching that yielded a functionalist approach to political order. Such functionalism might provide the foundations for a case on behalf of toleration, as in the writings of Marsiglio of Padua from the early fourteenth century. In his major work, the *Defensor pacis* (*The Defender of Peace*), Marsiglio, posits the material welfare and harmony of society as the chief goal of the political community, and this is best achieved when all of the goods and services necessary for bodily human existence were exchanged in an orderly fashion (Nederman 1995). Thus, those who adopted supposedly heretical views in matters of faith, while they could be detached from the spiritual community of the church, ought not to be excluded thereby from interactions with fellow citizens involving purely earthly needs. It remained beyond the power of clerics, in Marsiglio's view, to regulate the social and economic exchanges that were required or useful for maintaining the corporeal existence of the orthodox and the heterodox alike. Rather, only the community itself enjoyed competence to determine how temporal human conduct should be governed. Religious disputes per se constituted an inappropriate basis for determining who deserved to be excluded from or punished by secular society (see Nederman 2000, 69–84).

In a later work, the *Defensor minor*, Marsiglio, confirms his earlier claim that the priesthood lacks any rightful power whatsoever to declare any member of the church anathema: "Inasmuch as this authority must involve coercion over goods or persons or both, and thus must be applied (however moderately) in this world by the civil power, such authority never pertains to priests." Excommunication has a coercive dimension precisely because it imposes upon the sinner "the punishment of exile" and it removes "the wealth and income" by which one sustains oneself and one's family (Marsiglio 1993, 10.3). The excommunicate stands outside of the temporal community as well as the spiritual one. Hence, like all other applications of coercive authority, the decision to remove a person from the civil association through excommunication can only be the determination of the whole body of citizens or its appointed executives. Indeed, Marsiglio poses the further question of "whether it is expedient to separate heretics from, or deprive them of, the fellowship of believers" (Marsiglio 1993, 10.5). In other words, he wonders about the validity of excommunication at all. Is it even appropriate that those who decline to accept the established tenets of religious dogma should be anathematized? To answer this question, Marsiglio examines the purpose of excommunication. It cannot be the case that individuals are anathematized for the sake of compelling them to accept dogma. Marsiglio denies that nonbelievers can ever truly or effectively be coerced into accepting the faith: It is not a tenet of Christianity that "any individual ought to be compelled to profess the Christian faith." This is a view that he employs explicitly against the practice of crusading: "If a foreign journey is made or will be made in order to subdue or restrain infidels for the sake of the Christian faith, then such a foreign journey would in no way seem to be meritorious" (Marsiglio 1993, 7.3). Thus, if the aim of excommunication is the coercion of heretics to return to the faith, this enterprise is likewise unjustified (Marsiglio 1993, 15.7). Compulsion is not to be employed as a means to return the heterodox to the faith.

Consequently, the only valid reason for excommunication must be the protection of the eternal souls of orthodox believers. Marsiglio (1993, 10.5) admits that "heretics and other infidels ... are to be shunned, especially in connection with domestic or social relations, or cohabitation or conversation, concerning those matters which pertain to the preservation of the rituals of the faith, ... lest they taint the remaining believers." He quotes several biblical passages in support of the practice of excommunication on these grounds. But he immediately emphasizes that the separation of the believer from the heretic should occur in connection with spiritual matters only: "This is to be understood in regard to belief and the observance of the rituals of the faith, rather than in regard to other domestic or civil intercourse." There is neither a scriptural nor a rational basis for extending the spiritual prohibition to the temporal domain of communal life.

Marsiglio's defense of this claim assumes his functionalist conception of society. He points out that the final cause of human law and its coercive force "is the tranquility and finite happiness of this world," with the result that such precepts shape "human beings insofar as they are disposed and affected towards tranquility and power and many other [earthly] things" (Marsiglio 1993, 15.5). If excommunication were to encompass temporal as well as spiritual affairs, then the legitimate concerns of public order and welfare would be disturbed. Indeed, the very purpose of excommunication, the well-being of the faithful, would be undermined. By denying intercommunication of a purely secular nature between the orthodox and nonbelievers of all sorts, it is the faithful themselves who will be harmed: They will not be able to take advantage of those material benefits which constitute the very foundation of communal life. It is a violation of the social bond, the very law of nature that joins human beings together, to deprive anyone (let alone orthodox Christians) of:

> civil comforts and associations, such as by purchasing bread, wine, meat, fish, pots or clothes from them [persons guilty of heresy], if they abound in such items and others of the faithful lack them. This is likewise also true of the rest of the functions and comforts to which they might possibly be judged susceptible in connection with their positions or civil duties and services. For otherwise this punishment would redound in like fashion or for the most part to innocent believers. (Marsiglio 1993, 15.6)

The extension of excommunication to civil association constitutes for Marsiglio an attack on the most basic principle of community rooted in the interchange of functions. Neither orthodox Christians nor religious dissenters would be permitted to perform those tasks which form the basis of their citizenship. Inevitably, the functional breakdown of the community would occur, and intranquillity would ensue. Hence, functionalism supports a thoroughgoing policy of the toleration of heretics and other religious dissidents in all temporal dimensions. Persecution destroys the natural and necessary communal order.

Nationalism

Another theoretical framework that cradled a policy of toleration during the Latin Middle Ages was the growing acceptance of the divinely inspired naturalness of human diversity. In earlier Christian times, thinkers such as St. Augustine had castigated the signs of human difference – for example, the plurality of languages – by proclaiming them to be a token of God's punishment of mankind's wickedness. By contrast, many medieval Latin thinkers (under the influence of Aristotelian science as well as the emerging realities of European sociopolitical organization) came to view differences of identity stemming from region or place of birth – denoted by terms such as *natio* and *gens* – as a wholly natural phenomenon, consonant with the divine plan for salvation. Diversity of climate, terrain, and physical resources quite reasonably produce divergent qualities of character, temperament, and social organization. These are not to be reviled or suppressed but respected as a feature of the wondrous pluralism of God's creation. Implicit in the assertion of natural human difference was a measure of social and cultural toleration. As Kate Forhan (1996, 69) has argued in connection with one medieval theorist of nationality, Christine de Pizan, "The idea of nationalism can prepare an environment conducive to the growth of tolerance." If the "nation" reflects a divine design, it represents the height of impiety to seek to impose uniformity upon diverse peoples and ways of life.

Natioalism as a source of tolerant attitudes coalesced in a treatise by the ecclesiastical reformer and eventual cardinal, Nicholas of Cusa, entitled *De pace fidei* (*On the Peace of Faith*), composed in 1453. Nicholas constructs an explicit bridge from the national differences to a diversity of religious practices and forms of worship. *De pace fidei* laments and condemns persecutions stemming from religious diversity and calls for a peaceful harmonization of discordant faiths, motivated by a sincere desire to see all of the world's peoples reconciled in amiable coexistence. He admits the intractability of political and cultural divisions, yet he proposes that this is a strength rather than a weakness of humanity, even suggesting that "national" diversity may in fact serve to enhance reverence for God. Ultimately, Nicholas (1990, 7, 13, 62) adopts the view that, given the ineliminable character of social differences, religious concord can only be achieved in a partial and muted fashion – "one religion in a variety of rites," to use his now-famous phrase. *De pace fidei* in effect reverses the principle of Christian universalism by constructing a kind of sociology of religious toleration: Since earthly nations can never be reduced to a single universal order, many aspects of divergent confessions must be respected for the sake of peace.

De pace fidei purports to recount a vision experienced by Nicholas himself in which God determines to hold a conclave of wise men for the purpose of achieving universal settlement of disputes about matters of faith. God calls together into dialogue delegates from "the individual provinces and sects of the world" (Nicholas 1990, 4). Nicholas acknowledges that human cultures necessarily diverge according to time and place. As he remarks, "In the sensible world nothing remains stable and, because of time, opinions and conjectures as well as languages and interpretations vary as things transitory" (Nicholas 1990, 9). Although Nicholas consistently maintains that there is only a single ultimate truth in central religious doctrines, he is aware that understandings of that truth are bound to change and diverge due to the fragility of human intelligence and the particular patterns of cultural practice. Thus, for instance, "difference in the manner of speech" produces distinctive confessions and rites, even if the true meaning which each religion intends to convey is identical (Nicholas 1990, 29). Religious rites, Nicholas (1990, 52) says, "have been instituted and received as sensible signs of the truth of faith. But signs are subject to change; not however that which is signified." Differing cultural and linguistic contexts demand the expression of the same idea – in this case, the desirability of the afterlife – according to usages and expectations appropriate to their specific conditions.

Nicholas regards such historical particularity as unavoidable. Having explained the intractable character of historicity, he admits, "Yet the way it is with the earthly human condition, a longstanding custom that is taken as having become nature is defended as truth. Thus, not insignificant dissensions occur when each community prefers its faith to another" (Nicholas 1990, 6). Religion in this sociocultural sense is regarded to be a purely conventional phenomenon, flowing from the traditions and rituals that have accrued within a society as the result of contingent historical usage and the requirements of inequality. This frames the salient dilemma of *De pace fidei*: how to cope with matters of "rite," that is, the socially conditioned practices that distinguish worship among different faiths (Nicholas 1990, 50–51). (Nicholas counts circumcision, baptism, marriage, the Eucharist, and other Christian sacraments among such rites.) In his view, once faith as the chief source of salvation "is acknowledged, the variety of rites will not be a cause of turbulence" (Nicholas 1990, 51–52). He avers that "it is very often necessary to condescend to human weakness if it does not offend against eternal salvation. For to seek conformity in all things is rather to disturb the peace" (Nicholas 1990, 61). This is not to suggest that he does not express a preference for Christian rites in cases where conformity can be achieved, as conceded to the Tartar with regard to the value of circumcision (Nicholas 1990, 56). But he recognizes that, given the demands of diversity, mutual global respect for a "variety of rites" is more likely to produce the elimination of cross-cultural conflict (Nicholas 1990, 56). As a matter of principle, he declares, "Where no conformity in manner can be found, nations should be permitted their own devotional practices and ceremonies" (Nicholas 1990, 62).

Nicholas in fact finds virtue in the necessity of religious diversity. A variation of rites according to differences among nations is capable of promoting worship, he holds, by permitting a sort of creative competition among the peoples of the world (Nicholas 1990, 7). If human beings worship in a manner appropriate to their traditions and customs, that is, they will take pride in their confession and will be more inclined to praise and serve God. Nicholas thus approaches the equation of local religious ritual with national self-awareness; a people acknowledges itself to be such through the practice of its own distinctive forms of worship: "A certain diversity will perhaps even increase devotion when each nation will strive to make its own rite more splendid through zeal and diligence in order thus to surpass another and so to obtain greater merit with God and praise in the world" (Nicholas 1990, 62). Note that the purpose of a variation of rites is not simply religious in character; it redounds to the earthly glory and reputation of diverse peoples. Nicholas conveys a vision of a tolerant internationalism in which differences in worship are treated not as sources of hostility but as the basis for mutual dignity and respect among nations.

Dialogue

Dialogue as a specific mode of conceptualizing cross-cultural understanding has a long history both in and outside the West, perhaps most notably in the inter-religious dialogues composed in great numbers by Latin Christians (but also Jews and Muslims) during the Middle Ages (Lutz-Bachmann and Fidora 2004, 10–39). It may come as a surprise to discover that medieval thinkers produced a large and diverse body of writings that recounted conversations (usually, although not entirely, imagined) between medieval Christians and non-Western and/or non-Christian interlocutors. Inter-religious debates had debuted in the patristic era, pioneered by such writers as Minucius Felix, Justin Martyr, and Tertullian. Christian authors of the High Middle Ages (not to mention the Jews and Muslims who also employed the genre) thus simply revived an established format (Remer 1998). For this group of medieval authors, the tenets of Christianity, not to mention the lessons of philosophy and history, suggested that differences in belief ought to be addressed from the standpoint of patience and charity, manifested throughout dialogue and discussion.

Thus, the very period in which the rise of persecution has been detected also witnessed an upsurge in writings that took the form of inter-religious (and often intercultural) dialogue, that is, a discussion between persons of different faiths and/or sects directed toward the discovery of truth or, at least, a common ground.

Medieval inter-religious and intercultural writings, generally speaking, shared a certain confidence in a basic universal human reason and hence in the possibility of achieving some form of mutual understanding. At the same time, these dialogues persistently demonstrated recognition of the limitations of human reason and of the discourse that it facilitated, reminding their readers of the sometimes ineluctable quality of difference and of the many obstacles to the attainment of mutual understanding. Intercultural dialogues during the Middle Ages were a diverse lot in terms of their purpose, logic, and structure. They reveal that there could be multiple valid reasons to engage in exchange with nonorthodox and non-Christian perspectives. While some dialogues were merely aimed at rational demonstration of the truth of Christianity and thus conversion, others sought to achieve the mutual edification of participants, as well as their critical self-reflection and reciprocal accommodation and respect.

For illustrative purposes, one may concentrate on Ramon Llull's thirteenth-century *Liber de gentili et tribus sapientibus* (*Book of the Gentile and the Three Wise Men*) (1985; see Bidese et al. 2005 and Fidora 2004). It narrates the tale of three wise men – a Jew, a Christian, and a Saracen – who set off on a walk together and attempt to apply a wholly rational method for comparing their respective beliefs. Acknowledging that "we cannot agree by means of authorities," they propose to "try to come to some agreement by means of demonstrative and necessary reasons" (Llull 1985, 1:116). With a despondent Gentile as their judge, they "debate before him and... each give[s] his arguments as best he could, so that he [the Gentile] could see which of them was on the path to salvation" (Llull 1985, 1:149). The Epilogue to the *Liber*, in which final judgment is to be proclaimed, is filled with intriguing ambiguity. Having listened closely to the respective discourses of the Jew, the Christian, and the Moslem and having understood each of their teachings so precisely that they praise him, the Gentile has clearly come to his final decision. The three wise men, however, take their leave before judgment is rendered, saying that, in order for each to be free to choose his own religion, they preferred not knowing which religion he would choose: "And all the more so since this is a question we could discuss amongst ourselves to see, by force of reason and by means of our intellects, which religion it must be that you will choose. And if, in front of us, you state which religion it is that you prefer, then we would not have such a good subject of discussion nor such satisfaction in discovering the truth" (Llull 1985, 1:300–301). In closing, the wise men bemoan the harm that comes from inter-religious strife and agree upon the desirability of achieving concordance. They ascribe the diversity of confessions to earthly causes, such as the deference human beings pay to "the faith in which they found themselves, and in which they were raised by their parents and ancestors," as well their love "of temporal possessions" (Llull 1985, 1: 301–302). Ultimately, they agree to the perpetual continuation of their dialogue: "Would you like to meet once a day and ... have our discussions until all three of us have only one faith, one religion, and until we can find some way to honor and serve one another, so that we can be in agreement?" (Llull 1985, 1:309). The dialogue closes with a consensus on this proposal, assigning "a time and place for their discussions, as well as how they should honor and serve one another, and how they should dispute... Each of the three wise men went home and remained faithful to his promise" (Llull 1985, 1:308). The latter words are the final ones of Llull's narrative, to which only a short coda is appended in which the author expresses hope that he has adequately illuminated a rational method "for entering into union with and getting to know strangers and friends" (Llull 1985, 1:304). It is hard to imagine how any conception of open, unconstrained dialogical engagement could be more forbearing.

Mysticism

Finally, and perhaps surprisingly to some, the mystical dimensions of religious experience also yield the basis for the principled defense of toleration. This is not an especially new observation. A number of years ago, Gustav Mensching argued for the presence of what he called an "intrinsic" or "inner," as distinct from a "political" or a "rationalistic," conception of tolerance located in the experience of mystical truth. Mensching's main insight was that many mystics recognize the immanence and omnipresence of God in being and thus assert the requirement that all that exists must be respected and given its due, because in that way the divine itself is worshiped (Mensching 1971, 64–75). Mysticism posits truth, but a truth that is all-embracing and that may, in extreme cases, embrace all creation as ready for salvation. In Pseudo-Dionysius the Areopagite, for instance, the stages of mystical experience lead to the encounter with God in all things, which in turn are recognized to be God's appearances (*theophanias*). The journey to mystical insight entails a readiness to forbear differing or dissenting visions, since these, too, reflect elements of the divine plan of creation.

This theme resonates with a range of mystics writing during the Middle Ages. Meister Eckart's condemnation of intolerance seems typical:

> ... God never tied man's salvation to any pattern. Whatever possibilities inhere in any pattern of life inhere in all, because God has given it so and denied it to none. One good way does not conflict with another and people should know that they are wrong; seeing or hearing of some good man that his way is not like their own, they say that his is just so much lost labor. Because that person's life pattern does not please them, they decry it, together with his good intentions. That is not right! We ought rather to observe the ways of other good people and despise none of them. (Quoted from Mensching 1971, 73)

Such teaching, derived from a mystical conception of the unity and goodness of divine creation, may be encountered throughout the Western Christian tradition. As Mensching notes, the poetry composed in the environs of the high medieval Hohenstaufen court often reflects the oneness of the universe mediated through God. Wolfram von Eschenbach places this sentiment in the mouth of one of his characters, and Walther von der Vogelweide admonishes, "Many call you Father, but he who does not take me for a brother speaks the stern words with a weak spirit. ... Christians, Jews and heathens all serve Him who upholds every living wondrous thing" (Mensching 1971, 78). Doubtless many aspects of twelfth- and thirteenth-century neo-Platonism in theology and philosophy lend support to this view. Even after the Reformation, mystics such as Jacob Boehme found considerable warrant for privileging peaceful forbearance in the name of fulfilling God's plan. This extended not merely to various Christian confessions but even to non-Christian sects (Mensching 1971, 75–76). Indeed, among all the approaches to tolerance that we find in medieval Christian thought, the path of mysticism was perhaps the least exceptional and most widely embraced and propounded.

Summary and Future Directions

Granted that the premodern Christian West was not an entirely open society in either practice or theory, when judged by post-Enlightenment standards, neither was it the closed and monolithic "persecuting society" that it has regularly been portrayed as. Rather, the Latin Middle Ages harbored plenty of opportunities to pursue and defend different understandings of religious faith without necessarily suffering exclusion or suppression – or worse. Many expressions of dissent from religious authority, as we have seen, occurred in a relatively closed and essentially academic sphere. Some, however, had public and even popular dimensions. The unitary *Respublica Christiana* was at best an aspiration of medieval life – an ideal perhaps so revered because it seemed so unattainable – beneath the surface of which may be perceived diverse strands of thought and practice. None of this is to gloss over the difficulties and dangers associated with resistance to the rigid uniformity esteemed by the Roman church during the Middle Ages. Yet, an appreciation of the context may help to explain the ability of some people to criticize and resist dull devotion to the image of a single universal faith, governance, and culture and thus to consider strategies for coping with the worlds of difference that dotted the religious landscape, a view for which Albrecht Classen (2018) forcefully argues.

In particular, observance of persistent deep divisions, intellectual as well as cultural, in the beliefs held by Christians as well as non-Christians, led some of the most learned and sophisticated authors of the Middle Ages to articulate principles to explain and justify the existence of diverse forms of human life, rather than simply seeking the elimination of all such differences. In criticizing the practices of intolerance and the bases of their legitimacy, some medieval thinkers began to conceive of toleration as a subject worthy of theoretical reflection and as a permanent and necessary feature of the social and intellectual landscape. Once confronted with the ineliminable diversity of human life and the practical impossibility (and perhaps undesirability) of strictly and narrowly enforced religious conformity, possibilities opened up ways in which people holding divergent beliefs and engaging in diverse practices might nonetheless live together. The germ of tolerance should thus be sought in times far earlier than those conventionally considered. Recognizing this, scholars of toleration moving forward are tasked with at least two major responsibilities: first, seeking yet further approaches to tolerant thought and practice generated in the medieval world, and second, demonstrating the relevance and applicability of these approaches to contemporary discussion of tolerance (see Nederman 2016).

References

Augustine of Hippo St (1958) On Christian doctrine (trans: Robertson DW Jr). Bobbs-Merrill, Indianapolis
Augustine of Hippo St (1962) Political writings (ed: Paolucci H). Regenry, Chicago
Bejczy I (1997) *Tolerantia*: a medieval concept. J Hist Ideas 5:365–384
Bidese E, Fidora A, Renner P (eds) (2005) Ramon Lull und Nikolas von Kues: eine Begegnung im Zeichen der toleranz. Brepols, Turnhout
Bolgar RR (1954) The classical heritage and its beneficiaries. Cambridge University Press, Cambridge, MA
Bollermann K, Nederman CJ (2014) Standing in Abelard's shadow: Gilbert of Poitiers, the 1148 council of Rheims, and the politics of ideas. In: Bollermann K, Izbicki TM, Nederman CJ (eds) Religion, power and resistance from the eleventh to the sixteenth centuries: playing the Heresy Card. Palgrave/Macmillan, New York
Bruschi C, Biller P (2003) Texts and the repression of medieval heresy. York Medieval Press, York
Classen A (2018) Toleration and tolerance in medieval European literature. Routledge, London
Cochrane CN (1957) Christianity and classical culture. Oxford University Press, Oxford
Cohen MR (1994) Under cross and crescent: the Jews in the Middle Ages. Princeton University Press, Princeton
Constable G (1982) Renewal and reform in religious life. In: Benson RL, Constable G (eds) Renaissance and renewal in the twelfth century. Harvard University Press, Cambridge, MA
Constable G (1996) The reformation of the twelfth century. Cambridge University Press, Cambridge
de Ste Croix GEM (1974a) Why were the early Christians persecuted? In: Finley MI (ed) Studies in ancient society. Routldge and Kegan Paul, London
de Ste Croix GEM (1974b) Rejoinder. In: Finley MI (ed) Studies in ancient society. Routledge and Kegan Paul, London
Denry DG, Ghosh K, Zeeman N (2014) Uncertain knowledge: skepticism, relativism, and doubt in the Middle Ages. Brepols, Turnhout
Elukin J (2007) Living together, living apart: rethinking Jewish-Christian relations in the Middle Ages. Princeton University Press, Princeton
Feldman LH (1993) Jew and Gentile in the ancient world. Princeton University Press, Princeton
Fichtenau H (1998) Heretics and scholars in the high middle ages, 1000–1200. Pennsylvania State University Press, University Park
Fidora A (2004) Ramon Llull – Universaler Heilswille und universale Vernuft. In: Lutz-Bechmann-M, Fidora A (eds) Juden, Christen und Muslime: Religionsdialoge in Mittelalter. Wissenschaftliche Buchgesllschift, Darmstadt
Forhan KL (1996) Respect, independence and virtue: a medieval theory of toleration in the works of Christine de Pizan. In: Nederman CJ, Laursen JC (eds) Difference and dissent. Rowman and Littlefield, Lanham
Frassetto M (ed) (2006) Heresy and the persecuting society in the Middle Ages. Brill, Leiden
Frassetto M, Blanks DR (1999) Western views of Islam in medieval and early modern Europe. St. Martin's Press, New York
Frend WHC (1965) Martyrdom and persecution in the early church. Clarendon Press, Oxford

Garnsey P (1984) Religious toleration in classical antiquity. In: Shiels WJ (ed) Persecution and toleration. Blackwell, Oxford
Godthardt F (2011) Marsilius von Padua und der Romzug Ludwigs des Bayern. V&R unipress, Göttingen
Grellard C (2013) Jean de Salisbury et la renaissance médiévale du scepticisme. Les Belles Lettres, Paris
Hamilton B (1981) The medieval inquisition. Holmes & Meier, London
Haren M (1992) Medieval thought, 2nd edn. University of Toronto Press, Toronto
John of Salisbury (1990) Policraticus: of the frivolities of courtiers and the footprints of philosophers (ed and trans: Nederman CJ). Cambridge University Press, Cambridge
Jolivet J (1988) The Arabic inheritance. In: Dronke P (ed) A history of twelfth-century western philosophy. Cambridge University Press, Cambridge
Kelly HA (2019) The fourth Lateran *ordo* on inquisition adapted to the prosecution of heresy. In: Prudlo DH (ed) A companion to heresy inquisitions. Brill, Leiden
Ladner G (1982) Terms and ideas of renewal. In: Benson RL, Constable G (eds) Renaissance and renewal in the twelfth century. Harvard University Press, Cambridge, MA
Ladurie L (1974) Montaillou: promised land of error. Random House, New York
Laursen JC, Nederman CJ (eds) (1998) Beyond the persecuting society: religious toleration before the Enlightenment. University of Pennsylvania Press, Philadelphia
Leff G (1968) Paris and Oxford Universities in the thirteenth and fourteenth centuries. Wiley, New York
Llull R (1985) The book of the gentile and the three wise men. In: Bonner A (ed and trans) The selected works of Ramon Llull (1232–1216), 2 vols. Princeton University Press, Princeton
Lutz-Bechmann M, Fidora A (eds) (2004) Juden, Christen und Muslime: Religionsdialoge in Mittelalter. Wissenschaftliche Buchgesllschift, Darmstadt
Mann VB, Glick TF, Dodds JD (eds) (1992) Convivencia: Jews, Muslims, and Christians in medieval Spain. George Braziller, New York
Marsiglio of Padua (1993) Writings on the Empire: Defensor minor and De translatione Imperii (ed and trans: Nederman CJ). Cambridge University Press, Cambridge
Mensching G (1971) Tolerance and truth in religion. University of Alabama Press, Alabama
Mews CJ (1995a) Philosophy and theology 1100–1150: the search for harmony. In: Gaspari F (ed) Le XII siècle: Mutations et renouveau en France dans le première molti. Le Léopard d'Or, Paris
Mews CJ (1995b) Peter Abelard. Variorum, London
Moore RI (1987) The formation of a persecuting society: power and deviance in Western Europe. Blackwell, Oxford, pp 950–1250
Moore RI (2007) The formation of a persecuting society: power and deviance in Western Europe, 950–1250, 2nd edn. Blackwell, Oxford
Moore RI (2012) The war on heresy. Harvard University Press, Cambridge, MA
Moss C (2013) The myth of persecution: how early Christians invented the story of martyrdom. Harper One, New York
Murray A (1971) Piety and impiety in thirteenth century Italy. Stud Church Hist 8:83–106
Murray A (1974) Religion among the poor in thirteenth century France. Traditio 30:285–324
Murray A (2015) Excommunication and conscience in the Middle Ages. Oxford University Press, Oxford
Nederman CJ (1995) Community and consent: the secular political theory of Marsiglio of Padua's *Defensor pacis*. Rowman and Littlefield, Lanham
Nederman CJ (2000) Worlds of difference: European discourses of toleration c.1100–c.1550. Pennsylvania State University Press, University Park
Nederman CJ (2013) Toleration in medieval Europe: theoretical principles and historical lessons. In: Muldoon J (ed) Bridging the medieval/modern divide: medieval themes in the world of the reformation. Ashgate, Farnham
Nederman CJ (2016) Medieval toleration through a modern lens: a 'judgmental' view. Oxf Stud Mediev Philos 4:1–26

Nederman CJ, Laursen JC (eds) (1996) Difference and dissent: theories of tolerance in medieval and early modern Europe. Rowman and Littlefield, Lanham

Nicholas of Cusa (1990) Nicholas of Cusa on interreligious harmony (ed and trans: Biechler JE, Bond HL). Mellen Press, Lewiston

Nirenberg D (1996) Communities of violence: persecution of minorities in Middle Ages. Princeton University Press, Princeton

Ozment S (1980) The age of reform, 1250–1550: an intellectual and religious history of late medieval and reformation Europe. Yale University Press, New Haven

Pakter W (1988) Medieval canon law and the Jews. Gremler, Ebelsbach

Patschovasky A, Zimmermann H (eds) (1998) Toleranz im Mittelalter. Thorbecke, Sigmaringen

Prudlo DS (2019) A companion to heresy inquisitions. Brill, Leiden

Remer G (1998) Ha-Me'iri's theory of religious toleration. In: Laursen JC, Nederman CJ (eds) Beyond the persecuting society: religious toleration before the enlightenment. University of Pennsylvania Press, Philadelphia

Richards J (1990) Sex, dissonance and damnation: minority groups in the Middle Ages. Routledge, London

Richards DAJ (1996) Toleration and the struggle against prejudice. In: Heyd D (ed) Toleration: an elusive virtue. Princeton University Press, Princeton

Rubenstein RE (2003) Aristotle's children: how Christians, Muslims, and Jews rediscovered ancient wisdom and illuminated the Middle Ages. Harcourt, New York

Schaefer P (1997) Judeophobia. Harvard University Press, Cambridge, MA

Sherwin-White AN (1974) Amendment. In: Finley MI (ed) Studies in ancient society. Routledge and Kegan Paul, London

Shogimen T (2007) Ockham and political discourse in the late Middle Ages. Cambridge University Press, Cambridge

Solari E (2013) Contornos de la tolerancia medieval. Ideas valores 63:73–97

Stow KR (1992) Alienated minority: the Jews of medieval Latin Europe. Harvard University Press, Cambridge, MA

Strayer JR (1980) The reign of Philip the fair. Princeton University Press, Princeton

Svensson M (2011) A defensible conception of toleration in Aquinas? Thomist 75:291–308

Turchetti M (1991) Religious concord and political tolerance in sixteenth- and seventeenth- century France. Sixteenth Century J 22:15–25

Vodola E (1986) Excommunication in the Middle Ages. University of California Press, Berkeley

Waugh SL, Diehl PD (eds) (1997) Christendom and its discontents: exclusion, persecution, and rebellion, 1000–1500. Cambridge University Press, Cambridge

Williams S (2004) The secret of secrets. University of Michigan Press, Ann Arbor

Early Modern Arguments for Toleration

49

Andrew R. Murphy

Contents

Introduction	994
Toleration: Conceptual, Political, and Historical Dimensions	995
Toleration in Seventeenth-Century England	997
Antitolerationist Arguments	999
Case Study: The Career of William Penn	1000
Summary and Future Directions	1004
References	1006

Abstract

Although institutional arrangements that ensured protection for unpopular or controversial minority groups appear across a range of historical contexts, scholars have long focused on the early modern period as particularly important in the history of toleration. Originating in debates over the rights of dissenters from legally established or socially dominant churches, the vocabulary and institutional practices associated with religious toleration assumed greater sophistication in sixteenth- and seventeenth-century Europe. This chapter explores the main lines of argumentation in seventeenth-century England as both significant in its own right and influential in shaping future debates over the rights of dissenting and marginalized groups. After a few introductory remarks about the conceptual dimensions of religious toleration, I lay out the primary arguments advanced by tolerationists, as well as those presented by their opponents. I then focus on one particular individual, William Penn, theorist of religious liberty in England and, later, founder of the colony of Pennsylvania, where he hoped to put his

---

A. R. Murphy (✉)
Department of Political Science, Virginia Commonwealth University, Richmond, VA, USA
e-mail: amurphy5@vcu.edu

© The Author(s), under exclusive licence to Springer Nature Switzerland AG 2022
M. Sardoč (ed.), *The Palgrave Handbook of Toleration*,
https://doi.org/10.1007/978-3-030-42121-2_4

tolerationist principles into practice. I conclude with some brief reflections on the role played by religious toleration in the larger struggles for more expansive understandings of liberty in the modern world.

Keywords

Toleration · Penn, William · Locke, John · Liberty of conscience · Conscience · Restoration · Persecution · Religious liberty · Cromwell, Oliver

Introduction

The concept of toleration – its connection with related terms like tolerance, religious freedom, and liberty of conscience and its associated practices and institutional manifestations – has a long historical and philosophical pedigree and continues to engage theorists and practitioners of politics around the world. As the chapters in this volume make abundantly clear, toleration is a complex and multifaceted concept, related in subtle ways, at various times and in various places, to a host of related phenomena: liberalism, skepticism, relativism, justice, fear, dignity, respect, recognition, reasonableness, power, and domination, to name just a few. It thus raises a host of questions about the intersection of personal characteristics and the institutions of state and civil society. I have written on many of these topics elsewhere (see, e.g., Murphy 2016, Chap. 7; 2001, Chaps. 7, 8; Murphy 1997a, b) and will not repeat here what I have said in other works. My goal in this chapter is to offer a brief overview of the historical origins of tolerationist argument in one formative historical period – early modern England, which in many ways set the stage for debates that continue to this day – and reflect on some of the resonances that those debates hold for ongoing questions of political theory and practice.

For a variety of reasons – some intellectually sound, others historically contingent – many accounts of early modern toleration begin and end with John Locke's 1689 *Letter Concerning Toleration* (Locke [1689] 1983). Locke's *Letter*, written some years earlier and published in the wake of the Toleration Act's passage, inaugurated a lengthy debate with Anglican divine Jonas Proast and led Locke's arguments to grow from a pithy original edition of about 60 pages to more than 350 in the *Third Letter* (Vernon 1997; Wolfson 1997). To some extent, the focus on Locke is understandable, given his influence on Jefferson and the American founders a century later and his place in the philosophical canon more generally. There are serious drawbacks, however, to this "Locke obsession" (Laursen and Nederman 1998, 2), since a long and robust discourse of toleration (alongside, not surprisingly, an equally long and robust discourse of uniformity and antitoleration) characterized English and European political debate decades before Locke was even born. The achievement of some measure of toleration in England – during the Civil Wars and Protectorate, under James II after 1687 and, with the Act's passage, after 1689 – represented a momentous and bitterly contested accomplishment, often accompanied by a desire for Protestant unity and the simultaneous realization that the costs of achieving such unity were not worth paying. In the Conclusion, I touch briefly on the ways in which toleration in religion led to broader arguments over inclusion and exclusion along a number of other dimensions. But first, I offer a few preliminary comments about toleration as a concept. (Given the wide range of treatments of toleration in this volume, I shall keep these remarks to a minimum.)

Toleration: Conceptual, Political, and Historical Dimensions

In political terms, toleration generally refers to the protection of dissenting, unpopular, unorthodox, or marginalized individuals and groups in society. Rooted, etymologically, in the Latin verb "tolerare" – to endure or put up with – toleration has always carried with it an implication of conflict, disagreement, disapproval, and permission, a complex blend of rejection and acceptance, and a calculation on the part of its proponents that the price of suppression outweighed any gains that it might yield. For instance, ruling elites might view a controversial religious sect's doctrine or practices as fundamentally erroneous and misguided, while nonetheless endorsing the rights of its adherents to profess it free of legal penalties. The achievement of toleration in any given society, then, involves a willingness on the part of individuals or governments to provide protections for unpopular groups, even groups they themselves might consider deeply mistaken.

Every theorist of toleration has assumed limits to what is tolerable. The most famous of these, of course, is Locke's exclusion of Catholics and atheists from his scheme of toleration in the *Letter*. But Locke was hardly unique, and the vast majority of tolerationists during his time also considered those groups beyond the pale and, quite literally, intolerable. (Forst [2013, 23–25] refers to such determinations as toleration's "rejection component.") Vexed debates about the proper *extent* of toleration characterized the early modern conflicts I shall explore below, and a wide range of views gained support in these debates. Some supported the rights of certain Dissenters (those who would affirm the Trinity, e.g., or swear loyalty oaths), while others sought a more ambitious regime of toleration that extended protections to a far wider swath of the population. Still others sought "comprehension," or the expansion of established church doctrine to encompass theologically orthodox Dissenters, a route distrusted by more radical actors who considered it a dangerous precedent that gave the appearance of leniency while maintaining a hard line against those who could not conform. And moving outside of the ecclesiastical realm, it bears emphasizing that toleration in religion was compatible with a range of restrictions on behavior perceived as immoral: William Penn's 1679 *Address to Protestants* called on the civil magistrate to act against, among other things, "drunkenness, whoredoms and fornication . . . [and] profuse gaming," which threatened to bring God's judgment on the land (Penn 1679, 7).

Toleration is closely related to a number of other terms – e.g., religious liberty and liberty of conscience – with the latter of these terms attempting to ground political protections for dissenters on the less ambiguous theoretical footing of natural right (Coffey 2020). Compared with more expansive terms like "recognition" or "acceptance," toleration is fairly minimal. As a species of what Isaiah Berlin (1958) has called "negative liberty" – characterized largely by noninterference, or the absence of external constraint – it has historically tended to fall somewhere between persecution on the one hand and full liberty and equality on the other. Forst (2013, Chap. 1) highlights a series of paradoxes of toleration and offers four conceptions ranging from bare permission to mutual esteem.

Because of its minimalist nature, contemporary audiences often consider toleration a rather uninspiring ideal toward which to aspire, particularly when compared to the expansive understandings of respect and affirmation that characterize more recent understandings of identity and difference (Brown 2009). Nor is this view of toleration as unduly minimal merely a recent phenomenon: as George Washington put it in 1790,

> It is now no more that toleration is spoken of, as if it were the indulgence of one class of people that another enjoyed the exercise of their inherent natural rights. For happily the Government of the United States, which gives to bigotry no sanction, to persecution no assistance requires only that they who live under its protection should demean themselves as good citizens, in giving it on all occasions their effectual support. (Washington 1790)

(Whether or not the United States really did offer "to bigotry no sanction" is another question entirely; see, e.g., Wenger (2017) and Sehat (2010).) The idea of toleration as leniency offered at the discretion of a ruling party and subject to revocation at any time seems a far cry from what Washington calls "the exercise of their inherent natural rights." Yet as we shall see, this minimalist term has played a key role in the protracted struggle on behalf of broader understandings of rights for unpopular minorities. Tolerationist politics seeks to provide a sort of foothold for such groups, as they seek to carve out a protected social space for themselves; it represents an acknowledgment of the reality and the permanence of diversity in contemporary societies. (In this sense, a minimal term like toleration may require extensive government action to safeguard unpopular groups from violence at the hands of hostile fellow citizens.) It often, though by no means always, serves as a springboard toward efforts at more far-reaching protections. Indeed, as I point out in the Conclusion, the sort of toleration enshrined in the 1689 Toleration Act, partial though it was, proved to be the first step in a long and difficult struggle for inclusion on the part of a wider range of groups in English society.

Scholars often trace the roots of modern toleration to early modern Europe. Such debates took place within the contexts of post-Reformation European Christianity and the emergence of European nation-states, and addressed questions of the rights of dissenters from socially dominant or legally established churches. In the specific contexts I shall be discussing in this chapter, toleration generally involved political guarantees for those whose religious beliefs and/or practices placed them outside an established or dominant church, that is, an end to jailing, fines, or other punishments for refusal to conform to that church, and some minimal freedom of assembly and speech (for proselytizing and gathered worship). Certainly, tolerationist systems of various sorts had existed in prior times and places: under the Roman Empire (recall

Gibbon's famous claim that "The various modes of worship, which prevailed in the Roman world, were all considered by the people, as equally true; by the philosopher, as equally false; and by the magistrate, as equally useful" [Gibbon 1776, Chap. 2]); in the Ottoman millet system, where religious communities received a measure of autonomy to order their own affairs (Barkey and Gavrilis 2016); and in the work of medieval thinkers who envisioned adherents of diverse religions peacefully coexisting (Nederman 2001). But sixteenth- and seventeenth-century Europe saw two important and relatively simultaneous developments: the coalescence and increasing sophistication of arguments in favor of religious toleration and the political-military victory of tolerationist forces and, thus, the implementation of a measure of toleration in France under the Edict of Nantes, in England under Cromwell, in the Dutch Republic, and in other places across the Continent (see Kaplan 2007; Lecler 1960; Coffey 2000, Walsham 2006). The aftermath of those developments of the mid-seventeenth century continued to reverberate down through the Restoration in 1660, to the Revolution of 1688, and beyond.

Toleration in Seventeenth-Century England

The 1640s saw an outbreak of political and religious violence across the kingdoms of England, Scotland, and Ireland, violence that both reflected pre-existing dynamics and produced powerful arguments about toleration and religious dissent. A confluence of political events during those years led to the triumph of a tolerationist regime under Cromwell and reshaped the political and ecclesiastical landscape in profound ways. These arguments were not only important in their own right, in affecting tens of thousands of believers across the realm as well as the nascent colonial empire in North America and the Caribbean; they also set the stage for parallel debates during the Restoration, debates that included Locke's important contribution. (In what follows, I sketch out the broad contours of the arguments; for more comprehensive and detailed treatments, see Walsham (2006), Coffey (2000), and Murphy (2001, 2016).)

The debate over toleration in England, it must be emphasized, was a *Christian* argument, advanced in a Christian society. More specifically, it was a Protestant argument advanced against the backdrop of a robust Counter-Reformation and English concerns about geopolitical concerns about French and Spanish aspirations for domination in Europe and beyond. Virtually all English Protestants assumed that Catholicism represented not merely theological error but political tyranny, and deep-seated anti-Catholicism drove Puritan opposition within the Church of England during the early seventeenth century as well as Parliamentary opposition to royal policy in the years leading up to the outbreak of the Civil Wars. The legacy of anti-Catholicism in English society included the beheading of one king (Charles I) and the abdication of another (James II), to say nothing of the paranoia and unrest that convulsed the realm during the "Popish Plot" during 1678–1681 (see, e.g., Hibbard 1983; Miller 1973).

Appeals to the Christian Gospels, not surprisingly, formed a powerful part of tolerationists' rhetorical arsenal, and they drew on a wide range of Scriptures to denounce compulsion in matters of religion, including Jesus' rebuke of force (Matthew 26:52, Luke 9:54–55), the parable of the wheat and tares (Matthew 13), and his assertion that the Kingdom of God was not of this world (John 6:15 and 18:36). They also invoked the early church, primarily through references to Paul's epistles, including his exhortation, "Let every man be fully persuaded in his own mind" (Romans 14: 5), his emphasis on the dichotomy between spiritual and carnal realms (II Corinthians 10:4), and his injunction that Christians proceed with one another in a spirit of meekness and charity (II Timothy 2:24–26, Ephesians 4). As a corollary of these theological and Scriptural arguments, tolerationists often sought to identify a small number of core Christian doctrines to which all groups could subscribe, as a way of sidestepping complex doctrinal differences and emphasizing agreement on basics.

Alongside these Scriptural arguments, tolerationists also put forward an important *epistemological* argument about the nature of belief itself. On this understanding, belief could not be forced because it was a faculty of the understanding and not of the will. Persecution was not only wrong on Scriptural grounds, but it was also doomed to fail: one could force people to behave in certain ways (attend an established church, profess creeds, and so on), but the inner realm of belief – the heart of true religion – lay beyond the reach of governmental power. As Locke would later put it, "All the life and power of true religion consist in the inward and full persuasion of the mind; and faith is not faith without believing. Whatever profession we make. . . if we are not fully satisfied in our own mind. . .such profession. . .far from being any furtherance, are indeed great obstacles to our salvation" ([1689] 1983, 26–27). Persuasion and preaching, not coercion and persecution, represented the proper way to deal with spiritual errors. Tolerationists separated the understanding from the will and placed matters of religion and belief in the former, thereby ruling out attempts at religious compulsion.

In endorsing liberty of conscience and emphasizing the importance of sincere belief, tolerationists sought to develop a new and enhanced understanding of the conscience itself, in which subjective assent played an increasingly important role. Such a view represented a distinct departure from the reigning notion, which dated back to Aquinas, who had synthesized previous elaborations by Jerome, Bonaventure, Philip the Chancellor, and Peter Lombard. (For an overview, see Langston (2001).) In this orthodox conception, conscience represented the voice of God within an individual, and thus one could sin against one's conscience by transgressing God's law. In other words, it was possible for an individual to have an *erroneous conscience*, to hold as right some action that was, in fact, wrong. By contrast, early modern tolerationists began to stress a more subjective aspect of the term, in which one sinned by going against the conscience even if one's substantive beliefs were mistaken. They did not generally contest the notion that conscience could err, but instead sought political protections for individuals with erroneous consciences, so long as they comported themselves peacefully with their neighbors and obeyed the civil law. Even if an individual's religious beliefs were demonstrably erroneous,

William Penn argued in 1681, coercion remained unjustified, "for though their consciences be blind, yet they are not to be forced; such compulsion giveth no sight, neither do corporal punishments produce conviction" (1681, 10).

Finally, but no less importantly, tolerationists presented a number of *pragmatic and prudential arguments*. In a nation that had been divided by religion for more than a century, the prospect of finally settling differences and arriving at some sort of modus vivendi retained a strong attraction. On this account, persecution needlessly divided the populace, set neighbors against neighbors, prevented the government from making use of the talents of all its subjects, and destroyed the economy. Built upon the notion of a political community as a site of diverse human activities, with civil government responsible for the smooth functioning and harmonious oversight of them all, this view called for a dramatic restriction of the civil magistrate's powers over religious affairs. Roger Williams argued for conceptualizing the church as "like unto a corporation, society, or company of East India or Turkey merchants" within the larger society. Only when the health of the state was threatened by the activities of any of these "companies" was the magistrate justified in intervening in their affairs. In the preface to *The Bloudy Tenent*, Williams maintained that "all civil states...are proved essentially civil, and therefore not judges, governors, or defenders of the spiritual or Christian state and worship" (Williams [1644] 1867, 73; 3). To a realm in the throes of religious and political discord and civil war, tolerationists preached that granting toleration to Dissenters would promote peace and prosperity, often pointing to the neighboring Netherlands as an example of a political community where many faiths coexisted peacefully within a single state. Not only could such a state survive, but it could prosper and thrive, as Dutch economic power made abundantly clear.

Antitolerationist Arguments

In canvassing the arguments for toleration offered in this historical setting, it is worth remembering that the social and political ideal that tolerationists proposed was neither self-evident nor universally endorsed. Antitolerationists too possessed a robust Scriptural arsenal in endorsing religious uniformity, including Jesus's call for the apostles to "be one; as thou, Father, art in me, and I in thee" (John 17:21) and Paul's enjoining of Christians to unity (I Corinthians 1:10, II Corinthians 13:11). They went further into the Scriptures as well; in their attempt to construct a seamless Biblical case supporting the civil magistrate's duty to promote true religion and restrain heretics and blasphemers, advocates of uniformity cast their Scriptural nets even more broadly, evoking the expansive powers over religion possessed by kings of Israel.

Behind opposition to toleration lay profound fears about social order and concerns about anarchy, licentiousness, and social upheaval. In such a view, the fruits of political and religious dissent (rebellion, civil war, regicide) were plain to see for anyone who had followed events in England. If, as tolerationists claimed, compulsion in religious affairs was not acceptable, their opponents found it difficult to see how coercion of any sort could be acceptable in any area of human endeavor, making calls for toleration little more than endorsements of lawlessness and disorder. In addition, if freedom of belief was what tolerationists really wanted, then they already had it, since individuals could freely believe or disbelieve any piece of religious dogma they so chose. No one disputed the fact that thought should be free, and no one proposed punishing individuals for their beliefs. As Hobbes had put it in *Leviathan*, Chap. 37: "A private man has always the liberty (because thought is free), to believe, or not believe in his heart, those acts that have been given out for miracles." But, Hobbes continued, "when it comes to confession of that faith, the private reason must submit to the public" (Hobbes 1652 [1994], 300). What Dissenters wanted, their opponents pointed out, was not strictly speaking liberty of conscience – which after all was an internal judge of individual action – but rather a virtually unlimited liberty of action and behavior.

Case Study: The Career of William Penn

For the remainder of this chapter, I focus on one particular individual, William Penn (1644–1718), whose career as an activist and theorist of toleration evolved into a further role as proprietor of the American colony of Pennsylvania. Penn's thought predated Locke by more than a decade, and he played a central role in Restoration toleration debates, although he fell out of the public eye for years following the 1688 Revolution due to his association with James II. The campaign for toleration after 1660 continued in much the same vein as the aforementioned 1640s movement, with proponents arguing that individuals and groups ought to be free to follow their consciences not only in the narrow essentials of religious worship but in the many ways in which issues of conscience bear on public life. (Quakers like Penn refused to swear oaths in legal settings, show deference to social "superiors," and support armed forces with public funds, practices that further stretched the notion of "liberty of conscience" as well as "religious practice.") In contrast to theorists like Locke, Penn not only articulated principles of religious liberty in England: after 1681, he actually governed an American colony and attempted to put those principles into practice. Thus, Penn's political thought represents a marriage of tolerationist political theory with political practice, in the concrete experience of colonization in the Atlantic imperial context. (For overviews of Penn's thought, see Dunn (1967) and Murphy (2016).)

Although the political landscape shifted markedly with the Restoration in 1660, the main strands of argument regarding toleration remained broadly similar to those that had characterized the Civil War years. Scriptural arguments, increasingly explicit about their Protestant bases in the face of concern about the Catholic sympathies of Charles II and the overt Catholicism of James II, emphasized the sanctity of conscience and the right of even erroneous consciences to be free from coercion. Restoration tolerationists continued to reference Jesus's claim that his kingdom was not of this world, the parable of the tares and wheat, and Paul's exhortation that whatever is not of faith is sin; and to press the epistemological argument that true religion resides in inner conviction and was thus impervious to physical coercion, and thus doomed to fail. Historical or political arguments invoked the ancient English constitution and Magna Carta, seeking to build a dichotomy between religious identity on the one hand and political membership on the other. And pragmatic arguments, as before, emphasized the economic prosperity and civil peace that toleration would yield after years of religious strife.

Yet as in the past, tolerationists continued to face an uphill battle. Their critics powerfully evoked the 1640s and 1650s (in living memory), when Dissenters had pushed forward a civil war that led to regicide and Cromwell's imposed tolerationist regime. The view that civil rulers were charged with overseeing their realm's religious affairs, if not for the protection of pure doctrine then at least for the preservation of peace and order, remained powerful in the aftermath of such unrest and violence. Coercion might not able to effect a change in belief, antitolerationists conceded, but it could nonetheless play a role in forcing individuals to reconsider erroneous beliefs and thus come to accept true ones. (For a fuller account of the Restoration antitolerationist arguments, see Goldie (1991a, b).)

No one personified the Restoration antitolerationist cause like Samuel Parker, the Archdeacon of Canterbury (and, later, Bishop of Oxford). Parker's 1670 *A discourse of ecclesiastical politie* (Parker 1670), a ferocious polemic, advanced a bitter and often ad hominem attack on toleration and framed the religious, political, and philosophical case for religious orthodoxy and political uniformity in its most uncompromising form. The success of tolerationist arguments, Parker insisted, would surely lead to a repeat of the events of the 1640s and 1650s, when, under religious pretenses, an armed faction made war on legitimate authority, executed a king, and initiated a decade of army rule. Claims to liberty of conscience, he insisted, were little more than a demand to be free from any law an individual found irksome. Like many opponents of toleration, Parker refused to take talk of "conscience" seriously at all, seeing it as merely a mask for disloyalty or rebellion, and he denounced those who made a pretext of religious scruple while plotting to undermine both church and state. Given human fallibility and the likelihood of self-deception, it was virtually impossible to know ahead of time what sorts of consequences might ensue from granting the kind of liberty they sought: terms like chaos, anarchy, licentiousness, disorder, and confusion are ubiquitous in the antitolerationist literature. Parker claimed that "to exempt religion and the consciences of men from the authority of the supreme power is...to expose the peace of kingdoms to every wild and fanatick pretender, who may, whenever he pleases...thwart and unsettle government without control" (1670, 14–15).

William Penn published his first and most systematic defense of toleration, *The Great Case of Liberty of Conscience*, in 1670; he revised a second edition for publication while confined in London's Newgate prison for unauthorized preaching (Penn 1670a). *The Great Case* synthesizes the major tolerationist arguments in circulation at the time, denouncing persecution as contrary to the spirit of Christianity, Scripture, nature and reason, principles of good government, and the testimony of dozens of statesmen and church leaders. Penn defined liberty of conscience as "the free and uninterrupted exercise of our consciences, in that way of worship, we are most clearly persuaded, God requires us to serve Him in" (1670a, 4) and expanded on this brief definition by explaining that by liberty of conscience, he meant

> not only a mere liberty of the mind...but the exercise of ourselves in a visible way of worship, upon our believing it to be indispensibly required at our hands. . . . Yet...not to ...abet any contrivance destructive of the government and laws of the land, tending to matters of an external nature . . . but so far only, as it may refer to religious matters, and a life to come, and consequently wholly independent of . . . secular affairs. . . .

This broad understanding of liberty of conscience entailed an expanded definition of persecution: not simply the "requiring of us to believe this to be true, or that to be false...but...any coercive let or hindrance to us, from meeting together to perform those religious exercises which are according to our faith and persuasion" (1670a, 11–12).

In other words, liberty of conscience includes freedom not only of belief but also of action. He understood such liberty not merely as an individual right, but as a collective one that also incorporated several other rights: most particularly, freedoms of assembly and speech. Meeting with others serves an integral purpose to the exercise of individual conscience, and a commitment to free speech protected the liberty to preach and proselytize. Political theorists both then and ever since have recognized the centrality of this cluster of related rights, from John Milton to John Stuart Mill and down to Rawlsian liberals in our own time (Milton 1644; Mill 1859, esp. Chap. 1; Rawls 1971, 1993). In keeping with Penn's expanded notion of conscience went an expansive category of persecution, which he understood as encompassing any "coercive let or hindrance" to meeting for religious worship. To be concerned about persecution and toleration required attending not only to large-scale and graphic punishments like whipping, imprisonment, fining, and seizure of goods but also to the many ways in which early modern ecclesiastical and political authorities could interfere with Dissenters' religious exercise.

The Great Case thus attacked persecution along the main lines of tolerationist argument that had been circulating in England for decades: it represented an egregious interference with God's sovereignty over the human conscience; it interposed human authority between the individual and his or her God and "directly invade[s] divine prerogative...divest[s] the almighty of a due, proper to none besides himself . . . [and] enthrones man as king over conscience, the alone just claim and privilege of his creator" (1670a, 12, 13). Persecution was fundamentally un-Christian, as well, and Penn offered a range of familiar Scriptures, from the parable of the wheat and tares and the Golden Rule to Paul's exhortations to the Ephesians to bear meekly with others and his remarks in Romans that each believer should be convinced in his own mind. In sum, for Penn, persecution represented "the overthrow of the whole Christian religion" (1670a, 15, 21–22).

As mentioned above, the tolerationist movement in England was never simply about Christianity: it was a more specifically Protestant discourse and intertwined with long-standing English anti-Catholicism. Protestants persecuting other Protestants "overturns the very ground of [their] retreat from Rome" and puts them in the place formerly occupied by their Catholic persecutors, Penn lamented (1670a, 6). Denunciations of Roman Catholics were de rigueur among English tolerationists, who remained almost unanimous in their view that Catholics ought not to be tolerated. Penn shared his compatriots' deep distrust of Catholics, although he attempted to step back from its harshest implications, suggesting in *A seasonable caveat against popery* that Catholics whose political loyalty could be guaranteed might be granted some measure of toleration (Penn 1670b, 4, 32).

Penn also invoked the epistemological argument mentioned above, maintaining that persecution was based on a misapprehension about the structure of human psychology and the way that humans understand and interpret the world. God "has given [humanity] both senses corporeal and intellectual, to discern things and their differences, so as to assert or deny from evidences and reasons proper to each....Faith in all acts of religion is necessary: now in order to believe, we must first will; to will, we must first judge; to judge anything, we must first understand" (1670a, 19, 20). For religion to be salvific for any individual, it must be the product of mature understanding and deliberate consideration. And since belief resided in the understanding and not the will, persecution was bound simply *not to work*. In other words, "the understanding can never be convinced, nor properly submit, but by such arguments, as are rational, persuasive, and suitable to its own nature. . . . Force may make an hypocrite, 'tis faith grounded upon knowledge, and consent, that makes a Christian" (1670a, 22). The physical punishments delivered by punitive measures are powerless to effect the real inner change at the heart of true religion. (Such a position of the workings of belief would later be put, most famously, by Locke in his *Letter Concerning Toleration*: "Such is the nature of the understanding, that it cannot be compelled to the belief of anything by outward force" (Locke [1689] 1983, 27).)

Along with a reconstructed notion of conscience and its liberty, Penn presented a reconstructed view of the proper domain of government, which he called "an external order of justice, or the right and prudent disciplining of any society, by just laws" (23). Key to this understanding of the proper role of government was a distinction between two types of law. Fundamental law (e.g., Magna Carta) was "indispensable and immutable" and must not be abrogated under any circumstances. It functioned to preserve essential liberties like liberty, property, and representation and secured Englishmen from the exercise of arbitrary power. Superficial laws on the other hand ("temporary and alterable," passed by particular parliaments for the ordering of everyday life) were contingent and must change with the times (1670a, 24). Penn's distinction between fundamental and superficial law enabled him to argue that the changes he sought were not reckless innovations but rather a return to time-honored constitutional values.

Like his contemporaries, Penn emphasized the importance of civil peace and economic prosperity as evidence of the desirability of toleration. Penal laws "are so far from benefiting the country, that the execution of them will be the assured ruin of it, in the revenues, and consequently, in the power of it" (1670a, 27). If government is charged with promoting the common good, persecution undermines that goal, especially when considering how crucial Dissenters are to the nation's trade. And finally, Penn offered further evidence of the happy coincidence of the people and the ruler's interests: an extensive list of historical figures – from figures in classical antiquity to Church Fathers to European statesmen to England's own martyred King, Charles I – who had tolerated religious dissent in their midst and reaped the benefits (1670a, Chap. 6).

With the publication of the second edition of *The Great Case*, William Penn had articulated all the main philosophical, theological, and political arguments about toleration and liberty of conscience that would constitute his mature theory of toleration. He was also well on his way to establishing himself as a rising young figure in the Society of Friends and a national figure on the English political scene. He continued to develop additional dimensions of the argument for toleration, however, and was particularly influential in the early years of the Quaker Meeting for Sufferings, formed in October 1675 and charged with gathering information about the persecution faced by members of the Society of Friends. That year he published *The Continued Cry of the Oppressed* (Penn 1675), a collection of detailed accounts of persecution suffered by Quakers. In marked contrast to *The Great Case*, with its systematic presentation of arguments against persecution, *The Continued Cry* presented something rather different: an extensive listing of towns and counties across England and Wales, and the sufferings inflicted on peaceful Quakers in each one, often rendered in highly specific (and moving) detail. Stoking moral outrage and sympathy over the practices that supported a persecuting society – imprisonment, fines, whipping, banishment, seizure of property, and so on – was a central element of Penn's developing theory of toleration during the 1670s and of the broader Quaker movement to elicit public sympathy and, perhaps, eventual changes in religious policy.

Yet those hopes were to be dashed, and by the end of that decade, as a political crisis gripped England and Quakers faced continuing persecution, Penn hit upon a new idea: an American colony where adherents of many religions might live in peace, mutually committed to each other's welfare even while each worshipped as they saw fit. He parlayed a debt from the Crown into a massive American land grant and sailed for America in 1682. In Penn's vision, Pennsylvania would serve as a place where Quakers could live their lives in accord with their consciences (no established church and no swearing of oaths, to name just two). He also sought to encourage "sober people of all sorts" to join in the colonizing enterprise, and Pennsylvania soon became a destination for those seeking refuge from persecution as well as the expanded economic opportunities that American colonization promised (Soderlund 1983; Frost 1990). The story of the subsequent development of Pennsylvania society lies beyond the scope of this chapter, but it is worth noting, by way of conclusion, that Penn's struggle to balance his commitment to liberty of conscience with his responsibilities as colonial proprietor was an ongoing one. Penn struggled, with some success but also a great deal of disappointment, to translate principles articulated in England to new and different American realities (see Murphy 2019).

Summary and Future Directions

The arguments over religious toleration explored in this chapter are, on the one hand, highly restricted, advocating for the liberty of one type of Christians to worship as they see fit, against the resistance of another type of Christians, in several discrete

European contexts. (They are also rather abbreviated: a more comprehensive treatment would range across England and the Continent and include names like Erasmus, Castellio, and Bayle in addition to Williams, Locke, and Penn [Guggisberg 1983; Jordan 1932–1940].) Yet by providing a toehold for dissenters to exist with some measure of security, they provided a protected social space from which such groups could advocate for fuller notions of liberty (for themselves and/or others). In England, for example, the Toleration Act of 1689 left in place a number of restrictions on Dissenters like Penn and his fellow Quakers. The religious liberty granted by the Toleration Act was far less extensive than had existed during Cromwell's Protectorate during the 1650s, not to mention that extended by James II's Declaration of Indulgence. The Act required dissenting congregations to apply to Anglican bishops for licenses and to leave their doors unlocked during worship services. Penal laws for nonattendance of Anglican services, though suspended, remained on the books. The Test Act remained in effect, barring Catholics and non-Trinitarian Protestants from serving in public office and posts in the major universities.

That said, the groundwork laid by the Toleration Act in turn made possible the continuation of the movement for a more robust understanding of liberty of conscience. It was an extended and by no means easy process. In subsequent years, milestones of the ongoing struggle for greater liberty included the passage of the Affirmation Act (1695), Sacramental Test Act (1828), Catholic Relief Act (1829), and Jews Relief Act (1858), each of which gradually removed barriers to officeholding in Parliament. In the American case, although expansive understandings of religious liberty have always struggled against a dominant Protestant ethos in the broader culture, much twentieth-century jurisprudence has generally moved in the direction of a greater solicitousness toward claims of religious exercise, broadening the notion of "exercise" to include observation of the Sabbath (*Sherbert v Verner*, 1964) and conscientious objections to war (*US v Seeger*, 1968). Courts also broadened the idea of "burden" to include not merely political repression but also denial of unemployment benefits (again, *Sherbert*). (Then again, such expansions are hardly set in stone, as more recent decisions (e.g., *Smith* [1990], *Hosanna-Tabor* [2012]) have made abundantly clear.)

Nor should we assume, of course, that the history of religious toleration in early modern Europe is the only important context from which we can learn. Comparative historical studies of other traditions hold great promise to explore the ways in which a broader range of non-Christian societies have navigated difference in their midst. If Christian thinkers built their notions of liberty of conscience upon their understandings of conscience, then investigating the degree to which analogous concepts exist in non-Christian contexts might represent a fruitful direction of inquiry. Although all major religious traditions possess notions of right conduct and moral self-examination, it is important to keep languages and symbol systems within which non-Christian religions embed their concepts distinct from the Christian theological categories that gave rise to the standard notion of conscience. Searching for "equivalences" – say, a Buddhist or Hindu "version" of conscience – is inherently controversial (Despland 1995; but cf. Chryssides, in Hoose 1999). On the other hand, an appreciation of the many different criteria by which adherents of various religious traditions examine their own behavior and decisions – the ways in which they may broadly parallel each other, and the ways in which they depart from each other – promises a productive comparison of Christian debates over liberty of conscience with an expansive range of other virtues, practices, and beliefs.

Even many of its defenders will admit that toleration is an "old-fashioned ideal" (Gray 1995, 27); yet its benefits should not be overlooked. The cessation of violence between groups with long histories of strife and the extension of basic political protections to unpopular minorities are concrete social goods, even if they originate in very narrow ways. Debates over the degree to which tolerationist discourses might inform contemporary issues, for example, marriage equality, continue to characterize the scholarship on these topics (e.g., Gill 2012). Toleration thus represents a necessary, though not always sufficient, political achievement. Its defenders, from the seventeenth century down to our own day, recognize that political theory and practice involve the gradual, often halting, and always contested extension of civil and political rights. In that process, the tradition of toleration continues to play a central role in the ongoing struggle for human freedom and dignity.

References

Barkey K, Gavrilis G (2016) The Ottoman Millet system: non-territorial autonomy and its contemporary legacy. Ethnopolitics 15(1):24–42

Berlin I (1958) Two concepts of liberty. Clarendon Press, Oxford

Brown W (2009) Regulating aversion: tolerance in the age of identity and empire. Princeton University Press, Princeton

Chryssides GD (1999) Buddhism and conscience. In: Hoose J (ed) Conscience in world religions. Gracewing, Leominster

Coffey J (2000) Persecution and toleration in Protestant England 1558–1689. Routledge, Abingdon

Coffey J (2020) How religious freedom became a natural right: the case of post-Reformation England. In: van der Tol MDC, Brown C, Adenitire J, Kempson ES (eds) From toleration to religious freedom: cross-disciplinary perspectives. Peter Lang, Berlin

Despland, Michael ([1987] 1995). Conscience. In: Eliade M (ed) The encyclopedia of religion. Macmillan, New York

Dunn MM (1967) William Penn: politics and conscience. Princeton University Press, Princeton

Forst R (2013) Toleration in conflict: past and present. Transl Croni C. Cambridge University Press, Cambridge

Frost JW (1990) A perfect freedom: religious liberty in Pennsylvania. Cambridge University Press, New York

Gibbon E (1776) The history of the decline and fall of the Roman Empire, vol I. Strahan and Cadell, London

Gill ER (2012) An argument for same-sex marriage: religious freedom, sexual freedom, and public expressions of civic equality. Georgetown University Press, Washington, DC

Goldie M (1991a) The theory of religious intolerance in Restoration England. In: Grell OP, Israel JI, Tyacke N (eds) From persecution to toleration: the glorious revolution and religion in England. Oxford University Press, New York, pp 331–368

Goldie M (1991b) The political thought of the Anglican revolution. In: Beddard R (ed) The revolutions of 1688: the Andrew Browning lectures. Clarendon Press, Oxford, pp 102–136

Gray J (1995) Toleration: a post-liberal perspective. In: Enlightenment's wake: politics and culture at the close of the modern age. Routledge, London

Guggisberg HR (1983) The defence of religious toleration and religious liberty in early modern Europe: arguments, pressures, and some consequences. Hist Eur Ideas 4:35–50

Hibbard C (1983) Charles I and the Popish Plot. The University of North Carolina Press, Chapel Hill

Hobbes T (1652 [1994]) In: Curley E (ed) Leviathan. Hackett, Indianapolis, 1994

Jordan WK (1932–1940) The development of religious toleration in England, 4 vols. Harvard University Press, Cambridge, MA

Kaplan BJ (2007) Divided by faith: religious conflict and the practice of toleration in early modern Europe. Harvard University Press, Cambridge, MA

Langston D (2001) Conscience and other virtues. Penn State University Press, University Park

Laursen JC, Nederman CJ (eds) (1998) Beyond the persecuting society: religious toleration before the enlightenment. University of Pennsylvania Press, Philadelphia

Lecler J (1960) Toleration and the reformation, 2 vols. Transl Westlow TL. Longmans, London

Locke J (1689 [1983]) A letter concerning toleration. Hackett Publishing, Indianapolis

Mill JS (1859) On liberty. London

Miller J (1973) Popery and politics 1660–1688. Cambridge University Press, Cambridge

Milton J (1644) Areopagitica. London

Murphy AR (1997a) Tolerance, toleration, and the liberal tradition. Polity 29(4):593–623

Murphy AR (1997b) The uneasy relationship between social contract theory and religious toleration. J Polit 59:368–392

Murphy AR (2001) Conscience and community: revisiting toleration and religious dissent in early modern England and America. Penn State University Press, University Park

Murphy AR (2016) Liberty, conscience, and toleration: the political thought of William Penn. Oxford University Press, New York

Murphy AR (2019) William Penn: a life. Oxford University Press, New York

Nederman CJ (2001) Worlds of difference: European discourses of toleration, c. 1100–c.1500. Penn State University Press, University Park

Parker S (1670) A discourse of ecclesiastical politie. London

Penn W (1670a) The great case of liberty of conscience. London

Penn W (1670b) A seasonable caveat against popery. London

Penn W (1675) The continued cry of the oppressed. London

Penn W (1679) An address to Protestants upon the present conjuncture. London

Penn W (1681) A brief examination and state of liberty spiritual. London

Rawls J (1971) A theory of justice. Harvard University Press, Cambridge, MA

Rawls J (1993) Political liberalism. Columbia University Press, New York

Sehat D (2010) The myth of American religious freedom. Oxford University Press, New York

Soderlund J (ed) (1983) William Penn and the founding of Pennsylvania: a documentary history. University of Pennsylvania Press, Philadelphia

Vernon R (1997) The career of toleration: John Locke, Jonas Proast, and after. McGill-Queens University Press, Montreal

Walsham A (2006) Charitable hatred: tolerance and intolerance in England, 1500–1700. University of Manchester Press, Manchester

Washington G. Letter to the Hebrew congregation at Newport. 18 Aug 1790. http://teachingamericanhistory.org/library/document/letter-to-the-hebrew-congregation-at-newport/

Wenger T (2017) Religious freedom: the contested history of an American ideal. University of North Carolina Press, Chapel Hill

Williams R (1644) The bloudy tenent of persecution. London

Wolfson A (1997) Toleration and relativism: the Locke-Proast exchange. Rev Politics 59:213–231

Thomas Hobbes and the Conditionality of Toleration

50

J. Judd Owen

Contents

The Conditionality of Toleration	1011
The Contingency of Toleration on Enlightenment	1015
References	1021

Abstract

It is widely accepted today that toleration is a defining characteristic of liberalism. But this assumption leads to a conceptual impasse, since liberalism, like all regimes, is compelled at some point to be intolerant of forces that would overturn it. Liberalism cannot be the opposite of absolutism, as liberals today assume, if it rests on its own absolutism. The political thought of Thomas Hobbes is invaluable for sorting out this paradox. Hobbes is often considered illiberal by those who fail to recognize liberalism's own absolutism and who therefore fail to recognize that toleration was indeed a goal of Hobbes, although a goal that is necessarily secondary to peace and security. Hobbes makes explicit what liberals today tend to obscure. But Hobbes's alleged intolerance is also partly explained by the fact that he perceived the need for a profound religious and cultural transformation – popular "enlightenment" – before toleration could be secured.

Keywords

Hobbes · Toleration · Absolutism · Religion · Enlightenment

Liberalism is founded on the notions of individual rights and limited government. It is widely accepted today that, as a consequence of these foundational principles, toleration is a defining characteristic of liberalism. For a government to be

J. J. Owen (✉)
Department of Political Science, Emory University, Atlanta, GA, USA
e-mail: jjowen@emory.edu

considered liberal, in this view, it must be tolerant, in the sense of maintaining robust protections for a broad range of individual freedoms understood as inherent and inviolable rights. It is the inviolability of these rights that limits a liberal government. A government that does not protect a broad range of such rights, particularly if it curbs them for the sake of maintaining governmental authority, is not liberal but instead what is taken to be the opposite of liberal, viz., "absolutist."

But making toleration a defining principle of liberalism brings with it certain paradoxes, since liberalism repeatedly finds itself in a position where these freedoms must be curbed and some intolerance is required. When liberals oppose absolutist forces such as fascism, communism, and theocracy – not only with words but when necessary with the force of law and arms – they are justified in opposing what threatens the regime of liberalism itself. But cannot fascists, communists, and theocrats say that their own intolerances serve to protect their own regimes? Must not liberalism too circumscribe what it can and cannot tolerate? Isn't liberalism itself, therefore, in some sense absolutist? If so, then liberalism is not the opposite of absolutism but a peculiar form of it, and the attempt to define liberalism in terms of toleration proves inadequate, if not conceptually incoherent. Such considerations have led one shrewd critic to conclude that "liberalism doesn't exist" (Fish 1994, 138).

If making toleration the defining characteristic of liberalism leads to a conceptual impasse, how else can we articulate the peculiar character of liberal absolutism and do so in a way that does justice to the value that liberalism does seem to place on toleration? Is it simply a matter of the degree of toleration – a quantitative rather than qualitative difference? But then what quantity of toleration would define liberalism? And could any regime type whatever then be considered liberal when (but only so long as) it met some quantitative threshold? Must not liberalism instead be marked by some qualitative difference, some set of principles? But what set of principles would be more fundamental to liberalism than toleration?

Help in sorting out the paradoxes surrounding liberal toleration, and thus the character of liberalism, can be found in considering the philosophy of the great seventeenth-century political thinker, Thomas Hobbes. Hobbes's works are widely regarded as massively influential on the liberal tradition since his political doctrine is founded on natural human equality and individual rights, bases governmental authority on the consent of the governed, and limits the purpose of governmental authority to an unprecedented degree. And yet, despite these clearly liberal features, his own status as a liberal theorist is profoundly controversial. How could this be? At the heart of the controversy is the strong impression that Hobbes was indifferent, if not hostile, to toleration. This impression stems from the extraordinary power that he grants the sovereign over, e.g., religion and the press, and his emphatic denial of a right of conscience. Thus commentators have supposed there to be a disjunction between the founding principles of Hobbes's doctrine and the conclusions he drew from those principles. "The paradox of Hobbism," says Deborah Baumgold, lies "in its derivation of absolutist conclusions from liberal-individualistic principles of natural right, consent, and individual self-interest" (Baumgold 1988, 133–134).

This paradox lingers, despite the fact that Hobbes is renowned for the clarity and rigor of his thought.

In fact, however, Hobbes did seek to secure the greatest possible scope of private liberty, or what we now call toleration, which requires in the first place the peace and security that only an effective sovereign authority can provide. If Hobbes does grant the sovereign extraordinary power, he does so with a view to an extraordinarily limited purpose, beyond which the sovereign has no interest whatever. Hobbes is revealing of the often-hidden character of liberalism, because liberal toleration is always dependent on, and therefore limited by, liberalism's own absolutism. Liberal rights are always qualified and conditional. For Hobbesian liberalism, toleration is desirable and indeed a necessary feature of an enlightened society. Toleration is therefore, in a qualified sense, a principle of Hobbesian liberalism as well. But toleration is emphatically conditional on the capacity of the government to maintain peace, and that capacity must be absolute. Our accounts of liberalism today typically put the absolutism that qualifies toleration in the background, if they don't obscure it altogether, whereas Hobbes never lets us forget it. The liberal view that looks askance at Hobbes wishes to claim toleration as an unconditional right. But the inevitable untenability of such unconditional rights allows us to see that Hobbes's liberalism is not so much opposed to contemporary liberalism as it is more clear-sighted about the necessary relation between toleration and absolutism and about the necessarily secondary or contingent nature of toleration.

The Conditionality of Toleration

In order to understand Hobbes's teaching on toleration, i.e., the realm of individual freedom within political society, we must approach it by way of his teaching on human freedom more generally. We begin from the most famous part of Hobbes's political teaching: the state of nature. According to Hobbes, human beings by nature are not, as Aristotle supposed, political animals, nor are some human beings more naturally suited to govern than others. Political life is thoroughly artificial, and to understand human nature, we must imagine human beings prior to or outside of all political society – without government, without law, and without law enforcement. The natural condition of humankind is pure anarchy. This so-called state of nature for human beings is one of absolute freedom, in the sense that human beings are naturally equal and equally possess the unlimited right to do whatever they see fit, particularly with a view to their own preservation. And preservation in the state of nature is the paramount concern, because the natural condition is one of scarcity and intense competition among individuals who are equal not only in right but in power, leading to a war of each against all the rest. Life in the state of nature, as Hobbes famously says, is "poor, solitary, nasty, brutish, and short" (*Leviathan* 13.9). There can be no lasting trust between human beings, and none of the goods of society can get off the ground. Moreover, the universal individual right to preservation means that justice and injustice have no place in the state of nature. Hobbes thus teaches that the state of absolute freedom, i.e., of universal natural right, is a relentlessly terrible condition for everyone. Recognition of the horrors of the state of nature and its causes makes recognition of the only feasible solution possible. The naturally absolute freedom of unlimited right must be artificially abolished. Individuals must surrender to a man-made sovereign power as much of their rights as is necessary to secure their own preservation. In surrendering their natural absolute freedom, they consent to give the sovereign power they have created the authority to make laws over them and the power to enforce those laws.

Hobbes supposed that the implications of the state of nature cannot be driven home forcefully enough, precisely because the solution is artificial and our natures strongly incline toward absolute freedom for ourselves individually. But this is not to say that the solution to the state of nature does not appeal to our natural love of freedom, since in the state of nature, absolute and universal freedom, practically speaking, means a vanishingly small realm of *actual freedom*. Freedom de jure means almost no freedom de facto: "that right of all men to all things is in effect no better than if no man had a right to anything" (*Elements of Law* 14.10). Surrendering natural rights to a sovereign power means the ability to enjoy for the first time actual freedom, in a condition of peace and security, which in turn allows for the first time trust of and cooperation with our fellow human beings and all the goods of society that can result.

Despite this promise of freedom in fact, Hobbes was evidently wary of supporting his teaching through appeals to liberty, to rights claimed against sovereign power, fearing that such appeals could easily be exploited to undermine the necessary obedience to the sovereign on which practical liberty depends. More characteristic is his appeal to our fear of the reversion back to the state of nature that is implied in what he hopes to have shown to be the irrational desire for absolute liberty that we share with all other human beings. And this leads to the many passages that understandably have led many interpreters to see Hobbes as hostile to toleration. He expressly rejects, for example, that allegedly bedrock liberal principle of freedom of conscience. Hobbes anticipates the objection that his doctrine means "the loss of liberty," since "the subject may no more govern his own actions according to his own discretion and judgment, or, (which is all one) conscience, as the present occasions from time to time shall dictate; but must be tied to do according to [the sovereign] will only.... But," Hobbes responds, "this is really no inconvenience."

> For...it is the only means by which we have any possibility of preserving ourselves; for if every man were allowed this liberty of following his conscience, in such difference of consciences, they would not live together in peace an hour. But it appeareth a great inconvenience to every man in particular, to be debarred of this liberty, because every one apart considereth it as in himself, and not as in the rest; by which means, liberty appeareth in the likeness of rule and government over others; for where one man is at liberty, and the rest bound, there that one hath the government. Which honour, he that understandeth not so much, demanding by the name simply of liberty, thinking it a great grievance and injury to be denied it. (*Elements of Law* 24.2)

Since our consciences disagree, the right of conscience of one could only mean the abolition of the right of conscience of others. Alternatively, to claim an *equal* right of conscience for all would mean the anarchic clash of consciences and a return to the state of nature.

The same point has been made with sufficient clarity by the US Supreme Court decision in the landmark case of *Reynolds v. U.S.* (1879), in which the court confronted a challenge from Mormons to a federal ban on polygamy. In *Reynolds*, the court rejected the Mormon appeal to the right to free exercise under the First Amendment, declaring that "[a] party's religious belief cannot be accepted as justification for conduct that is made punishable by the law of the land. To permit such justification would be to make the professed doctrines of religious belief superior to the law of the land," and "government could only exist in name under such circumstances." Consider too Abraham Lincoln's defense of his suspension of the writ of habeas corpus during the Civil War: "the Constitution is not, in its application, in all respects the same, in cases of rebellion or invasion involving the public safety, as it is in time of profound peace and public security" (Lincoln 1992, 280). Similarly, John Rawls, one of the leading theorists of contemporary liberalism, says: Liberal rights are always followed by an asterisk.

> Assume that tolerant sects have the right not to tolerate the intolerant in at least one circumstance, namely, when they sincerely and with reason believe that intolerance is necessary for their own security. This right follows readily enough since, as the original position defined, each would agree to the right of self-preservation.... The situation presents a practical dilemma which philosophy alone cannot resolve. Whether the liberty of the intolerant should be limited to preserve freedom under a just constitution depends on the circumstances." (Rawls 1971, 218–219)

The character of Hobbes's liberalism can be seen more clearly in this regard in light of Locke's account of executive prerogative. Locke is easily recognizable as a liberal to us because he explicitly identifies a realm of individual rights that would serve as a check on governmental power. But he also is compelled to grant to the executive the power to violate that realm in cases where the public safety demands it. The magistrate, Locke says, must have "the power to act according to discretion, for the public good, without the prescription of the law, and sometimes even against it" (*Second Treatise of Government* §160). His example is the destruction of a row house to stop the spread of fire. Locke argues that when such discretion is truly necessary for the public good, the public can easily recognize the situation and accept it, while expecting a speedy return to the status quo ante. Nevertheless, he acknowledges that no line can be drawn circumscribing liberties that circumstances may not require to be crossed.

Where Hobbes differs from Locke, and from most of the liberal tradition that followed, is in his claim that it is imprudent to try to draw that line (by law), which one can know in advance may have to be crossed. Drawing such a line amounts to foreswearing publicly the use of some sovereign power. "From whence it comes to pass," Hobbes warns, "that, when the exercise of the power laid by is for the public safety to be resumed, it hath the resemblance of an unjust act, which disposeth great numbers of men (when occasion is presented) to rebel" (*Leviathan* 29.3). Hobbes fears the threat to the public safety that may result, under Locke's plan, when the public sees (or some meddlesome ambitious individuals decry) the sovereign acting illegally and hence (the people may assume or be led to believe) illegitimately. Locke might respond that such legal limitations on sovereign power are necessary in the first place in order for the people to submit willingly to the public authority. But that is a question of strategy for the same goal rather than a disagreement about the goal.

What, then, is the goal of Hobbesian liberalism? For Hobbes, as for other liberals, political society requires the surrender of liberty and obedience to the law. But for Hobbes, as for other liberals, that surrender of liberty is not choice worthy in itself but is instead the necessary means to peace among individuals with unavoidably conflicting opinions and interests. Moreover, for Hobbes, as for other liberals, it does not suffice to say that the goal is *mere* peace and security. Hobbes says that the "office," i.e., the duty, of the sovereign is "the procuration of the safety of the people," but he immediately adds: "But by safety here is not meant a bare preservation, but also all other contentments of life, which every man by lawful industry, without danger or hurt to the commonwealth shall acquire to himself" (*Leviathan* 23.9). It is the sovereign's duty to secure "commodity of living" for the people, which "consists in liberty and wealth. By liberty I mean, that there be no prohibition without necessity of anything to any man, which was lawful to him in the law of nature; that is to say, that there be no restraint of natural liberty, but what is necessary for the good of the commonwealth" (*Elements of Law* 28.4). The state of nature is indeed the worst state for human beings, where natural freedom is the problem and the artificial Leviathan is the solution. But the state of nature also, in a way, provides the goal of the Leviathan state: the maximum natural freedom that can be safely enjoyed (cf. Owen 2005, 137–140).

Hobbes is indeed the father of the liberal philosophy of limited government, understood as government existing for the extremely limited purpose of the material well-being of individuals as individuals. All governments must of course take into account the low aims of material well-being to some extent. What distinguishes Hobbesian liberalism is in making these low ends the sole measure and purpose of government. Government can limit itself to these low ends, Hobbes supposed, because the natural ends of human beings are low. Human beings have no ends nobler than their own material well-being and otherwise wish to be left alone. Under this doctrine of limited government, subjects are free to do whatever they please in any area not explicitly addressed by the law: "since all the motion and actions of the citizens have never been circumscribed by law, nor can be circumscribed because of their variety, it is necessary that the things that are neither commanded nor prohibited be almost infinite; and each can do them or not at his own discretion" (*De Cive* 13.15, my translation). These are "[t]hat part of natural right which is allowed and left to the citizens by the civil laws." That is, they are part of each man's freedom left over from the state of nature, and in some sense unleashed by the civil laws. Natural rights should be limited only insofar as they are harmful – harmful to the public safety, rather than to one's soul. Hobbes states: "it is contrary to the duty of those who rule and have authority to make law that there be more laws than conduces to the good of the citizens and civic body." As for the "harmless liberties, [these] the rulers are obligated to preserve for their citizens by the natural law" (*De Cive* 13.15).

Now, natural law for Hobbes, to be clear, does not involve a moral obligation in the sense of a duty to do something regardless of whether it is to one's own advantage. On the contrary, Hobbesian natural laws are "conclusions of theorems concerning what conduceth to the conservation and defense" of oneself (*Leviathan* 15.41). Hobbes always builds on what he assumed was the most solid ground of self-interest. When Hobbes instructs the sovereign in natural law, he is advising him on how to best preserve his rule. The sovereign will best preserve his rule by respecting human nature and preserving the greatest sphere of individual liberty that is compatible with civil peace. For Hobbes, the *enlightened self-interest* of the sovereign would be a surer basis for limited government than any bill of rights written on paper could ever be. The success of the Hobbesian project depends on an enlightened sovereign, i.e., a sovereign trained in Hobbesian political science. So too it requires an enlightened populace, and it is here – with the question of popular "enlightenment" – that we arrive at a genuine and profound disagreement between Hobbesian and contemporary liberalism (cf. *Leviathan* 31.41, *Elements of Law* 29.8).

The Contingency of Toleration on Enlightenment

Even if the case we have laid out above for Hobbes as a liberal friend of toleration is sound, it remains insufficient. For Hobbes does, in fact, advocate censorship of opinions by the sovereign. Indeed, he advocates a concerted effort by the sovereign to indoctrinate the people, not only in the principles of his political science but also in a variety of religious doctrines. Indeed, although he grants the sovereign considerable latitude with regard to the governance of religion, he seems to take for granted that the sovereign will dictate both religious doctrine and religious practice. It is true that Hobbes is not indifferent to the sort of religion to be established. He spends considerable effort reinterpreting Christianity to suit his ends, and the character of that reinterpretation helps to illuminate his ends, as we shall see below. Nevertheless, even if we accept that Hobbes favored toleration of the maximum individual freedom that can be safely enjoyed, does he not evidently think that the range of individual freedom that can be safely enjoyed is too narrow? Has the history of liberal societies not shown that Hobbes was far too cautious in permitting individual freedom and that *in practice* his doctrine is more authoritarian than tolerant?

In order to consider this question, it is necessary to pull back from the level of Hobbes's political doctrine in the abstract and situate it in its historical context. First, we must recognize that the question of toleration in seventeenth-century England and Europe more generally was almost wholly one of *religious* toleration. To be more precise, it was a question of whether and to what extent the state would tolerate religions other than the established ones. That some religion must be established was almost universally accepted. To be still more precise, it was a question of whether and to what extent the established sect of the Christian religion should tolerate other sects of the Christian religion. Policies of toleration varied and shifted amid ceaseless controversy and grievances, to say nothing of revolutions (and feared revolutions) in church establishment that might occur with a change of the sovereign. Struggles over questions of religious establishment and toleration were a prime cause of the English Civil War, the prospect and then actuality of which were, as is generally agreed, very much on Hobbes's mind as he was developing and articulating his doctrine over the span of several decades of the seventeenth century. The various policies of toleration were an unstable feature of a deeper instability, and Hobbes did not suppose that a policy of toleration would solve the fundamental problem, since many sectarians that might be tolerated were not themselves tolerant of other sects. If toleration was to be possible, it would depend on a deeper transformation.

Liberalism, then, did not invent toleration. Prior to liberal toleration, there was toleration rooted in competing claimants to orthodoxy and orthopraxy and toleration of heterodoxy and heteropraxy, to say nothing of heresy and apostasy. Such toleration was clearly secondary to orthodoxy and therefore limited, often severely. But, as the previous section shows, toleration being of secondary value to and limited by some other principle cannot be what distinguishes liberal toleration from religious orthodox toleration of heterodoxy. Nor does it indicate what is distinctive in the liberal solution to the problem of religiopolitical instability.

There was another model of toleration of which Hobbes was aware and which brings us closer to his approach. We can call it classical toleration, owing to the fact that examples would have been found in the classical world. Hobbes says that the policy on religion in Rome, as he claims was the case in the other pagan commonwealths, had as its goal "only to keep the people in obedience and peace" (*Leviathan* 12.20). "And therefore the Romans," he says, "that had conquered the greatest part of the then known world, made no scruple of tolerating any religion whatsoever in the city of Rome itself, unless it had something in it that could not consist with their civil government" (*Leviathan* 12.21). The Roman policy thus appears to accord with Hobbes's teaching. He then adds, however, the following observation: "nor do we read that any religion was there forbidden, but that of the Jews, who (being the peculiar kingdom of God) thought it unlawful to acknowledge subjection to any mortal king or state whatever." Hobbes's assertion here is surprising, since he can expect his reader to be aware of another religion besides Judaism that was suppressed by the Romans: Christianity. Why might Hobbes have avoided pointing out that Christianity had, like Judaism, posed a problem for the Roman policy of toleration? And what are the implications of this avoidance for his own views on a policy of toleration in an era, not of multiple polytheistic religions as in the pagan world, but of competing interpretations of the same monotheistic religion?

In approaching these questions, we must expand on Hobbes's account of the Roman policy on religion, for it was not simply one of toleration, and indeed he mentions Roman toleration only after enumerating four characteristics of Roman religion and pagan religion generally. First and foremost, "the first founders and legislators of commonwealths among the Gentiles" took care "to imprint in [the] minds [of the people] a belief that those precepts which they gave concerning religion might not be thought to proceed from their own device, but from the dictates of some god or other spirit (or else that they themselves were of a higher nature than mere mortals, that their laws might the more easily be received)" (*Leviathan* 12.20). These first founders and legislators observed in the people a superstitious fear of imaginary invisible powers and set out to "nourish, dress, and form it into laws, and to add to it, of their own invention, any opinion of the causes of future events by which they thought they should be able to govern others, and make unto themselves the greatest use of their powers" (*Leviathan* 11.27). Pagan religion, on this account, was an essentially secular political instrument for governing an ignorant and therefore superstitious people.

To some extent, Hobbes did seek to return to the pagan model in his reinterpretation of Christianity. Like the pagans, Hobbes begins with the paramount need for peace and obedience to the sovereign, and toleration is secondary to those ends. Accordingly, like the pagans, his religious policy does not begin with toleration but begins instead with what he frankly admits is civil religion (*Leviathan* 42.71 & 80). That is, religion is conceived wholly as a political instrument, advanced by the sovereign power and for the sake of peace. And here in particular, Hobbes is likely to appear distinctly illiberal, in his promotion of state-mandated religious conformity rather than toleration of religious pluralism.

But, to repeat, the character of this state-mandated religion is crucial to understanding Hobbes's purpose, which in turn will put us back on the path of liberalism. Although Hobbes's promotion of a state-mandated religion for obvious reasons causes him to appear unfriendly to religious pluralism, his interpretation of Christianity has the most minimal requirements for a religion that could still be called Christian. All that is required for salvation, according to Hobbesian Christianity, is (1) obedience to the sovereign and (2) belief that Jesus was the Christ, while leaving unclear what it means for him to have been the Christ and even what it means to be saved. The theological disputes that divide the sects, he claims, concern matters that are unknowable (which is why controversies about them go perennially unresolved). Only what is unambiguously taught by reason and by Scripture will be required, and in Hobbes's reading there is very little that is unambiguous in Scripture. Disagreement about the unknowable and hence inessential does not run afoul of Hobbesian Christianity, *provided one does not mistake the unknowable for the essential and confuse one's own private opinion for knowledge that warrants imposition on others.*

Hobbesian Christianity is then, in a sense, inherently pluralistic, insofar as it tolerates disagreement about the unknowable and inherently contentious matters of faith that divide believers. Indeed, any disagreement is tolerated so long as the primary requirement of obedience to the sovereign is maintained, recalling that the sovereign is concerned with private opinion only insofar as it issues in disobedience. Beyond that the sovereign is utterly indifferent to the beliefs of his subjects. Hobbesian Christianity thus might seem to encompass the sectarian divisions as much as possible. Hobbes's minimalist "big tent" Christianity would be adapted by later liberals such as Locke and Thomas Jefferson (see Owen 2015). It is a form of liberal Christianity. We are now in a position to see why, near the end of his extensive treatment of religion in Parts III & IV of *Leviathan*, he says that "the independency of the primitive Christians, to follow Paul, or Cephas, or Apollos, every man as he liketh best … if it be without contention and without measuring the doctrine of Christ by our affection to the person of his minister … is perhaps the best" (*Leviathan* 47.20). And we are only a step away from the unambiguously liberal principle that says to believers: believe and worship as you see fit, so long as you do not seek to impose your private belief and worship on others. Your being tolerated is contingent on your being tolerant.

But the pluralism of Hobbesian Christianity must be qualified; or rather, the qualification already stated (the proviso highlighted above) must be unpacked. For the proviso entails not mistaking the unknowable for the essential, which in turn entails accepting that the controversial matters dividing Christians are in fact matters of private belief, not of knowledge, and therefore not authoritative over those who disagree with one's private beliefs about them. The ostensible pluralism of Hobbesian Christianity rests in fact on *a new consensus* regarding the profound limits of human understanding of theological matters. More precisely, the new consensus entails a new disposition, for which the substantive matters, disagreement over which makes for ostensible pluralism, fade in importance if they do not disappear from view altogether. Here again, it is precisely an apparently illiberal feature of Hobbes's doctrine that is potentially revealing of liberalism as such. For we may suppose that liberalism asks nothing substantive of religious believers: your beliefs and practices can remain wholly intact, *provided* you tolerate the beliefs and practices of others. Hobbes forces us to ask whether this proviso is as insubstantial as it claims to be and whether some such conformity as Hobbes thought necessary always lies hidden within liberal "pluralism" (cf. Owen 2001, 121–127).

In the previous section, we showed that toleration for Hobbes was secondary to and dependent on peace and security. In this section, we are coming to see that toleration for Hobbes was, in addition, secondary to and dependent on a widespread transformation of popular opinion, or what has come to be known as popular "enlightenment." The pagan policy of religious toleration was premised on religious indifference, if not unbelief, on the part of the founders. Hobbes (who saw himself as a sort of founder; cf. *De Cive*, Epistle Dedicatory, *Leviathan* 31.41) shared that indifference or unbelief, but unlike the pagan founders, he confronted competing monotheistic claimants to the true orthodoxy akin to those that had proved inherently resistant to accepting Roman authority. The pagan solution simply did not meet the challenge of Christian sectarianism, which, Hobbes thought, required a more radical solution. Pacifying Christian sectarianism required a radical transformation of popular belief in the direction of the indifference or unbelief of the pagan founders. It therefore required advancing enlightenment, in the sense of prioritizing knowable (real) worldly goods and evils over unknowable (imaginary) otherworldly goods and evils. Only then could the prospects of the worldly good of civil peace and the worldly evil of the state of nature reliably outweigh the prospects of heaven and hell. Only then could fear of the visible power of the sovereign outweigh fear of the invisible power of God (cf. *Leviathan* 38.1 with 17.1). For the sovereign can possess a monopoly of worldly rewards and punishments in the commonwealth, but he remains potentially vulnerable if some ambitious troublemaker is able to manipulate belief in greater otherworldly rewards and punishments. A people that had been properly educated by a sovereign who himself had been enlightened by Hobbes would prove resistant to such manipulation. For such a people would not only be trained in the basics of natural causation, including the wholly natural causes of dreams and visions, but also in the basics of human nature, instilling a suspicion of the vainglorious motives of the ambitious. Such a people would be more cynical than gullible when confronted with would-be religious authorities.

This last point leads to an obvious puzzle. Would such a people who took a cynical view of would-be religious authority not also take a cynical view of the religious authority of the sovereign? Does not Hobbesian Christianity, precisely insofar as it is a vehicle of enlightenment, work to undermine itself? This puzzle forces us to acknowledge that, although Hobbes exerts considerable effort elaborating and defending his interpretation of Christianity, he allows the sovereign broad latitude with respect to policy regarding religion. The sovereign has the right to establish whatever religion he sees fit – including Roman Catholicism (*Leviathan* 42.80) or a non-Christian religion (*Leviathan* 43.23). The established religion can be tolerant or intolerant, as peace requires. But these do not exhaust the possibilities, since the sovereign may also establish no religion at all, "where many sorts of worship be allowed, proceeding from the different religions of private men" (*Leviathan* 31.37). This last possibility, which to liberals today seems the very soul of moderation, would likely have appeared the most radical and risky to Hobbes's contemporaries, since, as Hobbes observes, it means "that the commonwealth is not of any religion at all."

The fact that Hobbes does not openly advocate this option – the thoroughly secular, tolerant state – does not mean that he did not think it better than the established religion he did advocate, for he may not have thought the better option feasible. Hobbes is clearly no idealist, after all. But there is another possibility, viz., that he did think the best option feasible, but not feasible at present. We have already cited Hobbe's speculation in the final chapter of *Leviathan* that the toleration of early Christianity is "perhaps the best" (*Leviathan* 47). That speculation is the culmination of a lengthy account of the history of the Church, where he casts his opponents (exemplified by, but not limited to Roman Catholics) as those who "pretend the kingdom of God to be of this world, and thereby to have a power [i.e. a power over the affairs of the world] therein distinct from the civil state" (*Leviathan* 47.34). The effects of this politically pernicious doctrine cannot be eliminated easily or quickly. The property of these enemies of civil order, "together with their ambition, [has grown] to such a height as the violence thereof openeth the eyes which the wariness of their predecessors had before sealed up, and makes men by too much grasping let go all (as Peter's net was broken by the struggling of too great a multitude of fishes), whereas the impatience of those that strive to resist such encroachment before their subjects eyes are opened did but increase the power they resisted" (*Leviathan* 47.18, emphasis added). The "knot[s] upon [the people's] liberty" were tied over several hundred years and must be unraveled over time and by way of opening the people's eyes (*Leviathan* 47.20).

We say that Hobbes was no idealist, but he clearly entertained extraordinary ambition for his political project. He claimed to have been the first to have reduced politics and morals to a science on a par with geometry and physics. Classical political philosophers had but glimpsed the principles of their science as "showing a bit through the clouds" (*De Cive*, Preface 2). The promise of Hobbes's political science, on the other hand, is this: "[I]f the patterns of human action were known with the same certainty as the relations of magnitude in figures, ambition and greed, whose power rests on the false opinions of the common people [vulgi] about right and wrong, would be disarmed, and the human race would enjoy such a secure peace that (apart from conflicts over space as the population grew) it seems unlikely that it would ever have to fight again" (*De Cive* Epistle 6). And, as Hobbes says elsewhere, "the common people [vulgus] are educated little by little" (*Opera Philosophica* 2:128). He recognized that "opinions which are gotten by education, and in length of time are made habitual, cannot be taken away by force, and upon the sudden: they must therefore be taken away also, by time and education" (*Elements of Law* 28.8). The first step must be an enlightened sovereign, who will require Hobbes's doctrine to be taught in universities, whose students will then pass it down to the people, among whom, he says, "I am not totally without hope that some day . . . this doctrine, made more tolerable by custom, will be commonly received for the public good" (*Leviathan*, Latin version, 31.41). The thoroughly secular state will lead to a thoroughly secular society, and "toleration" will be secured on a universal indifference or unbelief to what would be tolerated (cf. Owen 2015, 54–56).

Hobbes was engaged in what David Johnston calls a "politics of cultural transformation" (Johnston 1986). Inhabitants of liberal societies today are heirs to, and indeed at least partially products of, that admittedly incomplete transformation. Liberals who take that transformation for granted fail to appreciate what was required to effect it in the first place. This permits them the luxury of mistaking the fruits of that transformation, such as a safe policy of toleration, for the defining characteristics of liberalism. It allows them to suppose that liberal societies, societies in which people generally accept the principles of liberalism, are pluralistic. It permits them not to recognize their own rejection of ideas antithetical to liberalism as forms of intolerance, such as when John Rawls draws the circle of liberal toleration so as to include only "reasonable pluralism," where reasonableness is measured by acceptance of liberal principles (Rawls 1996, 37). This is not to accuse Rawls of some failure to adhere to liberal principles but rather to say that Hobbes, precisely in those features of his thought that are likely to appear today as illiberal, in fact serves to clarify the true character of liberalism.

The resistance to recognizing the true character of liberalism in Hobbes's doctrine may stem from an aversion to its stark individualism and materialistic hedonism (cf. Owen 2005, 144–48). Hobbes's account of human nature and political society can hardly be described as noble and inspiring. Liberals today no longer see individual rights as, in the Hobbesian doctrine, elements of the self-centered unsociability of human beings, or toleration in its original negative sense of bearing or putting up with something we suppose is bad or disagreeable. For latter-day liberalism, the notions of toleration and individual liberty have clearly taken on an air of nobility of the sort that Hobbes is ever seeking to deflate. This aversion to the baseness of Hobbes's doctrine is understandable and human, but it may blind liberals to the distance between the noble self-conception that would replace that doctrine and the way of life manifestly fostered by liberal society liberal society in fact, a way of life in keeping with that doctrine. And even though this aversion implies a dissatisfaction with that way of life, it can also blind liberals to the inherent, and indeed perennial, vulnerabilities of liberalism stemming from that way of life. And one blind to those inherent vulnerabilities is not in the best position to protect liberalism from the perennial existential threats that it faces and will continue to face so long as human nature longs for something higher than what liberalism is built to deliver.

References

Baumgold D (1988) Hobbes's political theory. Cambridge University Press, New York
Fish S (1994) There's no such thing as free speech. Oxford University Press, New York
Johnston D (1986) The rhetoric of leviathan: Thomas Hobbes and the politics of cultural transformation. Princeton University Press, Princeton
Lincoln A (1992) The portable Lincoln. Penguin, New York
Owen JJ (2001) Religion and the demise of liberal rationalism: the foundational crisis of the separation of church and state. University of Chicago Press, Chicago
Owen JJ (2005) The tolerant Leviathan: Hobbes and the paradox of liberalism. Polity 37(1):130–148
Owen JJ (2015) Making religion safe for democracy: transformation from Hobbes to Tocqueville. Cambridge University Press, New York
Rawls J (1971) A theory of justice. Harvard University Press, Cambridge, MA
Rawls J (1996) Political liberalism. Columbia University Press, New York

John Locke and Religious Toleration

51

John William Tate

Contents

Introduction	1024
Locke and His Times	1025
John Locke and Anthony Ashley Cooper	1027
Locke and the Revolution of 1688	1028
A Letter Concerning Toleration	1029
Three "Considerations" for Toleration	1030
The "Consent Argument"	1031
The "Truth Argument"	1034
Limitations of the "Truth Argument"	1036
The "Rationality Argument"	1037
Rationality Argument I	1039
Rationality Argument II	1040
Rationality Argument III	1043
Locke's Skepticism	1044
Skepticism Argument I	1045
Skepticism Argument II	1049
"True Interests," "Use and Necessity," and "Corruption and Pravity"	1053
Locke, Proast, and Religious Diversity	1055
The "Skepticism" and "Rationality" Arguments	1056
Interpretive Issues	1056
Locke's Pragmatic Argument for Toleration	1060
Locke and the "Moral Challenge" of Toleration	1062
Locke and the Limits of Toleration	1063
"Atheists" and "Catholics"	1064
Dividing Locke from God	1066
"Things Indifferent"	1070

J. W. Tate (✉)
Discipline of Politics and International Relations, Newcastle Business School, College of Human and Social Futures, University of Newcastle, Newcastle, NSW, Australia
e-mail: john.Tate@newcastle.edu.au

© The Author(s), under exclusive licence to Springer Nature Switzerland AG 2022
M. Sardoĉ (ed.), *The Palgrave Handbook of Toleration*,
https://doi.org/10.1007/978-3-030-42121-2_43

Conclusion	1072
Summary and Future Directions	1073
References	1073

Abstract

This chapter focuses on the distinct arguments that John Locke advanced to justify toleration of the religious liberties of individuals, not least outward liberty of religious expression, where such toleration was to be engaged in by English state authorities. We shall see that these arguments for toleration were premised on either normative or pragmatic considerations. The chapter shall also investigate the limits that Locke sought to impose on such toleration, where such limits distinguished between those whose outward religious liberties ought to be permitted and those whose outward liberties, in specific circumstances and for specific reasons, ought to be proscribed. Locke was careful to ensure that the justifications he advanced for these limits on religious toleration were distinctly non-religious in nature, centered on "civil" concerns and interests (such as civil peace and state security) that all within society could conceivably endorse irrespective of their religious convictions. This was because Locke was fully aware of the divisions and upheavals that religious differences could produce within the England of his time, and he was therefore eager to provide a basis for civil and political coexistence, between those of rival faiths, which did not depend on the endorsement of any specific religious convictions.

Keywords

Toleration · Individual rights · Consent · Legitimacy · Obligation · Natural law · Religion · Catholicism · Skepticism · Atheism

Introduction

This chapter focuses on the arguments that John Locke advanced in favor of religious toleration, to be undertaken by English state authorities, as a means of responding to the religious diversity and division that existed within late seventeenth-century English society. Locke also discussed toleration as a practice that arises between individuals and churches, but the focus of this chapter concerns toleration undertaken by state authorities. Locke's arguments for toleration relied on either normative or pragmatic commitments.

The chapter begins by contextualizing Locke in his time and place. It then discusses his transition, early in his intellectual career, from an anti-tolerationist to a pro-tolerationist position. It then analyzes his most comprehensive pro-toleration text, *A Letter Concerning Toleration*, published anonymously in 1689. Within this text, Locke advanced three "considerations" (or arguments) for toleration, which I have elsewhere dubbed the "truth," "rationality," and "consent" arguments. The chapter then identifies Locke's fourth "consideration" for toleration, which emerges most comprehensively in his later writings in the context of his debate with the Anglican clergyman, Jonas Proast, and which I have dubbed the "skepticism argument." The "skepticism argument" draws on the same premises as the "truth argument" but with wider implications encompassing those engaged in the exercise of state authority rather than those merely subject to it. All of these are normative arguments for toleration. I also discuss the key pragmatic argument that Locke advances for toleration, premised on material concerns centered on civil peace and state security.

The focus of the chapter then shifts to the "moral challenge" with which toleration confronts devout religious believers and how Locke, a devout religious believer himself, sought to overcome this "challenge." Following this, the chapter identifies the "limits" which Locke sought to impose on toleration, dividing that which was to be permitted from that which, in his view, ought to be proscribed. We see how Locke was careful to justify these "limits" in non-religious terms, centered on the "civil" interests all within society shared. Locke did this because he was aware of the deep divisions, arising on the basis of religion, that existed within the English society of his time and so knew that no civil or political agreement (and no justification of the exercise of political power) premised on shared religious convictions, was likely to elicit widespread assent. Further, he knew that any such agreement, based on such a religious consensus, would itself inflict onerous impositions on the religious liberty of those dissenting from this consensus – Locke, by the time he adopted a pro-tolerationist position, being of the view that, wherever possible, religion should be a matter left to the liberty of the individual, and therefore "to every man's self," and not something imposed (or prescribed) by society or the state (Locke 1993a: 423. See also Locke 1993a: 393, 394, 396, 403, 405–406, 410–412, 421–423, 427; Locke 1993b: 187–189, 190–191, 195). In this way, the chapter seeks to show how those Locke scholars who have sought to immerse Locke's political philosophy within his religious theology, identifying Locke's deep personal religious convictions or theological opinions as fundamental to his political prescriptions, miss what is essential in Locke's politics, because they fail to perceive the extent to which Locke sought to distance the justifications of his political philosophy from such matters. The discussion of "things indifferent," at the end of the chapter, is one among a number of aspects of Locke's political philosophy, touched upon in the chapter, which seeks to show this "distancing" process. Finally, please note that when Locke refers to the "magistrate" he is using this as a short-hand description of those authorities, within a polity, who exercise authorized political authority.

Locke and His Times

John Locke was born in England in 1632, and his younger years coincided with the English Civil War. As he put it, "I no sooner perceived myself in the *world* but I found myself in a storm" (Locke 1967a: 119). Most of Locke's adult years were lived in the midst of the English Restoration, which began when Charles II returned to England in 1660 to take up the throne of his beheaded father. But Locke's later years, in the 1680s, were characterized by a self-imposed exile in Holland, to escape prosecution for his involvement in the Whig opposition to Charles II in the last years of that monarch's reign. The end of this decade saw Locke return to England, in the wake of the Revolution of 1688, as a distinguished associate of the new ruling regime headed by William and Mary.

The English Restoration, beginning in 1660, was characterized by the re-establishment of the Church of England as the official religion of the English state, whose primacy was sustained by legally imposed disabilities on rival faiths (Fraser 1980: 191–192; 215–218). The English Restoration Parliament was dominated by Anglicans who sought to re-affirm the religious ascendancy of the Church of England over Puritan sects whose members they identified with the anti-royalist forces of the Civil War (Trevelyan 1956: 24, 26–27). Between 1661 and 1665, Parliament passed a series of legislative statutes that would become known to posterity as the "Clarendon Code," seeking to impose legal, civil and religious disabilities on these Puritans (now known as "Dissenters" due to their unwillingness to conform to the outward rites of the Church of England), many of whom, in response, sought refuge in the New World (Trevelyan 1956: 24, 26–27; Ashcraft 1986: 22; Fraser 1980: 215–218). The result was a regime of religious intolerance emanating from the official sources of Church and state. As Mark Goldie puts it:

> Restoration England was a persecuting society. It was the last period in English history when the ecclesiastical and civil powers endeavoured systematically to secure religious uniformity by coercive means. (Goldie 1991: 331)

When the Restoration began, Locke was an academic resident of Oxford University and a definite supporter of this official religious intolerance, which he believed was necessary for the maintenance of political and social order in England after the upheavals of the pre-Restoration years (Locke 1967a: 118–122). At this time, Locke wrote (but did not publish) what became known as the *Two Tracts on Government* (1660–1662) in response to the advocacy of a fellow Oxford academic, Edward Bagshaw, for limited religious toleration of Dissenters in England (Abrams 1967: 4–5). Locke repudiated this ideal, insisting that as toleration would allow for the open expression of religious differences, the experience of the preceding decades suggested that this would be the precondition for upheaval and discord:

> I know not whether experience (if it may be credited) would not give us some reason to think that were this part of *freedom* contended for here by our *author* generally indulged in *England* it would prove only a *liberty* for *contention, censure* and *persecution* and turn us loose to the *tyranny* of a *religious rage*. (Locke 1967a: 120)

The reason why Locke perceived the open expression of religious differences, which toleration makes possible, as such a threat to civil and political order resided in what he believed to be the propensity of religion to produce vociferous disagreement and dissent between rival adherents, often over the most minor matters:

And he must confess himself a stranger to England that thinks that *meats* and *habits*, that *places* and *times* of worship etc., would not be as sufficient occasion of hatred and quarrels amongst us, as *leeks* and *onions* and other *trifles* described in that satire by Juvenal was amongst them, and be distinctions able to keep us always at a distance, and eagerly ready for like violence and cruelty as often as the *teachers* should alarm the *consciences* of their zealous votaries and direct them against the adverse party. (Locke 1967a: 121)

Yet for a number of reasons and in a variety of ways that I have discussed in detail elsewhere (see Tate 2016a: Chaps. 2 and 3; Tate 2017; Tate 2021), Locke, by 1667, had jettisoned the anti-tolerationist position that he had advanced in the *Two Tracts* and shifted to a pro–tolerationist point of view. This point of view was first expressed in detail in *An Essay Concerning Toleration*, which was written by Locke in 1667, only a few years after the *Two Tracts*, but again, unpublished in his lifetime. Within this pro-tolerationist text, we shall see that Locke insisted that the English ruling authorities should tolerate the outward expression of those religious beliefs or practices which (in Locke's view) did not harm the material interests of the state or civil society (irrespective of the opinion of these ruling authorities concerning the religious "truth" or "falsity" of those beliefs).

John Locke and Anthony Ashley Cooper

Locke's arguments for religious toleration (and its limits) are advanced in a series of written contributions produced over more than three decades. Aside from minor and occasional pieces, these begin with *An Essay Concerning Toleration* (1667) and extend to *A Letter Concerning Toleration* (1689). They culminate in Locke's debate with the Anglican clergyman, Jonas Proast, in which Locke seeks to defend the content of *A Letter Concerning Toleration*, often line-by-arduous-line, in the *Second*, *Third*, and *Fourth Letters for Toleration* (1690, 1692, 1704). This debate with Proast extended to the end of Locke's life, the *Fourth Letter for Toleration* remaining incomplete in 1704, the year of Locke's death. For an analysis of the Locke/Proast debate, see Tate (2016a), Tate (2016b), Vernon (1997), Wolfson (2010), Goldie (1991), Goldie (1999b), Goldie (2002), and Nicholson (1991).

In each of these later stages in his career, we see Locke developing and building on his arguments for toleration, some of which he first advanced in detail in *An Essay Concerning Toleration* in 1667. This was the year that Locke left Oxford and entered Exeter House, the household of Anthony Ashley Cooper, later the first Earl of Shaftesbury. Ashley, at this time, was an ardent advocate of toleration for Dissenters (but not Catholics) in England and an active opponent of the Clarendon Code recently passed by the English Parliament (Cranston 1952: 620; Cranston 1957: 107).

There has been much speculation about the extent to which Locke's volte-face on the subject of toleration – opposing it in his *Two Tracts on Government* but affirming it a few years later in *An Essay Concerning Toleration* – was due to the influence of Ashley himself. The *Essay*, at times, directly addresses itself to political authorities in England to whom it refers in the second person. Some have even proposed that the addressee is Charles II himself (Marshall 1996: 49; Milton and Milton 2010: 49). Consequently, there has been some suggestion that perhaps Locke wrote this text for Ashley's own political purposes, with Ashley seeking to persuade Charles II to offer some alleviation to Dissenters from the Clarendon Code (Cranston 1952: 621; Laslett 1965: 41–43; Cranston 1987: 103; Wootton 1993: 18). Others, however, have disputed this or at least declared that the evidence is insufficient to support any categorical conclusion that Locke wrote the *Essay* for Ashley's political purposes (Dunn 1969: 28–30; Marshall 1996: 49; Milton and Milton 2010: 27, 49, 50, 52). On this debate surrounding the *Essay* and its progenitive influences, see Tate (2016a: 61–69).

Nevertheless, irrespective of the precise lines of influence leading to *An Essay Concerning Toleration*, it is safe to say that Ashley had a profound influence on Locke's intellectual development when it came to matters of toleration. As Maurice Cranston writes:

> I have searched in vain for evidence of Locke's holding liberal views before his introduction to Lord Shaftesbury in 1666. There is much to show that Locke held such views soon afterwards; and I cannot help wondering if he learned them from Shaftesbury. For it is certainly not the case, as I have seen it sometimes suggested, that Shaftesbury learned his liberalism from Locke. Shaftesbury had been famous since before the Restoration for his advocacy of toleration... However, if Locke did learn the principle of religious toleration from Shaftesbury, he was a quick and ready pupil. Within a year of their meeting, and before he had installed himself in Shaftesbury's home as a domestic physician and philosopher, Locke was writing the first of several essays on toleration. (Cranston 1952: 620. See also Cranston 1957: 111; Ashcraft 1987: 21)

Locke and the Revolution of 1688

John Locke came late to toleration debates. These debates had emerged in Europe in the sixteenth century, in which religious toleration, engaged in by state authorities, was seen as one means, among others, whereby these authorities could respond to the reality of religious difference and division within their borders. Such division was a product of the sixteenth-century Reformation, which split much of Europe into rival camps of Catholic and Protestant. By the time Locke was writing about toleration, in the second half of the seventeenth century, this division, and the civil strife and conflict that it often engendered, had become entrenched. Locke was well aware of this. As he put it very late in his life:

> The horrid cruelties that in all ages, and of late in our view, have been committed under the name, and upon the account of religion, give so just an offence and abhorrence to all who have any remains, not only of religion, but humanity left, that the world is ashamed to own it. (Locke 1963a: 262)

Locke was in exile in Holland for much of the 1680s, having sought refuge across the Channel to escape prosecution for his role in the opposition to Charles II in which

Locke's patron, Anthony Ashley Cooper (now the Earl of Shaftesbury) and his supporters had sought to bar the succession of Charles' Catholic brother, the Duke of York (later James II) to the English throne (Laslett 1965: 44–45; Ashcraft 1986: Chap. 8). Locke was close to the new ruling authorities who replaced James II after the Revolution of 1688. He had returned to England from Holland in February 1689 as part of the same maritime convoy as the Princess Mary, having been asked by Lord Mordaunt to "take care of his wife on her passage with the Princess from The Hague" (Locke 1957).

Yet despite this proximity to ascendant state power, Locke was nothing if not politically cautious. He sought to ensure that two of his key texts, published in 1689 and widely associated with the Revolution of 1688 – the *Two Treatises of Government* and *A Letter Concerning Toleration* – were published anonymously, and he was extremely angry when his friend, Philip van Limborch, a Professor of Divinity at the Arminian or Remonstrant Church at Amsterdam, revealed to others his authorship of the *Letter* (Locke 1968. See also Tate 2016a: 22–23).

Peter Laslett, referring to the inordinate lengths to which Locke went to conceal his authorship of the *Two Treatises of Government*, has declared that such "exasperating attempts" at concealment "can only be called abnormal, obsessive" and suggest "a peculiarity in Locke's personality as a man and in his personality as an author" (Laslett 1965: 18). However, Laslett also tells us that Locke's Whig associate, Algernon Sidney, had had his *Discourses Concerning Government* brought against him as evidence in his trial for treason in the wake of his involvement in the Rye House Plot against Charles II - Sidney ultimately suffering execution (Laslett 1965: 45). Laslett tells us that Locke was also associated with those involved in this plot (Laslett 1965: 44–45), and his *Two Treatises of Government* was, like Sidney's *Discourses*, an argument in favor of government based on popular consent. Given these circumstances, perhaps Locke's caution was not as "abnormal," "obsessive," or "peculiar" as it first seems. After all, after decades as a close associate of the Earl of Shaftesbury, Locke himself would have been fully aware of the fickle winds of political fortune. Even the revolutionary settlement of 1688 may not, to Locke's cautious eyes, have appeared permanent or irreversible, and he may have wanted to conceal his past in order not to incriminate his future. Peter Nicholson has made this point:

> The Toleration Act had now been passed (May 1689)... Locke surely would have regarded the degree of toleration established as precarious, after his lifetime experience of political upheaval and reversal (it is only with hindsight that the revolutionary settlement can be viewed as inaugurating stability). (Nicholson 1991: 171. See also Laslett 1965: 79)

A Letter Concerning Toleration

John Locke's arguments in favor of toleration are most widely associated with *A Letter Concerning Toleration* – one of the two texts, published in 1689, identified above, whose authorship Locke was so eager to keep secret. The text was written by

Locke while in exile in Holland in the 1680s and at a time of significant reversals for the cause of toleration in Europe. Louis XIV had revoked the *Edict of Nantes* in 1685, which had been enacted by his grandfather, Henry IV, in 1598, granting a measure of toleration to French Protestants, known as Huguenots. Civil disabilities continued against Dissenters in England on the basis of the earlier legislated Clarendon Code. All in all, at the time Locke was writing *A Letter Concerning Toleration*, the political portents did not augur well for religious toleration in Europe.

The initial circumstances of publication of the *Letter* were outside of Locke's knowledge and control. The original document was simply a private letter that Locke had written to his Dutch friend, Philip van Limborch, while in Holland. James Tully outlines the material provenance of the *Letter* as follows:

> *A Letter Concerning Toleration* is a translation of the *Epistola de Tolerantia*, a letter written in Latin by John Locke to his close friend Philip van Limborch, a Dutch Arminian, during the winter months of 1685. At the time Locke was a political exile in Amsterdam, living underground in the home of Dr. Egbert Veen under an assumed name in order to elude extradition and persecution for his part in the revolutionary activity for toleration in England in 1679–83. The *Epistola de Tolerantia* was first published anonymously and without Locke's knowledge in May, 1689, in Gouda, after Locke had returned to England in the wake of William of Orange's conquest of the English throne in the winter of 1688. William Popple, a fellow radical Whig and religious dissenter, translated the *Epistola de Tolerantia* into English, wrote a preface... and had it published by the Whig publisher, Awnsham Churchill, anonymously, yet with Locke's knowledge, as *A Letter Concerning Toleration* in October 1689. A second corrected edition appeared in March 1690. (Tully 1983: 1. See also Klibansky 1968: ix, xvi–xvii, xix–xxiii; Ashcraft 1986: 475–76)

Three "Considerations" for Toleration

Although Locke wrote *A Letter Concerning Toleration* in Latin, we can accept the English translation as representative of his views given it was this translation that he defended, at times line by line, in his debate with the Anglican clergyman, Jonas Proast. Within *A Letter Concerning Toleration*, Locke does advance a distinctly Christian argument for religious toleration, premised on biblical authority. At the center of this argument is the following proposition: "The toleration of those that differ from others in matters of religion is so agreeable to the Gospel of Jesus Christ, and to the genuine reason of mankind, that it seems monstrous for men to be so blind, as not to perceive the necessity and advantage of it in so clear a light" (Locke 1993a: 393. See also Locke 1993a: 431).

However elsewhere in *A Letter Concerning Toleration*, Locke advances three other arguments, quite distinct from biblical authority, in favor of religious toleration, and it is upon these (or variations of these) that he places the greatest emphasis. Locke refers to these as his three "considerations" why "all the power of civil government relates only to men's civil interests, is confined to the care of the things of this world, and has nothing to do with the world to come," and therefore why government should not interfere with (but instead "tolerate") religious differences when these do not significantly impact on the material interests of governmental authorities in maintaining either civil peace or state security (Locke 1993a: 394, 396). These three "considerations" are articulated in the *Letter* by what I have elsewhere called, respectively, Locke's "consent," "truth," and "rationality" arguments for toleration (Tate 2016a: Chap. 5; Tate 2009: 766–773; Tate 2010a: 991–993). We shall now consider each of these "considerations" in turn.

The "Consent Argument"

Locke's first "consideration" for toleration I have dubbed the "consent argument" (Tate 2016a: 136–38; Tate 2009: 770–773; Tate 2010a: 990–991). This argument for toleration draws, for its plausibility, on the same model of government that Locke advances in the *Two Treatises of Government*. Within that model, Locke insists on a basic equation between "consent," "legitimacy," and "obligation." Governments, he insisted, are only *legitimate* if they arise from the *consent* of the governed, and individuals are only *obligated* to obey government if government is *legitimate* in this respect. As Locke puts it:

> For no Government can have a right to obedience from a people who have not freely consented to it: which they can never be supposed to do, till either they are put in a full state of Liberty to chuse their Government and Governors, or at least till they have such standing Laws, to which they have by themselves or their Representatives, given their free consent, and also till they are allowed their due Property, which is so to be Proprietors of what they have, that no body can take away any part of it without their own consent, without which, Men under any Government are not in the state of Free-men, but are direct Slaves under the Force of War (Locke 1965: II § 192. See also Locke 1965: II § 15, 95, 99, 112, 117, 119, 122, 134, 171, 175, 198, 212, 216, 227)

Locke insisted, in the *Two Treatises*, that civil society and government arose from individuals in an original "state of nature" engaging in an act of common agreement (or "compact"), via their mutual "consent," to enter civil society and create government, but only for specific reasons and specific purposes, centered on their material safety and security and also the security of their fundamental liberties (Locke 1965: II § 13, 14, 21, 87, 89, 90, 94, 95–99, 101, 104, 106, 112, 122, 123, 124, 127, 131, 134, 136, 137, 171, 192, 222). These purposes for which government is created, Locke argued, constitute the limits within which government authority can be legitimately exercised, because within Locke's model, as outlined in the *Two Treatises*, government only has a "commission," arising from the consent of those subject to its jurisdiction, to engage in activity which falls within the purposes for which it was established and to which such persons have agreed (Locke 1965: II § 83, 123, 124, 131, 134, 135, 149, 171, 222. See also Locke 1993a: 393–94, 422–423). As Locke put it:

> *Political Power* is that Power which every Man, having in the state of Nature, has given up into the hands of the Society, and therein to the Governours, whom the Society hath set over it self, with this express or tacit Trust, That it shall be imployed for their good, and the

preservation of their Property....So that the *end and measure of this Power*... can have no other *end or measure*, when in the hands of the Magistrate, but to preserve the Members of that Society in their Lives, Liberties, and Possessions; and so cannot be an Absolute, Arbitrary Power over their Lives and Fortunes, which are as much as possible to be preserved. (Locke 1965: II § 171. See also Locke 1965: II § 131, 135, 149, 222; Locke 1963b: 119, 121; Locke 1993a: 423; Locke 1993b: 186, 192, 193, 195)

The concerns of material safety and security for which, according to Locke, individuals first agreed to enter civil society, constitute their "civil" interests, centered on what Locke describes as their "Lives, Liberties and Estates" (Locke 1965: II § 87, 123, 209, 222) (or in the passage above, as their "Lives, Liberties, and Possessions") and it is in relation to these "civil interests" that Locke insists government authority can be legitimately exercised (not least, for the protection of these "interests" from arbitrary intrusion by others) (Locke 1965: II, § 87–89, 123, 124, 131, 134–139, 142, 149, 171, 222; Locke 1993a: 393, 394, 411, 422–23). Government authority does *not*, however, extend to religious matters, Locke declares, because individuals, in any original agreement to enter civil society and create government, would not have ceded to government any authority over such matters, governments being in no better position to judge these matters than these individuals themselves:

[I]n all societies instituted by man, the ends of them can be no other than what the institutors appointed; which I am sure could not be their spiritual and eternal interest. For they could not stipulate about these one with another, nor submit this interest to the power of the society, or any sovereign they should set over it. (Locke 1963b; 121. See also Locke 1963b: 119; Locke 1993a: 422; Locke 1993b: 189)

Locke therefore arrives at the following conclusion in *A Letter Concerning Toleration*, limiting the authority of government, and the ends it is entitled to pursue, to "civil" interests, centered on material concerns, and explicitly excluding religion from these, leaving the latter to the liberty of the individual:

These things being thus explained, it is easy to understand to what end the legislative power ought to be directed, and by what measures regulated; and that is the temporal good and outward prosperity of the society; which is the sole reason of men's entering into society, and the only thing they seek and aim at in it... For the political society is instituted for no other end but only to secure every man's possession of the things of this life. The care of each man's soul, and of the things of heaven, which neither does belong to the commonwealth nor can be subjected to it, is left entirely to every man's self. (Locke 1993a: 423. See also Locke 1993b: 186, 192, 193, 195)

Locke's "consent argument" for toleration, which he advances within *A Letter Concerning Toleration*, draws strongly on these propositions, and those earlier outlined in the *Two Treatises*. The "consent argument" presupposes, for its plausibility, Locke's assumption that government authority arises from the "consent" of those subject to it and that this authority is limited, in terms of its legitimate jurisdiction, to the purposes for which such "consent" is given. Because these purposes do not include religion, Locke is able to arrive at the conclusion, within the "consent argument," that the jurisdiction of government does not extend to individuals' religious beliefs or practices, with the result that "[t]he care...of every man's soul belongs unto himself, and is to be left unto himself" (Locke 1993a: 405–06. See also Locke 1993a: 393, 394, 396, 403, 405, 411, 412, 421–22, 422, 422–23, 423). It is on these grounds, Locke concludes, that state authorities ought not to interfere with, and therefore ought to "tolerate," religious differences, so long as these do not significantly impact on the state or society's material concerns centered on civil peace or state security. Locke articulates his "consent" argument for toleration, in these terms, as follows:

> [T]he care of souls is not committed to the civil magistrate, any more than to other men. It is not committed unto him, I say, by God; because it appears not that God has ever given any such authority to one man over another as to compel anyone to his religion. Nor can any such power be vested in the magistrate by the consent of the people, because no man can so far abandon the care of his own salvation as blindly to leave it to the choice of any other, whether prince or subject, to prescribe to him what faith or worship he shall embrace. (Locke 1993a: 394. See also Locke 1963a: 212; Locke 1993b: 189; Locke 2004d: 276).

One of the most significant features of the "consent argument" is the extent to which it is underwritten by an ideal of individual liberty. Locke did advance an ideal of individual liberty as early as the *Two Tracts on Government*, but in that text it was an ideal that was limited to an inward liberty of conscience only (Locke 1967a: 127–130, 165, 167; 1967b: 214, 225, 238–239), individuals being expected, in terms of their outward behavior, to engage in a complete obedience to the constituted governmental authorities (Locke 1967a: 119–123, 129–130, 152, 159; Locke 1967b: 212, 220, 226–227, 238–239). Nevertheless, even in that early antitolerationist text, Locke expressed a normative commitment to individual liberty, declaring that "[b]esides the submission I have for *authority* I have no less a love of *liberty* without which a *man* shall find himself less happy than a *beast*" (Locke 1967a: 120).

By the time of Locke's *Two Treatises of Government*, such was Locke's commitment to the ideal of individual liberty that (in contrast to the *Two Tracts*) he countenanced an individual right of resistance to government in those instances where individuals believed governments were irretrievably transgressing the liberties for whose protection they, or their predecessors, had first consented to and created government in the first place (Locke 1965: II § 135, 149, 155, 164, 168, 171, 172, 202–210, 212, 220–222, 225–228, 231, 232, 239, 242, 243; Locke 1993a: 424). Locke's right of resistance receives its rationale from Locke's idea of individual "consent" which, we saw, is the public and political expression of an individual's liberty, and thereby a source of legitimacy for government, in which individuals agree to incur civic obligations of obedience, but only in return for fundamental guarantees from government, not least concerning the security of their liberties (Locke 1965: II § 123–124, 131, 134–138, 171, 222). It is when individuals believe those guarantees have been irretrievably and irreversibly violated that resistance to government may become (in the minds of individuals) a legitimate (if not necessarily a prudent) option (see Locke 1965: II § 21, 168, 212, 241, 242. On prudence, see

Locke 1965: II § 168, 207–209, 223, 225, 230). There has been much debate within the Locke literature as to whether Locke intended his conception of "consent" and "resistance," within the *Two Treatises*, to apply to *all* members of civil society or only a "political class" of property-holders, and the extent to which he intended his ideas of individual rights and liberty to apply to women as much as men. All of these are important debates but are not discussed here.

Locke recognized that individuals themselves have a personal commitment to their liberty, not least because of its relationship to human dignity, Locke declaring that "so chary is human nature to preserve the liberty of that part wherein lies the dignity of a man, which could it be imposed on would make him but little different from a beast" (Locke 1993b: 204). He therefore understood that "[m]en commonly in their voluntary changes do pursue liberty and enthusiasm, wherein they are still free and at their own disposal, rather than give themselves up to the authority and impositions of others" (Locke 1993b: 203). It is in terms of this normative commitment to individual liberty, and the model of the origins and legitimacy of government outlined in the *Two Treatises*, that Locke's "consent argument" must be understood.

The "Truth Argument"

Locke's second "consideration" for toleration I have dubbed the "truth argument" (Tate 2016a: 127–134; Tate 2009: 767–768; Tate 2010a: 992–93). Like the "consent argument," the "truth argument" directly opposes the propensity of state authorities, in Locke's time, to impinge upon the religious liberties of those subject to their jurisdiction by imposing on them the religion which these authorities endorse, instead insisting that choices concerning religious belief and practice ought to be left to individuals alone. A key element of the "truth argument" is the assumption, central to a revealed religion such as Christianity, that individuals must embrace the "true religion" (the religion acceptable to God) in order to ensure their eternal salvation.

Locke, at one point in the *Letter*, refers to the "one truth, one way to heaven," thereby indicating a belief that there is a single "true religion" necessary for individual salvation (Locke 1993a: 396). Elsewhere, at a number of other points, he again affirms this view (Locke 1993a: 407, 408; Locke 1963a: 320, 326, 327, 328, 332–333, 356, 422; Locke 1963b: 133). However at another point in the *Letter*, Locke suggests that such an exclusive conception of the means of salvation is merely an excuse for persecution, since "if there were several ways that lead thither, there would not be so much as a pretence left for compulsion" (Locke 1993a: 406).

Locke, in his *Third Letter for Toleration*, provides a definition of "true religion," but one that capaciously and circularly defines "true religion" and "salvation" in terms of each other. As he puts it, "For that, and that alone, is the one only true religion, without which nobody can be saved, and which is enough for the salvation of every one who embraces it. And therefore whatever is less or more than this, is not the only true religion" (Locke 1963a: 422).

The key propositions upon which the "truth argument" rests are as follows. Firstly, there is a "true religion" which individuals must embrace if they wish to achieve eternal salvation. However, given that religious belief arises from individual faith, not indubitable knowledge, individuals have no guarantee as to what that "true religion" is (for Locke's arguments as to why we can only possess a "faith" in, not a knowledge of, "true religion," see the discussion below). As such, because individuals have no indubitable knowledge of the "true religion," they have no guarantee that the "orthodox" religion which state authorities seek to impose on them *is* the "true religion," capable of securing their eternal salvation. Given that state authorities can give no guarantee of this either (they too having no "knowledge" of the "true religion") and further, given that these state authorities are not able to pay the price of everlasting perdition which might arise for such individuals if the state forces upon them a "false" religion (see Locke 1993a: 407–408; Locke 1993b: 188), the "truth argument" concludes that individuals should resist any attempt by state authorities to impose religion upon them. As Locke states:

> [T]he care of the salvation of men's souls cannot belong to the magistrate, because, *though the rigour of laws and the force of penalties were capable to convince and change men's minds*, yet would not that help at all to the salvation of their souls. For there being but one truth, one way to heaven, what hopes is there that more men would be led into it, if they had no other rule to follow but the religion of the court, and were put under a necessity to quit the light of their own reason; to oppose the dictates of their own consciences; and blindly to resign up themselves to the will of their governors, and to the religion which either ignorance, ambition, or superstition had chanced to establish in the countries where they were born? (Locke 1993a: 395–96. Emphasis added. See also Locke 1993a: 407, 408; Locke 1993b: 188–89)

I have dubbed this line of argument the "truth argument" because it rests on the propositions that (i) religious "truth" is necessary to our eternal salvation; (ii) it is not possible to have indubitable knowledge of such religious "truth" with the result that we should be skeptical of any individual or authority's claim to have privileged access to this "truth"; and therefore (iii) we should resist the attempt of these authorities to impose such "truths" on us. The "truth argument" therefore provides (on the basis of these propositions) reasons why we should resist the attempts of state authorities (or indeed any others) to impose on us obligations of religious belief and practice that we have not freely affirmed ourselves. Indeed Locke goes even further and, discarding proposition (ii) above, declares that even if it were the case that state authorities possessed knowledge of the "true religion," and so the path to salvation, it is still not safe for the individual to follow such dictates unless they themselves sincerely believe the religion in question to be "true":

> But after all, the principal consideration, and which absolutely determines this controversy, is this: although the magistrate's opinion in religion be sound, and the way that he appoints be truly evangelical, yet if I be not thoroughly persuaded thereof in my own mind, there will be no safety for me in following it. No way whatsoever that I shall walk in, against the dictates of my conscience, will ever bring me to the mansions of the blessed. ...Faith only, and inward sincerity, are the things that procure acceptance with God. ...[W]hatsoever may

be doubtful in religion, yet this at least is certain, that no religion which I believe not to be true, can be either true or profitable unto me. . ...And therefore, when all is done, [individuals] must be left to their own consciences. (Locke 1993a: 410. My addition. See also Locke 1993a: 394, 395, 399, 402, 411; Locke 1993b: 189; Locke 2004d: 276)

Of course, when it comes to "eternal salvation," there is a negative complimentarity in the previous two passages quoted above. In the first, Locke declares that, our "sincerity" notwithstanding, salvation is denied us if the religion that the state authorities impose on us (and which we affirm) is not "true." In the second, he tells us that irrespective of the "truth" of the state's religion, salvation is denied us if our embrace of such a religion is not "sincere."

Further, it might be argued that this focus on "sincerity" constitutes an entirely separate "consideration" for toleration, distinct from those identified earlier, based on the "sincerity" of individual religious belief and its necessity for eternal salvation. After all, it might be argued, Locke's other "considerations" for toleration are premised on entirely different concerns. The "consent argument" is premised on the fact that state authorities have no authorization to impose religion on those subject to their jurisdiction; the "truth argument" is premised on the fact that we cannot be certain that the religion the state authorities seek to impose is "true"; and the "rationality argument" (considered below) is premised on the fact that the coercive means by which state authorities sometimes seek to impose religion cannot alter individual belief. But I have refrained from advancing, as an addition to these three "considerations" for toleration, a "sincerity argument," because the requirement of sincere belief for eternal salvation is a necessary (but not sufficient) condition of all three "considerations" identified above. The fact that our religious beliefs must be "sincere" is one reason why we would not confer on state authorities any authority to impose such beliefs on us ("consent argument"); and why our absence of certainty that the state possesses the "true religion" is a reason for us to resist its impositions in this regard ("truth argument"); and why the fact that "force" is incapable of instilling such "sincere" belief ("rationality argument") is a relevant "consideration" why the state should adopt a policy of toleration instead.

Limitations of the "Truth Argument"

What should be apparent is that although the "truth argument" might be persuasive in convincing individuals to resist the attempts of state authorities to impose religious obligations upon them, it has serious shortcomings as an argument for toleration (see Tate 2016a: 131–32). Toleration, after all, is the practice which (in this context) is engaged in by state authorities, not by the individuals who seek to resist state authority. Although the skepticism concerning knowledge of "true religion," at the center of the "truth argument," might convince individuals to resist state authority, it is unlikely to convince state authorities not to impose religion by force. After all, as Locke tells us, "the religion of every prince is orthodox to himself" (Locke 1993a: 416). The imposition of the state's religious doctrine, therefore, if the reason for this imposition is to ensure (in the mind of state authorities) the eternal salvation of those subject to their jurisdiction (as opposed to such imposition being intended to secure purely pragmatic ends such as civil peace or state security) is likely to be underwritten by sufficient certitude, concerning "true religion," on the part of state authorities, as to be impervious to such skepticism.

Consequently, if state authorities are seeking to impose a particular religion upon those subject to their jurisdiction because they believe it necessary for eternal salvation (something a seventeenth-century "prince" might do but something unlikely to occur among modern liberal democratic governments) the skepticism of those upon whom they seek to impose this religion is unlikely to shake their righteous convictions. On the other hand, if state authorities are imposing a particular religion, insisting that those subject to their jurisdiction ought to outwardly conform to it, for the sake of purely secular and pragmatic concerns – to ensure material ends such as civil peace or state security – then considerations of "true religion" (and the skepticism associated with it) are irrelevant to their purposes. This is because if the imposition of outward religious conformity upon a population is necessary (in the view of state authorities) for the maintenance of civil peace or state security, this does not require that the religion, whose outward observance is imposed, be "true," or that it be sincerely embraced by those upon whom it is imposed, or that it lead to their salvation. Rather, it only requires that such outward conformity be complied with by those upon whom it is imposed, thereby rendering it effective in reducing the incidents of religious conflict likely to threaten civil peace or state security. In such circumstances, the "truth argument," and the skepticism upon which it is based, has even less cogency as a means of convincing state authorities to tolerate than when such authorities impose religious uniformity for the sake of salvationist ends, because when states are seeking to secure secular ends, the key terms of the "truth argument" ("true religion" and "skepticism" concerning anyone's knowledge of it) are irrelevant to them.

Consequently, the "truth argument" is an argument whose potency arises from the interest of those subject to state authority in ensuring their eternal salvation and so underwrites their determination to resist state attempts to intrude upon their religious choices by force. However, as expressed by Locke in *A Letter Concerning Toleration*, it is *not* an argument that addresses the assurance of state authorities concerning the "truth" of the religion *they* seek to advance or their willingness to impose this religion by the use of force. It is, for this reason, not an argument that is sufficient to convince state authorities to engage in religious toleration.

The "Rationality Argument"

Locke's third "consideration" for toleration I have dubbed the "rationality argument" (see Tate 2016a: 135; Tate 2009: 763–768; Tate 2010a: 991). The term "rationality" draws strongly on Jeremy Waldron who believes that this "consideration" constitutes Locke's "main line of argument" for toleration within *A Letter Concerning Toleration* (Waldron 1988: 61, 62, 65, 79–80, 81–82; Waldron 2002: 210). Locke's "rationality argument" advances the proposition that state authorities should not seek to use outward force as a means of instilling sincere religious belief upon those subject to their jurisdiction, because such force is unable to achieve such ends - individual belief, in terms of either its sincerity or content, being impervious to the use of such force (Locke 1993a: 395). Force is therefore (to use Waldron's term) "irrational" as a means to achieve such ends, and so state authorities, recognizing their impotence in this regard, should instead seek to tolerate the religious beliefs and practices of those subject to their jurisdiction (see Waldron 1988: 66–67). As Waldron puts it:

> The crux of the argument - the step which dominates it and on which everything else depends - is the claim that religious belief cannot be secured by the coercive means characteristic of state action. This is the essence of Locke's challenge to the rationality of religious persecution: that what the persecutors purport to be up to is something that, in the nature of the case, they cannot hope to achieve. (Waldron 1988: 67)

Waldron is indeed correct that Locke advances such an argument in *A Letter Concerning Toleration*. As Locke states:

> [T]he care of souls cannot belong to the civil magistrate, because his power consists only in outward force; but true and saving religion consists in the inward persuasion of the mind, without which nothing can be acceptable to God. And such is the nature of the understanding that it cannot be compelled to the belief of anything by outward force. Confiscation of estate, imprisonment, torments, nothing of that nature can have any such efficacy as to make men change the inward judgement that they have framed of things. (Locke 1993a: 395. See also Locke 1993a: 399, 402, 420; Locke 1993b: 189, 192–193, 204–205, 206)

Locke's "rationality argument" is therefore premised on the epistemic claim, expressed in the passage above, that it is the "nature of the understanding that it cannot be compelled to the belief of anything by outward force" (see also Locke 1967a: 127–130, 165, 167; Locke 1967b: 214; Locke 1993a: 395, 399, 402, 420; Locke 1993b: 187–89, 192–93, 204–206). It is Locke's view that it is only upon an individual's "will" (as distinct from their "understanding") that such "outward force" can have an impact, the "understanding" not arising from, and therefore not being affected by, a person's will (Locke 1967b: 238–239; Locke 1967a: 127–128). As Locke puts it in the *Letter*, "For it is absurd that things should be enjoined by laws which are not in men's power to perform. And to believe this or that to be true, does not depend upon our will" (Locke 1993a: 420). Because "understanding and assent" is "not to be wrought upon by force," the result, Locke insists (as early as the *Two Tracts*) is that "rigour" (the use of force) "cannot work an internal persuasion" (Locke 1967a: 127, 128).

If it is the case that force can have no effect upon the understanding, and therefore on what we believe or disbelieve, then Locke is correct to conclude that any attempt to directly coerce belief by the use of such force is futile and therefore (to use Waldron's term once more) "irrational." Locke is of the view that "toleration" by the state is but the removal of "outward force," with the result that toleration arises once the state recognizes the futility of force, when used for such purposes, and so abandons it:

> Force, you allow, is improper to convert men to any religion. Toleration is but the removing that force. (Locke 1963b: 62)

Locke advanced this same "rationality argument" in *An Essay Concerning Toleration*, declaring that "punishment and fear may make men dissemble, but, not convincing anybody's reason, cannot possibly make them assent" (Locke 1993b: 206). On this basis, he concluded:

> [N]o man ought to be forced to renounce his opinion or assent to the contrary, because such a compulsion cannot produce any real effect to that purpose for which it is designed. It cannot alter men's minds; it can only force them to be hypocrites, and by this way the magistrate is so far from bringing men to embrace the truth of his opinion of that, as that he only constrains them to lie for their errors. (Locke 1993b: 192. See also Locke 1993b: 204–205)

In each case, Locke's "rationality argument" advances the proposition that the state's use of force is futile (and so "irrational") if the purpose of that force is to alter the sincere beliefs of those subject to it. The consequence of the "rationality argument" is that state authorities ought therefore to agree to tolerate what they cannot alter.

Rationality Argument I

While the "rationality argument" is one of Locke's three "considerations" for toleration, what should be apparent is that it is only effective as an argument for toleration in specific circumstances. The "rationality argument" only has cogency if state authorities, in forcibly imposing religious conformity, are seeking to do so in order to alter the sincere beliefs of those subject to their jurisdiction (perhaps for salvationist ends). The "rationality argument" applies in such circumstances because force can then be identified as "irrational" for this purpose (belief being impervious to the use of such force) with the result that toleration is a reasonable alternative. If, on the other hand, state authorities are imposing such religious observances, and demanding outward conformity to them, to secure pragmatic (i.e. secular) ends (such as civil peace or state security), then the "rationality argument" lacks cogency because state authorities, in such contexts, are not seeking to use force in order to alter inner belief, but rather are seeking to use it to direct outward behavior (see Locke 1963b: 73, 99; Locke 1967a: 128). Such outward behavior, Locke tells us, is governed by the "will" (as distinct from the "understanding") and so is amenable to the use of such force (Locke 1967a: 128; Locke 1967b: 238–39). Such force is not, therefore, "irrational" when used for such purposes, and the terms of the "rationality argument" therefore do not apply.

We see, therefore, that the cogency of the "rationality argument" depends not only on the means that the state deploys to achieve its ends (i.e., whether these means include the use of force). It also depends on the reasons or purposes (i.e. ends) for which those means are deployed.

Jeremy Waldron insists that the "rationality" argument is an argument governed entirely by this second consideration, where "what matters for Locke's purposes is not coercion as such or its effects, but the reasons that motivate it" (Waldron 1988, 77). It is on this basis that Waldron can conclude that Locke's "rationality argument" falls short as a robust means of securing (via toleration) individual religious liberty. He does so by arguing that the "rationality argument" is concerned with individual liberty only in a residual or indirect sense, the prohibitions it places on the state (and therefore the realm it leaves to the liberty of the individual) being the product not of any direct concern with individual liberty but rather a concern with the "reasons" or "purposes" for which the state deploys the coercive means at its disposal. On this basis, Waldron describes Locke's "rationality argument" as follows:

> Locke's...argument is directed not against coercion *as such*, but only against *coercion undertaken for certain reasons* and with certain ends in mind. The argument concerns the rationality of the would-be persecutor and his purposes; it is concerned about what happens to his rationality when he selects means evidently unfitted to his ends...The religious liberty for which Locke argues is [therefore] defined *not* by the actions permitted on the part of the person whose liberty is in question, but by the motivations it prohibits on the part of the person who is in a position to threaten the liberty...Thus it is not a right to freedom of worship as such, but rather, and at most, a right not to have one's worship interfered with for religious ends. (Waldron 1988: 76–77. My addition. See also Tate 2016a: 108–119)

Rationality Argument II

Waldron's contestation that Locke's "rationality argument" has only incidental outcomes for individual liberty, based on the "reasons" for which it is "irrational" for state authorities to employ force, would reveal considerable shortcomings in *A Letter Concerning Toleration* as a document in defence of such liberty if Waldron was correct, in his earlier claim above, that this argument constitutes the "main line of argument" that Locke provides for toleration within this text. However as I have argued elsewhere, Waldron is in error on this point (Tate 2009: 762–778, Tate 2010a: 989–997; Tate 2016a: 108–119). Far from the "rationality argument" constituting the "main line of argument" in the *Letter*, we have seen that Locke, within the *Letter*, provides three separate "considerations" for toleration, only one of which is the "rationality argument." Further, as the following demonstrates, Locke, in the *Letter*, explicitly subordinates the "rationality argument" to one of his other "considerations" for toleration (the "truth argument") and, in his debate with Jonas Proast in the years following the publication of the *Letter*, ultimately abandons the "rationality argument," relying, in this debate, on his other "considerations" for toleration instead. All of this indicates that, contrary to Waldron, the "rationality argument" is very far from being Locke's "main line of argument" for toleration.

We have seen that the basic condition of the "rationality argument," upon which its cogency depends, is Locke's empirical claim that it is not possible, on the basis of "outward force," to alter inner belief. Yet in the italicized section of the first Locke passage that appears in "The 'Truth Argument'" section above, Locke concedes, within the *Letter*, that these conditions of the "rationality argument" may not apply – that it might, in other words, be possible, in some circumstances, for "the rigour of laws and the force of penalties" to "convince and change men's minds." Yet he immediately couples this, in the same passage above, with the proposition that although in such circumstances the "rationality argument" would no longer be sustained, another "consideration" for toleration (the "truth argument") would apply in its place. In this way, Locke "subordinates" the "rationality argument" to the "truth argument" within the *Letter*.

Indeed, in his later *Letters for Toleration*, in which Locke defends the content of *A Letter Concerning Toleration* in an ongoing debate with the Anglican clergyman, Jonas Proast, Locke not only subordinates the "rationality argument" to his other "considerations" for toleration but explicitly abandons it in the face of Proast's repeated insistence that there are some circumstances in which "outward force" can alter inner belief.

Proast agrees with Locke that "outward force" cannot alter inner belief in any direct sense, declaring "I readily grant that Reason and Arguments are the only proper Means, whereby to induce the Mind to assent to any Truth, which is not evident by its own Light; and that Force is very improper to be used to that end *instead* of Reason and Arguments. For who knows not, That *the nature of the Understanding is such, that it cannot be Compelled to the Belief of any thing by outward Force?*" (Proast 1999a: 27. See also Proast 1999b: 65). However, Proast advocates the "indirect" use of force as a means of persuasion, declaring that "though Force be not proper to *convince the Mind*, yet it is not *absolutely impertinent in this case*, because it may...do some service towards the bringing men to embrace the Truth which must save them, by bringing them to *consider those Reasons and Arguments which are proper to convince the Mind, and which without being forced, they would not consider*" (Proast 1999b: 65). To this end, Proast declares:

> But notwithstanding this, *if Force be used, not in stead of Reason and Arguments, i.e.* not to convince by its own proper Efficacy (which it cannot do), but onely to bring men to consider those Reasons and Arguments which are proper and sufficient to convince them, but which, without being forced, they would not consider: who can deny, but that *indirectly* and *at a distance*, it does some service toward the bringing men to embrace that Truth, which otherwise, either through Carelessness and Negligence they would never acquaint themselves with, or through Prejudice they would reject and condemn unheard, under the notion of Errour? (Proast 1999a: 27. See also Proast 1999a: 29–30)

Mark Goldie has identified this line of reasoning by Proast with St. Augustine, and declares it was a "ubiquitous..... argument," advanced by Anglican divines during the Restoration period to justify their refusal of toleration to Dissenters – such divines declaring that if the "will" is directed (via the use of force) to attend to "Reasons and Arguments" for religious "truth," then the "understanding" (although itself not directly amenable to the use of force) may eventually come to embrace such "truth" voluntarily and of its own accord, thereby saving individuals from theological error and so ensuring their eternal salvation (see Goldie 1991: 363, 364–365; Tate 2016a: 152–153).

Locke ultimately abandons the "rationality argument," in the face of such propositions advanced by Proast, and does so in two ways. Firstly, just as in *A Letter Concerning Toleration*, where (as we have seen above) Locke concedes that it might be possible, in some circumstances, for "the rigour of laws and the force of penalties" to "convince and change men's minds," so in the *Second Letter for Toleration*, Locke concedes Proast's contention that there may be times when force, employed "indirectly" and "at a distance," is capable of producing conditions which alter inner belief (Locke 1963b: 67–70, 77, 78). In each case, the "rationality argument" is vitiated because its basic premise (that force is incapable of altering inner belief) no longer applies. Locke insists, however, that, in most cases, the preponderant weight of evidence is that the use of force will *not* be capable of producing such outcomes, or at least not without incurring inordinate adverse consequences, with the result that, in this second circumstance, another version of the "rationality argument" will apply, at least in broad terms, because the use of force, in such circumstances, will still be "irrational" if leading to such consequences:

> And therefore you will do well hereafter not to build so much on the usefulness of force, applied your way, your indirect and at a distance usefulness, which amounts but to the shadow and possibility of usefulness, but with an overbalancing weight of mischief and harm annexed to it. For upon a just estimate, this indirect, and at a distance, usefulness, can directly go for nothing; or rather less than nothing. (Locke 1963b: 79–80)

Secondly, Locke abandons the "rationality argument" by insisting, in the following passage, that state authorities are unlikely to use "outward force" as a means to alter inner belief in any case. Instead, he tells us, state authorities are likely to use such force only to secure outward "compliance" with the state's religious demands, perhaps for the sake of the secular ends of civil peace or state security identified above. We saw that, in such circumstances, the individual's will (as distinct from their understanding) might be amenable to such force – since it is the will, rather than the understanding, which is necessary for such outward "compliance." Once again, because the use of force is capable of attaining its ends in such circumstances, the terms of the "rationality argument" no longer apply and so the argument itself is vitiated. As Locke puts it:

> I think those who make laws, and use force, to bring men to church-conformity in religion, seek only the compliance, but concern themselves not for the conviction of those they punish; and so never use force to convince. (Locke 1963b: 73. See also Locke 1963b: 99; Locke 1967a: 127–128)

But Locke in no way believes that this abandonment of the "rationality argument" significantly weakens his case for toleration (as would be the case if Jeremy Waldron was correct that this argument constituted the "main line of argument" that Locke provided to this end). On the contrary, just as in *A Letter Concerning Toleration* above, Locke insists in his debate with Proast that if the "rationality argument" does not apply, his other "considerations" for toleration will apply in its place:

> [A]llowing that even force could work upon them, and magistrates had authority to use it in religion, then the argument you mention is not "the only one in that letter, of strength to prove the necessity of toleration"…For the argument of the unfitness of force to convince men's minds being quite taken away, either of the other would be a strong proof for toleration. (Locke 1963b: 67. See also Locke 1963b: 80, 111–112)

Rationality Argument III

Along with Jeremy Waldron, John Dunn and Mark Goldie have assumed that the fundamental premise of the "rationality argument" (the inefficacy of force as a means of altering inner belief) was the primary point at issue between Locke and Proast in their debate (see Tate 2016a: 153–157, 159–161). Goldie declares that "[t]he debate between the two men was conducted on an apparently narrow front. No general theory of toleration was at issue. The topic was the efficacy of coercion on behalf of 'true religion'. Reliable knowledge of the 'true religion' was taken as the starting point: what was contested was whether the civil magistrate could or should use physical pressure to bring people to that religion" (Goldie 1999a: 24. See also Goldie 1999b: 40; Goldie 1991: 363–364). Similarly, John Dunn, referring to the proposition that "[i]ndividual religious behaviour, if it is to attain its end, is necessarily defined by subjective conviction" and "[s]uch conviction cannot in principle be generated by governmental action," declared that "[t]his claim was at the heart of Locke's controversy with Jonas Proast" (Dunn 1969: 33, 33n. See Tate 2016a: 153–157, 159–61). Given Goldie and Dunn assume that "the efficacy of coercion on behalf of 'true religion'" is the primary point at issue in the debate between Locke and Proast, then, like Waldron, Goldie and Dunn must also assume that Proast's success in forcing Locke to concede, in their engagement, that "outward force" is capable, in some circumstances, of altering inner belief, is conclusive evidence that Proast comprehensively refuted the primary case for toleration that Locke sought to advance in that debate (see Waldron 1988: 61, 62, 65, 83, 84; Dunn 1969: 33n; Goldie 1991: 364n, 366–367; Goldie 1999a: 24).

Such a view is, in my opinion, deeply mistaken (see Tate 2016a: 153–161). Among the reasons why this is so is the fact that, as Locke makes clear above, even if the "rationality argument" has been comprehensively refuted, he believed that his other "considerations" for toleration would apply in its place. As such, contrary to Goldie, Dunn and Waldron, a refutation of Locke's "rationality argument" was not a refutation of Locke's case for toleration *tout court*. Just as Locke made this point clear to Proast in the last passage quoted above, he does so again as follows:

> And you tell us, "the whole strength of what that letter urged for the purpose of it, lies in this argument," which I think you have no more reason to say, than if you should tell us, that only one beam of a house had any strength in it, when there are several others that would support the building, were that gone. (Locke 1963b: 67)

Locke's Skepticism

We saw above that a skepticism concerning any individual or institution's claim to possess knowledge of "true religion" was the key condition of Locke's "truth argument." However as will be made clear below, skepticism plays a much wider role in Locke's case for religious toleration. It is in this context that we may refer to Locke's fourth "consideration" for toleration – the "skepticism argument."

Locke makes reference to the religious diversity of his own time when he states: "[I]n this great variety of ways that men follow, it is still doubted which is this right one" (Locke 1993a: 407). He also makes reference to the pervasive religious disagreement which was the corollary of this diversity when he declares: "[H]owever he came by his religion, there is scarce anyone to be found who does not own himself satisfied that he is in the right," with the result that "[t]he great dispute in all this diversity of opinions is where the truth is" (Locke 1963b: 102; Locke 2004a: 247. See also Locke 1993b: 205). What is apparent in Locke's advancement of the "truth argument" in the *Letter*, and in his engagement with Jonas Proast (discussed further below), is that Locke does not believe it is possible for individuals to resolve this disagreement by determining "where the truth is" – i.e., by applying a criterion of "true religion" that will distinguish who is in possession of the "true religion" and who is not. This is because Locke does not believe such a criterion to be accessible to human beings, God alone being the ultimate judge of "true religion" (Locke 1993a: 401–402). Such opinions are a characteristic feature of Locke's skepticism. While we have seen that Locke, at times, concedes that there is a "true religion" (the religion necessary for salvation), he is skeptical of anyone's claim to possess indubitable knowledge of it as well as anyone's claim to know the means by which such knowledge might be attained. All such propositions concerning "true religion," Locke insists, are matters of "faith," not knowledge, and therefore cannot be determined with categorical or veridical certainty (Locke 1963a: 144, 402, 424; Locke 1963c: 558, 559, 563). It is therefore on the basis of this religious skepticism that Locke insists that there is no indubitable criterion by which disputes concerning "true religion" can be authoritatively decided or resolved (see Locke 1963a: 296–297, 332–334, 419–420, 424, 425; Locke 1963b: 65, 76–77, 78, 88–91, 100, 102, 111, 114, 119, 130; Locke 1963c: 561, 562; Locke 1993a: 401–02).

The result of this inability to reach authoritative conclusions concerning "true religion," Locke believes, is that in matters of religion, "diversity of opinions... cannot be avoided" (Locke 1993a: 431), and this because "[m]en in all religions have equally strong persuasions" (Locke 1963c: 561), a genuine belief that they are "in the right" (Locke 1993b: 205), and yet there is no authoritative means to decide between them. The consequence of this inability to determine who is in possession of the "true religion," Locke declares, is that "every one is orthodox to himself" (Locke 1993a: 390), with the result that "every one is here judge for himself, what is right" (Locke 1963b: 135. See also Locke 1963c: 561; Locke 1993a: 393, 394, 396, 403, 405, 405–06, 411, 412, 421–423).

However not all aspects of religion, in Locke's opinion, are subject to such skepticism. Locke believed that knowledge of the *existence* of God was possible on the basis of human reason. As Locke put it in *An Essay Concerning Human Understanding*:

> [T]he knowledge of a GOD, be the most natural discovery of humane Reason. (Locke 1975: Bk. I, ch. iv, § 17, p. 95. See also Locke 2004b: 278–79; Tate 2013a: 152–153)

But Locke makes a distinction between such matters of "natural theology," arising on the basis of the judgments of "humane Reason," and "divine revelation" with its associated claims of "true religion" (Locke 1963a: 424). It is the latter which is the province of "revealed religion," and upon which are based salvationist claims (Locke 1963a: 424). It is in relation to "revealed religion," and therefore "true religion," we have seen, that Locke believes knowledge is not possible, all such matters being subject to "faith" (Locke 1963a: 144, 402, 424; Locke 1963c: 558, 559, 563). The fact that such knowledge is not available means that differences between individuals, concerning "true religion," are not only unavoidable but also (as we have seen above) irresolvable, there being no indubitable criterion by which such disputes can be authoritatively decided.

Locke's skepticism concerning claims to "true religion" arose, in part, as a result of the constituent features of "revealed" religion itself. The "divine revelation" upon which such "revealed" religion depends (such as, in the case of Christianity, the resurrection of Jesus Christ – see Locke 1963a: 144) itself depends, Locke insists, "upon particular matters of fact, whereof you were no eye–witness, but were done many ages before you were born.... And if so, by what principles of science they can be known to any man now living?" (Locke 1963a: 424. See also Locke 1963a: 144, 402, 422). The result, Locke concludes, is (once again) that knowledge of "truth" in such contexts is not possible, "faith" being all that is available in such matters (Locke 1963a: 144, 402, 422, 424; Locke 1963c: 558, 559, 563). As Locke puts it:

> [W]hatever is not capable of demonstration, as such remote matters of fact are not, is not, unless it be self-evident, capable to produce knowledge, how well grounded and great soever the assurance of faith may be wherewith it is received; but faith it is still, and not knowledge; persuasion, and not certainty. This is the highest the nature of the thing will permit us to go in matters of revealed religion, which are therefore called matters of faith: a persuasion of our minds, short of knowledge, is the last result that determines us in such truths. It is all God requires in the Gospel for men to be saved. (Locke 1963a: 144)

Skepticism Argument I

It was on the basis of such skepticism concerning knowledge of "true religion" that Locke arrived, during his debate with Jonas Proast in the *Second*, *Third*, and *Fourth Letters for Toleration*, at what I shall call his fourth "consideration" for toleration – the "skepticism argument" (see Tate 2016a: Chap. 9; Tate 2016b: 670–72; Tate 2010b: 960). The "skepticism argument" is distinct from the "truth argument." Both rely, for their foundational premise, on the proposition that knowledge of "true religion" is not possible (such matters invariably being subject to faith) with the result that we should be skeptical concerning anyone's claim to possession of such knowledge. But whereas the "truth argument" is an argument whose potency arises from the interest of those subject to state authority in ensuring their eternal salvation, and so their incentive in resisting state attempts to intrude upon their religious beliefs by force, the "skepticism argument" seeks to provide reasons why those possessing state authority should not use force to coerce such beliefs but rather should tolerate them instead, leaving matters of religion (when these do not impinge upon secular state concerns) to the choices of individuals.

The core proposition of the "skepticism argument" is that if those in possession of state authority lack indubitable knowledge of what constitutes the "true religion," they lack an authoritative basis to justify, on the grounds of such "truth," the imposition of religious beliefs or practices upon others by the use of force. I argued, in the case of the "truth argument," that such skepticism concerning religious "truth" is likely to convince those subject to state authority to resist all attempts by state authorities to impose such "truths" on them. But that it is unlikely to convince state authorities themselves not to impose such "truth" if they are convinced of its veracity, and therefore of their own righteousness. The "skepticism argument," therefore, goes further than the "truth argument" by seeking to make up this deficit and persuade those in possession of state authority not to impose such "truth" by force and instead to engage in toleration. We shall see below that one way in which it does so is that, in addition to arguing that state authorities, due to their absence of knowledge of "true religion," have no warrant, on the basis of such "truth," for imposing their religion on others by force, it also points to the unacceptable aggregate consequences if all state authorities seek to do this. As Locke explains further below, since state authorities embrace, between them, a wide diversity of religions, many at odds with each other, with the result that not all of them can be "true," and since there is only "one truth, one way to heaven," if all state rulers imposed their religions upon their populaces by force, this would be detrimental, in the aggregate, to the advance of "true religion" and the salvation of souls.

We saw above that Proast advocated the use of force in matters of religion, applied "indirectly" and "at a distance," as a means of instilling, in those subject to state authority, sincere religious belief, but he did so only in the case of what he conceived to be the "true religion" (i.e. the religion capable of "bringing men" to "Salvation") (Proast 1999a: 28, 31–32, 34, 36; Proast 1999b: 59, 63–68, 82, 85, 86, 104, 105, 108, 109, 111, 121). As Proast put it: "[I]f Force so applied as is above mentioned, may, in such sort as has been said, be serviceable to the bringing men to receive and embrace Truth; there can be no reason assigned, why this should not hold with respect to the Truths of Religion, as well as with respect to any other Truths whatsoever" (Proast 1999a: 27). Further, Proast had no doubt about his capacity to declare his own religion (the Church of England) to be "true." As he put it, "For if my *Church* be *in the right*; and my Religion be the true; why may I not all along suppose it to be so?" (Proast 1999b: 85. See also Proast 1999b: 50). He therefore justified the use of force in matters of religion only in those circumstances where the religion was "true" and therefore necessary for individual salvation:

> [I]f...there be one true Religion, and no more; and that may be known to be the onely true religion by those who are of it; and may by them to be manifested to others, in such sort as has been said: then 'tis altogether as plain, that it may be very reasonable and necessary for some men to change their Religion; and that it may be made to them to be so. And then if such men will not consider what is offer'd, to convince them of the Reasonableness and Necessity of doing it; it may be very fit and reasonable, for any thing you have said to the contrary, in order to the bringing them to Consideration, to require them under convenient Penalties, to forsake their false Religions, and to embrace the true. (Proast 1999b: 86. See also Proast 1999a: 27; Proast 1999b: 65)

Mark Goldie points to how such appeal to religious "truth" as justification for religious coercion was widespread among Anglican authorities in the Restoration period, the use of force upon Dissenters being "premised on an assumption of an objectively known true religion" (Goldie 1991: 361). To this extent, Goldie says, Proast's position is "the sharpest formulation of a ubiquitous Restoration argument" (Goldie 1991: 363).

Proast believed the Anglican religion, endorsed by English state authorities, to be the "true religion" (Proast 1999b: 50) and, further, as we have seen above, declared that it is possible to *know* this religion to be "true." One means by which such knowledge is possible, Proast insists, is a "third sort or degree of Perswasion," which, he says, arises in the minds of individuals in the case of "true religion" and "true religion" only, and which amounts to "Full Assurance" or "Knowledge" of its "truth," leaving "no reasonable Doubt in an attentive and unbyas'd mind," thereby enabling individuals to distinguish "true religion" from all other religions on this basis (Proast 1999c: 121. See also Tate 2016a: 157–59). It is precisely this assumption – that knowledge of "true religion" is possible – which, we have seen, Proast advances to legitimate the English state's use of force for "the promoting True Religion and the Salvation of Souls."

On the basis of what I have called his "skepticism," Locke explicitly seeks to refute these propositions as advanced by Proast. To this end, Locke addresses Proast's conception of a "third sort or degree of Perswasion" which (Proast tells us above) amounts to "Full Assurance" or "Knowledge" of the "true religion." In response to this proposition, Locke again insists that there is a categorical distinction between "belief" (or "faith") on the one hand and "knowledge" on the other, which cannot be bridged by the degree of "Assurance" of either – "for knowledge upon strict demonstration is not belief or persuasion, but wholly above it" (Locke 1963c: 559). In this respect, Locke insists that the "boundaries" between "knowledge and belief" "must be kept and their names not confounded" (Locke 1963c: 558), and the reason is because (as Locke explains above) "revealed religion" does not give rise to "truth" propositions amenable to knowledge, but only to faith. Further, the "Full Assurance" that Proast believes arises from his "third sort or degree of Perswasion" is again, according to Locke, no indication of its "truth," since such "Assurance" is equally capable of arising in relation to "false" religions, individuals being "as positive and peremptory in Error as in Truth" (Locke 1975: Book IV, ch. xix, §11, p. 703). As Locke put it:

> Another false supposition you build upon is this, that the true religion is always embraced with the firmest assent. There is scarce any one so little acquainted with the world, that hath not met with instances of men most unmoveably confident, and fully assured in a religion which was not the true. (Locke 1963c: 563)

The result, Locke says, is a fundamental divide between "faith" and "knowledge" when it comes to matters of "revealed religion":

> [B]elieving in the highest degree of assurance is not knowledge...[and]...whatever is not capable of demonstration is not, unless it be self-evident, capable to produce knowledge, how well grounded and great soever the assurance of faith may be wherewith it is received. (Locke 1963c: 558)

In this way, Locke's skepticism challenges, at its core, Proast's claim that knowledge of "true religion" is possible, and further, challenges his insistence that, on the basis of this knowledge, state authorities are justified in using force (applied "indirectly" and "at a distance") to impose this religion on those subject to their jurisdiction. Locke rejects these propositions on the grounds that, no indubitable criterion of "true religion" being available, no knowledge of "true religion" is possible, with the result that anybody's assertion of "religious truth," as a justification for the use of force, is equally capable of being countered by a similar (and equally contestable) claim arising from others:

> For whose is really the true religion, yours or his, being the matter in contest betwixt you, your supposing can no more determine it on your side, than his supposing on his; unless you can think you have a right to judge in your own cause. You believe yours to be the true religion, so does he believe his: you say you are certain of it; so, says he, he is: you think you have "arguments proper and sufficient" to convince him, if he would consider them; the same thinks he of his. If this claim, which is equally on both sides, be allowed to either, without any proof; it is plain he, in whose favour it is allowed, is allowed to be judge in his own cause, which nobody can have a right to be, who is not at least infallible. (Locke 1963a: 419)

It is precisely such irresolvable contestation that Locke draws upon to arrive at the conclusion of his "skepticism argument" – that because there is no indubitable criterion to determine the "true religion," there is no legitimate reason for exercising the use of force in its name, and toleration, by state authorities, of the diverse religions of those subject to their jurisdiction, is the only acceptable alternative. As Locke puts it to Proast:

> Men in the wrong way are to be punished: but who are in the wrong way is the question. You have no more reason to determine it against one who differs from you, than he has to conclude against you, who differ from him: no, not though you have the magistrate and the national church on your side. For, if to differ from them be to be in the wrong way, you, who are in the right way in England, will be in the wrong way in France. Every one here must be judge for himself. (Locke 1963b: 89. See also Locke 1963a, 419, 420; Locke 1963c, 561)

Proast, at one point in the debate, accuses Locke of precisely the sort of skepticism Locke is advancing in the passages above (Proast 1999b: 85). And Locke (no doubt because of the stigma and opprobrium attaching to any charge of religious skepticism in the seventeenth century) denies this accusation (Locke 1963a: 419. See also Locke 1963a: 415; Tate 2016a: 227–31; Tate 2016b: 671). But it is clear that Locke is advancing precisely the skepticism, in matters of religion, of which Proast accuses him, with the result, Locke insists, that "true and false" in such matters, "when we suppose them for ourselves, or our party, in effect, signify just nothing, or nothing to the purpose" (Locke 1963b: 90). It is on the basis of such skepticism that Locke declares that Proast ought to advance his case "without supposing all along your church in the right, and your religion the true; which can no more be allowed to you in this case, whatever your church or religion be, than it can be to a papist or a Lutheran, a Presbyterian or anana baptist; nay, no more to you, than it can be allowed to a Jew or a Mahometan" (Locke 1963a: 111). After all, Locke declares, "no...church...which claims not infallibility, can require any one to take the testimony of any church, as a sufficient proof of the truth of her own doctrine" (Locke 1963b: 90).

Mark Goldie declared above that "[r]eliable knowledge of the 'true religion' was taken as the starting point" of Locke and Proast's debate (Goldie 1999a: 24) and further declares that, within this debate, "limited attention [was] paid to the larger question of the inroads of skepticism upon the idea of 'true religion'" (Goldie 1991: 364. See also Goldie 2010: xvi; Tate 2016a: 156–57, 159–61). However, we have seen that nothing could be further from the truth. As the above makes clear, both Locke and Proast focused significant attention on this question as it is Locke's insistence on the *absence* of such "reliable knowledge" which allows him to directly challenge Proast's advocacy of the use of force, applied "indirectly" and "at a distance," in matters of religion, and also provides Locke with the basis for both his "truth argument" and his "skepticism argument" in favour of toleration (see Tate 2016a: 127–34, 156–61; Tate 2016b: 670–71). In other words, it is precisely this question of whether "reliable knowledge of the 'true religion'" is possible which most deeply divides Locke from Proast.

Skepticism Argument II

Jeremy Waldron has engaged with Locke's skepticism as it is applied by Locke to his arguments for toleration. Referring to a passage in *A Letter Concerning Toleration* in which Locke declares that any entitlement of a state ruler to forcibly impose their religion, on the grounds that it is the "true religion," must be an entitlement which applies to *all* state rulers, whether Christian or non-Christian, the "civil power" being "the same everywhere" (Locke 1993a: 416), Waldron responds:

> Notice that this is a good argument only against the following rather silly principle: (P1) that the magistrate may enforce *his own* religion or whatever religion *he thinks* is correct. It is not a good argument against the somewhat more sensible position (P2) that a magistrate may enforce the religion, whatever it may be, which is *in fact* objectively correct. It may, of course, be difficult to tell, and perhaps impossible to secure social agreement about, whether

the view that the magistrate believes is correct is in fact the correct view...But opposition to intolerance based on awareness of these difficulties is not opposition to intolerance as such, but only opposition to particular cases of it. (Waldron 1988: 72)

Waldron's statement has plausibility if it is indeed possible that those in possession of state authority are capable (at the very least, in principle) of determining which religion "is *in fact* objectively correct" and distinguishing this religion, on the basis of which the use of force is justifiable, from all others. But if this is not possible, then all that those in possession of state authority are left with is Waldron's "silly principle," wherein state rulers seek to impose the religion which they merely "think" to be correct.

Needless to say, the point of Locke's "skepticism argument" is that it is indeed only Waldron's "silly principle" which is available to state rulers or anyone else, indubitable knowledge of "true religion" not being a possibility. The result, therefore, is that from Locke's perspective, Waldron's distinction between P1 and P2 cannot be sustained, because no state ruler (or anyone else) possesses the knowledge of which religion "is *in fact* objectively correct" to make P2 a possibility. In this context, all that state rulers are left with are the circumstances of P1, in which they enforce their "own religion" or whatever religion they "think is correct":

[I]f the magistrates of the world cannot know, certainly know, the true religion to be the true religion...then that which gives them the last determination herein must be their own belief, their own persuasion. (Locke 1963a: 143. See Locke 1963a: 145; Locke 1963c: 567)

Locke's declaration that the "civil power is the same everywhere" (Locke 1993a: 402, 416) leads him to the conclusion that if one state ruler is purported to have the entitlement to impose his or her religion by force, on the grounds that it is the "true religion," then *all* state rulers have this entitlement, given that "the religion of every prince is orthodox to himself" (Locke 1993a: 416), and there is no indubitable criterion of "true religion" to decide between them (Locke 1963a: 143–146, 163, 184, 205, 213, 262, 365, 370, 374, 378, 382, 398, 399, 402, 408–409; Locke 1963c: 505–506, 514, 535–536, 541, 555–556). The result is that "at Geneva.... he may extirpate, by violence and blood the religion which is there reputed idolatrous" and, in another country, "by the same rule," another state ruler may "oppress the reformed religion; and, in India, the Christian" (Locke 1993a: 416).

Locke advances the opinion that the vast majority of the religions, both Christian and non-Christian, endorsed by state rulers of his time, are in fact "false." As he puts it, "[T]he national religions of the world are, beyond comparison, more of them false or erroneous, than such as have God for their author, and truth for their standard" (Locke 1963b: 78. See also Locke 1963b: 76–77, 80, 100, 114, 118, 119; Locke 1963c: 567; Locke 1993a: 396). Locke can presumably only arrive at this conclusion on the basis of the following assumptions. Firstly he tells us, the "lords of the earth... differ... vastly" on "religious matters" (Locke 1993a: 407) with many of them at odds on this issue ("there are more pagan, Mahometan, and erroneous princes in the world, than orthodox" – Locke 1963b: 114). However as there is but "one truth, one way to heaven," the vast majority of diverse (and contrary) religions endorsed by state rulers cannot all be instances of this "truth."

It is on the basis of these propositions that Locke then advances the element of the "skepticism argument" meant to convince state rulers to tolerate in a way the "truth argument" could not. This element of the "skepticism argument" arises from the following premises (outlined above): (i) if any single state ruler has an entitlement to enforce their religion upon their populace on the grounds that it is "true," then all state rulers have this entitlement, the "civil power" being "the same everywhere"; (ii) yet if there is "one truth, one way to heaven," and the vast majority of state rulers in the world endorse religions that are "false or erroneous," this general entitlement will have deleterious consequences for the advancement of "true religion" in the aggregate, with the result that toleration is the preferable alternative:

> And now I desire it may be considered, what advantage this supposition of force, which is supposed put into the magistrate's hands...to be used in religion, brings to the true religion, when it arms five hundred magistrates against the true religion, who must unavoidably in the state of things in the world act against it, for one that uses force for it. (Locke 1963c: 566. See also Locke 1963a: 145–6, 147–148, 163, 184, 205, 213, 374, 378; 1963c: 500, 535–536, 567; Locke 1963b: 76–7, 78, 114; Locke 1993a: 396)

Locke makes the same point elsewhere in his debate with Proast, this time pointing to the deleterious consequences for the advancement of "true religion" given that Christianity is a minority religion among state rulers:

> But yet it is...hard for me, I confess, and I believe for others, to conceive how you should think to do any service to truth and the Christian religion, by putting a right into Mahometans' or heathens' hands to punish Christians...since there are more pagan, Mahometan, and erroneous princes in the world, than orthodox; truth, and the Christian religion, taking the world as we find it, is sure to be more punished and suppressed, than error and falsehood. (Locke 1963b: 114)

Such is Locke's articulation, in his debate with Proast, of what I have called the "skepticism argument." However Locke shows an awareness of this argument as early as *A Letter Concerning Toleration*, where (on the basis of the same assumptions that he advances in his debate with Proast) he points to the deleterious aggregate consequences of state rulers claiming an entitlement to impose on their populace the religion that they believe to be "true":

> In the variety and contradiction of opinions in religion, wherein the princes of the world are as much divided as in their secular interests, the narrow way would be much straitened: one country alone would be in the right, and all the rest of the world would be put under an obligation of following their princes in the ways that lead to destruction; and that which heightens the absurdity, and very ill suits the notion of a deity, men would owe their eternal happiness or misery to the places of their nativity. (Locke 1993a: 396)

Such propositions are meant to convince state rulers to engage in toleration in a way the "truth argument" could not, because they show the negative aggregate consequences of a single entitlement (the right of those in possession of state authority to impose by force the religion that they believe to be "true") that, however much any individual ruler may claim this entitlement exclusively for themselves, is also available to all the others. It is the "skepticism argument," with its insistence that there is no indubitable criterion of "true religion" capable of distinguishing between those state rulers in possession of "true religion" and those who are not, which is the vehicle by which Locke arrives at these conclusions.

Proast responds to such conclusions by denying their aggregate implications. He insists that he was not advancing the proposition that "any Magistrate, who upon weak and deceitful grounds believes a False Religion to be true" is entitled to use force to impel others to their religion (Waldron's "silly principle"), but only the Magistrate "who upon just and sufficient grounds believes his Religion to be true" (Proast 1999c: 121). In other words, he insists that the deleterious aggregate outcomes Locke identifies above do not follow from his position because he never authorized *all* magistrates to advance their religion by force, only those possessing the "true religion" (Proast 1999b: 54, 66; Proast 1999c: 121. See also Proast 1999a: 36; Tate 2016a: 176–178). Locke's response is that Proast cannot avoid, via such a distinction, the "aggregate" consequences Locke outlines above, because, there being no criterion of "true religion" available, there is no means to decide which magistrates fall into the "true religion" category Proast identifies and which into the other. The result is that any such attempt to distinguish between magistrates, and their use of force, on this basis, is (according to Locke) a "useless distinction":

> [I]f the magistrate be to use force only for promoting the true religion, he can have no other guide but his own persuasion of what is the true religion, and must be led by that in his use of force, or else not use it at all in matters of religion. If you take the latter of these consquences, you and I are agreed: if the former, you must allow all magistrates, of whatsoever religion, the use of force to bring men to theirs, and so be involved in all those ill consequences which you cannot it seems admit, and hope to decline by your *useless distinction* of force to be used, not for any, but for the true religion. (Locke 1963a: 145–146. Emphasis added)

It is therefore Locke's "skepticism" concerning knowledge of "true religion," along with his beliefs (themselves a matter of faith) that (i) there is "one truth, one way to heaven," and (ii) that the vast bulk of the "national religions of the world" are "false or erroneous," that allow him to advance this "aggregate" version of his skepticism argument, enabling him to reach conclusions concerning the deleterious consequences if *all* magistrates seek to impose their religion by force. It is on the basis of these conclusions that he is thereby able to present toleration as a preferable alternative. We see, therefore, how this "aggregate" version of the "skepticism argument" relies on the same skeptical premise (that knowledge of "true religion" is not possible) that informs the "truth argument," but leads to a pro-tolerationist position much wider in its application, capable of incorporating those in possession of state authority, rather than (as in the case of the "truth argument") those merely subject to it.

"True Interests," "Use and Necessity," and "Corruption and Pravity"

Besides the debate between Locke and Proast as to whether God himself has authorized the magistrate to use force, "indirectly" and "at a distance," in matters of religion (see Tate 2016a: 206–220), there are three additional arguments that Proast advances to justify his proposition that the magistrate is entitled to use force for such purposes. Each is important since they elucidate Locke's defence of toleration in response.

In one argument, Proast seeks to directly confront Locke's "truth" and "consent" arguments by insisting that because eternal salvation is in the "true Interest" of individuals (Proast 1999a: 35), and the magistrate is in possession of "true religion," then government is entitled to use force to that end (Proast 1999a: 33, 35; Proast 1999b: 95, 97, 103, 114, 114–115), even against the "inclination" of those subject to such authority (and therefore without their consent) (Proast 1999a: 35). In this way, governments can ensure that such individuals act according to "Reason and sound Judgement" in such matters (Proast 1999a: 35. See Tate 2016a: 184–186).

On these grounds (contra Locke's "truth argument"), Proast is able to argue that individuals do not have an "interest" in resisting the magistrate's impositions in matters of religion (the magistrate being in possession of the "true religion") nor (contra Locke's "consent argument") is there a need to elicit their "consent" to justify such impositions. Of course, such propositions can only be sustained by Proast's assumption that it is possible for the magistrate to *know* he or she is in possession of the "true religion," thereby legitimating their impositions to this end. It is this assumption that Locke explicitly denies.

Another position advanced by Proast is his view that the "Corruption and Pravity of Humane Nature" is such that "true religion" will not "prevail by its own Light and Strength" against false religions without "the Assistance of the Powers in being" (Proast 1999b: 46–47). Toleration, by precluding this "Assistance," and allowing individuals to pursue their religious interests unhindered, enables this "Corruption and Pravity" to proliferate, with the result that (in Proast's words) "true religion" will not be in "any way a gainer" by toleration (Proast 1999a: 26. See also Proast 1999b: 48, 49, 50, 52, 73, 89, 101; Tate 2016a: 211–215). It is for this, among other reasons, that Proast insists that God Himself has assigned to magistrates an authority to impose this "Assistance" on those subject to their jurisdiction in order to prevent such outcomes (Proast 1999b: 70, 74, 75, 76, 78, 81, 90, 95, 99, 100, 101, 102; Tate 2016a: 215–220). The result is that individuals should not be left to "their own Consciences" in matters of religion (Proast 1999b: 52).

Such an argument again assumes that the magistrate is in possession of the "true religion," and can *know* this religion to be "true," since only such knowledge can justify the "Assistance" the magistrate gives to this "true religion" by the use of force, applied "indirectly" and "at a distance." Once again, such knowledge is precisely what Locke denies, insisting that although there may be but "one truth, one way to heaven," we have no indubitable means of determining what this "truth" or this "way" is.

A third basis of justification for the magistrate's use of force, in matters of religion, is Proast's appeal to the "use" and "necessity" of this force – i.e., its efficacy as a means of altering the inner beliefs of those upon whom it is applied, thereby enabling them to embrace the "true religion." Proast insists that the efficacy of this force, as a means of achieving its intended ends, is, in and of itself, a source of legitimation of those ends, and of the magistrate's entitlement to pursue them:

> And certainly, if there be so great *Use* and *Necessity* of outward Force (duly temper'd and applied) for the promoting True Religion and the Salvation of Souls, as I have endeavoured to shew there is; this is as good an Argument, to prove there is somewhere a Right to use such Force for that purpose, as the utter *Uselessness* of Force (if that could be made out) would be, to prove that no body has any such Right. (Proast 1999a: 31–32. See also Proast 1999b: 69, 80, 82, 85, 95, 112–114, 119–122, 134; Proast 1999c: 162. See also Tate 2016a: 125–127, 139 note 5 and 10)

Jeremy Waldron draws on precisely such a legitimation of the use of force in what he calls the "modal" definition of the state (Waldron 1988: 64–65). Here, the state is justified in its use of force if such force is capable of achieving its ends, and this because, according to this "modal" definition, the legitimacy of the ends the state is entitled to pursue is entirely dependent on the efficacy of the means it possesses to achieve them (Waldron 1988: 63–67). It is precisely such a conception of the state and its use of force that underwrote Waldron's account of the "rationality argument" as advanced by Locke in the *Letter*, and further, it is precisely such a conception of the state that Waldron seeks to *ascribe* to Locke (Waldron 1988: 65–67. See also Tate 2016a: 115–117). Needless to say, Waldron's declaration that Locke embraces a "modal" definition of the state assists Waldron in his claim that the "rationality argument" is the "main line of argument" Locke seeks to advance for toleration in the *Letter* (see Tate 2016a: 110–119).

Yet Locke, in his debate with Proast, explicitly repudiates the justification of the use of force that Proast advances in the passage above, and which Waldron seeks to ascribe to him in the form of a "modal" definition of the state. To do so, Locke draws on the same premises that he utilized to underwrite his "consent argument." This includes the equation we saw Locke establish between "consent," "legitimacy," and "obligation," and his claim that the state is only entitled to pursue those purposes or ends for which it has elicited the "consent" of those subject to its jurisdiction, with the result that its use of force is only "legitimate" if directed to those ends. Here (contrary to Proast's account above and also Waldron's "modal" definition of the state) the efficacy of the use of force (its capacity to achieve its ends) does not determine the legitimacy of those ends or the legitimacy of the use of force to achieve them. Rather, Locke is clear that the justification of the state's use of force is dependent on the prior legitimacy of the ends to which such force is directed, and which such force seeks to achieve, such ends only being legitimate if they fall within the prescribed sphere of authority (or "commission") which the state has been assigned by the "consent" of those subject to its jurisdiction. Such assumptions are evident in Locke's following response to Proast where Locke explicitly repudiates the justification of the use of force that Proast (and Waldron) identify above:

> But suppose force, applied your way, were as useful for the promoting true religion, as I suppose I have showed it to be the contrary; it does not from hence follow that it is lawful and may be used. . . ..Granting force, as you say, indirectly and at a distance, useful to the salvation of men's souls; yet it does not therefore follow that it is lawful for the magistrate to use it: because. . .the magistrate has no commission or authority to do so. . . ..For though it be a good argument; it is not useful, therefore not fit to be used; yet this will not be good logic; it is useful, therefore anyone has a right to use it. (Locke 1963b: 80. See Locke 1963a: 162, 214, 218; Locke 1963b: 69, 80, 82, 85, 112–114, 119–122, 134; Tate 2016a: 125–127, 181–184)

In this way, Locke makes clear that even if the state possesses means that are capable of achieving their ends (thereby rendering them, in Waldron's terms, "rational" for that purpose) this does not confer a legitimacy upon those means, or the ends to which they are directed, unless the state has been authorized to pursue such ends. Only then do such ends fall within the "commission" of the magistrate and therefore within the sphere of his or her legitimate authority (on "commission" see Locke 1963b: 80, 112, 113, 119–122, 126, 134; Locke 1963a: 164, 166–167, 169). Indeed, it is precisely such a chain of reasoning that ensures that Locke's "consent argument" for toleration retains its validity even if the "rationality argument," as a result of Proast identifying means capable of achieving their ends (i.e. altering inner belief), is vitiated. This is because the "consent argument" makes clear that the discovery of "rational" means (i.e., means capable of achieving their ends) has no implications either for the legitimacy of those means or the ends to which they are directed. Further, Locke points out that the "consent argument" retains its validity even if the conditions of the "truth argument" are undermined (as a result of the magistrate possessing knowledge of the "true religion") because even if the magistrate possessed such knowledge, he or she (as explained above) would have no "commission" to impose such "truth" on those subject to his or her jurisdiction.

> But supposing all the truths of the Christian religion necessary to salvation could be so known to the magistrate, that, in his use of force for the bringing men to embrace these, he could be guided by infallible certainty; yet I fear this would not serve your turn, nor authorize the magistrate to use force to bring men in England, or any where else, into the communion of the national church. (Locke 1963a: 145. See also Locke 1963a: 214–215, 387, 425; Locke 1993a: 402; Tate 2016a: 242–245)

Locke, Proast, and Religious Diversity

Thus we see the profound divide between Locke and Proast, arising from their differing opinion as to whether knowledge of "true religion" is possible, and also whether, on this basis, those in possession of state authority are entitled to use force to impose this "truth" on those subject to their jurisidiction. This difference also led them to draw fundamentally different conclusions, concerning toleration, in response to the religious diversity endemic within the England of their time.

Locke, we saw, not only believed that such diversity "cannot be avoided," but that it should be tolerated by those state authorities within whose jurisdiction it fell. Proast, by contrast, saw things very differently. He argued that as God would not deceive those who diligently seek his "truth" (Proast 1999a: 28), then "no Man can fail of finding the way of Salvation, who seeks it as he ought" (Proast 1999a: 28). The result, he insisted, is that if all individuals displayed such diligence, then "as there is indeed but one true Religion, so there could be no other Religion but that in the world" (Proast 1999a: 28). But as there are "many Religions in the World" and "only one of them can be true," the very fact of this diversity is clear evidence that "all Men have not sought the Truth in this matter, with that application of mind, and that freedom of Judgement, which was requisite to assure their finding it" (Proast 1999a: 28). Thus, the magistrate's use of force is needed to ensure this (Proast 1999a: 29–30).

We see, therefore, that the religious diversity within seventeenth century England that Locke identifies as reason for toleration, is utilized by Proast to reach the opposite conclusion (see Tate 2016a: 180–181). And the reason for this, above all else, is that Proast believes that the "true religion" can be known, and that the state's use of force, if applied effectively, can reduce this diversity by ensuring a convergence upon this "truth." Once again, we see the profound divide that arises between Locke and Proast based on their differing opinions as to whether knowledge of "true religion" is possible.

The "Skepticism" and "Rationality" Arguments

Like the "rationality argument," the "skepticism argument" depends, for its cogency, on state authorities using "outward force" to impose religion for the sake of salvationalist ends. This is because it is only when such ends are pursued that the concepts at the center of the "rationality argument" (sincere religious belief) and at the center of the "skepticism argument" ("true religion") have the import and relevance to state authorities capable of convincing them to alter their activity on the basis of these respective concerns. Consequently, it is only in such circumstances that those engaging in the use of such force will be likely to be amenable to the propositions advanced by either argument.

On the other hand, if state authorities apply force to matters of religion for purely secular ends (such as civil peace or state security), sincere belief and religious "truth" are rendered irrelevant as considerations. The result is that both the "skepticism" and "rationality" arguments, in such circumstances, lose their cogency as "considerations" for toleration. The "consent argument," however, retains its cogency in these circumstances, because irrespective of whether the state is imposing force, in matters of religion, for secular or salvationist ends, Locke still requires that it have a "commission" to do so, arising from the "consent" of the governed, and the absence of such "commission" means that the exercise of such force does not fall within the scope of the state's legitimate authority.

Interpretive Issues

We saw above that some Locke scholars have not perceived the role that skepticism plays in Locke's "considerations" for toleration. However, other interpretive issues have also arisen in the Locke literature as a result of an incomplete understanding of

Locke's position on toleration. These concern (a) the purposes that purportedly underwrite Locke's engagement on the topic of toleration (i.e., the reasons for which he advocated toleration as the preferred policy of governments); and (b) Locke's attitude to the state authorities engaged in the forcible imposition of religious uniformity (and the persecution associated with this) and his attitude to those subject to such punitive processes. We will consider each of these issues in turn.

We saw above that Mark Goldie was mistaken in his assumption that Locke and Proast were in fact in agreement that "reliable knowledge" of "true religion" was possible, when in fact it was on this matter that they were most deeply divided throughout their debate. It is precisely because Professor Goldie does not perceive Locke's "skepticism" on this matter, and its importance in his case for toleration, that he can collapse the distance between Locke and Proast in this way, insisting that "[r]eliable knowledge of the 'true religion' was taken" by each of them as the "starting point" of their debate (Goldie 1999a: 24. See also Goldie 1991: 364).

However, Professor Goldie also collapses the distance between Locke and Proast in another way. This concerns the respective purposes that underwrite their positions on the topic of toleration. Once more, his capacity to do so arises from his failure to perceive how Locke's skepticism is one key factor imposing a division between them. Proast's purposes, we have seen above, are clearly directed to finding both the means and the justification whereby all those subject to the jurisdiction of the English state can be brought within the auspices of the Anglican religion, on the grounds that the Anglican religion is the "true religion," that it can be *known* to be the "true religion," and that it can therefore be confirmed as indispensable to individual salvation. Proast conveys such certainties to Locke as follows:

> But as to my *supposing* that the *National Religion now in* England, *back'd by the Publick Authority of the Law*, is the *onely true Religion*; if you own...that there is but *one* true Religion, I cannot see how you your self can avoid *supposing* the same. For you own your self of the Church of *England*; and consequently you own the *National Religion now* in England, to be *the true Religion*; for that is her Religion. And therefore if you believe there is but *one* true Religion; there is no help for it, but you must suppose, with me, that the *National Religion now in* England, *back'd with the Publick Authority of the Law, is the onely true Religion*. (Proast 1999b: 50)

But Mark Goldie attributes the same purpose to Locke, insisting that Locke also seeks to bring all believers to the "true religion," merely differing from Proast about the appropriate means to do so (Locke eschewing all means of force to achieve this end). Describing the Locke/Proast debate, Goldie makes this point as follows:

> Noting that Locke concedes that there *is* a "true religion," the ensuing debate almost wholly concerns the efficacy of compulsion on its behalf. Hence their battle was fought on a narrow front, with limited attention paid to the larger question of the inroads of skepticism upon the idea of "true religion". This has the effect (quite properly) of portraying Locke not as a defender of a secular, sceptical pluralism, but as a Low Church Anglican who differs about the best means to bring people to true religion. (Goldie 1991: 363–64)

Elsewhere, Goldie again attributes the same salvationist purpose to Locke, insisting that the "premises" of *A Letter Concerning Toleration* "are rooted in Christian evangelism," it being an "essay in *evangelical* tolerance," with the result that its "argument" is "grounded in the question: What are the legitimate means at the disposal of Christians to bring the wayward to the truth?" (Goldie 2010: xi–xii). Indeed, Goldie's identification of Locke with Christian evangelism itself depends on his earlier assumption that Locke's position is largely devoid of religious skepticism. This is because Christian evangelicism, in its assumption that there is a religious "truth" that can be known and to which individuals can be "brought," is not consistent with any application of skepticism to such "truths." Consistent with this, Goldie, in describing the content of *A Letter Concerning Toleration*, declares: "In keeping with Locke's evangelical premise in the *Letter*, there is a limited role for skepticism" (Goldie 2010: xvi).

It is true that Locke upheld a right of individuals to exhort, encourage, and admonish each other on matters of religion, but he strictly distinguished this from any attempt at coercion on the grounds that "all force and compulsion are to be forborne," and "[n]obody is obliged...to yield obedience...further than he himself is persuaded," because each individual "has the supreme and absolute authority of judging for himself" (Locke 1993a: 421–22. See also Locke 1993a: 395, 399, 405; Locke 1993b: 195). Hence Locke was willing to condone evangelical activity on the part of others, so long as it remained within such limits.

However Locke's writings on toleration are in no way underwritten by an "evangelical" strategy of their own, to "bring people to true religion," or the "wayward to the truth," such as Professor Goldie seeks to ascribe to him above. Such a strategy, involving convergence on a singular religious "truth," would only be possible for Locke if knowledge of the "true religion" (and therefore the correct path to individual salvation) was itself possible, with the result that the religion to which "people" ought to be "brought" could be authoritatively identified. But we have seen that it was precisely this possibility that Locke repeatedly denied in his writings, the absence of such knowledge providing the foundation for two of his "considerations" for toleration. Indeed, we have seen that Locke declared that "true and false...when we suppose them for ourselves, or our party," in matters of religion, "in effect, signify just nothing, or nothing to the purpose" (Locke 1963b: 90) - a proposition which is entirely at odds with the sort of "evangelical" strategy which Goldie seeks to ascribe to him above. Further, Locke, in the *Third Letter for Toleration*, directly denies that the Church of England has any exclusive claim to being the "only true religion" (Locke 1963a: 320, 326, 327, 328, 332–334, 422, 423), thereby again casting doubt on the "Low Church Anglican" position that Goldie attributes to him in one of the passages above. Finally, the fact that Locke insists, in the *Letter*, that when it comes to religion, "diversity of opinions...cannot be avoided" (Locke 1993a: 431), and this because "everyone is orthodox to himself" (Locke 1993a: 390), would seem to be at odds with the possibility of a convergence upon one "true religion," such as an "evangelical" strategy of "bringing people to true religion" or the "wayward to the truth," of the type Goldie identifies above, would seem to presume.

Professor Goldie correctly recognizes, in his account of *A Letter Concerning Toleration* above, that the sort of skepticism we have attributed to Locke is inconsistent with the "evangelical" strategy he ascribes to him, the presence of one "limiting" any "role" that might be played by the other. But it is only because Professor Goldie does not perceive the wider presence of this skepticism in Locke's arguments for toleration, and its centrality in his debate with Proast, that he can associate Locke with Proast in an "evangelical" strategy which skepticism would render an impossibility (see Tate 2016a: 159–161).

Other counterintuitive (and highly erroneous) interpretations of Locke's political philosophy arise from similar shortcomings in fully perceiving the arguments Locke advanced in his advocacy of toleration. We saw that Jeremy Waldron was of the view that the "rationality argument" constituted the "main line of argument" Locke advanced for toleration in *A Letter Concerning Toleration*. The inability to perceive, within the *Letter*, Locke's alternative arguments for toleration meant that Professor Waldron was of the view that Locke had failed in his attempt to advance his case against Proast once Proast had refuted the "rationality argument" by showing that force, used "indirectly" and "at a distance," did have some impact on inner belief (Waldron 1988: 81, 83, 84).

But what is much more remarkable is the wider perspective that Waldron adopts, concerning Locke and his purposes, on the basis of his belief that Locke advanced only the "rationality argument" as the "main line of argument" for toleration in the *Letter*. We saw above that Waldron described the "rationality argument" as concerned with "the rationality of the would-be persecutor and his purposes," it being focused on "what happens to his rationality when he selects means evidently unfitted to his ends." He therefore insisted the "rationality argument" was only indirectly concerned with questions of individual liberty. It is on the basis of this analysis of the "rationality argument" that Waldron then arrives at the extraordinary conclusion that Locke himself, in the *Letter*, identified with the "interests" of "persecutors" (those denying toleration) and not those subject to their persecution, and so did not advance, within this text, a moral case *against* intolerance or persecution at all. Describing the "rationality argument," Waldron makes these points as follows:

> At this point, what one misses above all in Locke's argument is a sense that there is anything *morally* wrong with intolerance, or a sense of any deep concern for the *victims* of persecution or the moral insult that is involved in the attempt to manipulate their faith. What gives Locke's argument its *peculiar structure and narrowness* is that it is, in the end, an argument about agency rather than an argument about consequences. It appeals to and is concerned with the interests of the persecutors and with the danger that, in undertaking intolerant action, they may exhibit a less than perfect rationality. Addressed as it is to the persecutors in *their* interests, the argument has nothing to do with the interests of the victims of persecution as such; rather those interests are addressed and protected only incidentally as a result of what is, in the last resort, prudential advice offered to those who are disposed to oppress them. (Waldron 1988: 85. Emphasis added)

That Locke, in exile in Holland, seeking to escape persecution by the English state authorities for his role in the political opposition to Charles II, and watching the shadows of intolerance extend across Europe, could, in the text he was composing in hiding at this time, have identified with the "interests" of "persecutors," is counterintuitive to say the least. It is also a profoundly mistaken conclusion to reach and completely misidentifies Locke's purposes in *A Letter Concerning Toleration* (see Tate 2016a: Chap. 4; Tate 2009: 777–778; Tate 2010a: 999–1001).

However, Waldron is only able to arrive at this extraordinary conclusion concerning Locke and his purposes as a result of the "peculiar structure and narrowness" of his own interpretation of *A Letter Concerning Toleration*. We have seen that he has a truncated conception of the arguments Locke advances in this text, perceiving in them only one primary secular argument for toleration – what we have called the "rationality argument." It is within the context and in terms of this argument that Waldron falsely ascribes to Locke, in the passage above, an identification with the "interests" of "persecutors." However Locke's other arguments for toleration within that text, based on "truth" and "consent," fully identify Locke's interests and sympathies with those subject to persecution and provide reasons why such persecution should be resisted and why it should not take place. It is in this respect that Locke expresses, within the *Letter*, the "moral wrong" associated with intolerance and articulates a "deep concern" for its victims. A more comprehensive reading of *A Letter Concerning Toleration*, therefore, makes clear why any conclusion that Locke, within that text, identified with the "interests" of "persecutors," and did not advance a "moral" case against intolerance and persecution, is deeply in error (see Tate 2016a: 108–119).

Locke's Pragmatic Argument for Toleration

We saw above that there are specific conditions in the context of which the "skepticism" and "rationality" arguments for toleration lose their cogency. In particular, this arises in circumstances in which those in possession of state authority forcibly impose on the religious beliefs and practices of those subject to their jurisdiction for the sake of purely secular ends, centered on civil peace or state security. In such cases, the "skepticism" and "rationality" arguments lose their cogency because, when the state is seeking such ends, matters of "sincere belief" ("rationality argument") or "true religion" ("skepticism argument") are irrelevant. Equally, we saw that the "truth argument" loses its cogency in such circumstances, but we also saw that it falls short as a robust argument for toleration. The one "consideration," among Locke's normative arguments for toleration, that retains its cogency in such circumstances is the "consent argument," since its premises do not rely on "sincere belief" or "true religion." Equally, Locke's pragmatic argument for toleration retains its cogency in such circumstances because it is directed to precisely these secular concerns, centered on civil peace and state security – the pragmatic argument insisting that toleration is a more effective means for the state to achieve such ends than the use of force in matters of religion.

Locke advances this pragmatic argument in *An Essay Concerning Toleration*. It can be summarised as follows. If (i) state authorities wish to secure civil peace or state security, then (ii) if the use of force by the state, in matters of religion, is likely to produce more upheaval than it will quell, due to the resistance it will provoke, then (iii) toleration of religious differences (and therefore the avoidance of such force) is the most prudent policy for state authorities to adopt, since (iv) it is precisely such toleration which will be more conducive than force, in such circumstances, to securing the material ends of civil peace and state security (Locke 1993b: 192–93, 197–98, 204–07; Locke 1993a: 427–30, 431–32. See also Tate 2016a: ch. 3). Addressing himself directly to state authorities, Locke advances this argument as follows:

> [I]f the magistrate chance to find the dissenters so numerous as to be in a condition to cope with him, I see not what he can gain by force and severity when he thereby gives them the fairer pretence to embody and arm, and make them all unite the firmer against him...People, therefore, that are so shattered into different factions are best secured by toleration, since being in as good a condition under you as they can hope for under any, 'tis not like[ly] they should join to set up any other, whom they cannot be certain will use them so well. But if you persecute them you make them all of one party and interest against you, tempt them to shake off your yoke and venture for a new government. (Locke 1993b: 200, 207. See also Locke 1993b: 197–98; Locke 1993a: 428–430)

Indeed, Locke goes further with his pragmatic argument for toleration and insists that even if state authorities are successful in eradicating visible religious differences, by the forcible imposition of outward religious conformity, with the result that this appears to quell upheaval and ensure civil peace, it is not conducive to state security, since it produces subterranean resentments that may arise at a later date:

> But, after all this, could persecution...drive all dissenters within the pale of the Church, it would not thereby secure but more threaten the government, and make the danger as much greater as it is to have a false, secret, but exasperated enemy, rather than a fair, open adversary. For punishment and fear may make men dissemble, but, not convincing anybody's reason, cannot possibly make them assent to the opinion, but will certainly make them hate the person of their persecutor, and give them the greater aversion to both. (Locke 1993b: 206. See Locke 1993b: 192–193, 204–207)

Finally, Locke argues that state authorities' attempts, via "persecution," to "drive all dissenters within the pale of the Church," far from achieving this outcome, will, if sufficiently relentless, and confronting sufficient resistance, destroy recalcitrant dissenters altogether. As Locke puts it: "[T]here is scarce an instance to be found of any opinion driven out of the world by persecution, but where the violence of it at once swept away all the professors too..." (Locke 1993b: 204). Locke identifies such an outcome as perverse, referring to "the extreme absurdity they are guilty of, who, under pretence of zeal for the salvation of souls, proceed to the taking away their lives" (Locke 1963b: 72. See also Locke 1993a: 392, 405). Locke therefore concludes: "If, therefore, violence be to settle uniformity, 'tis in vain to mince the matter: that severity which must produce it cannot stop short of the total destruction and extirpation of all dissenters at once" (Locke 1993b: 208. See also Locke 1963a: 264–265, 285, 286, 288, 380; Locke 1963b: 77, 107–109).

It is precisely the perversity of such outcomes, arising from the forcibile imposition of religion, that, along with the other assumptions outlined above, underwrites Locke's pragmatic argument for toleration and renders it a practical, and preferable, alternative to persecution. In each case, toleration is justified because it, rather than the use of force, is perceived as the more effective means, in a context of religious diversity, for the state to avoid upheaval and ensure civil peace and state security. Locke expresses a similar outlook in *A Letter Concerning Toleration* when he states: "It is not the diversity of opinions (which cannot be avoided), but the refusal of toleration to those that are of different opinions (which might have been granted), that has produced all the bustles and wars that have been in the Christian world upon account of religion" (Locke 1993a: 431). I have discussed in a separate chapter how pragmatic arguments for toleration are qualitatively different to arguments for toleration arising from normative premises (see the chapter ▶ "Toleration and Religion").

Locke and the "Moral Challenge" of Toleration

Locke's skepticism concerning knowledge of "true religion" not only provides him with "considerations" for toleration in the form of the "truth" and "skepticism" arguments. It also makes possible some other outcomes, necessary for religious toleration, quite distinct from this. I have pointed out, in another chapter in this book, how toleration constitutes, for the religiously devout, a "moral challenge" (see the chapter ▶ "Toleration and Religion"). This is because toleration demands that they not interfere with religious beliefs and practices with which they disagree, and may even perceive as heretical or blasphemous, and so a danger to the eternal salvation of others. To tolerate such beliefs and practices, thereby enabling their proselytization, is (from the perspective of the devout) a "moral challenge," because such toleration places the immortal souls of others in danger. John Rawls gave expression to this outlook as follows:

> During the wars of religion people were not in doubt about the nature of the highest good, or the basis of moral obligation in divine law. These things they thought they knew with the certainty of faith, as here their moral theology gave them complete guidance. The problem was rather: How is society even possible between those of different faiths? What can conceivably be the basis of religious toleration? For many there was none, for it meant the acquiescence in heresy about first things and the calamity of religious disunity. Even the earlier proponents of toleration saw the division of Christendom as a disaster, though a disaster that had to be accepted in view of the alternative of unending religious civil war. (Rawls 2005: xxiii-xxiv)

Skepticism allowed Locke, himself a devout Christian, to avoid this "moral challenge of toleration," thereby helping to make possible his advocacy of religious toleration for faiths he did not share. It is true that Locke identifies some religious doctrines and practices as "false and absurd" (Locke 1993a: 420). But given that he lacks an authoritative criterion of "true religion," such judgments concerning "falsity" and "absurdity" can only be matters of belief, not knowledge, on his part. Consequently, because he has no indubitable criterion of religious "truth," Locke was never caught in the moral dilemma (as were those described by Rawls in the passage above) of having to negotiate the limits of toleration in terms of how far that which demanded toleration fell short of "true religion." Instead, he could argue (as he does below) that the limits of toleration should be determined solely in terms of "civil" concerns, rather than considerations of religious "truth." Such a position was only possible because Locke could avoid (as a result of his skepticism) considerations of religious "truth" altogether, thereby escaping the "moral challenge of toleration."

Locke and the Limits of Toleration

The scope of toleration is demarcated by the boundary between that which is permitted and that which, falling outside the limits of toleration, is proscribed. Locke made clear that such limits of toleration should not be determined by any considerations of religious "truth," wherein, for instance, a belief or practice is denied toleration because it is at odds with "true religion." Instead, Locke insists that the only relevant considerations for determining the limits of toleration should be wholly secular – these being the "civil interests," centered on matters such as civil peace or state security, which, we saw above, Locke believed were the sole concern of government and the only purpose for which those subject to its jurisdiction have ceded to it authority. Locke makes this secular justification of toleration's limits, in terms of such "civil interests," very clear in both *An Essay Concerning Toleration* and *A Letter Concerning Toleration* (Locke 1993a: 415–417, 424–426; Locke 1993b: 186, 192–195). Locke explicitly repudiated religious "truth" as a criterion for determining the limits of toleration, instead insisting that these limits should be determined by "civil" interests, as follows:

> [T]he magistrate ought not to forbid the preaching or professing of any speculative opinions in any Church, because they have no manner of relation to the civil rights of the subjects. If a Roman Catholic believe that to be really the body of Christ which another man calls bread, he does no injury thereby to his neighbour. If a Jew do not believe the New Testament to be the Word of God, he does not thereby alter anything in men's civil rights. If a heathen doubt of both Testaments, he is not therefore to be punished as a pernicious citizen. The power of the magistrate, and the estates of the people, may be equally secure, whether any man believe these things or no. I readily grant that these opinions are false and absurd. *But the business of laws is not to provide for the truth of opinions, but for the safety and security of the commonwealth, and of every particular man's goods and person.* And so it ought to be. For truth certainly would do well enough, if she were once left to shift for herself. (Locke 1993a: 420. Emphasis added. See also Locke 1993b: 187–88, 189–90, 190–91)

Because he repudiates religious "truth" as a criterion for determining the limits of toleration (i.e., those matters which ought to be proscribed) Locke is willing to endorse the toleration of religious practices, such as idolatry, that, as a sincere

Christian, he would certainly have believed to be an abomination in the eyes of God. And he does so precisely because such practices have no adverse effect on "civil interests" – what he elsewhere calls the "necessity of the state and the welfare of the people" (Locke 1993b: 193) – which alone, for Locke, constitute a potential limit on toleration:

> But idolatry (say some) is a sin, and therefore not to be tolerated. If they said it were therefore to be avoided, the inference were good. But it does not follow that, because it is a sin, it ought therefore to be punished by the magistrate...The reason is, because [it is] not prejudicial to other men's rights, nor [does it] break the public peace of societies. (Locke 1993a: 417. My addition. See also Locke 1993b: 187, 189, 195–196)

Yet religious practices that do transgress these "civil interests" (what Locke calls, in the passage above, "public peace" and "other men's rights") are subject, in the *Letter*, to proscription. So, for instance, Locke declares that "animal sacrifice," as a religious practice, if it has no adverse civil effects, ought to be tolerated (Locke 1993a: 415) – even though, again, as a sincere Christian, he would have clearly perceived this to be an abomination in the eyes of God (see Locke 1993a: 413). But should animal sacrifice interfere with "civil" concerns, such as public food supplies, then Locke insists it ought to be denied toleration and subject to proscription (Locke 1993a: 415). Equally, he denies toleration to those who, on antinomian grounds, seek to elevate their own spiritual injunctions above the civil and legal obligations to which all (according to the rule of law) must abide, thereby "arrogat[ing] to themselves, and to those of their own sect, some peculiar prerogative...opposite to the civil right of the community" (Locke 1993a: 425).

Once again, therefore, we see that the limits of toleration are determined by the "civil interests" that, for Locke, fall within the legitimate purview of the magistrate's authority (such purview not encompassing matters of "religious truth"). Locke therefore insists that the sole concern of state authorities, in determining what ought to be subject to religious toleration, is not the intrinsic religious merits of the belief or practice under consideration, but only its external impact upon "civil" concerns, toleration being possible if "the commonwealth receive no prejudice, and that there be no injury done to any man, either in life or estate" (Locke 1993a: 415).

"Atheists" and "Catholics"

Consequently, when Locke sought to deny toleration to atheists, in both *A Letter Concerning Toleration* and the earlier *An Essay Concerning Toleration*, he did not do this, as John Dunn, John Gray, and Ian Harris claim, because he believed (i) such atheism was at odds with "the clear priority of an individual's duty to worship God" (Dunn 1997: 520; cf. Dunn 1991: 287–88); (ii) atheists were "unholy" because they denied the "theism," and therefore the belief in natural law, which Locke (according to Harris) made a condition of legitimate participation within the "Commonwealth" (Harris 2013: 62–63, 94–98); or (iii) religious "truth" had been "found" and Locke "was not confident that persuasion" (as distinct from proscription) would "lead" atheists toward this "truth" (Gray 2000: 2). On the contrary, Locke denied toleration to atheists on the basis of the same "civil" (as distinct from religious) concerns that he identifies above, insisting that "belief of a deity...being the foundation of all morality," atheists, lacking such "morality," are "incapable of all society" (Locke 1993b: 188) and cannot be trusted to abide by their "[p]romises, covenants and oaths," these being (Locke tells us) the "bonds of human society" (Locke 1993a: 426). For further discussion of Locke and atheism, see Tate (2010b: 960–61), Tate (2010c: 145–47), Tate (2012: 225) Tate (2013a: 154–55), and Tate (2016a: 93–94).

Locke denied toleration to Catholics in *An Essay Concerning Toleration* for equally "civil" (as distinct from religious) reasons – insisting, among other things, that Catholics were a risk to the security of the state because they "owe a blind obedience to any infallible pope who hath the keys of their consciences tied to his girdle" and who "can upon occasion dispense with all their oaths, promises, and the obligations they have to their prince, especially being (in their sense) a heretic, and arm them to the disturbance of the government" (Locke 1993b: 202–203. See also Locke 1993b: 197). He also denied toleration to Catholics because they, he alleged, when they possess authority, deny toleration to others, it being "unreasonable that any should have a free liberty of their religion who do not acknowledge it as a principle of theirs that nobody ought to persecute or molest another because he dissents from him in religion," with the result that the magistrate, "by tolerating any who enjoy the benefit of this indulgence which at the same time they condemn as unlawful...only cherishes those who profess themselves obliged to disturb his government as soon as they shall be able" (Locke 1993b; 202).

In each case, it is on the basis of his perception of the "civil" consequences of the Catholic religion, rather than the religious doctrines of that religion itself, that Locke denies toleration to Catholics. Indeed, in the *Essay*, Locke explicitly pointed out that he was *not* advocating, in the case of Catholics, the "persecution of conscientious men for their religion," nor were Catholics being "punished" merely for their "consciences" (Locke 1993b: 203), but instead for the "other doctrines" (described above) that they "mix" with their "religious worship" and "speculative opinions" and which (in their potential consequences) are "absolutely destructive to the society wherein they live" (Locke 1993b: 197). It is on the basis of this distinction that Locke, in the *Essay* and *Letter*, can at times engage in the apparently contradictory process of coupling the purely religious elements of Catholic worship (such as his reference to "bread" and the "body of Christ" in the penultimate quote above) with other beliefs and practices which, he insists, are not harmful to society or state and which, he thereby concludes, are deserving of toleration (see Locke 1993a: 420, 430; Locke 1993b: 189) – Jeremy Waldron thereby mistakenly concluding, on the basis of such statements in the *Letter*, that Locke, by that time, was willing to tolerate Catholics (Waldron 2002: 218–223). What Locke was tolerating was not Catholics as such but those aspects of Catholic worship that did not have adverse "civil" consequences. Indeed, in *An Essay Concerning Toleration*, where Waldron would concede Locke clearly did deny toleration to Catholics, Locke again, at one point, couples Catholic worship with other practices which, he says, "if they be done sincerely and out of conscience," are deserving of toleration (Locke 1993b: 189). For further discussion of Locke and Catholicism, see Tate (2010b: 960–61), Tate (2010c: 147), Tate (2012: 225), Tate (2013b: 824), and Tate (2016a: 85–86, 93).

Locke, in the *Letter*, denies toleration to "Mahometans" on similar grounds to Catholics in the *Essay*, insisting that although such individuals might fall within the jurisdiction of a Christian magistrate, yet they "yield blind obedience to the Mufti of Constantinople, who himself is entirely obedient to the Ottoman emperor," with the result that, in "deliver[ing] themselves up to the protection and service of another prince," the magistrate, by according them toleration, "give[s] way to the settling of a foreign jurisdiction in his own country" (Locke 1993a: 426). Again, it is the "civil" consequences of Mahometan doctrines, rather than anything intrinsic to those doctrines themselves, which are the object of proscription.

In each case, concerning idolaters, atheists, Catholics, "Mahometans," and practitioners of animal sacrifice, we see that the limits of toleration, demarcating that which is permitted from that which is proscribed, are determined solely by the "civil" concerns which fall within the purview of legitimate state authority. Religious concerns, in particular the "truth" of these religious doctrines, fall outside that purview, and are, for Locke, irrelevant to the determination of these limits – the "business of laws" being not to "provide for the truth of opinions" but the "safety and security of the commonwealth, and of every particular man's goods and person" (Locke 1993a: 420).

Dividing Locke from God

It is true, as John Dunn tells us, that Locke, in the *Two Treatises*, declares "that men belong to their divine Creator and that their rights and duties in this earthly life derive from his ownership of them and from the purposes for which he fashioned them. The law of nature articulates these purposes as rationally intelligible authoritative commands" (Dunn 1991: 294). Locke makes clear in the *Two Treatises* that it is our equal status as God's "creatures" that defines our freedom and equality in relation to each other (Locke 1965: II, § 4, 6, 22, 54, 87), and it is natural law (itself a reflection of the will of God) which determines our natural rights and therefore the entitlements (and duties) that we possess in relation to each other (Locke, 1965: II, § 6, 8, 22, 87, 128, 135, 142, 195; Locke 2004c: 117–120, 124, 125; Tate 2013a: 150–151; Tate 2013b: 826; Tate 2016a: 4–5).

But it is with the transition from a "state of nature" to "civil society" that we perceive Locke explicitly seeking to distance, by the time of his *Two Treatises of Government*, his political philosophy from theological or religious considerations. It is true that Locke premised natural law, and the natural rights that he believed arose from it, on the will of God (see Locke, 1965: II, § 6, 8, 135, 142, 195; Locke 2004c: 117–120, 124, 125; Tate 2013a: 150–51; Tate 2013b: 826; Tate 2016a: 4–5). He also perceived natural law as continuing to have a normative status within civil society, beyond a pre-civil and pre-political state of nature (Locke 1965: II § 12, 134, 135, 142, 171, 195). But Locke also made clear that one of the reasons individuals engaged in mutual agreements, within the state of nature, to inaugurate civil society and establish governments, was because natural law was not an effective means of governance in the state of nature. The reason, Locke said, was because it was "unwritten, and so no where to be found but in the minds of Men," meaning it lacked an "establish'd Judge," capable of determining its import and application in any specific circumstance, thereby rendering each individual "Judge, Interpreter, and Executioner" of natural law, "and that in his own Case," with the result that it "serves not, as it ought, to determine the Rights, and fence the Properties of those that live under it..." (Locke, 1965: II § 136. See Locke, 1965: II § 13, 21, 87–90, 123–31, 134–36, 171, 222; Locke, 2004c: 86, 92, 94, 96, 110, 111–113, 120–121).

Further, when it came to the actual inauguration of civil societies, in the mutual agreement ("compact") of individuals, and the governments which arose from such agreement, Locke went to great lengths in his debate with Jonas Proast to insist that such "[c]ommonwealths, or civil societies and governments" are (in the words of St. Peter) "the contrivance and institution of man," not God (Locke 1963b: 121. See also Locke 1963a: 223–224; Tate 2016a: 206–211). In this, we can see the extent to which Locke had moved from his earlier *Two Tracts on Government* and *An Essay Concerning Toleration* where (independent of those times that he explicitly reserved judgment on the question) the authority of government was said to derive from God, not "man" (Locke 1967b: 223, 226, 227, 228; Locke 1993b: 192, 193, 195, 201. Cf. Locke 1967a: 122–123; 150, 174–175; Locke 1967b: 230–232; Locke 1993b: 186–187). Indeed it was on this question – whether "commonwealths, civil societies and governments" were instituted by God or "man" – that Locke and Proast were in deep disagreement (Proast 1999a: 32, 34; Proast 1999b: 98–99; Locke 1963a: 223–224; Tate 2016a: 206–211), and we can see the extent to which Locke desired to separate his political philosophy from theological considerations in his attempt to refute Proast's proposition that God, not "man," was at the foundation of these institutions (see Locke 1963a: 223–224, Tate 2016a: 209–211). Ultimately, Locke reluctantly conceded (in response to Proast's critique) that *both* God (as the author of natural law) and "man" reside at these foundations, insofar as it is natural law that initially authorizes individuals to "compact" with each other to form civil society and government. As Locke put it: "men in the corrupt state of nature might be authorized and required by reason, the law of nature, to avoid the inconveniences of that state" and inaugurate civil societies and governments "under such agreements as they should think fit," with the result that "though it be true, those powers that are, are ordained of God; yet it may nevertheless be true, that the power any one has, and the ends for which he has it, may be by the contrivance and appointment of men" (Locke 1963a: 224. See Tate 2016a: 206–211).

Locke's reluctance to concede that "commonwealths, or civil societies and governments" arose from anything other than the "contrivance and institution of man" was a dispute that Locke was always destined to lose given that he himself concedes, in the *Two Treatises of Government*, the role of natural law (and therefore the will of God) in the foundation and normative direction of civil society and government (see Locke 1965: II § 12, 134, 135, 142, 195) – although it is unclear how natural law provides this normative direction, in any indubitable sense, given Locke's account (provided above) of the contestation surrounding its application in many specific circumstances (see Tate 2017). Nevertheless Locke's acknowledgement of the role of natural law, in this respect, means we must always distinguish between matters of natural theology (in this case, natural law) which Locke, in his engagement with Proast, was unable to separate from civil society and government, and matters of religion (centered on ideas of revealed "truth" and salvation) which Locke did seek to separate from civil society and government, confining such matters to individual conscience and voluntary church attendance. However that Locke was willing to engage in this dispute with Proast, seeking to remove "God" entirely from what he insisted was the "contrivance and institution of man," shows the extent to which, in all relevant respects, Locke was eager to distance his political philosophy from religious (or even theological) concerns.

One reason Locke was so concerned to remove religious concerns from such considerations, and instead replace them with "civil" interests, was so the justification and exercise of political authority was capable of being endorsed by all individuals, irrespective of their religious convictions (in terms of which, Locke knew, they were deeply divided). Individuals were capable of such endorsement because, their religious differences notwithstanding, Locke assumed they all shared common "civil" interests, these being the interests which (as explained above) they (or their predecessors) first left the state of nature and inaugurated civil society and government to ensure, and it was on the basis of these that Locke believed political agreement was possible.

Consequently, those Locke scholars such as John Dunn, Ian Harris, Jeremy Waldron, or Timothy Stanton who seek to advance a "theological" interpretation of Locke's political philosophy, thoroughly immersing both its intent and its content in Locke's theological convictions, miss what is essential within this philosophy and also what is distinctive about it (see Tate 2012; Tate 2013a; Tate 2016a, 98–99 (note 69), 262 (note 1); Tate 2017).

John Dunn declared that "[Locke's] thinking in its entirety was shaped and dominated by a picture of the earthly setting of human life as a created order, an order designed and controlled by an omnipotent, omniscient and also, mercifully, benevolent deity: the God of the Christians" (Dunn 1990: 11. See also Dunn 1991: 294–95). It was on this basis that Professor Dunn declared that "I simply cannot conceive of constructing an analysis of any issue in contemporary political theory around the affirmation or negation of anything which Locke says about political matters," and this because of the "intimate dependence of an extremely high proportion of Locke's arguments for their very intelligibility, let alone plausibility, on a series of theological commitments" (Dunn 1969: x–xi. See Tate 2013a: 135–37).

Ian Harris and Timothy Stanton believe that Locke perceives the legitimacy and purpose of government as residing, ultimately, in "God's intentions" or "God's purposes" for humankind, not least the duty of each individual to worship God (Harris 2013: 60–62, 63, 72, 77, 89, 92, 94, 96–98, 104; Stanton 2006: 90; Stanton 2011: 19–22; Stanton 2012: 232). This means that, despite their intention to separate, within Locke's political thought, the realm of "respublica"" from the realm of "ecclesia" (Harris 2013: 59–63, 72–79, 88; Stanton 2011: 18–22; Stanton 2013: 53–54), Harris and Stanton can never conceive of "respublica" (and the authority of government that arises from it) as existing for entirely secular purposes, centered on "civil" interests, because they believe Locke ultimately subordinates all political authority to the divine purposes, referred to above, centered on God's "intentions" or "purposes" for humankind (see Harris 2013: 60, 62, 63, 72–79, 81–82, 92–94; Stanton 2006: 90–92, 94, 95; Stanton 2011: 20–21; Stanton 2012: 230; Tate 2012, 2016a: 98–99, 2017). Despite this, Harris and Stanton still seek to square their circle, insisting that Locke's conception of political authority is characterised by *both* the "secular" *and* the "divine" – which results, at times, in elliptical processes of locution in which political authority is presented as being *both* "divine" *and* "secular" all at the same time. An example might be Stanton's declaration that, for Locke, "the state's purposes could be conceived in terms of *divine* requirements with a purely *secular* bearing" (Stanton 2006: 90. Emphasis added). At other times their explanations of Locke's conception of political authority draw strongly on the "divine," as in Harris' account of Locke's proscription of atheists above.

Jeremy Waldron, in his most recent writings on Locke, follows Dunn, Harris, and Stanton in seeking to deeply immerse Locke's political philosophy in his theology (see Waldron 2002; Waldron 2005). Indeed, Professor Waldron himself acknowledges this lineage when he states:

> I have learned more from John Dunn's study of Locke than from anyone else's; indeed it was Professor Dunn who set me off on this project with his startling claim that "Jesus Christ (and Saint Paul) may not appear in person in the text of [Locke's] *Two Treatises* but their presence can hardly be missed when we come upon the normative creaturely equality of all men in virtue of their shared species-membership." (Waldron 2005: 498. My addition. See also Waldron 2002: 12)

Yet while Waldron acknowledges the influence of Dunn, the means by which Waldron grounds Locke's political philosophy in his theology is quite distinct from that of Dunn, Harris, or Stanton. Waldron relies on a reading of Locke's political philosophy which draws heavily on Locke's *An Essay Concerning Human Understanding*, and it is on the basis of this interpretation that he insists that the "theological content" within Locke's political philosophy "cannot simply be bracketed off as a curiosity" but rather both the theology and the political philosophy (on key normative issues like Locke's concept of "equality") are "intricately related" (Waldron 2002: 81, 82).

Professor Waldron's attempt to interpret Locke's political philosophy through the prism of *An Essay Concerning Human Understanding* is a highly innovative and interesting approach to Locke's *oeuvre*. But as I have sought to point out in detail elsewhere, the conclusions Professor Waldron reaches concerning the coextensive relationship between Locke's political philosophy and his theology cannot, in my opinion, be sustained. The first reason for this is due to problems of textual interpretation and analysis that Waldron encounters arising from his attempt to couple Locke's argument in *An Essay Concerning Human Understanding* with political texts like the *Two Treatises of Government* (see Tate 2013a: 137–50). The second reason is that Waldron's attempt to immerse Locke's political philosophy in his theology misses what we have seen above is Locke's concerted attempts to push matters in the opposite direction, distancing his political philosophy from these theological concerns (see Tate 2013a: 149–56).

"Things Indifferent"

John Locke was certainly a sincere Christian (see Locke 1993a: 421). However, we have seen that he went to great lengths to separate many of the propositions he advanced within his political philosophy (and the practices of toleration that arise from them) from the "truth" of Christian theology or even theological "truths" in general (see Tate 2010b: 958–64; Tate 2010c: 141–47; Tate 2012; Tate 2013a; Tate 2013b: 823–27; Tate 2016a: 4–5, 206–11, 251–55; Tate 2017). Indeed, in line with Locke's proposition, within his political philosophy, that political authority is inaugurated for entirely "civil" purposes and is limited to those purposes, he perceived all matters of religion and theology as falling within the authority of government only insofar as they impact on these "civil" purposes, and to the extent that they do not, he believed they ought to be left to the discretion of individuals. To this end, Locke insisted that every action of government needs to treat all that with which it comes into contact as "things indifferent" – devoid of any religious or theological significance and of concern to government solely insofar as government believes it impacts on "civil" purposes – with the result that government should not enact laws "but because the necessity of the state and the welfare of the people called for them" (Locke 1993b: 192, 193; Locke 1967b: 221, 222–23. See also Locke 1993b: 188, 191, 195; Locke 1993a: 393, 394, 411, 417, 420, 422, 423, 423–24). Indeed, we can see this "indifference" requirement applying in Locke's animal sacrifice example within the *Letter*. He insists that if government does prohibit such sacrifice for the sake of public food supplies, then it is the "slaughter" of animals (a secular practice and therefore a "thing indifferent"), not their religious "sacrifice," that is prohibited, with the result that "the law is not made about a religious but a political matter" (see Locke 1993a: 415).

On these same grounds, Locke insists (in the italicized section of the passage below) that religious "truth" is not a relevant factor that ought to inform the actions of government, it being unrelated to the "civil" purposes which constitute the "care of the commonwealth":

> [T]he magistrate cannot take away these worldly things from this man, or party, and give them to that; nor change property amongst fellow-subjects (no, not even by a law) for a cause that has no relation to the end of civil government - I mean, for their religion, which, *whether it be true or false*, does no prejudice to the worldly concerns of their fellow-subjects, which are the things that only belong unto the care of the commonwealth. (Locke 1993a: 423–424. Emphasis added)

In this way, we see that although Locke was forced to concede to Proast that (in line with the position Locke himself advances in the *Two Treatises*) matters of natural law were inextricably entwined with the foundations of civil society and government, nevertheless Locke sought to ensure that matters of religious belief, including their "truth" and "falsity," were fundamentally separated from and rendered irrelevant to the justification and exercise of political authority, thereby consigning these non-secular matters (in all cases where, in the opinion of state authorities, they did not impact on the "civil" concerns of government) to the "conscience" (and therefore liberty) of individuals (Locke 1993a: 393, 394, 396, 403, 405–406, 410, 411, 412, 421–423; Locke 1963b: 89, 114, 135).

Indeed even in the case of natural law, magistrates must presumably abide by the injunction that their authority is confined to "civil" matters. Although Locke in the *Two Treatises* identified natural law as a continuing norm within civil society, any attempt on the part of the magistrate to appeal directly to this norm, perhaps as a justification for the exercise of political authority (as in Ian Harris' account of the proscription of atheists above), would fall short of Locke's requirement that the magistrate only exercise authority for "civil" purposes. Why? Because in invoking the imprimatur of natural law, the magistrate would be appealing overtly to the "divine" (the "will of God") rather than the "civil" (the "necessity of the state and the welfare of the people") as the reason (and therefore the legitimation) for the public exercise of political authority. Locke makes clear in the *Essay* that it is considerations of the "civil" rather than the "divine" which must, in all such respects, direct, and justify, the magistrate's exercise of political authority, stating: "This I only note....to show how much the good of the commonwealth is the standard of all human laws when it seems to limit and alter the obligation even of some of the laws of God, and change the nature of vice and virtue" (Locke 1993b: 196). Once more, therefore, we see how Locke's requirement that magistrates confine their authority solely to "civil" purposes distances Locke's political philosophy from religious (or in this case, "theological") commitments, even if Locke, in his account of natural law and its relationship to political authority, sometimes implies the contrary (see Locke 1965: II § 12, 134, 135, 142, 195).

It was government toleration of individual conscience, and its visible outcomes in terms of religious expression and practice, which made possible the coexistence of government authority and individual religious liberty within Locke's political philosophy. Of course, such coexistence does not always arise, with individuals and state authorities inevitably, at times, disagreeing as to whether a religious matter does or does not impact significantly on "civil" concerns and therefore does or does not fall within the realm of state authority at the expense of individual conscience. In those instances where such conflict becomes intractable, Locke, in the *Essay*, accords individuals a right of "civil disobedience" (allowing them to disobey the magistrate but obliging them to accept the magistrate's penalty for their disobedience) (Locke 1993b: 193–94; Locke 1993a: 423). However by the time of the *Letter*, Locke implicitly condones (in line with the explicit terms of the *Two Treatises of Government*) a full-blown right of resistance to government in instances where individuals believe their liberties (religious or otherwise) are irretrievably threatened (Locke 1993a: 424, 432).

Conclusion

It is precisely because government, within Locke's political philosophy, is required to treat all matters falling within its jurisdiction as "things indifferent," and therefore of concern solely in terms of the "civil" matters which are government's sole responsibility, that Locke believed it could entirely ignore matters of religious "truth," thereby tolerating not only "Presbyterians," "Independents," "Anabaptists," "Arminians," and "Quakers" but also "pagans" and "Jews" (Locke also confusingly includes "Mahometans" in this list, his earlier proscription of them notwithstanding – perhaps these being the "Mahometans" who do *not* "yield blind obedience to the Mufti of Constantinople") (Locke 1993a: 431). Equally, just as the *scope* of toleration extends to include such faiths, so, we have seen, its *limits* exclude atheists, "Mahometans" and Catholics – again for the same "civil" reasons.

We have seen that one reason Locke sought to rigorously confine his political philosophy to such "civil" parameters was because he knew that any religious justification of political authority would be incapable of eliciting broad-based consent – individuals being fundamentally divided on matters of religion – and further, because he knew such religious justification would impinge on the liberty of individuals by making religious agreement a condition of political legitimacy. By removing religion entirely from the concerns of government (unless, in the view of government, it gave rise to "civil" consequences), Locke could preserve individual liberty, by removing religion from the public sphere of state authority and confining it to the realm of individual conscience and voluntary church attendance. Equally, via the "civil" justification of political authority, he could legitimate processes of government, in a context of religious diversity, because all individuals could conceivably endorse these processes, based on the "civil" interests they all shared, their religious differences notwithstanding.

Locke's four "considerations" for toleration, like his political philosophy as a whole, must therefore be understood within this wider context – this being Locke's understanding of the deep (and potentially volatile) religious differences of his time and his desire to exclude these from the justifications of his political philosophy. But these elements of Locke's political philosophy must also be understood in terms of Locke's normative commitment to individual liberty which, although present as early as the *Two Tracts*, widened to include, among other things, Locke's endorsement of individual choice concerning outward religious expression. For Locke, therefore, the ineradicable presence of religious diversity was as much an expression of individual liberty to be affirmed, as a political problem (involving the threat of conflict and disorder) that his political philosophy was designed to contain.

Locke's prime political purpose, throughout his political writings, was therefore to reconcile the government authority he understood as necessary for civil peace and state security with the individual liberty that he conceived as fundamental to human dignity, and to do so without producing the twin "scourges" of "tyranny" or "anarchy," the one arising from an excess of governance relative to liberty and the other arising from a deficiency of the same (Locke 1967a: 119). Over the course of decades, we saw, Locke shifted concerning the extent to which he believed an expansion of individual liberty (and therefore an extension of toleration) was consistent with the maintenance of the government authority necessary for civil peace and state security. Indeed, we saw that by the time of the publication of the *Two Treatises of Government*, Locke (in the wake of his association with the revolutionary activity of the Earl of Shaftesbury) was willing to concede a right of resistance to government authority, exercised by individuals hitherto subject to this authority, when such individuals perceived government as fundamentally threatening the individual liberties which government was inaugurated to protect, thereby overturning this balance between liberty and authority altogether.

But toleration is a practice, when engaged in by government, that occurs within the confines of an established rule of law, and therefore exists short of this exercise of resistance, and the "state of war" to which it gives rise. Toleration assumes both an entitlement of individuals to exercise their liberty but also (ceteris paribus) an obligation on the part of individuals to submit to the limits government places on this liberty for the sake of civil peace and state security. Of course, the demarcation, in specific instances, between such permission and proscription will often be a matter of ongoing contestation between individuals and government. But (short of Locke's "state of war") some *modus vivendi* between the two is necessary if individual liberty is to coexist with civil peace and state security. In this respect, toleration, when practiced by governments, is a means by which Locke sought to achieve that mutual accommodation between individual liberty and government authority which was one of the primary objects of his political philosophy throughout his intellectual career.

Summary and Future Directions

John Locke is one of the seminal seventeenth-century sources of the eighteenth-century Enlightenment and the liberal tradition. He is also associated, in the minds of many scholars, with the American Founding, the Bill of Rights, and other foundational sources of American government. Finally, he made a significant contribution to debates on religious toleration which first emerged in the Reformation era. For all these reasons, Locke's political philosophy will continue to remain of interest to scholars around the world for generations to come.

References

Abrams P (1967) John Locke as a Conservative. In: Locke J, Abrams P (eds) Two tracts on government. Cambridge University Press, Cambridge, pp 3–29
Ashcraft R (1986) Revolutionary politics and Locke's two treatises of government. Princeton University Press, Princeton
Ashcraft R (1987) Locke's two treatises of government. Allen and Unwin, London
Cranston M (1952) The politics of John Locke. Hist Today 2(9):619–622
Cranston M (1957) John Locke. A Biography. Longmans, Green and Co., London
Cranston M (1987) John Locke and the case for toleration. In: Mendus S, Edwards D (eds) On toleration. Clarendon Press, Oxford, pp 101–121

Dunn J (1969) The political thought of John Locke. Cambridge University Press, Cambridge

Dunn J (1990) What is living and what is dead in the political theory of John Locke? In: Dunn J (ed) Interpreting political responsibility: Essays 1981-1989. Polity Press, Cambridge, pp 9–25

Dunn J (1991) The concept of 'trust' in the politics of John Locke. In: Rorty R, Schneewind JB, Skinner Q (eds) Philosophy in history. Essays on the historiography of philosophy. Cambridge University Press, Cambridge, pp. 279–301

Dunn J (1997) The claim to freedom of conscience: freedom of speech, freedom of thought, freedom of worship? In: Dunn J, Harris I (eds) Locke, vol II. Edward Elgar, Cheltenham, pp 510–532

Fraser A (1980) King Charles II. Macdonald Futura Publishers, London

Goldie M (1991) The theory of religious intolerance in restoration England. In: Grell OP, Israel JI, Tyacke N (eds) From persecution to toleration: the glorious revolution and religion in England. Clarendon Press, Oxford, pp 331–368

Goldie M (1999a) Introduction to Jonas proast, 'the argument of the letter concerning toleration briefly consider'd and answer'd'. In: Goldie M (ed) The reception of locke's politics. Vol. 5. The Church, dissent and religious toleration 1689-1773, Pickering and Chatto, London, p. 24

Goldie M (1999b) Introduction to Jonas Proast, 'A Third letter concerning toleration: in defense of the argument of the letter concerning toleration, briefly consider'd and answer'd'. In: Goldie M (ed) The Reception of Locke's Politics. Vol. 5. The Church, dissent and religious toleration 1689-1773, Pickering and Chatto, London, p. 40

Goldie M (2002) John Locke, Jonas Proast and Religious Toleration 1688-1692. In: Walsh J, Haydon C, Taylor S (eds) The Church of England c.1689-c.1833; From Toleration to Tractarianism. Cambridge University Press, Cambridge, pp 143–171

Goldie M (2010) Introduction. In: Locke J (ed) A letter concerning toleration and other writings. Liberty Fund, Indianapolis, pp ix–xxiii

Gray J (2000) Two faces of liberalism. Polity Press, Cambridge

Harris I (2013) John Locke and natural law: free worship and toleration. In: Parkin J, Stanton T (eds) Natural law and toleration in the early enlightenment. Oxford University Press, Oxford, pp 60–105

Klibansky R (1968) Preface. In: Locke J (ed) Epistola de Tolerantia. A Letter on Toleration (trans: Gough JW). Clarendon Press, Oxford, pp vii–xliv

Laslett P (1965) Introduction. In: Locke J, Laslett P (eds) Two treatises of government. New American Library, New York, pp 15–148

Locke J (1957) Letter from John Locke to Philip van Limborch, February 5, 1689, MSS. Ba. 256h. In: Cranston M (ed) John Locke. A Biography. Longmans, Green and Co., London, p 307

Locke J (1963a) A third letter for toleration. In: John Locke, the works of John Locke, vol VI. Scientia Verlag, Aalen, pp 141–546

Locke J (1963b) A second letter concerning toleration. In: J Locke, the works of John Locke, vol VI. Scientia Verlag, Aalen, pp 61–137

Locke J (1963c) A fourth letter for toleration. In: J Locke, the works of John Locke, vol VI. Scientia Verlag, Aalen, pp 549–574

Locke J (1965) In: Laslett P (ed) Two treatises of government. New American Library, New York

Locke J (1967a) First tract on government: translation. In: Locke J, Abrams P (eds) Two tracts on government. Cambridge University Press, Cambridge, pp 117–181

Locke J (1967b) Second tract on government: translation. In: Locke J, Abrams P (eds) Two tracts on government. Cambridge University Press, Cambridge, pp 210–241

Locke J (1968) Letter from John Locke to Philip van Limborch, 22 April/2 May 1690, MS Locke c. 24, f. 155. In: Raymond Klibansky, Preface. In: J Locke, Epistola de Tolerantia. A Letter on Toleration (trans: Gough JW) Clarendon Press, Oxford, pp xxiii–xxiv

Locke (1975) An essay concerning human understanding. Ed. Peter H. Nidditch. Clarendon Press, Oxford.

Locke J (1993a) A letter concerning toleration. In: Locke J, Wootton D (eds) Political writings. Penguin, London, pp 390–436

Locke J (1993b) An essay concerning toleration. In: Locke J, Wootton D (eds) Political writings. Penguin, London, pp 186–210

Locke J (2004a) Toleration B. In: Locke J, Goldie M (eds) Political essays. Cambridge University Press, Cambridge, pp 246–248

Locke (2004b) Religion. In: Locke J, Goldie M (ed) Politicalessays. Cambridge University Press, Cambridge, pp. 278–80

Locke J (2004c) Essays on the law of nature. In: Locke J, Goldie M (eds) Political essays. Cambridge University Press, Cambridge, pp 79–133

Locke J (2004d) Toleration D. In: Locke J, Goldie M (eds) Political essays. Cambridge University Press, Cambridge, pp. 276–77

Marshall J (1996) John Locke. Resistance, religion and responsibility. Cambridge University Press, Cambridge

Milton JR, Milton P (2010) General introduction. In: Locke J, Milton JR, Milton P (eds) An Essay concerning toleration and other writings on law and politics 1667-1683. Clarendon Press, Oxford, pp 1–161

Nicholson P (1991) John Locke's later letters on toleration. In: Horton J, Mendus S (eds) John Locke. A Letter concerning toleration in focus. Routledge, London, pp 163–187

Proast J (1999a) The Argument of the letter concerning toleration, briefly consider'd and answer'd. In: Goldie M (ed) The reception of locke's politics. Vol. 5. The Church, dissent and religious toleration 1689-1773. Pickering and Chatto, London, pp 25–37

Proast J (1999b) A Third letter concerning toleration: in defense of the argument of the letter concerning toleration, briefly consider'd and answer'd. In: Goldie M (ed) The Reception of locke's politics. Vol. 5. The Church, dissent and religious toleration 1689-1773. Pickering and Chatto, London, pp 41–116

Proast J (1999c) A Second letter to the author of the three letters for toleration, from the Author of the argument of the letter concerning toleration, briefly consider'd and answer'd, and of the defense of it. In: Goldie M (ed) The Reception of locke's politics. Vol. 5. The Church, dissent and religious toleration 1689-1773. Pickering and Chatto, London, pp 119–128

Rawls J (2005) Political liberalism, exp edn. Columbia University Press, New York

Stanton T (2006) Locke and the politics and theology of toleration. Political Stud 54(1):84–102

Stanton T (2011) Authority and freedom in the interpretation of Locke's political theory. Political Theory 39(1):6–30

Stanton T (2012) On (Mis)interpreting Locke: a reply to Tate. Political Theory 40(2):229–236

Stanton T (2013) Natural law, nonconformity and toleration: two stages on Locke's way. In: Parkin J, Stanton T (eds) Natural law and toleration in the early enlightenment. Oxford University Press, Oxford, pp 35–57

Tate JW (2009) Locke and toleration: defending Locke's Liberal credentials. Philos Soc Criticism 35(7):761–791

Tate JW (2010a) Locke, rationality and persecution. Pol Stud 58(5):988–1008

Tate JW (2010b) A sententious divide: erasing the two faces of liberalism. Philos Soc Criticism 36(8):953–980

Tate JW (2010c) Toleration, neutrality and historical illiteracy. J Eur Stud 40(2):129–157

Tate JW (2012) Locke, god and civil society: a response to Stanton. Political Theory 40(2):222–228

Tate JW (2013a) Dividing Locke from god: the limits of theology in Locke's political philosophy. Philos Soc Criticism 39(2):133–164

Tate JW (2013b) 'We cannot give one millimetre'? Liberalism, enlightenment and diversity. Pol Stud 61(4):816–833

Tate JW (2016a) Liberty, toleration and equality: John Locke, Jonas Proast and the letters concerning toleration. Routledge, New York

Tate JW (2016b) Toleration, skepticism and blasphemy: John Locke, Jonas Proast and Charlie Hebdo. Am J Polit Sci 60(3):664–675

Tate JW (2017) Locke, toleration and natural law: a reassessment. Eur J Polit Theo 16(1):109–121

Tate JW (2021) John Locke and the 'problem' of toleration. In: Drerup J, Schweiger G (eds) Toleration and the challenges to liberalism. Routledge, New York, pp 13–35

Trevelyan GM (1956) The English revolution 1688-1689. Oxford University Press, Oxford
Tully J (1983) Introduction. In: Locke J, Tully J (eds) A letter concerning toleration. Hackett Publishing Co., Indianapolis, pp 23–58
Vernon R (1997) The career of toleration. John Locke, Jonas Proast and After. McGill-Queens University Press, Montreal
Waldron J (1988) Locke: toleration and the rationality of persecution. In: Mendus S (ed) Justifying toleration: conceptual and historical perspectives. Cambridge University Press, Cambridge, pp 61–86
Waldron J (2002) God, Locke and equality: Christian foundations in Locke's political thought. Cambridge University Press, Cambridge
Waldron J (2005) Response to critics. Rev Polit 67(3):495–513
Wolfson A (2010) Persecution or toleration: an explication of the Locke-Proast quarrel, 1689-1704. Lexington Books, Lanham
Wootton D (1993) Introduction. In: Locke J, Wootton D (eds) Political writings. Penguin, London, pp 7–122

"Stop Being So Judgmental!": A Spinozist Model of Personal Tolerance

52

Justin Steinberg

Contents

Introduction	1078
Tolerance as a Personal Virtue	1079
Spinoza on Intolerance	1080
Being Judgmental	1080
Intolerance and Disagreement	1082
Spinoza on Becoming Less Judgmental	1083
Suspension: The Official Account	1083
Suspension as Ambivalence or Persistent Vacillation	1084
Restricting the Scope of One's Judgments	1085
Spinoza on Tolerating Disagreement	1086
Non-contemptuous Engagement and Suspending Reactive Attitudes	1087
Sincere Engagement	1089
Toleration, Trust, and the State	1090
Conclusion	1091
References	1092

Abstract

This chapter considers the challenges to, and the resources for, cultivating a personal capacity for tolerance, according to the writings of Benedict Spinoza (1632–1677). After articulating two main components of personal tolerance, I examine the features of Spinoza's theory of cognition that make the cultivation of tolerance so difficult. This is followed by an analysis of Spinoza's account of overcoming intolerant tendencies. Ultimately, I argue that the capacity of individuals to be tolerant depends crucially on the establishment of conditions of trust, conditions that are conspicuously lacking in many modern democracies.

J. Steinberg (✉)
Brooklyn College and CUNY Graduate Center, New York, NY, USA
e-mail: jsteinberg@brooklyn.cuny.edu

© The Author(s), under exclusive licence to Springer Nature Switzerland AG 2022
M. Sardoč (ed.), *The Palgrave Handbook of Toleration*,
https://doi.org/10.1007/978-3-030-42121-2_50

Keywords

Disagreement · Judgment · Skepticism · Toleration · Trust

Introduction

In contemporary American culture, being judgmental is commonly regarded as a social vice. On the one hand, this seems to make good sense: the trait of being judgmental resembles other social vices like close-mindedness and arrogance. Still, there is something odd about the label, since, taken literally, being judgmental does not seem bad *per se*. We want to be fair, accurate, discriminating judges, not to refrain from judging altogether. And even if we accept that "being judgmental" is simply the vice of being *unduly* or *inappropriately* critical, one might still worry that admonitions against being judgmental are inapt since judgments do not fall under our direct voluntary control (see discussion in Elgin 2010). In response to this, one might maintain that while it is not under one's immediate voluntary control to refrain from being unduly critical, it is under one's distal control such that one can over time develop a habit or state of character of avoiding unduly critical judgment. This leaves one to answer how.

One philosopher who recognized the challenge, as well as the benefits, of becoming less judgmental was Benedict Spinoza (1632–1677). He denied the existence of a free will and advanced a fully deterministic account of judgment formation as an alternative to Descartes's voluntaristic model. While his account seems less equipped to explain how one can suspend one's judgment (2p49s), he declares that the power to suspend judgment is a "rare virtue" (TP 7/27). (References to English translations are to Benedict de Spinoza, *The Collected Works of Spinoza*. Vol. 1–2, translated and edited by Edwin Curley (1985, 2015). I adopt the following abbreviations for the *Ethics*: Numerals refer to parts; "p" denotes proposition; "c" denotes corollary; "d" denotes demonstration; "D" denotes definition; "DA" denotes Definition of the Affects; "s" denotes scholium (e.g. 3p59s refers to *Ethics*, part 3, proposition 59, scholium). References to the Tractatus Theologico-Politicus open with an abbreviated reference to the work – TTP – followed by the chapter and section in the Curley translation For instance, TTP 3.28; G III, 50 refers to Chap. 3, section 28. References to the Tractatus Politicus open with an abbreviated reference to the work – TP – followed by the chapter and section. For instance, TP 4/1 refers to chapter 4, section 1. All references to the Latin are to *Spinoza Opera*, edited by Carl Gebhardt.) This is of a piece with his general promotion of toleration. While much attention has been paid to Spinoza's defense of political toleration (e.g., Laursen 1996; Rosenthal 2001, 2003; Steinberg 2010), one can also find in Spinoza the basis of an intriguing, if overlooked, defense of tolerance as a personal virtue.

The structure of this chapter is as follows. I open with an explication of two main components of personal tolerance. This is followed by an examination of the features of Spinoza's theory of cognition that make the cultivation of tolerance so difficult. From there, I consider Spinoza's account of overcoming intolerant tendencies. Ultimately, the capacity of individuals to be tolerant depends crucially on the establishment of social conditions or civic relations. Regrettably, the conditions that foster tolerance are conspicuously lacking in many modern democracies today.

Before commencing, a quick note about method. While this chapter is largely about Spinoza, it is not a work of scholarship. I do not enter into interpretative disputes, but rather present Spinoza's views as directly as possible so as to show how they illuminate the challenges for, and prospects of, personal tolerance. I refer to the resulting model as "Spinozist" to flag that it is something of a reconstruction.

Tolerance as a Personal Virtue

There are at least two components to being personally tolerant: (1) responding to perceived disagreement in a non-dismissive way. We may refer to this as *being tolerant of disagreement* (see section "Spinoza on Tolerating Disagreement" for a further explication); (2) not proliferating disputes or treating every variation of opinion as a disagreement. For convenience, we may refer to this component as *not being judgmental*. To see why being tolerant requires both of these components, let us take them up in turn.

Typically, personal tolerance is theorized as a way of responding to disagreement. Where there is no disagreement, either because interlocutors agree or because variance of opinion is recognized as a matter of mere preference, the question of toleration seems not to arise. Two people may enjoy different genres of music, admire different character traits, and adopt different modes of life, but if both regard these as matters of taste or arational preferences, the issue of toleration is not an issue. For example, if I, as a beer lover, ask you whether you would prefer beer or wine with dinner, and you express your preference for wine, I can hardly be said to be exhibiting tolerance when I pour you a glass of wine. Tolerating another's preference implies that one regards it with disapproval (see e.g., Mendus 1988). (To be sure, one can be *in*tolerant of another's views when these are matters of mere taste or arbitrary allegiance. One team's fans may despise another team and their fans, even while acknowledging that the conditions that led her to be a fan of that particular team were the result of accidents of birthplace or upbringing.) Toleration is, at least in part, an attitude that one adopts in relation to beliefs or activities of which one disapproves.

But being tolerant requires more than just adopting a certain attitude in relation to those beliefs and activities of which one disapproves. To see this, imagine someone who thinks that it is morally repugnant to eat eggplant on Wednesdays, but who is willing to tolerate – however this is spelled out – those who violate this principle. There is good reason to question whether this person is really tolerant. Being tolerant seems to require that one subjects one's own judgments of disapproval to scrutiny, so as not to form judgments with undue haste and misplaced intensity and so as not to proliferate disputes or regard every variance of opinion as a form of contestation. Somewhat more demandingly, we might say that one who is tolerant does not judge others' beliefs or activities disapprovingly without warrant. She is not dogmatic or arrogant. Put more positively, it is the mark of the tolerant person that she tends to recognize when her prereflective evaluations are ungrounded or rooted in contingent features of her personal history. In light of this, we may say that toleration includes the tendency to be self-critical in forming evaluative judgments and modest about the scope of these judgments. I will call this aspect of personal toleration *being non-judgmental*, as I think that it captures much of the value that lies behind the admonition against being judgmental.

What follows is an examination of Spinoza's resources for cultivating the trait of tolerance. As we will see in the next section, the challenge for Spinoza is considerable, since his views about judgment-formation – which are at least somewhat plausible in their own right – imply that we are judgmental by nature, and judgmental in ways that conduce to intolerance of disagreement. Moreover, some have thought that being committed to a certain set of values entails disapproving of competing value systems, even when one, at some level, recognizes the legitimacy of these other views. This is expressed forcefully by Joseph Raz, who writes:

> Skills and character traits cherished by my way of life are a handicap for those pursuing one or another of its alternatives. I value long contemplation and patient examination: these are the qualities I require in my chosen course. Their life, by contrast, requires impetuosity, swift responses, and decisive action, and they despise the slow contemplative types as indecisive. They almost have to. To succeed in their chosen way, they have to be committed to it and to believe that the virtues it requires should be cultivated at the expense of those which are incompatible with them. They therefore cannot regard those others as virtues for them... Conflict is endemic. Of course, pluralists can step back from their personal commitments and appreciate in the abstract the value of other ways of life. But this acknowledgment coexists with, and cannot replace, the feelings of rejection and dismissiveness. Tension is an inevitable concomitant of value pluralism. And it is a tension without stability, without a definite resting-point of reconciliation of the two perspectives. (1995, 180)

On Raz's analysis, though one can adopt a disengaged and tolerant perspective, one cannot fully reconcile this perspective with one's engaged perspective (for a rich discussion of possible responses, see Wong 2006, Ch. 9). We may refer to this as Raz's challenge. While Spinoza admits that evaluative commitment tends to promote dismissiveness toward competing perspectives and that the more fundamental the evaluation is to one's belief-system, the less open one will be to tolerating it. But he would deny that toleration is merely a function of the shallowness of the dispute; being tolerant is a disposition that can be developed. Before we develop the Spinozistic account of personal tolerance, we must explore the psychological *problem* of tolerance.

Spinoza on Intolerance

Being Judgmental

On Spinoza's account of cognition, we are doubly judgmental by nature. The first sense in which we are judgmental is that our ideas are intrinsically belief-like. Spinoza's view of belief-formation is advanced as an alternative to the Cartesian view, according to which beliefs or judgment arise through the concurrence of two distinct faculties: the intellect and the will. On the Cartesian account, the intellect supplies the content, and the will assents to, rejects, or suspends judgment about this content. Spinoza denies that we have a free faculty of will that enables us to adopt a stance in relation to an idea. Rather, he thinks that ideas have an intrinsic force, such that the volitional attitude is baked into the idea, as it were: "In the mind there is no volition, or affirmation and negation, except that which the ideas involves insofar as it is an idea" (2p49). Affirmation in particular has a kind of pride of place: to have an idea is, in the first instance, to affirm its content, from which it follows that: "if the mind perceived nothing else except [a] winged horse, it would regard it as present to itself, and would not have any cause of doubting its existence" (2p49s). This renders us credulous by nature, tending to accept straightaway what we read and hear and to retain traces of past beliefs even after they have been debunked. Put somewhat differently, we are judgmental by nature, forming beliefs first and asking questions later. In recent decades, this so-called belief-default or "Spinozan" view has been defended by psychologists and philosophers of cognition (see Gilbert 1991; Gilbert et al. 1993; Mandelbaum 2014; Egan 2008).

There is a second, and perhaps more germane, sense in which we are judgmental by nature on Spinoza's account, which concerns *evaluative* judgments. To see why we are judgmental in this sense, we must examine Spinoza's account of the character of evaluative judgments. He grounds evaluative judgments in desire, claiming that "each one, from his own affect, judges, or evaluates, what is good and what is bad, what is better and what is worse, and finally, what is best and what is worst" (3p39s) and that "because each one judges from his own affect what is good and what is bad, what is better and what worse (see P39S) it follows that men can vary as much in judgment as in affect" (3p51s). Evaluative judgments covary with affects, and affects are in some sense prior to judgments.

The nature of the priority relationship is clarified in *Ethics* 4, where Spinoza asserts that: "The cognition of good and evil is *nothing but* an affect of joy or sadness, insofar as we are conscious of it" (4p8). In claiming that the cognition – or representation – of good and evil is "nothing but" an affect, insofar as we are conscious of it, Spinoza is signaling an explanatory reduction of evaluative judgments to the consciousness of an affect, which Spinoza claims is "not really distinguished from the affect itself" (4p8d). The crucial point here is that, according to Spinoza, evaluative judgments are constituted by affects themselves.

Affects are at once representations of changes in one's "power of acting" (3 GDA) and of some object or putative cause (2a3; 3p56). And while it is possible to represent objects non-affectively (2a3; 3 Post 1), given the manifold ways in which past experiences and associations inform our affective responses to things, our ideas of things will almost always include an affective component.

Joining together the preceding threads, we may say that we typically perceive the world affectively and consequently evaluatively. Since we naturally and automatically respond to what we perceive in affective ways, and since these affects themselves constitute judgments, we are naturally and automatically evaluatively engaged with the world (see Shapiro 2012). Even when we would prefer not to be moved by our affects – as for instance when they arise out of implicit associations and stereotypes – and even when we consciously disavow them, affects reveal our valuations, our judgments. Consequently, we are by nature judgmental in ways, and to degrees, that exceed our direct control.

In light of this, one might wonder whether the exhortation not to be judgmental can be voluntarily observed, since we simply cannot suspend our evaluative judgments or restrain our emotions through fiat. As we will see in section "Spinoza on Becoming Less Judgmental," Spinoza is keen to show that we can exercise distal and partial control over our wayward emotional responses, so that can become less judgmental in the pejorative sense.

Intolerance and Disagreement

According to Spinoza, in addition to being judgmental by nature, we are also prone to be intolerant of those with whom we disagree. To see this, we need to fill out a bit more of Spinoza's social psychology, one foundational principle of which is the so-called imitation of affects: "If we imagine a thing like us, toward which we have had no affect, to be affected with some affect, we are thereby affected with a like affect" (3p27). From the principle it follows that we tend to emulate the desires of others (3 DA xxxiii), emulation being the conative side of imitation. And since affects (including desires) constitute evaluate judgments, it follows that, other things being equal, we love what others love, desire what others desire, and regard as good what others regard as good.

One might think that imitation and emululation would tend to convergence of judgments. The desire for esteem plays an enormous role in one's motivational economy, encouraging one to regulate one's behavior to comport with social norms. However, Spinoza also claims that "from the same property of human nature from which it follows that men are compassionate [i.e., from the imitation of affects], it also follows that the same men are envious and ambitious" (3p32s). Envy arises when the imitation of affects contributes to a sense of deprivation, as when imitating another's joy at some accomplishment, say admission into a prestigious program, intensifies one's own sense of failure (e.g., being denied admission into the same program). More important for this account is Spinoza's analysis of ambition, which he construes as the striving that "everyone should love what he loves, and hate what he hates" (3p31c). Ambition, or the striving for others to defer to one's judgment, arises from imitation of affects for the following reason. When we disagree with others, *ceteris paribus*, we undergo a "vacillation of mind" (3p17, 3p31d), leaving us torn between contrary affects, and, in turn, judgments. Spinoza regards such dissonance as unstable (5a1). And while dissonance could be reduced by modifying one's own antecedent attitude and deferring to others, we are generally disinclined to defer because we are ideologically protective, or averse to modifying our own judgments (see Steinberg 2018a). The more deeply entrenched one's affect or evaluative attitude is, the more resistant one will be to adapt, since modifying such judgments will require extensive revision to one's belief system.

The upshot is that we are naturally ambitious, seeking to have others defer to us rather than vice versa. Since one's interlocutors are equally prone to ambition, all disputing parties are likely to resist revising their beliefs, leading to protracted disputation and deep internal dissonance, tending ultimately toward contemptuous dismissal. Contempt or hatred overcomes the dissonance problem since it overrides the imitative process that begets dissonance in the first place (3p27d; 3p23). Hating those with whom one disagrees – or delegitimating their perspective – enables one to retain one's viewpoint without internal conflict. There is thus a strong tendency to be intolerant of disagreement, especially with respect to matters of significance. While this account, as sketched, remains overly simplistic, the basic psychodynamics are not particularly implausible.

Tying this together with the conclusion of the previous section, we see that we are judgmental by nature and prone to hatred when disagreements persist. The dreary conclusion is that we are naturally prone toward intolerance. Still, we are not condemned to this condition. To see this, we will turn now to his account of how we come to be less judgmental.

Spinoza on Becoming Less Judgmental

Suspension: The Official Account

Since, on Spinoza's account, being judgmental makes us prone to agonistic disagreements, we can appreciate why he would declare that the capacity to suspend judgment is a "rare virtue" (TP 7/27). Still, one might wonder how suspension of judgment is possible on his account, since all ideas are belief-like in structure. Spinoza's account of suspension of judgment is advanced in the very passages in which he articulates his account of belief-formation: "when we say that someone suspends judgment, we are saying nothing but that he sees that he does not perceive the thing adequately. Suspension of judgment, therefore, is really a perception, not [an act of] free will" (2p49s). Here I think that Spinoza is being a bit imprecise, since the second-order perception of the inadequacy of the first-order perception is not really *itself* the suspension – a claim that would conflict with his view that ideas are belief-like. Rather, his point seems to be that the second-order idea offsets the force of the first-order idea, resulting in suspension (see Steinberg 2018b). This is suggested in the continuation of the "winged horse" passage noted above in which he claims that while we initially affirm the existence of a thing that we perceive, we doubt its existence when we form a further idea that holds the initial idea in check. While belief is the default cognitive stance, doubt arises when one has some further idea that functions as a kind of counterweight to the initial idea. And the paradigm case is that of forming a higher-order, or reflective, idea that challenges the credentials of the initial idea. The main features of this model of doubt as suspension between two opposing ideas have deep historical roots, resembling the Pyrrhonian account of skeptical suspension as equipollence, or balanced tension between appearances.

In light of this official suspension-through-reflection model, we can better appreciate the importance of Spinoza's sustained critique of ordinary unreflective moral judgments, which arise on the basis of confused, anthropocentric thinking. As he puts it, in the first instance, people judge things to be "good or evil, sound or rotten and corrupt, as they are affected by it" (1 App). Evaluative predicates, "indicate nothing positive in things, considered in themselves" (4 Preface; cf. 1app). And while Spinoza attempts to offer a well-grounded, nonarbitrary version of evaluative concepts, he clearly thinks that we ought not to give credence to our passions, which are unreliable guides to happiness and virtue.

Spinoza wishes to cultivate in his reader a healthy mistrust of our prereflective intuitions or automatic affective responses to things. If we can imprint on our mind the principle or maxim that passions are unreliable guides to the good, we may be able to neutralize their force before they are deeply embedded within our belief-system (see Huebner 2009). But, as Spinoza concedes, the ability to suspend judgment in this way is a *rare* virtue, since it is not easy to adopt a habit of checking one's intuitions or affects. It requires that one develop self-critical habits of thought, which is cognitively demanding and which is at odds with our natural ideological protectiveness.

Suspension as Ambivalence or Persistent Vacillation

Elsewhere in Spinoza's writings we find the basis for a somewhat different conception of suspension, one that perhaps better captures the interpersonal dimensions of "not being judgmental." The crucial concept here is one that we have already introduced: vacillation. When Spinoza introduces the notion of doubt, he presents it as a vacillation between opposing ideas (2p44s). This conception of doubt applies, *mutatis mutandis*, to evaluative attitudes, as when one oscillates between opposing affects (3p17s). On this account, suspension of judgment is just a state of non-commitment resulting from two counterbalanced ideas, where counterbalancing is understood diachronically, with the mind lurching back and forth, but never so decisively to express a proper judgment (see Steinberg 2018b). This is a somewhat different version of equipollence.

This account captures a form of suspension that can arise as a result of peer disagreement. The question of how to respond to peer disagreement has been the basis of a lively debate in epistemology. Some hold that the proper response to acknowledged peer disagreement is to accord the peer's position equal weight, resulting in an erosion in one's confidence, perhaps to the point of suspending one's judgment in the absence of further evidence (Christensen 2009; Elga 2007; Elgin 2010; Vavova 2014). This is often referred to as the conciliatory view. Others think that one should, at least to considerable degree, retain in one's judgment. This is often referred to as the steadfast view (see Kelly 2005). Rather than attempting to adjudicate this dispute here, I will simply situate Spinoza's position in relationship to it.

Spinoza's analysis of disagreement is fundamentally psychological rather than normative. As indicated above, he is interested in our tendency to imitate and internalize the evaluative judgments of our interlocutors. Here we should qualify his account in a couple of respects. First, a qualification about scope. Spinoza claims that we imitate those whom we imagine to be *like oneself*. This vague construal allows for different ranges of empathy. One important respect in which another may be like oneself – which Spinoza admittedly does not take up explicitly – is in terms of epistemic capacities and level of expertise. If part of how we modulate representations of likeness is in terms of epistemic capacities, we can make sense of why disagreement often yields disruptive forms of ambivalence. When an evaluative disputant is perceived as an equal, one is prone undergo destabilizing vacillation. In this sense, Spinoza is a kind of descriptive conciliationist, articulating a form of what David Wong has called "moral ambivalence," defined as "the phenomenon of coming to understand and appreciate the other side's viewpoint to the extent that our sense of the unique rightness of our own judgments gets destabilized" (Wong 2006, 102). Indeed, on an idealized version of this account, we might say that vacillation, or doubt, is a necessary consequence of regarding a disputant's view as just as authoritative as one's own, so that remaining steadfast in one's judgment in the face of disagreement is evidence that one does not fully acknowledge the other as one's peer.

Because we are ideologically protective, we tend to seek to reduce the discomfort of dissonance by impugning the perspective of the other. As Catherine Elgin puts it, in order for disputants to retain their judgments, they "must construe each other as irrational" (2010, 66). But while we tend to be ideologically protective, we are not destined to be. By coming to appreciate the incapacitating effects of ideological protection, we may be able to resist the impulse to discredit. To make this effective, one must imprint upon one's mind this further idea that the impulse to discredit incapacitates, so that this is ready at hand when discrediting ideas arise, rendering us ambivalent rather than intolerant (for a version of this method, see 5p10s). It is not easy to resist the impulse to dismiss, especially when successful resistance yields only an unsatisfying ambivalence. But perhaps this is the most important upshot of this analysis: if we are to curtail our tendency toward being judgmental and dismissive toward others, we must also be prepared to endure affronts to our pride and disruptions to our confidence and cognitive consonance.

Restricting the Scope of One's Judgments

The aforementioned ways of becoming less judgmental involve eroding the power of one's reflexive and ill-begotten judgments. One might wonder, though, if there are ways to avoid being unduly judgmental without sacrificing one's evaluative commitments. Can one remain affectively engaged (i.e., committed to one's own valuations) *and* personally tolerant, or does toleration require the suspension of judgment? This brings us back to Raz's challenge.

One rather straightforward way in which one can judge without being judgmental in the pejorative sense is by restricting the scope of one's judgment. For Spinoza, even well-founded deployments of evaluative predicates like "good" and "evil" are always indexed to a striving agent. And while he thinks that the most important goods – namely, on his highly intellectualist conception of morality, forms of knowledge – are common to all human beings (4p36; 4p26), he allows for variation among individuals with respect to other goods (e.g., material and social goods) which are often the source of dispute. The utility of various objects, courses of acting, ways of relating to others, and modes of living in general vary according to one's temperament or disposition such that "one and the same thing can, at the same time, be good, and bad, and also indifferent. For example, music is good for one who is melancholy, bad for one who is mourning, and neither good nor bad to one who is deaf" (*Ethics* 4 Preface). Since we are often not sufficiently well acquainted with others' temperaments to make very informed determinations about particular goods for them, we have reason in these instances to restrict the scope of our evaluative judgments.

This comports with a strand of Spinoza's analysis of religious toleration. On his account, faith should be understood in functional terms, as that set of beliefs that encourage obedience to God through loving one's neighbor (TTP 14.13–23). By defining faith functionally, Spinoza allows that the beliefs that constitute one person's faith may differ from the beliefs that constitute another's. And while he advances seven "doctrines of the universal faith," or basic religious precepts on which everyone can agree (TTP 14.24ff), even here he allows that these doctrines are so general as to admit a wide range of understanding, and that each person ought to "interpret them for himself, as it seems to him easier for him to accept them without hesistation, with complete agreement of the heart, so that he may obey God wholeheartedly" (TTP 14.32). Because human temperaments vary, the beliefs that are conducive to piety may differ between individuals, and it is the individual herself that is best positioned to make these determinations.

These arguments dovetail nicely with the suspension-through-reflection account, according to which we should rigorously scrutinize our evaluative judgments so as not to put credence in arbitrary and unreliable passions. Here the point is that even when we are confident about what is good for us, we should acknowledge the variability among human temperaments and not be overly confident that what is good for us is good for others. By acknowledging that not every variance of opinion is the grounds of a disagreement we avoid proliferating disputes and so resist the tendency toward being judgmental.

Spinoza on Tolerating Disagreement

In the preceding section, we considered three ways in which Spinoza thinks that we can resist the tendency to be judgmental: by reflecting on the inadequacy of many of our automatic evaluative responses, by embracing the ambivalence that arises through peer disagreement, and by restricting the scope of our judgments. In this section, we will examine how, on Spinoza's account, toleration is possible when one is evaluatively committed *and* there is persistent disagreement.

Non-contemptuous Engagement and Suspending Reactive Attitudes

While Spinoza regards many of our ordinary evaluative judgments as inadequate and unreliable, some of our evaluative judgments will remain credible even after careful scrutiny. Though we cannot trust the issuances of our passions, rational moral judgments are self-certifying, lying beyond all doubt (2p43s). And a great many of our particular ethical judgments fall in between the extremes of wholly unreliable passions and absolutely certain rational judgments, as somewhat credible, but disputable positions (see Kisner 2011; Steinberg 2014). How does Spinoza think that one should relate to others when one's ethical judgments persist in the face of scrutiny and disagreement?

To answer this, I propose that we consider some underappreciated remarks from Spinoza's discussion of impermissible speech in TTP 20, where he examines not only the content of the speech, but also the motives that prompt and animate it. Here, as elsewhere, he singles out speech motivated by "deception [*dolo*], anger [*ira*], [and] hatred [*odio*]" (TTP 20.14) for exemption from the scope of permissible expression on the grounds that these affects are distinctly anathema to civic agreement (see TTP 16.9; TTP 16.12–13; TTP 20.12). Since the way that deception undermines agreement is somewhat distinct from how hatred and anger do, we will treat them separately, beginning with hateful, angry – that is, contemptuous – speech.

According to Spinoza, hate is a uniquely destructive affect (4p45). It is itself a form of suffering or sadness (3 DA vii), and its expression breeds more hate and more suffering, keeping individuals locked in a negative feedback cycle (3p40; 3p43). While some of us might think that contemptuous disagreement can play a constructive role in firming up the convictions of the righteous and galvanizing social change, Spinoza evidently does not. Engaging others contemptuously does nothing to dislodge the offending views; it only inflames them.

At the social level, widespread hateful disagreement fractures society and undermines the very bedrock of the state, security, as "[t]here is no one who lives among hostilities, hatreds, anger and deceptions, who does not live anxiously" (TTP 16.13). Spinoza particularly has in mind the rancorous diatribes of preachers and clerics who target freethinkers. Since, on Spinoza's account, faith and piety are expressed through loving one's neighbor, it is in fact hateful religious zealots who are the true heretics: "faith condemns as heretics and schismatics only those who teach opinions which encourage obstinacy, hatred, quarrels and anger" (TTP 14.39).

We see from this that Spinoza's notion of personal toleration is rather more demanding than the conception of "mere civility" that Teresa Bejan has recently explored in connection with the work of Roger Williams. Williams was a firebrand protestant who went on to settle and found Providence Plantations and Rhode Island after being banished from the Massachusetts Bay Colony for his strident advocacy of puritanical ideals. Having experienced persecution himself, Williams advocated broad freedom of religious expression, including expressions of antipathy for other religions as a tool of evangelizing. The notion of mere civility, on Bejan's analysis, was that of being able to live together and converse even with those with whom one rather vehemently disagrees. Williams's minimal sense of civility as willingness to continue to engage with others does not require respectful or polite disagreement. Indeed, as Bejan puts it, it allows for "peremptory contradiction, dogmatic and unwanted counsels, expressions of disgust, or sharp rebukes" (2017, 65).

Spinoza certainly allowed for a degree of contentious dispute. In his critique of despotic rule in which dissent is thoroughly quelled, he writes that if one calls such a condition "peace," then "nothing is more wretched for me than peace. No doubt there are more, and more bitter, quarrels between parents and children than between masters and slaves" (TP 6/4). But whereas Williams regarded denunciations and insults as compatible with his conception of civility, Spinoza believed that hostile, hate-fueled disputes are destructive to civil life, which is why he includes "venting one's anger" among seditious forms of speech (TTP 20.21).

To overcome the contemptuous affects that deep disagreement engenders one must seek to make others intelligible. When others express themselves in ways that strike one as utterly indefensible, one must try to comprehend them, rather than critique, condemn, or deride them. This is a theme that runs throughout Spinoza's writing. Necessitarian metaphysics encourages us "to hate no one, to disesteem no one, to mock no one, to be angry at no one, to envy no one" (2p49s), recognizing instead that human passions "follow with the same necessity and force of Nature as the other singular things" (3 Preface). Unfortunately, even philosophers typically treat human affects "as vices, which men fall into by their own fault. That's why they usually laugh at them, weep over them, censure them, or (if they want to seem particularly holy) curse them" (TP 1/1). On Spinoza's view, those who ridicule or condemn others are themselves in the grips of passions that are rooted in confused beliefs about free will and moral responsibility.

In contrast to those who ridicule or scorn, Spinoza advocates simply trying to understand people as they are, dispassionately (TP 1/1). In P.F. Strawson's terms, Spinoza advocates adopting something like a dispassionate, objective attitude in the face of strong disagreement, rather than yielding to participant reactive attitudes like blame and indignation, which are themselves confused, irrational affects (4p51s; 4p45). While P.F. Strawson famously doubts that one could consistently adopt a dispassionate perspective on the basis of some general metaphysical principle like necessitarianism (1993b, 55), Spinoza would counter that while it is certainly not easy to take up this objective attitude, it can be achieved over time through a meditative, cognitive therapy (cf. G Strawson 1993a, 99–100). And he sought to practice what he preached, declaring in response to the needless bloodshed of the Second Anglo-Dutch war that: "these turmoils move me, neither to laughter nor even to tears, but to philosophizing and to observing human nature better. For I do not think it right for me to mock nature, much less to lament it, when I reflect that men, like all other things, are only a part of nature" (Ep. 30 to Oldenburg). Through meditating on the necessity of things and striving to make one's interlocutors intelligible, one can shed the feelings of contempt and dismissiveness without sacrificing one's evaluative commitments.

Sincere Engagement

On Spinoza's account, working to suspend reactive attitudes vis-à-vis those whom we regard as confused or misguided need not imply interpersonal disengagement. Ultimately, what we seek is intelligibility. When the opinions of others are not at all rationally intelligible to us, we are forced to take up a kind of third-person scientific approach to understanding them. In other instances of disagreement, though, the views of others will be to some degree rationally intelligible to us, or at least there will be reason to believe that they could be made so through deliberative engagement. The more intelligible another's view is, the less contempt – and the more dissonance – one will feel. Still, disagreement breeds discontent, which is why, according to Bejan, Hobbes calls for silence or nonengagement in the case of fundamental disputes (see Bejan 2017).

Spinoza rejects this approach, advocating instead for sincere engagement with others, partially on the grounds that it is extremely difficult to consistently suppress one's views (3p2s; TTP 20.8), but more importantly because suppressing one's true opinions undermines the trust or good faith [*fides*] on which civic harmony depends. He writes that if the state sought to restrict expression, "the necessary consequence would be that every day men would think one thing and say something else. The result? The good faith especially necessary in a Republic would be corrupted. Abominable flattery and treachery would be encouraged, as would deceptions and the corruption of all liberal studies" (TTP 20.27; Cf. TTP 20.45). While Spinoza is here discussing state censorship, the same considerations apply to self-censorship: suppressing one's views out of fear or aversion to conflict impedes intellectual progress and erodes the conditions of trust on which the health of the republic depends.

To engage others sincerely is to avoid tactical or temperamental peacekeeping. One who is deeply conflict averse might not denounce a view that she finds enraging, but it would be misleading to claim that her silence constitutes tolerance. And one who, in the midst of a political disagreement over dinner proposes that disputants drop the subject, might well be acting tactfully, but in calling for silence (say, in the form of "agreeing to disagree") she is not displaying tolerance. To be sure, there are cases where it makes good prudential sense to avoid disputes; but avoidance tendencies are not a mark of tolerance. On the contrary, toleration requires the willingness to express one's own sincere views and to listen charitably to the reasons behind opposing view.

Spinoza's defense of the freedom to philosophize is ultimately a defense of a certain kind of deliberative practice, that of engaging others in good faith and without contempt. In a well-governed state, people can "openly hold different and contrary opinions, and still live in harmony" (TTP 20.37). Deception and disengagement undermine genuine harmony; sincere, non-contemptuous disagreement need not. Provided then that one has checked one's hate and anger, the appropriate response to disagreement – the *tolerant* response – is to engage the other sincerely, in good faith.

Toleration, Trust, and the State

Still, in order to engage in sincere, non-contemptuous disagreement, a certain baseline of trust must be established. Put somewhat differently, expressions of disagreement not only contribute to trust, they require it. If I doubt the sincerity of your motives, suspecting that you are not at all amenable to persuasion, I will tend to withhold my views and to withdraw from the exchange, preempting any sort of productive dispute. And to the extent that one continues to debate in conditions of distrust, one is likely to react defensively and dismissively. Consequently, so long as general conditions of distrust or suspicion obtain, even well-intended actors are not likely to satisfy the conditions of Spinozist tolerance, since their motivation to engage with the other sincerely and non-contemptuously will be disabled. Tolerance requires trust. But how is trust between disputants established?

A certain degree of trust may be secured between disputants when the discussion is bound by salient, narrowly specified, common aims. (Note: much depends on the level of specificity with which we understand commonality. Two educators may share a concern with the development of their students, but if they have vastly different understandings of how development is to be understood and measured, they may well struggle to remain sincerely, non-contemptuously engaged.) Where the dispute is framed from within common project, disputants have at least some reason to assume that the exchange is founded in good faith. David Wong expresses something like this point in his response to Raz's challenge, maintaining that disagreement need not engender feelings of dismissiveness, provided that they are expressed against a background of commonality or cooperation. Consequently, he emphasizes the value of civic rituals that bind society even while allowing for disagreement, seeing contemporary democratic practices like voting and citizen juries as according with Mencius's aim of reconciling harmony and fragmentation (Wong 2006, 266–272).

We have seen that Spinoza himself seems to think that disagreement is compatible with harmony (though, to be sure, pure agreement is preferable (see Lord 2017; James 1996; contrast with Del Lucchese 2009)). Like Wong, he seems to think that this typically requires the establishment of a social bond that enables one to countenance disagreement non-dismissively. We see this informing Spinoza's analysis of cooperation and agreement and his defense of republicanism more broadly. The state aims to promote cooperation, or a sense of partaking in a common project, which underwrites civic trust (Steinberg 2019; Steinberg 2018a). And widespread trust will not be achieved unless the state actively roots out sources of discord and hate and establishes participatory institutions and conditions of relative equality (Steinberg 2018a, Chs. 6–7).

Ultimately, since toleration of disagreement is expressed through sincere, non-contemptuous engagement, which requires trust, and since trust itself depends on the establishment of cooperative civil conditions, we are led to the conclusion that personal toleration is inexorably a political problem. To be sure, even in the absence of pervasive conditions of trust, one might be able to tolerate disputes with a small circle of friends (see Spinoza's exchange with his friend Hugo Boxel, Ep. 53–54).

But to be tolerant toward a few does not make one tolerant, any more than being generous toward a few makes one generous. The conclusion that the state plays a crucial role in establishing the conditions that enable individuals to be tolerant is of a piece with Spinoza's more general observation that virtues and vices are fundamentally dependent on the institutions and laws of a state (TP 5/2–5/3).

Conclusion

We have now seen that, on Spinoza's view, while people tend to be judgmental and to be intolerant toward those with whom we disagree, these tendencies can be checked in a variety of ways that involve acquiring habits of thinking and reacting that are at odds with our inclinations to give credence to our automatic evaluative responses, to resist revision, and to dismiss or disengage from those with whom we disagree. Instead, if we are to be tolerant, we must critically scrutinize our judgments, welcome destabilizing challenges, work toward making opposing views intelligible, and seek to engage others sincerely. It should be apparent from all of this that it is quite difficult to become tolerant. And, I have argued, it is not something that lies entirely under one's control, since it depends on the establishment widespread social trust, which seems to be in short supply today.

Let me conclude with a reflection on how the preceding bears on a recent stir among intellectuals, especially on the American left. On July 7, 2020, over a hundred and fifty prominent writers, academics, and artists – most of whom are broadly left-leaning – signed an open letter to *Harper's Magazine* decrying what they perceive as leftist intolerance that seeks to silence and punish dissent. Predictably, the signatories were subsequently accused of seeking to protect the status quo under the false mantle of freedom of speech. Spinoza would likely regard the intractability of this dispute – which is, ostensibly, a kind of meta-dispute, a dispute about how we dispute – as a reflection of civic dysfunction rooted in distrust. The signatories distrust their opponents, taking them to be censorious and dismissive interlocutors who seek to silence what they find disagreeable, a suspicion that they took to be validated by the critical responses to the letter. And the letter's critics distrust the motives of signatories, assuming that the appeal to free speech is really just a cover for preserving their own privileged social positions. Critics suspect that what the signatories really want is not really free speech, but deference.

Leaving aside the merits of the competing claims, I think that it is fair to say that this debate is characterized by distrust. And if such distrust pervades internecine debates on the American left, the prospect of sincere and non-contemptuous disagreement across the political spectrum is vanishingly small. What, then, are we to do? We can push for structural political change, the kind of change that diminishes power disparities that contributes to distrust and obstructs political cooperation. We can also work to be less judgmental and to engage in tolerant disagreement within circles of good faith, even if we are likely to find these circles to be quite confined. And where conditions of suspicion seem to forestall sincere, non-contemptuous engagement, we can at least try to make others intelligible so as not to participate in noxious and unproductive disagreement that deepens civic distrust.

References

Bejan T (2017) Mere civility: disagreement and the limits of toleration. Harvard University Press, Cambridge, MA
Christensen D (2009) Disagreement as evidence. Philos Compass 4(5):756–767
Del Lucchese F (2009) Conflict, power, and multitude in Machiavelli and Spinoza: tumult and indignation. Continuum, London/New York
Egan A (2008) Seeing and believing: perception, belief formation, and the divided mind. Philos Stud 140(1):47–63
Elga A (2007) Reflection and disagreement. Nous 41(3):478–502
Elgin C (2010) Persistent disagreement. In: Feldman R, Warfield T (eds) Disagreement. Oxford University Press, Oxford
Gilbert D (1991) How mental systems believe. Am Psychol 46(2):107–119
Gilbert D, Tafarodi R, Malone P (1993) You can't not believe everything you read. J Pers Soc Psychol 65(2):221–233
Huebner B (2009) Troubles with stereotypes for Spinozan minds. Philos Soc Sci 39(1):63–92
James S (1996) Power and difference: Spinoza's conception of freedom. J Polit Philos 4(3):207–228
Kelly T (2005) The epistemic significance of disagreement. In: Szabo Gendler T, Hawthorne J (eds) Oxford studies in epistemology, vol 1. Oxford University Press, Oxford, pp 167–196
Kisner M (2011) Spinoza on human freedom. Cambridge University Press, Cambridge, MA
Laursen J (1996) Spinoza on toleration. In: Nederman C, Laursen J (eds) Difference and dissent: theories of toleration in medieval and early modern Europe. Rowman and Littlefield, Lanham, pp 185–204
Lord B (2017) Disagreement in the political philosophy of Spinoza and Rancière. Proc Aristot Soc 117(1):61–80
Mandelbaum E (2014) Thinking is believing. Inquiry 57(1):55–96
Mendus S (1988) Introduction. In: Mendus S (ed) Justifying toleration. Cambridge University Press, Cambridge, MA, pp 1–19
Raz J (1995) Ethics in the public domain: essays in the morality of law and politics. Oxford University Press, New York
Rosenthal M (2001) Tolerance as a virtue in Spinoza's Ethics. J Hist Philos 39(4):535–557
Rosenthal M (2003) Spinoza's republican argument for toleration. J Polit Philos 11(3):320–337
Shapiro L (2012) How we experience the world: passionate perception in Descartes and Spinoza. In: Pickavé M, Shapiro L (eds) Emotion and reason in early modern philosophy. Oxford University Press, Oxford, pp 193–216
Spinoza B (1985, 2015) The collected works of Spinoza, vols I–II (ed and trans: Curley E). Princeton University Press, Princeton
Steinberg J (2010) Spinoza's curious defense of toleration. In: Melamed Y, Rosenthal M (eds) Spinoza's theological–political treatise: a critical guide. Cambridge University Press, Cambridge, MA, pp 210–230
Steinberg J (2014) Following a recta ratio vivendi: the practical utility of Spinoza's dictates of reason. In: Kisner M, Youpa A (eds) The ethics of Spinoza's ethics. Oxford University Press, Oxford, pp 178–196
Steinberg J (2018a) Spinoza's political psychology: the taming of fortune and fear. Cambridge University Press, Cambridge, MA
Steinberg J (2018b) Two puzzles concerning Spinoza's conception of belief. Eur J Philos 26(1): 261–282

Steinberg J (2019) Spinoza on bodies politic and civic agreement. In: Armstrong A, Green K, and Sangiacomo A (eds) Spinoza and relational autonomy: being with others. Edinburgh University Press, pp 132–148

Strawson G (1993a) On 'freedom and resentment'. In: Martin Fischer J, Ravizza M (eds) Perspectives on moral responsibility. Cornell, Ithaca, pp 67–100

Strawson P (1993b) Freedom and resentment. In: Martin Fischer J, Ravizza M (eds) Perspectives on moral responsibility. Cornell, Ithaca, pp 45–66

Vavova K (2014) Moral disagreement and moral skepticism. Philos Perspect 28(1):302–333

Wong D (2006) Natural moralities: a defense of pluralistic relativism. Oxford University Press, Oxford

Toleration and Liberty of Conscience

Jon Mahoney

Contents

Two Models of Toleration and Liberty of Conscience	1096
Toleration, Neutrality, and Religious Equality	1101
Three Challenges	1107
Summary and Future Directions	1111
References	1112

Abstract

This chapter examines some central features to liberal conceptions of toleration and liberty of conscience. The first section briefly examines conceptions of toleration and liberty of conscience in the traditions of Locke, Rawls, and Mill. The second section considers contemporary controversies surrounding toleration and liberty of conscience with a focus on neutrality and equality. The third section examines several challenges, including whether nonreligious values should be afforded the same degree of accommodation as religious values, whether liberty of conscience requires a secular state, and how bias impedes understandings of toleration and liberty of conscience. The chapter concludes with brief comments on future directions for research on toleration and liberty of conscience. One is exploring toleration and liberty of conscience in non-Western contexts; another is exploring ways that varieties of religious and political identity impact conceptions of toleration and liberty of conscience.

Keywords

Toleration · Liberty of conscience · The harm principle · Neutrality · Fairness · Liberalism · Rights · Religious minorities · Nonreligious conscience · Secularism · Political authority

---

J. Mahoney (✉)
Department of Philosophy, Kansas State University, Manhattan, KS, USA
e-mail: jmahoney@ksu.edu

© The Author(s), under exclusive licence to Springer Nature Switzerland AG 2022
M. Sardoč (ed.), *The Palgrave Handbook of Toleration*,
https://doi.org/10.1007/978-3-030-42121-2_19

Liberty of conscience is central to liberal conceptions of toleration. One tradition that runs from John Locke (1983) through John Rawls (2005) holds that liberty of conscience is a fundamental right. A conception of the person as free and equal is a primary moral basis for toleration on this view. John Stuart Mill (1978) represents another tradition. On his view, utility is the moral basis for toleration and liberty of conscience. Both collective and individual interests are best promoted by a policy of toleration that extends to religious among other value commitments. The limits to liberty are set by the harm principle: toleration extends to beliefs and actions that do not cause or pose a significant risk of harm to others. Political philosophers in both traditions claim that liberty of conscience is a fundamental feature to a liberal conception of toleration.

Recent proposals on how modern, diverse, and multireligious states can best honor their commitments to toleration and liberty of conscience are often efforts to adapt ideas from traditional liberal thought to contemporary political and legal contexts. Two influential views are the neutrality and equality approaches to liberty of conscience (Patten 2017; Nussbaum 2008). Defenders of neutrality claim that a tolerant state is one whose policies are neutral toward religious values and practices. Others claim that toleration is best realized by a commitment to religious equality, one that treats each religious practice and conviction without favoritism or prejudice. Some argue that since religious values as a class are special, a liberal state can give some preferential treatment to religious exemption claims. Critics of this view reasonably argue that for reasons of fairness a tolerant state will treat religious and nonreligious values with equal regard (Leiter 2012; Perry 2018).

This chapter proceeds as follows. Section "Two Models of Toleration and Liberty of Conscience" briefly sets out main ideas in the Locke, Rawls, and Mill traditions on toleration and liberty of conscience. Section "Toleration, Neutrality, and Religious Equality" examines contemporary neutrality and equality approaches to toleration and liberty of conscience. Section "Three Challenges" considers three challenges. First is the claim that toleration should mean the same thing for religious and nonreligious convictions. Second, whether liberal toleration requires a secular state. Third, the legitimate worry that prevailing conceptions of toleration and liberty of conscious are objectionably exclusionary. Section "Future Directions" concludes with a brief comment on issues for future research and reflection.

Two Models of Toleration and Liberty of Conscience

In its contemporary form the Locke–Rawls paradigm holds that citizens and government must tolerate the religious convictions of persons whatever their content, unless such convictions imperil the rights of others. Although there is common ground within this tradition of liberalism, it is important to highlight some important differences.

Locke famously claimed that atheists, Catholics, and "Turks" ought not to be tolerated because they cannot be trusted to honor a social contract between citizens to uphold rights to life, liberty, and property (Locke 1983). On this view, atheists are excluded from the group of persons to be tolerated because, fearing no divine sanctions for breaking their promises, they are unreliable partners to a social contract. If you cannot trust an atheist to keep her or his promise then you cannot trust an atheist to comply with the terms of one of the most important promises of all, the social contract. Catholics on Locke's view are conflicted, as are "Turks," which is Locke's conflation of Muslims with Muslim citizens of the Ottoman state. The political loyalty of a Catholic or "Turk" to a liberal state, according to Locke, will be mitigated by their loyalty to the Papacy or the Ottoman Sultan.

On a charitable interpretation Locke is committed to something like the following loyalty test: Do they endorse a view at odds with the essential requirements for a social contract between citizens committed to a liberal state? If "yes," toleration does not extend to them. Citizens can reasonably be expected to endorse a model of political authority whose jurisdictional authority over civil affairs is not compromised by the authority of a religious institution. Yet in actuality Locke formulates the limits of toleration in a way that affirms preexisting prejudices as well as seriously misinformed beliefs about political and religious authority within Islam.

Locke's conception of political morality also explicitly depends on his conception of Christian morality. Locke states that his *Letter Concerning Toleration* expresses "my thoughts about the mutual toleration of Christians" (Locke 1983: 23). The political morality that is the basis for his account of political authority, liberty, and equality is a Christian conception of natural law.

Contemporary liberals in the Lockean tradition defend more inclusive conceptions of toleration and seek in general to extend the limits of toleration as far as possible within the boundaries of basic rights. Robert Nozick's (1974) famous construal of negative rights as side-constraints offers a model on how to formulate this idea: there are some things a person can do on the basis of his/her religious convictions that no one has a right to interfere with. Toleration understood in this way will not be objectionably exclusionary in the way Locke's position was. Yet we'll see in section "Three Challenges" that challenging issues remain for any attempt to defend an inclusive conception of toleration.

After his turn to political liberalism Rawls (2005) sought to present the case for liberal toleration in a way that could unite as many persons who are committed to fair terms for social cooperation as possible. Toleration extends, up to a point, to political philosophy itself. Provided someone is willing to seek fair terms for social cooperation in a state committed to treating each citizen as free and equal, he/she is to be tolerated. Someone's commitment to a minority or any religion is irrelevant in the sense that anyone willing to abide by the fair terms for social cooperation is entitled to liberty of conscience and the full protections of an inclusive tolerant state.

One important difference between Locke and Rawls centers on whether adherence to a religious tradition by itself is good evidence that someone is or is not committed to respecting the terms of the social contract. For Locke it is. For Rawls it is not. The fact that citizens committed to coexisting in a liberal state have widely diverging views about religion, moral, political, and other values, is a compelling reason to accommodate rather than alienate – as Locke's liberalism does – those who accept fair terms for social cooperation. Greater sensitivity toward the fact of pluralism has led to new ways of thinking about the moral basis for toleration. One result of this is the realization that a commitment to the idea of all persons as free and equal requires a conception of toleration that is more inclusive.

Despite philosophical differences it is appropriate to refer to a tradition in liberal thought as the Locke–Rawls paradigm. Like any tradition, liberalism is internally pluralistic. Yet this pluralism does not mean there are no meaningful ways to highlight common ground between Locke and Rawls. For example, political philosophers in this tradition can agree that how we think about toleration and liberty of conscience should be compatible with the idea of persons as free and equal. By contrast, utility is the basis for toleration according to Mill.

Mill characterizes liberty of conscience in a way that encompasses freedom of thought in general (Mill 1978). Persons can express themselves on all matters unless when doing so they cause harm or pose an immanent risk of harm to other persons. Liberty of conscience is part of a more general defense of liberty that includes religious, cultural, political, and artistic freedoms. The moral basis for this view is utility: protecting the liberty of the individual serves both our own and society's interests in maximizing happiness. Moreover, like his predecessor Bentham, Mill's conception of political morality is secular. Utility, according to Mill, is not in opposition to religion, nor does it depend upon a religious morality. The case for liberal toleration is further bolstered by a recognition of the "progressive" potential in human nature, which for Mill consists of an open-ended potential for moral, political, and cultural improvement (Rawls 2007: 301–303). Toleration is important in part because it serves this permanent interest of both the individual and the human community.

Liberty and other liberal values form a core part of what Mill termed "the principles of the modern world." These principles include liberty, marriage equality, equal treatment under law, and freedom of occupation (Mill 2007; Rawls 2007: 297). The toleration required by the liberty principle is understood by Mill to be part of a set of principles that work to advance the interests of all persons in an open society.

A central component of Mill's approach to toleration and liberty of conscience is a strong anti-paternalism. Neither government nor citizens are permitted to use coercion to stop persons from exercising their liberty of conscience on grounds that such restrictions are in the interest of those whose freedom is curtailed. For example, in his interesting discussion of Mormon polygamy Mill announces his own objections, targeting in particular the patriarchy within Mormon marriage practices (Mill 1978). Yet Mill defends a classical liberal standpoint by distinguishing coercive intervention from the free expressing of attitudes about the practices that are tolerated. Citizens are free to state their positions on nearly any topic. When they express opposition to a religious practice on grounds that it is patriarchal, they do not violate the requirement to tolerate something they object to. Mill does not conflate toleration with endorsement. Citizens are free to try to persuade, cajole, and argue with their fellow citizens about how they choose to exercise their liberty. By contrast, when the state prohibits freely constituted marriage practices that a majority finds repulsive, and when the harm principle does not authorize intervention, liberty is replaced by tyranny, whether of the majority or of some other power that lacks a moral justification for its coercive intervention.

That liberty is not a license to dominate others is central to the harm principle. Liberty imposes a strong duty of noninterference that is defeasible only when persons harm or pose a significant risk of harm to others. A practice that results in nonconsensual domination should not be tolerated. Yet when citizens claim they wish to freely exercise their liberty in ways that many find objectionable, the burden for intervening to prohibit should be on those who want to intervene, and not those who want to exercise their liberty.

Mill's view differs from the Locke–Rawls paradigm in three important respects. The first is that utility rather than a moral conception of the person is the moral basis for liberty of conscience. Instead of invoking the intrinsic worth of persons Mill, like other utilitarians, claims that the primary moral value is happiness. Liberty of conscience and other liberal principles are grounded in utility. The second is that harm to others rather than denying an inviolable moral status of the person is the criterion for deciding when to restrict liberty of conscience. Harm to others is a common variable in both traditions of liberal thought, yet the conception of harm that justifies coercive intervention differs across the two traditions. Mill emphasizes harm to the welfare of other persons, whereas the Locke–Rawls tradition emphasizes the intrinsic moral worth of persons, which is taken to be the basis for fundamental rights. Rights are important to a Millian conception of toleration, yet rights are grounded in utility and limited by the harm principle. Rights occupy a different space in the moral architecture of the two traditions of liberalism. A third important difference concerns the moral basis for the political authority that enforces liberal values, including toleration and liberty of conscience. Mill follows Hume (2015) and others in rejecting social contract theory. According to the noncontractarian liberal, political authority is justified when exercised according to the right political values, such as liberty and equality. The social contract tradition of which Locke and Rawls are paradigm figures claims that some form of consent – real, tacit, or hypothetical – is a condition for political authority, including the authority to enforce a right to liberty of conscience. The contractarian and noncontractarian liberal traditions thus disagree about the basis for the political authority to enforce a commitment to toleration and liberty of conscience. Noncontractarian liberals agree that consent plays an important role in a liberal society, for example, in commerce and in decisions about whether to join a religious community. Yet the idea of a social contract as the basis for political authority is rejected.

The harm principle can be invoked in ways that do not depend on Mill's utilitarian liberalism. For example, some contemporary positions appeal to a rights-based rather than utility-based conception of liberty. Others such as Feinberg (1984: 18) defend a conception of harm that can justify coercive intervention without taking a stand on whether the moral basis for this conception is utility, rights based, or contractarian. Cohen (2014) develops a theory of toleration in the tradition of Feinberg which extends the anti-paternalism implied by the harm principle to a range of contemporary debates. This more recent work has shown that one can creatively combine ideas from different conceptions of liberal political values.

Though the focus here has been on Mill's version, the harm principle can be adapted to different conceptions of liberal political morality.

On matters of law and policy there is a lot of common ground between liberals who affirm different conceptions of liberal values. Liberal political philosophers typically favor a civil libertarian conception liberty of conscience. Mormons, Muslims, Zoroastrians, atheists, and others should be tolerated with respect to their various faiths, convictions, and traditions. They also typically agree that government should not promote sectarian religious viewpoints. On matters of conscience, most liberals will concur that toleration requires a religiously nonsectarian state, the accommodation of nontraditional and minority religious viewpoints, as well as liberty of conscience for nonreligious values.

The features to liberal thought that hold across traditions of liberalism help to explain the relative agreement on a number of policies designed to protect liberty of conscience. For example, it is unlikely that a liberal political philosopher will endorse forcing religious citizens to make public pledges to secular symbols if such citizens object on religious grounds. Liberal political philosophers will also oppose obstructionist efforts on the part of citizens or government to make it harder for religious minorities to build a place of worship or to engage in religious practices. Tyranny of the majority was a special concern of Mill in part because he recognized that democratic states are often dominated by majorities who are able to use their power in ways advantageous to themselves and harmful to minorities. The treatment of Mormons and Catholics in the nineteenth-century America (Smith 2015), and Muslims today in both Europe and the USA, confirms the salience of Mill's concern. Moreover, an immigration policy that makes it harder for members of one religious group to migrate for travel, study, or residency is on its face intolerant in ways liberal political philosophers oppose.

Those in the Rawlsian tradition hold that to protect against the tyranny of the majority formal recognition of basic rights is not sufficient. The fair value of liberty will not be realized if relations between citizens are marked by significant status and material inequalities. Likewise, toleration does not require permitting people to opt out of policies that serve a compelling state interest, such as immunizing a population from polio. From the standpoint of liberal toleration polio and polygamy differ. Polio is a threat that is hard to protect against without a vaccine, and unvaccinated persons pose a risk to those too young for a vaccine or those who receive defective vaccines. There is no analogy here with polygamy because "protecting oneself from the harm of polygamy" is a matter of choice in a way to protecting oneself from communicable diseases that others may carry. To be sure, some idealizations are being made here about marriage. In a gender inegalitarian society, other factors are on the scale. A feminist liberal perspective can offer guidance on whether the conditions for consent in marriage are reasonably satisfied or not (Brake 2012). Likewise, both the harm principle and the idea of persons as free an equal will weigh the interests of third parties, including children, whether the issue is public health, marriage, or any number of other examples that generate conflicts between what people claim they have a liberty to do and the limits of toleration.

The discussion here is not meant to be a contribution to Locke, Mill, or Rawls scholarship, but is instead a highlighting of central features to liberal conceptions of toleration and liberty of conscience. We can better understand contemporary debates by appreciating how they draw from ancestral versions of the liberal values that animate contemporary debates. In that respect historical trends in liberalism are important to how toleration and liberty of conscience are examined here. The sketch just provided is framed with an eye toward contemporary debates, which is the focus of the rest of the chapter.

Toleration, Neutrality, and Religious Equality

Section "Two Models of Toleration and Liberty of Conscience" briefly considered representative positions on toleration and liberty of conscience from the history of liberal thought. Even granting that some ideas are settled, such as persons hold moral claims against many forms of coercion that restrict their liberty, there are a number of controversies about how best to realize toleration and liberty of conscience. Some controversies concern how liberal states try to promote toleration and protect liberty of conscience through law. For example, by what criterion can we judge someone's complaint that their liberty of conscience has not been respected? When does accommodating one person or group create an unfair burden for another person or group? Does the American practice of giving preferential treatment to exercises in religious over nonreligious conscience violate equal treatment? One way to grapple with these questions is by proposing neutrality as a criterion for evaluating state policy. A second is to defend religious equality as the best way to protect citizens from religious intolerance.

This section considers contemporary views on neutrality and religious equality that emphasize how different principles can work together in the service of toleration. Neutrality and religious equality are not mutually exclusive, although at times they will be considered separately in what follows. One can argue, for example, that state neutrality is a means to the realization of religious equality. Just as political philosophers argue in different ways for priority relations between principles (e.g., fair equality of opportunity over the difference principle) this architecture is also possible for principles within a conception of toleration.

To motivate thinking about neutrality and equality we can consider an example. Suppose we claim that an immigration policy that severely restricts immigration from a number of Muslim majority states is objectionable. Perhaps we claim such a policy too closely resembles the discredited Chinese exclusion policies in late nineteenth- and early twentieth-century America (Mahoney 2019). One way to express this judgment is to claim that the policy is intolerant because it fails to treat prospective Muslim immigrants in the same way it treats prospective Christian immigrants. On its face such a policy looks like an instance of official religious inequality. By contrast, one might defend the policy by showing the intent behind the policy has nothing to do with religious identity, but instead some other factor, such as national security. If there are unusually high numbers of bogus passports that are difficult to detect, a lawmaker might invoke this as a reason for greater scrutiny for visa applicants from some countries. On this view, if the reasons for the policy are what matter, and if these reasons are neutral towards religious groups, the disparate impact would not imply the policy is illegitimate. One issue here is deciding which is more salient when assessing a claim to neutrality: intent or impact. Which should be emphasized might depend on other factors, such as whether the state in question has a history of objectionably exclusionary policies that disfavor members of a religious group affected by the policy. In such cases, the suspicion level that a state is attempting to defend its policy in bad faith is elevated. A conception of toleration should give us resources to expose bad faith efforts to invoke what is presented as a fair principle, but which is really an effort at rationalization in order to confer "legitimacy" on an objectionable policy. Recent accounts of neutrality and religious equality are offered in part to address practical questions like these.

In the contemporary context Alan Patten (2014, 2017) defends one of the most compelling conceptions of neutrality. His view bases the idea of neutrality on fair equality of opportunity for self-determination (FOSD). This formulation has the virtue of making clear that neutrality is not a foundational principle. Rather, neutrality serves its purpose by helping us determine whether state policy treats each of its citizens as they deserve to be treated. A recent defense of religious equality is defended by Martha Nussbaum (2008). On her view religious toleration is required in part because the capacity for liberty of conscience deserves appraisal respect (Leiter 2012; Maclure 2018). On this view, there are good moral reasons to treat religious conscience in a way that affirms its intrinsic value. Nussbaum uses examples from American political and legal history to illustrate success and failure stories. She favors the religious exemption model sometimes affirmed in First Amendment jurisprudence according to which religious exemption claims should sometimes be accommodated.

Neutrality is not foundational to a liberal conception of morality, because it depends upon a more basic set of principles (Patten 2014). Like toleration, which depends on a concept of the person, utility, or some other basic value, neutrality is a "normatively dependent concept" (Forst 2017: 1). For example, on Patten's view fair equality of opportunity is prior to neutrality. Thinking about neutrality in relation to other political values helps us see how a neutrality standard can serve as a basis for evaluating law and policy. Consider a policy that prohibits slaughtering animals within city limits. Posed abstractly, "is the policy legitimate?" might seem straightforward if we are envisioning the policy as motivated to stop animal cruelty. Rationales for the policy could include: public health, limiting cruelty to animals, or regulating the production of meat products. Each on its own looks like a permissible reason for a policy. Yet suppose there is a religious minority committed to the ritual slaughter of chickens. If those whose religious practices are curtailed by the policy claim that their right to liberty of conscience is unfairly restricted, how should we reply? A neutrality test might help us decide how best to answer. For example, if there is reason to believe the lawmakers' motives included a bias against the religious minority whose practices are curtailed by the law, we see the policy in a different light. From this perspective it looks like the state is formulating public policy in a manner that hides the policy's actual rationale. Public health might remain a compelling public policy reason for the law. Yet a neutrality test would highlight the objectionable motives of the lawmakers, which might suffice to invalidate the policy.

If we opt for a neutrality approach to evaluating law and policy, we need to be clear about which aspects of public policy are subject to review by a neutrality test. Does neutrality apply to the motives behind state policy? Or are the effects of a policy more salient? We can imagine a public health policy, such as one prohibiting the slaughter of animals within city limits, adopted by lawmakers in good faith who harbor no bias against a religious group. From the standpoint of toleration this would matter. Yet so would the impact of the policy on religious citizens. If impact is more salient than purpose, neutrality will protect a wider range of expressions of religious freedom. To illustrate, let's consider another example.

Consider a federal education law that requires parents to ensure their children receive an adequate formal education, either in a school or at home. Whatever the adequacy standard (e.g., high school diploma or equivalency, minimum competency across a range of subjects) suppose the law is adopted on grounds that each citizen is entitled to a fair opportunity to pursue forms of employment that requires skilled labor, etc. Such a policy adopted on the basis of an educational adequacy approach to state education policy can meet a neutrality of intent test. Yet its effects will not be neutral across religious communities if one or more religious community believes that such a policy conflicts with religious obligation. Neutrality of effect is a possible test for the fairness of such a policy. Yet since neutrality is not a fundamental political value, there might be other considerations in a case like this, such as fair equality of opportunity for children. If the education policy was motivated by and satisfies a fair equality of opportunity standard, and if this is judged to be a legitimate policy aim on grounds that children have rights to opportunities that would be undermined were the exemption granted, the religious objection to the policy is much weaker. By contrast, suppose lawmakers developed an educational adequacy standard during a period of great social hostility towards a religious group who would have to modify its religious practices to comply with the adequacy standard. Would that impact the legitimacy of the policy?

Patten defends three ideas that are helpful as a guide to these issues. First, neutrality "is a constraint that has genuine weight and reflects significant liberal values, but it sometimes gives way to other considerations" (Patten 2014: 106). Second, Patten proposes a neutral treatment conception of neutrality. On this view, "The state violates this requirement when, relative to an appropriate baseline, its policies are more accommodating of some considerations of the good than they are of others" (Patten 2014: 113). Third, a person "should be given the most extensive opportunity to pursue and fulfil her ends that is justifiable given the reasonable claims of others" or FOSD (Patten 2017: 208).

When we make a judgment about a state-religion policy we should consider both the reasons for it and its effects. To do this we need some standard. FOSD is one proposal. A reason counts as neutral when it is consistent with FOSD. This does not mean that all such reasons are sufficient to vindicate the policy; there are other political values that weigh in. An education policy that serves a legitimate aim such as fair equality of opportunity might conflict with another legitimate aim such as protecting the liberty of parents to make decisions about their children's education on the basis of religious convictions. Judgments about cases like this will reflect views about which values weigh in and whether some such values override claims to religious freedom.

FOSD is egalitarian in the following sense. FOSD is prior to neutrality. FOSD is among the considerations that a policy that satisfies neutrality must be compatible with; if a law satisfies neutrality but not FOSD, then the law could be opposed. For instance, a state policy that grants religious parents exemptions from a state education policy might pass a neutrality test, yet run afoul of FOSD. If students have a right to an adequate education, one that does not block opportunities for pursuing higher education for instance, then limiting parental discretion in this context may be justified.

FOSD likewise assigns a degree of responsibility to citizens for how they exercise their conscience. For example, the accommodation of a religious practice is not always cost free. Conscientious objector status, exemptions from health care policies, exemptions from motorcycle helmet laws, and tax relief alter the distribution of financial and other shared burdens. FOSD can help us navigate between those practices we should tolerate on grounds of liberty of conscience, and those we need not on grounds that doing so will impose an unfair burden on someone else.

A recent American Supreme Court verdict shows why these issues matter. In *Masterpiece Cakeshop* (2018) the Court ruled in favor of a business owner who refused to produce a wedding cake for a same-sex couple. At the state level the business owner was found to be in violation of the state of Colorado's anti-discrimination policy. However, this initial verdict was judged by many to be problematic. Much of the political opposition to the Colorado verdict reflected both anti-gay bias and confusion about the salience of liberty of conscience in the context of for-profit commercial activity. Yet a legitimate concern is that agents of the state whose role is to enforce anti-discrimination policy had expressed religious bias about a business owner who declined to make a wedding cake for a same-sex couple. What is the right way to handle a case in which representatives of the state express intolerant attitudes towards the religious convictions of its citizens in the course of enforcing an otherwise legitimate state policy? One option is to rule in favor of the business owner without striking down the anti-discrimination policy, which is how the Court ruled. Yet the Court could have both made clear that expressions of religious bias by agents of the state are inappropriate, while at the same time upholding an anti-discrimination policy designed to reduce harms to an historically oppressed group (Macedo 2019). Claims for either position will not be resolved by appealing to the idea of toleration alone. Patten's framework pays off because it offers a way to think through conflicts with a principle, FOSD, that specifies how to give a number considerations, including equality and liberty of conscience, and their due.

Martha Nussbaum argues for a conception toleration and liberty of conscience based on the idea of religious equality. On her view, the tradition of religious equality in the American context serves as a model, albeit with the important qualification that we need to acknowledge the many failures to honor religious equality in practice when religious bigotry undermines the realization of religious equality. Moreover, Nussbaum does not oppose developing this model in a way that is more inclusive, for example, by expanding the idea of conscience to include nonreligious convictions. A secular citizen whose moral convictions put her at odds with a legitimate state policy should not be dismissed simply because the convictions are not religious. Religious exemptions have a special place in Nussbaum's view, however, in part because past instances of religious intolerance should inform our commitment to religious toleration, in particular, intolerance against religious minorities such as Mormons, Catholics, and Jews.

The central ideas in Nussbaum's position can be summarized as follows:

1. Conscience is a source of purpose and meaningful conceptions of how to live.
2. A free conscience permits persons to explore questions about the meaning of life unhindered by others and the state.
3. Conscience has intrinsic value, in the same way that the capacity for autonomy has intrinsic value.
4. Although not all values arrived at from liberty of conscience are religious values – e.g., a secular moral argument for pacifism can ground a legitimate exemption claim against mandatory service in the military – many authentic deliverances of conscience are religious, and religious convictions are often the target of state-sponsored oppression and intolerance by citizens. Therefore, religious values hold a special place among the values people affirm and religious conscience serves as a model for the kinds of value commitments that merit special protection from government (Nussbaum 2008: 22–26).

Religious equality means that government should be neutral between religions and refrain from taking sides, for example, between Christianity and Islam. This puts a strong burden on government to refrain from adopting policies that impact persons because of their religious identity.

A religious equality approach such as Nussbaum's offers a strong counterpoint to a recent Supreme Court decision that effectively blocks immigration from a number of Muslim majority countries. In *Trump* v *Hawaii* (2018) the US Supreme Court argued that despite President Trump's numerous anti-Muslim comments, both before and during his presidency, the government had made an effective case for the policy on national security grounds. The court further claimed that both legal precedent and the Constitution favor great deference to the executive branch regarding its judgments about national security. It is worth noting that although a claim about religious equality might not override a national security argument in every instance, in this one a commitment to religious equality offers a compelling counterpoint. In actuality the claim in favor of the restrictive immigration policy is an effort by government to rationalize religious bigotry with a pretense of claiming national security is the primary concern (Mahoney 2019). One clear piece of evidence in favor of this assessment is the gratuitous last-minute addition of two non-Muslim majority states – Venezuela and N. Korea – to the visa ban.

The idea of religious equality is built around this above-mentioned conception of conscience that is central to Nussbaum's project. In practice this means that a legitimate state can refrain from endorsing a sectarian religious viewpoint while at the same time affirming the value of religion as such. Sometimes American First Amendment jurisprudence has followed this model, and this is the conception of religious equality that Nussbaum seeks to defend as one that is suitable for a liberal theory of toleration.

Like Patten, Nussbaum is clear about priority relations among the considerations in play when we think about toleration and liberty of conscience. Religious equality is prior to neutrality. Stated quickly the order of ideas here runs from liberty of conscience to religious equality, and then to neutrality. Though the content of her view differs from Patten's view which adapts a way of thinking about equality from theories of distributive justice, the architecture in both views is similar in the sense that each affirms that equality is more basic than neutrality. It is a requirement of justice that government affirm a conception of religious equality. Neutrality is an instrument for realizing a more fundamental principle; it is an instrument in the sense that it helps us consider whether reasons for a law or policy are consistent with a commitment to religious equality.

Nussbaum's position has the merit of highlighting social status inequalities that often harm unpopular religious minorities. A state that affirms an ideal of religious equality, especially when its legal practice has a longstanding tradition of granting religious exemptions, can reform both its legal and political culture in ways that render its commitment to religious toleration more inclusive and more egalitarian. In the American context a clear example is the difference in social status that is conferred by various forms of religious identity. Mainline Protestant Christianity has something akin to an unofficial "first among equals" status. Mormon, Muslim, and Native American religious identities often correlate with barriers to numerous opportunities which Episcopalian or Presbyterian citizens, for example, can take for granted. The legitimate fairness concerns raised by those who oppose favoritism towards religious over nonreligious convictions that conflict with state policy should not detract from the ongoing effort to reduce the effects of religious bias.

Some liberals oppose exemptions (Barry 2001) while others oppose preferential treatment of religious convictions. (Leiter 2012; Maclure 2018; Perry 2018). Brian Barry argued that when a citizen has a strong argument against being required to comply with a law, this is a reason to rescind the law. A religious citizen who makes a compelling argument against having to comply with a law on grounds of religious freedom is thus really providing a compelling reason for the claim that the law is illegitimate. Those who oppose favoritism towards religion but not exemptions claim that whether a state accommodates a religious practice at odds with state policy ought not to depend on whether the reasons citizens have for endorsing the practices are religious or nonreligious. Nussbaum's position is much closer to the exemption paradigm that informs American law. American law does not exclude nonreligious exemptions, yet it favors religious over nonreligious exemption claims as a matter of legal practice.

Three Challenges

This section explores challenging questions that can be posed to liberal conceptions toleration and liberty of conscience. First, how can we formulate a conception of liberty of conscience that is not objectionably biased in favor of some kinds of values over others? Second, should liberals claim that toleration and liberty of conscience require a secular state? Third, what is best strategy for proponents of toleration and liberty of conscience to mitigate the problem of bias and exclusion?

Liberty of Conscience: Which Values Matter? In American law there is a tradition of favoritism for religious over nonreligious exemption requests. Legal precedent is not uniform, but it does lean toward preferential treatment of religious over nonreligious exemption claims. Recent statutory law, such as the 1993 Religious Freedom Restoration Act (RFRA) puts a higher burden on policy which conflicts with religious convictions. If a religious citizen objects to having to comply with a policy for religious reasons RFRA says the burden is on government to show that the policy that is being contested serves a "compelling state interest" and imposes less of a burden on the practices of the claimant than alternative policy options. This level of accommodation is not guaranteed for nonreligious claimants. Since the mid-1960s as commentators have noted (Greenawalt 2006; Nussbaum 2008) the trajectory in American law is towards a more inclusive conception of liberty of conscience, one that still privileges religious over nonreligious convictions, but overtime to a lesser extent than in the past.

Switching perspectives from law to political morality there are a range of positions on religious exemptions (Vallier and Weber 2018). Much of the most recent work on exemptions has been devoted to showing that equality and fairness support a conception of toleration that is neutral between religious and nonreligious values. Many who favor granting exemptions argue the state should not favor religious over nonreligious exemption requests. This model is preferable to one that grants special privileges for religious exemption claims, although it too is open to objections.

Suppose we claim that toleration is best honored if we adopt a conscience principle according to which citizens can sometimes be entitled to special legal accommodations. Watching the World Cup and conscientious objection to military service, for religious or secular moral reasons, might seem to most persons to reflect nonmoral and moral values, respectively. Yet as Simon Cabulea May (2017) shows there are a range of kinds of commitments that include nonmoral value commitments that are central to persons' conceptions of the good. Citizens can pursue scientific, artistic, intellectual, athletic, and other activities with an earnest conviction that a life with meaning requires unhindered opportunity to pursue such activities. Why should their efforts to pursue values in the service of a meaningful life be treated as less weighty simply because such values are not picked out by a conscience principle that gives priority to moral over nonmoral values? Lacking a clear basis for sorting values into those which are important and those which are trivial, we will be left with a dilemma: either we unfairly exclude some exemption requests that should be taken seriously, or we face a slippery slope that will be too inclusive. Moreover, authorizing the state to adopt a principle according to which some value commitments are trivial while others are profound comes at the risk of permitting government to adopt a sectarian position on matters about which reasonable citizens can disagree.

There is reason for skepticism about a conscience principle that is neutral between religious and moral convictions, because it leaves important questions unsettled. If we attempt to address this worry by claiming the conscience principle should treat equally any meaning-conferring conviction, regardless of the kind of value, the gain in inclusivity will be accompanied by new worries. The legal impact of adopting an inclusive conscience principle would require asking whether a distinction between significant and trivial values can be fairly applied, and if so, how such a standard might be developed.

We can partly address worries about how to specify which values the conscience principle makes eligible as the basis for exemptions by adopting Patten's idea of equal treatment and fair opportunity for self-determination. Patten's FOSD is neutral between kinds of values. It specifies limits to accommodation in terms of costs that must be shouldered by others. Expecting citizens to bear some responsibility for their pursuits, religious or otherwise, is one way to mitigate what might reasonably be claimed to be an unfairness. However, can FOSD provide guidance on how to distinguish an exemption request that would enable watching the World Cup from an exemption request that would enable someone to ride a motorcycle without a helmet because a helmet conflicts with a religious obligation to wear a turban? If one worker has to forgo a day off so that his/her coworker can watch the World Cup, is he/she unreasonably burdened? If a Sikh is permitted to ride a motorcycle without a helmet is his risk of incurring higher medical expenses an unfair burden placed on others? The kind of value invoked could be ignored with a conception of toleration instead being guided by the idea that each is entitled to a fair pursuit of any kind of value. Many will be unsatisfied with this approach insofar as it accommodates accommodation requests for what many will regard as trivial pursuits. Whether the liberal state should declare something like "one person's mere preference is another's life-defining project" is an interesting and open question.

We can consider multiple policy options. For example, labor policies that specify the legitimate reasons for time-off from work must be in place to accommodate the conscience principle. Or raising insurance premiums for those who forgo safety measures for reasons of conscience. Nevertheless, once it is claimed that toleration favors exemptions, questions about fairness and inclusivity are inevitable. This does not mean we should abandon the exemption approach to liberty of conscience altogether. Doing so on grounds that there will be intractable disagreement over which kinds of exemption claims have merit arguably represents a sour-grapes approach to the political reality of hard cases. Yet the hard questions concerning whether all, some – and if so which and why – values can support reasonable exemption claims remain.

Does Toleration Require a Secular State? In his recent book *Islam and the Secular State* an-Na'im claims, "In order to be a Muslim by conviction and free choice...I need a secular state" (2008:1). An-Na'im defends a Lockean argument, albeit a version that is more inclusive than Locke's own position. The main principles in an-Na'im's view include first, the thesis that authentic religious conviction is incompatible with state enforcement of religious doctrine. Second, religious authority does not have jurisdictional authority over the civil affairs that states exist to project. Third, persons can disagree about religion yet coexist as equal citizens. Fourth, those Muslims who choose to abide by principles of Sharia can do so voluntarily. Yet no one has the right to compel others to comply with religious obligations. Though most liberal political philosophers do not engage questions about toleration and liberty of conscience in Muslim majority contexts (exceptions include Hashemi 2009; March 2009; Stepan 2014), an-Na'im's position represents a familiar liberal position on toleration and liberty of conscience adapted to Muslim majority societies.

Is a state that does not exercise its authority on the basis of secular values necessarily intolerant? To address this, it is important to bear some distinctions in mind. One is the difference between a just and a legitimate state. If we interpret an-Na'im's claim to mean that a fully just state will be a secular state, his position is plausible from the standpoint of a liberal conception of toleration. A just state is fully compliant with liberal political morality. Real states fall short of this standard. If any states have the moral authority to coerce, they must be authorized to do so despite this fact. This is one reason why contemporary liberal philosophers distinguish justice from political legitimacy (May 2009; Rawls 2005). A state is legitimate when it exercises power on the basis of principles that reasonable persons – or some other proposed baseline that is lower than what an ideally just state will be based upon – can accept. For example, a legitimate state is committed to restricting religious liberty only when doing so is viewed as necessary to protect the status of citizens as free and equal, or on the basis of the harm principle. It will not seek to oppress religious minorities. Yet a state with these commitments may fall short – up to a point which will be left vague here – without forfeiting its political authority. There are many controversies about legitimacy and political authority (Huemer 2012), yet many accept that legitimacy is a lower standard than justice.

From the Rawlsian standpoint an-Na'im's claim about religious toleration and the secular state is appropriate when we are thinking about the conditions for a just state. Yet as Alfred Stepan (2001) and Simon Cabulea May (2009) have shown, Stepan from a social science perspective, May from a philosophical perspective, there are multiple variations on the configuration of religious and political authority within legitimate states. When political legitimacy is the baseline, the secular requirement is less stringent. A religious democracy understood as a state that protects religious freedom yet adopts some policies that reflect a majority religious viewpoint, according to this view, can qualify as legitimate. Alternatively put, such a state need not be liable to revolution simply because it is a religious democracy. Details will matter here, yet some actual transitional states and May's hypothetical example of religious democracy are compelling counterexamples to the claim that secularism is a condition for political legitimacy.

A second important consideration concerns what is meant by a secular state. An-Na'im's view is that a tolerant secular state is one that upholds the principle of liberty of conscience. In his words:

> The separation of Islam and the state is necessary for Muslims to uphold their genuine beliefs and to live accordingly....Historically, religious leaders were either enticed to cooperate with the political agenda of rulers or coerced to do so to avoid facing harsh consequences, as illustrated by the inquisition....I am calling for the separation of Islam from the state, which means that those who control the state cannot use its coercive powers to enforce their own beliefs. (An-Na'im 2008: 56)

A familiar nontechnical idea of a theocracy or state whose purported authority is rooted in a conception of religious authority is incompatible with this idea of a secular state. Yet we need a conception of political authority that is more fine-grained than one that distinguishes a just state from a theocracy. If we accept a distinction between just and legitimate state as presented above, then an-Na'im's argument can be charitably construed as supporting the conclusion that a fully just state will be a secular state.

Bias and Exclusion in Conceptions of Toleration and Liberty of Conscience. A third challenge concerns objectionable limits to liberty of conscience that are supported by persons or states that claim to be committed to toleration. Liberal conceptions of toleration need to consider how biases or insensitivities to unfairness are often unacknowledged. There are both theoretical and practical dimensions to this problem. As a matter of theory, the following is a useful starting point for thinking about toleration and liberty of conscience with this concern in mind:

> Sometimes one hears reference made to the so called Enlightenment project of finding a philosophical secular doctrine, one founded on reason and yet comprehensive....Whether there is or ever was such an Enlightenment project...political liberalism...and justice as fairness as a form thereof has no such ambitions. As I have said, political liberalism takes for granted not simply pluralism but the fact of reasonable pluralism; and beyond this it supposes that of the main existing reasonable comprehensive doctrines, some are religious. (Rawls 2005: xvii)

According to the conception of political morality the later Rawls endorsed, toleration applies, up to a point, to political philosophy itself (Rawls 2005). This means that those committed to the idea of persons as free and equal should accept that commitments to the values a legitimate state will rest upon can be affirmed for a variety of reasons from a variety of perspectives. Pluralism applies to political philosophy's account of what counts as a legitimate state. More recent work has taken this idea further by exploring, for example, the relevance of political liberalism in Islam, as well as to non-Western contexts (Kim 2014) that have long traditions of construing political morality in collectivistic rather than individualistic terms.

Practical challenges to efforts to avoid bias in conceptions of toleration are equally important. Liberal political philosophers are always revising, often too slowly, their understanding of how to reconfigure the limits of toleration in order to reduce unfairness, biases that led to unjust exclusion, and to accommodate new moral insights that reveal unnoticed insensitivities in prevailing accounts. The effort to remedy mistakes rooted in prejudice and failures to acknowledge groups and individuals with interests that have a reasonable claim to be accommodated and affirmed as equal should be a central focus of how we understood toleration. Locke's failures with respect to atheists and Catholics may have been largely remedied in subsequent liberal theory. Yet it is the failures to address ways that contemporary understandings of toleration and liberty of conscience are compromised by unnoticed unfairness that should occupy us most when looking at the present, and towards the future. Neutrality tests, Patten's FOSD, Nussbaum's religious equality approach, and other conceptions of toleration can be evaluated in light of how well they fare in light of how other conceptions of toleration have failed. Liberal Muslims like an-Na'im make a valuable contribution by encouraging us to think about toleration from the standpoint of religious yet non-Christian citizens.

Constraints on moral imagination from outright prejudice to subtle sources of bias that persist in spite of good faith efforts to overcome them provide compelling reasons to insist that whichever conception of toleration we adopt we should do so with the full recognition that the political project of realizing toleration is never finished. Given traditions of bias in law and political culture, liberty of conscience, especially for those whose values and religious practices fall outside what is imagined to be "paradigmatic conceptions of religiosity" or "meaningful pursuits" should framed in a way that puts this concern at the center.

Summary and Future Directions

There are many ways ideas about toleration and liberty of conscience can be developed beyond what has been considered here. This concluding section will briefly state two examples. One is to expand contexts to include the many perspectives on politics and toleration that fall outside typical discussions within liberal political philosophy. For example, in addition to considering toleration and liberty of conscience in different religious contexts as an-Na'im has proposed, recent work in comparative philosophy promises to make an important contribution to how liberal political philosophers think about toleration and liberty of conscience. Other contexts include those where prevailing conceptions of political morality are collectivistic rather than individualistic. Toleration and liberty of conscience as considered in this chapter fits squarely within a tradition of political morality based on the idea of value individualism: the idea that the individual person has rights or interests that merit special protections in the form of moral principles and law. Yet in the liberal tradition value individualism reflects the impact of Protestant Christianity, among other sources. Whether liberal conceptions of political morality can or should be adapted to the many global contexts in which religious and political history differ from the European experience is a pressing issue (Buchanan 2013: 249–274; Kim 2014).

A second way work on toleration and liberty of conscience can be advanced further by exploring ways that identity and politics inform citizens' and governments' willingness to extend toleration to each person and group. For example, in the American context, the dominant Protestant religious identity, in addition to attitudes about race and ethnicity, informs many persons' attitudes about toleration and liberty of context (Kazi 2019). Attitudes about Islam in the American context cannot be separated from the dominant religious identity. When "we are a Christian nation" is endorsed in contexts where national identity is at stake, the conflation of a legal status with a religious identity signals a desire to deny equal status to those with the "wrong kind" of religious identity. When expressed inwardly to the domestic context, this has the effect of calling into question the loyalty of religious citizens who embrace a minority identity, such as "Muslim-American." When expressed outwardly, for example, towards refugees, visa applicants, or international students, this attitude becomes a basis for exclusion.

Consider attempts to draw an analogy between 9/11 and the Japanese attack on Pearl Harbor. Though a bad analogy, one reason this is politically effective is that religious identity is often conflated with nationality. In the crudest form attitudes that rest on this conflation are expressed in slogans such as, "Islam hates us" or "we are at war with Islam." The analogy between a Muslim community center in Manhattan and a Japanese community center in Pearl Harbor was endorsed by many, because of this conflation of religious identity with nationality (Gutterman and Murphy 2015). Politics and reality do not meet here: Islam is not a nation; no state committed an act of war against the USA on 9/11, and no political authority represents the world's nearly two billion Muslim population. Yet prevailing attitudes that in part reflect America's dominant religious identity, along with an undercurrent of fear of Islam, combine to reinforce a status inequality for American Muslims. Toleration and liberty of conscience as a matter of principle are of course opposed to this politics. Political philosophers can engage this issue by exploring ways that identity and politics impact how people think about toleration. When "nationality" or some other category is really a proxy for "Muslim" or any other religious group those who defend toleration and liberty of conscience must develop a clear and effective counter narrative to the political discourses that serve objectionable efforts to exclude.

References

An-Na'im AA (2008) Islam and the secular state. Cambridge, MA. Harvard University Press
Barry B (2001) Culture and equality: an egalitarian critique of multiculturalism. Cambridge, MA. Harvard University Press
Brake E (2012) Minimizing marriage: marriage, morality, and the law. New York, NY. Oxford University Press
Buchanan A (2013) The heart of human rights. New York, NY. Oxford University Press
Cohen AJ (2014) Toleration. Cambridge, UK. Polity Press
Feinberg J (1984) Harm to others. Oxford, UK. Oxford University Press
Forst R (2017) Religion, reason, and toleration: Bayle, Kant – and US. In: Laborde C, Bardon A (eds) Religion in liberal political philosophy. Oxford, UK. Oxford University Press, pp 249–261
Greenawalt K (2006) Religion and the constitution: Vol. 1 Religious free-exercise. Princeton, NJ. Princeton University Press

Gutterman D, Murphy A (2015) Political religion and religious politics: navigating identities in the United States. New York, NY. Routledge
Hashemi N (2009) Islam, secularism and liberal democracy: toward a democratic theory for Muslim societies. Oxford, UK. Oxford University Press
Huemer M (2012) The problem of political authority: an examination of the right to coerce and the duty to obey. London, UK. Palgrave
Hume D (2015) Of the social contract. Library of Alexandria
Kazi N (2019) Islamophobia, race, and global politics. Louisville, CO. Rowman and Littlefield
Kim S (2014) Confucian democracy in East Asia: theory and practice. Cambridge, UK. Cambridge University Press
Leiter B (2012) Why toleration religion? Princeton, NJ. Princeton University Press
Locke J (1983) A letter concerning toleration (ed: Tully J). Indianapolis, IN. Hackett
Macedo S (2019) Liberalism beyond toleration: religious exemptions, civility, and the ideological other. Philos Soc Criticism:370–389
Maclure J (2018) Conscience, religion, and exemptions: an egalitarian view. In: Vallier K, Weber M (eds) Religious exemptions. Oxford, UK. Oxford University Press, pp 9–20
Mahoney J (2019) Wedding cakes and Muslims: religious freedom and politics in contemporary American legal practice. Politoligia 1:25–36
March A (2009) Islam and liberal citizenship: the search for an overlapping consensus. Oxford, UK. Oxford University Press
Masterpiece Cakeshop v Colorado Civil Rights Commission (2018) No. 16–111, 584 U.S.
May SC (2009) Religious democracy and the liberal principle of legitimacy. Philos Public Aff 37(2):136–170
May SC (2017) Exemptions for conscience. In: Laborde C, Bardon A (eds) Religion in liberal political philosophy. Oxford, UK. Oxford University Press, pp 191–203
Mill JS (1978) On liberty, 8th edn. Indianapolis, IN. Hackett
Mill JS (2007) On the subjection of women (ed: Ryan A). New York, NY. Penguin Classics
Nozick R (1974) Anarchy, state, and utopia. Cambridge, MA. Harvard University Press
Nussbaum M (2008) Liberty of conscience: a defense of America's tradition of religious equality. New York, NY. Basic Books
Patten A (2014) Equal recognition: the moral foundations of minority rights. Princeton, NJ. Princeton University Press
Patten A (2017) Religious exemptions and fairness. In: Laborde C, Bardon A (eds) Religion in liberal political philosophy. Oxford, UK. Oxford University Press, pp 204–219
Perry M (2018) On the constitutionality and political morality of granting conscience-protecting exemptions to only to religious believers. In: Vallier K, Weber M (eds) Religious exemptions. Oxford, UK. Oxford University Press, pp 21–36
Rawls J (2005) Political liberalism. New York, NY. Columbia University Press
Rawls J (2007) Lectures on the history of political philosophy (ed: Freeman S). Cambridge, MA. Harvard University Press
Religious Freedom Restoration Act (1993)
Smith DT (2015) Religious persecution and order in the United States. Cambridge, UK. Cambridge University Press
Stepan A (2001) Religion, democracy, and the 'twin tolerations'. J Democr 11(4):37–57
Stepan A (2014) Muslims and toleration: unexamined contributions to the multiple secularisms of modern democracies. In: Stepan A, Taylor C (eds) Boundaries of toleration. New York, NY. Columbia University Press, pp 267–296
Trump v Hawaii (2018) No. 17–965, 584 U.S.
Vallier K, Weber M (2018) Religious exemptions. Oxford, UK. Oxford University Press

Tolerating Racism and Hate Speech: A Critique of C.E. Baker's "Almost" Absolutism

54

Raphael Cohen-Almagor

Contents

Introduction 1116
The Liberal Free Speech Principle 1117
The Liberty Model 1119
The Autonomy Argument 1121
The Promotional Approach 1129
    Rejection of Content Neutrality 1129
    Accepting Some Form of Perfectionism 1129
    Balancing 1130
    Denying Legitimacy 1131
    Excluding Incitement and Profound Offense from the Free Speech Principle 1131
Conclusion 1133
References 1134

Abstract

This chapter takes issue with C.E. Baker's stance that the Free Speech Principle should protect even the most harmful and vile expression because such protection would promote individual self-government, enhance personal autonomy, and promote critical thinking. It is argued that a balance needs to be struck between these goods and the impact of the speech in question on its target group. The protection of free speech cannot be offered in isolation from its wider consequences, not only those that affect the speaker but also those that affect those whom the speaker intended to influence. Furthermore, the content of the speech

---

Gratitude is expressed to Tim Scanlon, Wayne Sumner, Bhikhu Parekh, Steve Newman, and Eric Heinze for their most constructive comments on earlier drafts.

R. Cohen-Almagor (✉)
University of Hull, Hull, UK
e-mail: r.cohen-almagor@hull.ac.uk

© The Author(s), under exclusive licence to Springer Nature Switzerland AG 2022
M. Sardoĉ (ed.), *The Palgrave Handbook of Toleration*,
https://doi.org/10.1007/978-3-030-42121-2_8

should be evaluated on its face value. Incitement and grave offenses, morally on a par with physical harm, should be excluded from the Free Speech Principle.

Keywords

Autonomy · Baker · Balancing · Freedom of expression · Hate · Mill

Introduction

On Saturday, October 27, 2018, Robert Bowers opened fire on the Tree of Life synagogue in Pittsburgh, murdering 11 people and injuring 6 others in what is believed to be the deadliest attack on the Jewish community in the history of the United States. Bowers told a SWAT officer that he wanted all Jews to die because Jews were committing genocide to his people (Croft and Ahmed 2018). Bowers had spawned his hatred for Jews over the social media, especially on Gab, a social network with a far-right following. Inspection of the Gab account in his name showed months of anti-Semitic and racist posts that had been allowed to remain online. Bowers believed that Jews are "children of satan," responsible for the ills of the world and for things he did not appreciate, first and foremost, immigration to America. He also believed that the Holocaust did not exist. On June 21, 2018, Bowers wrote, "Lord, make me fast and accurate. Let my aim be true and my hand faster than those who would seek to destroy me. Grant me victory over my foes and those that wish to do harm to me and mine. Let not my last thought be 'If only I had my gun' and Lord if today is truly the day that You call me home, let me die in a pile of brass" (Dearden 2018).

Not for the first time, this tragedy showed that there is a direct link between hate speech and hate crime (Cohen-Almagor 2015). Not for the first time, incitement was allowed on the free highway without disruption. Not for the first time, people who were intent to embark on a shooting spree declared their intentions prior to the massacre, but nothing was done to avert the plan (Cohen-Almagor and Haleva-Amir 2008). In the United States, the combination of the first and second amendments proves, time and again, to be lethal. Words can hurt. Words can wound. Words can lead to destructive action. There is a strong link between hate speech and hate crime. Sweeping liberal protection of free speech might undermine the very foundations of democracy and cost human lives.

This chapter offers critical analysis of a specific strand in the liberal free speech theory. It takes issue with C.E. Baker's very liberal stance that holds that the Free Speech Principle should protect even the most harmful and vile expression because such protection would promote individual self-government, enhance personal autonomy, and promote critical thinking. It is argued that a balance needs to be struck between these goods and the impact of the speech in question on its target group. The protection of free speech cannot be offered in isolation from its wider consequences, not only those that affect the speaker but also those that affect those whom the speaker intends to influence. Furthermore, against the American liberal stance that endorses content neutrality, it is argued that the content of the speech should be evaluated on its face value when we come to decide the scope of tolerance.

The decision about what is mere advocacy, hence legitimate, and what constitutes illegitimate incitement is not a simple one. Liberals argue that statements like "Blacks should climb trees in Africa," "Pakis should return to Pakistan," "Jews are money hungry," "Zionism equals racism," "France is only for the French," "All Nigerians are criminals," "Israel is Apartheid State," "Thai women are whores," or "All Arabs are dirty" – none of which is a fragment of my imagination – are all problematic and deeply offensive, yet are also advocacy. The Free Speech Principle shields all of them. It is only when the speech directly invokes violence that it becomes problematic. Speech is more problematic when the target is more and more specific, and it is even more problematic in circumstances where a direct link can be established between the violent speech and violent action. Liberals are reluctant to ban speech. Consequently, the scope of tolerance encompasses many problematic speeches that might provoke violence (Cohen-Almagor 2006). This is especially true in the United States, the land of the free and of the First Amendment (Abrams 2017; Stone and Bollinger 2018). The United States is willing to pay a high price for maintaining freedom of expression. No other country in the world is willing to pay such a price.

Under the influence of J.S. Mill's (1948) writings, the consequentialist reasoning has been adopted and further developed by many liberal thinkers. Liberals conflate different argumentation to make the strongest possible protection of free expression. They are worried that government might stifle free speech for partisan, political interests (Wood 1969; Henthoff 1992; Abrams 2017). We indeed should be worried about government's tendency to abuse its powers. We had seen that this fear is founded. Past experience has shown that different governments used their powers not only in legitimate ways. Sometimes they were tempted to abuse their powers to promote partisan interests and to undermine their opposition (Cohen-Almagor 2016).

Following my critique of Baker, the balancing method is explained and then boundaries to free expression are delineated. It is argued that incitement and grave offenses, morally on a par with physical harm, should be excluded from the Free Speech Principle.

The Liberal Free Speech Principle

During the past two centuries, liberal reasoning about the boundaries of freedom of expression has been *en vogue* in the western world. Liberals warn that if we restrict speech, this might lead to an increasing tendency toward law and order legislation (Skillen 1982); to the creation of undergrounds (Dorsen 1988; Neier 1979; Baker 1978, 2012); to outburst of violence, rage, aggression, and use of illegal means (Baker 2009: 152, 2012); to abuse of power on part of the government (Scanlon 1979, 2003; Schauer 1982, 2000); to more censorship (Bollinger and Stone 2002;

Dworkin 2009; Reidy 2013); or to a less tolerant society (Bollinger 1986, 2010; Richards 1986, 1988).

In the United States, trust in government used to be high up until the 1950s, but a string of events from then on has eroded that trust. As a result of the "Red Scare" and the Cold War between the United States and the Soviet Union, Senator Joseph McCarthy directed investigations toward Hollywood and the intellectual community. During the McCarthyism period (1947–1957) basic civil rights of out-of-favor individuals were harmed by the government (Fried 1996; Schreker 2001; Oshinsky 2005). In the late 1950s and early 1960s, as the United States was recovering from McCarthyism, public trust in government was relatively high, but the trust in government declined in the late 1960s (Alford 2001: 30). The Vietnam War (1959–1975) further eroded public trust, and the Watergate scandal in the early 1970s that resulted in the resignation of President Richard Nixon in August 1974 (the only resignation of a US president) certainly did not relax the growing suspicions toward government. Mismanagement of the economy did not help, and George W. Bush's "war on terror," including the war waged on Iraq for unclear motives, has further undermined the American public trust in its government. Thus, public trust in government has plummeted from 73% in 1958 to 58% in 1973 and continued to drop to 19% in 2013. According to the Pew Research Report, in 2014, 24% of Americans said they were content with the federal government (PewResearch 2014).

The United States is known to hold the most tolerant view in the democratic world on hate speech, but pays a price for tolerating hate as some of those speeches translate into hate crimes. But American liberals hold that there is no need to panic or to be afraid of such vile ideas. Instead, we need to expose the falsity of hatred and educate to tolerance and equal liberties for all.

The American Civil Liberties Union (ACLU), among other organizations, has supported the rights of racist and anti-Semitic organizations, most notoriously the Ku Klux Klan (KKK) and the American National Socialist Party, to speak, to demonstrate, to march, and to organize (*Collin v. Smith* 1978; *Village of Skokie v. National Socialist Party of America* 1978; Neier 1979). In their defense of radical political groups, the ACLU and others have not claimed that the words, pictures, and symbols of such groups have no negative consequences. The constitutional protection accorded to the freedom of speech is not based on a naïve belief that speech can do no harm, but based on the confidence that the benefits society reaps from the free flow and exchange of ideas outweigh the costs society endures by allowing reprehensible and even dangerous ideas. Free speech activists acknowledged that the racist images and discourse of these groups might offend and harm the targeted individuals, might corrupt the level and nature of civic discourse, and might increase the probability of hate crimes. Yet, the admission of speech's causal propensities and harmful consequences has not lessened the strength of the Free Speech Principle. The Nazis and the KKK have free speech rights not because what they say is harmless, but despite their harmful expressions (Schauer 2000; Newman 2004). In Virginia v. Black (2003), the Supreme Court declared the Virginia cross-burning statute unconstitutional because it discriminated on the basis of content and viewpoint. This ruling was widely criticized (Gey 2004). Liberals who argue for the protection of racist and hateful speech see this kind of speech as the litmus case for tolerance. After all, tolerance is precisely about challenging expressions, not pleasantries.

Those who challenge this stand question why should the racist, who wishes to deny equal status and respect to others due to their race, be entitled to equal status and respect. They argue that the racist is excluding himself from the liberal shield by denying equality for all. But liberals insist on maintaining our high standards and on not becoming "like them". Believing that the liberal standards are right, correct, just and true, liberals think that through the battles of words and the free market of opinions the liberal truth will eventually gain the upper hand over the vile speech. This is Ronald Dworkin's view. Dworkin (1983, 1985, 1986, 2002), Cohen, Nagel, and Scanlon (1977) and Barker (1999) see any infringement by the state on the content of speech as denying the equality of citizens (see Cohen-Almagor 2019). Liberals are willing to take risk and pay some price in adhering to their noble principles. They think that the liberal state should respect the rights of racist speakers to "contribute" to the society's "moral climate" although they acknowledge that the racists actually undermine the moral climate. Liberals may even argue that we have an obligation to listen to the racist diatribes and then choose our response. We may choose to ignore them because such diatribes do not deserve our attention, or we may decide to confront the racist ideas with our benevolent ideas and persuade the racist, or others who listen to the debate, in the truism of the liberal moral ideas.

The Liberty Model

In his writings, Ed Baker developed the liberty model. He acknowledges the following:

- Speech may seriously harm others (Baker 1978: 997, 1989: 55, 1997: 987).
- Hate speech causes many real harms, many real injuries (Baker 2008: 22, 2009: 143, 156).
- The seriousness of harms caused by speech should never be underestimated (Baker 1997: 987).
- Racist speech can impose brutal injuries in individual incidents (Baker 1997: 987) and has the potential of stimulating further harms (Baker 2008: 6).
- Racist speech does not respect others' equality or dignity (Baker 2008: 5).
- Historical accounts show that racist hate speech was prominent in periods leading to genocide (Baker 2008: 9).

Given this set of assumptions, one wonders why Baker protects hate speech. To offset the above assumptions, Baker advances a series of counter-arguments:

- People "ought to have the legal option to engage in harm-causing expression" (Baker 1997: 989).
- There are many forms of harmful speech that are not subject to legal regulations, including parents who generally "cannot be jailed for speech that leads their kids to hire psychologists later in life" (Baker 1997: 988, 2009: 157).

- Protection of speech is essential to democracy (Baker 1989: 28–33, 2009: 145).
- Prevention of harm does not justify limits on liberty (Baker 1997: 996, 1011–1012).
- In the spirit of John Stuart Mill, prohibition of hate speech might result in truth that we hold as sterile dogma, ineffective as people do not have an opportunity to justify and explain the truth (2009: 151–152, 156; 2012: 72, 78).
- Regulation is not an effective, or the most effective, response (Baker 1997: 989).
- Moreover, hate speech regulation is more likely to contribute to genocidal events and racial violence than to reduce them (Baker 2008: 1, 2009: 140, 2012: 79).

Baker (1978: 997) explains that harms caused by speech normally do not justify a restriction. Speech harms only occur to the extent people mentally adopt perceptions or attitudes (Baker 1978: 998). No one has the right to decide what the speaker should say or believe. Restricting speech because the listener may adopt certain perceptions "disrespects the responsibility and freedom of the listener" (Baker 1978: 998). This is an interesting argument. Baker does not speak about speaker's responsibility, and he applies liberal paternalism to argue that speech limitations disrespect the listener's freedom where the listener may believe that her freedom would be enriched with the imposition of such limitations. Baker's free speech stance is also manifested in his argument that the listener "has a right to demand that the government not prohibit the listener from receiving or using information" (Baker 1978: 1007). But the listener does not have a right to demand that the government prohibit certain information.

Baker's thesis (1978) is that the First Amendment protects a broad realm of non-violent and noncoercive activity. Speech is not merely communicative but also creative; therefore, it requires the broadest possible protection. Baker (1978: 1002) argues that only three types of speech are not protected: (1) speech that causes or attempts to cause physical injury to another person or property; (2) speech designed to disrespect and distort the integrity of another's mental processes; and (3) speech not chosen by the speaker and which cannot be attributed to the speaker's manifestation of her substantive values. Examples of unprotected types of speech include fraud, perjury, blackmail, espionage, and treason. Unclear why all forms of hate speech are protected as they may violate types 1 and 2. The puzzle grows as Baker states in the same article (Baker 1978: 1009) that as long as speech "represents the freely-chosen expression of the speaker while depending for its power on the free acceptance of the listener and is not used in the context of violent or coercive activity, freedom of speech represents a charter of liberty for noncoercive action." This is an acceptable argument but unclear why, then, Baker defends hate speech. Does Baker think that all forms of hate speech are non-violent and noncoercive? What does Baker have in mind when he protects what he calls "hate speech"?

Baker's 1996 "First Amendment and the Internet" does not say a word about hate speech. In later writings, Baker (2008: 1, 2012: 79) argues that hate speech regulation is more likely to contribute to genocidal events and racial violence than to reduce them. No evidence is provided to substantiate this claim. In order to persuade that hate regulation is wrong and harmful, Baker reminds us of American history, when courts regularly approved limitations on free speech. However, his examples have little to do, if at all, with hate speech. Baker (2008: 2, 2012: 59) speaks of speech favoring socialism, communism, and anarchism. His discussions lack focus.

In his studies, Baker often uses two methods to promote his free speech agenda: the either–or method and the lumping method. Baker (2009: 151, 2012: 73) suggests, for instance, that more active and effective opposition to racism is likely to come from social practices "of not tolerating racist expression than from laws making it illegal." Baker does not explain why we need to choose between these two alternatives. Many liberal democracies opt to use both social practices and laws in fighting down racism. They use education to promote a tolerant and pluralist culture, and they also resort to hate speech regulations. To convince his readers, Baker also lumps together different forms of speech that at one point or another were subject to regulation. He hammers the same arguments time and again (Baker 2008, 2009, 2012) without examining concrete cases in which hate speech had resulted in hate crimes. Unfortunately, these do exist, especially in the land of the First Amendment. Baker is not interested to engage with such cases. Instead, he reminds us of unjustifiable restrictions on communist and anarchist speech as if these are relevant to the discussion on hate speech.

The Autonomy Argument

The liberty theory is based on the premise that the community must respect individual autonomy as an end in itself (Baker 1980: 822). The Autonomy Argument is the key in Baker's defense of freedom of expression. Baker argues that a central aim of democracies is to promote substantive autonomy. By *substantive* autonomy Baker (2008: 5, 2009: 143, 2012: 64) means the actual capacity and opportunities a person has "to lead the best, most meaningful self-directed life possible." Democracy is the only political order that embodies a normative principle of equal respect for people's right to be engaged in self-determination activities (Baker 2009: 146, 2012: 67). Democracy acts illegitimately when its rules and actions are inconsistent with respect for individual autonomy, for equality, and for liberty. It is unjust to restrict hate speech (Baker 2009: 152). Our commitment to democracy requires protection of political speech and public discourse (Baker 1997: 1015, 2009: 145). Baker (1989: 59, 1997: 992, 2009: 142) argues that respect for personhood, for agency, and for autonomy requires that individuals be permitted to be themselves. Democracy embodies liberty, and liberty is fundamental (Baker 1989: 30, 278, 1997: 1020). This idea was originally presented by John Stuart Mill (1948; 1973; 1975, and 1976) who argued that the duty to oneself means self-respect and self-development. The duties we have to ourselves are not socially obligatory, unless circumstances make them at the same time duties to others. Pursuing a utilitarian argument, Mill (1948, Chap. 4) constantly struggled to establish a distinction between self- and other-regarding conduct, wishing to secure the freest possible sphere for self-regarding conduct, but Mill was forced to acknowledge that paternalism may be warranted even in matters that concern the self (Cohen-Almagor 2012).

Baker is far less paternalistic than Mill and far more suspicious of the government. With Justice William O. Douglas, he would argue that the Constitution was designed to take the government off the backs of people (William O. Douglas Quote 2019). The government's role, according to Baker (2009), is limited to ensuring that individuals can present themselves and their values to others. Its legitimacy is dependent on the ability to promote individual autonomy. The content of expression is immaterial. The law must respect the freedom of the racist to express her views (Baker 2008: 9, 2009: 146, 2012: 67). Racist hate speech is as legitimate as respectful speech. Both types of speech embody the speaker's view of the world and express her values. As the government is to take the speaker's autonomy and her self-development very seriously, all forms of speech should be protected. Legal restrictions on racist or hate speech are prohibited because they violate the speaker's formal autonomy. Dworkin (2009) expressed a similar view.

Thus, while Baker (1997: 987) writes that the seriousness of harms caused by speech should never be underestimated, he does not seriously consider the interests of the audience, of the bystander, and of the society at large. In his liberty model, these are secondary. In the forefront are considerations relating to the speaker's autonomy, and the government should provide her with all the possibilities to cultivate her ideas and to promote her values, even if those values are vile and come at the expense of the values of other members of society. Baker assumes that capacities to speak in society are equal, and people, as speakers, are always able to promote their values and ideas. People choose whether they are to be offended by hate speech. It is up to them to take notice of the speaker's words or to ignore those words.

I wonder whether the issue is that simple. Consider the following. Rebecca is a Holocaust survivor. On Holocaust Remembrance Day, she is invited to the local radio station to tell her personal story including the years she spent at the notorious Auschwitz death camp. At the radio studio, she is told that David was invited as well. David is known for his uncompromising belief that the Holocaust was fabricated by Jews to blackmail the world in order to establish the State of Israel. Rebecca has no choice but to listen to David who, inter alia, argued that Auschwitz was a country club; that women like Rebecca "dined and wined" in Auschwitz, had parties, and enjoyed the resort's swimming pools. David in effect told his audience, including Rebecca, that she is a liar. She, and others, invented the greatest fabrication story in history and that she even went the extra mile by carving numbers on her arm, alleging that this was part of a plan to dehumanize her. Now, is it really up to Rebecca to decide whether she should be offended by these claims? Can she decide *not* to be offended and then she would not?

I think not. This scenario is not a fragment of my imagination. It is loosely based on a real event that took place in Canada in 1987, when Sabina Citron, of the Holocaust survivors organization, was invited to speak on a CBC radio show, hosted by David Schatzky, in which people can phone in to talk on whether the notorious Holocaust denial Ernst Zündel deserved a new trial. Citron was invited to the studio to explain her position and to answer questions, and she agreed to do so after receiving assurance that she would be spared the need to confront Zündel. He would not be invited. But against this agreement, Zündel was invited to speak on the program. Citron was interviewed for approximately the same length of time (6 min) that was given to Zündel. Citron had to hear him saying things like "Germans are innocent of the charge of genocide against the Jews ... Sabina Citron's friends, and Sabina Citron herself, had every opportunity during that seven-and-a-half-week trial, Mr. Shatsky (sic), to bring us the orders for the extermination of the Jews. They cannot because there is none" (Full text of Background and Detailed Chronology of Ernst Zuendel Persecution 1996). After her interview, against the agreement, Citron was not allowed to respond to callers. When she found she could not answer callers, Citron stormed off the radio studio.

Citron was forced to speak on the same program with Zündel who denied her Holocaust ordeal. It was a horrifying and traumatic experience which has tormented Citron for years. We discussed the issue 16 years later, in 2003 (Cohen-Almagor 2013), and she was still very much under the impression of that event. She described it in detail and was still very angry with the CBC for the insensitive way they handled the issue. Schatzky and his producers failed to recognize the ethical problem they had orchestrated; they did not try to minimize harm but rather gave voice to a bigot so he could torment "the Jew" with his brute lies, denying Citron's past and circulating via a respectable media program hateful ideas, distorted history, and false news. That this episode was so traumatic for Citron is hardly surprising. When a group of American Nazis attempted to march in Skokie, one of the suburbs of Chicago, inhabited mostly by Jews, some hundreds of them being survivors of Nazi concentration camps, there were testimonies by psychologists on the possible injuries many Jews would suffer as a result of the march. They argued that this speech act might be regarded as the equivalent of a physical assault (Cohen-Almagor 2005; Keneally 2018).

Baker points out that (a) the values underlying the right to free speech are values not themselves derived from the speech's harmlessness, and therefore are not undercut by the speech's harmfulness, and (b) that almost all the harm that free speech does is mediated casually by mental processes of the audience. Per Mill's (1948: 114) famous example in *On Liberty*, harm is done when a speaker asserts before an agitated crowd assembled outside the house of a corn dealer that corn dealers are starvers of the poor. This constitutes incitement to violence. But, Baker (1997: 991) asserts, the house might be set ablaze not because of the speech, but because of action. The crowd chose to be agitated, accepted the incitement, and followed it to its destructive outcome. The speaker contributes only through "mental mediation." The hearer must determine a response. The response need not necessarily be harmful. Any consequences involved in the listener's response must be attributed in the end to the listener. The result is a right of the speaker to present her viewpoint even if the assimilation by the listener leads to or constitutes serious harm. Baker (1997: 992) does not take any notice of the corn dealer's interests and his safety and security. His care for the protection of freedom of expression outweighs the protection of life and security of the target of incitement.

Baker (1997: 990–993) maintains that a speaker's racial epithet harms the hearer only through her understanding of the message. Baker reiterates that harm depends on mental mediation. The hearer must determine a response. Baker is oblivious to the concept of vulnerability. He consistently fails to grasp just how vulnerable targeted groups in society are. He fails to understand that the issue is not merely of strong-willed individuals who are capable of choosing the right response: they have several options: to be offended, to suffer psychological harm, to ignore, to take something positive from the hateful slur, to learn from it, and so on. But sometimes the pain is so strong, so immediate, so penetrating, and so instant that this luxury of choosing a response is absent. Such choice is in the mind of strong-willed liberals like Baker. It is not a mental process readily available to targeted minorities who wish to have equal standing in society and feel that they need to fight for it, still.

In this context Jeremy Waldron (2012: 171) notes that to the extent that the message conveyed by the racist already puts the target group on the defensive, and distracts them from the ordinary business of life, to that extent the racist speech has already succeeded in one of its destructive aims. Waldron (2012: 165) rightly notes that it remains the case that hate speech damages the dignity and reputation of individuals in vulnerable groups (Waldron 2010); it undermines the public good of socially furnished assurance with which the dignity of ordinary people is supported; it remains the case that the hateful disclosure of racist attitudes through public speech defaces and pollutes the environment in which members of vulnerable groups have to live their lives and bring up their children.

Baker sees a direct connection between freedom of expression and one's autonomy: preventing a speaker from articulating her opinion directly limits her autonomy. The value of autonomy requires respect and protection of all viewpoints, notwithstanding how harmful those might be. Baker speaks in terms of values: value of free expression and value of autonomy. Granted that in the lofty realm of ideas, all should be permissible. But when we need to weigh the tangible consequences of ideas, things are becoming much more complex and problematic. It is unclear, for instance, why we need to protect the autonomy of a speaker who declares her aim "to eradicate society from the gay disease" or who draws a comparison between cancer and certain people, saying we should fight them as we fight cancer.

At times, Baker's (2008: 5, 2009: 143) argument becomes muddled and incoherent when he argues that hate speech does not interfere with or contradict anyone else's formal autonomy (by which Baker means formal equality) even if the speech does cause injuries "that sometimes include undermining others' substantive autonomy." Unclear on what basis Baker makes this point. A majority that espouses racism and hate against minorities create conditions for discrimination that might undermine the position of these minorities in society. A relevant distinction is between *formal citizenship and full citizenship*. Minorities in such an environment may possess formal citizenship yet lack full citizenship. Elsewhere, it is argued (Cohen-Almagor and Wattad 2018) that this is the situation of the Arab-Palestinian minority in Israel.

Baker (2008: 4) argues that the state respects people's autonomy if it allows people to express their own values – "no matter what these values are and irrespective of how this expressive content harms other people." This statement is contested. Most liberal democracies introduce restrictions on expressive content when it might harm other people. The United States imposes restrictions on some forms of harmful speech, such as defamation and fraud. Where hate speech is concerned, the *Schenck* (1919) and *Brandenburg* (1969) precedents prohibit incitement. The constitutional tools do exist for American courts to regulate hate speech where it rises to the level of incitement or constitutes an imminent threat of harm. Furthermore, most liberal democracies have adopted some forms of hate speech regulations (Bleich 2011a, b; Waldron 2012; Cohen-Almagor 2016; Article 19 2018). Arguing that Australia, Austria, Belgium, Canada, France, Germany, Italy, Switzerland, and the United Kingdom, among other countries, respect people's autonomy less than the United States requires a detailed explanation, which Baker does not provide.

Baker fails to provide an iron-clad reasoning to convince us that the autonomy of the speaker and her right to freedom of expression should always enjoy precedence over competing values. Practically speaking, upholding autonomy as a general shield for any opinion is very dangerous. We need to address the ethical meaning of the speech in question, the circumstances, and the likely consequences of the utterance: Why should we tolerate manifestly unethical expressions ("A dead nigger is a good nigger"; "Jews are good for the gas industry"; "rape is exciting both for the rapist and for the woman")? What is the likelihood that the dangerous views might translate into discriminatory and harmful action? What are the consequences of unrestricted tolerance?

Baker (2008: 16, 2009: 152, 2012: 73, 77) argues that by causing racism to go underground, speech prohibitions are likely to obscure the extent of the problem as well as the location or the social carriers of the problem. It might also undermine the liberal-democratic culture of society. He further argues that speech prohibitions can increase racist individuals' or groups' sense of oppression and, thereby, their rage and belief that they must act. Their frustration might lead them to violence.

I wonder why Baker takes this trouble of providing consequentialist reasoning when his view is essentially principled as is evident in his discussion of formal autonomy. He objects to free speech legislation. Baker (2008:1, 2009: 139, 2012: 57) identifies himself as an advocate of "almost absolute protection of free speech." It does not occur to him that racism might oppress minorities and that unregulated hate speech might exacerbate and excite speakers to translate their harmful speech into harmful action. Contra Baker, one may argue that free racist speech might increase the likelihood that racism will be expressed in overt violence. Spiral of hatred can motivate and push bigots into action. Violent speech may lead to violent action. The argument expressed by many American liberals including Baker (2012), Meiklejohn (1961, 1965), Emerson (1970), Bollinger (1986), and Dworkin (2011) that hate speech legislation might lead to a less tolerant society is thus contested. It can equally be argued that allowing hate mongers to disseminate their views freely undermines tolerance and human rights protection.

As for the fear of undergrounds, it is unclear what is less damaging: to allow freely aired bigotry in public or drive it underground. Waldron argues that we actually want to isolate the bigots rather than permit them contact and coordination.

True, there is a cost involved as transparency is lost, but it is not at all clear that driving the hateful message underground is altogether a bad thing (Waldron 2012: 95–96). Furthermore, as Parekh (2012: 52, 2017) notes, when extremist groups go underground, they are denied the oxygen of publicity and the aura of legitimacy and respectability. This makes it harder for them to link with like-minded people.

Baker offers three "empirical suppositions" against hate speech regulation: speech prohibitions will be ineffective, regulation of hate speech "may affirmatively contribute to the rise of racist genocidal cultures or polities," and a key element in the most effective strategy of preventing the rise of such a culture is to provide for more robust protection of speech. Curiously, although Baker (2012: 78–79) claims these are "empirical suppositions," he does not bring any empirical evidence to substantiate his claims.

Mere unsubstantiated assertions are no substitute for careful reasoning, but Baker (2009: 156, 2012: 78) tends to resort to them to press his argument. He writes that prohibition laws "would not have, or perhaps rather might not have prevented" the genocide in Rwanda "or elsewhere." This statement raises many questions. First, how does Baker know? Is he an expert on Rwanda's culture and politics? On what basis does he say this? Second, what does he mean by "or elsewhere"? Does he mean that prohibition laws never work and resorting to them is never helpful? Did he conduct a comprehensive survey to substantiate this assertion? If he did, then it is something that he is not confident enough to report. No references are provided. If he did not, then this is simply a sloppy line of argumentation.

In his 2009 article, Baker writes, "Many countries that have experienced the worst racist violence have, in fact, had such prohibitions without successfully preventing racist or genocidal results" (p. 147). Baker substantiates this claim with a footnote which says, "I was told at the conferences were this paper was presented that both Rwanda before the genocide and Nazi and pre-Nazi Germany are examples." Baker saw no reason to substantiate their saying with research.

In his articles, Baker consistently makes pro-speech and anti-regulation hypotheses without testing them. Thus, Baker (2008: 12) hypothesizes that at earlier stages legal prohibitions would not be effective against relevant forms of hate speech and at later stages enforcement will not occur, will be counter-productive, or will focus on the wrong targets. As an empirical matter, Baker (2008: 14; 2009: 150) "suspects" that free speech prohibitions will not be effective at reducing the chances of horrendous results. He also "suspects" that provisions on hate speech will exacerbate problems and increase the likelihood of horrendous results, and Baker (2009: 152) speculates that hate speech prohibitions may do little. Researchers should avoid speculations and substantiate them with concrete evidence. Likewise, having "suspicions" is a good trigger for conducting research, but Baker is more an ideologue than a social scientist. He does not conduct investigations aimed at substantiating or refuting his assumptions. Baker does not analyze the effectiveness of hate speech legislation in liberal democracies nor does he consider sporadic episodes of hate speech that led to hate crimes that resulted in multiple deaths. Making hypotheses without testing them is a curious practice.

Baker (2012: 79) dismissed the Harm Argument by saying that racism is not the only speech that causes harm. But why does it matter? Does the fact that other forms of speech create harm justify inaction regarding another form of speech that creates harm? Most staggeringly, Baker expresses very little sympathy for those who will pay the price for the tolerance he preaches.

Baker (2008: 19, 2009: 154, 2012: 76–77) does not trust government to do the right thing. He thinks that restrictive laws are likely to be abused by those in power. He raises the slippery-slope argument according to which those in power will draw the lines and shape the legitimate and illegitimate categories of speech in a way that would suit their partisan political interests. Their opponent's speech will be regarded as hate speech beyond the scope of tolerance.

In response, the slippery-slope argument does not really address the justifications for free speech prohibitions. All it does is to warn against employing it carelessly (Schauer 1985; Volokh 2003). Indeed, we must be strict with free speech limitations and prescribe them only when it is appropriate so as to prevent its cynical misuse in prohibiting freedom of expression. Prescribing boundaries to freedom of expression requires a painstaking effort, involving careful consideration and lucid articulation, so as to avoid sliding down the slope and allowing room for illiberal interpretations that would broaden it unnecessarily. Checks and balances on governmental decisions should be maintained. But the fear of abuse should not compel us to ignore the problems of racism and hate speech. Speculative fears of something that might happen in the future should not make us silent in face of tangible threats, here and now, voiced against vulnerable communities.

Baker (2009: 157) concludes that given (in his mind) the lack of adequate evidence for any certainty about "the guess whether suppression or freedom provides the best security," wisdom requires that choice favor liberty. "For this reason," Baker (2009: 157) maintains, recognizing that the guess may turn out to be wrong, he "would rather have hazarded the guess that justifies a concern with the circumstances and future of humanity." It is unclear why guessing is required. Many European countries have cautionary laws designed to protect against the harms of hate speech. These restrictive regulations stem from the belief that all people are worthy of respect and deserve dignity. Some people deserve protections against those who abuse their free speech privileges. All European democracies, without exception, do not permit bigots the wide scope for speech that they enjoy in the United States. It is hard to imagine, for instance, that the British authorities would allow an explicit "British Nazi Party," under the swastika flag, the right to organize on its soil. The United States is the only country in the world that permits the operation of a Nazi party. In 2017, the Southern Poverty Law Center named 121 American neo-Nazi organizations all over the United States. On average, US residents experienced approximately 250,000 hate crime victimizations each year between 2004 and 2015, of which about 230,000 were violent hate victimizations. The number of total and violent hate crime victimizations did not change significantly from 2004 to 2015 (Masucci and Langton 2017). In his writings, Baker does not mention or examine even one of those hate crime incidents.

A study conducted by the Southern Poverty Law Center shows that between 2009 and 2014 nearly 100 people have been murdered by active users of one American hate website, Stormfront.org (Beirich 2014; Dickson 2014). The incidents include the killing of three Pittsburgh police officers by Richard Poplawski in 2009. Two years later, in 2011, Anders Behring Breivik's murderous journey in which he detonated a truck bomb in front of a government building in Oslo, killing 8, and then went on a shooting spree in Utoya Island, murdering 69 others. In May 2012, Jason Todd Ready killed four people before killing himself. That same month, Eric Clinton Kirk Newman, also known as Luca Rocco Magnotta, was accused of torturing and dismembering a Chinese immigrant; 3 months later, Wade Michael Page shot and killed six people at a Sikh temple before killing himself during a shootout with police. In 2014, between 200,000 and 400,000 Americans visited Stormfront every month (Stephens-Davidowitz 2014), and it has been said to have more than 300,000 registered users (Hatewatch 2017). The site openly promotes racial violence and was used, along with dailystormer.org, to organize and encourage participation in the fatal "Unite the Right" rally (Lawyers' Committee for Civil Rights Under Law 2017).

On August 12, 2017, James Alex Fields Jr. rammed his car into a crowd of anti-fascist protesters united against the "Unite the Right" white supremacist rally in Charlottesville, Virginia. Fields killed 32-year-old Heather Heyer and injured dozens other. Prior to this attack, Fields associated himself with the alt-right movement, which includes white supremacists and neo-Nazis. On his Facebook account, Fields regularly posted photos that expressed support for Nazism, fascism, and racism. Photos showed Fields with members of "Vanguard America" (https://national vanguard.org/), a neo-Nazi group that is part of the "Nationalist Front" (https://www.nfunity.org/). A silver lining resulting from the Charlottesville tragedy is that many Internet Service Providers and Web-Hosting Companies that were friendly to racial propaganda, acting in an irresponsible akrasian way (i.e., acting against one's better judgment), have now ousted from their servers websites associated with white supremacism and neo-Nazism (Associated Press 2017). Stormfront was briefly shut down in August 2017, but reopened in October 2017 (Schulberg et al. 2017). Such a poisonous website would not enjoy the protection of, for instance, British and German laws.

I have criticized Baker for his near absolutism, for stretching the Free Speech Principle widely to cover almost all forms of expression, and for emphasizing the speakers' interests at the expense of their targets. To be constructive, an alternative approach is suggested, one that harnesses the interests of speakers, of targets, of audiences, and of society at large. Speech comes with costs, and these costs should not be ignored (Schauer 2000). In his constructive comments on an earlier draft of this chapter, Wayne Sumner asked when does hate speech rise to the level of incitement? Must it be directly causally linked to an actual hate crime? Sumner rightly thinks this requirement is too demanding. Is it then enough that the speech might give rise to such a crime? But then the criterion is not demanding enough and would justify a near total ban on any form of hate speech. We need to define a middle ground between the two extremes. This is my task in the last part of this chapter.

The Promotional Approach

The promotional approach (PA) is based on several foundations: (1) rejection of content neutrality; (2) acceptance of some form of perfectionism; (3) balancing; (4) denying legitimacy; and (5) excluding incitement and profound offense from the Free Speech Principle.

Rejection of Content Neutrality

Conceptually, the concept of content neutrality emphasizes diversity and plurality. Diversity entails openness and more opportunities for living a valuable and richer life. Pluralism is perceived indispensable for having the potential for a good life. Methodologically, the idea of neutrality is placed within the broader concept of anti-perfectionism. The implementation and promotion of conceptions of the good, though worthy in themselves, are not regarded as a legitimate matter for governmental action. The fear of exploitation, of some form of discrimination, leads to the advocacy of plurality and diversity. Consequently, governments are not to act in a way that might favor some ideas over others. No single belief about moral issues and values should guide all, and therefore, each has to enjoy autonomy and to hold her ideals freely.

The concept of anti-perfectionism comprises the "political neutrality principle" and the "exclusion of ideals" doctrine (Cohen-Almagor 1994). The "political neutrality principle" holds that policies should seek to be neutral regarding ideals of the good. It requires governments to ensure that their actions do not help acceptable ideals more than unacceptable ones; to see to it that their actions will not hinder the cause of false ideals more than they do that of true ones. The "exclusion of ideals" doctrine does not tell governments what to do. Rather it forbids them to act for certain reasons. The doctrine holds that the fact that some conceptions of the good are true or valid should never serve as justification for any action. Neither should the fact that a conception of the good is false, invalid, unreasonable, or unsound be accepted as a reason for a political or other action. The doctrine prescribes that governments refrain from using one's conception of the good as a reason for state action. They are not to hold partisan (or non-partisan) considerations about human perfection to foster social conditions (Raz 1986, pp. 110–111).

Accepting Some Form of Perfectionism

Advocates of content neutrality, in their striving to convince us of the necessity of the doctrine, are conveying the assumption that the decision regarding the proper policy is crucial because of its grave consequences. Content neutrality entails pluralism, diversity, freedom, public consensus, non-interference, vitality, and so on. If we do not adhere to neutrality, then we might be left with none of these virtues. This picture leads to the rejection of subjectivity (or perfectionism), while my view suggests a rival view that observes conduct of policies on a continuous scale between strict perfectionism, on the one hand, and complete neutrality, on the other hand. The policy to be adopted does not have to be either the one or the other. It could well take the middle ground, allowing plurality and diversity without resorting to complete neutrality, involving some form of perfectionism without resorting to coercion. For perfectionism does not necessarily imply exercise of force, nor does it impose the values and ideals of one or more segments of society on others, or strive to ensure uniformity, as neutralists fear. On this issue, my view comes close to that of Joseph Raz (1986). The PA is advocated elsewhere (Cohen-Almagor 2012a).

Balancing

A nuanced approach, one that tries to balance between competing interests, aiming at a calculus of costs, is the goal. Balancing does more justice to individuals and to society at large than Baker's near absolutist and insensitive approach. This adjudication method was adopted by many courts in the world, including the American and the Israeli courts (Pinto 2012). In the United States, in a letter to Elliot Richardson (February 29, 1952), Judge Learned Hand (Jordan and Dworkin 2013) wrote that cases should be decided ad hoc by balancing the opposing considerations and should be left to Congress. In another letter to Justice Felix Frankfurter (February 10, 1958), Hand reiterated that "values are incommensurables and the business of legislation is to strike such a balance that it will be as well accepted, by and large, as is possible, given the prevailing conventions" (Jordan and Dworkin 2013; for further discussion, see Holmes 1920, Frankfurter 1956; Cardozo 2012).

President of the Israel Supreme Court, Aharon Barak (2000), explained that behind balancing lies the understanding that not all principles are equally important in the eyes of society and that when legislative guidance is lacking, the court must appraise the relative social importance of the different principles. Barak (2000: 176) wrote, "Just as there is no person without his shadow, there is no principle without its weight. Establishing the balance on the basis of weight means giving a social estimate of the relative importance of the different principles."

Barak's views have been guiding my thinking for many years. For Barak, it is only natural that the balance changes from one case to another, according to the nature of the conflicting values. Freedom of expression needs to be weighed against the no-less-important values of personal reputation and dignity. A uniform standard must not be adopted; rather, varying standards should be adopted, according to the weight of the conflicting values and the particular circumstances of the case. The results of balancing vary according to the substance and character of the conflicting values.

Baker himself is not a fan of balancing. This is because any process that involves the weighing of interests is extremely subjective. Ad hoc balancing fails to provide effective protection, argues Baker (1980: 849), because of the systematic features of the legal order. The balancing is done in accordance with the judge's social class, and especially at times of conflict or crisis, anyone who is connected with the perceived threat might suffer a loss of freedom. Thus, absolute rules "are necessary to avoid accordion-like protection" (ibid.).

Denying Legitimacy

At the start of this chapter, several hateful expressions are noted. While they are disturbing and may trigger great discomfort, it is argued that they are still protected under the Free Speech Principle. Balancing between liberty and tolerance, on the one hand, and the offense and inconvenience, on the other hand, caused by these expressions, should be included within the scope of tolerance. Generally speaking, advocacy is protected speech.

Having said that, we should distinguish between legal and other forms of reaction to such expressions. While liberal democracies should not legislate to bar such hateful advocacy, they can work to deny them legitimacy in the public sphere. In society, there are moral norms that are of no less importance than the law. Through the education system, the media, and other channels of communication, liberal democracies can denounce such expressions, conferring them a shameful status and making people understand that these have no place in a decent society. These are not-to-be-said expressions, contra the values of the nation and its moral *raison d'être*. My promotional approach holds that the *raison d'être* of liberal democracy is founded upon two principles: respect for others, in the sense of treating citizens as equals, and not harming others, in the sense that we should address attempts made to harm others, either physically or psychologically. Accordingly, restrictions on liberty may be prescribed when threats of immediate violence are voiced against some individuals or groups and also when the expression in question is intended to inflict psychological offense, morally on a par with physical harm (Cohen-Almagor 2005).

Excluding Incitement and Profound Offense from the Free Speech Principle

Liberal democracies exclude incitement to violence from the Free Speech Principle. The United States also accepts that incitement is outside the First Amendment. As this issue is explained in detail elsewhere (Cohen-Almagor 2017), it will not be elaborated here.

The second exception is more controversial as offense is perceived as a problematic ground to warrant restriction. *Most cases* in which the expression "offense to sensibilities" is used do not involve the type of behavior that causes emotional incapacity, a sort of assault on the person's sensibilities (Feinberg 1985; Cohen-Almagor 2006, Chaps. 4–5; Pinto 2010: Smits 2016, Chap. 8). The reference here is to profound offense, formulating the offense to sensibilities argument as possible grounds for restricting free expression when the expression might cause severe damage to the target person/s. The task of definition is truly problematic because of the difficulty in assessing emotional and psychological offense. At the same time, we should acknowledge that certain expressions under certain circumstances might hurt no less than physical harm. An irreversible offense to the sensibilities of a person, which brings that person to a state of shock or constant dejection, is arguably more harmful than injury to one's arm or leg, or irreversible damage to one's kidneys. While a person can live without a limb or a kidney, one might lose the taste for life if the offense to sensibilities is devastating and irreversible. In extreme cases, it can cause the victims to lose their human dignity. Thus, we must not avoid discussion of the Offense to Sensibilities Argument, but rather invest more efforts to set defensible criteria for restriction. Instead of being discouraged from the outset, we must make greater, more rigorous attempts to find sensible solutions.

My line of reasoning places the individual at the center in examining whether the individual needs protection from certain expressions because they might offend one's emotional and spiritual system. The Offense to Sensibilities Argument *in and of itself* can serve as grounds for restricting freedom of expression in extreme cases when the offense is severe; even more so when the target group (individual or individuals) cannot avoid being exposed to the offense, and the consequences of the offense might be destructive. The factors that must be taken into account are the content of the expression, the manner of expression, the duration and intensity of the offense, the frequency of the offense, the intentions of the speaker, the circumstances which include the avoidability standard and the presence of mitigating factors, and the consequences of speech. Examples to prohibition on grounds of profound offense include Nazi marches in Jewish neighborhoods, introducing a pig head in front of a synagogue, KKK cross-burning in front of a home of an African-American family, statements like "All Muslims are terrorists and pigs," and promoting the sales of Salman Rushdie's *The Satanic Verses* in front of a mosque.

It is incumbent on those who restrict speech on grounds of profound offense to examine *all* the above factors. While it is possible to think of cases in which not all these factors exist and we might still prohibit certain expressions (e.g., astute politicians may not explicitly admit that their intention is to hurt the target group), we still require to examine all these factors when we consider prohibition on grounds of causing profound offense.

Whenever we come to restrict speech, the onus for limiting free expression is always with the one who wishes to limit expression. Concrete evidence should be produced to justify restriction. The speech must be dangerous and/or harmful. The danger and/or harm cannot be implicit or implied. If speech would be prohibited only because its danger might be implied from an unclear purpose that is opened for interpretations, then the scope for curtailing fundamental democratic rights is too broad, and the slippery-slope syndrome becomes tangible. The implicit way is not the path that liberals should tread on when pondering restricting of freedom of expression. This does not mean that we should not be vigilant in protecting our democracy. But mere suspicion, "bad tendency" (*Gitlow v. New York* 1925; see Rabban 1999; Bollinger and Stone 2002) will not do to override basic freedoms. The American Supreme Court explicitly overruled the bad tendency test in *Brandenburg v. Ohio* (1969).

Conclusion

In a democracy, people must enjoy absolute freedom to advocate and debate ideas, but this is so long as they refrain from abusing this freedom to attack the rights of others or their status in society as human beings and equal members of the community. The freedom of one should be balanced and weighed against the freedom of others. Boundless liberty is a recipe for anarchy. Democracy is founded on two basic principles: respect for others and not harming others. The first stems from Kantian ethics. It speaks of respecting people as rational beings and of autonomy in terms of self-legislation (Kant 1997). The second is derived from Mill's (Mill 1948) philosophy. We respect the rights of individuals so long as they do not harm others. For Mill, harmful conduct should be restricted when the speech or action in question warrant it in accordance with a consequentialist balancing-of-interests test. These principles are the lighthouse according to which democratic morality and policies are formed. *There is* right and wrong. There is a standard, a moral compass that guides our reasoning. Not all views have equal standing in society, just as not all actions have equal standing. As we know it is wrong to kill another person, we also know it is wrong to incite others to kill. Absolute content neutrality should be replaced by the promotional approach which follows the principles of respecting others and not harming others. It is the democratic duty to protect third parties, vulnerable people. Indeed, often the litmus test for the extent of democratization of any given society is the status of its minorities. The more equal the minorities are, enjoying equal standing in society like any other member, the more democratic the society usually is.

Baker (and also Scanlon 1977, 1979, 1995, 2003, and n/d, unpublished paper; Meiklejohn 1965, 1966, 2000) endorses viewpoint-neutrality especially when social and political speech is concerned. Like Tribe (1988: 790), Baker believed that if the First Amendment means anything, it means that government has no power to restrict expression because of its message, ideas, subject matter, or content. Certain expressions might be evil and dangerous, but we still should tolerate them, notwithstanding what we think of those expressions and notwithstanding the price that we, as a society, may require to pay.

People, as rationale and moral beings, can recognize evil when they see it and argue on moral grounds that certain kinds of speech are beyond tolerance. Anti-Semitic and Islamophobic assertions are, of course, political, aimed to bring societal changes. Yet most people would not defend speakers who hold "Jews are good for gas chambers" or "Good Arabs are dead Arabs." Baker would not like such expressions but would ultimately allow them due to his overriding suspicion of government. The permissibility of such expressions derives from Baker's unwillingness to grant governments the power to regulate speech on certain grounds.

Limitations on freedom of expression should be crafted with great care. Boundaries to freedom of expression should be introduced with cautiousness and due process. Once the speech is designed to harm others, it becomes questionable. Questions then arise about its legitimacy. The state ought to weigh the costs of allowing hate speech as well as the risks involved and balance these against the costs and risks to democracy and free speech associated with censorship. Baker does recognize that harmful speech has costs and his near absolutism dictates that these costs must be borne by the victims of the harmful speech. This view is contested. Instead, a balancing approach is endorsed. Balancers of free expression insist on proving a direct link between the harmful expression and the resulting harmful action: the government has to establish a nexus of harm linking the proscribed utterance to some grave and imminent threat of tangible injury. This would require that the government perform a contextual analysis drawing on empirical data. Who was harmed? How were they harmed? What are the competing interests and how do we balance between them? It is similar to what we demand of the plaintiff in a libel case. And if the argument also brings in society's right of self-defense, then we should seek evidence of a real threat to individuals and/or social stability.

References

Abrams F (2017) The Soul of the first amendment. New Haven: Yale University Press

Alford JR (2001) We're all in this together. The decline of trust in government, 1958–1996. In: Hibbing JR, Theiss-Morse E (eds) What is it about government that Americans dislike? Cambridge University Press, Cambridge

Article 19 (2018) Responding to 'hate speech': comparative overview of six EU countries. Article 19, London. https://www.article19.org/wp-content/uploads/2018/03/ECA-hate-speech-compilation-report_March-2018.pdf

Associated Press (2017) Neo-Nazi site's publisher says he's got no home on Internet. NY Times (August 16). https://www.nytimes.com/aponline/2017/08/16/us/ap-us-neo-nazi-website-sued.html

Baker CE (1978) Scope of the first amendment freedom of speech. UCLA Law Rev 25:964–1040

Baker CE (1980) Press rights and government power to structure the Press. U Miami Law Rev 34: 819–889

Baker CE (1989) Human liberty and freedom of speech. Oxford University Press, New York

Baker CE (1996) First amendment and the Internet: will free speech principles applied to the media apply here? J Civil Rights Econ Dev 11(3):Article 17

Baker CE (1997) Harm, liberty and free speech. South Calif Law Rev 70:979–1020

Baker CE (2008) Hate speech. University of Pennsylvania Law School, Faculty Scholarship, Paper 198:1–23

Baker CE (2009) Autonomy and hate speech. In: Hare I, Weinstein J (eds) Extreme speech and democracy. Oxford University Press, Oxford, pp 139–157

Baker CE (2012) Chap 3 Hate speech. In: Herz M, Molnar P (eds) The content and context of hate speech. Cambridge University Press, New York

Barak A (2000) Freedom of expression and its limitations. In: Cohen-Almagor R (ed) Challenges to democracy: essays in honour and memory of Isaiah Berlin. Ashgate Publishing Ltd., Aldershot, pp 167–188

Barker P (ed) (1999) Living as equals. Oxford University Press, New York

Beirich H (2014) Frazier Glenn Miller, Longtime Anti-Semite, Arrested in Kansas Jewish Community center murders. splcenter.org (April 13)

Bleich E (2011a) The rise of hate speech and hate crime laws in liberal democracies. J Ethn Migr Stud 37(6):917–934

Bleich E (2011b) The freedom to be racist? Oxford University Press, New York

Bollinger LC (1986) The tolerant society. Clarendon Press, Oxford

Bollinger LC (2010) Uninhibited, Robust, and Wide-open: a free press for a new century. Oxford University Press, New York

Bollinger LC, Stone GR (eds) (2002) Eternally vigilant: free speech in the modern era. University of Chicago Press, Chicago

Brandenburg v. Ohio, 395 U.S. 444 (1969)

Cardozo BN (2012) The paradoxes of legal science. Columbia University Press, New York, p 1956

Cohen M, Nagel T, Scanlon T (eds) (1977) Equality and preferential treatment. Princeton University Press, Princeton

Cohen-Almagor R (1994) The boundaries of liberty and tolerance. The University Press of Florida, Gainesville

Cohen-Almagor R (2005) Speech, media, and ethics: the limits of free expression. Palgrave Macmillan, Houndmills/New York

Cohen-Almagor R (2006) The scope of tolerance: studies on the costs of free expression and freedom of the Press. Routledge, London/New York

Cohen-Almagor R (2012) Between autonomy and state regulation: J.S. Mill's elastic paternalism. Philosophy 87(4):557–582

Cohen-Almagor R (2012a) Content net neutrality – a critique. In: Demir H (ed) Luciano Floridi's philosophy of technology: critical reflections. Springer, Dordrecht, pp 151–167

Cohen-Almagor R (2013) Freedom of expression v. social responsibility: holocaust denial in Canada. J Mass Media Ethics 28(1):42–56

Cohen-Almagor R (2015) Confronting the Internet's dark side: moral and social responsibility on the free highway. Cambridge University Press and Woodrow Wilson Center Press, New York/Washington, DC

Cohen-Almagor R (2016) Hate and racist speech in the United States – a critique. Philos Public Iss 6(1):77–123. http://fqp.luiss.it/2016/11/29/hate-and-racist-speech-in-the-united-states-a-critique/

Cohen-Almagor R (2017) JS Mill's boundaries of freedom of expression: a critique. Philosophy 92: 565–596

Cohen-Almagor R (2019) Racism and hate speech – a critique of Scanlon's contractual theory. First Amendment Stud 53:41–66

Cohen-Almagor R, Haleva-Amir S (2008) Bloody Wednesday in Dawson College – the story of Kimveer Gill, or why should we monitor certain websites to prevent murder. Stud Ethics Law Technol 2(3):Article 1. Available at: http://works.bepress.com/raphael_cohen_almagor/1

Cohen-Almagor R, Wattad MS (2018) The legal status of Israeli-Arabs/Palestinians. GNLU Law Soc Rev 1:1–28

Collin v. Smith, 578 F.2d 1197 (7th Cir.), cert. denied 439 U.S. 915 (1978)

Croft J, Ahmed S (2018) The Pittsburgh synagogue shooting is believed to be the deadliest attack on Jews in American history, the ADL says. CNN (October 28). https://edition.cnn.com/2018/10/27/us/jewish-hate-crimes-fbi/index.html

Dearden L (2018) Gab: inside the social network where alleged Pittsburgh synagogue shooter posted final message. The Independent (October 28). https://www.independent.co.uk/news/world/americas/pittsburgh-synagogue-shooter-gab-robert-bowers-final-posts-online-comments-a8605721.html

Dickson C (2014) Where white supremacists breed online. The Daily Beast (April 17). http://www.thedailybeast.com/articles/2014/04/17/where-white-supremacists-breed-online.html?utm_medium=email&utm_source=newsletter&utm_campaign=cheatsheet_afternoon&cid=newsletter%3Bemail%3Bcheatsheet_afternoon&utm_term=Cheat%20Sheet

Dorsen N (1988) Is there a right to stop offensive speech? The case of the Nazis at Skokie. In: Gostin L (ed) Civil liberties in conflict. Routledge, London/New York, pp 122–135

Douglas, William O. Quote (2019). http://izquotes.com/quote/52709

Dworkin RM (1983) Why liberals should believe in equality. New York Rev Books (February 3)

Dworkin RM (1985) A matter of principle. Clarendon Press, Oxford

Dworkin R (1986) Introduction. In: Dworkin RM (ed) The philosophy of law. Oxford University Press, Oxford, pp 14–15

Dworkin RM (2002) Sovereign virtue: the theory and practice of equality. Harvard University Press, Cambridge, MA

Dworkin R (2009) Foreword. in Ivan Hare and James Weinstein (eds.), Extreme speech and democracy. Oxford: Oxford University Press, pp. v–ix

Dworkin R (2011) Justice for hedgehogs. Cambridge, MA, Belknap

Emerson TI (1970) The system of freedom of expression. Random House, New York

Feinberg J (1985) Offense to others. Oxford University Press, New York

Frankfurter F (1956) Of law and men: papers and addresses of Felix Frankfurter 1939–1956. Harcourt Brace, New York

Fried A (1996) McCarthyism, the great American Red Scare. Oxford University Press, New York

Full text of "Background and Detailed Chronology of Ernst Zuendel Persecution (1996). https://www.archive.org/stream/BackgroundAndDetailedChronologyOfErnstZuendelPersecutionEN199693P./Background%20and%20Detailed%20Chronology%20of%20Ernst%20Zuendel%20Persecution%20(EN,%201996,%2093%20p.)_djvu.txt

Gey SG (2004) A few questions about cross burning, intimidation, and free speech. Florida State University College of Law, Public Law Research Paper, 106

Gitlow v. New York, 268 U.S. 652 (1925)

Hatewatch Staff (2017) Waning storm: Stormfront.org loses its domain (August 29). https://www.splcenter.org/hatewatch/2017/08/29/waning-storm-stormfrontorg-loses-its-domain

Henthoff N (1992) Free speech for me – but not for thee: how the American left and right relentlessly censor each other. Harper Collins, New York

Holmes OW (1920) Collected legal papers. Harcourt Brace and Howe, New York

Jordan C, Dworkin R (2013) Reason and imagination: the selected correspondence of learned hand. Oxford University Press, New York

Kant I (1997) Critique of practical reason. Cambridge University Press, Cambridge

Keneally M (2018) Skokie: the legacy of the would-be Nazi march in a town of Holocaust survivors. *ABC News* (June 22). https://abcnews.go.com/US/skokie-legacy-nazi-march-town-holocaust-survivors/story?id=56026742

Lawyers' Committee for Civil Rights Under Law (2017) Stormfront.com website shut down following successful action By National Civil Rights Organization (August 26). https://plus.google.com/u/0/+LaurenWeinstein/posts/MwpNHuFqGeK

Masucci M, Langton L (2017) Hate crime victimization, 2004–2015. U.S. Department of Justice: Office of Justice Programs Bureau of Justice Statistics (June). Washington: U.S. Department of Justice

Meiklejohn A (1961) The first amendment is an absolute. Supreme Court Rev 245–266

Meiklejohn A (1965) Political freedom. Oxford University Press, New York

Meiklejohn A (1966) Freedom of speech. In: Radcliff P (ed) Limits of liberty. Wadsworth Publishing Co., Belmont, pp 19–26

Meiklejohn A (2000) Free speech and its relation to self-government. Lawbook Exchange, Union

Mill JS (1948) On liberty, in utilitarianism, liberty, and representative government. J. M. Dent, London. Everyman's edition

Mill JS (1973) Dissertations and discussions, vol I, II. Haskell House Publishers., New York

Mill JS (1975) Three essays. Oxford University Press, Oxford

Mill JS (1976) Law and libel and liberty of the Press. In: Williams GL (ed) John Stuart Mill on politics and society. Fontana, Glasgow, pp 143–169

Neier A (1979) Defending my enemy. E.P. Dutton, New York

Newman SL (2004) American and Canadian perspectives on hate speech and the limits of free expression. In: Newman SL (ed) Constitutional politics in Canada and the United States. State University of New York Press, Albany, pp 153–173

Oshinsky DM (2005) A conspiracy so immense: the world of Joe McCarthy. Oxford University Press, New York

Parekh B (2012) Is there a case for banning hate speech? In: Herz M, Molnar P (eds) The content and context of hate speech. Cambridge University Press, New York, pp 37–56

Parekh B (2017) Limits of free speech. Philosophia 45(3):931–935

PewResearch (2014) Public trust in government: 1958–2014. http://www.people-press.org/2014/11/13/public-trust-in-government/
Pinto M (2010) What are offences to feelings really about? A new regulative principle for the multicultural era. Oxf J Leg Stud 30(4):695–723
Pinto M (2012) Offences to religious feelings in Israel: a theoretical explication of an exceptional legal doctrine. Ethnicities 12(2):233–248
Rabban D (1999) Free speech in its forgotten years, 1870–1920. Cambridge University Press, Cambridge
Raz R (1986) The morality of freedom. Clarendon Press, Oxford
Reidy P (2013) Ronald Dworkin: a new map of censorship. *Xindex* (February 14). http://www.indexoncensorship.org/2013/02/ronal-dworkin-free-speech-censorship/
Richards DAJ (1986) Toleration and the constitution. Oxford University Press, NY
Richards DAJ (1988) Toleration and free speech. Philos Public Aff 17(4):323–336
Scanlon TM (1977) A theory of freedom of expression. In: Dworkin RM (ed) The philosophy of law, pp 161–162. Reprinted from *Philosophy & Public Affairs*, 1(2) (Winter 1972): 204–226
Scanlon TM (1979) Freedom of expression and categories of expression. Univ Pittsburgh Law Rev 40(3):519–550
Scanlon TM (1995) Content regulation reconsidered. In: Lichtenberg J (ed) Democracy and the mass media. Cambridge University Press, New York, pp 331–339
Scanlon T (2003) The difficulty of tolerance. Cambridge University Press, Cambridge
Scanlon TM (n/d) Moral rights and constitutional rights (unpublished paper)
Schauer F (1982) Free Speech: A Philosophical Enquiry. New York: Cambridge University Press
Schauer F (1985) Slippery slopes. Harvard Law Rev 99:361–383
Schauer F (2000) The cost of communicative tolerance. In: Cohen-Almagor R (ed) Liberal democracy and the limits of tolerance. University of Michigan Press, Ann Arbor, pp 28–42
Schenck v. United States, 249 *U.S.* 47 (1919)
Schreker EW (2001) The age of McCarthyism. St. Martin's, Bedford
Schulberg J, Liebelson D, Craggs T (2017) The Neo-Nazis are back online. Huffington Post (October 3). http://www.huffingtonpost.com/entry/nazis-are-back-online_us_59d40719e4b06226e3f46941?m8d
Skillen A (1982) Freedom of speech. In: Graham K (ed) Contemporary political philosophy. Cambridge University Press, Cambridge, England, pp 139–159
Smits K (2016) Applying political theory. Palgrave, London
Southern Poverty Law Center, "Neo-Nazi", SPLC (2017). https://www.splcenter.org/fighting-hate/extremist-files/ideology/neo-nazi
Stephens-Davidowitz S (2014) The data of hate. *New York Times* (July 12). http://www.nytimes.com/2014/07/13/opinion/sunday/seth-stephens-davidowitz-the-data-of-hate.html
Stone GR, Bollinger LC (eds) (2018) The free speech century. Oxford University Press, New York
Tribe LH (1988) American constitutional law. Foundation Press, New York
Village of Skokie v. National Socialist Party of America, 69 Ill. 2d 605, 373 N.E.2d 21 (1978)
Virginia v. Black, 123 S. Ct. 1536 (2003)
Volokh E (2003) The mechanisms of the slippery slope. Harv Law Rev 116:1026–1137
Waldron J (2010) Dignity and defamation: the visibility of hate. Harv Law Rev 123:1596–1657
Waldron J (2012) The harm in hate speech. Harvard University Press, Cambridge, MA
Wood GS (1969) The creation of the American Republic, 1776–1787. University of North Carolina Press, Chapel Hill

Toleration of Free Speech: Imposing Limits on Elected Officials

55

Amos N. Guiora

Contents

Introduction 1140
    Preface 1140
    Looking to the Future 1142
    Proud Boys 1142
COVID and Its Impact on Tolerance-Intolerance 1143
Free Speech 1144
Tolerance-Intolerance in the Context of Free Speech 1145
Speech of National Leaders 1147
Two Different Political Regimes 1148
The United States and Israel Today 1150
Social Media 1153
Qualified Immunity 1154
Enough Is Enough 1156
Summary and Future Directions 1157
References 1158

Abstract

Tolerance is a nuanced issue, inevitably raising concerns regarding tolerant of what and whom. There is a sense of subjective judgment in the tolerance-intolerance debate; the terminology reflects particular norms, mores, customs, and traditions. What one might perceive as a healthy and tolerable challenging of existing acceptable "ways," another would not tolerate because of the very challenge it poses to society. That split between tolerance-intolerance applies to both speech and conduct. It reflects everyday tensions, challenges, and conflict. In examining the tolerance-intolerance debate in the speech context there are a number of assumptions integral to a robust, liberal democracy: the freedom of speech is given a wide swath, whereby courts broadly protect the freedom of

A. N. Guiora (✉)
S.J. Quinney College of Law, University of Utah, Salt Lake City, UT, USA
e-mail: amos.guiora@law.utah.edu

© The Author(s), under exclusive licence to Springer Nature Switzerland AG 2022
M. Sardoĉ (ed.), *The Palgrave Handbook of Toleration*,
https://doi.org/10.1007/978-3-030-42121-2_55

speech guaranteed in constitutions and legislation. While the speech may make certain sectors of the population uncomfortable, may be perceived as offensive, courts are tolerant of such speech provided it does not morph-transition into the realm of incitement.

National leaders have significant power when they speak. The scope of this chapter is limited to analyzing the extent to which national leaders' speech should be tolerated. Donald Trump and Bibi Netanyahu both provide salient examples regarding the extent to which speech should be tolerated. Both Netanyahu and Trump have used social media to great effect. The way that social media facilitates the spread of misinformation plays must be taken into account when analyzing the importance of contemporary leaders speech. In addition, the level to which qualified immunity and the freedom of speech should apply to elected officials comes under question. This chapter analyzes the extent to which qualified immunity should apply and the level of tolerance that the speech of leaders should be afforded.

Keywords

Free speech · Donald Trump · Bibi Netanyahu · Incitement · Code words · Tolerating intolerance · Social media · Qualified immunity

Introduction

Preface

These lines are written in late November/early December 2020, weeks after the Presidential election. Under normal circumstances, shortly after the final results were made public, one candidate would congratulate the other candidate on a hard fight, acknowledging the will of the people. It is an understatement to suggest the election, much less one of the candidates, met traditional American normative behavior. The refusal of President Trump to concede the election results will, in all probability, not impact the final result. Court after court, state and federal alike, have dismissed Trump's demands for re-counts, cancellation of votes cast, and other legal efforts best described as futile. That is the polite version.

What Trump and his "all star team" (the air quotes are meant to reflect deep sarcasm) of attorney's, led by former NYC Mayor Rudy Gulliani and including extreme right wing conspiracy theorists, are doing – whether deliberately or not – is undermining democracy and casting doubt on the legitimacy of the future Presidency of Joe Biden. In "Trump-land" the efforts are bearing fruit as a significant percentage of the "base" agree with Trump that Biden's victory reflects fraud on a scale never seen before in the annals of American political history.

Judicial decisions, whether by federal judges nominated by Democratic or Republican Presidents, notwithstanding President Trump continues to deliberately undermine the democratic process, with ramifications for democracy. While his motivations are the subject of endless inquiry, speculation, and long-distance psycho-analyzing, they are not the focus of the present inquiry. That shall be left to others. What is of great interest to this study is analyzing the extent to which speech of an elected national leader should be tolerated. When this project was undertaken (summer, 2020) there was much food for fodder; after all, the two national leaders to be examined at length – Trump and Israeli Prime Minister – provide significant material for analysis and examination in this effort to determine the relationship between the speech of a national leader and incitement.

The weeks following the November 3, 2020, election could fill books regarding the speech of what appears to be a President on the edge and an unhinged legal team, seemingly speaking on his behalf. It is necessary to distinguish between THE leader and the leaders' minions and mouthpieces.

Both Trump and Netanyahu are enabled, surrounded, and cheered on by bulldogs/pit bulls who all too readily do their masters bidding. While "shame on them" is the apt phrase, they are not of concern. One can but hope they will fade into the wood paneling of their respective offices and that history will point a long and sharp finger at them…if they ever make it to the pages of history as they are, ultimately, inconsequential albeit harmful in the present moment. In focusing on Netanyahu and Trump, thereby casting asunder their respective coteries, as unrepentant, harmful, and distasteful, one question must be asked: should the speech of the national leader be limited. As a spoiler alert, this can only be answered in the affirmative. As a second spoiler alert, this proposal contains a mechanism for doing so.

This proposal is not "personal" in that it is neither directed at Trump nor Netanyahu. It is directed at any elected national leader who incites, potentially endangering individuals and/or members of specific racial, ethnic, and minority groups. While that is precisely what both do, the recommendation to limit their free speech under the guise of qualified immunity must not be understood as a one-off, but rather applicable to any elected national leader who conducts themselves in a similar manner. To perceive the recommendation as "personal" is to miss its essence. One must not underestimate – willingly or otherwise – the power of an elected leader's speech. While political theatre is recognized as legitimate, while both Trump and Netanyahu have mastered showmanship to a level none of their opponents can come close to mastering, while their embellishments are recognized as part of their personal and political makeup, there are lines the law must not tolerate being crossed.

The line of tolerance-intolerance explored in the pages ahead must be understood on two distinct levels: speech that can be understood as incitement to violence and speech that intends to undermine democracy. The former endangers individuals, while the latter is a threat to the collective. Trump's post-election behavior manifests both; Netanyahu's consistent attacks against Israeli Arabs and democratic institutions mirror that.

An important caveat is in order: There is no intention to engage in a mis-placed comparison, as some have suggested, between these two leaders and leaders of dark regimes, whether Mussolini or Hitler. Those comparisons must be rejected, though Hitler came to power by democratic means. However, that path of comparison between US-Israel and Germany-Italy is rejected outright.

The focus is on leaders in a democracy where democratic institutions and principles, primarily checks and balances and separation of powers, empowered by accountability and transparency are the guiding lights, whether in spirit or law. It is for that very reason that the other two branches of government – the legislature and the courts – must step forward, acknowledging that an unfettered executive (quoting Justice Jackson in Youngstown) must be subject to restraint when their words and/or actions endanger democracy and/or vulnerable members of society. That, after all, what both Trump and Netanyahu do; year after year, speech after speech, tweet after tweet, post after post.

The classic words of the iconic rock group, The Who, must ring loud in our ears: "we're not going to take it." Our as is said at Passover, "da-ye-nu" meaning, "enough."

Looking to the Future

President Trump lost the 2020 election. Prime Minister Netanyahu will eventually retire, be convicted, be replaced as the head of the Likud Party, or become President (elected by the Knesset, Parliament), and no longer serve as Prime Minister. This shall be left to historians to assess their years as President and Prime Minister. What is, when holding a crystal ball is seeking to ascertain whether their influence extends to future leaders of their respective parties. Will future Republicans openly denounce science and use Twitter to negotiate foreign policy? Will future Israeli prime ministers continue to incite against Israel Arabs and froth against democratic institutions, norms, and values? The questions are not posed in the abstract. Quite the opposite, for it is undeniable that Trump and Netanyahu's words – which can be interpreted as incitement and undermining democracy – are warmly received by their supporters. Whether their successors will similarly resonate is open question. Precisely for that reason, the legal model proposed whereby their speech is understood as incitement that must be limited must be viewed not only through the lens of today but also the perspective of tomorrow.

Proud Boys

"Proud Boys, stand back and stand by."

President Trump's response to a question about his willingness to denounce white supremacy in the first 2020 Presidential Debate sparked immediate backlash. Rather than condemn right-wing hate groups, the President chose instead to blame "antifa and the left" for recent racial unrest. His remarks about the Proud Boys caused the group to embrace that phrase online. After the debate, the President condemned the Proud Boys and other white supremacist groups.

However, the damage was already done: the Proud Boys had received national attention and what some might consider an endorsement from the US President. The endorsement – or at least its perception – must not be considered exclusively in the abstract. As shown by recent events, whether the killing of Heather Heyer in Charlottesville, Virginia, or the (fortunately) thwarted plans to kidnap and murder Michigan Governor, Gretchen Whitmer, white supremacists are feeling emboldened.

That they pose a serious danger is irrefutable; that they are capable of causing great harm cannot be doubted. The connection – direct or indirect – between President Trump's words and the actions of white supremacists is an issue that demands attention. That is one of the purposes of this undertaking. That same examination regarding a connection between the words of a national leader and the violent actions in their heed is relevant to Israeli Prime Minister Benjamin (Bibi) Netanyahu who engages in rhetoric similar to Trump in angrily, if not dangerously, delegitimizing the "other." After all, Netanyahu refers to Israelis protesting against him as "anarchists," his wife (of whom much could be written) intimates that the demonstrators are drug users, and his son (of whom even more could be written) posted a "photo-shopped" picture of demonstrators defecating outside the Prime Minister's residence.

The intent, of the Prime Minister and his family, was to cast unlimited, unbridled, and unhinged aspersions against the tens (if not hundreds) of thousands of Israelis who have protested these past months. The right to protest is guaranteed in Israel; Netanyahu's (and his family and others) efforts to angrily delegitimize the demonstrations go well beyond accepted norms of political verbiage. The question is whether their speech must be deemed intolerable, and therefore limited. That same question applies to President Trump.

To help us undertake this discussion, this chapter shall be constructed as follows: Sections "COVID and Its Impact on Tolerance-Intolerance," "Free Speech," "Tolerance-Intolerance in the Context of Free Speech," "Speech of National Leaders," "Different Political Regimes," "The United States and Israel Today," "Social Media," "Qualified Immunity," "Enough Is Enough," and "Looking Ahead: Areas for Future Research."

COVID and Its Impact on Tolerance-Intolerance

To suggest the present is a complicated time would rank as one of the classic understatements. As these lines are written (Fall, 2020), the world is confronted with an epidemic whose final impact is but a guessing game. The President of the United States was diagnosed with COVID and hospitalized. Other members of the White House and re-election campaign were diagnosed, as was The First Lady.

The overwhelming costs to national economies, small businesses, public health systems, families, and educational institutions struggling to implement workable alternatives to working remotely and in-class instruction have yet to be fully measured. The same applies to our societal fabric, political structures, and personal mental and physical health. The impact on the global economy is staggering. The challenges to already stressed public services are overwhelming. How this will end is unclear; the long-term damage is largely unknown. What societies, cultures, and institutions will look like in the years ahead is uncertain; what can be expected from government and the services we are accustomed to receiving has yet to be determined for we are in the throes of an extraordinary crises.

The race to develop a vaccine seems to be much more an ultra-marathon than a "regular" marathon. Industries have collapsed, iconic stores have permanently shuttered their doors, how we live is being redefined, and traditional means of communicating and conducting basic human interaction is undergoing significant changes. How much of this will be regained once a vaccine is developed and society is able to regain its footing remains to be seen. To assume we can go back to where we were, to what we were, to as we were is a bet one takes with significant risks and much hesitation.

Were the COVID challenge not sufficiently taxing, we are, today, confronted with a toxic brew of rising nationalism, bordering on xenophobia, fueled by the combustible trilogy of racism-fear-hatred, propelled by national leaders whose willingness to play to their political base knows, literally, no bounds. That is, while COVID is, at present, the most pressing issue, the question of national leaders who inflame, if not incite, deserves our attention and merits concern. President Trump's words were not the first time he articulated sympathy, if not support, for white supremacists. While political considerations may dictate Trump's response, in the violence that swept across America's streets following the murder of George Floyd by Minneapolis Police Officers show, yet again, that words matter and have consequences.

Free Speech

That recognition draws attention in examining free speech, particularly the limits of free speech of elected officials directed at public servants and minority groups that embolden violence. Restated: to what degree should intolerance be tolerated for that is the essence of speech whose result – whether intended or unintended – is violence. The question is not posed in the abstract but rather under the harsh glare of a deeply troubling reality: national leaders in liberal democracies not guided by traditional norms of speech, mores, and behaviors. The combination of fake news, instrumental use of people, situations, vulnerabilities, and unbridled cynicism reflecting political reality under the looming specter of incitement is the reality. These words are not written lightly, for the accusation of "incitement" implies criminal conduct, punishable in accordance with relevant criminal codes.

Nevertheless, that is the question to unravel in examining President Trump and Prime Minister Netanyahu. While previous leaders have conducted themselves in a non-normative manner – Trump and Netanyahu are not the first – both function in liberal democracies, not authoritarian regimes, subject to checks and balances, separation of powers, and the rule of law.

Notwithstanding important differences between the political regimes and institutions in the United States and Israel, there are sufficient similarities between the two countries that justify examining the two leaders under the same microscope.

This is not a matter of a round hole and square peg; rather, this is scrutinizing the words of two leaders in democratic regimes whose words demand attention when considering the extent to which their unrelenting intolerance must be tolerated. As these lines are written (in Israel), there is much concern that violence is a real possibility in the face of demonstrations against Netanyahu. According to Nahum Barnea, one of Israel's most respected commentators:

> Every attempt by police to stamp out protests, such as in Jerusalem and Tel Aviv at the weekend, only exacerbates the situation and sends more people onto the streets. It is not too far-fetched to believe that these popular protests will explode into open rebellion. For the first time since the creation of the state, Israel could experience civil revolt on a mass scale. The first seeds of this are already visible on social media.

In a nutshell, both Trump and Netanyahu are riding the wave – which they have helped create, foster, and exacerbate and from which both benefit – a rise in angry nationalism that challenges, if not weakens, democratic principles and values. The danger of the challenge is heightened when the public's attention is, understandably, focused on a pandemic to which both Trump and Netanyahu have overwhelmingly failed to develop coherent responses. In Netanyahu's case, this failure – stunning by all accounts – has played an important role in demonstrations across the country, resulting in increasingly antidemocratic emergency regulations combined with incendiary language by Netanyahu and his cohorts.

Neither are merely bystanders in this most disturbing trend of intolerance. Quite the opposite for both are perpetrators, challenging the limits of tolerance with a seemingly calculated indifference regarding the consequences of their speech. The weakening of democratic principles and institutions is an inevitable consequence; it is not far-fetched to suggest this result would be met approvingly by both.

Distinct from broad-based, traditional freedom of speech discussions, this focus is narrow, but critical: democratically elected public officials, and the extent to which their speech should be tolerated. The question is whether that speech should be limited and whether the fact the speaker is a national leader in a democracy means all their speech is to be tolerated or whether there is a need to impose limits.

Tolerance-Intolerance in the Context of Free Speech

Tolerance is a nuanced issue, inevitably raising concerns regarding tolerant of what and whom. The Merriam-Webster dictionary defines "tolerance" as the permitted deviation from the norm. Conversely, intolerance would be defined as that which is not tolerated. Some of the most divisive issues in recent America today, such as abortion and same-sex marriage, have revolved around the concept of tolerance. There is a sense of subjective judgment in the tolerance-intolerance debate; the terminology reflects particular norms, mores, customs, and traditions. What one might perceive as a healthy and tolerable challenging of existing acceptable "ways," another would not tolerate because of the very challenge it poses to society.

That split between tolerance-intolerance applies to both speech and conduct. It reflects everyday tensions, challenges, and conflict. In examining the tolerance-intolerance debate in the speech context there are a number of assumptions integral to a robust, liberal democracy: the freedom of speech is given a wide swath, whereby courts broadly protect the freedom of speech guaranteed in constitutions and legislation. While the speech may make certain sectors of the population uncomfortable, may be perceived as offensive, courts are tolerant of such speech provided it does not morph-transition into the realm of incitement.

By enabling the speaker to benefit from significant leeway, courts reflect a broad tolerance of free speech, even if the speech reflects intolerance of others. That is, a speaker whose speech is offensive (and thereby intolerant) will be protected by the courts provided the content stays within the boundaries of speech that does not incite or, in some jurisdictions, is not deemed to be "hate speech." Tolerating intolerance is, in many ways, the essence of a democracy; it reflects a society open to challenges, stridency, discomfort, and competing perspectives. Nowhere is that more subject to scrutiny and disagreement than when examined under the microscope of free speech.

In both the United States and Israel free speech is given extraordinary respect; police, prosecutors, and courts are extremely hesitant to curtail a speaker's right. That respect is, historically, extended to national leaders who are understood to enjoy, literally, unlimited free speech.

The US Supreme Court weighed in on a very similar issue regarding free speech in the context of punishing criminal libel. Here, Illinois had passed a criminal statute that criminalized publishing any sort of text that portrayed individuals as inferior based on their race, creed, or religion when that portrayal exposes members of that group to derision or contempt. The petitioner in this case who had placed lithographs in public places depicting "depravity, criminality, unchastity, or lack of virtue of citizens of Negro race and color" challenged his conviction under this statute as too vague under the Due Process clause of the 14th Amendment. The court recognized that the history of racial tensions that plagued Illinois provided ample reasoning for the implementation of this statute. The law was passed in 1917, at a time when tensions ran high due to the influx of immigrants and African Americans arriving to work at factories in Illinois. The court upheld petitioner's conviction based on libel law. The defense to libel is that the speech was made with "good motives and justifiable ends." Finding neither one of those elements, the court reasoned that petitioner's case did not merit 14th Amendment protection.

Within the context of the present issue of restricting free speech of elected officials, tolerance follows a similar pattern. However, the restrictions imposed on elected officials often are ignored as a result of the deep polarization in American politics.

This comment insinuates two different and disturbing elements of the President's relationship with the Proud Boys: he feels like they respect him enough to listen to him and he wants them to "stand-by." In the context of the 2020 Black Lives Matter protests and calls for racial equality, this level of blatant disregard for the tension felt throughout the nation likely should merit censorship.

The racially tense atmosphere that inflicted Illinois in 1917 mirrors today. Speech in this environment can lead to conflict. President Trump's tacit endorsement of the Proud Boys actions will likely lead to further violence. Already, the Proud Boys have seen the President's comments as a call to action.

Speech of National Leaders

Examples of national leaders whose speech raises legitimate concern regarding the extent to which its intolerance should be tolerated include Brazilian President Bolsonaro, President Duterte of the Philippines, the late President of Venezuela Chavez, President Lukashenko of Belarus, Turkish President Erdogan, and Hungarian Prime Minister Orban. However, as controversial, if not problematic, as these national leaders are, they are not the primary focus of this analysis.

In focusing exclusively on Trump and Netanyahu, excluded are US Cabinet members, Israeli Government Ministers, US Members of Congress, and Members of Knesset (the Israeli Parliament). The reason for this goes to the heart of this chapter: the intolerance-tolerance debate in the free speech context is most compellingly understood when examining the words of *the* national leader.

Otherwise the full impact of their words and their direct meaning will be lost; more than that, broadening the range of speakers (beyond the national leader) enables establishing layers that provide cover for the national leader. That well-known model, time-tested over the years, whereby politicians create buffers between their words and their consequences, must be rejected in suggesting national leaders be held legally accountable for their words. Bully pulpit is a term associated with President Theodore Roosevelt:

> Theodore Roosevelt used what he called the "bully pulpit" ("bully" meaning "wonderful" and "pulpit" meaning "a preaching position") to spread his ideas and solve problems. He said: "I suppose my critics will call that preaching, but I have got such a bully pulpit!" His use of the bully pulpit contributed to the greatest expansion of federal power in the country's history to that time.

The phrase suggests a national leader setting the national agenda, directly communicating with the public on matters of importance. It conjures images of a national leader, similar to President Franklin D. Roosevelt, speaking in an unfiltered manner to the body politic. That model of the national leader, communicating directly, enables us to examine *their* speech when analyzing its impact on the public.

In examining only the speech of national leaders the focus of this chapter is deliberately limited, reflecting rejection of determined efforts to hide behind others, to deflect, to distract, and to spin. Given the centrality of the executive – even if subject to checks and balances and separation of powers – the focus is exclusively on the national leader whose influence is greater than other politicians or public figures.

That is not to suggest that others do not engage in rhetoric that mirrors, or mimics, that of the national leader, the national leader in a democracy must be held to a different standard with responsibilities and expectations distinct from other elected officials. The words and actions of a national leader are held to a different standard, understood by the public to have greater significance and impact than other politicians. The amount of media coverage, social media commentary, attention paid to the national leader justifies an exclusive focus on a President or Prime Minister, distinct from others.

Both Trump and Netanyahu, regardless of the constant drumbeat of their deeply troubling rhetoric, are quick to "pass the buck" deflecting attention from themselves consistently pointing a finger at their enemies, imagined or otherwise and ignoring the consequences of their speech. That has been their *modus operandi*; it has served them well in galvanizing their respective political bases. Because both dominate their respective national landscapes, the efforts to deflect blame from themselves must be understood for what it is: an effort to protect themselves and dismiss any accusation their speech must be perceived as inciting hatred and violence. Both are skilled at deflection and conveying a sense of innocence regarding the tone and tenor of their words; it is a practiced response, recalling the *Mad Magazine* cover, "What me worry."

As this chapter shall show, for Netanyahu this is a time-tested model that politically has served him well. Trump's ability to frame an issue, to seize the moment – regardless of how crassly or offensive – played was significant to his 2016 victory. Few politicians are as skilled at "tagging" an opponent as Trump, whether "crooked Hillary" or "Sleepy Joe"; similarly few politicians so adeptly communicate with their base, phrases such as "lock her up" and "build the wall" resonate emotionally and viscerally. Netanyahu adopts the same tact, delegitimizing demonstrators calling for his immediate resignation, by referring to them as "anarchists" and "lefties," a catch-all term Netanyahu uses to disparage the political left, the media, and the "elites."

Trump and Netanyahu are their own best spokesmen, even though they have "mouthpieces" willing to do their dirty-work. To do otherwise is to miss the essence of their personalities, leadership styles, and the dangers they pose. The word "danger" is used deliberately, for that is how their words must be understood.

Two Different Political Regimes

While the United States and Israel are two very different regimes, the similarities – both are vibrant, robust, rugged democracies – warrant comparing their respective national leaders. Perhaps at first blush comparing the two countries seems a stretch; after all, one is the world's super-power with a population of over 300 million, the other a small country of 9 million.

The differences, obviously, extend well beyond mere numbers: while both are democracies, the political regimes are very different. Israel is a parliamentary democracy, predicated on a party system, whereby there is no direct election of members of Knesset. To form a government requires cobbling together a coalition of 61 MK's (the Knesset is comprised of 120 MK's); for a party to be seated in the Knesset it must pass a certain threshold of votes; this is intended to decrease the number of small parties. Votes for parties that do not pass the threshold are, literally, discarded.

The Prime Minister is the head of the largest party of the coalition; there is no requirement by law that the largest party in the coalition received the most votes in the election. The question is which party garners the largest number of recommenders to the President (a largely ceremonial office) who is entrusted with inviting the head of that party to form a government. The invitation is time-limited; if the party is unable to form a government, then the President invites the head of the second largest party to form a government. This process can drag on for an extended period of time; in the interim, the government that was in power before the election continues as "transition" government. Once the government is formed, the parties not included in the ruling coalition comprise the opposition; the MK who is the head of the largest party in the opposition is the head of the opposition.

The notion of two major parties, akin to the US system, existed in the past; however, over the years party affiliation/party consistency has, largely, eroded. While LIKUD (Netanyahu's party) is consistently the largest or second largest party, LABOR-MA'ARACH which used to be the largest party (in an earlier iteration it founded the State) has all but disappeared. In its place have risen – and fallen – parties that have sought to fill the void in the political center. Other than LIKUD, sectoral parties representing Orthodox, religious, Israeli-Arabs, and Russian immigrant voters have the most durability.

A small left-wing party is in the opposition. Elections are not held on a regular basis – as an example, there have been three elections in the last 2 years – but rather as a result of a vote of no-confidence or a snap election with the intent to re-structure the sitting government. The threat of a snap election is a mechanism for the majority party in the coalition to ensure "discipline" on key votes in the Knesset; the issue in question can be both of great import or seemingly insignificant.

Checks and balances and separation of powers are a mainstay of the Israeli system, particularly because of a unique institution that does not exist in the United States. The Israeli Supreme Court, in addition to sitting as a Supreme Court (similar to the United States) also sits as a High Court of Justice (HCJ). The HCJ hears cases brought against the government by any individual who feels aggrieved by a present or future government decision. There is no standing requirement for filing a petition; the right to file petitions extends to Palestinian's living in the West Bank for whom the standing requirement has been similarly waived. The HCJ acts as the most powerful restraint on government decision-making; watch dog groups regularly file petitions on a wide range of issues. From a political perspective, in broad terms, the center-left views the HCJ as the last bastion of democracy whereas the right views the HCJ as intervening-interfering in government decision making.

The Knesset, in contrast to the SC-HCJ, does not act as a restraint on government policy; that is understandable given that its composition reflects that of the government. The strength of the Knesset in the spirit of checks and balances depends on the aggressiveness and robustness of the opposition; however, as determined as the opposition may be, its power is ultimately limited. Knesset committees exercise minimal influence and power.

Government ministers are MK's (or in certain situations only Ministers) from the coalition parties; they are slotted by the Prime Minister who is the final arbitrator regarding ministerial appointments. The appointments are predicated on political calculations rather than experience or skill based. In addition, the larger the coalition, the more Ministers and Deputy Ministers; there is no law restricting the number of Ministers a Prime Minister can appoint.

This is obviously different from the US political regime; there are significant distinctions between a parliamentary system and the US Republic-Federal form of government. Nevertheless, the differences notwithstanding, there are four core similarities enabling comparison between the two leaders: both countries are robust, vigorous liberal democracies; checks and balances and separation of powers are guaranteed in both systems; elections (while different in manner and practice) are fair with a citizen's right to vote guaranteed, and basic rights protected whether in a Constitution or Basic Laws. For this reason, the discussion primarily focuses on these two political leaders.

The United States and Israel Today

The legitimacy of comparing Trump and Netanyahu is enhanced by the fact that both consistently use nationalist rhetoric to inflame extremists, thereby accentuating the critical question of the limits of tolerating intolerance. Trump and Netanyahu provide fertile ground for examining the extent to which their speech should be tolerated; both consistently engage in speech that pushes the envelope, and both are highly skilled at speaking to their respective bases in a manner guaranteed to ensure their support and commitment.

Both inflame, enhance rift among different sectors of the public, and engage in deliberate minimizing of the legitimacy of the "other." While that may be ascribed to the art of politics, the question is whether that is incitement and therefore is speech that must not be tolerated. Careful observers of Netanyahu, regardless of their political affiliation, will be the first to consistently note how sophisticated, educated, and worldly he is; those terms would not be ascribed to Trump. What they share in common is a ready willingness to discard any semblance of the truth; the *Washington Post* "Pinocchio test" is readily and all-too often applicable to both.

The two share a trait essential to this analysis: they are divisive, push the envelope, and present their positions and perspectives in stark, un-nuanced language that is, primarily, directed at their respective base. Neither "play" to the traditional, middle ground of safe and cautious politics, and both are intent on painting their respective paradigms in clear, unequivocal language. Both are skilled in presenting their opinions, both well understand visceral politics, both subscribe to the "take no prisoners" school of politics, eschewing moderate, deliberate language. While their respective political fates are unclear at the time of this writing, this conclusion may be drawn from their years in office.

A major difference between Netanyahu and Trump is their manner of delivery. Netanyahu generally delivers his messages with relative restraint and political decorum. Conversely, Trump tweets out messages with seemingly little to no filter. "When the looting starts, the shooting starts." This message, sent directly from Trump's authorized Twitter account, harkened back to 1967 Miami when Miami's Police Chief Walter Headley threatened civil rights protestors in Florida with violence. Twitter flagged Trump's Tweet as having "violated the Twitter Rules about glorifying violence."

Both instances show a leader attempting to rally his base by demonizing an unpopular political opponent. Trump's tweet about the Black Lives Matter movement also demonstrates his understanding of what he needs to say to motivate his base. By framing the Black Lives Matter protest as "looting" and the protestors as "thugs" Trump stokes the fires racial unrest already present in America.

Both countries are mired in deep political divide, political and societal tension, angry voices, protests, clear fault lines between government and judiciary, identification of opposition as the "other, provocative labelling of the media, civil servants, and presumed enemies." There is one important distinction: the violence that has marked the American street in the past months has not been replicated in Israel.

While weekly demonstrations against Netanyahu are loud and engaged, and arrests have been made, the violence has been limited to a handful of instances. In addition, the looting in the United States in the past months is not part of the Israeli protest movements. That is not to say violence has not marked Israeli society in the past, the most obvious example is the November 4, 1995, assassination of Prime Minister Rabin by a Jewish religious extremist. A caveat is in order: this discussion addressing Israel will not address the Israel-Palestinian conflict in the West Bank and Gaza Strip, but rather focus on Israeli politics exclusively.

Both Netanyahu and Trump portray themselves as outsiders, fighting elites and the much-discussed "deep state." While Trump is a relative newcomer to politics, Netanyahu has been an active participant in Israeli politics since the early 1990's. Trump's positioning of himself as the "outsider" reflects his years long business experience primarily in New York, arguing he has never been "inside the Beltway," both literally and figuratively. Netanyahu's outsider claim is far more difficult to parse, fueled by a decades old family myth that is factually incorrect. Notwithstanding the fallacy at the core of the claim, Netanyahu has religiously stuck to the outsider label, positioning himself as fighting Israel's elites. This is of great importance when examining his speech and the extent to which it should be tolerated.

The adherence to the theme of the outsider fighting the deep state, media, and elites defines much of their politics; both Trump and Netanyahu focus – if not denigrate – on the "other," often a strawman argument identifying who they claim – without any basis in fact – poses a grave and immediate danger to national security, public safety, and the public good. Whether there is any validity to the claim is not their primary focus, rather the emphasis is on the identification – targeting – of a group (or individual) who the public must understand seeks to undermine the broader, at-risk public. It is the classic "us-them" political narrative, previously implemented by regimes, primarily in Europe, that caused extraordinary harm to their publics, particularly the identified "them." In exploring the tolerance-intolerance question, the us-them narrative is most important. For both Netanyahu and Trump this is a crucial piece of their political positioning and a mainstay of how they communicate.

Netanyahu would not, at least publicly, stoop (for there is no other word) to Trump's mocking of a physically challenged reporter or mock a respected war hero such as John McCain or as Jeffrey Goldberg reported in *The Atlantic* refer to American's killed in action disparagingly or question why efforts must be made to find soldier's Missing in Action. Nevertheless, Trump consistently engages in unrelenting attacks against those identified as threats to himself, his family, and his political fortunes.

Both Trump and Netanyahu use a politically unpopular group in order to further their own political agendas. Israel's unique situation as the setting of an unresolved conflict provides Netanyahu with plenty of source material to dehumanize his political unpopular group: the Arabs. "The Arabs want to annihilate us all – women, children, and men," stated a message from Netanyahu's Facebook page. Netanyahu's use of demonizing Israeli-Arabs, and delegitimizing political parties willing to enter a coalition with Israeli-Arab parties, serves a clear (from his perspective) political purpose.

Similarly, Trump's speech reflects a growing unrest in America as changing demographics begin to change the political landscape. Trump managed to turn a group of scraggly refugees coming to America for asylum into a fear of invasion. This demonization of immigrants plays to Trump's base by instilling paranoia and fear. This fear of demographic change has played out with horrific results. The 2019 El Paso shooting claimed the lives of three people and injured many more. Police discovered that this shooter had posted racist propaganda on Facebook prior to his attack.

The three examples are deeply intertwined and his speech, coded or otherwise, must be understood accordingly. This is similar to how Trump perceives the political arena and accordingly interacts with the public. There is, however, one important difference: while Trump is his most effective spokesman – through Twitter, brief interactions with the press, or political rallies – Netanyahu has at his disposal political allies willing to be, for lack of a better term, his pit bulls only too eager to attack when ordered. While Netanyahu uses social media akin to Trump (Facebook not Twitter), he rarely – if ever – engages with the press or directly with the public in face-to-face interactions. Obviously, he meets with Israeli citizens but that is largely limited to meetings in the Prime Minister's Office on specific issues. The manner in which Trump, whether on the campaign trail or otherwise, prefers direct engagement is largely alien to Netanyahu, unrelated to the present pandemic.

That was not always the case.

Netanyahu as a member of the opposition to Prime Minister Rabin was arguably the most vociferous in the aftermath of the signing of the Oslo Peace Accords in September 1993. It was, after all, Netanyahu who stood on a balcony in Zion Square in Jerusalem when demonstrators held pictures of Prime Minister dressed in a keffiyeh and in an SS uniform.

While at least one Member of the Knesset was sufficiently dismayed by the pictures that he left the balcony, Netanyahu did not, claiming later he did not see the placard. Were that not enough, Netanyahu participated – actually led – a mock funeral of Zionism, in protest of the Peace Accords. It was not by chance that Rabin's widow, Leah, refused to shake Netanyahu's hand at the funeral. Whether Netanyahu engaged in incitement against Rabin is an open question; given that as a Member of Knesset he enjoys Parliamentary immunity, the point, from that perspective, is moot as there was no demand to undertake the process to "waive" his immunity. That said, there is much to be learned from Netanyahu's conduct almost 30 years ago in examining his actions today.

Netanyahu has used his position as a "global statesman" with the ability to influence Trump as a bargaining tool to obtain qualified immunity. Netanyahu sought to gain qualified immunity from charges of fraud, breach of trust, and bribery. He failed to receive this from the Knesset.

It is not an exaggeration or mischaracterization to suggest that Netanyahu skirts the edges of tolerable speech, careful not to cross the line into unequivocal incitement. After all, he did not call on Yigal Amir (Rabin's assassin) to fire the bullets in Rabin's back nor did he condone the act afterwards, thereby encouraging others to follow suit. On the other hand, on election day xx March 2015, Netanyahu warned his base that the election might be lost given that, "the Arabs are voting in droves." The reference to Israeli-Arabs, who make up 21% of the Israeli population, was nothing but unmitigated racism that is akin to Trump's reference to "all Mexicans are rapists" or the so-called Muslim ban.

There is much in common with these three examples: they reflect a rational-based decision to directly target a minority group in an effort to curry favor with their electoral base. Putting aside the rough and tumble nature of Israeli politics that would make most non-Israeli's gasp, Netanyahu had one intent in his statement: warn the base of the direct electoral threat posed by 15% of their fellow citizens. While he subsequently back tracked when heavily criticized by President Obama, fair to assume no Israeli placed an ounce of credence in the "apology" (quotation marks deliberate).

Netanyahu is very careful in his language, meaning he meets the test of, "means what he says, says what he means" which is why the "apology" was dismissed. What is important and demands attention is whether the phrase "the Arabs are voting in droves" is aggressive campaigning, hours before the polls close, thereby merely skirting the line of incitement or did it cross the line of tolerable speech. That very question applies to Trump's persistent characterization of political opponents – real or imagined – in highly inflammatory language. Whether it was claiming a Federal judge could not be impartial because he was "Mexican."

Social Media

Traditionally, the concept of limiting a President's speech has not been explored. Social media has provided a platform that allows Trump to say what he thinks at any given moment. This allows Trump to dictate what the press reports on him. By tweeting out his opinions on elected officials, other countries' leaders, and political opponents without regard to the time of day or night, Trump ensures that the press will focus on what he has to say.

Past presidents have not had access to the level of technology available to Trump. If Nixon had Twitter, surely Watergate would have been covered differently. If Lincoln had Instagram, perhaps #GettysburgAddress would have been trending. Public perception of these historical figures would also likely have been different if they had the same capability that Trump has to send his thoughts out into the world. Even President Obama, one year into his first term, existed in a world where only 970 million people had social media profiles. Comparatively, one year into Trump's presidency, 2.65 billion people were using social media. This dramatic increase in social media has redefined how politicians' speech is received.

While it will remain impossible to conclusively prove Trump's speech directly leads to violence, his Tweets and other actions on social media provide validation to supporters who, arguably, otherwise would not have feel validation. This extra exposure to the Internet also provokes an additional issue that has caught national attention: how a President speaks behind closed doors. The infamous Hollywood Access tapes exposed an incredibly derogatory aspect of Trump that caused extreme discomfort among voters. While he was not yet a public official, this element of derogatory speech done in private speaks to the changing elements of public speech in the era of social media.

Qualified Immunity

Qualified Immunity applies to elected officials so long as their conduct does not lead to illegal activity or the infringement of others' rights. Generally, unless a government official knew or should have known that their actions were illegal, they are not liable. Therefore, to analyze qualified immunity in the context of leaders' speech, one must first analyze whether Trump's actions have led to any sort of illegal activity or an infringement of rights. Speech, as a concept, is exceptionally difficult to link to action without an express call to action from a leader. Much of Trump's speech throughout his presidency provided him with plausible deniability that makes linking the actions of his followers to his own speech very difficult. In Trump's case, the wide accessibility of social media provides a plethora of examples of his speech.

Trump's Twitter account gives him unfettered access to millions of followers around the world. Within seconds, he can reach a massive audience in ways that are reactionary and instantaneous. Therefore, this chapter will analyze Trump's tweets and the corresponding response that they received as a measurement for the impact Trump's speech has on his listeners.

In the 2020 presidential election, Trump's ability to tweet to his many followers led to the spread of misinformation about mail-in ballots and their legitimacy. At one point, Trump tweeted out, "STOP THE COUNT," in what was largely viewed as an attempt to win the election by failing to count all of the ballots. Nearly a month after the election, Trump tweeted "RIGGED ELECTION!" further insinuating that the election process was fraudulent. This disregard for the electoral process resulted in some of his supporters harassing ballot counters by chanting "STOP THE COUNT." This same sentiment was reiterated when Trump's fundraising team sent out an email to supporters calling for his "fiercest and most loyal defenders" to stop the Democrats from "stealing the election."

His message to "Stop the Count" became a rallying cry to his supporters around the nation when it became apparent that if all ballots were counted, Trump would lose the election. Protestors gathered around vote counting centers, following Trump's request to "Stop Democrats from stealing the election." These protests reiterated the same points that Mr. Trump had spewed through his tweet. Many chanted "Stop the Vote" in Detroit, while others in Arizona cried, "Stop the Steal."

These protests show the best example of correlation between Trump's tweets and the resultant actions. Without any evidence of fraud, Trump repeatedly encouraged his followers to question the results of the election. A Politico poll found that in the weeks following the election, approximately 70% of Republicans believed that the election was not free or fair. This is a dramatic rise from the 35% of Republicans who believed that the election was not free or fair prior to the election. A YouGov poll held over a week after the election similarly showed that four in five Trump supporters believed that Fraud changed the outcome of the election nationally.

In the weeks following the election, Trump continued to tweet about how the election was fraudulently conducted, citing sources like Breitbart news to back up his claim. This continuous onslaught of questioning the election was met with fact checking by Twitter and other news sources, much to Mr. Trump's dismay. Twitter began marking his claims about election fraud as "disputed" often within minutes of him uploading the tweet. Fox News cut away from White House Press Secretary Kayleigh McEnany when she began making unsubstantiated claims about voter fraud. Neil Cavuto, the Fox News anchor who cut off the conference, said "I can't in good conscience continue to show this."

This push to censor the president indicated a recognition among media organizations that Trump's speech could potentially incite further protests or violence. This, lamentably, did not occur earlier in his presidency when Trump made misleading or dangerous claims such as suggesting injecting bleach as a cure for COVID-19. Mr. Trump would later backtrack that statement, arguing that he was being sarcastic. However, this rise in public censorship of Mr. Trump's comments help illustrate why any sort of qualified immunity should not apply to a national figure's free speech.

The claims regarding election fraud show that Mr. Trump was willing to undermine one of the most important functions of a free democracy: the peaceful transfer of power. He publicly asked his supporters to fight back against the election results and his supporters have openly embraced his vitriolic rhetoric. Speech should not provide a vehicle for politicians to openly question science and the democratic process without consequences. A politician should not be able to hide behind the shield of qualified immunity when their speech has such far reaching impact. A politician's speech and any resulting illegal action that flow from the speech should be subjected to intense scrutiny and swift retribution.

Enough Is Enough

To conclude: with a warm nod to Peter Townshend the great lead guitarist and songwriter for The Who; he said the following of the song, "We're Not Going to Take It":

> It was about the rabble in general, how we, myself as part of them, were not going to take fascism, were not going to take dreary, dying politics; were not going to take things the way they were, the way they always had been and that we were keen to change things.

That applies to what underlies this proposal: calling attention to the dangers of tolerating speech whose danger lurks under the surface, with the potential to percolate ever present. Social media significantly enhances the boiling point. While it is most unfortunate that Mark Zuckerberg – the manifestation of ignorance, blind greed, and sheer stupidity – refuses to recognize the power of social media that reality cannot be ignored. Quite the opposite. Because of the manner in which leaders such as Trump and Netanyahu effectively use the extraordinary platform social media – such as Facebook – "enough is enough" is the most obvious conclusion. While there are multiple layers to this declaration, the focus has been twofold: analyzing when the speech of THE (Caps deliberate), elected national leader in a democracy needs to be limited and the recommended means for doing so. Trump and Netanyahu are prime examples of leaders whose speech, were this proposal to be adopted, would be limited.

They have more than earned that distinction. There is no reason the body politic should tolerate their incitement and endangerment of democracy. Tolerating their intolerance may be viewed with favor by those advocating tolerance of all speech; however, that tolerance is not cost-free, quite the opposite. Possible danger to individuals and institutions alike outweighs tolerance for free, unfettered speech. Otherwise democracy fails to protect itself; doing so in the name of democracy is self-destructive or inherently idiotic. There are no words more fitting to finish this discussion than Goebbels,

> We enter parliament in order to supply ourselves, in the arsenal of democracy, with its own weapons. If democracy is so stupid as to give us free tickets and salaries for this bear's work, that is its affair. We do not come as friends, nor even as neutrals. We come as enemies. As the wolf bursts into the flock, so we come.

We recall Hitler did exactly as Goebbels protended, any German to claim surprise at the calamity that awaited them was engaging in deliberate self-delusion. That is not to suggest that the consequences of failing to act against the incitement of THE elected national leader portends a recurrence of Germany 1932–1945 but it is, indeed, intended to signal with a bright orange flag of caution regarding the consequences of failing to impose limits on tolerance. Allowing intolerance to carry the day is fraught with danger; articulating the limits of tolerance is an essential duty of democratic institutions intent on protecting themselves.

At is core, that is the essence of this proposal.

Summary and Future Directions

In this chapter a number of important issues have been raised regarding the free speech in general and limiting speech of national leaders in particular. The discussion is intended to encourage discussion regarding legal measures that could be imposed in developing qualified immunity for the speech of those leaders; the basis for the proposal is a recognition that tolerating intolerant speech results, potentially, in incitement with violence a distinct possibility.

Given that, it is hoped that this chapter will directly contribute to research that examines the mechanisms for implementing qualified immunity focused on national leaders. Doing so requires researching the history of immunity for national leaders and analyzing case law where questions of immunity where discussed. To ensure a rich and full discussion, it is recommended that court decisions addressing immunity-qualified from distinct jurisdictions be examined. While the chapter focused on Trump and Netanyahu, the question examined goes well beyond the United States and Israel.

For that reason, it is recommended that researchers analyze the speech of additional leaders in determining whether qualified immunity is relevant to additional political cultures and the means by which legislators may address the question, specific to their nation. Opposition is to be expected to such a proposal; therefore, scholars and others would be encouraged to research past experiences (legislative history) in order to develop counterarguments. In highlighting the importance of qualified immunity, it is understood that researching constitutional law is particularly important with an emphasis on comparative constitutional law focusing on the free speech and justifications for limits.

As highlighted by Trump and Netanyahu, social media has become the dominant form of mass communication replacing traditional media. Given the extraordinary unregulated reach of social media, scholars and policy makers are encouraged to explore means imposing limits (akin to FCC) on social media. Mark Zuckerberg's congressional testimony graphically demonstrated the need to develop regulatory mechanisms for it is clear FACEBOOK will deflect all efforts to engage in self-policing. Restricting forums for national leaders who incite, including Netanyahu and Trump, is an effective means to limit their reach. That effort is most effective when combined with legal efforts focused on qualified immunity. The two-pronged effort similarly demands attention of scholars.

Addressing these issues would significantly contribute to a better understanding of how to implement – legislatively and jurisprudentially – qualified immunity that would minimize tolerating intolerant free speech that incites to violence. Under the umbrella of tolerance – the essence of this notable project – this effort is necessary to protect those harmed by speech that incites.

References

*Professor of Law, S.J. Quinney College of Law, University of Utah; I wish to thank Austin Weenig, Quinney Fellow, S.J. Quinney College of Law, University of Utah (J.D. expected, 2022) for his outstanding contribution to this project and M (identity known to me), Avner de Shalit and Rebekah Wightman, J.D. for their insightful comments on earlier drafts

Archive of Political Emails (2020) https://politicalemails.org/messages/293741

Associated Press and Reuters (2020) Israel's Netanyahu officially indicted in court on corruption charges. Available at https://www.nbcnews.com/news/world/netanyahu-pulls-request-immunity-ahead-trump-plan-unveiling-n1124466

Barbara Sprunt (2020) The history behind 'When the looting starts, the shooting starts'. Available at https://www.npr.org/2020/05/29/864818368/the-history-behind-when-the-looting-starts-the-shooting-starts

Barnea N (2020) Playing politics with coronavirus could result in open revolt in Israel. Available at https://www.ynetnews.com/article/ryaESIu8D

BBC News (2020) Coronavirus: outcry after Trump suggests injecting disinfectant as treatment. Available at https://www.bbc.com/news/world-us-canada-52407177

Beauharnais v. Illinois, 343 U.S. 250, 251, 72 S. Ct. 725, 728, 96 L. Ed. 919, 924, 1952 U.S. LEXIS 2799, *1.

Bill of Rights Institute. Federal power: Theodore Roosevelt. Available at https://billofrightsinstitute.org/educate/educator-resources/lessons-plans/presidents-constitution/federal-power-theodore-roosevelt/

Brown D (2019) Remember vine? These social networking sites defined the past decade. Available at https://www.usatoday.com/story/tech/2019/12/19/end-decade-heres-how-social-media-has-evolved-over-10-years/4227619002/

Bryon Wolf Z (2018) Trump's attacks on Judge Curiel are still jarring to read. Available at https://www.cnn.com/2018/02/27/politics/judge-curiel-trump-border-wall/index.html

Catherine Kim (2020) Poll: 70 percent of republicans don't think the election was free and fair. Available at https://www.politico.com/news/2020/11/09/republicans-free-fair-elections-435488?nname=politico-nightly&nid=00000170-c000-da87-af78-e185fa700000&nrid=0000014e-f10a-dd93-ad7f-f90f318e0001&nlid=2670445

Cathey L, Keneally M (2020) A look back at Trump's comments perceived by some as inciting violence. Available at https://abcnews.go.com/Politics/back-trump-comments-perceived-encouraging-violence/story?id=48415766

Cillizza C (2020) Why it's impossible to believe Trump simply misspoke about the Proud Boys. Available at https://www.cnn.com/2020/09/30/politics/white-supremacy-trump-proud-boys-charlottesville-kkk-david-duke/index.html

Conger K (2020) Twitter says it labeled 0.2% of all election-related tweets as disputed. Available at https://www.nytimes.com/2020/11/12/technology/twitter-says-it-labeled-0-2-of-all-election-related-tweets-as-disputed.html

D'Anna J (2019) 'This Anglo man came to kill Hispanics': after El Paso shooting, will race motivate more violence? Available at https://www.usatoday.com/story/news/nation/2019/08/06/el-paso-texas-shooting-race-motivate-more-violence/1934948001/

Frankovic K (2020) President Trump and his supporters agree on not accepting the election results – for now. Available at https://today.yougov.com/topics/politics/articles-reports/2020/11/13/trump-voters-election-results-poll

Funke D (2020) In context: what Donald Trump said about disinfectants, sun and coronavirus. Available at https://www.politifact.com/article/2020/apr/24/context-what-donald-trump-said-about-disinfectant-/

Garcia HF (2020) How to understand Trump's incendiary language – and how to combat it. Available at https://www.salon.com/2020/06/22/how-to-understand-donald-trumps-incendiary-language%2D%2Dand-how-to-combat-it/

Hall M (2018) He said what? Available at https://www.insidehighered.com/views/2018/10/10/president-trumps-use-social-media-and-why-we-cant-ignore-it-opinion

Haltiwanger J (2020) Fox news cuts away from Trump's press secretary as she pushes baseless claims of election fraud. Available at https://www.businessinsider.com/fox-news-cut-trump-press-secretary-false-election-fraud-video-2020-11

Hammerstrom M "What, me worry?" The timeless wisdom of Alfred E. Neuman. Available at https://aalliancecollects.com/2020/01/08/what-me-worry-the-timeless-wisdom-of-alfred-e-neuman/

Hudson DL Jr. Qualified immunity. Available at https://www.mtsu.edu/first-amendment/article/1560/qualified-immunity#:~:text=Qualified%20immunity%20protects%20government%20officials,she%20was%20doing%20was%20unlawful

Kershner I (2020) Israel's coronavirus lockdown fuels protest, violence and confusion. Available at https://www.nytimes.com/2020/10/05/world/middleeast/israel-coronavirus-lockdown.html

Murphy P (2020) Trump's debate call out bolsters proud boys. Available at https://www.cnn.com/2020/09/30/politics/proud-boys-trump-debate-trnd/index.html

Neuman S (2020) Trump now says he'll 'condemn all white supremacists' after failing to at debate. https://www.npr.org/sections/live-updates-protests-for-racial-justice/2020/10/01/919375470/trump-now-says-he-condemns-all-white-supremacists-after-declining-to-at-debate

Quotes by Paul Joseph Goebbels. Available at http://www.quoteland.com/author/Paul-Joseph-Goebbels-Quotes/4814/

Romero S et al (2020) In a year of protest cries, now it's 'Count every vote!' and 'Stop the steal!'. Available at https://www.nytimes.com/2020/11/05/us/election-protests-vote-count.html

Rucker P et al (2020) 20 days of fantasy and failure: inside Trump's attempt to overturn the election. The Washington Post. Available at https://www.washingtonpost.com/politics/trump-election-overturn/2020/11/28/34f45226-2f47-11eb-96c2-aac3f162215d_story.html?wpmk=1&wpisrc=al_trending_now_alert-politics%2D%2Dalert-national&utm_campaign=wp_news_alert_revere_trending_now&utm_medium=email&utm_source=alert&location=alert&pwapi_token=eyJ0eXAiOiJKV1QiLCJhbGciOiJIUzI1NiJ9.eyJjb29raWVuYW1lIjoid3BfY3J0aWQiLCJjb29raWV2YWxlIjoiNTk2Y2VlM2RhZTdlOGE0NGU3ZmNlMTg4IiwidGFnIjoiM0BfbWV3c19hbGVydF9yZXZlcmVfdHJlbmRpbmdfbm93IiwidXJsIjoiaHR0cHM6Ly93d3cud2FzaGluZ3RvbnBvc3QuY29tL3BvbGl0aWNzL3RydW1wLWVsZWN0aW9uLW92ZXJ0dXJuLzIwMjAvMTEvMjgvMzRmNDUyMjYtMmY0Ny0xMWViLTk2YzItYWFjM2YxNjIyMTVkX3N0b3J5Lmh0bWw_d3Btaz0xJndwaXNyYz1hbF90cmVuZGluZ19ub3dfX2FsZXJ0LXBvbGl0aWNzJTJEJTJEYWxlcnQtbmF0aW9uYWwLXBvbGljaWVzL3RydW1wLWVsZWN0aW9uLW92ZXJ0dXJuLzIwMjAvMTEvMjgvMzRmNDUyMjYtMmY0Ny0xMWViLTk2YzItYWFjM2YxNjIyMTVkX3N0b3J5Lmh0bWw.N6Ds2t1bIdiSSgvxgtsEX0YVrfc5bxQScPn0QKsgbYc

Salas v. Carpenter, 980 F.2d 299, 310 (5th Cir.1992)

Tarnopolsky N (2019) As election nears, Netanyahu intensifies his rhetoric against Israel's Arab population. Available at https://www.latimes.com/world-nation/story/2019-09-14/netanyahu-election-israel-arab-population

The Voting Rights Act of 1965 Pub. L. 89-110, 79 Stat. 437

The Who. We're not gonna take it. Available at https://www.youtube.com/watch?v=b58NmMybJEk

Trump D (@realdonaldtrump), Twitter (November 5, 2020a, 7:12 AM) https://twitter.com/realdonaldtrump/status/1324353932022480896

Trump D (@realdonaldtrump), Twitter (November 6, 2020b, 12:23 AM) https://twitter.com/realDonaldTrump/status/1324613375213621248

Trump D (@realdonaldtrump), Twitter (November 20, 2020c, 6:53 AM) https://twitter.com/realDonaldTrump/status/1329784812257890306

Trump D (@realdonaldtrump), Twitter (November 25, 2020d, 10:45 AM) https://twitter.com/realDonaldTrump/status/1331655154492448770

Index

A
Abortion, 430, 434
Abstraction, 550–553
Academic dispute, 976–978
Academic skepticism, 370
Acceptability, 251
Acceptance, 500–505, 509, 512, 513, 516, 521, 523, 528–530, 536
 component, 76, 94, 236
Acceptingness, 705
Accommodation, 57, 60, 63, 68, 521, 525–527, 529, 532, 537
Accommodative toleration, 501, 507–510
Ackerman, B., 316
Active toleration, 656, 663, 665–669
Adjudication method, 1130
Advocacy, 1117, 1129, 1131
Aggression, 1117
Agonistic respect, 901
Agrarian populism, 657
A Letter Concerning Toleration, 1029–1030
Alt-right, 1128
Altruism, 688
Ambition, 1082
American Civil Liberties Union (ACLU), 1118
Anarchism, 1121
An Essay Concerning Toleration, 810
Anger, 677–678, 680
Anglican(s), 638, 642, 645
 religion, 1057
Anglo-American political theory, 544
Anti-fascist protesters, 1128
Anti-perfectionism, 1129
Anti-tolerationist arguments, 999
Apostasy, 480, 481, 486, 488, 493
Appraisal respect, 294, 643
Aquinas, Thomas, 805
Arab Christian tribe, 464

Arabic tribes, 464
Arbitrary power, 213, 215
Aristotelian virtues, 761
Arneson, R., 309
Art of separation, 647
Ashers and *Masterpiece*, 835
Asymmetry, 624, 628
Atheism, 1064
 accusation of, 889
 Marxism-Leninism than with, 898
 negative, 888–892
 positive, 892–896
 revolutionary, 897
 superiority of, 899
Augustine of Hippo, 804, 805
Autonomy, 97, 326, 327, 329–331, 345
 sceptics, 963
Autonomy argument
 anti-fascist protesters, 1128
 concept of vulnerability, 1124
 democracy, 1121
 duties, 1121
 formal, 1125
 freedom of expression, 1121, 1124
 future of humanity, 1127
 government's role, 1122
 harmful speech, 1125
 legal restrictions, 1122
 mental mediation, 1124
 minorities, 1124
 physical assault, 1123
 prohibition laws, 1126
 slippery-slope argument, 1127
 substantive, 1121, 1124
 suspects, 1126
 upholding, 1125
Autonomy-based toleration, 715–717
Avramenko's approach, 728

B
Bad tendency, 1132
Baker
 autonomy argument, 1121–1128
 critique, 1117
 hypothesizes, 1126
 liberty model, 1119–1121
 values, 1124
Balancing, 1130, 1131
Balint, P., 312
Barak, Aharon, 1130
Basic rights, 162–164, 166
Basolateral amygdala (BLA), 677
Benhabib, Seyla, 770
Berlin, Isaiah, 94
Bernstein, Richard, 372
Blake, Michael, 183, 184
Blasphemy, 584, 597–600
Bowers, Robert, 1116
Brahman, 466
Breivik, Anders Behring, 1128
British Nazi Party, 1127
Brute hospitality, 762, 763
Brute tolerance, 761, 762
Buddhism, 469, 470
 Ashoka, 471
  Pillar Edicts, 471
  Rock Edicts, 471
 the Buddha, 469
 dharma, 472
 Tipitaka, 469
Burdens of judgment, 98
Burqa, 594–597
Burwell vs. Hobby Lobby Stores, Inc (2014), 834
Butterfield, Herbert, 817

C
Calculable responsibility, 281
Calvin, John, 876, 877
Canadian society, 715
Cannata v. Catholic Diocese of Austin (2012), 841
Carroll, Lewis, 857
Castellio, Sebastian, 874, 877, 878, 883, 884
Catholicism, 814
Catholics, 638, 639, 642, 645, 1065, 1066
Cavanaugh, William, 859–861
Chan, J., 320, 321
Character, 267, 270, 272, 274
Choice-protecting rights, 152, 156, 158, 160, 162

Christianity, 978–979
Christian missionaries, 468
Churchill, Robert Paul, 131
Citron, Sabina, 1122, 1123
Civil peace, 367
Civil rights, 485, 491, 495
Classical liberalism, 287
Classical toleration, 954
 agency challenge, 955
 inappropriateness, 957
 in liberal education, 954–955
 scope challenge, 956
Close personal relationships
 condition of caring, 739, 740
 friendship, 740, 741
 lovers' individual identities, 741
 romantic love, 741
 toleration, 742–754
Code words, 1152
Coexistence, 214, 217
 conception, 17
Cognition, 1078, 1080, 1081
Cohen, Andrew Jason, 799
Cohen, G.A., 310
Cold-bloodedness, 727
Cold War, 1118
Collective exemptions
 basic interests, 841
 communicative injury, 843–844
 domination, 844–846
 justification of, 836–838
 material objection, 842–843
 objection to, 838–840
 religion, discrimination and, 833–836
 severity and baseline puzzle, 846–848
 third-party injuries, 841–848
Collective mindset, 712–714
Committedness, 705
Communicative injury, 843–844
Communism, 1121
Communitarian philosophies, 760
Compassion and toleration, 778–781
 acts and omissions, 786–787
 moral virtues, 790–794
 power, 787–790
 reasons for, 781–786
Complex emotions, 676, 677
Comprehensive doctrines, 303, 304, 318
Compulsory education, 911
Conception of the good, 301, 303, 308, 314–316, 321
Conceptualization, 233, 242, 244
Conceptual positivism, 854–856, 858, 869

Condescending argument, 957
Conflict, 500, 502, 506, 508, 516
Confucianism, 457, 458
   Analects, 457, 459
   Confucian Golden Rule, 458
   Confucius, 459
   Mencius, 457
   positive approach, 461
   ren, 459
   rites, 459
   self-restraint, 460
   sympathy, 460
   taught, 459
   Xunxi, 457
Conscience, 994, 995, 998, 1000–1002, 1004, 1005
   principle, 1107–1108
Conscientious exemptions, 342
   and neutrality, 353–360
   toleration, 345–353
Consensus, 422, 429
Consent, 1024, 1029, 1031–1033, 1060, 1072
Consequentialist reasoning, 1117, 1125
Constitutional law, 192, 194, 198, 200, 202–204, 206, 207
Constructivist contractarianism, 865
Contact hypothesis, 941
Contact theory, 693–695
Content-based restrictions, 152
Content neutrality, 1117, 1129
Content-neutral restrictions, 152
Contractarianism, 855, 864, 865, 868–870
Conversion therapy, 685
Cooper, Anthony Ashley, 1027
Cosmetic genital surgery, 259
Cosmopolitanism, 767, 769, 770, 772
Cranston, Maurice, 1028
Crisis, 500, 501, 512–515
Critical thinking, 1116
Critique of toleration, 4
Cromwell, Oliver, 997, 1001, 1005
Culture, 556, 557
   diversity, 522

D
Decent non-liberal society, 449
Deepfakes, 691
Degrees of toleration, 238–240
Democracy, 337, 510, 512, 514, 517, 939, 947, 1121
Democratic institutions, 1142

Democratic tolerance, justification of education, 944–948
Democratizing knowledge, 692–693
Denying legitimacy, 1131
Deontological reason, 199
Derrida, Jacques, 821
Despotism, 293, 295
Devaney v. Kilmartin, 2015, 841
Dharma, 472
Dialogue, 986–988
Difference, 521–525, 528, 531–533, 536, 537
Dignity, 270, 273, 543, 545, 551, 1124, 1127, 1130, 1132
Disagreement, 421–424, 435, 500, 502, 507
Disapproval, 73, 79, 81–82, 86
Discipline and Punish, 860
Discrimination, 907, 1124, 1129
   against religion, 833–836
Discursive control, 216
Discursive principle of justice, 685
Disgust, 676–678, 682
Dislike, 76, 80, 82–84, 89
Dispositional tolerance, 34
Dissenters, 638
Diverse diversities, 646
Diversity, 4, 6, 521–524, 527, 529–535
Dixon, Scott, 875
Domination
   internalized, 211–216
   Pettit's classical republican conception of, 216
   and public expression of difference, 553–555
   recognition and abstraction, 550–553
Double standards, 258
Douglas, William O., Justice, 1122
Dunn, John, 1068
Duty of civility, 682–684
Duty of recognition, 154
Dworkin, R., 301, 308, 320, 565, 1119

E
Education, 906, 909–915, 917, 922
   adequacy approach, 1103
   system, 1131
Education for tolerance
   aims, 930
   for children, 930
   democratic virtue and aim of, 932–934
   description, 929
   as education of emotions, 935–941
   and epistemic virtues, 941–944

Eileen Flynn v. Sister Mary Anna Power and The Sisters of the Holy Faith 1985, 835
Emotion(s), 675–678
  incapacity, 1131
Empathy, 686–688, 778, 780–785, 787, 790, 792–794
Emperor Akbar, 465
Empirical suppositions, 1126
Employment Non-Discrimination Act, 711
Endurance, 223
Enlightenment, 1018
  liberalism, 287
Epistemic arguments for tolerance
  Mill's argument, 113–117
  taxonomy of, 112–113
Epistemic division, 426–433
Epistemic values, 110, 112–113, 117, 126
Epistemic virtues, 112, 126, 711–715
Epistemological problem, 729
Equality, 522, 524, 529, 543, 544, 552, 559
Erroneous conscience, 998
Esteem, 547–550, 555, 556
  conception, 18–19
Ethical conception of toleration, 746
Ethical reasons, 744
Ethics and Education, 912
European culture, 860
European democracies, 1127
Evolutionary processes, 118
Exclusion of ideals, 1129
Extreme perfectionism, 320

F
Fair equality of opportunity for self-determination (FOSD), 1102, 1104, 1108
Fairness, 1103, 1107, 1108
Faith, 424, 425, 430
Fake news, 125
Family, 738, 739, 741, 747, 754
Fascism, 1128
Fear
  and distress, 689–690
  and empathy, 686–688
  enmity, and Us/theming, 678–680
  and intolerance, 692–693
  neurosciences of, 675–678
Federal Maritime Commission v. South Carolina State Ports Authority, 571
Female circumcision, 250, 253

First Amendment, 1117, 1120, 1121, 1131, 1133
First-order tolerance, 284
Fish, Stanley, 822
Forbearance tolerance, 133, 134, 136–138, 140–143, 146, 829, 830, 832
Foreign policy, 446, 448–452
Formal autonomy, 1125
Formal citizenship, 1124
Formal equality, 18
Forst, Rainer, 623–626
Forst's approach, 731
Foucault, Michel, 860
France Télécom, 578
Frankfurter, Felix, Justice, 1130
Freedom, 329, 331
  of conscience, 575
  de jure, 1012
  of thought, 165
Freedom of expression
  and autonomy, 1124, 1125
  Baker's defence, 1121
  cynical misuse, 1127
  en vogue, 1117
  limitations, 1133
  maintaining, 1117
  personal reputation and dignity, 1130
  protection, 1123
  restricting, 1132
Freely-chosen expression, 1120
Free speech, 113, 580
  intolerance, 1145
  liberal democracies, 1144
  limitations, 1127
  of national leaders, 1147
  prohibitions, 1127
  role in demonstrations, 1145
  social media, 1153
  tolerance-intolerance, 1146
Free Speech Principle
  excluding incitement and profound offence, 1131, 1132
  liberal, 1117–1119
  PA, 1129–1132
  partisan, 1117
  political interests, 1117
  problematic, 1117
  stretching, 1128
Free speech theory, 1116
French revolution, 888, 891, 894, 896, 897
Friendship, 738–740, 747, 748, 751, 753
Full citizenship, 1124

Fullinwider, R.K., 280
Functionalism, 982–984
Future of humanity, 1127

G
Gadamer, Hans-Georg, 859
Galeotti, Anna, 918, 919
Galeotti, Elisabetta, 376
Galeotti's model, 830
Gallala, I., 915, 918
General/specific distinction, 133, 134, 136
Genocidal events, 1120
Genocide, 1126
German Federal Constitutional Court, 919
Gewirth, A., 916
Glen Newey, 131
Golden Rule, 763, 764, 768, 769
Goldie, Mark, 804
Good, 367
  affirmation, 367–369
  orientation, 369–370
Governmentality, 211, 214
Graham, Gordon, 375
Gray, John, 131
Griffiths, Paul, 862
Group autonomy model, 480–484
Group polarization, 966
Group rights, 481

H
Habermas, Jürgen, 94
Habits-based morality, 280
Haefeli, Evan, 856
Halberstam, Joshua, 908
Harassment, 578
Harm, 778, 779, 781–783, 786–790, 792–794
  principle, 1099–1100, 1109
Harmful speech, 1119
Hate
  crime, 1116, 1118, 1126, 1127
  speech legislation, 1125
Hate speech, 89–90, 1116, 1119–1122, 1124–1128, 1133
  democratic world, 1118
  prohibitions, 1126
  racist, 1122
  regulation, 1120, 1121, 1125, 1126
  toleration, 714–715
Hayden, P., 920
Helicopter parent, 708
Helping, 695–696

Hence legitimate, 1117
Herder, 468
Heresy, 973–976
Heyd, David, 821
Heyman, Steven, 151, 153–156
Hick, John, 859
Hierarchical model of tolerance, 284
High Court of Justice (HCJ), 1149
Hinduism, 465
  Bhavagad Gita, 467
  Brahman, 466
  definition, 466
  Jain/Buddhist, 467
  Jews, 467
  missionary activities, 468
  pluralism, 466
Historical inquiry, 855
Historical positivism, 854–856, 869
Hobbes, Thomas, 859, 864, 866, 867
Hobbesian Christianity, 1017–1018
Hobbesian liberalism, 1011
  goals of, 1014
Hobbesian natural laws, 1015
Hobby Lobby, 835, 841, 846
Holocaust Remembrance Day, 1122
Holocaust survivors, 1122
Honor, 266, 269
Horizontal tolerance, 191, 192, 194, 201, 207
Horton, John, 500, 503, 516, 764, 765, 768, 772, 821
Hospitality and toleration, 759–760
  brute tolerance, brute hospitality and moral choice, 761–763
  mere toleration, modus vivendi and liberal toleration, 764–767
  moral argument, in existential need and compassion, 768–769
  political argument, 769–772
Hubris syndrome, 692
Human dignity
  description, 564–567
  toleration for sake of, 567–576
Human fallibility, 421–426
Humanity, 270–272, 274
Human rights, 565
  and toleration, 910–921
Hume, David, 365

I
Idealism, 289–292
Identity(ies), 178, 182, 366, 549, 552, 556
Imagination, 1122

Incitement, 1116, 1117, 1123, 1125, 1129, 1131–1132, 1141, 1142, 1144, 1150, 1153, 1156, 1157
Inclusive multiculturalism, 760, 765, 769
Indifference, 132, 133, 135, 136–140, 146
    and toleration, 388–389
Individual autonomy, 184, 484–487
Individuality, 326
Individual rights, 914, 1058
Inequality, 689, 690, 820
Inquisition, 977
Insufficiency argument, 957
Integrated inhibition mechanism, 687
Intellectual autonomy, 705
Interest-based theory, 157
Intergroup contact theory, 962
International toleration, 180
    and liberal foreign policy, 448–452
Interpersonal deliberation, 151
Intolerable, 78–81
Intolerance, 78–81, 131, 133, 135, 137, 142–144, 654–658, 660–662, 665, 669–671, 907, 914
    logic of, 638–639
    and relativists, 384
Intolerant neighborhood, 716–717
Intolerant parent, 707, 708
Intrinsic value, 791
Islamic philosophy, 461
    Prophet, 463
    Qur'an, 464
    tolerance, 465
    toleration, 462

J
Jewish community, 1116
Jews, 972, 979
John Locke, 135, 456
John of Salisbury, 980
Jones, Peter, 252, 801, 802
Justice, 315, 729, 933
    distributive, 308–310
    principles of political, 318
    Rawls's theory of, 302–304
Justice and toleration, 616
    Forst's conception, 623–626
    political inclusion, 626–631
    Rawls' conception, 620–623
Justification of toleration, 5, 6, 16, 19
Justificatory neutrality, 428

K
Kant, Immanuel, 365, 371, 589, 590, 592, 598, 604, 759, 770–772
Kantian ethics, 264, 270, 565, 703, 1133
Kantian model of tolerance, 731
Kierkegaard, Søren, 874, 879–882
Kinds of reasons, 744, 745, 748, 749, 751, 754
Ku Klux Klan (KKK), 1118, 1132
Kuyper, Abraham, 874, 879, 881, 882
Kymlicka, Will, 913

L
Laborde, Cécile, 917
Larmore, C., 318
Laslett, Peter, 1029
Law and toleration
    apex courts, 191–194
    neutrality, 195–201
    respect, 201–206
Learned Hand, Judge, 1130
Lee v. Ashers Baking Company, 2018, 834
Legal restrictions, 1122
Legal toleration, 195
    categories of, 197–199
    implications of, 200–201
    pragmatic justifications for, 199–200
Legitimacy, 1031, 1068, 1126
Lessnoff, Michael, 864
Letter Concerning Toleration, 863, 867
Levine, Alan, 854
Liberal(s), 1117
    citizenship, 572
    democracy(ies), 151, 152, 250, 441, 444, 510–515, 680–682, 926, 929, 939, 940, 1131
    education, 953
    model of toleration, 83–84
    neutralist's theory of toleration, 285
    neutrality, 332
    perfectionist justification, 946
    political toleration, 332
    science, 118–120
    standards, 1119
    theory, 765, 768
    thinkers, 1117
    toleration, 349, 640, 760, 766, 767
Liberal-democratic culture of society, 1125
Liberal Free Speech Principle, 1117–1119

Liberalism, 6, 94, 134, 314, 329, 332, 334–336, 433, 501–503, 510–512, 530, 533, 534, 618, 621, 765, 767–770, 772, 854, 1009, 1028, 1096, 1098, 1100, 1110
  characteristics of, 1010
  Hobbesian, 1011, 1014
Liberating tolerance, 183
Libertarian status-based theory of rights, 161–166
Liberty, 330, 366, 367
  model, 1119–1122
  rights, 760
Liberty of conscience, 995, 998, 1000–1002, 1004, 1005, 1096
  bias and exclusion in, 1110–1111
  challenges, 1107–1108
  Mill's approach, 1098–1101
Lillian Ladele v. London Borough of Islington, 2008, 834
Limits of toleration, 6, 93
Linguistic legislation, 49
Little v. Wuerl, 1991, 836
Locke, John, 94, 314, 367, 589, 590, 605, 804, 810, 814–816, 854, 863–870, 878, 883, 994, 995, 997, 998, 1000, 1027, 1070, 1071
  A Letter Concerning Toleration, 1029–1030
  consent argument, for toleration, 1031–1033
  early life, 1025
  interpretive problems, 1056–1060
  limits of toleration, 1063–1064
  moral challenge, of toleration, 1062–1063
  pragmatic argument, for toleration, 1060–1062
  rationality argument, for toleration, 1037–1043
  Restoration, 1026
  Revolution of 1688, 1028–1029
  scepticism, 1043–1052
  truth argument, for toleration, 1034–1037
Lorde, Audre, 175
Love, 739–742, 744, 746, 747, 749–754
Luca Rocco Magnotta, 1128
Lumping method, 1121

M
MacIntyre, Alasdair, 371, 858
Marakesh compact, 666, 668, 669
Marcuse, H., 177, 178, 183, 185, 187

Marketplace of ideas, 119, 122, 123
Marsiglio of Padua, 979, 982
Martha Nussbaum, 94
Martinez v. Spain, 2014, 836
McCabe, David, 501, 510
McCarthyism period (1947-1957), 1118
Medieval persecution, 804–806
Mental mediation, 1123, 1124
Mere tolerance, 637
Mere toleration, 759, 764–770
Metatheism, 902
Method of avoidance, 420, 428, 429
Migration crisis, 655
Mill, John Stuart, 94, 110, 314, 587, 588, 812, 817, 1117, 1120–1122, 1133
  collective and individual epistemic virtues, 126
  epistemic arguments for tolerance, 113–117
Millet system, 463
Mill's approach, 1098–1101
Milton, John, 859, 869
Mindsight
  case of tolerant parents, 704–709
  description, 701
  prohibition of hate speech, 711–715
Minority(ies), 210, 211, 214, 216, 218, 222, 522, 523, 525–527, 529, 535, 537, 1124
Models of toleration
  group autonomy model, 480–484
  individual rights and autonomy, 484–487
Moderate perfectionism, 320
Modern toleration, 954
  and assimilative pressure, 962–964
  in liberal education, 960–962
Modus vivendi, concept of
  accommodative toleration, 507–510
  conflict and power, 502
  liberal democracies, context of, 510–515
  peaceful coexistence, 501
  political arrangements, 504
  political virtues or attitudes, 505
  traditional conception of toleration, 506–507
  universal minimal morality, 503
Modus vivendi, 315, 759, 764–769, 771, 772
Moksa/nirvana, 467
Montefiore, A., 307
Moral climate, 1119
Moral conception, 746

Moralism, 278
  and anti-moralism, 279–282
  modes in theories of toleration, 282–289
Moral judgment, 356, 357
  and toleration, 326–331
Moral law, 729
Moral offenses, 266–268
  and professional offenses, 266–268
Moral reasons, 330, 744
Moral toleration, 762
Moral virtue, 343, 344, 780, 790–792, 794, 907
Multicultural hospitality, 760
Multiculturalism, 963
  integrated societies, 587
  liberal democracies, 588
  principles, 588
Multiculturalism and toleration, 520, 534–537
  as descriptive concepts and normative ideals, 527–529
  diversity, 521–523
  justifications, 529–530
  as modes of accommodation, 525–527
  multiculturalism challenge to liberal toleration, 530–532
  policies, 534
  as positive and negative attitudes to difference, 523–525
Multiculturalist sensibility, 534
Murphy, Andrew, 857, 858
Muslim(s), 636, 640
  headscarves, 640
Mysticism, 988–989

N

Nationalism, 984–986
Natural law, 573, 1066, 1067
  contractarianism, 865
Natural rights theory, 157, 1066
Nazi Germany, 1126
Nazism, 1128
Negative atheism, 888–892
Neglectful parent, 707, 708
Neo-Nazism, 1128
Netanyahu, Bibi, 1142–1145, 1147, 1148, 1150–1154, 1156, 1157
Neuroscience, 675–678
Neuroscientific research, 781
Neutralism, 300
  and perfectionism, 320
Neutrality, 31–32, 250–253, 259, 331, 332, 334–338, 342, 343, 347, 353–356, 680–682, 1101–1104, 1106
  of aim, 311
  Balint, P. and Pattern, A., 312–314
  and distibutive justice, 308–310
  of effect, 307, 311
  and judicial integrity, 357–359
  justification, 311, 314–317
  law, 195–201
  objection, 232, 233
  and public policy, 310–312
  and toleration, 359–360
  of treatment, 313
Neutral liberalism, 353
Neutral state, 302
  democracy of, 305
  liberal idea of, 300
  policies of, 313
Newey, Glen, 137, 142, 145, 374, 801
Nicholas of Cusa, 979, 985
Nicomachean Ethics, 761
Niqab, 594–597
Noncoercive action, 1120
Noncoercive activity, 1120
Non-discrimination, 915
Non-domination, 216–221
  and toleration, 221–224, 398, 406–408
Nonideal theory, 289
Non-interference, 82, 84, 86, 521, 524, 526, 528, 530, 531, 533, 801–803, 811, 814
Non-judgmentalism, 280
Non-religious conscience, 1101
Non-tolerant people, 721
Non-violent activity, 1120
Normative conception of toleration, 932
Normative multiculturalism, 527
Norms, 1142
Nozickean status-based theory of rights, 151, 164
Nuanced approach, 1130

O

Objection, 521, 523–526, 528, 531–533, 535–537
  component, 76, 78, 93, 231, 232
Obligation, 1031, 1035, 1036, 1062, 1065
O'Conner and Weatherall's models, 125
Offense(s), 265–266
  to sensibilities, 1131
On Liberty, 1123
Ottoman(s), 461
  millet system, 463, 480–484
  Ottoman Empire, 461
  Sultan Mehmed II, 462
  Sultan Süleyman the Magnificent, 464
  toleration, 463

P

Pagan policy of religious toleration, 1018
Paradoxes, of toleration, 100–106, 683, 762, 909–910
   The Paradox of Drawing the Limits, 102
   The Paradox of Moral Toleration, 95
   The Paradox of Self-Destruction, 100
   The Paradox of the Tolerant Racist, 104
Parekh, B., 832
Passive toleration, 656, 662–665
Paternalism, 1120, 1121
Patten, A., 313
Peace, 444, 445, 770
Peaceful society, 427
Pedagogical toleration, 954, 964–967
Penn, William, 1000–1004
Perfectionism, 320, 1129, 1130
Perfectionist state, 300
Permission, 217, 221
   conception, 16–17
Perpetual Peace, 770
Persecution, 810, 811, 971–973, 996, 998, 999, 1002–1004
   medieval, 804–806
   Protestant, 806–808
Personal autonomy, 946
Personal reputation and dignity, 1130
Personal sovereignty, 573–575
Personal tolerance, 953, 1078–1080
Pew Research Report, 1118
Philosophical inquiry, 855
Physical assault, 1123
Physical harm, 1117
Pierre Bayle, 95
Pity, 778, 780–785, 787, 790, 792, 793
Pluralism, 3, 6, 28, 175–177, 326, 332, 337, 364, 393, 446–448, 568, 569, 729, 944–945, 1098, 1110
   as an empirical reality, 376–377
   as a normative ideal, 378–379
   and Reformation, 875–877
   and relativism, 377, 379–380
   and toleration, 380–381
Pluralist culture, 1121
Political authority, 1099, 1109
Political autonomy, 444–446, 931, 946
Political change, 174–186
Political equality, 18
Political inclusion, 626–631
Political institutions, 166–168
Political liberalism, 332, 426, 427, 434, 487–492, 621
Political life, 1011
Political moralism, 289

Political neutrality, 302, 314, 316
   principle, 1129
Political philosophy, 759, 760, 769
Political populism, 657
Political realism, 289
Political reasons, 744
Political recognition, 333
Political regimes, 1148–1150
Political toleration, 133, 152, 159, 160, 532, 818–821, 932, 953
   forbearance tolerance, 137
   indifference, 136–137
   respect, 138
   state power, 142
   as substantive neutrality, 331–337
   symmetry thesis, 142–145
   The Neutrality Challenge, 131–132, 138–140
   understanding state objection, 140–141
Popper, Karl, 94
Populism, 512, 514
   agrarian, 657
   political, 657
Populist intolerance
   active toleration, 665–669
   hospitality and classical passive toleration, 662–665
   and migration crisis, 655
Positive atheism, 892–896
Power, 521, 524, 526–528, 530, 779, 783, 785, 787–790
   condition, 76, 82
Pragmatic conception of toleration, 745
Pragmatic reasons, 195, 196, 199, 200, 207, 744
Pragmatism, 809–812
Pre-emption of toleration, 250
Prefrontal cortex, 674, 676–678
Pre-Nazi Germany, 1126
Principle of free speech, 288
Principle of natural liberty, 292
Probability, 421, 422
Procedural liberalism, 545
Prohibition, 234
   laws, 1126
Promisel's approach, 728
Promotional approach (PA), 1129–1132
   accepting some form of perfectionism, 1129, 1130
   balancing, 1130, 1131
   denying legitimacy, 1131
   excluding incitement and profound offence from the Free Speech Principle, 1131, 1132
   rejection of content neutrality, 1129

Proselytization, 486, 488, 493
Protestant(s), 462
    persecution, 806–808
    political authorities, 815
    Reformation, 807
    tradition, 874, 877–879
Protestantism, 810, 812, 874, 878, 883
Proud Boys, 1142
Psychology of toleration, 701, 702, 709, 716
Public discourse, 150
Publicity, 1126
Public judgment, 422, 423
Public reason, 318, 319, 429
Public reasoning, 690–692
Public schools, 911, 912, 922
    parents' religious beliefs, 911–912
    wearing of Islamic headscarves, 915–921
Public toleration, 856
Public trust, 1118
Pyrrhonian skepticism, 370
Pyrrho of Elis, 370

Q
Qualified immunity, 1154–1156
Qualitative equality, 18
Quong, Jonathan, 151, 156–159

R
Racial violence, 1120, 1128
Racism, 641, 1121, 1124, 1125, 1127, 1128
    and hate speech (*see* Hate speech)
Rage, 1117
Rainer Forst, 95
Ramon Llull, 979, 987
Rational dialogue, 316
Rawls, John, 94, 178–181, 183, 301–305, 308, 319, 373, 376, 479–480, 483, 487–492, 564, 575, 620–623, 764
Rawls's approach, 451
Raz, Joseph, 97, 1080
Realpolitik, 812, 817, 818
Reasonable disagreement, 315
Reasonableness
    description, 420
    epistemic division and public reason in Rawls, John, 426–433
    public debate, 434–435
Reasonable pluralism, 98
Reasons of love, 744
Rebecca, 1122

Recognition, 84–86, 286, 332–334, 337, 522, 524–526, 531, 534–537, 542, 618, 619, 622, 625–632
    abstraction and domination, 550–553
    modes of, 547
    respect, 271, 294, 643, 684–686
    vs. toleration, 555–557
    withcultural differences, 548–550
    withpolitics of difference, 544–545
Recognition-denying speech, 151, 155
Reconciliation strategy, 571
Red Scare, 1118
Reflective self-consciousness, 704, 705
Reform, 974
Reformation, 798, 803, 804, 806, 812–813, 817, 818, 874–877
    liberalism, 288
Refugees, 654, 656, 657, 662–665, 667–670
Relativization, 14
Relativism, 364, 365, 370–374, 376, 391–393
    and toleration, 381–384
    and value pluralism, 379–380
Religion, 232, 239, 240, 424–426, 479, 489, 1025, 1026, 1032–1039, 1043–1047, 1049, 1050, 1056–1058, 1060, 1062, 1063, 1070–1072
Religion and toleration, 803–804
    limits of toleration, 813–814
    medieval persecution, 804–806
    moral challenge of toleration, 808–809
    political toleration, 818–821
    pragmatism, 809–812
    Protestant persecution, 806–808
    Reformation, 812–813
Religious accommodations, 829
    characterization, 835
    toleration, neutrality and, 829–833
Religious diversity, 522, 1044
Religious equality approach, 1105, 1111
Religious exemptions, 202, 204–206
Religious freedom, 194, 202–204, 207
Religious Freedom Restoration Act, 206
Religious institutionalism, 836, 863
Religious liberty, 995, 1000, 1005
Religiously-inspired discrimination, 833–836
Religious minority, 1102, 1106
Religious Reading, 862
Religious symbols, 915, 917–919
Religious toleration, 300, 302, 304, 854, 855, 857, 859, 861–863
Renaut, Alain, 917, 918
Repressive tolerance, 183, 282
Republic, 865

Residual prohibition principle, 292
Resilience, 223
Resourcism, 308, 309
Respect, 133, 138, 140, 141, 146, 264, 267, 269–270, 342–344, 348–351, 353, 356, 524, 525, 528, 531–534, 536, 537, 547–550, 555
  agonistic, 901
  blasphemy/free speech, 599, 600
  blasphemy, 597, 599, 600, 610
  burqa and niqab, 594–597
  contemporary liberals, 590, 591
  contested and contentious norm, 611
  contested term, 601–603
  definition, 584
  equal, 589
  evaluative spectrum, 609
  features *vs.* persons, 591–593
  Galeotti, 594
  intolerance, 603
  lack of, 899
  liberal tradition, 588–590, 611
  mutual exclusivity, 600, 601
  non-universalization, 606, 607
  policy, 585
  questions, 607–609
  rival, 598, 599
  vs. tolerance, 899
  universalization, 604–606
Respectability, 1126
Respect and toleration, law, 201–202
  alternative constitutional understandings, 202–204
  religious exemptions, 204–206
Respect conception, 17–18
Respect for others, 1131, 1133
Respect for persons
  Heyman's argument, 153–156
  libertarian status-based theory of rights, 161–166
  Quong's argument, 156–159
Respect for right, 55, 59, 64, 65, 67
Respect toleration, 216–221
  and justification, 401–404
Respublica Christiana, 970, 974, 989
Restoration, 997, 1000, 1001
R(E) v. Governing Body of JFS, 840
Revolutionary social change, 175
Reynolds v. U.S., (1879), 1013
Right to freedom of religion, 910, 915, 916, 920–922
Right to freedom of thought, 165
Right to recognition, 153

Right-wing authoritarianism (RWA), 690
Rig Veda, 466
Ritual circumcision, 256, 259
Ronald Dworkin's view, 1119
Rorty, Richard, 373
Roth, K., 920
Rules-based morality, 280
Rwanda genocide, 1126

S
Sandel, Michael, 912
Sarvepalli Radhakrishnan, 469
Satkunanandan, S., 281
Saxsena, M., 915
Scepticism, 315, 1044–1052
Second-personal agents, 684–686
Secularism, 1109
  vs. atheism, 896
Secularity, 917–919
Secure toleration, 222, 224
Self-censorship, 1089
Self-certainty, 281
Self-constitution, 544
Self-determination, 444–446
Self-development, 1122
Self-respect, 264, 272–274
Sex discrimination, 907
Skepticism, 62, 96, 364, 365, 376, 386, 387, 393, 980–982
  academic skepticism, 370
  Pyrrhonian skepticism, 370
  and toleration, 384–386
Skokie, 1123
Slippery-slope argument, 1127
Social change, 175
Social conflict, 765
Social contract theory of justice, 854, 864, 865, 868, 870
Social discrimination, 616
Social-dominance orientation (SDO), 689
Social groups, 176, 177, 179
Social identities, 546
Socialism, 1121
Social media, 1116, 1153
Social model of selfhood, 544
Social practices and laws, 1121
Social psychology, 1082
Social relations, 760
Socio-economic status (SES), 689–690
Southern Poverty Law Center, 1128
Sovereignty, 446–448

Soviet totalitarianism, 898
Speech
   harmfulness, 1123
   limitations, 1120
   opponent's, 1127
   prohibitions, 1125, 1126
   types, 1120
   unprotected types, 1120
Speech-act, 1123
Spinoza, Benedict, 1078, 1091
   belief-formation, 1080
   evaluative judgments, 1081
   intolerance of disagreement, 1082–1083
   religious toleration, analysis of, 1086
   sincere engagement, 1089
   suspension as ambivalence, 1084–1085
   toleration, trust and state, 1090–1091
St. Augustine, 972, 973, 984
Standing, 264, 268–269, 271
Stasi Commission, 918
State/Church, 424
State neutrality, 130, 131, 302–304, 316
State objection, 130, 140
State power, 130, 140, 142
State speech, 240–244
Status, 264, 267, 268, 273
Status-concept, 566
Stigma, 549, 550
Stormfront, 1128
Strong perfectionism, 458
Subordination, 213
Substantive autonomy, 1121, 1124
Supererogation, 67–69
Supererogatory, 307
Supremacism, 1128
Suspension-through-reflection model, 1083
Swami Vivekananda, 468
Symbolic genital cutting, 253, 254, 258
Symmetry thesis, 130, 140, 142–145
Sympathy, 778, 780–785, 787, 790, 792–794
Systematic theory of social recognition, 547

T
Taylor, Charles, 859, 861
Theism, 1064, 1070
The Myth of Religious Violence, 859
The Neutrality Challenge, 131–132, 138–140, 145, 146
The right to do wrong, 160
The Treaty of Galata, 462

Thomas Nagel, 97
Threats, 639
   cultural, 640
   normative, 640
   political, 640
Tolerance, 133–138, 140–146, 457, 1117–1119, 1125, 1127, 1131, 1133
   agent, 35
   as a personal virtue, 1079–1080
   atheistic, 902
   of atheists, 891
   attitude of, 33
   believed power, 47–49
   definition, 33
   dispositional, 34
   fundamental, 899
   vs. indifference, 724–725
   intentional, 35–36
   vs. intolerance, 730–733, 898
   issues in neutral and the virtue approach, 725
   moral reasons for, 725
   noninterference, 41–43
   object, 46–47
   objection component, 721
   opposition, 43–46
   paradox of tolerance, 726–727
   policy of, 898
   spirit of, 895
   tolerance-as-sheer-respect approach, 726
   universal, 896
   value, 36–41
   value-laden virtue approach, 723
   virtue approach, 722
Toleration, 11, 132–135, 174, 175, 178–186, 210, 212, 284, 326, 342–354, 356–361, 374–376, 456, 458, 542, 657–662, 799–803, 821, 823
   acceptance component, 13–14
   as a condition for respect, 569–571
   active, 665–669
   ad hoc agreement, 57
   as a "disposition", 389–393
   as a duty of civility, 682–684
   as a general political practice, 136–138
   among groups, 709–711
   approaches to, 282
   autonomy and conscience, 569–571
   beliefs and practices, 65
   bias and exclusion in, 1110–1111
   broad interpretations, 68
   Brown's conception of, 215

case of tolerant parents, 704–709
challenges, 1108–1110
characterizations, 68
classical, 954
close personal relationships, 742–754
coercing beliefs, 57
coexistence conception, 17
cognitive category, 57
concept and conceptions, 399–401
conditionality of, 1011–1015
conditions, 27, 366–367, 585, 586
consent argument, 1031–1033
considerateness and charity, 63
contingency on enlightenment, 1015–1020
contingent circumstances, 62
conversions, 645–649
definition, 24
discursive equality, idea of, 412–415
diversity, 29–30
emergence of European nation-states, 996
and equal civic status, 571–574
esteem conception, 18–19
fear and empathy, 686–688
female circumcision, 253, 257–261
formal components, 59–61
Foucauldian critique of, 214
and "good", 367–370
Hegelian process of *Aufhebung*, 66
history of, 547
and human rights, 910–921
and incongruence, 234–236
and "indifference", 25–27, 388–389
indulgence and condonation, 58
justice and equality, 69
justification, 16, 19, 642–645
lack of commitment, 56
language of, 2–7
and law (*see* Law and toleration)
liberal conceptions, 460
and liberal democracy, 680–682
liberal model, 83–84
liberal philosophy, 459
liberal polity, 252
liberal theory, 54, 65
limits of, 14–15, 813–814
local religions and cultures, 63
Locke-Rawls traditions on, 1096–1098
manifestations of white supremacism, 253
medieval persecution, 804–806
Mill's approach, 1098–1101
modern, 954

modus vivendi perspective (*see* Modus vivendi, concept of)
moral challenge, 808–809, 1062–1063
and moral judgment, 326–331
multiculturalism, 28, 29
negative and positive conceptions of, 285–287
and neutrality, 31–32, 304–307, 1101–1104
and nineteenth-century models of religious thought, 879–883
non-domination toleration, 406–408
normative justification, 54, 55
objection, 456
objection component, 12–13
one's own free will, 15
origin of doctrine of, 73–75
Ottoman millet system, 997
paradox and limitis of, 702–704
passive, 662–665
pedagogical, 954
Penn's political thought, 1000–1004
permission conception, 16–17
permissiveness, 30
pessimism, 31
pluralism, 28
political, 331–337, 818–821
political and personal dimensions of, 953
political definition, 995
political protections, 995
post-Reformation European Christianity, 996
power and non-domination, 404–406
practice, 54
pragmatic argument, 1060–1061
and pragmatism, 809–812
principle of, 28
Protestant persecution, 806–808
psychological dispositions, 58
psychology of virtue of, 701
public virtue, 700
quasi-moral attitude, 58
rationality argument, 1037–1043
reasonableness, 409–412
as recognition, 84–86, 555–557
religious equality, 1101–1104
Reformation, 812–813
relativism, 31, 381–384
in religion, 995
religious, 57, 547
resignation, 26–27
respect, 216–221, 269–270
respect conception, 17–18

Toleration (*cont.*)
   respect toleration and justification, 401–404
   robust discourse of, 994
   roles, 952
   for sake of dignity, 567–576
   in Seventeenth-Century England, 997–1000
   simple noninterference, 25–27
   and skepticism, 385–386
   social virtue of, 81–83
   state/individual, 587
   and state speech, 240–244
   supererogatory behaviour, 69
   thin and thick concepts, 55–56
   threats, 639–642
   tolerantia, 456
   tolerationist politics, 996
   and transformative liberalism, 236–240
   truth argument, 1034–1037
   and value pluralism, 380–381
   vertical and horizontal issues of, 86–87
   Western conception, 457, 460
   zero tolerance, 57
Toleration Act, 996
Tony and Susan Alamo Foundation v. Secretary of Labor, 1985, 842
Tradition, 854, 855, 858, 862, 863, 865–867, 869, 870
Traditionary inquiry, 858
Transformative liberalism, 235
   and toleration, 236–240
Tree of Life synagogue, 1116
Trinity Western University v. Law Society of Upper Canada (2018), 835
Trinity Western University v British Columbia College of Teachers (2001), 835
True tolerance, 726
Trump, Donald, 1142, 1144, 1145, 1147, 1148, 1150–1152, 1154, 1157
Trust, 966

U

'Umar ibn al-Khattab, 463
United States v. Lee, 1982, 842
Unite the Right, 1128
Upanishads, 466, 468
Upholding autonomy, 1125
U.S.-Israel relations, 1150–1153
Utilitarian-pragmatic toleration, 781
Utopophobia, 290, 291

V

Value(s), 1142
   of autonomy, 1124
   of free expression, 1124
   individualism, 1111
Value-laden virtue approach, 723
Value pluralism, 98
   and relativism, 379–380
   and toleration, 380–381
Vanguard America, 1128
Vedantic philosophy, 468
Vedenta, 466
Veritistic social epistemology framework, 122
Vernon, Richard, 385
Vertical toleration, 191, 192, 194–200, 207
Vietnam War (1959-1975), 1118
Viewpoint-based restrictions, 153, 169
Viewpoint neutrality, 151, 156, 159–161, 164–166, 168–170
Vinet, Alexandre, 874, 879–881, 884
Violence, 1117
Violent speech, 1125
Virtue epistemology, 701, 705
   explanatory and normative potential of, 710
   moral evaluation, 708
Virtue of tolerance, 111
Voltaire, 456
Vulnerability, concept of, 1124

W

Waldron, Jeremy, 571, 579, 800, 1069
Walzer, M., 180–183, 185
Weak perfectionism, 458
Welfarism, 308, 309
Western culture, 858
Williams, Roger, 864, 869, 1087
Wolff, Robert Paul, 175–177
Workplace accommodations, 829

Z

Zagorin, Perez, 805, 817
Zero tolerance, 907
Zionism equals racism, 1117
Zuckerberg, Mark, 1156, 1157
Zündel, Ernst, 1122
Zuolo, Federico, 249